Perl Cookbook™

Other Perl resources from O'Reilly

Related titles

Programming Perl

Learning Perl

CGI Programming with Perl

Computer Science & Perl
  Programming

Web, Graphics & Perl/Tk

Games, Diversions & Perl
  Culture

Programming Web Services
  with Perl

Perl 6 Essentials

Learning Perl Objects,
  References & Modules

Mastering Regular
  Expressions

Practical mod_perl

Perl Pocket Reference

Perl in a Nutshell

Perl Graphics Programming

**Perl Books
Resource Center**

perl.oreilly.com is a complete catalog of O'Reilly's books on Perl and related technologies, including sample chapters and code examples.

Perl.com is the central web site for the Perl community. It is the perfect starting place for finding out everything there is to know about Perl.

Conferences

O'Reilly & Associates brings diverse innovators together to nurture the ideas that spark revolutionary industries. We specialize in documenting the latest tools and systems, translating the innovator's knowledge into useful skills for those in the trenches. Visit *conferences.oreilly.com* for our upcoming events.

Safari Bookshelf (*safari.oreilly.com*) is the premier online reference library for programmers and IT professionals. Conduct searches across more than 1,000 books. Subscribers can zero in on answers to time-critical questions in a matter of seconds. Read the books on your Bookshelf from cover to cover or simply flip to the page you need. Try it today with a free trial.

SECOND EDITION

Perl Cookbook™

Tom Christiansen and Nathan Torkington

O'REILLY®

Beijing · Cambridge · Farnham · Köln · Paris · Sebastopol · Taipei · Tokyo

Perl Cookbook, Second Edition
by Tom Christiansen and Nathan Torkington

Published by O'Reilly Media, Inc., 1005 Gravenstein Highway North, Sebastopol, CA 95472.

O'Reilly Media, Inc. books may be purchased for educational, business, or sales promotional use. Online editions are also available for most titles (*safari.oreilly.com*). For more information, contact our corporate/institutional sales department: (800) 998-9938 or *corporate@oreilly.com*.

Editor:	Linda Mui
Production Editor:	Genevieve d'Entremont
Cover Designer:	Edie Freedman
Interior Designer:	David Futato

Printing History:

August 1998:	First Edition.
August 2003:	Second Edition.

ISBN-10: 0-596-00313-7
ISBN-13: 978-0-596-00313-5
[M]

Table of Contents

Foreword

They say that it's easy to get trapped by a metaphor. But some metaphors are so magnificent that you don't mind getting trapped in them. Perhaps the cooking metaphor is one such, at least in this case. The only problem I have with it is a personal one—I feel a bit like Betty Crocker's mother. The work in question is so monumental that anything I could say here would be either redundant or irrelevant.

However, that never stopped me before.

Cooking is perhaps the humblest of the arts; but to me humility is a strength, not a weakness. Great artists have always had to serve their artistic medium—great cooks just do so literally. And the more humble the medium, the more humble the artist must be in order to lift the medium beyond the mundane. Food and language are both humble media, consisting as they do of an overwhelming profusion of seemingly unrelated and unruly ingredients. And yet, in the hands of someone with a bit of creativity and discipline, things like potatoes, pasta, and Perl are the basis of works of art that "hit the spot" in a most satisfying way, not merely getting the job done, but doing so in a way that makes your journey through life a little more pleasant.

Cooking is also one of the oldest of the arts. Some modern artists would have you believe that so-called ephemeral art is a recent invention, but cooking has always been an ephemeral art. We can try to preserve our art, make it last a little longer, but even the food we bury with our pharoahs gets dug up eventually. So too, much of our Perl programming is ephemeral. This aspect of Perl cuisine has been much maligned. You can call it quick-and-dirty if you like, but there are billions of dollars out there riding on the supposition that fast food is not necessarily dirty food. (We hope.)

Easy things should be easy, and hard things should be possible. For every fast-food recipe, there are countless slow-food recipes. One of the advantages of living in California is that I have ready access to almost every national cuisine ever invented. But even within a given culture, There's More Than One Way To Do It. It's said in Russia that there are more recipes for borscht than there are cooks, and I believe it. My mom's recipe doesn't even have any beets in it! But that's okay, and it's more than okay. Borscht is a cultural differentiator, and different cultures are interesting, and educational, and useful, and exciting.

So you won't always find Tom and Nat doing things in this book the way I would do them. Sometimes they don't even do things the same way as each other. That's okay—again, this is a strength, not a weakness. I have to confess that I learned quite a few things I didn't know before I read this book. What's more, I'm quite confident that I still don't know it all. And I hope I don't any time soon. I often talk about Perl culture as if it were a single, static entity, but there are in fact many healthy Perl sub-cultures, not to mention sub-subcultures and supercultures and circumcultures in every conceivable combination, all inheriting attributes and methods from each other. It can get confusing. Hey, I'm confused most of the time.

So the essence of a cookbook like this is not to cook for you (it can't), or even to teach you how to cook (though it helps), but rather to pass on various bits of culture that have been found useful, and perhaps to filter out other bits of "culture" that grew in the refrigerator when no one was looking. You in turn will pass on some of these ideas to other people, filtering them through your own experiences and tastes, your creativity and discipline. You'll come up with your own recipes to pass to your children. Just don't be surprised when they in turn cook up some recipes of their own, and ask you what you think. Try not to make a face.

I commend to you these recipes, over which I've made very few faces.

—Larry Wall
June, 1998

Preface

The investment group eyed the entrepreneur with caution, their expressions flickering from scepticism to intrigue and back again.

"Your bold plan holds promise," their spokesman conceded. "But it is costly and entirely speculative. Our mathematicians mistrust your figures. Why should we entrust our money into your hands? What do you know that we do not?"

"For one thing," he replied, "I know how to balance an egg on its point without outside support. Do you?" And with that, the entrepreneur reached into his satchel and delicately withdrew a fresh hen's egg. He handed over the egg to the financial tycoons, who passed it amongst themselves trying to carry out the simple task. At last they gave up. In exasperation they declared, "What you ask is impossible! No man can balance an egg on its point."

So the entrepreneur took back the egg from the annoyed businessmen and placed it upon the fine oak table, holding it so that its point faced down. Lightly but firmly, he pushed down on the egg with just enough force to crush in its bottom about half an inch. When he took his hand away, the egg stood there on its own, somewhat messy, but definitely balanced. "Was that impossible?" he asked.

"It's just a trick," cried the businessmen. "Once you know how, anyone can do it."

"True enough," came the retort. "But the same can be said for anything. Before you know how, it seems an impossibility. Once the way is revealed, it's so simple that you wonder why you never thought of it that way before. Let me show you that easy way, so others may easily follow. Will you trust me?"

Eventually convinced that this entrepreneur might possibly have something to show them, the skeptical venture capitalists funded his project. From the tiny Andalusian port of Palos de Moguer set forth the *Niña*, the *Pinta*, and the *Santa María*, led by an entrepreneur with a slightly broken egg and his own ideas: Christopher Columbus.

Many have since followed.

Approaching a programming problem can be like balancing Columbus's egg. If no one shows you how, you may sit forever perplexed, watching the egg—and your program—fall over again and again, no closer to the Indies than when you began. This is especially true in a language as idiomatic as Perl.

This book isn't meant to be a complete reference book for Perl. Keeping a copy of *Programming Perl* handy will let you look up exact definitions of operators, keywords, functions, pragmata, or modules. Alternatively, every Perl installation comes with a voluminous collection of searchable, online reference materials. If those aren't where you can easily get at them, see your system administrator if you have one, or consult the documentation section at *http://www.perl.com*.

Neither is this book meant to be a bare-bones introduction for programmers who have never seen Perl before. That's what *Learning Perl*, a kinder and gentler introduction to Perl, is designed for. (If you're on a Microsoft system, you might prefer the *Learning Perl for Win32 Systems* version.)

Instead, this is a book for learning *more* Perl. Neither a reference book nor a tutorial book, *Perl Cookbook* serves as a companion book to both. It's for people who already know the basics but are wondering how to mix all those ingredients together into a complete program. Spread across 22 chapters and more than 400 focused topic areas affectionately called recipes, this task-oriented book contains thousands of solutions to everyday challenges encountered by novice and journeyman alike.

We tried hard to make this book useful for both random and sequential access. Each recipe is self-contained, but has a list of references at the end should you need further information on the topic. We've tried to put the simpler, more common recipes toward the front of each chapter and the simpler chapters toward the front of the book. Perl novices should find that these recipes about Perl's basic data types and operators are just what they're looking for. We gradually work our way through topic areas and solutions more geared toward the journeyman Perl programmer. Now and then we include material that should inspire even the master Perl programmer.

Each chapter begins with an overview of that chapter's topic. This introduction is followed by the main body of each chapter, its recipes. In the spirit of the Perl slogan of TMTOWTDI, *There's more than one way to do it*, most recipes show several different techniques for solving the same or closely related problems. These recipes range from short-but-sweet solutions to in-depth mini-tutorials. Where more than one technique is given, we often show costs and benefits of each approach.

As with a traditional cookbook, we expect you to access this book more or less at random. When you want to learn how to do something, you'll look up its recipe. Even if the exact solutions presented don't fit your problem exactly, they'll give you ideas about possible approaches.

Each chapter concludes with one or more complete programs. Although some recipes already include small programs, these longer applications highlight the chapter's principal focus and combine techniques from other chapters, just as any real-world program would. All are useful, and many are used on a daily basis. Some even helped us put this book together.

What's in This Book

Spread over five chapters, the first portion of the book addresses Perl's basic data types. Chapter 1, *Strings*, covers matters like accessing substrings, expanding function calls in strings, and parsing comma-separated data; it also covers Unicode strings. Chapter 2, *Numbers*, tackles oddities of floating-point representation, placing commas in numbers, and pseudo-random numbers. Chapter 3, *Dates and Times*, demonstrates conversions between numeric and string date formats and using timers. Chapter 4, *Arrays*, covers everything relating to list and array manipulation, including finding unique elements in a list, efficiently sorting lists, and randomizing them. Chapter 5, *Hashes*, concludes the basics with a demonstration of the most useful data type, the associative array. The chapter shows how to access a hash in insertion order, how to sort a hash by value, how to have multiple values per key, and how to have an immutable hash.

Chapter 6, *Pattern Matching*, includes recipes for converting a shell wildcard into a pattern, matching letters or words, matching multiple lines, avoiding greediness, matching nested or recursive patterns, and matching strings that are close to but not exactly what you're looking for. Although this chapter is one of the longest in the book, it could easily have been longer still—every chapter contains uses of regular expressions. It's part of what makes Perl Perl.

The next three chapters cover the filesystem. Chapter 7, *File Access*, shows opening files, locking them for concurrent access, modifying them in place, and storing filehandles in variables. Chapter 8, *File Contents*, discusses storing filehandles in variables, managing temporary files, watching the end of a growing file, reading a particular line from a file, handling alternative character encodings like Unicode and Microsoft character sets, and random access binary I/O. Finally, in Chapter 9, *Directories*, we show techniques to copy, move, or delete a file, manipulate a file's timestamps, and recursively process all files in a directory.

Chapters 10 through 13 focus on making your program flexible and powerful. Chapter 10, *Subroutines*, includes recipes on creating persistent local variables, passing parameters by reference, calling functions indirectly, crafting a switch statement, and handling exceptions. Chapter 11, *References and Records*, is about data structures; basic manipulation of references to data and functions are demonstrated. Later recipes show how to create elaborate data structures and how to save and restore these structures from permanent storage. Chapter 12, *Packages, Libraries, and Modules*, concerns breaking up your program into separate files; we discuss how to make variables and functions private to a module, customize warnings for modules, replace built-ins, trap errors loading missing modules, and use the *h2ph* and *h2xs* tools to interact with C and C++ code. Lastly, Chapter 13, *Classes, Objects, and Ties*, covers the fundamentals of building your own object-based module to create user-defined types, complete with constructors, destructors, and inheritance. Other recipes show examples of circular data structures, operator overloading, and tied data types.

The next two chapters are about interfaces: one to databases, the other to users. Chapter 14, *Database Access*, includes techniques for manipulating DBM files and querying and updating databases with SQL and the DBI module. Chapter 15, *Interactivity*, covers topics such as clearing the screen, processing command-line switches, single-character input, moving the cursor using *termcap* and *curses*, thumbnailing images, and graphing data.

The last portion of the book is devoted to interacting with other programs and services. Chapter 16, *Process Management and Communication*, is about running other programs and collecting their output, handling zombie processes, named pipes, signal management, and sharing variables between running programs. Chapter 17, *Sockets*, shows how to establish stream connections or use datagrams to create low-level networking applications for client-server programming. Chapter 18, *Internet Services*, is about higher-level protocols such as mail, FTP, Usenet news, XML-RPC, and SOAP. Chapter 19, *CGI Programming*, contains recipes for processing web forms, trapping their errors, avoiding shell escapes for security, managing cookies, shopping cart techniques, and saving forms to files or pipes. Chapter 20, *Web Automation*, covers non-interactive uses of the Web, such as fetching web pages, automating form submissions in a script, extracting URLs from a web page, removing HTML tags, finding fresh or stale links, and parsing HTML. Chapter 21, *mod_perl*, introduces mod_perl, the Perl interpreter embedded in Apache. It covers fetching form parameters, issuing redirections, customizing Apache's logging, handling authentication, and advanced templating with Mason and the Template Toolkit. Finally, Chapter 22, *XML* is about the ubiquitous data format XML and includes recipes such as validating XML, parsing XML into events and trees, and transforming XML into other formats.

What's New in This Edition

The book you're holding is thicker than its previous edition of five years ago—about 200 pages thicker. New material is spread across more than 80 entirely new recipes plus over 100 existing recipes that were substantially updated since the first edition. You'll also find two new chapters: one on mod_perl, Perl's interface to the popular Apache web server; the other on XML, an increasingly important standard for exchanging structured data.

Growth in this book reflects growth in Perl itself, from Version 5.004 in the first edition to v5.8.1 in this one. Syntactic changes to the core language are nevertheless comparatively few. Some include the spiffy our keyword to replace the crufty use vars construct for declaring global variables, fancier forms of open to disambiguate filenames with strange characters in them, and automatic allocation of anonymous filehandles into undefined scalar variables. We've updated our solutions and code examples to reflect these changes where it made sense to make use of the new features.

Several of Perl's major subsystems have been completely overhauled for improved functionality, stability, and portability. Some of these are relatively isolated, like the subsystems for threading (see Recipe 17.14) and for safe signals (see Recipe 16.17). Their applications are usually confined to systems programming.

More sweeping are the changes to Perl and to this book that stem from integrated support for Unicode characters. The areas most profoundly affected are strings (now with multibyte characters) and I/O (now with stackable encoding layers), so Chapters 1 and 8 include new introductory material to orient you to these sometimes confusing topics. These chapters also provide the bulk of recipes dealing with those specific topics, but this fundamental shift touches many more recipes throughout the book.

Another growth area for this book and Perl has been the welcome proliferation of many highly used and highly useful modules now released standard with the Perl core. Previously, these modules had to be separately located, downloaded, configured, built, tested, and installed. Now that they're included in the standard distribution, that's all taken care of when installing Perl itself.

Some new core modules are really pragmas that alter Perl's compilation or runtime environment, as demonstrated in Recipes like 1.21 ("Constant Variables"), 12.3 ("Delaying use Until Runtime"), and 12.15 ("Customizing Warnings"). Some are programmer tools to aid code development and debugging, like modules shown in Recipes 11.11 ("Printing Data Structures"), 11.13 ("Storing Data Structures to Disk"), 11.15 ("Coping with Circular Data Structures Using Weak References"), and 22.2 ("Parsing XML into a DOM Tree"). Others augment basic operations available on core data types, like those shown in Recipes 2.1 ("Checking Whether a String Is a Valid Number"), 4.13 ("Finding the First List Element That Passes a Test"), 4.18 ("Randomizing an Array"), 5.3 ("Creating a Hash with Immutable Keys or Values"), 8.7 ("Randomizing All Lines"), and 11.15 ("Coping with Circular Data Structures Using Weak References"). Finally, the networking modules have at last made their way into the core distribution, as seen throughout Chapter 18. We've probably not seen the last of this inward migration of modules.

Platform Notes

This book was developed using Perl release v5.8.1. That means major release 5, minor release 8, and patch level 1. We tested most programs and examples under BSD, Linux, and SunOS, but that doesn't mean they'll work only on those systems. Perl was *designed* for platform independence. When you use Perl as a general-purpose programming language, employing basic operations like variables, patterns, subroutines, and high-level I/O, your program should work the same everywhere that Perl runs—which is just about everywhere. The first two-thirds of this book uses Perl for general-purpose programming.

Perl was originally conceived as a high-level, cross-platform language for systems programming. Although it has long since expanded beyond its original domain, Perl continues to be heavily used for systems programming, both on its native Unix systems and elsewhere. Most recipes in Chapters 14 through 18 deal with classic systems programming. For maximum portability in this area, we've mainly focused on open systems as defined by the Portable Operating System Interface (POSIX), which includes nearly every form of Unix and numerous other systems as well. Most recipes should run with little or no modification on any POSIX system.

You can still use Perl for systems programming work even on non-POSIX systems by using vendor-specific modules, but these are not covered in this book. That's because they're not portable—and to be perfectly forward, because we have no such systems at our disposal. Consult the documentation that came with your port of Perl for any proprietary modules that may have been included. The *perlport*(1) manpage is a good start; its SEE ALSO section points to per-platform documentation, such as *perlmacos*(1) and *perlvms*(1).

But don't worry. Many recipes for systems programming should work on non-POSIX systems as well, especially those dealing with databases, networking, and web interaction. That's because the modules used for those areas hide platform dependencies. The principal exception is those few recipes and programs that rely upon multitasking constructs, notably the powerful fork function, standard on POSIX systems, but seldom on others. Mac OS X now supports fork natively, however, and even on Windows systems Perl now emulates that syscall remarkably well.

When we needed structured files, we picked the convenient Unix */etc/passwd* database; when we needed a text file to read, we picked */etc/motd*; and when we needed a program to produce output, we picked *who*(1). These were merely chosen to illustrate the principles—the principles work whether or not your system has these files and programs.

Other Books

If you'd like to learn more about Perl, here are some related publications that we (somewhat sheepishly) recommend:

Programming Perl, by Larry Wall, Tom Christiansen, and Jon Orwant; O'Reilly & Associates (Third Edition, 2000). This book is indispensable for every Perl programmer. Coauthored by Perl's creator, this classic reference is the authoritative guide to Perl's syntax, functions, modules, references, invocation options, and much more.

Mastering Algorithms with Perl, by Jon Orwant, Jarkko Hietaniemi, and John Macdonald; O'Reilly & Associates (2000). All the useful techniques from a CS algorithms course, but without the painful proofs. This book covers fundamental and useful algorithms in the fields of graphs, text, sets, and more.

Mastering Regular Expressions, by Jeffrey Friedl; O'Reilly & Associates (Second Edition, 2002). This book is dedicated to explaining regular expressions from a practical perspective. It not only covers general regular expressions and Perl patterns well, it also compares and contrasts these with those used in other popular languages.

Object Oriented Perl, by Damian Conway; Manning (1999). For beginning as well as advanced OO programmers, this book explains common and esoteric techniques for writing powerful object systems in Perl.

Learning Perl, by Randal Schwartz and Tom Phoenix; O'Reilly & Associates (Third Edition, 2001). A tutorial introduction to Perl for folks who are already programmers and who are interested in learning Perl from scratch. It's a good starting point if this book is over your head. Erik Olson refurbished this book for Windows systems, called *Learning Perl for Win32 Systems*.

Programming the Perl DBI, by Tim Bunce and Alligator Descartes; O'Reilly & Associates (2000). The only book on Perl's relational database interface, by the author of the DBI module.

CGI Programming with Perl, by Scott Guelich, Shishir Gundavaram, and Gunther Birznieks; O'Reilly & Associates (Second Edition, 2000). This is a solid introduction to the world of CGI programming.

Writing Apache Modules with Perl and C, by Lincoln Stein and Doug MacEachern; O'Reilly & Associates (1999). This guide to web programming teaches you how to extend the capabilities of the Apache web server, especially using the turbocharged mod_perl for fast CGI scripts and via the Perl-accessible Apache API.

Practical mod_perl, by Stas Bekman and Eric Cholet; O'Reilly & Associates (2003). A comprehensive guide to installing, configuring, and developing with mod_perl. This book goes into corners of mod_perl programming that no other book dares to touch.

The mod_perl Developer's Cookbook, by Geoff Young, Paul Lindner, and Randy Kobes; SAMS (2002). Written in a similar style to the Cookbook you hold in your hand, this book belongs on every mod_perl developer's desk. It covers almost every task a mod_perl developer might want to perform.

Beyond the Perl-related publications listed here, the following books came in handy when writing this book. They were used for reference, consultation, and inspiration.

The Art of Computer Programming, by Donald Knuth, Volumes I-III: "Fundamental Algorithms," "Seminumerical Algorithms," and "Sorting and Searching"; Addison-Wesley (Third Edition, 1998).

Introduction to Algorithms, by Thomas H. Cormen, Charles E. Leiserson, and Ronald L. Rivest; MIT Press and McGraw-Hill (1990).

Algorithms in C, by Robert Sedgewick; Addison-Wesley (1992).

The Art of Mathematics, by Jerry P. King; Plenum (1992).

The Elements of Programming Style, by Brian W. Kernighan and P.J. Plauger; McGraw-Hill (1988).

The UNIX Programming Environment, by Brian W. Kernighan and Rob Pike; Prentice-Hall (1984).

POSIX Programmer's Guide, by Donald Lewine; O'Reilly & Associates (1991).

Advanced Programming in the UNIX Environment, by W. Richard Stevens; Addison-Wesley (1992).

TCP/IP Illustrated, by W. Richard Stevens, et al., Volumes I–III; Addison-Wesley (1992-1996).

HTML: The Definitive Guide, by Chuck Musciano and Bill Kennedy; O'Reilly & Associates (Third Edition, 1998).

Official Guide to Programming with CGI.pm, by Lincoln Stein; John Wiley & Sons (1997).

Web Client Programming with Perl, by Clinton Wong; O'Reilly & Associates (1997).

The New Fowler's Modern English Usage, edited by R.W. Burchfield; Oxford (Third Edition, 1996).

Conventions Used in This Book

Programming Conventions

We give lots of examples, most of which are pieces of code that should go into a larger program. Some examples are complete programs, which you can recognize because they begin with a #! line. We start nearly all of our longer programs with:

```
#!/usr/bin/perl -w
use strict;
```

or else the newer:

```
#!/usr/bin/perl
use strict;
use warnings;
```

Still other examples are things to be typed on a command line. We've used % to show the shell prompt:

```
% perl -e 'print "Hello, world.\n"'
Hello, world.
```

This style represents a standard Unix command line, where single quotes represent the "most quoted" form. Quoting and wildcard conventions on other systems vary. For example, many command-line interpreters under MS-DOS and VMS require double quotes instead of single ones to group arguments with spaces or wildcards in them.

Typesetting Conventions

The following typographic conventions are used in this book:

Bold

is used exclusively for command-line switches. This allows one to distinguish for example, between the **-w** warnings switch and the -w filetest operator.

Italic

is used for URLs, manpages, pathnames, and programs. New terms are also italicized when they first appear in the text.

`Constant Width`

is used for function and method names and their arguments; in examples to show text that you enter verbatim; and in regular text to show literal code.

`Constant Width Bold Italic`

is used in examples to show output produced.

 Indicates a warning or caution.

Documentation Conventions

The most up-to-date and complete documentation about Perl is included with Perl itself. If typeset and printed, this massive anthology would use more than a thousand pages of printed paper, greatly contributing to global deforestation. Fortunately, you don't have to print it out, because it's available in a convenient and searchable electronic form.

When we refer to a "manpage" in this book, we're talking about this set of online manuals. The name is purely a convention; you don't need a Unix-style man program to read them. The *perldoc* command distributed with Perl also works, and you may even have the manpages installed as HTML pages, especially on non-Unix systems. Plus, once you know where they're installed, you can grep them directly.* The HTML version of the manpages is available on the Web at *http://www.perl.com/CPAN/doc/manual/html/*.

When we refer to non-Perl documentation, as in "See *kill*(2) in your system manual," this refers to the *kill* manpage from section 2 of the *Unix Programmer's Manual* (system calls). These won't be available on non-Unix systems, but that's probably okay,

---

* If your system doesn't have *grep*, use the *tcgrep* program supplied at the end of Chapter 6.

because you couldn't use them there anyway. If you really do need the documentation for a system call or library function, many organizations have put their manpages on the Web; a quick search of Google for *crypt(3) manual* will find many copies.

We'd Like to Hear from You

We have tested and verified the information in this book to the best of our ability, but you may find that features have changed (which may in fact resemble bugs). Please let us know about any errors you find, as well as your suggestions for future editions, by writing to:

O'Reilly & Associates, Inc.
1005 Gravenstein Highway North
Sebastopol, CA 95472
(800) 998-9938 (in the U.S. or Canada)
(707) 829-0515 (international or local)
(707) 829-0104 (FAX)

You can also send us messages electronically. To be put on the mailing list or request a catalog, send email to:

info@oreilly.com

To ask technical questions or comment on the book, send email to:

bookquestions@oreilly.com

There is a web site for the book, where we'll list errata and plans for future editions. Here you'll also find source code for the book's examples available for download so you don't have to type them in yourself. You can access this page at:

http://www.oreilly.com/catalog/perlckbk2/

For more information about this book and others, see the O'Reilly web site:

http://www.oreilly.com/

Acknowledgments for the First Edition

This book wouldn't exist but for a legion of people standing, knowing and unknowing, behind the authors. At the head of this legion would have to be our editor, Linda Mui, carrot on a stick in one hand and a hot poker in the other. She was great.

As the author of Perl, Larry Wall was our ultimate reality check. He made sure we weren't documenting things he was planning to change and helped out on wording and style.* If now and then you think you're hearing Larry's voice in this book, you probably are.

---

* And footnotes.

Larry's wife, Gloria, a literary critic by trade, shocked us by reading through every single word—and actually liking most of them. Together with Sharon Hopkins, resident Perl Poetess, she helped us rein in our admittedly nearly insatiable tendency to produce pretty prose sentences that could only be charitably described as lying somewhere between the inscrutably complex and the hopelessly arcane, eventually rendering the meandering muddle into something legible even to those whose native tongues were neither PDP-11 assembler nor Mediæval Spanish.

Our three most assiduous reviewers, Mark-Jason Dominus, Jon Orwant, and Abigail, have worked with us on this book nearly as long as we've been writing it. Their rigorous standards, fearsome intellects, and practical experience in Perl applications have been of invaluable assistance. Doug Edwards methodically stress-tested every piece of code from the first seven chapters of the book, finding subtle border cases no one else ever thought about. Other major reviewers include Andy Dougherty, Andy Oram, Brent Halsey, Bryan Buus, Gisle Aas, Graham Barr, Jeff Haemer, Jeffrey Friedl, Lincoln Stein, Mark Mielke, Martin Brech, Matthias Neeracher, Mike Stok, Nate Patwardhan, Paul Grassie, Peter Prymmer, Raphaël Manfredi, and Rod Whitby.

And this is just the beginning. Part of what makes Perl fun is the sense of community and sharing it seems to engender. Many selfless individuals lent us their technical expertise. Some read through complete chapters in formal review. Others provided insightful answers to brief technical questions when we were stuck on something outside our own domain. A few even sent us code. Here's a partial list of these helpful people: Aaron Harsh, Ali Rayl, Alligator Descartes, Andrew Hume, Andrew Strebkov, Andy Wardley, Ashton MacAndrews, Ben Gertzfield, Benjamin Holzman, Brad Hughes, Chaim Frenkel, Charles Bailey, Chris Nandor, Clinton Wong, Dan Klein, Dan Sugalski, Daniel Grisinger, Dennis Taylor, Doug MacEachern, Douglas Davenport, Drew Eckhardt, Dylan Northrup, Eric Eisenhart, Eric Watt Forste, Greg Bacon, Gurusamy Sarathy, Henry Spencer, Jason Ornstein, Jason Stewart, Joel Noble, Jonathan Cohen, Jonathan Scott Duff, Josh Purinton, Julian Anderson, Keith Winstein, Ken Lunde, Kirby Hughes, Larry Rosler, Les Peters, Mark Hess, Mark James, Martin Brech, Mary Koutsky, Michael Parker, Nick Ing-Simmons, Paul Marquess, Peter Collinson, Peter Osel, Phil Beauchamp, Piers Cawley, Randal Schwartz, Rich Rauenzahn, Richard Allan, Rocco Caputo, Roderick Schertler, Roland Walker, Ronan Waide, Stephen Lidie, Steven Owens, Sullivan Beck, Tim Bunce, Todd Miller, Troy Denkinger, and Willy Grimm.

And let's not forget Perl itself, without which this book could never have been written. Appropriately enough, we used Perl to build endless small tools to help produce this book. Perl tools converted our text in pod format into *troff* for displaying and review and into FrameMaker for production. Another Perl program ran syntax checks on every piece of code in the book. The Tk extension to Perl was used to build a graphical tool to shuffle around recipes using drag-and-drop. Beyond these, we also built innumerable smaller tools for tasks like checking RCS locks, finding duplicate words, detecting certain kinds of grammatical errors, managing mail folders with feedback from reviewers, creating program indices and tables of contents, and running text searches that crossed line boundaries or were restricted to certain sections—just to name a few. Some of these tools found their way into the same book they were used on.

Tom

Thanks first of all to Larry and Gloria for sacrificing some of their European vacation to groom the many nits out of this manuscript, and to my other friends and family—Bryan, Sharon, Brent, Todd, and Drew—for putting up with me over the last couple of years and being subjected to incessant proofreadings.

I'd like to thank Nathan for holding up despite the stress of his weekly drives, my piquant vegetarian cooking and wit, and his getting stuck researching the topics I so diligently avoided.

I'd like to thank those largely unsung titans in our field—Dennis, Linus, Kirk, Eric, and Rich—who were all willing to take the time to answer my niggling operating system and *troff* questions. Their wonderful advice and anecdotes aside, without their tremendous work in the field, this book could never have been written.

Thanks also to my instructors who sacrificed themselves to travel to perilous places like New Jersey to teach Perl in my stead. I'd like to thank Tim O'Reilly and Frank Willison first for being talked into publishing this book, and second for letting time-to-market take a back seat to time-to-quality. Thanks also to Linda, our shamelessly honest editor, for shepherding dangerously rabid sheep through the eye of a release needle.

Most of all, I want to thank my mother, Mary, for tearing herself away from her work in prairie restoration and teaching high school computer and biological sciences to keep both my business and domestic life in smooth working order long enough for me to research and write this book.

Finally, I'd like to thank Johann Sebastian Bach, who was for me a boundless font of perspective, poise, and inspiration—a therapy both mental and physical. I am certain that forevermore the Cookbook will evoke for me the sounds of BWV 849, now indelibly etched into the wetware of head and hand.

Nat

Without my family's love and patience, I'd be baiting hooks in a 10-foot swell instead of mowing my lawn in suburban America. Thank you! My friends have taught me much: Jules, Amy, Raj, Mike, Kef, Sai, Robert, Ewan, Pondy, Mark, and Andy. I owe a debt of gratitude to the denizens of Nerdsholm, who gave sound technical advice and introduced me to my wife (they didn't give me sound technical advice on her, though). Thanks also to my employer, Front Range Internet, for a day job I don't want to quit.

Tom was a great co-author. Without him, this book would be nasty, brutish, and short. Finally, I have to thank Jenine. We'd been married a year when I accepted the offer to write, and we've barely seen each other since then. Nobody will savour the final full-stop in this sentence more than she.

Acknowledgments for the Second Edition

We would like to thank our many tech reviewers, who gave generously of their time and knowledge so that we might look better. Some were formal reviewers who painstakingly plodded through endless drafts and revisions, while others were casual comrades roped into reading small excerpts related to their own particular expertise or interest. The bugs you don't find in this book are thanks to them. Those you do find were probably introduced after they reviewed it.

Just a few of these selfless people were Adam Maccabee Trachtenberg, Rafael Garcia-Suarez, Ask Björn Hansen, Mark-Jason Dominus, Abhijit Menon-Sen, Jarkko Hietaniemi, Benjamin Goldberg, Aaron Straup Cope, Tony Stubblebine, Michel Rodriguez, Nick Ing-Simmons, Geoffrey Young, Douglas Wilson, Paul Kulchenko, Jeffrey Friedl, Arthur Bergman, Autrijus Tang, Matt Sergeant, Steve Marvell, Damian Conway, Sean M. Burke, Elaine Ashton, Steve Lidie, Ken Williams, Robert Spier, Chris Nandor, Brent Halsey, Matthew Free, Rocco Caputo, Robin Berjon, Adam Turoff, Chip Turner, David Sklar, Mike Sierra, Dave Rolsky, Kip Hampton, Chris Fedde, Graham Barr, Jon Orwant, Rich Bowen, Mike Stok, Tim Bunce, Rob Brown, Dan Brian, Gisle Aas, and Abigail.

We'd also like to thank our patient and persistent editor, Linda Mui, who ran serious risk of getting herself committed as she tried to wrestle "the final edits" from us.

Tom

I would like to thank Larry Wall for making the programming world (and several others) a better place for all of us, Nathan for documenting the undocumented, and our editor, Linda Mui, for her indefatigable patience at herding her author cats of the Schrödinger clan ever onward. This book would not exist but for all three of them.

I would especially like to thank someone who is no longer here to read these words in print, words he would otherwise himself have shepherded: O'Reilly's longtime editor-in-chief and my friend, Frank Willison, gone from us two years now. His many erudite epistles are a thing of legend, carefully crafted treasures more dear to any writer than finest gold. Over our years of working together, Frank was a constant source of personal inspiration and encouragement. His easygoing cheer and charm, his broad learning and interests, and his sparkling wit—sometimes subtle, sometimes hilarious, and often both—made him more deserving of being called avuncular than anyone else I have ever known, and as such do I miss him. Thank you, Frank, wherever you are.

Nat

Henry David Thoreau wrote, "What is commonly called friendship is only a little more honor among rogues." If that be true, I have two honorable rogues to thank: Jon Orwant, who engineered my job at O'Reilly & Associates; and Linda Mui, who helped me keep it.

As with the first edition, the book in your hands wouldn't be there without Tom's drive, attention to detail, and willingness to tackle the hard stuff. Thanks for taking the Unicode bullet, Tom.

And finally, my family. Jenine nearly became a solo parent while I worked on this book. My heart broke when William sadly told a friend, "My daddy works and works—all day and all night," and again when one of Raley's first two-word sentences was "Daddy work." Thank you all.

## CHAPTER 1

Strings

He multiplieth words without knowledge.
—Job 35:16

1.0   Introduction

Many programming languages force you to work at an uncomfortably low level. You think in lines, but your language wants you to deal with pointers. You think in strings, but it wants you to deal with bytes. Such a language can drive you to distraction. Don't despair; Perl isn't a low-level language, so lines and strings are easy to handle.

Perl was *designed* for easy but powerful text manipulation. In fact, Perl can manipulate text in so many ways that they can't all be described in one chapter. Check out other chapters for recipes on text processing. In particular, see Chapters 6 and 8, which discuss interesting techniques not covered here.

Perl's fundamental unit for working with data is the scalar, that is, single values stored in single (scalar) variables. Scalar variables hold strings, numbers, and references. Array and hash variables hold lists or associations of scalars, respectively. References are used for referring to values indirectly, not unlike pointers in low-level languages. Numbers are usually stored in your machine's double-precision floating-point notation. Strings in Perl may be of any length, within the limits of your machine's virtual memory, and can hold any arbitrary data you care to put there—even binary data containing null bytes.

A string in Perl is not an array of characters—nor of bytes, for that matter. You cannot use array subscripting on a string to address one of its characters; use substr for that. Like all data types in Perl, strings grow on demand. Space is reclaimed by Perl's garbage collection system when no longer used, typically when the variables have gone out of scope or when the expression in which they were used has been evaluated. In other words, memory management is already taken care of, so you don't have to worry about it.

A scalar value is either defined or undefined. If defined, it may hold a string, number, or reference. The only undefined value is undef. All other values are defined, even numeric 0 and the empty string. Definedness is not the same as Boolean truth, though; to check whether a value is defined, use the defined function. Boolean truth has a specialized meaning, tested with operators such as && and || or in an if or while block's test condition.

Two defined strings are false: the empty string ("") and a string of length one containing the digit zero ("0"). All other defined values (e.g., "false", 15, and \$x) are true. You might be surprised to learn that "0" is false, but this is due to Perl's on-demand conversion between strings and numbers. The values 0., 0.00, and 0.0000000 are all numbers and are therefore false when unquoted, since the number zero in any of its guises is always false. However, those three values ("0.", "0.00", and "0.0000000") are *true* when used as literal quoted strings in your program code or when they're read from the command line, an environment variable, or an input file.

This is seldom an issue, since conversion is automatic when the value is used numerically. If it has never been used numerically, though, and you just test whether it's true or false, you might get an unexpected answer—Boolean tests never force any sort of conversion. Adding 0 to the variable makes Perl explicitly convert the string to a number:

```
print "Gimme a number: ";
0.00000
chomp($n = <STDIN>);   # $n now holds "0.00000";

print "The value $n is ", $n ? "TRUE" : "FALSE", "\n";
That value 0.00000 is TRUE

$n += 0;
print "The value $n is now ", $n ? "TRUE" : "FALSE", "\n";
That value 0 is now FALSE
```

The undef value behaves like the empty string ("") when used as a string, 0 when used as a number, and the null reference when used as a reference. But in all three possible cases, it's false. Using an undefined value where Perl expects a defined value will trigger a runtime warning message on STDERR if you've enabled warnings. Merely asking whether something is true or false demands no particular value, so this is exempt from warnings. Some operations do not trigger warnings when used on variables holding undefined values. These include the autoincrement and autodecrement operators, ++ and --, and the addition and concatenation assignment operators, += and .= ("plus-equals" and "dot-equals").

Specify strings in your program using single quotes, double quotes, the quoting operators q// and qq//, or here documents. No matter which notation you use, string literals are one of two possible flavors: interpolated or uninterpolated. Interpolation governs whether variable references and special sequences are expanded. Most are interpolated by default, such as in patterns (/regex/) and running commands ($x = `cmd`).

Where special characters are recognized, preceding any special character with a backslash renders that character mundane; that is, it becomes a literal. This is often referred to as "escaping" or "backslash escaping."

Using single quotes is the canonical way to get an uninterpolated string literal. Three special sequences are still recognized: ' to terminate the string, \' to represent a single quote, and \\ to represent a backslash in the string.

```
$string = '\n';                    # two characters, \ and an n
$string = 'Jon \'Maddog\' Orwant'; # literal single quotes
```

Double quotes interpolate variables (but not function calls—see Recipe 1.15 to find how to do this) and expand backslash escapes. These include "\n" (newline), "\033" (the character with octal value 33), "\cJ" (Ctrl-J), "\x1B" (the character with hex value 0x1B), and so on. The full list of these is given in the *perlop*(1) manpage and the section on "Specific Characters" in Chapter 5 of *Programming Perl*.

```
$string = "\n";                    # a "newline" character
$string = "Jon \"Maddog\" Orwant"; # literal double quotes
```

If there are no backslash escapes or variables to expand within the string, it makes no difference which flavor of quotes you use. When choosing between writing 'this' and writing "this", some Perl programmers prefer to use double quotes so that the strings stand out. This also avoids the slight risk of having single quotes mistaken for backquotes by readers of your code. It makes no difference to Perl, and it might help readers.

The q// and qq// quoting operators allow arbitrary delimiters on interpolated and uninterpolated literals, respectively, corresponding to single- and double-quoted strings. For an uninterpolated string literal that contains single quotes, it's easier to use q// than to escape all single quotes with backslashes:

```
$string = 'Jon \'Maddog\' Orwant';  # embedded single quotes
$string = q/Jon 'Maddog' Orwant/;    # same thing, but more legible
```

Choose the same character for both delimiters, as we just did with /, or pair any of the following four sets of bracketing characters:

```
$string = q[Jon 'Maddog' Orwant];   # literal single quotes
$string = q{Jon 'Maddog' Orwant};   # literal single quotes
$string = q(Jon 'Maddog' Orwant);   # literal single quotes
$string = q<Jon 'Maddog' Orwant>;   # literal single quotes
```

Here documents are a notation borrowed from the shell used to quote a large chunk of text. The text can be interpreted as single-quoted, double-quoted, or even as commands to be executed, depending on how you quote the terminating identifier. Uninterpolated here documents do not expand the three backslash sequences the way single-quoted literals normally do. Here we double-quote two lines with a here document:

```
$a = <<"EOF";
This is a multiline here document
```

```
    terminated by EOF on a line by itself
    EOF
```

Notice there's no semicolon after the terminating EOF. Here documents are covered in more detail in Recipe 1.16.

The Universal Character Code

As far as the computer is concerned, all data is just a series of individual numbers, each a string of bits. Even text strings are just sequences of numeric codes interpreted as characters by programs like web browsers, mailers, printing programs, and editors.

Back when memory sizes were far smaller and memory prices far more dear, programmers would go to great lengths to save memory. Strategies such as stuffing six characters into one 36-bit word or jamming three characters into one 16-bit word were common. Even today, the numeric codes used for characters usually aren't longer than 7 or 8 bits, which are the lengths you find in ASCII and Latin1, respectively.

That doesn't leave many bits per character—and thus, not many characters. Consider an image file with 8-bit color. You're limited to 256 different colors in your palette. Similarly, with characters stored as individual *octets* (an octet is an 8-bit byte), a document can usually have no more than 256 different letters, punctuation marks, and symbols in it.

ASCII, being the *American* Standard Code for Information Interchange, was of limited utility outside the United States, since it covered only the characters needed for a slightly stripped-down dialect of American English. Consequently, many countries invented their own incompatible 8-bit encodings built upon 7-bit ASCII. Conflicting schemes for assigning numeric codes to characters sprang up, all reusing the same limited range. That meant the same number could mean a different character in different systems and that the same character could have been assigned a different number in different systems.

Locales were an early attempt to address this and other language- and country-specific issues, but they didn't work out so well for character set selection. They're still reasonable for purposes unrelated to character sets, such as local preferences for monetary units, date and time formatting, and even collating sequences. But they are of far less utility for reusing the same 8-bit namespace for different character sets.

That's because if you wanted to produce a document that used Latin, Greek, and Cyrillic characters, you were in for big trouble, since the same numeric code would be a different character under each system. For example, character number 196 is a Latin capital A with a diaeresis above it in ISO 8859-1 (Latin1); under ISO 8859-7, that same numeric code represents a Greek capital delta. So a program interpreting numeric character codes in the ISO 8859-1 locale would see one character, but under the ISO 8859-7 locale, it would see something totally different.

This makes it hard to combine different character sets in the same document. Even if you did cobble something together, few programs could work with that document's text. To know what characters you had, you'd have to know what system they were in, and you couldn't easily mix systems. If you guessed wrong, you'd get a jumbled mess on your screen, or worse.

Unicode Support in Perl

Enter Unicode.

Unicode attempts to unify all character sets in the entire world, including many symbols and even fictional character sets. Under Unicode, different characters have different numeric codes, called *code points*.

Mixed-language documents are now easy, whereas before they weren't even possible. You no longer have just 128 or 256 possible characters per document. With Unicode you can have tens of thousands (and more) of different characters all jumbled together in the same document without confusion.

The problem of mixing, say, an Ä with a Δ evaporates. The first character, formally named "LATIN CAPITAL LETTER A WITH DIAERESIS" under Unicode, is assigned the code point U+00C4 (that's the Unicode preferred notation). The second, a "GREEK CAPITAL LETTER DELTA", is now at code point U+0394. With different characters always assigned different code points, there's no longer any conflict.

Perl has supported Unicode since v5.6 or so, but it wasn't until the v5.8 release that Unicode support was generally considered robust and usable. This by no coincidence corresponded to the introduction of I/O layers and their support for encodings into Perl. These are discussed in more detail in Chapter 8.

All Perl's string functions and operators, including those used for pattern matching, now operate on characters instead of octets. If you ask for a string's length, Perl reports how many characters are in that string, not how many bytes are in it. If you extract the first three characters of a string using substr, the result may or may not be three bytes. You don't know, and you shouldn't care, either. One reason not to care about the particular underlying bytewise representation is that if you have to pay attention to it, you're probably looking too closely. It shouldn't matter, really—but if it does, this might mean that Perl's implementation still has a few bumps in it. We're working on that.

Because characters with code points above 256 are supported, the chr function is no longer restricted to arguments under 256, nor is ord restricted to returning an integer smaller than that. Ask for chr(0x394), for example, and you'll get a Greek capital delta: Δ.

```
$char = chr(0x394);
$code = ord($char);
```

```
printf "char %s is code %d, %#04x\n", $char, $code, $code;
```

char Δ is code 916, 0x394

If you test the length of that string, it will say 1, because it's just one character. Notice how we said character; we didn't say anything about its length in bytes. Certainly the internal representation requires more than just 8 bits for a numeric code that big. But you the programmer are dealing with characters as abstractions, not as physical octets. Low-level details like that are best left up to Perl.

You shouldn't think of characters and bytes as the same. Programmers who interchange bytes and characters are guilty of the same class of sin as C programmers who blithely interchange integers and pointers. Even though the underlying representations may happen to coincide on some platforms, this is just a coincidence, and conflating abstract interfaces with physical implementations will always come back to haunt you, eventually.

You have several ways to put Unicode characters into Perl literals. If you're lucky enough to have a text editor that lets you enter Unicode directly into your Perl program, you can inform Perl you've done this via the use utf8 pragma. Another way is to use \x escapes in Perl interpolated strings to indicate a character by its code point in hex, as in \xC4. Characters with code points above 0xFF require more than two hex digits, so these must be enclosed in braces.

```
print "\xC4 and \x{0394} look different\n";
```

char Ä and Δ look different\n

Recipe 1.5 describes how to use charnames to put \N{*NAME*} escapes in string literals, such as \N{GREEK CAPITAL LETTER DELTA}, \N{greek:Delta}, or even just \N{Delta} to indicate a Δ character.

That's enough to get started using Unicode in Perl alone, but getting Perl to interact properly with other programs requires a bit more.

Using the old single-byte encodings like ASCII or ISO 8859-*n*, when you wrote out a character whose numeric code was *NN*, a single byte with numeric code *NN* would appear. What actually appeared depended on which fonts were available, your current locale setting, and quite a few other factors. But under Unicode, this exact duplication of logical character numbers (code points) into physical bytes emitted no longer applies. Instead, they must be encoded in any of several available output formats.

Internally, Perl uses a format called UTF-8, but many other encoding formats for Unicode exist, and Perl can work with those, too. The use encoding pragma tells Perl in which encoding your script itself has been written, or which encoding the standard filehandles should use. The use open pragma can set encoding defaults for all handles. Special arguments to open or to binmode specify the encoding format for that particular handle. The **-C** command-line flag is a shortcut to set the encoding on all (or just standard) handles, plus the program arguments themselves. The environment variables `PERLIO`, `PERL_ENCODING`, and `PERL_UNICODE` all give Perl various sorts of hints related to these matters.

1.1 Accessing Substrings

Problem

You want to access or modify just a portion of a string, not the whole thing. For instance, you've read a fixed-width record and want to extract individual fields.

Solution

The `substr` function lets you read from and write to specific portions of the string.

```
$value = substr($string, $offset, $count);
$value = substr($string, $offset);

substr($string, $offset, $count) = $newstring;
substr($string, $offset, $count, $newstring);  # same as previous
substr($string, $offset)          = $newtail;
```

The `unpack` function gives only read access, but is faster when you have many substrings to extract.

```
# get a 5-byte string, skip 3 bytes,
# then grab two 8-byte strings, then the rest;
# (NB: only works on ASCII data, not Unicode)
($leading, $s1, $s2, $trailing) =
    unpack("A5 x3 A8 A8 A*", $data);

# split at 5-byte boundaries
@fivers = unpack("A5" x (length($string)/5), $string);

# chop string into individual single-byte characters
@chars  = unpack("A1" x length($string), $string);
```

Discussion

Strings are a basic data type; they aren't arrays of a basic data type. Instead of using array subscripting to access individual characters as you sometimes do in other programming languages, in Perl you use functions like `unpack` or `substr` to access individual characters or a portion of the string.

The offset argument to `substr` indicates the start of the substring you're interested in, counting from the front if positive and from the end if negative. If the offset is 0, the substring starts at the beginning. The count argument is the length of the substring.

```
$string = "This is what you have";
#          +012345678901234567890  Indexing forwards  (left to right)
```

```
#            109876543210987654321- Indexing backwards (right to left)
#               note that 0 means 10 or 20, etc. above

$first  = substr($string, 0, 1);   # "T"
$start  = substr($string, 5, 2);   # "is"
$rest   = substr($string, 13);     # "you have"
$last   = substr($string, -1);     # "e"
$end    = substr($string, -4);     # "have"
$piece  = substr($string, -8, 3);  # "you"
```

You can do more than just look at parts of the string with substr; you can actually change them. That's because substr is a particularly odd kind of function—an *lvaluable* one, that is, a function whose return value may be itself assigned a value. (For the record, the others are vec, pos, and keys. If you squint, local, my, and our can also be viewed as lvaluable functions.)

```
$string = "This is what you have";
print $string;
This is what you have
substr($string, 5, 2) = "wasn't"; # change "is" to "wasn't"
This wasn't what you have
substr($string, -12)  = "ondrous";# "This wasn't wondrous"
This wasn't wondrous
substr($string, 0, 1) = "";       # delete first character
his wasn't wondrous
substr($string, -10)  = "";       # delete last 10 characters
his wasn'
```

Use the =~ operator and the s///, m//, or tr/// operators in conjunction with substr to make them affect only that portion of the string.

```
# you can test substrings with =~
if (substr($string, -10) =~ /pattern/) {
        print "Pattern matches in last 10 characters\n";
}

# substitute "at" for "is", restricted to first five characters
substr($string, 0, 5) =~ s/is/at/g;
```

You can even swap values by using several substrs on each side of an assignment:

```
# exchange the first and last letters in a string
$a = "make a hat";
(substr($a,0,1), substr($a,-1)) =
(substr($a,-1),  substr($a,0,1));
print $a;
take a ham
```

Although unpack is not lvaluable, it is considerably faster than substr when you extract numerous values all at once. Specify a format describing the layout of the record to unpack. For positioning, use lowercase "x" with a count to skip forward some number of bytes, an uppercase "X" with a count to skip backward some number of bytes, and an "@" to skip to an absolute byte offset within the record. (If the data contains Unicode strings, be careful with those three: they're strictly byte-oriented, and moving around by bytes within multibyte data is perilous at best.)

```
# extract column with unpack
$a = "To be or not to be";
$b = unpack("x6 A6", $a);  # skip 6, grab 6
print $b;
or not

($b, $c) = unpack("x6 A2 X5 A2", $a); # forward 6, grab 2; backward 5, grab 2
print "$b\n$c\n";
or
be
```

Sometimes you prefer to think of your data as being cut up at specific columns. For example, you might want to place cuts right before positions 8, 14, 20, 26, and 30. Those are the column numbers where each field begins. Although you could calculate that the proper unpack format is "A7 A6 A6 A6 A4 A*", this is too much mental strain for the virtuously lazy Perl programmer. Let Perl figure it out for you. Use the cut2fmt function:

```
sub cut2fmt {
    my(@positions) = @_;
    my $template   = '';
    my $lastpos    = 1;
    foreach $place (@positions) {
        $template .= "A" . ($place - $lastpos) . " ";
        $lastpos   = $place;
    }
    $template .= "A*";
    return $template;
}

$fmt = cut2fmt(8, 14, 20, 26, 30);
print "$fmt\n";
A7 A6 A6 A6 A4 A*
```

The powerful unpack function goes far beyond mere text processing. It's the gateway between text and binary data.

In this recipe, we've assumed that all character data is 7- or 8-bit data so that pack's byte operations work as expected.

See Also

The pack, unpack, and substr functions in *perlfunc*(1) and in Chapter 29 of *Programming Perl*; use of the *cut2fmt* subroutine in Recipe 1.24; the binary use of unpack in Recipe 8.24

1.2   Establishing a Default Value

Problem

You would like to supply a default value to a scalar variable, but only if it doesn't already have one. It often happens that you want a hardcoded default value for a variable that can be overridden from the command line or through an environment variable.

Solution

Use the || or ||= operator, which work on both strings and numbers:

```
# use $b if $b is true, else $c
$a = $b || $c;

# set $x to $y unless $x is already true
$x ||= $y;
```

If 0, "0", and "" are valid values for your variables, use defined instead:

```
# use $b if $b is defined, else $c
$a = defined($b) ? $b : $c;

# the "new" defined-or operator from future perl
use v5.9;
$a = $b // $c;
```

Discussion

The big difference between the two techniques (defined and ||) is what they test: definedness versus truth. Three defined values are still false in the world of Perl: 0, "0", and "". If your variable already held one of those, and you wanted to keep that value, a || wouldn't work. You'd have to use the more elaborate three-way test with defined instead. It's often convenient to arrange for your program to care about only true or false values, not defined or undefined ones.

Rather than being restricted in its return values to a mere 1 or 0 as in most other languages, Perl's || operator has a much more interesting property: it returns its first operand (the lefthand side) if that operand is true; otherwise it returns its second operand. The && operator also returns the last evaluated expression, but is less often used for this property. These operators don't care whether their operands are strings, numbers, or references—any scalar will do. They just return the first one that makes the whole expression true or false. This doesn't affect the Boolean sense of the return value, but it does make the operators' return values more useful.

This property lets you provide a default value to a variable, function, or longer expression in case the first part doesn't pan out. Here's an example of ||, which would set $foo to be the contents of either $bar or, if $bar were false, "DEFAULT VALUE":

```
$foo = $bar || "DEFAULT VALUE";
```

Here's another example, which sets $dir to be either the first argument to the program or "/tmp" if no argument were given.

```
$dir = shift(@ARGV) || "/tmp";
```

We can do this without altering @ARGV:

```
$dir = $ARGV[0] || "/tmp";
```

If 0 is a valid value for $ARGV[0], we can't use ||, because it evaluates as false even though it's a value we want to accept. We must resort to Perl's only ternary operator, the ?: ("hook colon," or just "hook"):

```
$dir = defined($ARGV[0]) ? shift(@ARGV) : "/tmp";
```

We can also write this as follows, although with slightly different semantics:

```
$dir = @ARGV ? $ARGV[0] : "/tmp";
```

This checks the number of elements in @ARGV, because the first operand (here, @ARGV) is evaluated in scalar context. It's only false when there are 0 elements, in which case we use "/tmp". In all other cases (when the user gives an argument), we use the first argument.

The following line increments a value in %count, using as the key either $shell or, if $shell is false, "/bin/sh".

```
$count{ $shell || "/bin/sh" }++;
```

You may chain several alternatives together as we have in the following example. The first expression that returns a true value will be used.

```
# find the user name on Unix systems
$user = $ENV{USER}
    || $ENV{LOGNAME}
    || getlogin( )
    || (getpwuid($<))[0]
    || "Unknown uid number $<";
```

The && operator works analogously: it returns its first operand if that operand is false; otherwise, it returns the second one. Because there aren't as many interesting false values as there are true ones, this property isn't used much. One use is demonstrated in Recipes 13.12 and 14.19.

The ||= assignment operator looks odd, but it works exactly like the other binary assignment operators. For nearly all of Perl's binary operators, $VAR OP= VALUE means $VAR = $VAR OP VALUE; for example, $a += $b is the same as $a = $a + $b. So ||= is used to set a variable when that variable is itself still false. Since the || check is a simple Boolean one—testing for truth—it doesn't care about undefined values, even when warnings are enabled.

Here's an example of ||= that sets $starting_point to "Greenwich" unless it is already set. Again, we assume $starting_point won't have the value 0 or "0", or that if it does, it's okay to change it.

```
$starting_point ||= "Greenwich";
```

You can't use or in place of || in assignments, because or's precedence is too low. $a = $b or $c is equivalent to ($a = $b) or $c. This will always assign $b to $a, which is not the behavior you want.

Don't extend this curious use of || and ||= from scalars to arrays and hashes. It doesn't work, because the operators put their left operand into scalar context. Instead, you must do something like this:

```
@a = @b unless @a;        # copy only if empty
@a = @b ? @b : @c;        # assign @b if nonempty, else @c
```

Perl is someday expected to support new operators: //, //=, and err. It may already do so by the time you read this text. These defined-or operators will work just like the logical-or operators, ||, except that they will test definedness, not mere truth. That will make the following pairs equivalent:

```
$a = defined($b) ? $b : $c;
$a = $b // $c;

$x = defined($x) ? $x : $y;
$x //= $y;

defined(read(FH, $buf, $count))  or  die "read failed: $!";
read(FH, $buf, $count)          err die "read failed: $!";
```

These three operators are already present in Perl release v5.9, which being an odd-numbered release, is an experimental version and not what you want in a production environment. It is expected to be in v5.10, which will be a stable release, and will most certainly be in Perl v6, whose release date has not yet been determined.

See Also

The || operator in *perlop*(1) and Chapter 3 of *Programming Perl*; the defined and exists functions in *perlfunc*(1) and Chapter 29 of *Programming Perl*

1.3   Exchanging Values Without Using Temporary Variables

Problem

You want to exchange the values of two scalar variables, but don't want to use a temporary variable.

Solution

Use list assignment to reorder the variables.

```
($VAR1, $VAR2) = ($VAR2, $VAR1);
```

Discussion

Most programming languages require an intermediate step when swapping two variables' values:

```
$temp    = $a;
$a       = $b;
$b       = $temp;
```

Not so in Perl. It tracks both sides of the assignment, guaranteeing that you don't accidentally clobber any of your values. This eliminates the temporary variable:

```
$a       = "alpha";
$b       = "omega";
($a, $b) = ($b, $a);          # the first shall be last -- and versa vice
```

You can even exchange more than two variables at once:

```
($alpha, $beta, $production) = qw(January March August);
# move beta        to alpha,
# move production to beta,
# move alpha        to production
($alpha, $beta, $production) = ($beta, $production, $alpha);
```

When this code finishes, $alpha, $beta, and $production have the values "March", "August", and "January".

See Also

The section on "List value constructors" in *perldata*(1) and on "List Values and Arrays" in Chapter 2 of *Programming Perl*

1.4   Converting Between Characters and Values

Problem

You want to print the number represented by a given character, or you want to print a character given a number.

Solution

Use ord to convert a character to a number, or use chr to convert a number to its corresponding character:

```
$num  = ord($char);
$char = chr($num);
```

The %c format used in `printf` and `sprintf` also converts a number to a character:

```
$char = sprintf("%c", $num);                    # slower than chr($num)
printf("Number %d is character %c\n", $num, $num);
Number 101 is character e
```

A C* template used with pack and unpack can quickly convert many 8-bit bytes; similarly, use U* for Unicode characters.

```
@bytes = unpack("C*", $string);
$string = pack("C*", @bytes);

$unistr = pack("U4",0x24b6,0x24b7,0x24b8,0x24b9);
@unichars = unpack("U*", $unistr);
```

Discussion

Unlike low-level, typeless languages such as assembler, Perl doesn't treat characters and numbers interchangeably; it treats *strings* and numbers interchangeably. That means you can't just assign characters and numbers back and forth. Perl provides Pascal's chr and ord to convert between a character and its corresponding ordinal value:

```
$value     = ord("e");    # now 101
$character = chr(101);    # now "e"
```

If you already have a character, it's really represented as a string of length one, so just print it out directly using print or the %s format in `printf` and `sprintf`. The %c format forces `printf` or `sprintf` to convert a number into a character; it's not used for printing a character that's already in character format (that is, a string).

```
printf("Number %d is character %c\n", 101, 101);
```

The pack, unpack, chr, and ord functions are all faster than `sprintf`. Here are pack and unpack in action:

```
@ascii_character_numbers = unpack("C*", "sample");
print "@ascii_character_numbers\n";
115 97 109 112 108 101

$word = pack("C*", @ascii_character_numbers);
$word = pack("C*", 115, 97, 109, 112, 108, 101);   # same
print "$word\n";
sample
```

Here's how to convert from HAL to IBM:

```
$hal = "HAL";
@byte = unpack("C*", $hal);
foreach $val (@byte) {
    $val++;                    # add one to each byte value
}
$ibm = pack("C*", @byte);
print "$ibm\n";                # prints "IBM"
```

On single-byte character data, such as plain old ASCII or any of the various ISO 8859 charsets, the ord function returns numbers from 0 to 255. These correspond to C's unsigned char data type.

However, Perl understands more than that: it also has integrated support for Unicode, the universal character encoding. If you pass chr, sprintf "%c", or pack "U*" numeric values greater than 255, the return result will be a Unicode string.

Here are similar operations with Unicode:

```
@unicode_points = unpack("U*", "fac\x{0327}ade");
print "@unicode_points\n";
102 97 99 807 97 100 101

$word = pack("U*", @unicode_points);
print "$word\n";
façade
```

If all you're doing is printing out the characters' values, you probably don't even need to use unpack. Perl's printf and sprintf functions understand a v modifier that works like this:

```
printf "%vd\n", "fac\x{0327}ade";
102.97.99.807.97.100.101

printf "%vx\n", "fac\x{0327}ade";
66.61.63.327.61.64.65
```

The numeric value of each character (that is, its "code point" in Unicode parlance) in the string is emitted with a dot separator.

See Also

The chr, ord, printf, sprintf, pack, and unpack functions in *perlfunc*(1) and Chapter 29 of *Programming Perl*

1.5   Using Named Unicode Characters

Problem

You want to use Unicode names for fancy characters in your code without worrying about their code points.

Solution

Place a use charnames at the top of your file, then freely insert "\N{*CHARSPEC*}" escapes into your string literals.

Discussion

The use charnames pragma lets you use symbolic names for Unicode characters. These are compile-time constants that you access with the \N{*CHARSPEC*} double-quoted string sequence. Several subpragmas are supported. The :full subpragma grants access to the full range of character names, but you have to write them out in full, exactly as they occur in the Unicode character database, including the loud, all-capitals notation. The :short subpragma gives convenient shortcuts. Any import without a colon tag is taken to be a script name, giving case-sensitive shortcuts for those scripts.

```
use charnames ':full';
print "\N{GREEK CAPITAL LETTER DELTA} is called delta.\n";
```

Δ *is called delta.*

```
use charnames ':short';
print "\N{greek:Delta} is an upper-case delta.\n";
```

Δ *is an upper-case delta.*

```
use charnames qw(cyrillic greek);
print "\N{Sigma} and \N{sigma} are Greek sigmas.\n";
print "\N{Be} and \N{be} are Cyrillic bes.\n";
```

Σ *and* σ *are Greek sigmas.*
Б *and* б *are Cyrillic bes.*

Two functions, charnames::viacode and charnames::vianame, can translate between numeric code points and the long names. The Unicode documents use the notation U+*XXXX* to indicate the Unicode character whose code point is *XXXX*, so we'll use that here in our output.

```
use charnames qw(:full);
for $code (0xC4, 0x394) {
    printf "Character U+%04X (%s) is named %s\n",
        $code, chr($code), charnames::viacode($code);
}
```

Character U+00C4 (Ä) is named LATIN CAPITAL LETTER A WITH DIAERESIS
Character U+0394 (Δ) is named GREEK CAPITAL LETTER DELTA

```
use charnames qw(:full);
$name = "MUSIC SHARP SIGN";
$code = charnames::vianame($name);
printf "%s is character U+%04X (%s)\n",
    $name, $code, chr($code);
```

MUSIC SHARP SIGN *is character U+266F (♯)*

Here's how to find the path to Perl's copy of the Unicode character database:

```
% perl -MConfig -le 'print "$Config{privlib}/unicore/NamesList.txt"'
```
/usr/local/lib/perl5/5.8.1/unicore/NamesList.txt

Read this file to learn the character names available to you.

See Also

The *charnames*(3) manpage and Chapter 31 of *Programming Perl*; the Unicode Character Database at *http://www.unicode.org/*

1.6   Processing a String One Character at a Time

Problem

You want to process a string one character at a time.

Solution

Use split with a null pattern to break up the string into individual characters, or use unpack if you just want the characters' values:

```
@array = split(//, $string);      # each element a single character
@array = unpack("U*", $string);   # each element a code point (number)
```

Or extract each character in turn with a loop:

```
while (/(.)/g) {          # . is never a newline here
        # $1 has character, ord($1) its number
    }
```

Discussion

As we said before, Perl's fundamental unit is the string, not the character. Needing to process anything a character at a time is rare. Usually some kind of higher-level Perl operation, like pattern matching, solves the problem more handily. See, for example, Recipe 7.14, where a set of substitutions is used to find command-line arguments.

Splitting on a pattern that matches the empty string returns a list of individual characters in the string. This is a convenient feature when done intentionally, but it's easy to do unintentionally. For instance, /X*/ matches all possible strings, including the empty string. Odds are you will find others when you don't mean to.

Here's an example that prints the characters used in the string "an apple a day", sorted in ascending order:

```
%seen = ( );
$string = "an apple a day";
foreach $char (split //, $string) {
    $seen{$char}++;
}
print "unique chars are: ", sort(keys %seen), "\n";
unique chars are:  adelnpy
```

These split and unpack solutions give an array of characters to work with. If you don't want an array, use a pattern match with the /g flag in a while loop, extracting one character at a time:

```
%seen = ();
$string = "an apple a day";
while ($string =~ /(.)/g) {
    $seen{$1}++;
}
print "unique chars are: ", sort(keys %seen), "\n";
unique chars are: adelnpy
```

In general, whenever you find yourself doing character-by-character processing, there's probably a better way to go about it. Instead of using index and substr or split and unpack, it might be easier to use a pattern. Instead of computing a 32-bit checksum by hand, as in the next example, the unpack function can compute it far more efficiently.

The following example calculates the checksum of $string with a foreach loop. There are better checksums; this just happens to be the basis of a traditional and computationally easy checksum. You can use the standard* Digest::MD5 module if you want a more robust checksum.

```
$sum = 0;
foreach $byteval (unpack("C*", $string)) {
    $sum += $byteval;
}
print "sum is $sum\n";
# prints "1248" if $string was "an apple a day"
```

This does the same thing, but much faster:

```
$sum = unpack("%32C*", $string);
```

This emulates the SysV checksum program:

```
#!/usr/bin/perl
# sum - compute 16-bit checksum of all input files
$checksum = 0;
while (<>) { $checksum += unpack("%16C*", $_) }
$checksum %= (2 ** 16) - 1;
print "$checksum\n";
```

Here's an example of its use:

```
% perl sum /etc/termcap
1510
```

If you have the GNU version of *sum*, you'll need to call it with the **--sysv** option to get the same answer on the same file.

```
% sum --sysv /etc/termcap
1510 851 /etc/termcap
```

---

* It's standard as of the v5.8 release of Perl; otherwise, grab it from CPAN.

Another tiny program that processes its input one character at a time is *slowcat*, shown in Example 1-1. The idea here is to pause after each character is printed so you can scroll text before an audience slowly enough that they can read it.

Example 1-1. slowcat

```
#!/usr/bin/perl
# slowcat - emulate a  s l o w  line printer
# usage: slowcat [-DELAY] [files ...]
$DELAY = ($ARGV[0] =~ /^-([.\d]+)/) ? (shift, $1) : 1;
$| = 1;
while (<>) {
    for (split(//)) {
        print;
        select(undef,undef,undef, 0.005 * $DELAY);
    }
}
```

See Also

The split and unpack functions in *perlfunc*(1) and Chapter 29 of *Programming Perl*; the use of expanding select for timing is explained in Recipe 3.10

1.7   Reversing a String by Word or Character

Problem

You want to reverse the words or characters of a string.

Solution

Use the reverse function in scalar context for flipping characters:

```
$revchars = reverse($string);
```

To flip words, use reverse in list context with split and join:

```
$revwords = join(" ", reverse split(" ", $string));
```

Discussion

The reverse function is two different functions in one. Called in scalar context, it joins together its arguments and returns that string in reverse order. Called in list context, it returns its arguments in the opposite order. When using reverse for its character-flipping behavior, use scalar to force scalar context unless it's entirely obvious.

```
$gnirts   = reverse($string);      # reverse letters in $string

@sdrow    = reverse(@words);       # reverse elements in @words

$confused = reverse(@words);       # reverse letters in join("", @words)
```

Here's an example of reversing words in a string. Using a single space, " ", as the pattern to split is a special case. It causes split to use contiguous whitespace as the separator and also discard leading null fields, just like *awk*. Normally, split discards only trailing null fields.

```
# reverse word order
$string = 'Yoda said, "can you see this?"';
@allwords    = split(" ", $string);
$revwords    = join(" ", reverse @allwords);
print $revwords, "\n";
this?" see you "can said, Yoda
```

We could remove the temporary array @allwords and do it on one line:

```
$revwords = join(" ", reverse split(" ", $string));
```

Multiple whitespace in $string becomes a single space in $revwords. If you want to preserve whitespace, use this:

```
$revwords = join("", reverse split(/(\s+)/, $string));
```

One use of reverse is to test whether a word is a palindrome (a word that reads the same backward or forward):

```
$word = "reviver";
$is_palindrome = ($word eq reverse($word));
```

We can turn this into a one-liner that finds big palindromes in */usr/dict/words*:

```
% perl -nle 'print if $_ eq reverse && length > 5' /usr/dict/words
deedeed
degged
deified
denned
hallah
kakkak
murdrum
redder
repaper
retter
reviver
rotator
sooloos
tebbet
terret
tut-tut
```

See Also

The split, reverse, and scalar functions in *perlfunc*(1) and Chapter 29 of *Programming Perl*; Recipe 1.8

1.8 Treating Unicode Combined Characters as Single Characters

Problem

You have a Unicode string that contains combining characters, and you'd like to treat each of these sequences as a single logical character.

Solution

Process them using \X in a regular expression.

```
$string = "fac\x{0327}ade";        # "façade"
$string =~ /fa.ade/;               # fails
$string =~ /fa\Xade/;              # succeeds

@chars = split(//, $string);       # 7 letters in @chars
@chars = $string =~ /(.)/g;        # same thing
@chars = $string =~ /(\X)/g;       # 6 "letters" in @chars
```

Discussion

In Unicode, you can combine a base character with one or more non-spacing characters following it; these are usually diacritics, such as accent marks, cedillas, and tildes. Due to the presence of precombined characters, for the most part to accommodate legacy character systems, there can be two or more ways of writing the same thing.

For example, the word "façade" can be written with one character between the two a's, "\x{E7}", a character right out of Latin1 (ISO 8859-1). These characters might be encoded into a two-byte sequence under the UTF-8 encoding that Perl uses internally, but those two bytes still only count as one single character. That works just fine.

There's a thornier issue. Another way to write U+00E7 is with two different code points: a regular "c" followed by "\x{0327}". Code point U+0327 is a non-spacing combining character that means to go back and put a cedilla underneath the preceding base character.

There are times when you want Perl to treat each combined character sequence as one logical character. But because they're distinct code points, Perl's character-related operations treat non-spacing combining characters as separate characters, including substr, length, and regular expression metacharacters, such as in /./ or /[^abc]/.

In a regular expression, the \X metacharacter matches an extended Unicode combining character sequence, and is exactly equivalent to (?:\PM\pM*) or, in long-hand:

```
(?x:                  # begin non-capturing group
        \PM           # one character without the M (mark) property,
```

```
                        #   such as a letter
        \pM             # one character that does have the M (mark) property,
                        #   such as an accent mark
        *               # and you can have as many marks as you want
    )
```

Otherwise simple operations become tricky if these beasties are in your string. Consider the approaches for reversing a word by character from the previous recipe. Written with combining characters, "année" and "niño" can be expressed in Perl as "anne\x{301}e" and "nin\x{303}o".

```
    for $word ("anne\x{301}e", "nin\x{303}o") {
        printf "%s simple reversed to %s\n", $word,
            scalar reverse $word;
        printf "%s better reversed to %s\n", $word,
            join("", reverse $word =~ /\X/g);
    }
```

That produces:

    année simple reversed to éenna
    année better reversed to eénna
    niño simple reversed to õnin
    niño better reversed to oñin

In the reversals marked as simply reversed, the diacritical marking jumped from one base character to the other one. That's because a combining character always follows its base character, and you've reversed the whole string. By grabbing entire sequences of a base character plus any combining characters that follow, then reversing that list, this problem is avoided.

See Also

The *perlre*(1) and *perluniintro*(1) manpages; Chapter 15 of *Programming Perl*; Recipe 1.9

1.9 Canonicalizing Strings with Unicode Combined Characters

Problem

You have two strings that look the same when you print them out, but they don't test as string equal and sometimes even have different lengths. How can you get Perl to consider them the same strings?

Solution

When you have otherwise equivalent strings, at least some of which contain Unicode combining character sequences, instead of comparing them directly, compare the results of running them through the NFD( ) function from the Unicode::Normalize module.

```
use Unicode::Normalize;
$s1 = "fa\x{E7}ade";
$s2 = "fac\x{0327}ade";
if (NFD($s1) eq NFD($s2)) { print "Yup!\n" }
```

Discussion

The same character sequence can sometimes be specified in multiple ways. Sometimes this is because of legacy encodings, such as the letters from Latin1 that contain diacritical marks. These can be specified directly with a single character (like U+00E7, LATIN SMALL LETTER C WITH CEDILLA) or indirectly via the base character (like U+0063, LATIN SMALL LETTER C) followed by a combining character (U+0327, COMBINING CEDILLA).

Another possibility is that you have two or more marks following a base character, but the order of those marks varies in your data. Imagine you wanted the letter "c" to have both a cedilla and a caron on top of it in order to print a ç̌. That could be specified in any of these ways:

```
$string = v231.780;
#   LATIN SMALL LETTER C WITH CEDILLA
#   COMBINING CARON

$string = v99.807.780;
#       LATIN SMALL LETTER C
#       COMBINING CARON
#       COMBINING CEDILLA

$string = v99.780.807
#       LATIN SMALL LETTER C
#       COMBINING CEDILLA
#       COMBINING CARON
```

The normalization functions rearrange those into a reliable ordering. Several are provided, including NFD( ) for canonical decomposition and NFC( ) for canonical decomposition followed by canonical composition. No matter which of these three ways you used to specify your ç̌, the NFD version is v99.807.780, whereas the NFC version is v231.780.

Sometimes you may prefer NFKD( ) and NFKC( ), which are like the previous two functions except that they perform *compatible* decomposition, which for NFKC( ) is then followed by canonical composition. For example, \x{FB00} is the double-f ligature. Its NFD and NFC forms are the same thing, "\x{FB00}", but its NFKD and NFKC forms return a two-character string, "\x{66}\x{66}".

See Also

The section on "The Universal Character Code" at the beginning of this chapter; the documentation for the Unicode::Normalize module; Recipe 8.20

1.10 Treating a Unicode String as Octets

Problem

You have a Unicode string but want Perl to treat it as octets (e.g., to calculate its length or for purposes of I/O).

Solution

The use bytes pragma makes all Perl operations in its lexical scope treat the string as a group of octets. Use it when your code is calling Perl's character-aware functions directly:

```
$ff = "\x{FB00}";            # ff ligature
$chars = length($ff);        # length is one character
{
  use bytes;                 # force byte semantics
  $octets = length($ff);     # length is two octets
}
$chars = length($ff);        # back to character semantics
```

Alternatively, the Encode module lets you convert a Unicode string to a string of octets, and back again. Use it when the character-aware code isn't in your lexical scope:

```
use Encode qw(encode_utf8);

sub somefunc;                # defined elsewhere

$ff = "\x{FB00}";            # ff ligature
$ff_oct = encode_utf8($ff);  # convert to octets

$chars = somefunc($ff);      # work with character string
$octets = somefunc($ff_oct); # work with octet string
```

Discussion

As explained in this chapter's Introduction, Perl knows about two types of string: those made of simple uninterpreted octets, and those made of Unicode characters whose UTF-8 representation may require more than one octet. Each individual string has a flag associated with it, identifying the string as either UTF-8 or octets. Perl's I/O and string operations (such as length) check this flag and give character or octet semantics accordingly.

Sometimes you need to work with bytes and not characters. For example, many protocols have a Content-Length header that specifies the size of the body of a message in octets. You can't simply use Perl's length function to calculate the size, because if the string you're calling length on is marked as UTF-8, you'll get the size in characters.

The use bytes pragma makes all Perl functions in its lexical scope use octet semantics for strings instead of character semantics. Under this pragma, length always returns the number of octets, and read always reports the number of octets read. However, because the use bytes pragma is lexically scoped, you can't use it to change the behavior of code in another scope (e.g., someone else's function).

For this you need to create an octet-encoded copy of the UTF-8 string. In memory, of course, the same byte sequence is used for both strings. The difference is that the copy of your UTF-8 string has the UTF-8 flag cleared. Functions acting on the octet copy will give octet semantics, regardless of the scope they're in.

There is also a no bytes pragma, which forces character semantics, and a decode_utf8 function, which turns octet-encoded strings into UTF-8 encoded strings. However, these functions are less useful because not all octet strings are valid UTF-8 strings, whereas all UTF-8 strings are valid octet strings.

See Also

The documentation for the bytes pragma; the documentation for the standard Encode module

1.11   Expanding and Compressing Tabs

Problem

You want to convert tabs in a string to the appropriate number of spaces, or vice versa. Converting spaces into tabs can be used to reduce file size when the file has many consecutive spaces. Converting tabs into spaces may be required when producing output for devices that don't understand tabs or think them at different positions than you do.

Solution

Either use a rather funny looking substitution:

```
while ($string =~ s/\t+/' ' x (length($&) * 8 - length($`) % 8)/e) {
    # spin in empty loop until substitution finally fails
}
```

or use the standard Text::Tabs module:

```
use Text::Tabs;
@expanded_lines  = expand(@lines_with_tabs);
@tabulated_lines = unexpand(@lines_without_tabs);
```

Discussion

Assuming tab stops are set every N positions (where N is customarily eight), it's easy to convert them into spaces. The standard textbook method does not use the Text:: Tabs module but suffers slightly from being difficult to understand. Also, it uses the $` variable, whose very mention currently slows down every pattern match in the program. This is explained in "Special Variables" in Chapter 6. You could use this algorithm to make a filter to expand its input's tabstops to eight spaces each:

```
while (<>) {
    1 while s/\t+/' ' x (length($&) * 8 - length($`) % 8)/e;
    print;
}
```

To avoid $`, you could use a slightly more complicated alternative that uses the numbered variables for explicit capture; this one expands tabstops to four each instead of eight:

```
1 while s/^(.*?)(\t+)/$1 . ' ' x (length($2) * 4 - length($1) % 4)/e;
```

Another approach is to use the offsets directly from the @+ and @- arrays. This also expands to four-space positions:

```
1 while s/\t+/' ' x (($+[0] - $-[0]) * 4 - $-[0] % 4)/e;
```

If you're looking at all of these 1 while loops and wondering why they couldn't have been written as part of a simple s///g instead, it's because you need to recalculate the length from the start of the line again each time rather than merely from where the last match occurred.

The convention 1 while CONDITION is the same as while (CONDITION) { }, but shorter. Its origins date to when Perl ran the first incredibly faster than the second. While the second is now almost as fast, it remains convenient, and the habit has stuck.

The standard Text::Tabs module provides conversion functions to convert both directions, exports a $tabstop variable to control the number of spaces per tab, and does not incur the performance hit because it uses $1 and $2 rather than $& and $`.

```
use Text::Tabs;
$tabstop = 4;
while (<>) { print expand($_) }
```

We can also use Text::Tabs to "unexpand" the tabs. This example uses the default $tabstop value of 8:

```
use Text::Tabs;
while (<>) { print unexpand($_) }
```

See Also

The manpage for the Text::Tabs module; the s/// operator in *perlre*(1) and *perlop*(1); the @- and @+ variables (@LAST_MATCH_START and @LAST_MATCH_END) in

Chapter 28 of *Programming Perl*; the section on "When a global substitution just isn't global enough" in Chapter 5 of *Programming Perl*

1.12   Expanding Variables in User Input

Problem

You've read a string with an embedded variable reference, such as:

```
You owe $debt to me.
```

Now you want to replace $debt in the string with its value.

Solution

Use a substitution with symbolic references if the variables are all globals:

```
$text =~ s/\$(\w+)/${$1}/g;
```

But use a double /ee if they might be lexical (my) variables:

```
$text =~ s/(\$\w+)/$1/gee;
```

Discussion

The first technique is basically to find what looks like a variable name, then use symbolic dereferencing to interpolate its contents. If $1 contains the string somevar, ${$1} will be whatever $somevar contains. This won't work if the use strict 'refs' pragma is in effect because that bans symbolic dereferencing.

Here's an example:

```
our ($rows, $cols);
no strict 'refs';                    # for ${$1}/g below
my $text;

($rows, $cols) = (24, 80);
$text = q(I am $rows high and $cols long);  # like single quotes!
$text =~ s/\$(\w+)/${$1}/g;
print $text;
I am 24 high and 80 long
```

You may have seen the /e substitution modifier used to evaluate the replacement as code rather than as a string. It's designed for situations where you don't know the exact replacement value, but you do know how to calculate it. For example, doubling every whole number in a string:

```
$text = "I am 17 years old";
$text =~ s/(\d+)/2 * $1/eg;
```

When Perl is compiling your program and sees a /e on a substitute, it compiles the code in the replacement block along with the rest of your program, long before the substitution actually happens. When a substitution is made, $1 is replaced with the string that matched. The code to evaluate would then be something like:

```
2 * 17
```

If we tried saying:

```
$text = 'I am $AGE years old';     # note single quotes
$text =~ s/(\$\w+)/$1/eg;          # WRONG
```

assuming $text held a mention of the variable $AGE, Perl would dutifully replace $1 with $AGE and then evaluate code that looked like:

```
'$AGE'
```

which just yields us our original string back again. We need to evaluate the result *again* to get the value of the variable. To do that, just add another /e:

```
$text =~ s/(\$\w+)/$1/eeg;         # finds my( ) variables
```

Yes, you can have as many /e modifiers as you'd like. Only the first one is compiled and syntax-checked with the rest of your program. This makes it work like the eval {BLOCK} construct, except that it doesn't trap exceptions. Think of it more as a do {BLOCK} instead.

Subsequent /e modifiers are quite different. They're more like the eval "STRING" construct. They don't get compiled until runtime. A small advantage of this scheme is that it doesn't require a no strict 'refs' pragma for the block. A tremendous advantage is that unlike symbolic dereferencing, this mechanism finds lexical variables created with my, something symbolic references can never do.

The following example uses the /x modifier to enable whitespace and comments in the pattern part of the substitute and /e to evaluate the righthand side as code. The /e modifier gives more control over what happens in case of error or other extenuating circumstances, as we have here:

```
# expand variables in $text, but put an error message in
# if the variable isn't defined
$text =~ s{
    \$                         # find a literal dollar sign
    (\w+)                      # find a "word" and store it in $1
}{
    no strict 'refs';          # for $$1 below
    if (defined ${$1}) {
        ${$1};                     # expand global variables only
    } else {
        "[NO VARIABLE: \$$1]"; # error msg
    }
}egx;
```

Once upon a time, long ago and far away, $$1 used to mean ${$}1 when it occurred within a string; that is, the $$ variable followed by a 1. This was grandfathered to work that way so you could more readily expand the $$ variable as your process ID to compose temporary filenames. It now always means ${$1}, i.e., dereference the contents of the $1 variable. We have written it the more explicit way for clarity, not correctness.

See Also

The s/// operator in *perlre*(1) and *perlop*(1) and Chapter 5 of *Programming Perl*; the eval function in *perlfunc*(1) and Chapter 29 of *Programming Perl*; the similar use of substitutions in Recipe 20.9

1.13   Controlling Case

Problem

A string in uppercase needs converting to lowercase, or vice versa.

Solution

Use the lc and uc functions or the \L and \U string escapes.

```
$big = uc($little);      # "bo peep" -> "BO PEEP"
$little = lc($big);      # "JOHN"    -> "john"
$big = "\U$little";      # "bo peep" -> "BO PEEP"
$little = "\L$big";      # "JOHN"    -> "john"
```

To alter just one character, use the lcfirst and ucfirst functions or the \l and \u string escapes.

```
$big = "\u$little";      # "bo"      -> "Bo"
$little = "\l$big";      # "BoPeep"  -> "boPeep"
```

Discussion

The functions and string escapes look different, but both do the same thing. You can set the case of either just the first character or the whole string. You can even do both at once to force uppercase (actually, titlecase; see later explanation) on initial characters and lowercase on the rest.

```
$beast   = "dromedary";
# capitalize various parts of $beast
$capit   = ucfirst($beast);      # Dromedary
$capit   = "\u\L$beast";         # (same)
$capall  = uc($beast);           # DROMEDARY
$capall  = "\U$beast";           # (same)
$caprest = lcfirst(uc($beast));  # dROMEDARY
$caprest = "\l\U$beast";         # (same)
```

These capitalization-changing escapes are commonly used to make a string's case consistent:

```
# titlecase each word's first character, lowercase the rest
$text = "thIS is a loNG liNE";
$text =~ s/(\w+)/\u\L$1/g;
print $text;
This Is A Long Line
```

You can also use these for case-insensitive comparison:

```
if (uc($a) eq uc($b)) { # or "\U$a" eq "\U$b"
    print "a and b are the same\n";
}
```

The *randcap* program, shown in Example 1-2, randomly titlecases 20 percent of the letters of its input. This lets you converse with 14-year-old WaREz d00Dz.

Example 1-2. randcap

```
#!/usr/bin/perl -p
# randcap: filter to randomly capitalize 20% of the letters
# call to srand( ) is unnecessary as of v5.4
BEGIN { srand(time( ) ^ ($$ + ($$<<15))) }
sub randcase { rand(100) < 20 ? "\u$_[0]" : "\l$_[0]" }
s/(\w)/randcase($1)/ge;
% randcap < genesis | head -9
boOk 01 genesis
001:001 in the BEginning goD created the heaven and tHe earTh.

001:002 and the earth wAS without ForM, aND void; AnD darkneSS was
        upon The Face of the dEEp. and the spIrit of GOd movEd upOn
        tHe face of the Waters.
001:003 and god Said, let there be ligHt: and therE wAs LigHt.
```

In languages whose writing systems distinguish between uppercase and titlecase, the ucfirst( ) function (and \u, its string escape alias) converts to *titlecase*. For example, in Hungarian the "dz" sequence occurs. In uppercase, it's written as "DZ", in title-case as "Dz", and in lowercase as "dz". Unicode consequently has three different characters defined for these three situations:

```
Code point  Written  Meaning
01F1        DZ       LATIN CAPITAL LETTER DZ
01F2        Dz       LATIN CAPITAL LETTER D WITH SMALL LETTER Z
01F3        dz       LATIN SMALL LETTER DZ
```

It is tempting but ill-advised to just use tr[a-z][A-Z] or the like to convert case. This is a mistake because it omits all characters with diacritical markings—such as diaereses, cedillas, and accent marks—which are used in dozens of languages, including English. However, correctly handling case mappings on data with diacritical markings can be far trickier than it seems. There is no simple answer, although if everything is in Unicode, it's not all that bad, because Perl's case-mapping functions do work perfectly fine on Unicode data. See the section on "Universal Character Code" in the Introduction to this chapter for more information.

See Also

The uc, lc, ucfirst, and lcfirst functions in *perlfunc*(1) and Chapter 29 of *Programming Perl*; \L, \U, \l, and \u string escapes in the "Quote and Quote-like Operators" section of *perlop*(1) and Chapter 5 of *Programming Perl*

1.14   Properly Capitalizing a Title or Headline

Problem

You have a string representing a headline, the title of book, or some other work that needs proper capitalization.

Solution

Use a variant of this tc( ) titlecasing function:

```
INIT {
    our %nocap;
    for (qw(
            a an the
            and but or
            as at but by for from in into of off on onto per to with
        ))
    {
        $nocap{$_}++;
    }
}

sub tc {
    local $_ = shift;

    # put into lowercase if on stop list, else titlecase
    s/(\pL[\pL']*)/$nocap{$1} ? lc($1) : ucfirst(lc($1))/ge;

    s/^(\pL[\pL']*) /\u\L$1/x;  # first  word guaranteed to cap
    s/ (\pL[\pL']*)$/\u\L$1/x;  # last word guaranteed to cap

    # treat parenthesized portion as a complete title
    s/\( (\pL[\pL']*) /(\u\L$1/x;
    s/(\pL[\pL']*) \) /\u\L$1)/x;

    # capitalize first word following colon or semi-colon
    s/ ( [:;] \s+ ) (\pL[\pL']* ) /$1\u\L$2/x;

    return $_;
}
```

Discussion

The rules for correctly capitalizing a headline or title in English are more complex than simply capitalizing the first letter of each word. If that's all you need to do, something like this should suffice:

```
s/(\w+\S*\w*)/\u\L$1/g;
```

Most style guides tell you that the first and last words in the title should always be capitalized, along with every other word that's not an article, the particle "to" in an infinitive construct, a coordinating conjunction, or a preposition.

Here's a demo, this time demonstrating the distinguishing property of titlecase. Assume the tc function is as defined in the Solution.

```
# with apologies (or kudos) to Stephen Brust, PJF,
# and to JRRT, as always.
@data = (
            "the enchantress of \x{01F3}ur mountain",
    "meeting the enchantress of \x{01F3}ur mountain",
    "the lord of the rings: the fellowship of the ring",
);

$mask = "%-20s: %s\n";

sub tc_lame {
    local $_ = shift;
    s/(\w+\S*\w*)/\u\L$1/g;
    return $_;
}

for $datum (@data) {
    printf $mask, "ALL CAPITALS",      uc($datum);
    printf $mask, "no capitals",       lc($datum);
    printf $mask, "simple titlecase",  tc_lame($datum);
    printf $mask, "better titlecase",  tc($datum);
    print "\n";
}

ALL CAPITALS         : THE ENCHANTRESS OF DZUR MOUNTAIN
no capitals          : the enchantress of dzur mountain
simple titlecase     : The Enchantress Of Dzur Mountain
better titlecase     : The Enchantress of Dzur Mountain

ALL CAPITALS         : MEETING THE ENCHANTRESS OF DZUR MOUNTAIN
no capitals          : meeting the enchantress of dzur mountain
simple titlecase     : Meeting The Enchantress Of Dzur Mountain
better titlecase     : Meeting the Enchantress of Dzur Mountain

ALL CAPITALS         : THE LORD OF THE RINGS: THE FELLOWSHIP OF THE RING
no capitals          : the lord of the rings: the fellowship of the ring
simple titlecase     : The Lord Of The Rings: The Fellowship Of The Ring
better titlecase     : The Lord of the Rings: The Fellowship of the Ring
```

One thing to consider is that some style guides prefer capitalizing only prepositions that are longer than three, four, or sometimes five letters. O'Reilly & Associates, for example, keeps prepositions of four or fewer letters in lowercase. Here's a longer list of prepositions if you prefer, which you can modify to your needs:

```
@all_prepositions = qw{
    about above absent across after against along amid amidst
    among amongst around as at athwart before behind below
    beneath beside besides between betwixt beyond but by circa
```

```
         down during ere except for from in into near of off on onto
         out over past per since than through till to toward towards
         under until unto up upon versus via with within without
};
```

This kind of approach can take you only so far, though, because it doesn't distinguish between words that can be several parts of speech. Some prepositions on the list might also double as words that should always be capitalized, such as subordinating conjunctions, adverbs, or even adjectives. For example, it's "Down by the Riverside" but "Getting By on Just $30 a Day", or "A Ringing in My Ears" but "Bringing In the Sheaves".

Another consideration is that you might prefer to apply the \u or ucfirst conversion by itself without also putting the whole string into lowercase. That way a word that's already in all capital letters, such as an acronym, doesn't lose that trait. You probably wouldn't want to convert "FBI" and "LBJ" into "Fbi" and "Lbj".

See Also

The uc, lc, ucfirst, and lcfirst functions in *perlfunc*(1) and Chapter 29 of *Programming Perl*; the \L, \U, \l, and \u string escapes in the "Quote and Quote-like Operators" section of *perlop*(1) and Chapter 5 of *Programming Perl*

1.15 Interpolating Functions and Expressions Within Strings

Problem

You want a function call or expression to expand within a string. This lets you construct more complex templates than with simple scalar variable interpolation.

Solution

Break up your expression into distinct concatenated pieces:

```
$answer = $var1 . func() . $var2;   # scalar only
```

Or use the slightly sneaky @{[LIST EXPR]} or ${ \(SCALAR EXPR) } expansions:

```
$answer = "STRING @{[ LIST EXPR ]} MORE STRING";
$answer = "STRING ${\( SCALAR EXPR )} MORE STRING";
```

Discussion

This code shows both techniques. The first line shows concatenation; the second shows the expansion trick:

```
$phrase = "I have " . ($n + 1) . " guanacos.";
$phrase = "I have ${\($n + 1)} guanacos.";
```

The first technique builds the final string by concatenating smaller strings, avoiding interpolation but achieving the same end. Because print effectively concatenates its entire argument list, if we were going to print $phrase, we could have just said:

```
print "I have ",  $n + 1, " guanacos.\n";
```

When you absolutely must have interpolation, you need the punctuation-riddled interpolation from the Solution. Only @, $, and \ are special within double quotes and most backquotes. (As with m// and s///, the qx( ) synonym is not subject to double-quote expansion if its delimiter is single quotes! $home = qx'echo home is $HOME'; would get the shell $HOME variable, not one in Perl.) So, the only way to force arbitrary expressions to expand is by expanding a ${ } or @{ } whose block contains a reference.

In the example:

```
$phrase = "I have ${\( count_em( ) )} guanacos.";
```

the function call within the parentheses is not in scalar context; it is still in list context. The following overrules that:

```
$phrase = "I have ${\( scalar count_em( ) )} guanacos.";
```

You can do more than simply assign to a variable after interpolation. It's a general mechanism that can be used in any double-quoted string. For instance, this example builds a string with an interpolated expression and passes the result to a function:

```
some_func("What you want is @{[ split /:/, $rec ]} items");
```

You can interpolate into a here document, as by:

```
die "Couldn't send mail" unless send_mail(<<"EOTEXT", $target);
To: $naughty
From: Your Bank
Cc: @{ get_manager_list($naughty) }
Date: @{[ do { my $now = `date`; chomp $now; $now } ]} (today)

Dear $naughty,

Today, you bounced check number @{[ 500 + int rand(100) ]} to us.
Your account is now closed.

Sincerely,
the management
EOTEXT
```

Expanding backquotes (``) is particularly challenging because you would normally end up with spurious newlines. By creating a braced block following the @ within the @{[ ]} anonymous array dereference, as in the last example, you can create private variables.

Although these techniques work, simply breaking your work up into several steps or storing everything in temporary variables is almost always clearer to the reader.

The Interpolation module from CPAN provides a more syntactically palatable covering. For example, to make elements of the hash %E evaluate and return its subscript:

```
use Interpolation E       => 'eval';
print "You bounced check number $E{500 + int rand(100)}\n";
```

Or to make a hash named %money call a suitably defined function of your choice:

```
use Interpolation money => \&currency_commify;

print "That will be $money{ 4 * $payment }, right now.\n";
```

expect to get something like:

> *That will be $3,232.421.04, right now.*

See Also

perlref(1) and the "Other Tricks You Can Do with Hard References" section in Chapter 8 of *Programming Perl*; the Interpolation CPAN module

1.16   Indenting Here Documents

Problem

When using the multiline quoting mechanism called a *here document*, the text must be flush against the margin, which looks out of place in the code. You would like to indent the here document text in the code, but not have the indentation appear in the final string value.

Solution

Use a s/// operator to strip out leading whitespace.

```
# all in one
($var = << HERE_TARGET) =~ s/^\s+//gm;
    your text
    goes here
HERE_TARGET

# or with two steps
$var = << HERE_TARGET;
    your text
    goes here
HERE_TARGET
$var =~ s/^\s+//gm;
```

Discussion

The substitution is straightforward. It removes leading whitespace from the text of the here document. The /m modifier lets the ^ character match at the start of each line in the string, and the /g modifier makes the pattern-matching engine repeat the substitution as often as it can (i.e., for every line in the here document).

```
($definition = << 'FINIS') =~ s/^\s+//gm;
    The five varieties of camelids
    are the familiar camel, his friends
    the llama and the alpaca, and the
    rather less well-known guanaco
    and vicuña.
FINIS
```

Be warned: all patterns in this recipe use \s, meaning one whitespace character, which will also match newlines. This means they will remove any blank lines in your here document. If you don't want this, replace \s with [^\S\n] in the patterns.

The substitution uses the property that the result of an assignment can be used as the lefthand side of =~. This lets us do it all in one line, but works only when assigning to a variable. When you're using the here document directly, it would be considered a constant value, and you wouldn't be able to modify it. In fact, you can't change a here document's value *unless* you first put it into a variable.

Not to worry, though, because there's an easy way around this, particularly if you're going to do this a lot in the program. Just write a subroutine:

```
sub fix {
    my $string = shift;
    $string =~ s/^\s+//gm;
    return $string;
}

print fix( << "END");
    My stuff goes here
END

# With function predeclaration, you can omit the parens:
print fix << "END";
    My stuff goes here
END
```

As with all here documents, you have to place this here document's target (the token that marks its end, END in this case) flush against the lefthand margin. To have the target indented also, you'll have to put the same amount of whitespace in the quoted string as you use to indent the token.

```
($quote = << '    FINIS') =~ s/^\s+//gm;
        ...we will have peace, when you and all your works have
        perished--and the works of your dark master to whom you would
        deliver us. You are a liar, Saruman, and a corrupter of men's
        hearts.  --Theoden in /usr/src/perl/taint.c
    FINIS
$quote =~ s/\s+--/\n--/;       #move attribution to line of its own
```

If you're doing this to strings that contain code you're building up for an eval, or just text to print out, you might not want to blindly strip all leading whitespace, because that would destroy your indentation. Although eval wouldn't care, your reader might.

Another embellishment is to use a special leading string for code that stands out. For example, here we'll prepend each line with @@@, properly indented:

```
if ($REMEMBER_THE_MAIN) {
    $perl_main_C = dequote << '    MAIN_INTERPRETER_LOOP';
        @@@ int
        @@@ runops() {
        @@@     SAVEI32(runlevel);
        @@@     runlevel++;
        @@@     while ( op = (*op->op_ppaddr)() ) ;
        @@@     TAINT_NOT;
        @@@     return 0;
        @@@ }
    MAIN_INTERPRETER_LOOP
    # add more code here if you want
}
```

Destroying indentation also gets you in trouble with poets.

```
sub dequote;
$poem = dequote << EVER_ON_AND_ON;
       Now far ahead the Road has gone,
          And I must follow, if I can,
       Pursuing it with eager feet,
          Until it joins some larger way
       Where many paths and errands meet.
          And whither then? I cannot say.
                --Bilbo in /usr/src/perl/pp_ctl.c
EVER_ON_AND_ON
print "Here's your poem:\n\n$poem\n";
```

Here is its sample output:

```
Here's your poem:

Now far ahead the Road has gone,
   And I must follow, if I can,
Pursuing it with eager feet,
   Until it joins some larger way
Where many paths and errands meet.
   And whither then? I cannot say.
      --Bilbo in /usr/src/perl/pp_ctl.c
```

The following dequote function handles all these cases. It expects to be called with a here document as its argument. It checks whether each line begins with a common substring, and if so, strips that off. Otherwise, it takes the amount of leading whitespace found on the first line and removes that much from each subsequent line.

```
sub dequote {
    local $_ = shift;
    my ($white, $leader);  # common whitespace and common leading string
    if (/^\s*(?:([^\w\s]+)(\s*).*\n)(?:\s*\1\2?.*\n)+$/) {
        ($white, $leader) = ($2, quotemeta($1));
```

```
    } else {
        ($white, $leader) = (/^(\s+)/, '');
    }
    s/^\s*?$leader(?:$white)?//gm;
    return $_;
}
```

If that pattern makes your eyes glaze over, you could always break it up and add comments by adding /x:

```
if (m{
        ^                       # start of line
        \s *                    # 0 or more whitespace chars
        (?:                     # begin first non-remembered grouping
            (                   #   begin save buffer $1
                [^\w\s]         #     one character neither space nor word
                +               #     1 or more of such
            )                   #   end save buffer $1
            ( \s* )             #   put 0 or more white in buffer $2
            .* \n               #   match through the end of first line
        )                       # end of first grouping
        (?:                     # begin second non-remembered grouping
            \s *                #   0 or more whitespace chars
            \1                  #   whatever string is destined for $1
            \2 ?                #   what'll be in $2, but optionally
            .* \n               #   match through the end of the line
        ) +                     # now repeat that group idea 1 or more
        $                       # until the end of the line
    }x
    )
{
    ($white, $leader) = ($2, quotemeta($1));
} else {
    ($white, $leader) = (/^(\s+)/, '');
}
s{
        ^                       # start of each line (due to /m)
        \s *                    # any amount of leading whitespace
          ?                     #   but minimally matched
        $leader                 # our quoted, saved per-line leader
        (?:                     # begin unremembered grouping
            $white              #   the same amount
        ) ?                     # optionalize in case EOL after leader
}{ }xgm;
```

There, isn't that much easier to read? Well, maybe not; sometimes it doesn't help to pepper your code with insipid comments that mirror the code. This may be one of those cases.

See Also

The "Scalar Value Constructors" section of *perldata*(1) and the section on "Here Documents" in Chapter 2 of *Programming Perl*; the s/// operator in *perlre*(1) and *perlop*(1), and the "Pattern Matching" section in Chapter 5 of *Programming Perl*

1.17   Reformatting Paragraphs

Problem

Your string is too big to fit the screen, and you want to break it up into lines of words, without splitting a word between lines. For instance, a style correction script might read a text file a paragraph at a time, replacing bad phrases with good ones. Replacing a phrase like *utilizes the inherent functionality of* with *uses* will change the length of lines, so it must somehow reformat the paragraphs when they're output.

Solution

Use the standard Text::Wrap module to put line breaks at the right place:

```
use Text::Wrap;
@output = wrap($leadtab, $nexttab, @para);
```

Or use the more discerning CPAN module, Text::Autoformat, instead:

```
use Text::Autoformat;
$formatted = autoformat $rawtext;
```

Discussion

The Text::Wrap module provides the `wrap` function, shown in Example 1-3, which takes a list of lines and reformats them into a paragraph with no line more than `$Text::Wrap::columns` characters long. We set `$columns` to 20, ensuring that no line will be longer than 20 characters. We pass `wrap` two arguments before the list of lines: the first is the indent for the first line of output, the second the indent for every subsequent line.

Example 1-3. wrapdemo

```
#!/usr/bin/perl -w
# wrapdemo - show how Text::Wrap works
@input = ("Folding and splicing is the work of an editor,",
          "not a mere collection of silicon",
          "and",
          "mobile electrons!");
use Text::Wrap qw($columns &wrap);
$columns = 20;
print "0123456789" x 2, "\n";
print wrap("    ", "  ", @input), "\n";
```

The result of this program is:

```
01234567890123456789
    Folding and
  splicing is the
  work of an
  editor, not a
```

```
mere collection
of silicon and
mobile electrons!
```

We get back a single string, with newlines ending each line but the last:

```
# merge multiple lines into one, then wrap one long line
use Text::Wrap;
undef $/;
print wrap('', '', split(/\s*\n\s*/, <>));
```

If you have the Term::ReadKey module (available from CPAN) on your system, you can determine your window size so you can wrap lines to fit the current screen size. If you don't have the module, sometimes the screen size can be found in $ENV{COLUMNS} or by parsing the output of the *stty*(1) command.

The following program tries to reformat both short and long lines within a paragraph, similar to the *fmt*(1) program, by setting the input record separator $/ to the empty string (causing <> to read paragraphs) and the output record separator $\ to two newlines. Then the paragraph is converted into one long line by changing all newlines and any surrounding whitespace to single spaces. Finally, we call the wrap function with leading and subsequent tab strings set to the empty string so we can have block paragraphs.

```
use Text::Wrap      qw(&wrap $columns);
use Term::ReadKey   qw(GetTerminalSize);
($columns) = GetTerminalSize();
($/, $\)  = ('', "\n\n");   # read by paragraph, output 2 newlines
while (<>) {                 # grab a full paragraph
    s/\s*\n\s*/ /g;          # convert intervening newlines to spaces
    print wrap('', '', $_); # and format
}
```

The CPAN module Text::Autoformat is much more clever. For one thing, it tries to avoid "widows," that is, very short lines at the end. More remarkably, it correctly copes with reformatting paragraphs that have multiple, deeply nested citations. An example from that module's manpage shows how the module can painlessly convert:

```
In comp.lang.perl.misc you wrote:
: > <CN = Clooless Noobie> writes:
: > CN> PERL sux because:
: > CN>    * It doesn't have a switch statement and you have to put $
: > CN>signs in front of everything
: > CN>    * There are too many OR operators: having |, || and 'or'
: > CN>operators is confusing
: > CN>    * VB rools, yeah!!!!!!!!!
: > CN> So anyway, how can I stop reloads on a web page?
: > CN> Email replies only, thanks - I don't read this newsgroup.
: >
: > Begone, sirrah! You are a pathetic, Bill-loving, microcephalic
: > script-infant.
: Sheesh, what's with this group - ask a question, get toasted! And how
: *dare* you accuse me of Ianuphilia!
```

into:

```
In comp.lang.perl.misc you wrote:
: > <CN = Clooless Noobie> writes:
: > CN> PERL sux because:
: > CN>    * It doesn't have a switch statement and you
: > CN>      have to put $ signs in front of everything
: > CN>    * There are too many OR operators: having |, ||
: > CN>      and 'or' operators is confusing
: > CN>    * VB rools, yeah!!!!!!!!! So anyway, how can I
: > CN>      stop reloads on a web page? Email replies
: > CN>      only, thanks - I don't read this newsgroup.
: >
: > Begone, sirrah! You are a pathetic, Bill-loving,
: > microcephalic script-infant.
: Sheesh, what's with this group - ask a question, get toasted!
: And how *dare* you accuse me of Ianuphilia!
```

simply via print autoformat($badparagraph). Pretty impressive, eh?

Here's a miniprogram that uses that module to reformat each paragraph of its input
stream:

```
use Text::Autoformat;
$/ = '';
while (<>) {
    print autoformat($_, {squeeze => 0, all => 1}), "\n";
}
```

See Also

The split and join functions in *perlfunc*(1) and Chapter 29 of *Programming Perl*; the
manpage for the standard Text::Wrap module; the CPAN module Term::ReadKey,
and its use in Recipe 15.6 and the CPAN module Text::Autoformat

1.18   Escaping Characters

Problem

You need to output a string with certain characters (quotes, commas, etc.) escaped.
For instance, you're producing a format string for sprintf and want to convert literal % signs into %%.

Solution

Use a substitution to backslash or double each character to be escaped:

```
# backslash
$var =~ s/([CHARLIST])/\\$1/g;

# double
$var =~ s/([CHARLIST])/$1$1/g;
```

Discussion

$var is the variable to be altered. The CHARLIST is a list of characters to escape and can contain backslash escapes like \t and \n. If you just have one character to escape, omit the brackets:

```
$string =~ s/%/%%/g;
```

The following code lets you do escaping when preparing strings to submit to the shell. (In practice, you would need to escape more than just ' and " to make any arbitrary string safe for the shell. Getting the list of characters right is so hard, and the risks if you get it wrong are so great, that you're better off using the list form of system and exec to run programs, shown in Recipe 16.2. They avoid the shell altogether.)

```
$string = q(Mom said, "Don't do that.");
$string =~ s/(['"])/\\$1/g;
```

We had to use two backslashes in the replacement because the replacement section of a substitution is read as a double-quoted string, and to get one backslash, you need to write two. Here's a similar example for VMS DCL, where you need to double every quote to get one through:

```
$string = q(Mom said, "Don't do that.");
$string =~ s/(['"])/$1$1/g;
```

Microsoft command interpreters are harder to work with. In Windows, *COMMAND.COM* recognizes double quotes but not single ones, disregards backquotes for running commands, and requires a backslash to make a double quote into a literal. Any of the many free or commercial Unix-like shell environments available for Windows will work just fine, though.

Because we're using character classes in the regular expressions, we can use - to define a range and ^ at the start to negate. This escapes all characters that aren't in the range A through Z.

```
$string =~ s/([^A-Z])/\\$1/g;
```

In practice, you wouldn't want to do that, since it would pick up a lowercase "a" and turn it into "\a", for example, which is ASCII BEL character. (Usually when you mean non-alphabetic characters, \PL works better.)

If you want to escape all non-word characters, use the \Q and \E string metacharacters or the quotemeta function. For example, these are equivalent:

```
$string = "this \Qis a test!\E";
$string = "this is\\ a\\ test\\!";
$string = "this " . quotemeta("is a test!");
```

See Also

The s/// operator in *perlre*(1) and *perlop*(1) and Chapter 5 of *Programming Perl*; the quotemeta function in *perlfunc*(1) and Chapter 29 of *Programming Perl*; the discussion of HTML escaping in Recipe 19.1; Recipe 19.5 for how to avoid having to escape strings to give the shell

1.19   Trimming Blanks from the Ends of a String

Problem

You have read a string that may have leading or trailing whitespace, and you want to remove it.

Solution

Use a pair of pattern substitutions to get rid of them:

```
$string =~ s/^\s+//;
$string =~ s/\s+$//;
```

Or write a function that returns the new value:

```
$string = trim($string);
@many   = trim(@many);

sub trim {
    my @out = @_;
    for (@out) {
        s/^\s+//;          # trim left
        s/\s+$//;          # trim right
    }
    return @out == 1
            ? $out[0]    # only one to return
            : @out;      # or many
}
```

Discussion

This problem has various solutions, but this one is the most efficient for the common case. This function returns new versions of the strings passed in to it with their leading and trailing whitespace removed. It works on both single strings and lists.

To remove the last character from the string, use the chop function. Be careful not to confuse this with the similar but different chomp function, which removes the last part of the string contained within that variable if and only if it is contained in the $/ variable, "\n" by default. These are often used to remove the trailing newline from input:

```
# print what's typed, but surrounded by > < symbols
while (<STDIN>) {
    chomp;
    print ">$_<\n";
}
```

This function can be embellished in any of several ways.

First, what should you do if several strings are passed in, but the return context demands a single scalar? As written, the function given in the Solution does a somewhat silly thing: it (inadvertently) returns a scalar representing the number of strings passed in. This isn't very useful. You *could* issue a warning or raise an exception. You could also squash the list of return values together.

For strings with spans of extra whitespace at points other than their ends, you could have your function collapse any remaining stretch of whitespace characters in the interior of the string down to a single space each by adding this line as the new last line of the loop:

```
s/\s+/ /g;                # finally, collapse middle
```

That way a string like " but\t\tnot here\n" would become "but not here". A more efficient alternative to the three substitution lines:

```
s/^\s+//;
s/\s+$//;
s/\s+/ /g;
```

would be:

```
$_ = join(' ', split(' '));
```

If the function isn't passed any arguments at all, it could act like chop and chomp by defaulting to $_. Incorporating all of these embellishments produces this function:

```
# 1. trim leading and trailing white space
# 2. collapse internal whitespace to single space each
# 3. take input from $_ if no arguments given
# 4. join return list into single scalar with intervening spaces
#     if return is scalar context

sub trim {
    my @out = @_ ? @_ : $_;
    $_ = join(' ', split(' ')) for @out;
    return wantarray ? @out : "@out";
}
```

See Also

The s/// operator in *perlre*(1) and *perlop*(1) and Chapter 5 of *Programming Perl*; the chomp and chop functions in *perlfunc*(1) and Chapter 29 of *Programming Perl*; we trim leading and trailing whitespace in the getnum function in Recipe 2.1

1.20   Parsing Comma-Separated Data

Problem

You have a data file containing comma-separated values that you need to read, but these data fields may have quoted commas or escaped quotes in them. Most spreadsheets and database programs use comma-separated values as a common interchange format.

Solution

If your data file follows normal Unix quoting and escaping conventions, where quotes within a field are backslash-escaped "like \"this\"", use the standard Text::ParseWords and this simple code:

```
use Text::ParseWords;
sub parse_csv0 {
    return quotewords("," => 0, $_[0]);
}
```

However, if quotes within a field are doubled "like ""this""", you could use the following procedure from *Mastering Regular Expressions*, Second Edition:

```
sub parse_csv1 {
    my $text = shift;      # record containing comma-separated values
    my @fields = ();

    while ($text =~ m{
        # Either some non-quote/non-comma text:
        ( [^"',] + )

         # ...or...
         |

         # ...a double-quoted field: (with "" allowed inside)

         " # field's opening quote; don't save this
          (   now a field is either
           (?:     [^"]    # non-quotes or
             |
                   ""       # adjacent quote pairs
           ) *  # any number
          )
         " # field's closing quote; unsaved

    }gx)
    {
      if (defined $1) {
          $field = $1;
      } else {
          ($field = $2) =~ s/""/"/g;
      }
      push @fields, $field;
    }
    return @fields;
}
```

Or use the CPAN Text:CSV module:

```
use Text::CSV;
sub parse_csv1 {
```

```
        my $line = shift;
        my $csv = Text::CSV->new();
        return $csv->parse($line) && $csv->fields();
    }
```

Or use the CPAN Tie::CSV_File module:

```
    tie @data, "Tie::CSV_File", "data.csv";

    for ($i = 0; $i < @data; $i++) {
        printf "Row %d (Line %d) is %s\n", $i, $i+1, "@{$data[$i]}";
        for ($j = 0; $j < @{$data[$i]}; $j++) {
            print "Column $j is <$data[$i][$j]>\n";
        }
    }
```

Discussion

Comma-separated input is a deceptive and complex format. It sounds simple, but involves a fairly complex escaping system because the fields themselves can contain commas. This makes the pattern-matching solution complex and rules out a simple split /,/. Still worse, quoting and escaping conventions vary between Unix-style files and legacy systems. This incompatibility renders impossible any single algorithm for all CSV data files.

The standard Text::ParseWords module is designed to handle data whose quoting and escaping conventions follow those found in most Unix data files. This makes it eminently suitable for parsing the numerous colon-separated data files found on Unix systems, including *disktab*(5), *gettytab*(5), *printcap*(5), and *termcap*(5). Pass that module's quotewords function two arguments and the CSV string. The first argument is the separator (here a comma, but often a colon), and the second is a true or false value controlling whether the strings are returned with quotes around them.

In this style of data file, you represent quotation marks inside a field delimited by quotation marks by escaping them with backslashes "like\"this\"". Quotation marks and backslashes are the only characters that have meaning when backslashed. Any other use of a backslash will be left in the output string. The standard Text::ParseWords module's quotewords() function can handle such data.

However, it's of no use on data files from legacy systems that represent quotation marks inside such a field by doubling them "like""this""". For those, you'll need one of the other solutions. The first of these is based on the regular expression from *Mastering Regular Expressions,* Second Edition, by Jeffrey E. F. Friedl (O'Reilly). It enjoys the advantage of working on any system without requiring installation of modules not found in the standard distribution. In fact, it doesn't use any modules at all. Its slight disadvantage is the risk of sending the unseasoned reader into punctuation shock, despite its copious commenting.

The object-oriented CPAN module Text::CSV demonstrated in the next solution hides that parsing complexity in more easily digestible wrappers. An even more elegant solution is offered by the Tie::CSV_File module from CPAN, in which you are given what appears to be a two-dimensional array. The first dimension represents each line of the file, and the second dimension each column on each row.

Here's how you'd use our two kinds of parse_csv subroutines. The q( ) is just a fancy quote so we didn't have to backslash everything.

```
$line = q(XYZZY,"","O'Reilly, Inc","Wall, Larry","a \"glug\" bit,",5,"Error, Core
Dumped");
@fields = parse_csv0($line);
for ($i = 0; $i < @fields; $i++) {
    print "$i : $fields[$i]\n";
}
```

```
0 : XYZZY
1 :
2 : O'Reilly, Inc
3 : Wall, Larry
4 : a "glug" bit,
5 : 5
6 : Error, Core Dumped
```

If the second argument to quotewords had been 1 instead of 0, the quotes would have been retained, producing this output instead:

```
0 : XYZZY
1 : ""
2 : "O'Reilly, Inc"
3 : "Wall, Larry"
4 : "a \"glug\" bit,"
5 : 5
6 : "Error, Core Dumped"
```

The other sort of data file is manipulated the same way, but using our parse_csv1 function instead of parse_csv0. Notice how the embedded quotes are doubled, not escaped.

```
$line = q(Ten Thousand,10000, 2710 ,,"10,000","It's ""10 Grand""", baby",10K);
@fields = parse_csv1($line);
for ($i = 0; $i < @fields; $i++) {
    print "$i : $fields[$i]\n";
}
```

```
0 : Ten Thousand
1 : 10000
2 :  2710
3 :
4 : 10,000
5 : It's "10 Grand", baby
6 : 10K
```

See Also

The explanation of regular expression syntax in *perlre*(1) and Chapter 5 of *Programming Perl*; the documentation for the standard Text::ParseWords module; the section on "Parsing CSV Files" in Chapter 5 of *Mastering Regular Expressions*, Second Edition

1.21 Constant Variables

Problem

You want a variable whose value cannot be modified once set.

Solution

If you don't need it to be a scalar variable that can interpolate, the use constant pragma will work:

```
use constant AVOGADRO => 6.02252e23;

printf "You need %g of those for guac\n", AVOGADRO;
```

If it does have to be a variable, assign to the typeglob a reference to a literal string or number, then use the scalar variable:

```
*AVOGADRO = \6.02252e23;
print "You need $AVOGADRO of those for guac\n";
```

But the most foolproof way is via a small tie class whose STORE method raises an exception:

```
package Tie::Constvar;
use Carp;
sub TIESCALAR {
    my ($class, $initval) = @_;
    my $var = $initval;
    return bless \$var => $class;
}
sub FETCH {
    my $selfref = shift;
    return $$selfref;
}
sub STORE {
    confess "Meddle not with the constants of the universe";
}
```

Discussion

The use constant pragma is the easiest to use, but has a few drawbacks. The biggest one is that it doesn't give you a variable that you can expand in double-quoted strings. Another is that it isn't scoped; it puts a subroutine of that name into the package namespace.

The way the pragma really works is to create a subroutine of that name that takes no arguments and always returns the same value (or values if a list is provided). That means it goes into the current package's namespace and isn't scoped. You could do the same thing yourself this way:

```
sub AVOGADRO( ) { 6.02252e23 }
```

If you wanted it scoped to the current block, you could make a temporary subroutine by assigning an anonymous subroutine to the typeglob of that name:

```
use subs qw(AVOGADRO);
local *AVOGADRO = sub () { 6.02252e23 };
```

But that's pretty magical, so you should comment the code if you don't plan to use the pragma.

If instead of assigning to the typeglob a reference to a subroutine, you assign to it a reference to a constant scalar, then you'll be able to use the variable of that name. That's the second technique given in the Solution. Its disadvantage is that typeglobs are available only for package variables, not for lexicals created via my. Under the recommended use strict pragma, an undeclared package variable will get you into trouble, too, but you can declare the variable using our:

```
our $AVOGADRO;
local *AVOGADRO = \6.02252e23;
```

The third solution provided, that of creating your own little tie class, might appear the most complicated, but it provides the most flexibility. Plus you get to declare it as a lexical if you want.

```
tie my $AVOGADRO, Tie::Constvar, 6.02252e23;
```

After which this is okay:

```
print "You need $AVOGADRO of those for guac\n";
```

But this will get you in trouble:

```
$AVOGADRO = 6.6256e-34;    # sorry, Max
```

See Also

Recipe 1.15; Recipe 5.3; the discussion on folding constant subroutines toward the end of the section on "Compiling Your Code" in Chapter 18 of *Programming Perl*; the CPAN module Tie::Scalar::RestrictUpdates might give you some other ideas

1.22   Soundex Matching

Problem

You have two English surnames and want to know whether they sound somewhat similar, regardless of spelling. This would let you offer users a "fuzzy search" of names in a telephone book to catch "Smith" and "Smythe" and others within the set, such as "Smite" and "Smote".

Solution

Use the standard Text::Soundex module:

```
use Text::Soundex;
$CODE  = soundex($STRING);
@CODES = soundex(@LIST);
```

Or use the CPAN module Text::Metaphone:

```
use Text::Metaphone;
$phoned_words = Metaphone('Schwern');
```

Discussion

The soundex algorithm hashes words (particularly English surnames) into a small space using a simple model that approximates an English speaker's pronunciation of the words. Roughly speaking, each word is reduced to a four-character string. The first character is an uppercase letter; the remaining three are digits. By comparing the soundex values of two strings, we can guess whether they sound similar.

The following program prompts for a name and looks for similarly sounding names from the password file. This same approach works on any database with names, so you could key the database on the soundex values if you wanted to. Such a key wouldn't be unique, of course.

```
use Text::Soundex;
use User::pwent;

print "Lookup user: ";
chomp($user =<STDIN>);
exit unless defined $user;
$name_code = soundex($user);

while ($uent = getpwent()) {
    ($firstname, $lastname) = $uent->gecos =~ /(\w+)[^,]*\b(\w+)/;

    if ($name_code eq soundex($uent->name) ||
        $name_code eq soundex($lastname)   ||
        $name_code eq soundex($firstname)  )
    {
```

```
        printf "%s: %s %s\n", $uent->name, $firstname, $lastname;
    }
}
```

The Text::Metaphone module from CPAN addresses the same problem in a different and better way. The soundex function returns a letter and a three-digit code that maps just the beginning of the input string, whereas `Metaphone` returns a code as letters of variable length. For example:

```
                           soundex   metaphone

        Christiansen       C623      KRSXNSN
        Kris Jenson        K625      KRSJNSN

        Kyrie Eleison      K642      KRLSN
        Curious Liaison    C624      KRSLSN
```

To get the most of Metaphone, you should also use the String::Approx module from CPAN, described more fully in Recipe 6.13. It allows for there to be errors in the match and still be successful. The *edit distance* is the number of changes needed to go from one string to the next. This matches a pair of strings with an edit distance of two:

```
    if (amatch("string1", [2], "string2") { }
```

There's also an `adist` function that reports the edit distance. The edit distance between "Kris Jenson" "Christiansen" is 6, but between their Metaphone encodings is only 1. Likewise, the distance between the other pair is 8 originally, but down to 1 again if you compare Metaphone encodings.

```
use Text::Metaphone qw(Metaphone);
use String::Approx  qw(amatch);

if (amatch(Metaphone($s1), [1], Metaphone($s1)) {
    print "Close enough!\n";
}
```

This would successfully match both of our example pairs.

See Also

The documentation for the standard Text::Soundex and User::pwent modules; the Text::Metaphone and String::Approx modules from CPAN; your system's *passwd*(5) manpage; Volume 3, Chapter 6 of *The Art of Computer Programming*, by Donald E. Knuth (Addison-Wesley)

1.23 Program: fixstyle

Imagine you have a table with both old and new strings, such as the following:

Old words	New words
bonnet	hood
rubber	eraser
lorry	truck
trousers	pants

The program in Example 1-4 is a filter that changes all occurrences of each element in the first set to the corresponding element in the second set.

When called without filename arguments, the program is a simple filter. If filenames are supplied on the command line, an in-place edit writes the changes to the files, with the original versions saved in a file with a ".orig" extension. See Recipe 7.16 for a description. A **-v** command-line option writes notification of each change to standard error.

The table of original strings and their replacements is stored below __END__ in the main program, as described in Recipe 7.12. Each pair of strings is converted into carefully escaped substitutions and accumulated into the $code variable like the *popgrep2* program in Recipe 6.10.

A -t check to test for an interactive run check tells whether we're expecting to read from the keyboard if no arguments are supplied. That way if users forget to give an argument, they aren't wondering why the program appears to be hung.

Example 1-4. fixstyle

```
#!/usr/bin/perl -w
# fixstyle - switch first set of <DATA> strings to second set
#    usage: $0 [-v] [files ...]
use strict;
my $verbose = (@ARGV && $ARGV[0] eq '-v' && shift);
if (@ARGV) {
   $^I = ".orig";           # preserve old files
} else {
   warn "$0: Reading from stdin\n" if -t STDIN;
}
my $code = "while (<>) {\n";
# read in config, build up code to eval
while (<DATA>) {
  chomp;
  my ($in, $out) = split /\s*=>\s*/;
  next unless $in && $out;
  $code .= "s{\\Q$in\\E}{$out}g";
  $code .= "&& printf STDERR qq($in => $out at \$ARGV line \$.\\n)"
                                             if $verbose;
  $code .= ";\n";
```

Example 1-4. fixstyle (continued)

```
    }
    $code .= "print;\n}\n";
    eval "{ $code } 1" || die;
    __END__
    analysed         => analyzed
    built-in         => builtin
    chastized        => chastised
    commandline      => command-line
    de-allocate      => deallocate
    dropin           => drop-in
    hardcode         => hard-code
    meta-data        => metadata
    multicharacter   => multi-character
    multiway         => multi-way
    non-empty        => nonempty
    non-profit       => nonprofit
    non-trappable    => nontrappable
    pre-define       => predefine
    preextend        => pre-extend
    re-compiling     => recompiling
    reenter          => re-enter
    turnkey          => turn-key
```

One caution: this program is fast, but it doesn't scale if you need to make hundreds of changes. The larger the DATA section, the longer it takes. A few dozen changes won't slow it down, and in fact, the version given in Example 1-4 is faster for that case. But if you run the program on hundreds of changes, it will bog down.

Example 1-5 is a version that's slower for few changes but faster when there are many changes.

Example 1-5. fixstyle2

```perl
#!/usr/bin/perl -w
# fixstyle2 - like fixstyle but faster for many many changes
use strict;
my $verbose = (@ARGV && $ARGV[0] eq '-v' && shift);
my %change = ();
while (<DATA>) {
  chomp;
  my ($in, $out) = split /\s*=>\s*/;
  next unless $in && $out;
  $change{$in} = $out;
}
if (@ARGV) {
  $^I = ".orig";
} else {
  warn "$0: Reading from stdin\n" if -t STDIN;
}
while (<>) {
  my $i = 0;
  s/^(\s+)// && print $1;            # emit leading whitespace
```

Example 1-5. fixstyle2 (continued)

```perl
    for (split /(\s+)/, $_, -1) {    # preserve trailing whitespace
        print( ($i++ & 1) ? $_ : ($change{$_} || $_));
    }
}
__END__
analysed        => analyzed
built-in        => builtin
chastized       => chastised
commandline     => command-line
de-allocate     => deallocate
dropin          => drop-in
hardcode        => hard-code
meta-data       => metadata
multicharacter  => multi-character
multiway        => multi-way
non-empty       => nonempty
non-profit      => nonprofit
non-trappable   => nontrappable
pre-define      => predefine
preextend       => pre-extend
re-compiling    => recompiling
reenter         => re-enter
turnkey         => turn-key
```

This version breaks each line into chunks of whitespace and words, which isn't a fast operation. It then uses those words to look up their replacements in a hash, which is much faster than a substitution. So the first part is slower, the second faster. The difference in speed depends on the number of matches.

If you don't care about keeping the whitespace separating each word constant, the second version can run as fast as the first, even for a few changes. If you know a lot about your input, collapse whitespace into single blanks by plugging in this loop:

```perl
# very fast, but whitespace collapse
while (<>) {
  for (split) {
      print $change{$_} || $_, " ";
  }
  print "\n";
}
```

That leaves an extra blank at the end of each line. If that's a problem, you could use the technique from Recipe 16.5 to install an output filter. Place the following code in front of the while loop that's collapsing whitespace:

```perl
my $pid = open(STDOUT, "|-");
die "cannot fork: $!" unless defined $pid;
unless ($pid) {                 # child
      while (<STDIN>) {
      s/ $//;
      print;
    }
```

```
    exit;
}
```

1.24 Program: psgrep

Many programs, including *ps*, *netstat*, *lsof*, *ls -l*, *find -ls*, and *tcpdump*, can produce more output than can be conveniently summarized. Logfiles also often grow too long to be easily viewed. You could send these through a filter like *grep* to pick out only certain lines, but regular expressions and complex logic don't mix well; just look at the hoops we jump through in Recipe 6.18.

What we'd really like is to make full queries on the program output or logfile. For example, to ask *ps* something like, "Show me all processes that exceed 10K in size but which aren't running as the superuser" or "Which commands are running on pseudo-ttys?"

The *psgrep* program does this—and infinitely more—because the specified selection criteria are not mere regular expressions; they're full Perl code. Each criterion is applied in turn to every line of output. Only lines matching all arguments are output. The following is a list of things to find and how to find them.

Lines containing "sh" at the end of a word:

```
% psgrep '/sh\b/'
```

Processes whose command names end in "sh":

```
% psgrep 'command =~ /sh$/'
```

Processes running with a user ID below 10:

```
% psgrep 'uid < 10'
```

Login shells with active ttys:

```
% psgrep 'command =~ /^-/' 'tty ne "?"'
```

Processes running on pseudo-ttys:

```
% psgrep 'tty =~ /^[p-t]/'
```

Non-superuser processes running detached:

```
% psgrep 'uid && tty eq "?"'
```

Huge processes that aren't owned by the superuser:

```
% psgrep 'size > 10 * 2**10' 'uid != 0'
```

The last call to *psgrep* produced the following output when run on our system. As one might expect, only *netscape* and its spawn qualified.

FLAGS	UID	PID	PPID	PRI	NI	SIZE	RSS	WCHAN	STA	TTY	TIME	COMMAND
0	101	9751	1	0	0	14932	9652	do_select	S	p1	0:25	netscape
100000	101	9752	9751	0	0	10636	812	do_select	S	p1	0:00	(dns helper)

Example 1-6 shows the *psgrep* program.

Example 1-6. psgrep

```perl
#!/usr/bin/perl -w
# psgrep - print selected lines of ps output by
#          compiling user queries into code
use strict;
# each field from the PS header
my @fieldnames = qw(FLAGS UID PID PPID PRI NICE SIZE
                    RSS WCHAN STAT TTY TIME COMMAND);
# determine the unpack format needed (hard-coded for Linux ps)
my $fmt = cut2fmt(8, 14, 20, 26, 30, 34, 41, 47, 59, 63, 67, 72);
my %fields;                          # where the data will store
die << Thanatos unless @ARGV;
usage: $0 criterion ...
  Each criterion is a Perl expression involving:
   @fieldnames
  All criteria must be met for a line to be printed.
Thanatos
# Create function aliases for uid, size, UID, SIZE, etc.
# Empty parens on closure args needed for void prototyping.
for my $name (@fieldnames) {
  no strict 'refs';
  *$name = *{lc $name} = sub () { $fields{$name} };
}
my $code = "sub is_desirable { " . join(" and ", @ARGV) . " } ";
unless (eval $code.1) {
  die "Error in code: $@\n\t$code\n";
}
open(PS, "ps wwaxl |")              || die "cannot fork: $!";
print scalar <PS>;                   # emit header line
while (<PS>) {
  @fields{@fieldnames} = trim(unpack($fmt, $_));
  print if is_desirable();          # line matches their criteria
}
close(PS)                           || die "ps failed!";
# convert cut positions to unpack format
sub cut2fmt {
  my(@positions) = @_;
  my $template  = '';
  my $lastpos   = 1;
  for my $place (@positions) {
      $template .= "A" . ($place - $lastpos) . " ";
      $lastpos   = $place;
  }
  $template .= "A*";
  return $template;
}
sub trim {
  my @strings = @_;
  for (@strings) {
      s/^\s+//;
      s/\s+$//;
  }
  return wantarray ? @strings : $strings[0];
```

Example 1-6. psgrep (continued)

```
    }
    # the following was used to determine column cut points.
    # sample input data follows
    #1234567890123456789012345678901234567890123456789012345678901234567890 12345
    #        1         2         3         4         5         6         7
    # Positioning:
    #        8    14    20    26 30 34    41    47          59 63 67   72
    #        |     |     |     |  |  |     |     |           |  |  |    |
    __END__
    FLAGS    UID   PID  PPID PRI  NI   SIZE   RSS WCHAN       STA TTY  TIME COMMAND
      100      0     1     0   0   0    760   432 do_select    S   ?   0:02 init
      140      0   187     1   0   0    784   452 do_select    S   ?   0:02 syslogd
   100100    101   428     1   0   0   1436   944 do_exit      S   1   0:00 /bin/login
   100140     99 30217   402   0   0   1552  1008 posix_lock_  S   ?   0:00 httpd
        0    101   593   428   0   0   1780  1260 copy_thread  S   1   0:00 -tcsh
   100000    101 30639  9562  17   0    924   496              R  p1   0:00 ps axl
        0    101 25145  9563   0   0   2964  2360 idetape_rea  S  p2   0:06 trn
   100100      0 10116  9564   0   0   1412   928 setup_frame  T  p3   0:00 ssh -C www
   100100      0 26560 26554   0   0   1076   572 setup_frame  T  p2   0:00 less
   100000    101 19058  9562   0   0   1396   900 setup_frame  T  p1   0:02 nvi /tmp/a
```

The *psgrep* program integrates many techniques presented throughout this book. Stripping strings of leading and trailing whitespace is found in Recipe 1.19. Converting cut marks into an unpack format to extract fixed fields is in Recipe 1.1. Matching strings with regular expressions is the entire topic of Chapter 6.

The multiline string in the here document passed to die is discussed in Recipes 1.15 and 1.16. The assignment to @fields{@fieldnames} sets many values at once in the hash named %fields. Hash slices are discussed in Recipes 4.8 and 5.11.

The sample program input contained beneath __END__ is described in Recipe 7.12. During development, we used canned input from the DATA filehandle for testing purposes. Once the program worked properly, we changed it to read from a piped-in *ps* command but left a remnant of the original filter input to aid in future porting and maintenance. Launching other programs over a pipe is covered in Chapter 16, including Recipes 16.10 and 16.13.

The real power and expressiveness in *psgrep* derive from Perl's use of string arguments not as mere strings but directly as Perl code. This is similar to the technique in Recipe 9.9, except that in *psgrep*, the user's arguments are wrapped with a routine called is_desirable. That way, the cost of compiling strings into Perl code happens only once, before the program whose output we'll process is even begun. For example, asking for UIDs under 10 creates this string to eval:

```
eval "sub is_desirable { uid < 10 } " . 1;
```

The mysterious ".1" at the end is so that if the user code compiles, the whole eval returns true. That way we don't even have to check $@ for compilation errors as we do in Recipe 10.12.

Specifying arbitrary Perl code in a filter to select records is a breathtakingly powerful approach, but it's not entirely original. Perl owes much to the *awk* programming language, which is often used for such filtering. One problem with *awk* is that it can't easily treat input as fixed-size fields instead of fields separated by something. Another is that the fields are not mnemonically named: *awk* uses $1, $2, etc. Plus, Perl can do much that *awk* cannot.

The user criteria don't even have to be simple expressions. For example, this call initializes a variable $id to user *nobody*'s number to use later in its expression:

```
% psgrep 'no strict "vars";
        BEGIN { $id = getpwnam("nobody") }
        uid == $id '
```

How can we use unquoted words without even a dollar sign, like uid, command, and size, to represent those respective fields in each input record? We directly manipulate the symbol table by assigning closures to indirect typeglobs, which creates functions with those names. The function names are created using both uppercase and lowercase names, allowing both "UID < 10" and "uid > 10". Closures are described in Recipe 11.4, and assigning them to typeglobs to create function aliases is shown in Recipe 10.14.

One twist here not seen in those recipes is empty parentheses on the closure. These allowed us to use the function in an expression anywhere we'd use a single term, like a string or a numeric constant. It creates a void prototype so the field-accessing function named uid accepts no arguments, just like the built-in function time. If these functions weren't prototyped void, expressions like "uid < 10" or "size/2 > rss" would confuse the parser because it would see the unterminated start of a wildcard glob and of a pattern match, respectively. Prototypes are discussed in Recipe 10.11.

The version of *psgrep* demonstrated here expects the output from Red Hat Linux's *ps*. To port to other systems, look at which columns the headers begin at. This approach isn't relevant only to *ps* or only to Unix systems; it's a generic technique for filtering input records using Perl expressions, easily adapted to other record layouts. The input format could be in columns, space separated, comma separated, or the result of a pattern match with capturing parentheses.

The program could even be modified to handle a user-defined database with a small change to the selection functions. If you had an array of records as described in Recipe 11.9, you could let users specify arbitrary selection criteria, such as:

```
sub id()        { $_->{ID}   }
sub title()     { $_->{TITLE} }
sub executive() { title =~ /(?:vice-)?president/i }

# user search criteria go in the grep clause
@slowburners = grep { id<10 && !executive } @employees;
```

For reasons of security and performance, this kind of power is seldom found in database engines like those described in Chapter 14. SQL doesn't support this, but given Perl and small bit of ingenuity, it's easy to roll it up on your own.

## CHAPTER 2

Numbers

Anyone who considers arithmetical methods of
producing random digits is, of course, in a state of sin.
—John von Neumann (1951)

2.0 Introduction

Numbers, the most basic data type of almost any programming language, can be surprisingly tricky. Random numbers, numbers with decimal points, series of numbers, and conversion between strings and numbers all pose trouble.

Perl works hard to make life easy for you, and the facilities it provides for manipulating numbers are no exception to that rule. If you treat a scalar value as a number, Perl converts it to one. This means that when you read ages from a file, extract digits from a string, or acquire numbers from any of the other myriad textual sources that Real Life pushes your way, you don't need to jump through the hoops created by other languages' cumbersome requirements to turn an ASCII string into a number.

Perl tries its best to interpret a string as a number when you use it as one (such as in a mathematical expression), but it has no direct way of reporting that a string doesn't represent a valid number. Perl quietly converts non-numeric strings to zero, and it will stop converting the string once it reaches a non-numeric character—so "A7" is still 0, and "7A" is just 7. (Note, however, that the **-w** flag will warn of such improper conversions.) Sometimes, such as when validating input, you need to know whether a string represents a valid number. We show you how in Recipe 2.1.

Recipe 2.15 shows how to get a number from strings containing hexadecimal, octal, or binary representations of numbers such as "0xff", "0377", and "0b10110". Perl automatically converts numeric literals of these non-decimal bases that occur in your program code (so $a = 3 + 0xff will set $a to 258) but not data read by that program (you can't read "ff" or even "0xff" into $b and then say $a = 3 + $b to make $a become 258).

As if integers weren't giving us enough grief, floating-point numbers can cause even more headaches. Internally, a computer represents numbers with decimal points as floating-point numbers in binary format. Floating-point numbers are not the same as real numbers; they are an approximation of real numbers, with limited precision. Although infinitely many real numbers exist, you only have finite space to represent them, usually about 64 bits or so. You have to cut corners to fit them all in.

When numbers are read from a file or appear as literals in your program, they are converted from their textual representation—which is always in base 10 for numbers with decimal points in them—into an internal, base-2 representation. The only fractional numbers that can be exactly represented using a finite number of digits in a particular numeric base are those that can be written as the sum of a finite number of fractions whose denominators are integral powers of that base.

For example, 0.13 is one tenth plus three one-hundredths. But that's in base-10 notation. In binary, something like 0.75 is exactly representable because it's the sum of one half plus one quarter, and 2 and 4 are both powers of two. But even so simple a number as one tenth, written as 0.1 in base-10 notation, cannot be rewritten as the sum of some set of halves, quarters, eighths, sixteenths, etc. That means that, just as one third can't be exactly represented as a non-repeating decimal number, one tenth can't be exactly represented as a non-repeating binary number. Your computer's internal binary representation of 0.1 isn't exactly 0.1; it's just an approximation!

```
$ perl -e 'printf "%.60f\n", 0.1'
0.100000000000000005551115123125782702118158340454101562500000
```

Recipes 2.2 and 2.3 demonstrate how to make your computer's floating-point representations behave more like real numbers.

Recipe 2.4 gives three ways to perform one operation on each element of a set of consecutive integers. We show how to convert to and from Roman numerals in Recipe 2.5.

Random numbers are the topic of several recipes. Perl's rand function returns a floating-point value between 0 and 1, or between 0 and its argument. We show how to get random numbers in a given range, how to make random numbers more random, and how to make rand give a different sequence of random numbers each time you run your program.

We round out the chapter with recipes on trigonometry, logarithms, matrix multiplication, complex numbers, and the often-asked question: "How do you put commas in numbers?"

2.1 Checking Whether a String Is a Valid Number

Problem

You want to check whether a string represents a valid number. This is a common problem when validating input, as in CGI scripts, configuration files, and command-line arguments.

Solution

Compare it against a regular expression that matches the kinds of numbers you're interested in:

```
if ($string =~ /PATTERN/) {
    # is a number
} else {
    # is not
}
```

Or use the patterns provided by the CPAN module Regexp::Common:

```
if ($string =~ m{^$RE{num}{real}$}) {
    # is a real number
} else {
    # is not
}
```

Discussion

This problem gets to the heart of what we mean by a number. Even things that sound simple, like *integer*, make you think hard about what you will accept; for example, "Is a leading + for positive numbers optional, mandatory, or forbidden?" The many ways that floating-point numbers can be represented could overheat your brain.

Decide what you will and will not accept. Then, construct a regular expression to match those things alone. Here are some precooked solutions (the Cookbook's equivalent of just-add-water meals) for most common cases:

```
warn "has nondigits"        if      /\D/;
warn "not a natural number" unless /^\d+$/;               # rejects -3
warn "not an integer"       unless /^-?\d+$/;             # rejects +3
warn "not an integer"       unless /^[+-]?\d+$/;
warn "not a decimal number" unless /^-?\d+\.?\d*$/;       # rejects .2
warn "not a decimal number" unless /^-?(?:\d+(?:\.\d*)?|\.\d+)$/;
warn "not a C float"
        unless /^([+-]?)(?=\d|\.\d)\d*(\.\d*)?([Ee]([+-]?\d+))?$/;
```

These lines do not catch the IEEE notations of "Infinity" and "NaN", but unless you're worried that IEEE committee members will stop by your workplace and beat you over the head with copies of the relevant standards documents, you can probably forget about these strange forms.

If your number has leading or trailing whitespace, those patterns won't work. Either add the appropriate logic directly, or call the `trim` function from Recipe 1.19.

The CPAN module Regexp::Common provides a wealth of canned patterns that test whether a string looks like a number. Besides saving you from having to figure out the patterns on your own, it also makes your code more legible. By default, this module exports a hash called %RE that you index into, according to which kind of regular expression you're looking for. Be careful to use anchors as needed; otherwise, it will search for that pattern anywhere in the string. For example:

```
use Regexp::Common;
$string = "Gandalf departed from the Havens in 3021 TA.";
print "Is an integer\n"          if $string =~ / ^    $RE{num}{int} $ /x;
print "Contains the integer $1\n" if $string =~ /    ( $RE{num}{int} ) /x;
```

The following examples are other patterns that the module can use to match numbers:

```
$RE{num}{int}{-sep=>',?'}              # match 1234567 or 1,234,567
$RE{num}{int}{-sep=>'.'}{-group=>4}    # match 1.2345.6789
$RE{num}{int}{-base => 8}              # match 014 but not 99
$RE{num}{int}{-sep=>','}{-group=3}     # match 1,234,594
$RE{num}{int}{-sep=>',?'}{-group=3}    # match 1,234 or 1234
$RE{num}{real}                         # match 123.456 or -0.123456
$RE{num}{roman}                        # match xvii or MCMXCVIII
$RE{num}{square}                       # match 9 or 256 or 12321
```

Some of these patterns, such as square, were not available in early module versions. General documentation for the module can be found in the Regexp::Common manpage, but more detailed documentation for just the numeric patterns is in the Regexp::Common::number manpage.

Some techniques for identifying numbers don't involve regular expressions. Instead, these techniques use functions from system libraries or Perl to determine whether a string contains an acceptable number. Of course, these functions limit you to the definition of "number" offered by your libraries and Perl.

If you're on a POSIX system, Perl supports the POSIX::strtod function. Its semantics are cumbersome, so the following is a getnum wrapper function for more convenient access. This function takes a string and returns either the number it found or undef for input that isn't a C float. The is_numeric function is a frontend to getnum for when you just want to ask, "Is this a float?"

```
sub getnum {
    use POSIX qw(strtod);
    my $str = shift;
    $str =~ s/^\s+//;          # remove leading whitespace
    $str =~ s/\s+$//;          # remove trailing whitespace
    $! = 0;
    my($num, $unparsed) = strtod($str);
    if (($str eq '') || ($unparsed != 0) || $!) {
        return;
    } else {
        return $num;
    }
}

sub is_numeric { defined scalar &getnum }
```

The Scalar::Util module, newly standard as of Perl v5.8.1, exports a function called looks_like_number( ) that uses the Perl compiler's own internal function of the same name (see *perlapi*(1)). It returns true for any base-10 number that is acceptable to

Perl itself, such as 0, 0.8, 14.98, and 6.02e23—but not 0xb1010, 077, 0x392, or numbers with underscores in them. This means that you must check for alternate bases and decode them yourself if you want to permit users to enter such numbers, as in Example 2-1.

Example 2-1. Decode numbers

```
#!/usr/bin/perl -w
use Scalar::Util qw(looks_like_number);
print "$0: hit ^D (your eof character) to exit\n";
for (;;) {
    my ($on, $n);        # original string and its numeric value
    print "Pick a number, any number: ";
    $on = $n = <STDIN>;
    last if !defined $n;
    chomp($on,$n);
    $n =~ s/_//g;                        # allow 186_282.398_280_685
    $n = oct($n) if $n =~ /^0/;  # allow 0xFF, 037, 0b1010
    if (looks_like_number($n)) {
        printf "Decimal double of $on is %g\n", 2*$n;
    } else {
        print "That doesn't look like a number to Perl.\n";
    }
}
print "\nBye.\n";
```

See Also

The regular expression syntax in *perlre*(1) and Chapter 5 of *Programming Perl*; your system's *strtod*(3) manpage; the *perlapi*(1) manpage; the documentation for the CPAN module Regexp::Common, including the Regexp::Common::number manpage; the documentation for the standard POSIX and Scalar::Util modules (also in Chapter 32 of *Programming Perl*)

2.2   Rounding Floating-Point Numbers

Problem

You want to round a floating-point value to a certain number of decimal places. This problem arises from the same inaccuracies in representation that make testing for equality difficult (see Recipe 2.3), as well as in situations where you must reduce the precision of your answers for readability.

Solution

Use the Perl function sprintf, or printf if you're just trying to produce output:

```
# round off to two places
$rounded = sprintf("%.2f", $unrounded);
```

Or you can use other rounding functions described in the Discussion.

Discussion

Whether visible or not, rounding of some sort is virtually unavoidable when working with floating-point numbers. Carefully defined standards (namely, IEEE 754, the standard for binary floating-point arithmetic) coupled with reasonable defaults within Perl often manage to eliminate or at least hide these round-off errors.

In fact, Perl's implicit rounding on output is usually good enough so that it rarely surprises. It's almost always best to leave the numbers unrounded until output, and then, if you don't like Perl's default rounding, use printf or sprintf yourself with a format that makes the rounding explicit. The %f, %e, and %g formats all let you specify how many decimal places to round their argument to. Here's an example showing how all three behave; in each case, we're asking for a field that's 12 spaces wide, but with a precision of no more than four digits to the right of the decimal place.

```
for $n ( 0.0000001, 10.1, 10.00001, 100000.1 ) {
    printf "%12.4e %12.4f %12.4g\n", $n, $n, $n;
}
```

This produces the following output:

```
1.0000e-07        0.0000        1e-07
1.0100e+01       10.1000         10.1
1.0000e+01       10.0000           10
1.0000e+05   100000.1000        1e+05
```

If that were all there were to the matter, rounding would be pretty easy. You'd just pick your favorite output format and be done with it.

However, it's not that easy: sometimes you need to think more about what you really want and what's really happening. As we explained in the Introduction, even a simple number like 10.1 or 0.1 can only be approximated in binary floating-point. The only decimal numbers that can be *exactly* represented as floating-point numbers are those that can be rewritten as a finite sum of one or more fractions whose denominators are all powers of two. For example:

```
$a = 0.625;            # 1/2 + 1/8
$b = 0.725;            # 725/1000, or 29/40
printf "$_ is %.30g\n", $_ for $a, $b;
```

prints out:

```
0.625 is 0.625
0.725 is 0.724999999999999977795539507497
```

The number in $a is exactly representable in binary, but the one in $b is not. When Perl is told to print a floating-point number but not told the precision, as occurs for the interpolated value of $_ in the string, it automatically rounds that number to however many decimal digits of precision that your machine supports. Typically, this is like using an output format of "%.15g", which, when printed, produces the same number as you assigned to $b.

Usually the round-off error is so small you never even notice it, and if you do, you can always specify how much precision you'd like in your output. But because the underlying approximation is still a little bit off from what a simple print might show, this can produce unexpected results. For example, while numbers such as 0.125 and 0.625 are exactly representable, numbers such as 0.325 and 0.725 are not. So let's suppose you'd like to round to two decimal places. Will 0.325 become 0.32 or 0.33? Will 0.725 become 0.72 or 0.73?

```
$a = 0.325;              # 1/2 + 1/8
$b = 0.725;              # 725/1000, or 29/40
printf "%s is %.2f or %.30g\n", ($_) x 3 for $a, $b;
```

This produces:

```
0.325 is 0.33 or 0.325000000000000011102230246252
0.725 is 0.72 or 0.724999999999999977795539507497
```

Since 0.325's approximation is a bit above that, it rounds up to 0.33. On the other hand, 0.725's approximation is really a little under that, so it rounds down, giving 0.72 instead.

But what about if the number *is* exactly representable, such 1.5 or 7.5, since those are just whole numbers plus one-half? The rounding rule used in that case is probably not the one you learned in grade school. Watch:

```
for $n (-4 .. +4) {
    $n += 0.5;
    printf "%4.1f %2.0f\n", $n, $n;
}
```

That produces this:

```
-3.5 -4
-2.5 -2
-1.5 -2
-0.5 -0
 0.5  0
 1.5  2
 2.5  2
 3.5  4
 4.5  4
```

What's happening is that the rounding rule preferred by numerical analysts isn't "round up on a five," but instead "round toward even." This way the bias in the round-off error tends to cancel itself out.

Three useful functions for rounding floating-point values to integral ones are int, ceil, and floor. Built into Perl, int returns the integral portion of the floating-point number passed to it. This is called "rounding toward zero." This is also known as integer truncation because it ignores the fractional part: it rounds down for positive numbers and up for negative ones. The POSIX module's `floor` and `ceil` functions also ignore the fractional part, but they always round down and up to the next integer, respectively, no matter the sign.

```
use POSIX qw(floor ceil);
printf "%8s %8s %8s %8s %8s\n",
    qw(number even zero down up);
for $n (-6 .. +6) {
    $n += 0.5;
    printf "%8g %8.0f %8s %8s %8s\n",
            $n, $n, int($n), floor($n), ceil($n);
}
```

This produces the following illustrative table; each column heading shows what happens when you round the number in the specified direction.

number	even	zero	down	up
-5.5	-6	-5	-6	-5
-4.5	-4	-4	-5	-4
-3.5	-4	-3	-4	-3
-2.5	-2	-2	-3	-2
-1.5	-2	-1	-2	-1
-0.5	-0	0	-1	0
0.5	0	0	0	1
1.5	2	1	1	2
2.5	2	2	2	3
3.5	4	3	3	4
4.5	4	4	4	5
5.5	6	5	5	6
6.5	6	6	6	7

If you add up each column, you'll see that you arrive at rather different totals:

6.5	6	6	0	13

What this tells you is that your choice of rounding style—in effect, your choice of round-off error—can have tremendous impact on the final outcome. That's one reason why you're strongly advised to wait until final output for any rounding. Even still, some algorithms are more sensitive than others to accumulation of round-off error. In particularly delicate applications, such as financial computations and thermonuclear missiles, prudent programmers will implement their own rounding functions instead of relying on their computers' built-in logic, or lack thereof. (A good textbook on numerical analysis is also recommended.)

See Also

The `sprintf` and `int` functions in *perlfunc*(1) and Chapter 29 of *Programming Perl*; the `floor` and `ceil` entries in the documentation for the standard POSIX module (also in Chapter 32 of *Programming Perl*); we introduce the `sprintf` technique in Recipe 2.3

2.3 Comparing Floating-Point Numbers

Problem

Floating-point arithmetic isn't exact. You want to compare two floating-point numbers and know whether they're equal when carried out to a certain number of decimal places. Most of the time, this is the way you *should* compare floating-point numbers for equality.

Solution

Use `sprintf` to format the numbers to a certain number of decimal places, then compare the resulting strings:

```
# equal(NUM1, NUM2, PRECISION) : returns true if NUM1 and NUM2 are
# equal to PRECISION number of decimal places
sub equal {
    my ($A, $B, $dp) = @_;
    return sprintf("%.${dp}g", $A) eq sprintf("%.${dp}g", $B);
}
```

Alternatively, store the numbers as integers by assuming the decimal place.

Discussion

You need the equal routine because computers' floating-point representations are just approximations of most real numbers, as we discussed in the Introduction to this chapter. Perl's normal printing routines display numbers rounded to 15 decimal places or so, but its numeric tests don't round. So sometimes you can print out numbers that look the same (after rounding) but do not test the same (without rounding).

This problem is especially noticeable in a loop, where round-off error can silently accumulate. For example, you'd think that you could start a variable out at zero, add one-tenth to it ten times, and end up with one. Well, you can't, because a base-2 computer can't exactly represent one-tenth. For example:

```
for ($num = $i = 0; $i < 10; $i++) { $num += 0.1 }
if ($num != 1) {
    printf "Strange, $num is not 1; it's %.45f\n", $num;
}
```

prints out:

Strange, 1 is not 1; it's 0.99999999999999988897769753748434345957636833191

The $num is interpolated into the double-quoted string using a default conversion format of "%.15g" (on most systems), so it looks like 1. But internally, it really isn't. If you had checked only to a few decimal places, for example, five:

```
!equal($num, 1, 5)
```

then you'd have been okay.

If you have a fixed number of decimal places, as with currency, you can often side-step the problem by storing your values as integers. Storing $3.50 as 350 instead of 3.5 removes the need for floating-point values. Reintroduce the decimal point on output:

```
$wage = 536;                # $5.36/hour
$week = 40 * $wage;         # $214.40
printf("One week's wage is: \$%.2f\n", $week/100);
```

One week's wage is: $214.40

It rarely makes sense to compare more than 15 decimal places, because you probably only have that many digits of precision in your computer's hardware.

See Also

The sprintf function in *perlfunc*(1) and Chapter 29 of *Programming Perl*; the entry on $OFMT in the *perlvar*(1) manpage and Chapter 28 of *Programming Perl*; the documentation for the standard Math::BigFloat module (also in Chapter 32 of *Programming Perl*); we use sprintf in Recipe 2.2; Volume 2, Section 4.2.2 of *The Art of Computer Programming*

2.4 Operating on a Series of Integers

Problem

You want to perform an operation on all integers between X and Y, such as when you're working on a contiguous section of an array or wherever you want to process all numbers* within a range.

Solution

Use a for loop, or .. in conjunction with a foreach loop:

```
foreach ($X .. $Y) {
    # $_ is set to every integer from X to Y, inclusive
}

foreach $i ($X .. $Y) {
    # $i is set to every integer from X to Y, inclusive
}

for ($i = $X; $i <= $Y; $i++) {
    # $i is set to every integer from X to Y, inclusive
}

for ($i = $X; $i <= $Y; $i += 7) {
```

---

* Okay, integers. It's hard to find all the reals. Just ask Cantor.

```
    # $i is set to every integer from X to Y, stepsize = 7
}
```

Discussion

The first two approaches use a foreach loop in conjunction with the $X .. $Y construct, which creates a list of integers between $X and $Y. Now, if you were just assigning that range to an array, this would use up a lot of memory whenever $X and $Y were far apart. But in a foreach loop, Perl notices this and doesn't waste time or memory allocating a temporary list. When iterating over consecutive integers, the foreach loop will run faster than the equivalent for loop.

Another difference between the two constructs is that the foreach loop implicitly localizes the loop variable to the body of the loop, but the for loop does not. That means that after the for loop finishes, the loop variable will contain the value it held upon the final iteration. But in the case of the foreach loop, that value will be inaccessible, and the variable will hold whatever it held—if anything—prior to entering the loop. You can, however, use a lexically scoped variable as the loop variable:

```
foreach my $i ($X .. $Y)        { ... }
for (my $i=$X; $i <= $Y; $i++) { ... }
```

The following code shows each technique. Here we just print the numbers we generate:

```
print "Infancy is: ";
foreach (0 .. 2) {
    print "$_ ";
}
print "\n";

print "Toddling is: ";
foreach $i (3 .. 4) {
    print "$i ";
}
print "\n";

print "Childhood is: ";
for ($i = 5; $i <= 12; $i++) {
    print "$i ";
}
print "\n";
```

Infancy is: 0 1 2
Toddling is: 3 4
Childhood is: 5 6 7 8 9 10 11 12

See Also

The for and foreach operators in *perlsyn*(1) and the "For Loops" and "Foreach Loops" sections of Chapter 4 of *Programming Perl*

2.5 Working with Roman Numerals

Problem

You want to convert between regular numbers and Roman numerals. You need to do this with items in outlines, page numbers on a preface, and copyrights for movie credits.

Solution

Use the Roman module from CPAN:

```
use Roman;
$roman = roman($arabic);                    # convert to roman numerals
$arabic = arabic($roman) if isroman($roman);    # convert from roman numerals
```

Discussion

The Roman module provides both Roman and roman for converting Arabic ("normal") numbers to their Roman equivalents. Roman produces uppercase letters, whereas roman gives lowercase ones.

The module only deals with Roman numbers from 1 to 3999, inclusive. The Romans didn't represent negative numbers or zero, and 5000 (which 4000 is represented in terms of) uses a symbol outside the ASCII character set.

```
use Roman;
$roman_fifteen = roman(15);                      # "xv"
print "Roman for fifteen is $roman_fifteen\n";
$arabic_fifteen = arabic($roman_fifteen);
print "Converted back, $roman_fifteen is $arabic_fifteen\n";
```

Roman for fifteen is xv
Converted back, xv is 15

Or to print the current year:

```
use Time::localtime;
use Roman;
printf "The year is now %s\n", Roman(1900 + localtime->year);
```

The year is now MMIII

Now, if you happen to have Unicode fonts available, you'll find that code points U+2160 through U+2183 represent Roman numerals, including those beyond the typical ASCII values.

```
use charnames ":full";
print "2003 is ", "\N{ROMAN NUMERAL ONE THOUSAND}" x 2, "\N{ROMAN NUMERAL THREE}\n";
```
2003 is MMIII

However, the Roman module doesn't yet have an option to use those characters.

Believe it or not, there's even a CPAN module that lets you use Roman numerals in arithmetic.

```
use Math::Roman qw(roman);
print $a  = roman('I'); #  I
print $a += 2000;       #  MMI
print $a -= "III";      #  MCMXCVIII
print $a -= "MCM";      #  XCVIII
```

See Also

The Encyclopaedia Britannica article on "Mathematics, History Of"; the documentation with the CPAN modules Roman and Math::Roman; Recipe 6.23

2.6   Generating Random Numbers

Problem

You want to make random numbers in a given range, inclusive, such as when you randomly pick an array index, simulate rolling a die in a game of chance, or generate a random password.

Solution

Use Perl's rand function:

```
$random = int( rand( $Y-$X+1 ) ) + $X;
```

Discussion

This code generates and prints a random integer between 25 and 75, inclusive:

```
$random = int( rand(51)) + 25;
print "$random\n";
```

The rand function returns a fractional number, from (and including) 0 up to (but not including) its argument. We give it an argument of 51 to get a number that can be 0 or more, but never 51 or more. We take the integer portion of this to get a number from 0 to 50, inclusive (50.99999.... will be turned into 50 by int). We then add 25 to it to get a number from 25 to 75, inclusive.

A common application of this is the random selection of an element from an array:

```
$elt = $array[ rand @array ];
```

That's just like saying:

```
$elt = $array[ int( rand(0+@array) ) ];
```

Because rand is prototyped to take just one argument, it implicitly imposes scalar context on that argument, which, on a named array, is the number of elements in that array. The function then returns a floating-point number smaller than its argument and greater than or equal to zero. A floating-point number used as an array subscript implicitly undergoes integer truncation (rounding toward zero), producing in the end an evenly distributed, randomly selected array element to assign to $elt.

Generating a random password from a sequence of characters is similarly easy:

```
@chars = ( "A" .. "Z", "a" .. "z", 0 .. 9, qw(! @ $ % ^ & *) );
$password = join("", @chars[ map { rand @chars } ( 1 .. 8 ) ]);
```

We use map to generate eight random indices into @chars, extract the corresponding characters with a slice, and join them together to form the random password. This isn't a *good* random number, though, as its security relies on the choice of seed, which (in older versions of Perl) is based on the time the program started. See Recipe 2.7 for a way to better seed your random number generator.

See Also

The int, rand, map, and join functions in *perlfunc*(1) and Chapter 29 of *Programming Perl*; we explore random numbers further in Recipes 2.7, 2.8, and 2.9; we use random numbers in Recipe 1.13

2.7   Generating Repeatable Random Number Sequences

Problem

Every time you run your program, you get a different sequence of (pseudo-)random numbers. But you want a reproducible sequence, useful when running a simulation, so you need Perl to produce the same set of random numbers each time.

Solution

Use Perl's srand function:

```
srand EXPR;   # use a constant here for repeated sequences
```

Discussion

Making random numbers is hard. The best that computers can do, without special hardware, is generate "pseudo-random" numbers, which are evenly distributed in their range of values. These are generated using a mathematical formula, which means that given the same *seed* (starting point), two programs will produce identical pseudo-random numbers.

The srand function creates a new seed for the pseudo-random number generator. If given an argument, it uses that number as the seed. If no argument is given, srand uses a value that's reasonably difficult to guess as the seed.

If you call rand without first calling srand yourself, Perl calls srand for you, choosing a "good" seed. This way, every time you run your program you'll get a different set of random numbers. Ancient versions of Perl did not call srand, so the same program always produced the same sequence of pseudo-random numbers every time the program was run. Certain sorts of programs don't want a different set of random numbers each time; they want the same set. When you need that behavior, call srand yourself, supplying it with a particular seed:

```
srand( 42 );  # pick any fixed starting point
```

Don't call srand more than once in a program, because if you do, you'll start the sequence again from that point. Unless, of course, that's what you want.

Just because Perl tries to use a good default seed does not necessarily guarantee that the numbers generated are cryptographically secure against the most intrepid crackers. Textbooks on cryptography are usually good sources of cryptographically secure random number generators.

See Also

The srand function in *perlfunc*(1) and Chapter 29 of *Programming Perl*; Recipes 2.6 and 2.8; Bruce Schneier's excellent *Applied Cryptography* (John Wiley & Sons)

2.8 Making Numbers Even More Random

Problem

You want to generate numbers that are more random than Perl's random numbers. Limitations of your C library's random number generator seeds can sometimes cause problems. The sequence of pseudo-random numbers may repeat too soon for some applications.

Solution

Use a different random number generator, such as those provided by the Math::Random and Math::TrulyRandom modules from CPAN:

```
use Math::TrulyRandom;
$random = truly_random_value( );

use Math::Random;
$random = random_uniform( );
```

Discussion

The Perl build process tries to find the best C-library routine to use for generating pseudo-random numbers, looking at *rand*(3), *random*(3), and *drand48*(3). (This can be changed manually at build time, however.) The standard library functions are getting pretty good, but some ancient implementations of the rand function return only 16-bit random numbers or have other algorithmic weaknesses, and may therefore not be sufficiently random for your purposes.

The Math::TrulyRandom module uses inadequacies of your system's timers to generate the random numbers. This takes a while, so it isn't useful for generating a lot of random numbers.

The Math::Random module uses the randlib library to generate random numbers. It also includes a wide range of related functions for generating random numbers according to specific distributions, such as binomial, poisson, and exponential.

See Also

The srand and rand functions in *perlfunc*(1) and Chapter 29 of *Programming Perl*; Recipes 2.6 and 2.7; the documentation for the CPAN modules Math::Random and Math::TrulyRandom

2.9   Generating Biased Random Numbers

Problem

You want to pick a random value where the probabilities of the values are not equal (the distribution is not even). You might be trying to randomly select a banner to display on a web page, given a set of relative weights saying how often each banner is to be displayed. Alternatively, you might want to simulate behavior according to a normal distribution (the bell curve).

Solution

If you want a random value distributed according to a specific function—e.g., the Gaussian (Normal) distribution—consult a statistics textbook to find the appropriate function or algorithm. This subroutine generates random numbers that are normally distributed, with a standard deviation of 1 and a mean of 0:

```
sub gaussian_rand {
    my ($u1, $u2);  # uniformly distributed random numbers
    my $w;          # variance, then a weight
    my ($g1, $g2);  # gaussian-distributed numbers

    do {
        $u1 = 2 * rand() - 1;
```

```
        $u2 = 2 * rand() - 1;
        $w = $u1*$u1 + $u2*$u2;
    } while ($w >= 1 || $w == 0);

    $w = sqrt( (-2 * log($w))  / $w );
    $g2 = $u1 * $w;
    $g1 = $u2 * $w;
    # return both if wanted, else just one
    return wantarray ? ($g1, $g2) : $g1;
}
```

If you have a list of weights and values you want to randomly pick from, follow this two-step process: first, turn the weights into a probability distribution with weight_to_dist, and then use the distribution to randomly pick a value with weighted_rand:

```
# weight_to_dist: takes a hash mapping key to weight and returns
# a hash mapping key to probability
sub weight_to_dist {
    my %weights = @_;
    my %dist    = ();
    my $total   = 0;
    my ($key, $weight);
    local $_;

    foreach (values %weights) {
        $total += $_;
    }

    while ( ($key, $weight) = each %weights ) {
        $dist{$key} = $weight/$total;
    }

    return %dist;
}

# weighted_rand: takes a hash mapping key to probability, and
# returns the corresponding element
sub weighted_rand {
    my %dist = @_;
    my ($key, $weight);

    while (1) {                         # to avoid floating point inaccuracies
        my $rand = rand;
        while ( ($key, $weight) = each %dist ) {
            return $key if ($rand -= $weight) < 0;
        }
    }
}
```

Discussion

The gaussian_rand function implements the *polar Box Muller* method for turning two independent, uniformly distributed random numbers between 0 and 1 (such as rand returns) into two numbers with a mean of 0 and a standard deviation of 1 (i.e., a

Gaussian distribution). To generate numbers with a different mean and standard deviation, multiply the output of gaussian_rand by the new standard deviation, and then add the new mean:

```
# gaussian_rand as shown earlier
$mean = 25;
$sdev = 2;
$salary = gaussian_rand( ) * $sdev + $mean;
printf("You have been hired at \$%.2f\n", $salary);
```

The Math::Random module implements this and other distributions for you:

```
use Math::Random qw(random_normal);
$salary = random_normal(1, $mean, $sdev);
```

The weighted_rand function picks a random number between 0 and 1. It then uses the probabilities generated by weight_to_dist to see which element the random number corresponds to. Because of the vagaries of floating-point representation, accumulated errors in representation might mean we don't find an element to return. This is why we wrap the code in a while to pick a new random number and try again.

Also, the CPAN module Math::Random has functions to return random numbers from a variety of distributions.

See Also

The rand function in *perlfunc*(1) and Chapter 29 of *Programming Perl*; Recipe 2.6; the documentation for the CPAN module Math::Random

2.10   Doing Trigonometry in Degrees, Not Radians

Problem

You want your trigonometry routines to operate in degrees instead of Perl's native radians.

Solution

Convert between radians and degrees (2π radians equals 360 degrees):

```
use constant PI => (4 * atan2 (1, 1));

sub deg2rad {
    my $degrees = shift;
    return ($degrees / 180) * PI;
}
```

```
sub rad2deg {
    my $radians = shift;
    return ($radians / PI) * 180;
}
```

Alternatively, use the standard Math::Trig module:

```
use Math::Trig;

$radians = deg2rad($degrees);
$degrees = rad2deg($radians);
```

Discussion

If you're doing a lot of trigonometry, look into using either the standard Math::Trig or POSIX modules. They provide many more trigonometric functions than are defined in the Perl core. Otherwise, the first solution will define the rad2deg and deg2rad functions. The value of π isn't built directly into Perl, but you can calculate it to as much precision as your floating-point hardware provides. In the Solution, the PI function is a constant created with use constant. Instead of having to remember that π is 3. 14159265358979 or so, we use the built-in function call, resolved at compile time, which, besides sparing us from memorizing a long string of digits, is also guaranteed to provide as much accuracy as the platform supports.

If you're looking for the sine in degrees, use this:

```
# deg2rad and rad2deg defined either as above or from Math::Trig
sub degree_sine {
    my $degrees = shift;
    my $radians = deg2rad($degrees);
    my $result = sin($radians);

    return $result;
}
```

See Also

The sin, cos, and atan2 functions in *perlfunc*(1) and Chapter 29 of *Programming Perl*; the documentation for the standard POSIX and Math::Trig modules (also in Chapter 32 of *Programming Perl*)

2.11 Calculating More Trigonometric Functions

Problem

You want to calculate values for trigonometric functions like sine, tangent, or arccosine.

Solution

Perl provides only sin, cos, and atan2 as standard functions. From these, you can derive tan and all other trig functions (if you're intimately familiar with esoteric trig identities):

```
sub tan {
    my $theta = shift;

    return sin($theta)/cos($theta);
}
```

The POSIX module provides a wider range of trig functions:

```
use POSIX;

$y = acos(3.7);
```

The standard Math::Trig module provides a complete set of functions and supports operations on or resulting in complex numbers:

```
use Math::Trig;

$y = acos(3.7);
```

Discussion

The tan function will cause a division-by-zero exception when $theta is $\pi/2$, $3\pi/2$, and so on, because the cosine is 0 for these values. Similarly, tan and many other functions from Math::Trig may generate the same error. To trap these, use eval:

```
eval {
    $y = tan($pi/2);
} or return undef;
```

See Also

The sin, cos, and atan2 functions in *perlfunc*(1) and Chapter 29 of *Programming Perl*; the documentation for the standard Math::Trig module; we talk about trigonometry in the context of imaginary numbers in Recipe 2.14; we talk about the use of eval to catch exceptions in Recipe 10.12

2.12 Taking Logarithms

Problem

You want to take a logarithm in various bases.

Solution

For logarithms to base *e*, use the built-in log:

```
$log_e = log(VALUE);
```

For logarithms to base 10, use the POSIX module's log10 function:

```
use POSIX qw(log10);
$log_10 = log10(VALUE);
```

For other bases, use the mathematical identity:

$$\log_n(x) = \frac{\log_e(x)}{\log_e(n)}$$

where *x* is the number whose logarithm you want, *n* is the desired base, and *e* is the natural logarithm base.

```
sub log_base {
    my ($base, $value) = @_;
    return log($value)/log($base);
}
```

Discussion

The log_base function lets you take logarithms to any base. If you know the base you'll want in advance, it's more efficient to cache the log of the base instead of recalculating it every time.

```
# log_base as defined earlier
$answer = log_base(10, 10_000);
print "log10(10,000) = $answer\n";
log10(10,000) = 4
```

The Math::Complex module does the caching for you via its logn( ) routine, so you can write:

```
use Math::Complex;
printf "log2(1024) = %lf\n", logn(1024, 2); # watch out for argument order!
log2(1024) = 10.000000
```

even though no complex number is involved here. This is not very efficient, but there are plans to rewrite Math::Complex in C for speed.

See Also

The log function in *perlfunc*(1) and Chapter 29 of *Programming Perl*; the documentation for the standard POSIX and Math::Complex modules (also in Chapter 32 of *Programming Perl*)

2.13 Multiplying Matrices

Problem

You want to multiply a pair of two-dimensional arrays. Mathematicians and engineers often need this.

Solution

Use the PDL modules, available from CPAN. PDL is the *Perl Data Language*—modules that give fast access to compact matrix and mathematical functions:

```
use PDL;
# $a and $b are both pdl objects
$c = $a x $b;
```

Alternatively, apply the matrix multiplication algorithm to your two-dimensional array:

```
sub mmult {
    my ($m1,$m2) = @_;
    my ($m1rows,$m1cols) = matdim($m1);
    my ($m2rows,$m2cols) = matdim($m2);

    unless ($m1cols == $m2rows) {  # raise exception
        die "IndexError: matrices don't match: $m1cols != $m2rows";
    }

    my $result = [ ];
    my ($i, $j, $k);

    for $i (range($m1rows)) {
        for $j (range($m2cols)) {
            for $k (range($m1cols)) {
                $result->[$i][$j] += $m1->[$i][$k] * $m2->[$k][$j];
            }
        }
    }
    return $result;
}

sub range { 0 .. ($_[0] - 1) }

sub veclen {
    my $ary_ref = $_[0];
    my $type = ref $ary_ref;
    if ($type ne "ARRAY") { die "$type is bad array ref for $ary_ref" }
    return scalar(@$ary_ref);
}

sub matdim {
    my $matrix = $_[0];
```

```
    my $rows = veclen($matrix);
    my $cols = veclen($matrix->[0]);
    return ($rows, $cols);
}
```

Discussion

If you have the PDL library installed, you can use its lightning-fast manipulation of numbers. This requires far less memory and CPU than Perl's array manipulation. When using PDL objects, many numeric operators (such as + and *) are overloaded and work on an element-by-element basis (e.g., * is the so-called *scalar multiplication* operator). To get true matrix multiplication, use the overloaded x operator.

```
use PDL;

$a = pdl [
    [ 3, 2, 3 ],
    [ 5, 9, 8 ],
];

$b = pdl [
    [ 4, 7 ],
    [ 9, 3 ],
    [ 8, 1 ],
];

$c = $a x $b;  # x overload
```

If you don't have the PDL library, or don't feel like pulling it in for a small problem, you can always do the work yourself the good old-fashioned way.

```
# mmult( ) and other subroutines as shown earlier

$x = [
    [ 3, 2, 3 ],
    [ 5, 9, 8 ],
];

$y = [
    [ 4, 7 ],
    [ 9, 3 ],
    [ 8, 1 ],
];

$z = mmult($x, $y);
```

See Also

The documentation with the CPAN module PDL

2.14 Using Complex Numbers

Problem

Your application must manipulate complex numbers, as are often needed in engineering, science, and mathematics.

Solution

Either keep track of the real and imaginary components yourself:

```
# $c = $a * $b manually
$c_real = ( $a_real * $b_real ) - ( $a_imaginary * $b_imaginary );
$c_imaginary = ( $a_real * $b_imaginary ) + ( $b_real * $a_imaginary );
```

or use the Math::Complex module (part of the standard Perl distribution):

```
# $c = $a * $b using Math::Complex
use Math::Complex;
$c = $a * $b;
```

Discussion

Here's how you'd manually multiply 3+5i and 2-2i:

```
$a_real = 3; $a_imaginary = 5;          # 3 + 5i;
$b_real = 2; $b_imaginary = -2;         # 2 - 2i;
$c_real = ( $a_real * $b_real ) - ( $a_imaginary * $b_imaginary );
$c_imaginary = ( $a_real * $b_imaginary ) + ( $b_real * $a_imaginary );
print "c = ${c_real}+${c_imaginary}i\n";
```

```
c = 16+4i
```

and with Math::Complex:

```
use Math::Complex;
$a = Math::Complex->new(3,5);           # or Math::Complex->new(3,5);
$b = Math::Complex->new(2,-2);
$c = $a * $b;
print "c = $c\n";
```

```
c = 16+4i
```

You may create complex numbers via the cplx constructor or via the exported constant *i*:

```
use Math::Complex;
$c = cplx(3,5) * cplx(2,-2);            # easier on the eye
$d = 3 + 4*i;                           # 3 + 4i
printf "sqrt($d) = %s\n", sqrt($d);
```

```
sqrt(3+4i) = 2+i
```

The Math::Trig module uses the Math::Complex module internally because some functions can break out from the real axis into the complex plane—for example, the inverse sine of 2.

See Also

The documentation for the standard Math::Complex module (also in Chapter 32 of *Programming Perl*)

2.15 Converting Binary, Octal, and Hexadecimal Numbers

Problem

You want to convert a string (e.g., "0b10110", "0x55", or "0755") containing a binary, octal, or hexadecimal number to the correct number.

Perl understands numbers specified in binary (base-2), octal (base-8), and hexadecimal (base-16) notation only when they occur as literals in your programs. If they come in as data—such as by reading from files or environment variables, or when supplied as command-line arguments—no automatic conversion takes place.

Solution

Use Perl's hex function if you have a hexadecimal string like "2e" or "0x2e":

```
$number = hex($hexadecimal);        # hexadecimal only ("2e" becomes 47)
```

Use the oct function if you have a hexadecimal string like "0x2e", an octal string like "047", or a binary string like "0b101110":

```
$number = oct($hexadecimal);    # "0x2e" becomes 47
$number = oct($octal);          # "057"  becomes 47
$number = oct($binary);         # "0b101110" becomes 47
```

Discussion

The oct function converts octal numbers with or without the leading "0"; for example, "0350" or "350". Despite its name, oct does more than convert octal numbers: it also converts hexadecimal ("0x350") numbers if they have a leading "0x" and binary ("0b101010") numbers if they have a leading "0b". The hex function converts only hexadecimal numbers, with or without a leading "0x": "0x255", "3A", "ff", or "deadbeef". (Letters may be in upper- or lowercase.)

Here's an example that accepts an integer in decimal, binary, octal, or hex, and prints that integer in all four bases. It uses the oct function to convert the data from binary, octal, and hexadecimal if the input begins with a 0. It then uses `printf` to convert into all four bases as needed.

```
print "Gimme an integer in decimal, binary, octal, or hex: ";
$num = <STDIN>;
chomp $num;
exit unless defined $num;
$num = oct($num) if $num =~ /^0/; # catches 077 0b10 0x20
printf "%d %#x %#o %#b\n", ($num) x 4;
```

The # symbol between the percent and the three non-decimal bases makes `printf` produce output that indicates which base the integer is in. For example, if you enter the number 255, the output would be:

```
255 0xff 0377 0b11111111
```

But without the # sign, you would only get:

```
255 ff 377 11111111
```

The following code converts Unix file permissions. They're always given in octal, so we use oct instead of hex.

```
print "Enter file permission in octal: ";
$permissions = <STDIN>;
die "Exiting ...\n" unless defined $permissions;
chomp $permissions;
$permissions = oct($permissions);   # permissions always octal
print "The decimal value is $permissions\n";
```

See Also

The "Scalar Value Constructors" section in *perldata*(1) and the "Numeric Literals" section of Chapter 2 of *Programming Perl*; the oct and hex functions in *perlfunc*(1) and Chapter 29 of *Programming Perl*

2.16   Putting Commas in Numbers

Problem

You want to output a number with commas in the right places. People like to see long numbers broken up in this way, especially in reports.

Solution

Reverse the string so you can use backtracking to avoid substitution in the fractional part of the number. Then use a regular expression to find where you need commas, and substitute them in. Finally, reverse the string back.

```
sub commify {
    my $text = reverse $_[0];
```

```
$text =~ s/(\d\d\d)(?=\d)(?!\d*\.)/$1,/g;
return scalar reverse $text;
}
```

Discussion

It's a lot easier in regular expressions to work from the front than from the back. With this in mind, we reverse the string and make a minor change to the algorithm that repeatedly inserts commas three digits from the end. When all insertions are done, we reverse the final string and return it. Because reverse is sensitive to its implicit return context, we force it to scalar context.

This function can easily be adjusted to accommodate the use of periods instead of commas, as are used in many countries.

Here's an example of commify in action:

```
# more reasonable web counter :-)
use Math::TrulyRandom;
$hits = truly_random_value( );        # negative hits!
$output = "Your web page received $hits accesses last month.\n";
print commify($output);
Your web page received -1,740,525,205 accesses last month.
```

See Also

perllocale(1); the reverse function in *perlfunc*(1) and Chapter 29 of *Programming Perl*; the section "Adding Commas to a Number with Lookaround" in Chapter 2 of *Mastering Regular Expressions*, Second Edition

2.17   Printing Correct Plurals

Problem

You're printing something like "It took $time hours", but "It took 1 hours" is ungrammatical. You would like to get it right.

Solution

Use printf and the conditional operator (X ? Y : Z) to alter the noun or verb:

```
printf "It took %d hour%s\n", $time, $time == 1 ? "" : "s";

printf "%d hour%s %s enough.\n", $time,
        $time == 1 ? ""   : "s",
        $time == 1 ? "is" : "are";
```

Or use the Lingua::EN::Inflect module from CPAN, as described in the following Discussion.

Discussion

The only reason inane messages like "1 file(s) updated" appear is because their authors are too lazy to bother checking whether the count is 1 or not.

If your noun changes by more than an "-s", you'll need to change the printf accordingly:

```
printf "It took %d centur%s", $time, $time == 1 ? "y" : "ies";
```

This is good for simple cases, but you'll tire of writing it. This leads you to write funny functions like this:

```
sub noun_plural {
    local $_ = shift;
    # order really matters here!
    s/ss$/sses/                         ||
    s/([psc]h)$/${1}es/                 ||
    s/z$/zes/                           ||
    s/ff$/ffs/                          ||
    s/f$/ves/                           ||
    s/ey$/eys/                          ||
    s/y$/ies/                           ||
    s/ix$/ices/                         ||
    s/([sx])$/$1es/                     ||
    s/$/s/                              ||
                die "can't get here";
    return $_;
}
*verb_singular = \&noun_plural;    # make function alias
```

As you find more exceptions, your function will become increasingly convoluted. When you need to handle such morphological changes, turn to the flexible solution provided by the Lingua::EN::Inflect module from CPAN.

```
use Lingua::EN::Inflect qw(PL classical);
classical(1);                  # why isn't this the default?
while (<DATA>) {               # each line in the data
    for (split) {              # each word on the line
        print "One $_, two ", PL($_), ".\n";
    }
}
# plus one more
$_ = 'secretary general';
print "One $_, two ", PL($_), ".\n";

__END__
fish fly ox
species genus phylum
cherub radius jockey
index matrix mythos
phenomenon formula
```

That produces the following:

```
One fish, two fish.
One fly, two flies.
One ox, two oxen.
One species, two species.
One genus, two genera.
One phylum, two phyla.
One cherub, two cherubim.
One radius, two radii.
One jockey, two jockeys.
One index, two indices.
One matrix, two matrices.
One mythos, two mythoi.
One phenomenon, two phenomena.
One formula, two formulae.
One secretary general, two secretaries general.
```

Without calling classical, these lines would have come out different than in the previous output:

```
One phylum, two phylums.
One cherub, two cherubs.
One radius, two radiuses.
One index, two indexes.
One matrix, two matrixes.
One formula, two formulas.
```

This is just one of the many things the module can do. It also handles inflections or conjugations for other parts of speech, provides number-insensitive comparison functions, figures out whether to use *a* or *an*, and plenty more.

See Also

The "Conditional Operator" in *perlop*(1) and Chapter 3 of *Programming Perl*; the documentation with the CPAN module Lingua::EN::Inflect

2.18 Program: Calculating Prime Factors

The following program takes one or more integer arguments and determines the prime factors. It uses Perl's native numeric representation, unless those numbers use floating-point representation and thus lose accuracy. Otherwise (or if the program's **-b** switch is used), it uses the standard Math::BigInt library, thus allowing for huge numbers. However, it only loads this library if necessary. That's why we use require and import instead of use, which would unconditionally load the library at compile time instead of conditionally at runtime. This is not an efficient way to crack the huge integers used for cryptographic purposes.

Call the program with a list of numbers, and it will show you the prime factors of those numbers:

```
% bigfact 8 9 96 2178
8         2**3
```

```
9          3**2
96         2**5 3
2178       2 3**2 11**2
```

You can give it very large numbers:

```
% bigfact 2393220000000000000000000
+2393220000000000000000000 2**19 3 5**18 +39887

% bigfact 25000000000000000000000000000
+25000000000000000000000000000 2**24 5**26
```

The program is shown in Example 2-2.

Example 2-2. bigfact

```
#!/usr/bin/perl
# bigfact - calculate prime factors
use strict;
use integer;

our ($opt_b, $opt_d);
use Getopt::Std;

@ARGV && getopts('bd')          or die "usage: $0 [-b] number ...";

load_biglib() if $opt_b;

ARG: foreach my $orig ( @ARGV ) {
    my ($n, %factors, $factor);
    $n = $opt_b ? Math::BigInt->new($orig) : $orig;
    if ($n + 0 ne $n) { # don't use -w for this
        printf STDERR "bigfact: %s would become %s\n", $n, $n+0 if $opt_d;
        load_biglib();
        $n = Math::BigInt->new($orig);
    }
    printf "%-10s ", $n;

    # Here $sqi will be the square of $i. We will take advantage
    # of the fact that ($i + 1) ** 2 == $i ** 2 + 2 * $i + 1.
    for (my ($i, $sqi) = (2, 4); $sqi <= $n; $sqi += 2 * $i ++ + 1) {
        while ($n % $i == 0) {
            $n /= $i;
            print STDERR "<$i>" if $opt_d;
            $factors {$i} ++;
        }
    }

    if ($n != 1 && $n != $orig) { $factors{$n}++ }
    if (! %factors) {
        print "PRIME\n";
        next ARG;
    }
    for $factor ( sort { $a <=> $b } keys %factors ) {
        print "$factor";
```

Example 2-2. bigfact (continued)

```
        if ($factors{$factor} > 1) {
            print "**$factors{$factor}";
        }
        print " ";
    }
    print "\n";
}

# this simulates a use, but at runtime
sub load_biglib {
    require Math::BigInt;
    Math::BigInt->import();          #immaterial?
}
```

CHAPTER 3

Dates and Times

It is inappropriate to require that a time represented as
seconds since the Epoch precisely represent the number
of seconds between the referenced time and the Epoch.
—IEEE Std 1003.1b-1993 (POSIX) Section B.2.2.2

3.0   Introduction

Times and dates are important things to be able to manipulate. "How many users logged in last month?", "How many seconds should I sleep if I want to wake up at midday?", and "Has this user's password expired yet?" are common questions whose answers involve surprisingly non-obvious manipulations.

Perl represents points in time as intervals, measuring seconds past a point in time called *the Epoch*. On Unix and many other systems, the Epoch was 00:00 Jan 1, 1970, UTC (Universal Corrected Time).[*]

When we talk about dates and times, we often interchange two different concepts: points in time (dates and times) and intervals between points in time (weeks, months, days, etc.). Epoch seconds represent intervals and points in the same units, so you can do basic arithmetic on them.

However, people are not used to working with Epoch seconds. We are more used to dealing with individual year, month, day, hour, minute, and second values. Furthermore, the month can be represented by its full name or its abbreviation. The day can precede or follow the month. Because of the difficulty of performing calculations with a variety of formats, we typically convert human-supplied strings or lists to Epoch seconds, calculate, and then convert back to strings or lists for output.

Epoch seconds are an absolute number of seconds, so they don't take into account time zones or daylight saving times. When converting to or from distinct values,

---

[*] UTC is the preferred way to specify what used to be called GMT, or Greenwich Mean Time.

always consider whether the time represented is UTC or local. Use different conversion functions depending on whether you need to convert from UTC to local time or vice versa.

Perl's time function returns the number of seconds that have passed since the Epoch—more or less.* POSIX requires that time not include leap seconds, a peculiar practice of adjusting the world's clock by a second here and there to account for the slowing down of the Earth's rotation due to tidal angular-momentum dissipation. (See the *sci.astro* FAQ, section 3, at *http://sciastro.astronomy.net/sci.astro.3.FAQ.*) To convert Epoch seconds into distinct values for days, months, years, hours, minutes, and seconds, use the localtime and gmtime functions. In list context, these functions return a nine-element list, as shown in Table 3-1.

Table 3-1. Values (and their ranges) returned from localtime and gmtime

Variable	Values	Range
$sec	seconds	0–60
$min	minutes	0–59
$hour	hours	0–23
$mday	day of month	1–31
$mon	month of year	0–11, 0 = = January
$year	years since 1900	1–138 (or more)
$wday	day of week	0–6, 0 = = Sunday
$yday	day of year	0–365
$isdst	0 or 1	true if daylight saving is in effect

The values for seconds range from 0–60 to account for leap seconds; you never know when a spare second will leap into existence at the urging of various standards bodies.

From now on, we'll refer to a list of day, month, year, hour, minute, and seconds as DMYHMS, for no better reason than that writing and reading "distinct day, month, year, hour, minute, and seconds values" is wearisome. The abbreviation is not meant to suggest an order of return values.

Perl does *not* return a two-digit year value. It returns the year minus 1900, which just happens to be a two-digit number through 1999. Perl doesn't intrinsically have a Year 2000 problem, unless you make one yourself. (Your computer, and Perl, may have a 2038 problem, though, if we're still using 32 bits by that time.) Add 1900 to get the full year value instead of using the construct "20$year", or your programs will refer to the year as something like "20103". We can't pin down the year value's range, because it depends on how big an integer your operating system uses for Epoch seconds. Small integers mean a small range; big (64-bit) integers mean a very big range.

---

* Well, less actually. To be precise, 22 seconds less as of this writing.

In scalar context, localtime and gmtime return the date and time formatted as an ASCII string:

Fri Apr 11 09:27:08 1997

The standard Time::tm module provides a named interface to these values. The standard Time::localtime and Time::gmtime modules override the list-returning localtime and gmtime functions, replacing them with versions that return Time::tm objects. Compare these two pieces of code:

```
# using arrays
print "Today is day ", (localtime)[7], " of the current year.\n";
Today is day 117 of the current year.

# using Time::tm objects
use Time::localtime;
$tm = localtime;
print "Today is day ", $tm->yday, " of the current year.\n";
Today is day 117 of the current year.
```

To go *from* a list *to* Epoch seconds, use the standard Time::Local module. It provides the functions timelocal and timegm, both of which take a nine-element list and return an integer. The list's values have the same meaning and ranges as those returned by localtime and gmtime.

Epoch seconds values are limited by the size of an integer. If you have a 32-bit signed integer holding your Epoch seconds, you can only represent dates (in UTC) from Fri Dec 13 20:45:52 1901 to Tue Jan 19 03:14:07 2038 (inclusive). By 2038, it is assumed, computers will change to use larger integers for Epoch seconds. We hope. For operations on dates outside this range, you must use another representation or work from distinct year, month, and day values.

The Date::Calc and Date::Manip modules on CPAN both work from these distinct values, but be warned: years don't necessarily have 1900 subtracted from them the way the year value returned by localtime does, nor do months and weeks always start at 0. As always, consult the manpage of the appropriate module to make sure you're giving it what it expects and getting back from it what you expect. There's little more embarrassing than realizing you've calculated your company payroll based on a calendar that's 1,900 years in the past.

3.1   Finding Today's Date

Problem

You need to find the year, month, and day values for today's date.

Solution

Use localtime, which returns values for the current date and time if given no arguments. You can either use localtime and extract the information you want from the list it returns:

```
($DAY, $MONTH, $YEAR) = (localtime)[3,4,5];
```

or use Time::localtime, which overrides localtime to return a Time::tm object:

```
use Time::localtime;
$tm = localtime;
($DAY, $MONTH, $YEAR) = ($tm->mday, $tm->mon, $tm->year);
```

Discussion

Here's how you'd print the current date as "YYYY MM DD", using the non-overridden localtime:

```
($day, $month, $year) = (localtime)[3,4,5];
printf("The current date is %04d %02d %02d\n", $year+1900, $month+1, $day);
The current date is 2003 03 06
```

To extract the fields we want from the list returned by localtime, we take a list slice. We could also have written it as:

```
($day, $month, $year) = (localtime)[3..5];
```

This is how we'd print the current date as "YYYY-MM-DD" (in approved ISO 8601 fashion), using Time::localtime:

```
use Time::localtime;
$tm = localtime;
printf("The current date is %04d-%02d-%02d\n", $tm->year+1900,
    ($tm->mon)+1, $tm->mday);
The current date is 2003-03-06
```

The object interface might look out of place in a short program. However, when you do a lot of work with the distinct values, accessing them by name makes code much easier to understand.

A more obfuscated way that does not involve temporary variables is:

```
printf("The current date is %04d-%02d-%02d\n",
        sub {($_[5]+1900, $_[4]+1, $_[3])}->(localtime));
```

There is also strftime from the POSIX module discussed in Recipe 3.8:

```
use POSIX qw(strftime);
print strftime "%Y-%m-%d\n", localtime;
```

The gmtime function works just as localtime does, but gives the answer in UTC instead of your local time zone.

See Also

The localtime and gmtime functions in *perlfunc*(1) and Chapter 29 of *Programming Perl*; the documentation for the standard Time::localtime module

3.2   Converting DMYHMS to Epoch Seconds

Problem

You want to convert a date, a time, or both with distinct values for day, month, year, etc. to Epoch seconds.

Solution

Use the timelocal or timegm functions in the standard Time::Local module, depending on whether the date and time is in the current time zone or in UTC.

```
use Time::Local;
$TIME = timelocal($sec, $min, $hours, $mday, $mon, $year);
$TIME = timegm($sec, $min, $hours, $mday, $mon, $year);
```

Discussion

The built-in function localtime converts an Epoch seconds value to distinct DMY-HMS values; the timelocal subroutine from the standard Time::Local module converts distinct DMYHMS values to an Epoch seconds value. Here's an example that shows how to find Epoch seconds for a time in the current day. It gets the day, month, and year values from localtime:

```
# $hours, $minutes, and $seconds represent a time today,
# in the current time zone
use Time::Local;
$time = timelocal($seconds, $minutes, $hours, (localtime)[3,4,5]);
```

If you're passing month and year values to timelocal, it expects values with the same range as those which localtime returns. Namely, months start at 0, and years have 1900 subtracted from them.

The timelocal function assumes the DMYHMS values represent a time in the current time zone. Time::Local also exports a timegm subroutine that assumes the DMY-HMS values represent a time in the UTC time zone. Unfortunately, there is no convenient way to convert from a time zone other than the current local time zone or UTC. The best you can do is convert to UTC and add or subtract the time zone offset in seconds.

This code illustrates both the use of timegm and how to adjust the ranges of months and years:

```
# $day is day in month (1-31)
# $month is month in year (1-12)
```

```
# $year is four-digit year e.g., 1967
# $hours, $minutes and $seconds represent UTC (GMT) time
use Time::Local;
$time = timegm($seconds, $minutes, $hours, $day, $month-1, $year-1900);
```

As explained in the introduction, Epoch seconds cannot hold values before Fri Dec 13 20:45:52 1901 or after Tue Jan 19 03:14:07 2038. Don't convert such dates to Epoch seconds—use a Date:: module from CPAN, and do your calculations with that instead.

See Also

The documentation for the standard Time::Local module (also in Chapter 32 of *Programming Perl*); convert in the other direction using Recipe 3.3

3.3   Converting Epoch Seconds to DMYHMS

Problem

You have a date and time in Epoch seconds, and you want to calculate individual DMYHMS values from it.

Solution

Use the localtime or gmtime functions, depending on whether you want the date and time in UTC or your local time zone.

```
($seconds, $minutes, $hours, $day_of_month, $month, $year,
    $wday, $yday, $isdst) = localtime($time);
```

The standard Time::timelocal and Time::gmtime modules override the localtime and gmtime functions to provide named access to the individual values.

```
use Time::localtime;         # or Time::gmtime
$tm = localtime($TIME);      # or gmtime($TIME)
$seconds = $tm->sec;
# ...
```

Discussion

The localtime and gmtime functions return strange year and month values; the year has 1900 subtracted from it, and 0 is the month value for January. Be sure to correct the base values for year and month, as this example does:

```
($seconds, $minutes, $hours, $day_of_month, $month, $year,
    $wday, $yday, $isdst) = localtime($time);
printf("Dateline: %02d:%02d:%02d-%04d/%02d/%02d\n",
    $hours, $minutes, $seconds, $year+1900, $month+1,
    $day_of_month);
```

We could have used the Time::localtime module to avoid the temporary variables:

```
use Time::localtime;
$tm = localtime($time);
printf("Dateline: %02d:%02d-%02d-%04d/%02d/%02d\n",
    $tm->hour, $tm->min, $tm->sec, $tm->year+1900,
    $tm->mon+1, $tm->mday);
```

See Also

The localtime function in *perlfunc*(1) and Chapter 29 of *Programming Perl*; the documentation for the standard Time::localtime and Time::gmtime modules; convert in the other direction using Recipe 3.2

3.4   Adding to or Subtracting from a Date

Problem

You have a date and time and want to find the date and time of some period in the future or past.

Solution

Simply add or subtract Epoch seconds:

```
$when = $now + $difference;
$then = $now - $difference;
```

If you have distinct DMYHMS values, use the CPAN Date::Calc module. If you're doing arithmetic with days only, use Add_Delta_Days ($offset is a positive or negative integral number of days):

```
use Date::Calc qw(Add_Delta_Days);
($y2, $m2, $d2) = Add_Delta_Days($y, $m, $d, $offset);
```

If you are concerned with hours, minutes, and seconds (in other words, times as well as dates), use Add_Delta_DHMS:

```
use Date::Calc qw(Add_Delta_DHMS);
($year2, $month2, $day2, $h2, $m2, $s2) =
    Add_Delta_DHMS( $year, $month, $day, $hour, $minute, $second,
                $days_offset, $hour_offset, $minute_offset, $second_offset );
```

Discussion

Calculating with Epoch seconds is easiest, disregarding the effort to get dates and times into and out of Epoch seconds. This code shows how to calculate an offset (55 days, 2 hours, 17 minutes, and 5 seconds, in this case) from a given base date and time:

```
$birthtime = 96176750;              # 18/Jan/1973, 3:45:50 am
$interval = 5 +                     # 5 seconds
```

```
           17 * 60 +                      # 17 minutes
            2 * 60 * 60 +                 # 2 hours
           55 * 60 * 60 * 24;            # and 55 days
    $then = $birthtime + $interval;
    print "Then is ", scalar(localtime($then)), "\n";
    Then is Wed Mar 14 06:02:55 1973
```

We could have used Date::Calc's `Add_Delta_DHMS` function and avoided the conversion to and from Epoch seconds:

```
    use Date::Calc qw(Add_Delta_DHMS);
    ($year, $month, $day, $hh, $mm, $ss) = Add_Delta_DHMS(
        1973, 1, 18, 3, 45, 50, # 18/Jan/1973, 3:45:50 am
                    55, 2, 17, 5); # 55 days, 2 hrs, 17 min, 5 sec
    print "To be precise: $hh:$mm:$ss, $month/$day/$year\n";
    To be precise: 6:2:55, 3/14/1973
```

As usual, we need to know the range of values the function expects. `Add_Delta_DHMS` takes a full year value—that is, one that hasn't had 1900 subtracted from it. The month value for January is 1, not 0. Date::Calc's `Add_Delta_Days` function expects the same kind of values:

```
    use Date::Calc qw(Add_Delta_Days);
    ($year, $month, $day) = Add_Delta_Days(1973, 1, 18, 55);
    print "Nat was 55 days old on: $month/$day/$year\n";
    Nat was 55 days old on: 3/14/1973
```

See Also

The documentation for the CPAN module Date::Calc

3.5   Difference of Two Dates

Problem

You need to find the number of days between two dates or times.

Solution

If your dates are in Epoch seconds and fall in the range `Fri Dec 13 20:45:52 1901` to `Tue Jan 19 03:14:07 2038` (inclusive), subtract one from the other and convert the seconds to days:

```
    $seconds = $recent - $earlier;
```

If you have distinct DMYMHS values or are worried about the range limitations of Epoch seconds, use the Date::Calc module from CPAN. It can calculate the difference between dates:

```
    use Date::Calc qw(Delta_Days);
    $days = Delta_Days( $year1, $month1, $day1, $year2, $month2, $day2);
```

It also calculates the difference between a pair of dates and times:

```
use Date::Calc qw(Delta_DHMS);
($days, $hours, $minutes, $seconds) =
    Delta_DHMS( $year1, $month1, $day1, $hour1, $minute1, $seconds1,  # earlier
                $year2, $month2, $day2, $hour2, $minute2, $seconds2); # later
```

Discussion

One problem with Epoch seconds is how to convert the large integers back to forms that people can read. The following example shows one way of converting an Epoch seconds value back to its component numbers of weeks, days, hours, minutes, and seconds:

```
$bree = 361535725;       # 16 Jun 1981, 4:35:25
$nat  = 96201950;        # 18 Jan 1973, 3:45:50

$difference = $bree - $nat;
print "There were $difference seconds between Nat and Bree\n";
There were 265333775 seconds between Nat and Bree

$seconds    = $difference % 60;
$difference = ($difference - $seconds) / 60;
$minutes    = $difference % 60;
$difference = ($difference - $minutes) / 60;
$hours      = $difference % 24;
$difference = ($difference - $hours)  / 24;
$days       = $difference % 7;
$weeks      = ($difference - $days)   / 7;

print "($weeks weeks, $days days, $hours:$minutes:$seconds)\n";
(438 weeks, 4 days, 23:49:35)
```

Date::Calc's functions can ease these calculations. The Delta_Days function returns the number of days between two dates. It takes the two dates as a list: year, month, day. The dates are given chronologically—earliest first.

```
use Date::Calc qw(Delta_Days);
@bree = (1981, 6, 16);       # 16 Jun 1981
@nat  = (1973, 1, 18);       # 18 Jan 1973
$difference = Delta_Days(@nat, @bree);
print "There were $difference days between Nat and Bree\n";
There were 3071 days between Nat and Bree
```

The Delta_DHMS function returns a four-element list corresponding to the number of days, hours, minutes, and seconds between the two dates you give it.

```
use Date::Calc qw(Delta_DHMS);
@bree = (1981, 6, 16, 4, 35, 25);   # 16 Jun 1981, 4:35:25
@nat  = (1973, 1, 18, 3, 45, 50);   # 18 Jan 1973, 3:45:50
@diff = Delta_DHMS(@nat, @bree);
print "Bree came $diff[0] days, $diff[1]:$diff[2]:$diff[3] after Nat\n";
Bree came 3071 days, 0:49:35 after Nat
```

See Also

The documentation for the CPAN module Date::Calc

3.6   Day in a Week/Month/Year or Week Number

Problem

You have a date, either in Epoch seconds or as distinct year, month, etc. values. You want to find out what week of the year, day of the week, day of the month, or day of the year that the date falls on.

Solution

If you have Epoch seconds, the day of the year, day of the month, and day of the week are returned by localtime. The week of the year is easily calculated from the day of the year (but see the following discussion, as standards differ).

```
($MONTHDAY, $WEEKDAY, $YEARDAY) = (localtime $DATE)[3,6,7];
$WEEKNUM = int($YEARDAY / 7) + 1;
```

If you have distinct DMYHMS values, you can either convert them to Epoch seconds values as in Recipe 3.2 and then use the previous solution, or else use the Day_of_Week, Week_Number, and Day_of_Year functions from the CPAN module Date::Calc:

```
use Date::Calc qw(Day_of_Week Week_Number Day_of_Year);
# you have $year, $month, and $day
# $day is day of month, by definition.
$wday = Day_of_Week($year, $month, $day);
$wnum = Week_Number($year, $month, $day);
$dnum = Day_of_Year($year, $month, $day);
```

Discussion

The Day_of_Week, Week_Number, and Day_of_Year functions all expect years that haven't had 1900 subtracted from them and months where January is 1, not 0. The return value from Day_of_Week can be 1 through 7 (corresponding to Monday through Sunday) or 0 in case of an error (an invalid date, for example).

```
use Date::Calc qw(Day_of_Week Week_Number Day_of_Week_to_Text);

$year  = 1981;
$month = 6;          # (June)
$day   = 16;

$wday = Day_of_Week($year, $month, $day);
print "$month/$day/$year was a ", Day_of_Week_to_Text($wday), "\n";
## see comment above
```

```
$wnum = Week_Number($year, $month, $day);
print "in the $wnum week.\n";
```
6/16/1981 was a Tuesday
in week number 25.

The governing standard bodies of particular countries may have rules about when the first week of the year starts. For example, in Norway the first week must have at least 4 days in it (and weeks start on Mondays). If January 1 falls on a week with 3 or fewer days, it is counted as week 52 (or 53) of the previous year. In America, the first Monday of the year is usually the start of the first workweek. Given such rules, you may have to write your own algorithm, or at least look at the %G, %L, %W, and %U formats to the UnixDate function in Date::Manip.

See Also

The localtime function in *perlfunc*(1) and Chapter 29 of *Programming Perl*; the documentation for the CPAN module Date::Calc

3.7   Parsing Dates and Times from Strings

Problem

You read in a date or time specification in an arbitrary format but need to parse that string into distinct year, month, etc. values.

Solution

If your date is already numeric, or in a rigid and easily parsed format, use a regular expression (and possibly a hash mapping month names to numbers) to extract individual day, month, and year values, and then use the standard Time::Local module's timelocal and timegm functions to turn that into an Epoch seconds value.

```
use Time::Local;
# $date is "2003-02-13" (YYYY-MM-DD form).
($yyyy, $mm, $dd) = ($date =~ /(\d+)-(\d+)-(\d+)/);
# calculate epoch seconds at midnight on that day in this timezone
$epoch_seconds = timelocal(0, 0, 0, $dd, $mm-1, $yyyy);
```

For a more flexible solution, use the ParseDate function provided by the CPAN module Date::Manip, and then use UnixDate to extract the individual values.

```
use Date::Manip qw(ParseDate UnixDate);
$date = ParseDate($STRING);
if (!$date) {
    # bad date
} else {
    @VALUES = UnixDate($date, @FORMATS);
}
```

Discussion

The flexible ParseDate function accepts many formats. It even converts strings such as "today", "2 weeks ago Friday", "2nd Sunday in 1996", and "last Sunday in December", plus it understands the date and time format used in mail and news headers. It returns the decoded date in its own format: a string of the form "YYYYM-MDDHH:MM:SS". You could compare two such strings to compare the dates they represent, but arithmetic is difficult. We therefore use the UnixDate function to extract the year, month, and day values in a preferred format.

UnixDate takes a date (as returned by ParseDate) and a list of formats. It applies each format to the string and returns the result. A format is a string describing one or more elements of the date and time and the way that the elements are to be formatted. For example, %Y is the format for the year in four-digit form. Here's an example:

```
use Date::Manip qw(ParseDate UnixDate);

while (<>) {
    $date = ParseDate($_);
    if (!$date) {
        warn "Bad date string: $_\n";
        next;
    } else {
        ($year, $month, $day) = UnixDate($date, "%Y", "%m", "%d");
        print "Date was $month/$day/$year\n";
    }
}
```

See Also

The documentation for the CPAN module Date::Manip; we use this in Recipe 3.11

3.8   Printing a Date

Problem

You need to print a date and time shown in Epoch seconds format in human-readable form.

Solution

Call localtime or gmtime in scalar context, which takes an Epoch seconds value and returns a string of the form Tue July 22 05:15:20 2003:

```
$STRING = localtime($EPOCH_SECONDS);
```

Alternatively, the strftime function in the standard POSIX module supports a more customizable output format and takes individual DMYHMS values:

```
use POSIX qw(strftime);
$STRING = strftime($FORMAT, $SECONDS, $MINUTES, $HOUR,
                   $DAY_OF_MONTH, $MONTH, $YEAR, $WEEKDAY,
                   $YEARDAY, $DST);
```

The CPAN module Date::Manip has a UnixDate routine that works like a specialized form sprintf designed to handle dates. Pass it a Date::Manip date value. Using Date::Manip in lieu of POSIX::strftime has the advantage of not requiring a POSIX-compliant system.

```
use Date::Manip qw(UnixDate);
$STRING = UnixDate($DATE, $FORMAT);
```

Discussion

The simplest solution is built into Perl already: the localtime function. In scalar context, it returns the string formatted in a particular way:

Wed July 16 23:58:36 2003

This makes for simple code, although it restricts the format of the string:

```
use Time::Local;
$time = timelocal(50, 45, 3, 18, 0, 73);
print "Scalar localtime gives: ", scalar(localtime($time)), "\n";
```
Scalar localtime gives: Thu Jan 18 03:45:50 1973

Of course, localtime requires the date and time in Epoch seconds. The POSIX:: strftime function takes individual DMYMHS values plus a format and returns a string. The format is similar to a printf format: % directives specify fields in the output string. A full list of these directives is available in your system's documentation for strftime. The strftime function expects the individual values representing the date and time to be in the same range as those returned by localtime:

```
use POSIX qw(strftime);
use Time::Local;
$time = timelocal(50, 45, 3, 18, 0, 73);
print "strftime gives: ", strftime("%A %D", localtime($time)), "\n";
```
strftime gives: Thursday 01/18/73

All values are shown in their national representation when using POSIX::strftime. So, if you run it in France, your program would print "Sunday" as "Dimanche". Be warned: Perl's interface to the POSIX function strftime assumes the date falls in the current time zone.

If you don't have access to POSIX's strftime function, there's always the trusty Date:: Manip CPAN module, described in Recipe 3.6.

```
use Date::Manip qw(ParseDate UnixDate);
$date = ParseDate("18 Jan 1973, 3:45:50");
$datestr = UnixDate($date, "%a %b %e %H:%M:%S %z %Y");    # as scalar
```

```
print "Date::Manip gives: $datestr\n";
Date::Manip gives: Thu Jan 18 03:45:50 GMT 1973
```

See Also

The gmtime and localtime functions in *perlfunc*(1) and Chapter 29 of *Programming Perl*; *perllocale*(1); your system's *strftime*(3) manpage; the documentation for the POSIX module (also in Chapter 32 of *Programming Perl*); the documentation for the CPAN module Date::Manip

3.9   High-Resolution Timers

Problem

You need to measure time with a finer granularity than the full seconds that time returns.

Solution

The Time::HiRes module, which is included standard starting with the v5.8 release of Perl, encapsulates this functionality for most systems:

```
use Time::HiRes qw(gettimeofday);
$t0 = gettimeofday( );
## do your operation here
$t1 = gettimeofday( );
$elapsed = $t1 - $t0;
# $elapsed is a floating point value, representing number
# of seconds between $t0 and $t1
```

Discussion

Here's some code that uses Time::HiRes to time how long the user takes to press the Return key:

```
use Time::HiRes qw(gettimeofday);
print "Press return when ready: ";
$before = gettimeofday( );
$line = <STDIN>;
$elapsed = gettimeofday( ) - $before;
print "You took $elapsed seconds.\n";
```

```
Press return when ready:
You took 0.228149 seconds.
```

The module's gettimeofday function returns a two-element list representing seconds and microseconds when called in list context, or a single floating-point number combining the two when called in scalar context. You can also import its time function to replace the standard core version by that name; this always acts like scalar gettimeofday.

The module also provides usleep and ualarm functions, which are alternate versions of the standard Perl sleep and alarm functions that understand granularities of microseconds instead of just seconds. They take arguments in microseconds; alternatively, you can import the module's sleep and alarm functions, which take floating-point arguments in seconds, to replace the standard versions, which take integer arguments in seconds. For access to your system's low-level itimer routines (if you have them), setitimer and getitimer are also provided.

If your system doesn't support that module, you might try to poke around by hand using syscall. Compare Time::HiRes to the equivalent syscall code. (This example is included principally so that you can see an example of Perl's abstruse and archaic syscall function.)

```perl
require 'sys/syscall.ph';

# initialize the structures returned by gettimeofday
$TIMEVAL_T = "LL";
$done = $start = pack($TIMEVAL_T, (0,0));

# prompt
print "Press return when ready: ";

# read the time into $start
syscall(&SYS_gettimeofday, $start, 0) != -1
        || die "gettimeofday: $!";

# read a line
$line = <>;

# read the time into $done
syscall(&SYS_gettimeofday, $done, 0) != -1
      || die "gettimeofday: $!";

# expand the structure
@start = unpack($TIMEVAL_T, $start);
@done  = unpack($TIMEVAL_T, $done);

# fix microseconds
for ($done[1], $start[1]) { $_ /= 1_000_000 }

# calculate time difference
$delta_time = sprintf "%.4f", ($done[0]  + $done[1]  )
                                      -
                              ($start[0] + $start[1] );

print "That took $delta_time seconds\n";
Press return when ready:
That took 0.3037 seconds
```

It's longer because it's doing system calls in Perl, whereas Time::HiRes does them in C providing a single function. It's complex because directly accessing system calls peculiar to your operating system requires understanding the underlying C structures that the system call takes and returns. Some programs that come with the Perl distribution try to automatically calculate the formats to pack and unpack for you, if fed the appropriate C header file. In the example, *sys/syscall.ph* is a Perl library file generated with *h2ph*, which converts the *sys/syscall.h* header file into *sys/syscall.ph*, defining (among other things) &SYS_gettimeofday as a subroutine that returns the system call number of gettimeofday.

Here's another example of Time::HiRes, showing how you could use it to benchmark a sort (if you didn't care to use the standard Benchmark module):

```
use Time::HiRes qw(gettimeofday);
# take mean sorting time
$size = 2000;
$number_of_times = 100;
$total_time = 0;

for ($i = 0; $i < $number_of_times; $i++) {
    my (@array, $j, $begin, $time);
    # populate array
    @array = ( );
    for ($j=0; $j < $size; $j++) { push(@array, rand) }

    # sort it
    $begin = gettimeofday;
    @array = sort { $a <=> $b } @array;
    $time = gettimeofday-$begin;
    $total_time += $time;
}

printf "On average, sorting %d random numbers takes %.5f seconds\n",
    $size, ($total_time/$number_of_times);
On average, sorting 2000 random numbers takes 0.01033 seconds
```

See Also

The documentation for the Time::HiRes and Benchmark modules; the syscall function in *perlfunc*(1) and Chapter 29 of *Programming Perl*; your system's *syscall*(2) manpage

3.10 Short Sleeps

Problem

You need to sleep for less than a second.

Solution

Use the select( ) function, if your system supports it:

```
select(undef, undef, undef, $time_to_sleep);
```

Some systems don't support a four-argument select. The Time::HiRes module provides a sleep function that takes a floating-point number of seconds:

```
use Time::HiRes qw(sleep);
sleep($time_to_sleep);
```

Discussion

Here's an example of select. It's a simpler version of the program in Recipe 1.6. Think of it as your very own 300-baud terminal.

```
while (<>) {
    select(undef, undef, undef, 0.25);
    print;
}
```

Using Time::HiRes, we'd write it as:

```
use Time::HiRes qw(sleep);
while (<>) {
    sleep(0.25);
    print;
}
```

See Also

The documentation for the CPAN modules Time::HiRes and Benchmark; the sleep and select functions in *perlfunc*(1) and Chapter 29 of *Programming Perl*; we use the select function for short sleeps in the slowcat program in Recipe 1.6

3.11 Program: hopdelta

Have you ever wondered why it took so long for someone's mail to get to you? With postal mail, you can't trace how long each intervening post office let your letter gather dust in their back office. But with electronic mail, you can. The message carries in its header Received: lines showing when each intervening mail transport agent along the way got the message.

The dates in the headers are hard to read. You have to read them backwards, bottom to top. They are written in many varied formats, depending on the whim of each transport agent. Worst of all, each date is written in its own local time zone. It's hard to eyeball "Tue, 26 May 1998 23:57:38 -0400" and "Wed, 27 May 1998 05:04:03 +0100" and realize these two dates are only 6 minutes and 25 seconds apart.

The ParseDate and DateCalc functions in the Date::Manip module from CPAN can help this:

```
use Date::Manip qw(ParseDate DateCalc);
$d1 = ParseDate("Sun, 09 Mar 2003 23:57:38 -0400");
$d2 = ParseDate("Mon, 10 Mar 2003 05:04:03 +0100");
print DateCalc($d1, $d2);
+0:0:0:0:0:6:25
```

That's a nice format for a program to read, but it's still not what the casual reader wants to see. The *hopdelta* program, shown in Example 3-1, takes a mailer header and tries to analyze the deltas (difference) between each hop (mail stop). Its output is shown in the local time zone.

Example 3-1. hopdelta

```
#!/usr/bin/perl
# hopdelta - feed mail header, produce lines
#            showing delay at each hop.
use strict;
use Date::Manip qw (ParseDate UnixDate);

# print header; this should really use format/write due to
# printf complexities
printf "%-20.20s %-20.20s %-20.20s   %s\n",
        "Sender", "Recipient", "Time", "Delta";

$/ = '';                # paragraph mode
$_ = <>;                # read header
s/\n\s+/ /g;            # join continuation lines

# calculate when and where this started
my($start_from) = /^From.*\@([^\s>]*)/m;
my($start_date) = /^Date:\s+(.*)/m;
my $then = getdate($start_date);
printf "%-20.20s %-20.20s %s\n", 'Start', $start_from, fmtdate($then);

my $prevfrom = $start_from;

# now process the headers lines from the bottom up
for (reverse split(/\n/)) {
    my ($delta, $now, $from, $by, $when);
    next unless /^Received:/;
    s/\bon (.*?) (id.*)/; $1/s;         # qmail header, I think
    unless (($when) = /;\s+(.*)$/) {    # where the date falls
        warn "bad received line: $_";
        next;
    }
    ($from) = /from\s+(\S+)/;
    ($from) = /\((.*?)\)/ unless $from; # some put it here
    $from =~ s/\)$//;                   # someone was too greedy
    ($by)   = /by\s+(\S+\.\S+)/;        # who sent it on this hop
```

Example 3-1. hopdelta (continued)

```perl
    # now random mungings to get their string parsable
    for ($when) {
        s/ (for|via) .*$//;
        s/([+-]\d\d\d\d) \(\S+\)/$1/;
        s/id \S+;\s*//;
    }
    next unless $now = getdate($when);          # convert to Epoch
    $delta = $now - $then;

    printf "%-20.20s %-20.20s %s  ", $from, $by, fmtdate($now);
    $prevfrom = $by;
    puttime($delta);
    $then = $now;
}

exit;

# convert random date strings into Epoch seconds
sub getdate {
    my $string      = shift;
    $string         =~ s/\s+\(.*\)\s*$//;       # remove nonstd tz
    my $date        = ParseDate($string);
    my $epoch_secs  = UnixDate($date,"%s");
    return $epoch_secs;
}

# convert Epoch seconds into a particular date string
sub fmtdate {
    my $epoch = shift;
    my($sec,$min,$hour,$mday,$mon,$year) = localtime($epoch);
    return sprintf "%02d:%02d:%02d %04d/%02d/%02d",
                    $hour, $min, $sec,
                    $year + 1900, $mon + 1, $mday,
}

# take seconds and print in pleasant-to-read format
sub puttime {
    my($seconds) = shift;
    my($days, $hours, $minutes);

    $days    = pull_count($seconds, 24 * 60 * 60);
    $hours   = pull_count($seconds, 60 * 60);
    $minutes = pull_count($seconds, 60);

    put_field('s', $seconds);
    put_field('m', $minutes);
    put_field('h', $hours);
    put_field('d', $days);

    print "\n";
}
```

Example 3-1. hopdelta (continued)

```
# usage: $count = pull_count(seconds, amount)
# remove from seconds the amount quantity, altering caller's version.
# return the integral number of those amounts so removed.
sub pull_count {
    my($answer) = int($_[0] / $_[1]);
    $_[0] -= $answer * $_[1];
    return $answer;
}

# usage: put_field(char, number)
# output number field in 3-place decimal format, with trailing char
# suppress output unless char is 's' for seconds
sub put_field {
    my ($char, $number) = @_;
    printf " %3d%s", $number, $char if $number || $char eq 's';
}

=end
```

Sender	Recipient	Time		Delta	
Start	wall.org	09:17:12	1998/05/23		
wall.org	mail.brainstorm.net	09:20:56	1998/05/23	44s	3m
mail.brainstorm.net	jhereg.perl.com	09:20:58	1998/05/23	2s	

CHAPTER 4

Arrays

Works of art, in my opinion, are the only objects in the
material universe to possess internal order, and that is
why, though I don't believe that only art matters, I do
believe in Art for Art's sake.
—E.M. Forster

4.0   Introduction

If you are asked about the contents of your pockets, or the names of the first three
Greek letters, or how to get to the highway, you recite a list: you name one thing
after another in a particular order. Lists are part of your conception of the world.
With Perl's powerful list- and array-handling primitives, you can translate this world
view directly into code.

In this chapter, we'll use the terms *list* and *array* as the Perl language thinks of them.
Take ("alpha", "beta", "gamma"); that's a *list* of the names of the first three Greek letters, in order. To store that list into a variable, use an *array*, as in @greeks = ("alpha",
"beta", "gamma"). Both are ordered groups of scalar values; the difference is that an
array is a named variable, one whose array length can be directly changed, whereas a
list is a more ephemeral notion. You might think of an array as a variable and a list as
the values it contains.

This distinction may seem arbitrary, but operations that modify the length of these
groupings (like push and pop) require a proper array and not merely a list. Think of
the difference between $a and 4. You can say $a++ but not 4++. Likewise, you can say
pop(@a) but not pop (1,2,3).

The most important thing to glean from this is that Perl's lists and arrays are both
ordered groupings of scalars. Operators and functions that work on lists or arrays are
designed to provide faster or more convenient access to the elements than manual
access would provide. Since few actually deal with modifying the array's length, you
can usually use arrays and lists interchangeably.

You can't use nested parentheses to create a list of lists. If you try that in Perl, your lists get *flattened*, meaning that both these lines are equivalent:

```
@nested = ("this", "that", "the", "other");
@nested = ("this", "that", ("the", "other"));
```

Why doesn't Perl (usefully) just support nested lists directly? Although partially for historical reasons, this easily allows for operations (like print or sort) that work on arbitrarily long lists of arbitrary contents.

What happens if you want a more complex data structure, such as an array of arrays or an array of hashes? Remember that scalars aren't restricted to containing just numbers or strings; they can also hold references. Complex (multilevel) data structures in Perl are always put together using references. Therefore, what appear to be "two-dimensional arrays" or "arrays of arrays" are always implemented as arrays of array *references*, in the same way that two-dimensional arrays in C can be arrays of pointers to arrays.

Most recipes in this chapter don't care what you keep in your arrays; for example, the problem of merging two arrays is the same whether the arrays contains strings, numbers, or references. Some problems are intrinsically tied to the contents of your arrays; recipes for those are in Chapter 11. This chapter's recipes deal with generic arrays.

Let's have some more terminology. The scalar items in an array or list are called *elements*, which you access by specifying their position, or *index*. Indices in Perl start at 0. So, given this list:

```
@greeks = ( "alpha", "beta", "gamma" );
```

"alpha" is in the first position, but you'd access it as $greeks[0]. "beta" is in the second position, but you'd access it as $greeks[1]. This structure is doubly justified: the contrariness of computers, whose first representable number is 0, and the contrariness of language designers, who chose 0 because it is an *offset* into the array, not the *ordinal* number of the element.

4.1 Specifying a List in Your Program

Problem

You want to include a list in your program. This is how you initialize arrays.

Solution

You can write out a comma-separated list of elements:

```
@a = ("quick", "brown", "fox");
```

If you have a lot of single-word elements, use the qw( ) operator:

```
@a = qw(Meddle not in the affairs of wizards.);
```

If you have a lot of multiword elements, use a here document and extract lines:

```
@lines = (<< "END_OF_HERE_DOC" =~ /^\s*(.+)/gm);
    I sit beside the fire and think
    of all that I have seen,
    of meadow-flowers and butterflies
    and summers that have been;
END_OF_HERE_DOC
```

Discussion

The first technique is the one most commonly used, often because only small arrays are normally initialized as program literals. Initializing a large array would fill your program with values and make it hard to read, so such arrays either tend to be initialized in a separate library file (see Chapter 12), or else have their values read in from a file:

```
@bigarray = ();
open(FH, "<", "myinfo")    or die "Couldn't open myinfo: $!";
while (<FH>) {
    chomp;
    push(@bigarray, $_);
}
close(FH);
```

The second technique uses qw( ), one of several pseudo-functions in Perl used for quoting without having to resort to actual quotation marks. This one splits its string argument on whitespace to produce a list of words, where "words" in this instance means strings that don't contain any whitespace. The initial argument is not subject to interpolation of variables or (most) backslash escape sequences.

```
@banner = ('Costs', 'only', '$4.95');
@banner = qw(Costs only $4.95);
@banner = split(' ', 'Costs only $4.95');
```

You can use qw( ) only when each whitespace-separated argument is to be a distinct element in the return list. Be careful not to give Columbus four ships instead of three:

```
@ships = qw(Niña Pinta Santa María);          # WRONG
@ships = ('Niña', 'Pinta', 'Santa María');    # right
```

The third solution takes a here document, which is a single, multiline string, and applies a global pattern match to that string. The pattern /^\s*(.+)/ says to skip any whitespace at the start of the line, then capture everything through the end of each line. The /g modifier means to apply that match globally, and the /m modifier says to permit ^ to match not just at the beginning of the string, but also immediately after a newline, which, in a multiline string, is just what you need. Applying that technique to the ships example yields:

```
@ships = ( << "END_OF_FLOTILLA" =~ /^\s*(.+)/gm);
            Niña
            Pinta
            Santa María
END_OF_FLOTILLA
```

See Also

The "List Value Constructors" section of *perldata*(1); the "List Values and Arrays" section of Chapter 2 of *Programming Perl*; the "Quote and Quote-Like Operators" section of *perlop*(1); the s/// operator in *perlop*(1) and Chapter 5 of *Programming Perl*

4.2   Printing a List with Commas

Problem

You'd like to print out a list containing an unknown number of elements, placing an "and" before the last element and commas between each element if there are more than two.

Solution

Use this function, which returns the formatted string:

```
sub commify_series {
    (@_ == 0) ? ''                                    :
    (@_ == 1) ? $_[0]                                 :
    (@_ == 2) ? join(" and ", @_)                     :
                join(", ", @_[0 .. ($#_-1)], "and $_[-1]");
}
```

Discussion

It often looks odd to print out arrays:

```
@array = ("red", "yellow", "green");
print "I have ", @array, " marbles.\n";
print "I have @array marbles.\n";
I have redyellowgreen marbles.
I have red yellow green marbles.
```

What you really want it to say is, "I have red, yellow, and green marbles". The function given in the solution generates strings in that format. The word "and" is placed between the last two list elements. If there are more than two elements in the list, a comma is placed between every element.

Example 4-1 gives a complete demonstration of the function, with one addition: if any element in the list already contains a comma, a semicolon is used for the separator character instead.

Example 4-1. commify_series

```
#!/usr/bin/perl -w
# commify_series - show proper comma insertion in list output

# @lists is an array of (references to anonymous) arrays
@lists = (
```

Example 4-1. commify_series (continued)

```
        [ 'just one thing' ],
        [ qw(Mutt Jeff) ],
        [ qw(Peter Paul Mary) ],
        [ 'To our parents', 'Mother Theresa', 'God' ],
        [ 'pastrami', 'ham and cheese', 'peanut butter and jelly', 'tuna' ],
        [ 'recycle tired, old phrases', 'ponder big, happy thoughts' ],
        [ 'recycle tired, old phrases',
          'ponder big, happy thoughts',
          'sleep and dream peacefully' ],
    );

foreach $aref (@lists) {
    print "The list is: " . commify_series(@$aref) . ".\n";
}
# demo for single list
@list = qw(one two three);
print "The last list is: " . commify_series(@list) . ".\n";

sub commify_series {
    my $sepchar = grep(/,/ => @_) ? ";" : ",";
    (@_ == 0) ? ''                                      :
    (@_ == 1) ? $_[0]                                   :
    (@_ == 2) ? join(" and ", @_)                       :
                join("$sepchar ", @_[0 .. ($#_-1)], "and $_[-1]");
}
```

Here's the output from the program:

```
The list is: just one thing.
The list is: Mutt and Jeff.
The list is: Peter, Paul, and Mary.
The list is: To our parents, Mother Theresa, and God.
The list is: pastrami, ham and cheese, peanut butter and jelly, and tuna.
The list is: recycle tired, old phrases and ponder big, happy thoughts.
The list is: recycle tired, old phrases; ponder
    big, happy thoughts; and sleep and dream peacefully.
The last list is: one, two, and three.
```

As you see, we don't follow the ill-advised practice of omitting the final comma from a series under any circumstances. To do so introduces unfortunate ambiguities and unjustifiable exceptions. The examples shown would have claimed that we were the offspring of Mother Teresa and God, and would have had us eating sandwiches made of jelly and tuna fish mixed together atop the peanut butter.

See Also

Fowler's *Modern English Usage*; we explain the nested list syntax in Recipe 11.1; the grep function in *perlfunc*(1) and Chapter 29 of *Programming Perl*; the conditional operator ("?:") is discussed in *perlop*(1) and in the "Conditional Operator" section of Chapter 3 of *Programming Perl*

4.3   Changing Array Size

Problem

You want to enlarge or truncate an array. For example, you might truncate an array of employees that's already sorted by salary to list the five highest-paid employees. Or, if you know how big your array will get and that it will grow piecemeal, it's more efficient to grab memory for it in one step by enlarging just once than to keep pushing values onto the end.

Solution

Assign to $#ARRAY:

```
# grow or shrink @ARRAY
$#ARRAY = $NEW_LAST_ELEMENT_INDEX_NUMBER;
```

Assigning to an element past the end automatically extends the array:

```
$ARRAY[$NEW_LAST_ELEMENT_INDEX_NUMBER] = $VALUE;
```

Discussion

$#ARRAY is the number of the last valid index in @ARRAY. If we assign it a number smaller than its current value, we truncate the array. Truncated elements are lost forever. If we assign $#ARRAY a number larger than its current value, the array grows. New elements have the undefined value.

$#ARRAY is not @ARRAY, though. Although $#ARRAY is the last valid index in the array, @ARRAY (in scalar context, as when treated as a number) is the *number* of elements. $#ARRAY is one less than @ARRAY because array indices start at 0.

Here's some code that uses both. We have to say scalar @array in the print because Perl gives list context to (most) functions' arguments, but we want @array in scalar context.

```
sub what_about_that_array {
    print "The array now has ", scalar(@people), " elements.\n";
    print "The index of the last element is $#people.\n";
    print "Element #3 is `$people[3]'.\n";
}

@people = qw(Crosby Stills Nash Young);
what_about_that_array();
```

prints:

```
The array now has 4 elements.
The index of the last element is 3.
Element #3 is `Young'.
```

whereas:

```
$#people--;
what_about_that_array();
```

prints:

The array now has 3 elements.
The index of the last element is 2.
Element #3 is `'.

Element #3 disappeared when we shortened the array. If we'd turned on warnings (either with the **-w** command-line option to Perl or with use warnings inside the program), Perl would also have warned "use of uninitialized value" because $people[3] is undefined.

```
$#people = 10_000;
what_about_that_array();
```

prints:

The array now has 10001 elements.
The index of the last element is 10000.
Element #3 is `'.

The "Young" element is now gone forever. Instead of assigning to $#people, we could have said:

```
$people[10_000] = undef;
```

although this isn't exactly the same. If you have a three-element array, as in:

```
@colors = qw(red blue green);
```

and you undef its last element:

```
undef $colors[2];        # green is gone
```

you still have a three-element array; its last element is just undefined. If you pop the array, either via the function or manually by changing $#colors:

```
$last_color = $colors[ $#colors-- ];
```

then the array grows shorter by one element.

Perl arrays are not sparse. In other words, if you have a 10,000th element, you must have the 9,999 other elements, too. They may be undefined, but they still take up memory. For this reason, $array[time()], or any other construct that uses a very large integer as an array index, is a really bad idea. Use a hash instead.

See Also

The discussion of the $#ARRAY notation in *perldata*(1), also explained in the "List Values and Arrays" section of Chapter 2 of *Programming Perl*

4.4 Implementing a Sparse Array

Problem

An array with large, unoccupied expanses between occupied elements wastes memory. How do you reduce that overhead?

Solution

Use a hash instead of an array.

Discussion

If you assign to the millionth element of an array, Perl allocates a million and one slots to store scalars. Only the last element contains interesting data, leaving earlier ones each set to undef at a cost of four (or more) bytes per unoccupied slot.

In recent versions of Perl, if you grow an array by assigning either past the end or directly to $#ARRAY, you can distinguish these implicit undefs from those that would result from assigning undef there by using exists instead of defined, just as you would with a hash.

```
$#foo = 5;
@bar = ( (undef) x 5 ) ;

printf "foo element 3 is%s defined\n",
        defined $foo[3] ? "" : "n't";
printf "foo element 3 does%s exist\n",
        exists $foo[3] ? "" : "n't";
printf "bar element 3 is%s defined\n",
        defined $bar[3] ? "" : "n't";
printf "bar element 3 does%s exist\n",
        exists $bar[3] ? "" : "n't";

foo element 3 isn't defined
foo element 3 doesn't exist
bar element 3 isn't defined
bar element 3 does exist
```

However, you still waste a lot of space. That's because Perl's array implementation reserves a contiguous vector, one for each element up to the highest occupied position.

```
$real_array[ 1_000_000 ] = 1;      # costs 4+ megabytes
```

A hash works differently: you pay only for what you really use, not for unoccupied positions. Although a hash element costs somewhat more than an array element because you need to store both the value and its key, with sparse arrays, the savings can be astonishing.

```
$fake_array{ 1_000_000 } = 1;      # costs 28 bytes
```

What's the trade-off? Because a hash's keys aren't ordered, a little more work is needed to sort the numeric keys so you can handle their values in the same order as you would if they were stored as a real array. With an array, you'd just do this to process elements in index order:

```
foreach $element ( @real_array ) {
    # do something with $element
}
```

or this to process indices in ascending order:

```
foreach $idx ( 0 .. $#real_array ) {
    # do something with $real_array[$idx]
}
```

Using a hash representation, you should instead do either this to process elements in index order:

```
foreach $element ( @fake_array{ sort {$a <=> $b} keys %fake_array } ) {
    # do something with $element
}
```

or this to process indices in ascending order:

```
foreach $idx ( sort {$a <=> $b} keys %fake_array ) {
    # do something with $fake_array{$idx}
}
```

If you don't care about handling elements in a particular order, however, you don't need to go through all that. Just process the values according to their internal order, either like this:

```
foreach $element ( values %fake_array ) {
    # do something with $element
}
```

or like this:

```
# process indices in internal hash order
foreach $idx ( keys %fake_array ) {
    # do something with $fake_array{$idx}
}
```

If you're determined to use an array, two fairly specialized cases occasionally arise in which you can save substantial amounts of memory by using an alternate storage scheme. Both cases also apply to arrays that are densely populated, not just those that are mostly empty.

The first case shows up when you grow an array by repeatedly appending new elements until its subscripts become large. Because of how Perl reallocates memory for growing arrays, this can use up to four times the memory you really need. If you happen to know how big the array will (or might) eventually become, you can avoid this reallocation overhead either by storing the large subscripts first instead of the small ones:

```
for ($i = 10_000; $i >= 0; $i--) { $real_array[$i] = 1 }
```

or by presizing the array by assigning to the special $#ARRAY notation:

```
$#real_array = 10_000;
```

The second special case comes up when each array element holds nothing but a single one-bit value—essentially either a true or a false. For example, suppose you are keeping track of numbered USENET news articles, and you only need to know whether a given article number has been read. For situations like this, use a bit vector instead of a real array:

```
my $have_read = '';
for ($i = 10_000; $i >= 0; $i--) { vec($have_read, $i, 1) = 1 }
```

Then you can check to see whether a given article has been read this way:

```
if (vec($have_read, $artno, 1)) { .... }
```

See Also

The vec function in *perlfunc*(1) and in Chapter 29 of *Programming Perl*

4.5   Iterating Over an Array

Problem

You want to repeat a procedure for every element in a list.

Often you use an array to collect information you're interested in; for instance, login names of users who have exceeded their disk quota. When you finish collecting the information, you want to process it by doing something with every element in the array. In the disk quota example, you might send each user a stern mail message.

Solution

Use a foreach loop:

```
foreach $item (LIST) {
    # do something with $item
}
```

Discussion

Let's say we've used @bad_users to compile a list of users who are over their allotted disk quotas. To call some complain subroutine for each user, we'd use:

```
foreach $user (@bad_users) {
        complain($user);
}
```

Rarely is this recipe so simply applied. Instead, we often use functions to generate the list:

```
foreach $var (sort keys %ENV) {
    print "$var=$ENV{$var}\n";
}
```

Here we're using sort and keys to build a sorted list of environment variable names. If you use the list more than once, you'll obviously keep it around by saving in an array. But for one-shot processing, it's often tidier to process the list directly.

Not only can we add complexity to this formula by building up the list in the foreach, we can also add complexity by doing more work inside the code block. A common application of foreach is to gather information on every element of a list and then, based on that information, decide whether to do something. For instance, returning to the disk quota example:

```
foreach $user (@all_users) {
    $disk_space = get_usage($user);       # find out how much disk space in use
    if ($disk_space > $MAX_QUOTA) {        # if it's more than we want ...
        complain($user);                   # ... then object vociferously
    }
}
```

More complicated program flow is possible. The code can call last to jump out of the loop, next to move on to the next element, or redo to jump back to the first statement inside the block. Use these to say "no point continuing with this one, I know it's not what I'm looking for" (next), "I've found what I'm looking for, there's no point in my checking the rest" (last), or "I've changed some things, I'd better run this loop's calculations again" (redo).

The variable set to each value in the list is called a *loop variable* or *iterator variable*. If no iterator variable is supplied, the global variable $_ is used. $_ is the default variable for many of Perl's string, list, and file functions. In brief code blocks, omitting $_ improves readability. (In long ones, though, too much implicit use hampers readability.) For example:

```
foreach (`who`) {
    if (/tchrist/) {
        print;
    }
}
```

or combining with a while loop:

```
while (<FH>) {              # $_ is set to the line just read
    chomp;                  # $_ has a trailing \n removed, if it had one
    foreach (split) {       # $_ is split on whitespace, into @_
                            # then $_ is set to each chunk in turn
        $_ = reverse;       # the characters in $_ are reversed
        print;              # $_ is printed
    }
}
```

Perhaps all these uses of $_ are starting to make you nervous. In particular, the foreach and the while both give values to $_. You might fear that at the end of the foreach, the full line as read into $_ with <FH> would be forever gone.

Fortunately, your fears would be unfounded, at least in this case. Perl won't permanently clobber $_'s old value, because the foreach's iterator variable (here, $_) is automatically preserved during the loop. It saves away any old value on entry and restores it upon exit.

However, there is some cause for concern. If the while had been the inner loop and the foreach the outer one, your fears would have been realized. Unlike a foreach loop, the while (<FH>) construct clobbers the value of the global $_ without first localizing it! So any routine—or block for that matter—that uses this construct with $_ should declare local $_.

If a lexical variable (one declared with my) is in scope, the temporary variable will be lexically scoped, private to that loop. Otherwise, it will be a dynamically scoped global variable. To avoid strange magic at a distance, write this more obviously and more clearly as:

```
foreach my $item (@array) {
    print "i = $item\n";
}
```

The foreach looping construct has another feature: each time through the loop, the iterator variable becomes not a copy of but rather an *alias* for the current element. This means that when you change that iterator variable, you really change each element in the list:

```
@array = (1,2,3);
foreach $item (@array) {
    $item--;
}
print "@array\n";
0 1 2

# multiply everything in @a and @b by seven
@a = ( .5, 3 ); @b = ( 0, 1 );
foreach $item (@a, @b) {
    $item *= 7;
}
print "@a @b\n";
3.5 21 0 7
```

You can't change a constant, though, so this is illegal:

```
foreach $n (1, 2, 3) {
    $n **= 2;
}
```

This aliasing means that using a foreach loop to modify list values is both more readable and faster than the equivalent code using a three-part for loop and explicit indexing would be. This behavior is a feature, not a bug, that was introduced by design. If you didn't know about it, you might accidentally change something. Now you know about it.

For example, to trim leading and trailing whitespace in a hash, we take advantage of how the values function works: the elements of its return list really *are* the values of the hash, and changing these changes the original hash. Because we use s/// directly on the list returned by the values function without copying these into a variable, we change the real hash itself.

```
# trim whitespace in the scalar, the array, and in all
# the values in the hash
foreach ($scalar, @array, values %hash) {
    s/^\s+//;
    s/\s+$//;
}
```

For reasons hearkening back to the equivalent construct in the Unix Bourne shell, the for and foreach keywords are interchangeable:

```
for $item (@array) {  # same as foreach $item (@array)
    # do something
}

for (@array)     {   # same as foreach $_ (@array)
    # do something
}
```

This style often indicates that its author writes or maintains shell scripts, perhaps for Unix system administration. As such, their life is probably hard enough, so don't speak too harshly of them. Remember, TMTOWTDI. This is just one of those ways.

If you aren't fluent in Bourne shell, you might find it clearer to express "for each $thing in this @list" by saying foreach, to make your code look less like the shell and more like English. (But don't try to make your English look like your code!)

See Also

The "For Loops," "Foreach Loops," and "Loop Control" sections of *perlsyn*(1) and Chapter 4 of *Programming Perl*; the "Temporary Values via local" section of *perlsub*(1); the "Scoped Declarations" section of Chapter 4 of *Programming Perl*; we talk about local in Recipe 10.13; we talk about my in Recipe 10.2

4.6   Iterating Over an Array by Reference

Problem

You have a reference to an array, and you want to use a loop to work with the array's elements.

Solution

Use foreach or for to loop over the dereferenced array:

```
# iterate over elements of array in $ARRAYREF
foreach $item (@$ARRAYREF) {
    # do something with $item
}

for ($i = 0; $i <= $#$ARRAYREF; $i++) {
    # do something with $ARRAYREF->[$i]
}
```

Discussion

The solutions assume you have a scalar variable containing the array reference. This lets you do things like this:

```
@fruits = ( "Apple", "Blackberry" );
$fruit_ref = \@fruits;
foreach $fruit (@$fruit_ref) {
    print "$fruit tastes good in a pie.\n";
}
Apple tastes good in a pie.
Blackberry tastes good in a pie.
```

We could have rewritten the foreach loop as a for loop like this:

```
for ($i=0; $i <= $#$fruit_ref; $i++) {
    print "$fruit_ref->[$i] tastes good in a pie.\n";
}
```

Frequently, though, the array reference is the result of a more complex expression. Use the @{ EXPR } notation to turn the result of the expression back into an array:

```
$namelist{felines} = \@rogue_cats;
foreach $cat ( @{ $namelist{felines} } ) {
    print "$cat purrs hypnotically..\n";
}
print "--More--\nYou are controlled.\n";
```

Again, we can replace the foreach with a for loop:

```
for ($i=0; $i <= $#{ $namelist{felines} }; $i++) {
    print "$namelist{felines}[$i] purrs hypnotically.\n";
}
```

See Also

perlref(1) and *perllol*(1); Chapter 8 of *Programming Perl*; Recipe 11.1; Recipe 4.5

4.7   Extracting Unique Elements from a List

Problem

You want to eliminate duplicate values from a list, such as when you build the list from a file or from the output of another command. This recipe is equally applicable to removing duplicates as they occur in input and to removing duplicates from an array you've already populated.

Solution

Use a hash to record which items have been seen, then keys to extract them. You can use Perl's idea of truth to shorten and speed up your code.

Straightforward

```
%seen = ( );
@uniq = ( );
foreach $item (@list) {
    unless ($seen{$item}) {
        # if we get here, we have not seen it before
        $seen{$item} = 1;
        push(@uniq, $item);
    }
}
```

Faster

```
%seen = ( );
foreach $item (@list) {
    push(@uniq, $item) unless $seen{$item}++;
}
```

Similar but with user function

```
%seen = ( );
foreach $item (@list) {
    some_func($item) unless $seen{$item}++;
}
```

Faster but different

```
%seen = ( );
foreach $item (@list) {
    $seen{$item}++;
}
@uniq = keys %seen;
```

Faster and even more different

```
%seen = ( );
@uniq = grep { ! $seen{$_} ++ } @list;
```

Discussion

The question at the heart of the matter is "Have I seen this element before?" Hashes are ideally suited to such lookups. The first technique ("Straightforward") builds up the array of unique values as we go along, using a hash to record whether something is already in the array.

The second technique ("Faster") is the most natural way to write this sort of thing in Perl. It creates a new entry in the hash every time it sees an element that hasn't been seen before, using the ++ operator. This has the side effect of making the hash record the number of times the element was seen. This time we only use the hash for its property of working like a set.

The third example ("Similar but with user function") is similar to the second but rather than storing the item away, we call some user-defined function with that item as its argument. If that's all we're doing, keeping a spare array of those unique values is unnecessary.

The next mechanism ("Faster but different") waits until it's done processing the list to extract the unique keys from the %seen hash. This may be convenient, but the original order has been lost.

The final approach ("Faster and even more different") merges the construction of the %seen hash with the extraction of unique elements. This preserves the original order of elements.

Using a hash to record the values has two side effects: processing long lists can take a lot of memory, and the list returned by keys is unordered.

Here's an example of processing input as it is read. We use `who` to gather information on the current user list, then extract the username from each line before updating the hash:

```
# generate a list of users logged in, removing duplicates
%ucnt = ( );
for (`who`) {
    s/\s.*\n//;    # kill from first space till end-of-line, yielding username
    $ucnt{$_}++;  # record the presence of this user
}
# extract and print unique keys
@users = sort keys %ucnt;
print "users logged in: @users\n";
```

See Also

The "Foreach Loops" section of *perlsyn*(1) and Chapter 4 of *Programming Perl*; the keys function in *perlfunc*(1) and Chapter 29 of *Programming Perl*; the "Hashes" section of Chapter 2 of *Programming Perl*; Chapter 5; we use hashes in a similar fashion in Recipes 4.8 and 4.9

4.8   Finding Elements in One Array but Not Another

Problem

You want to find elements that are in one array but not another.

Solution

You want to find elements in @A that aren't in @B. Build a hash of the keys of @B to use as a lookup table. Then check each element in @A to see whether it is in @B.

Straightforward implementation

```
# assume @A and @B are already loaded
%seen = ();                  # lookup table to test membership of B
@aonly = ();                 # answer

# build lookup table
foreach $item (@B) { $seen{$item} = 1 }

# find only elements in @A and not in @B
foreach $item (@A) {
    unless ($seen{$item}) {
        # it's not in %seen, so add to @aonly
        push(@aonly, $item);
    }
}
```

More idiomatic version

```
my %seen;       # lookup table
my @aonly;      # answer

# build lookup table
@seen{@B} = ();

foreach $item (@A) {
    push(@aonly, $item) unless exists $seen{$item};
}
```

Loopless version

```
my @A = ...;
my @B = ...;

my %seen;
@seen {@A} = ();
delete @seen {@B};

my @aonly = keys %seen;
```

Discussion

As with nearly any problem in Perl that asks whether a scalar is *in* one list or another, this one uses a hash. First, process @B so that the %seen hash records each element from @B by setting its value to 1. Then process @A one element at a time, checking whether that particular element had been in @B by consulting the %seen hash.

The given code retains duplicate elements in @A. This can be fixed easily by adding the elements of @A to %seen as they are processed:

```
foreach $item (@A) {
    push(@aonly, $item) unless $seen{$item};
    $seen{$item} = 1;                      # mark as seen
}
```

The first two solutions differ mainly in how they build the hash. The first iterates through @B. The second uses a *hash slice* to initialize the hash. A hash slice is easiest illustrated by this example:

```
$hash{"key1"} = 1;
$hash{"key2"} = 2;
```

which is equivalent to:

```
@hash{"key1", "key2"} = (1,2);
```

The list in the curly braces holds the keys; the list on the right holds the values. We initialize %seen in the first solution by looping over each element in @B and setting the appropriate value of %seen to 1. In the second, we simply say:

```
@seen{@B} = ( );
```

This uses items in @B as keys for %seen, setting each corresponding value to undef, because there are fewer values on the right than places to put them. This works out here because we check for existence of the key, not logical truth or definedness of the value. If we needed true values, a slice could still shorten our code:

```
@seen{@B} = (1) x @B;
```

In the third solution, we make use of this property even further and avoid explicit loops altogether. (Not that avoiding loops should be construed as being particularly virtuous; we're just showing you that there's more than one way to do it.) The slice assignment makes any element that was in @A a key, and the slice deletion removes from the hash any keys that were elements of @B, leaving those that were only in @A.

A fairly common situation where this might arise is when you have two files and would like to know which lines from the second file either were or weren't in the first. Here's a simple solution based on this recipe:

```
open(OLD, $path1)        || die "can't open $path1: $!";
@seen{ <OLD> } = ( );
open(NEW, $path2)        || die "can't open $path2: $!";
while (<NEW>) {
    print if exists $seen{$_};
}
```

This shows the lines in the second file that were already seen in the first one. Use unless instead of if to show the lines in the second file that were *not* in the first.

Imagine two files, the first containing the lines:

```
red
yellow
green
blue
```

and the second containing:

```
green
orange
purple
black
yellow
```

The output using if would be:

```
green
yellow
```

and the output using unless would be:

```
orange
purple
black
```

You could even do this from the command line; given a suitable *cat*(1) program, it's easy:

```
% perl -e '@s{`cat OLD`}=(); exists $s{$_} && print for `cat NEW`'
% perl -e '@s{`cat OLD`}=(); exists $s{$_} || print for `cat NEW`'
```

You'd find that you just emulated these calls to the Unix fgrep(1) program:

```
% fgrep -Ff  OLD NEW
% fgrep -vFf OLD NEW
```

See Also

Hash slices are explained in *perldata*(1) and the "Variables" section of Chapter 2 of *Programming Perl*; Chapter 5; we use hashes in a similar fashion in Recipes 4.7 and 4.9

4.9   Computing Union, Intersection, or Difference of Unique Lists

Problem

You have a pair of lists, each holding unduplicated items. You'd like to find out which items are in both lists (*intersection*), one but not the other (*difference*), or either (*union*).

Solution

The following solutions need the listed initializations:

```
@a = (1, 3, 5, 6, 7, 8);
@b = (2, 3, 5, 7, 9);

@union = @isect = @diff = ();
%union = %isect = ();
%count = ();
```

Simple solution for union and intersection

```
foreach $e (@a) { $union{$e} = 1 }

foreach $e (@b) {
    if ( $union{$e} ) { $isect{$e} = 1 }
    $union{$e} = 1;
}
@union = keys %union;
@isect = keys %isect;
```

More idiomatic version

```
foreach $e (@a, @b) { $union{$e}++ && $isect{$e}++ }

@union = keys %union;
@isect = keys %isect;
```

Union, intersection, and symmetric difference

```
foreach $e (@a, @b) { $count{$e}++ }

@union = keys %count;
foreach $e (keys %count) {
    if ($count{$e} == 2) {
        push @isect, $e;
    } else {
        push @diff, $e;
    }
}
```

Indirect solution

```
@isect = @diff = @union = ();

foreach $e (@a, @b) { $count{$e}++ }

@union = keys %count;
foreach $e (keys %count) {
    push @{ $count{$e} == 2 ? \@isect : \@diff }, $e;
}
```

Discussion

The first solution most directly computes the union and intersection of two lists, neither containing duplicates. Two hashes are used to record whether a particular item goes in the union or the intersection. We put every element of the first array in the union hash, giving it a true value. Then, processing each element of the second array, we check whether that element is already present in the union. If it is, we put it in the intersection as well. In any event, it goes into the union. When we're done, we extract the keys of both the union and intersection hashes. The values aren't needed.

The second solution ("More idiomatic version") is essentially the same but relies on familiarity with the Perl (and *awk*, C, C++, and Java) ++ and && operators. By placing the ++ after the variable, we first look at its old value before incrementing it. The first time through it won't be in the union, which makes the first part of the && false, so the second part is consequently ignored. The second time that we encounter the same element, it's already present in the union, so we put it in the intersection.

The third solution uses just one hash to track how many times each element is seen. Once both arrays have their elements recorded in the hash, we grab those keys and put them in the union. Then we process those hash keys one at a time. Keys whose values are 2 were in both arrays, so they go in the intersection array. Keys whose values are 1 were in just one of the two arrays, so they go in the difference array. Elements of the output arrays are not in the same order as those in the input arrays.

The last solution, like the previous one, uses just one hash to count how many times each element is encountered. Here, though, we dynamically select one of two possible arrays by placing within the @{...} array-dereferencing block an expression whose evaluation yields a reference to whichever array is demanded by the situation.

In this recipe we compute the symmetric difference, not the simple difference. These are terms from set theory. A *symmetric difference* is the set of all elements that are members of either @A or @B, but not both. A *simple difference* is the set of members of @A but not @B, which we calculated in Recipe 4.8.

See Also

The "Hashes" section of Chapter 2 of *Programming Perl*; Chapter 5; we use hashes in a similar fashion in Recipes 4.7 and 4.8

4.10 Appending One Array to Another

Problem

You want to join two arrays by appending all elements of one to the other.

Solution

Use push:

```
# push
push(@ARRAY1, @ARRAY2);
```

Discussion

The push function is optimized for appending a list to the end of an array. You can take advantage of Perl's list flattening to join two arrays, but this results in significantly more copying than push:

```
@ARRAY1 = (@ARRAY1, @ARRAY2);
```

Here's an example of push in action:

```
@members = ("Time", "Flies");
@initiates = ("An", "Arrow");
push(@members, @initiates);
# @members is now ("Time", "Flies", "An", "Arrow")
```

To insert the elements of one array into the middle of another, use the splice function:

```
splice(@members, 2, 0, "Like", @initiates);
print "@members\n";
splice(@members, 0, 1, "Fruit");
splice(@members, -2, 2, "A", "Banana");
print "@members\n";
```

This is the output:

```
Time Flies Like An Arrow
Fruit Flies Like A Banana
```

See Also

The splice and push functions in *perlfunc*(1) and Chapter 29 of *Programming Perl*; the "List Values and Arrays" section of Chapter 2 of *Programming Perl*; the "List Value Constructors" section of *perldata*(1)

4.11   Reversing an Array

Problem

You want to reverse an array.

Solution

Use the reverse function:

```
# reverse @ARRAY into @REVERSED
@REVERSED = reverse @ARRAY;
```

Or process with a foreach loop on a reversed list:

```
foreach $element (reverse @ARRAY) {
    # do something with $element
}
```

Or use a for loop, starting with the index of the last element and working your way down:

```
for ($i = $#ARRAY; $i >= 0; $i--) {
    # do something with $ARRAY[$i]
}
```

Discussion

Called in list context, the reverse function reverses elements of its argument list. You can save a copy of that reversed list into an array, or just use foreach to walk through it directly if that's all you need. The for loop processes the array elements in reverse order by using explicit indices. If you don't need a reversed copy of the array, the for loop can save memory and time on very large arrays.

If you're using reverse to reverse a list that you just sorted, you should have sorted it in the correct order to begin with. For example:

```
# two-step: sort then reverse
@ascending = sort { $a cmp $b } @users;
@descending = reverse @ascending;

# one-step: sort with reverse comparison
@descending = sort { $b cmp $a } @users;
```

See Also

The reverse function in *perlfunc*(1) and Chapter 29 of *Programming Perl*; we use reverse in Recipe 1.7

4.12   Processing Multiple Elements of an Array

Problem

You want to pop or shift multiple elements at a time.

Solution

Use splice:

```
# remove $N elements from front of @ARRAY (shift $N)
@FRONT = splice(@ARRAY, 0, $N);

# remove $N elements from the end of the array (pop $N)
@END = splice(@ARRAY, -$N);
```

Discussion

The `splice` function allows you to add elements, delete elements, or both, at any point in an array, not just at the ends. All other operations that modify an array's length can also be written as a `splice`:

Direct method	Splice equivalent
push(@a, $x, $y)	splice(@a, @a, 0, $x, $y)
pop(@a)	splice(@a, -1)
shift(@a)	splice(@a, 0, 1)
unshift(@a, $x, $y)	splice(@a, 0, 0, $x, $y)
$a[$x] = $y	splice(@a, $x, 1, $y)
(@a, @a = ())	splice(@a)

Unlike pop and unshift, though, which always delete and return just one element at a time—and from the ends only—splice lets you specify the number of elements. This leads to code like the examples in the Solution.

It's often convenient to wrap these splices as functions:

```
sub shift2 (\@) {
    return splice(@{$_[0]}, 0, 2);
}

sub pop2 (\@) {
    return splice(@{$_[0]}, -2);
}
```

This makes their behavior more apparent when you use them:

```
@friends = qw(Peter Paul Mary Jim Tim);
($this, $that) = shift2(@friends);
# $this contains Peter, $that has Paul, and
# @friends has Mary, Jim, and Tim

@beverages = qw(Dew Jolt Cola Sprite Fresca);
@pair = pop2(@beverages);
# $pair[0] contains Sprite, $pair[1] has Fresca,
# and @beverages has (Dew, Jolt, Cola)
```

The `splice` function returns the elements it removed from the array, so `shift2` replaces the first two elements in @ARRAY with nothing (i.e., deletes them) and returns the two elements deleted. In `pop2`, the two elements at end of the array are removed and returned.

These two functions are prototyped to take an array reference as their argument to better mimic the built-in `shift` and `pop` functions. The caller doesn't pass in an explicit reference using a backslash. Instead, the compiler, having seen the array reference prototype, arranges to pass the array by reference anyway. Advantages to this approach include efficiency, transparency, and compile-time parameter checking. One disadvantage is that the thing passed in must look like a real array with a leading

@ sign, not just a scalar containing an array reference. If it did, you'd have to prepend an @, making it less transparent:

```
$line[5] = \@list;
@got = pop2( @{ $line[5] } );
```

This is another example of where a proper array and not a mere list is called for. The \@ prototype requires that whatever goes in that argument slot be an array. $line[5] isn't an array, but an array reference. That's why we need the "extra" @ sign.

See Also

The splice function in *perlfunc*(1) and Chapter 29 of *Programming Perl*; the "Proto-types" sections of *perlsub*(1) and Chapter 6 of *Programming Perl*; we use splice in Recipe 4.10

4.13   Finding the First List Element That Passes a Test

Problem

You want the first element in the list (or its index) that passes a test. Alternatively, you want to know whether any element passes the test. The test can be simple identity ("Is this element in the list?")[*] or more complex ("I have a list of Employee objects, sorted from highest salary to lowest. Which manager has the highest salary?"). Simple cases normally require only the value of the element, but when the array itself will be altered, you probably need to know the index number of the first matching element.

Solution

To find a matching value, use foreach to loop over every element, and call last as soon as you find a match:

```
my ($match, $found, $item);
foreach $item (@array) {
    if (CRITERION) {
        $match = $item;  # must save
        $found = 1;
        last;
    }
}
if ($found) {
    ## do something with $match
} else {
```

[*] But why didn't you use a hash then?

```
        ## unfound
    }
```

To find a matching index, use for to loop a variable over every array index, and call last as soon as you find a match:

```
my ($i, $match_idx);
for ($i = 0; $i < @array; $i++) {
    if (CRITERION) {
        $match_idx = $i;      # save the index
        last;
    }
}

if (defined $match_idx) {
    ## found in $array[$match_idx]
} else {
    ## unfound
}
```

The List::Util module, shipped standard with Perl as of v5.8 but available on CPAN for earlier versions, provides an even easier approach:

```
use List::Util qw(first);
$match = first { CRITERION } @list
```

Discussion

Lacking (until recently) a built-in mechanism to do this, we must write our own code to go through the list and test each element. We use foreach and for, and call last to ensure that we stop as soon as we find a match. Before we use last to stop looking, though, we save the value or index.

A common approach is to try to use grep here. But grep always tests all elements and finds all matches, so it's inefficient if you want only the first match. However, grep might still be faster. That's because there will be less source code if you use grep rather than writing your own loop. That means fewer internal Perl operations, and it is these that in practice often dominate runtimes.

Beyond a certain size of your data set, a loop that terminates early will still be faster—assuming it has the chance to do so. Empirical evidence suggests that for will be faster as long as you can exit before the first two-thirds of the list has been examined. It's worthwhile to know how to do that.

We have to set $match when we want the value of the first matching element. We can't just test $item at the end of the loop, because foreach automatically localizes the iterator variable and thereby prevents us from accessing the final loop value after the loop ends. See Recipe 4.5.

Here's an example. Assume that @all_emps holds a list of Employee objects, sorted in descending order by salary. We wish to find the highest paid engineer, who will be the first engineer in the array. We only want to print the engineer's name, so we want the value, not the index.

```
foreach $employee (@all_emps) {
    if ( $employee->category() eq 'engineer' ) {
        $top_engr = $employee;
        last;
    }
}
print "Highest paid engineer is: ", $highest_engineer->name(), "\n";
```

When we're searching and want only the index, we can save some code by remembering that $i will not be an acceptable array index if we don't find a match. This mainly saves us code space, as not doing an assignment doesn't really win much compared to the time spent testing list elements. It's more obscure, because it tests if ($i < @ARRAY) to check whether we found a match, instead of the more obvious defined test in the previous solution.

```
for ($i = 0; $i < @ARRAY; $i++) {
    last if CRITERION;
}
if ($i < @ARRAY) {
    ## found and $i is the index
} else {
    ## not found
}
```

The first function from List::Util encapsulates the logic from an entire loop into a convenient, easy-to-use function. It acts just like a short-circuiting form of the built-in grep function that stops as soon as a match is found. While running, each list element is in a localized $_ variable. For example:

```
$first_odd = first { $_ % 2 == 1 } @ARRAY;
```

Or rewriting the previous employee loop:

```
$top_engr = first { $_->category() eq 'engineer' } @all_emps;
```

See Also

The "For Loops," "Foreach Loops," and "Loop Control" sections of *perlsyn*(1) and Chapter 4 of *Programming Perl*; the grep function in *perlfunc*(1) and Chapter 29 of *Programming Perl*

4.14 Finding All Elements in an Array Matching Certain Criteria

Problem

From a list, you want only the elements that match certain criteria.

This notion of extracting a subset of a larger list is common. It's how you find all engineers in a list of employees, all users in the "staff" group, or all the filenames you're interested in.

Solution

Use grep to apply a condition to all elements in the list and return only those for which the condition was true:

```
@MATCHING = grep { TEST ($_) } @LIST;
```

Discussion

This could also be accomplished with a foreach loop:

```
@matching = ();
foreach (@list) {
    push(@matching, $_) if TEST ($_);
}
```

The Perl grep function is shorthand for all that looping and mucking about. It's not really like the Unix grep command; it doesn't have options to return line numbers or to negate the test, and it isn't limited to regular-expression tests. For example, to filter out just the large numbers from an array or to find out which keys in a hash have very large values:

```
@bigs = grep { $_ > 1_000_000 } @nums;
@pigs = grep { $users{$_} > 1e7 } keys %users;
```

Here's something that sets @matching to lines from the *who* command that start with "gnat ":

```
@matching = grep { /^gnat / } `who`;
```

Here's another example:

```
@engineers = grep { $_->position() eq "Engineer" } @employees;
```

It extracts only those objects from the array @employees whose position method returns the string Engineer.

You could have even more complex tests in a grep:

```
@secondary_assistance = grep { $_->income >= 26_000 &&
                               $_->income <  30_000 }
                        @applicants;
```

But at that point you may decide it would be more legible to write a proper loop instead.

See Also

The "For Loops," "Foreach Loops," and "Loop Control" sections of *perlsyn*(1) and Chapter 4 of *Programming Perl*; the grep function in *perlfunc*(1) and Chapter 29 of *Programming Perl*; your system's *who*(1) manpage, if it exists; Recipe 4.13

4.15   Sorting an Array Numerically

Problem

You want to sort a list of numbers, but Perl's sort (by default) sorts in ASCII order.

Solution

Use Perl's sort function and the <=> numerical comparison operator:

```
@sorted = sort { $a <=> $b } @unsorted;
```

Discussion

The sort function takes an optional code block, which lets you replace the default alphabetic comparison with your own subroutine. This comparison function is called each time sort has to compare two values. The values to compare are loaded into the special package variables $a and $b, which are automatically localized.

The comparison function should return a negative number if $a ought to appear before $b in the output list, 0 if they're the same and their order doesn't matter, or a positive number if $a ought to appear after $b. Perl has two operators that behave this way: <=> for sorting numbers in ascending numeric order, and cmp for sorting strings in ascending alphabetic order. By default, sort uses cmp-style comparisons.

Here's code that sorts the list of PIDs in @pids, lets the user select one, then sends it a TERM signal followed by a KILL signal. We use a code block that compares $a to $b with <=> to sort numerically:

```
# @pids is an unsorted array of process IDs
foreach my $pid (sort { $a <=> $b } @pids) {
    print "$pid\n";
}
print "Select a process ID to kill:\n";
chomp ($pid = <>);
die "Exiting ... \n" unless $pid && $pid =~ /^\d+$/;
kill('TERM',$pid);
sleep 2;
kill('KILL',$pid);
```

If you use $a <=> $b or $a cmp $b, the list will be sorted in ascending order. For a descending sort, all we have to do is swap $a and $b in the sort subroutine:

```
@descending = sort { $b <=> $a } @unsorted;
```

Comparison routines must be consistent; that is, they should always return the same answer when called with the same values. Inconsistent comparison routines lead to infinite loops or core dumps, especially in older releases of Perl.

You can also say sort SUBNAME LIST where SUBNAME is the name of a comparison subroutine returning -1, 0, or +1. In the interests of speed, the normal calling conventions are bypassed, and the values to be compared magically appear for the duration of the subroutine in the global package variables $a and $b. Because of the odd way Perl calls this subroutine, it may not be recursive.

A word of warning: $a and $b are set in the package active in the call to sort, which may not be the same as the one that the SUBNAME function passed to sort was compiled in! For example:

```
package Sort_Subs;
sub revnum { $b <=> $a }

package Other_Pack;
@all = sort Sort_Subs::revnum 4, 19, 8, 3;
```

This will silently fail (unless you have **-w** in effect, in which case it will vocally fail) because the sort call sets the package variables $a and $b in its own package, Other_Pack, but the revnum function uses its own package's versions. This is another reason why in-lining sort functions is easier, as in:

```
@all = sort { $b <=> $a } 4, 19, 8, 3;
```

For more on packages, see Chapter 10.

See Also

The cmp and <=> operators in *perlop*(1) and Chapter 3 of *Programming Perl*; the kill, sort, and sleep functions in *perlfunc*(1) and Chapter 29 of *Programming Perl*; Recipe 4.16

4.16   Sorting a List by Computable Field

Problem

You want to sort a list by something more complex than a simple string or numeric comparison.

This is common when working with objects ("sort by the employee's salary") or complex data structures ("sort by the third element in the array that this is a reference to"). It's also applicable when you want to sort by more than one key; for instance, sorting by birthday and then by name when multiple people share the same birthday.

Solution

Use the customizable comparison routine in sort:

```
@ordered = sort { compare( ) } @unordered;
```

You can speed this up by precomputing the field.

```
@precomputed = map { [compute( ),$_] } @unordered;
@ordered_precomputed = sort { $a->[0] <=> $b->[0] } @precomputed;
@ordered = map { $_->[1] } @ordered_precomputed;
```

And, finally, you can combine the three steps:

```
@ordered = map { $_->[1] }
           sort { $a->[0] <=> $b->[0] }
           map { [compute( ), $_] }
           @unordered;
```

Discussion

The use of a comparison routine was explained in Recipe 4.15. As well as using built-in operators like <=>, you can construct more complex tests:

```
@ordered = sort { $a->name cmp $b->name } @employees;
```

You often see sort used like this in part of a foreach loop:

```
foreach $employee (sort { $a->name cmp $b->name } @employees) {
    print $employee->name, " earns \$", $employee->salary, "\n";
}
```

If you're going to do a lot of work with elements in a particular order, it's more efficient to sort once and work from that:

```
@sorted_employees = sort { $a->name cmp $b->name } @employees;
foreach $employee (@sorted_employees) {
    print $employee->name, " earns \$", $employee->salary, "\n";
}
# load %bonus
foreach $employee (@sorted_employees) {
    if ( $bonus{ $employee->ssn } ) {
        print $employee->name, " got a bonus!\n";
    }
}
```

We can put multiple comparisons in the routine and separate them with ||. || is a short-circuit operator: it returns the first true value it finds. This means we can sort by one kind of comparison, but if the elements are equal (the comparison returns 0), we can sort by another. This has the effect of a sort within a sort:

```
@sorted = sort { $a->name cmp $b->name
                        ||
                 $b->age <=> $a->age } @employees;
```

This first considers the names of the two employees to be compared. If they're not equal, || stops and returns the result of the cmp (effectively sorting them in ascending order by name). If the names are equal, though, || keeps testing and returns the result of the <=> (sorting them in descending order by age). The result is a list that is sorted by name and by age within groups of the same name.

Let's look at a real-life example of sorting. First we fetch all system users, represented as User::pwent objects. Then we sort them by name and print the sorted list:

```
use User::pwent qw(getpwent);
@users = ( );
# fetch all users
while (defined($user = getpwent)) {
    push(@users, $user);
}
@users = sort { $a->name cmp $b->name } @users;
foreach $user (@users) {
    print $user->name, "\n";
}
```

We can have more than simple comparisons, or combinations of simple comparisons. This code sorts a list of names by comparing the *second* letters of the names. It gets the second letters by using substr:

```
@sorted = sort { substr($a,1,1) cmp substr($b,1,1) } @names;
```

and here we sort by string length:

```
@sorted = sort { length $a <=> length $b } @strings;
```

The sort function calls the code block each time it needs to compare two elements, so the number of comparisons grows dramatically with the number of elements we're sorting. Sorting 10 elements requires (on average) 46 comparisons, but sorting 1,000 elements requires 14,000 comparisons. A time-consuming operation like a split or a subroutine call for each comparison can easily make your program crawl.

Fortunately, we can remove this bottleneck by running the operation once per element prior to the sort. Use map to store the results of the operation in an array whose elements are anonymous arrays containing both the computed field and the original field. Then we sort this array of arrays on the precomputed field and use map to get the sorted original data. This map-sort-map concept is useful and common, so let's look at it in depth.

Let's apply map-sort-map to the sorting by string length example:

```
@temp   = map  {  [ length $_, $_ ]  } @strings;
@temp   = sort { $a->[0] <=> $b->[0] } @temp;
@sorted = map  {           $_->[1]   } @temp;
```

The first line creates a temporary array of strings and their lengths, using map. The second line sorts the temporary array by comparing the precomputed lengths. The third line turns the sorted temporary array of strings and lengths back into a sorted array of strings. This way, we calculate the length of each string only once.

Because the input to each line is the output of the previous line (the @temp array we make in line 1 is fed to sort in line 2, and that output is fed to map in line 3), we can combine it into one statement and eliminate the temporary array:

```
@sorted = map  { $_->[1] }
          sort { $a->[0] <=> $b->[0] }
          map  { [ length $_, $_ ] }
          @strings;
```

The operations now appear in reverse order. When you meet a map-sort-map, you should read it from the bottom up to determine the function:

@strings

> The last part is the data to be sorted. Here it's just an array, but later we'll see that this can be a subroutine or even backticks. Anything that returns a list is fair game.

map

> The map closer to the bottom builds the temporary list of anonymous arrays. This list contains the precomputed fields (length $_) and also records the original element ($_) by storing both in an anonymous array. Look at this map line to find out how the fields are computed.

sort

> The sort line sorts the list of anonymous arrays by comparing the precomputed fields. It won't tell you much, other than whether the list is sorted in ascending or descending order.

map

> The map at the top of the statement turns the sorted list of anonymous arrays back into a list of the sorted original elements. It will generally be the same for every map-sort-map.

Here's a more complicated example, which sorts by the first number that appears on each line in @fields:

```
@temp          = map  {    [ /(\d+)/, $_ ]  } @fields;
@sorted_temp   = sort { $a->[0] <=> $b->[0] } @temp;
@sorted_fields = map  {        $_->[1]       } @sorted_temp;
```

The regular expression mumbo jumbo in the first line extracts the first number from the line being processed by map. We use the regular expression /(\d+)/ in a list context to extract the number.

We can remove the temporary arrays in that code, giving us:

```
@sorted_fields = map  { $_->[1] }
                 sort { $a->[0] <=> $b->[0] }
                 map  { [ /(\d+)/, $_ ] }
                 @fields;
```

This final example compactly sorts colon-separated data, as from Unix's *passwd* file. It sorts the file numerically by the fourth field (group id), then numerically by the third field (user id), and then alphabetically by the first field (username).

```
print map  { $_->[0] }              # whole line
      sort {
              $a->[1] <=> $b->[1]  # gid
                ||
              $a->[2] <=> $b->[2]  # uid
                ||
              $a->[3] cmp $b->[3]  # login
           }
```

```
map { [ $_, (split /:/)[3,2,0] ] }
  `cat /etc/passwd`;
```

See Also

The sort function in *perlfunc*(1) and Chapter 29 of *Programming Perl*; the cmp and <=> operators in *perlop*(1) and Chapter 3 of *Programming Perl*; Recipe 4.15

4.17   Implementing a Circular List

Problem

You want to create and manipulate a circular list.

Solution

Use unshift and pop (or push and shift) on a normal array.

Procedure

```
unshift(@circular, pop(@circular));  # the last shall be first
push(@circular, shift(@circular));   # and vice versa
```

Discussion

Circular lists are commonly used to repeatedly process things in order; for example, connections to a server. The code shown previously isn't a true computer science circular list, with pointers and true circularity. Instead, the operations provide for moving the last element to the first position, and vice versa.

```
sub grab_and_rotate ( \@ ) {
    my $listref = shift;
    my $element = $listref->[0];
    push(@$listref, shift @$listref);
    return $element;
}

@processes = ( 1, 2, 3, 4, 5 );
while (1) {
    $process = grab_and_rotate(@processes);
    print "Handling process $process\n";
    sleep 1;
}
```

See Also

The unshift and push functions in *perlfunc*(1) and Chapter 29 of *Programming Perl*; Recipe 13.13

4.18   Randomizing an Array

Problem

You want to randomly shuffle the elements of an array. The obvious application is writing a card game, where you must shuffle a deck of cards, but it is equally applicable to any situation where you want to treat elements of an array in a random order.

Solution

Use the shuffle function from the standard List::Util module, which returns the elements of its input list in a random order.

```
use List::Util qw(shuffle);
@array = shuffle(@array);
```

Discussion

Shuffling is a surprisingly tricky process. It's easy to write a bad shuffle:

```
sub naive_shuffle {                          # DON'T DO THIS
    for (my $i = 0; $i < @_; $i++) {
        my $j = int rand @_;                 # pick random element
        ($_[$i], $_[$j]) = ($_[$j], $_[$i]); # swap 'em
    }
}
```

This algorithm is biased; the list's possible permutations don't all have the same probability of being generated. The proof of this is simple: take the case where we're passed a three-element list. We generate three random numbers, each of which can have three possible values, yielding 27 possible outcomes. There are only six permutations of the three-element list, though. Because 27 isn't evenly divisible by 6, some outcomes are more likely than others.

The List::Util module's shuffle function avoids this bias to produce a more randomly shuffled result.

If all you want to do is pick one random element from the array, use:

```
$value = $array[ int(rand(@array)) ];
```

See Also

The rand function in *perlfunc*(1) and Chapter 29 of *Programming Perl*; for more on random numbers, see Recipes 2.6, 2.7, and 2.8; Recipe 4.20 provides another way to select a random permutation

4.19   Program: words

Have you ever wondered how programs like *ls* generate columns of sorted output that you read down the columns instead of across the rows? For example:

```
awk         cp      ed      login   mount   rmdir   sum
basename    csh     egrep   ls      mt      sed     sync
cat         date    fgrep   mail    mv      sh      tar
chgrp       dd      grep    mkdir   ps      sort    touch
chmod       df      kill    mknod   pwd     stty    vi
chown       echo    ln      more    rm      su
```

Example 4-2 does this.

Example 4-2. words

```perl
#!/usr/bin/perl -w
# words - gather lines, present in columns

use strict;

my ($item, $cols, $rows, $maxlen);
my ($xpixel, $ypixel, $mask, @data);

getwinsize();

# first gather up every line of input,
# remembering the longest line length seen
$maxlen = 1;
while (<>) {
    my $mylen;
    s/\s+$//;
    $maxlen = $mylen if (($mylen = length) > $maxlen);
    push(@data, $_);
}

$maxlen += 1;                    # to make extra space

# determine boundaries of screen
$cols = int($cols / $maxlen) || 1;
$rows = int(($#data+$cols) / $cols);

# pre-create mask for faster computation
$mask = sprintf("%%-%ds ", $maxlen-1);

# subroutine to check whether at last item on line
sub EOL { ($item+1) % $cols == 0 }

# now process each item, picking out proper piece for this position
for ($item = 0; $item < $rows * $cols; $item++) {
    my $target = ($item % $cols) * $rows + int($item/$cols);
    my $piece = sprintf($mask, $target < @data ? $data[$target] : "");
    $piece =~ s/\s+$// if EOL();  # don't blank-pad to EOL
    print $piece;
    print "\n" if EOL();
}

# finish up if needed
print "\n" if EOL();
```

Example 4-2. words (continued)

```
# not portable -- linux only
sub getwinsize {
    my $winsize = "\0" x 8;
    my $TIOCGWINSZ = 0x40087468;
    if (ioctl(STDOUT, $TIOCGWINSZ, $winsize)) {
        ($rows, $cols, $xpixel, $ypixel) = unpack('S4', $winsize);
    } else {
        $cols = 80;
    }
}
```

The most obvious way to print out a sorted list in columns is to print each element of the list, one at a time, padded out to a particular width. Then when you're about to hit the end of the line, generate a newline. But that only works if you're planning on reading each row from left to right. If you instead expect to read it down each column, this approach won't do.

The *words* program is a filter that generates output going down the columns. It reads all input, keeping track of the length of the longest line seen. Once everything has been read in, it divides the screen width by the length of the longest input record seen, yielding the expected number of columns.

Then the program goes into a loop that executes once per input record, but the output order isn't in the obvious order. Imagine you had a list of nine items:

```
Wrong       Right
-----       -----
1 2 3       1 4 7
4 5 6       2 5 8
7 8 9       3 6 9
```

The *words* program does the necessary calculations to print out elements (1,4,7) on one line, (2,5,8) on the next, and (3,6,9) on the last.

To figure out the current window size, this program does an ioctl call. This works fine—on the system it was written for. On any other system, it won't work. If that's good enough for you, then good for you. Recipe 12.17 shows how to find this on your system using the *ioctl.ph* file, or with a C program. Recipe 15.4 shows a more portable solution, but that requires installing a CPAN module.

See Also

Recipe 15.4

4.20 Program: permute

Have you ever wanted to generate all possible permutations of an array or to execute some code for every possible permutation? For example:

```
% echo man bites dog | permute
```
dog bites man
bites dog man
dog man bites
man dog bites
bites man dog
man bites dog

The number of permutations of a set is the factorial of the size of the set. This number grows extremely fast, so you don't want to run it on many permutations:

```
Set Size          Permutations
1                 1
2                 2
3                 6
4                 24
5                 120
6                 720
7                 5040
8                 40320
9                 362880
10                3628800
11                39916800
12                479001600
13                6227020800
14                87178291200
15                1307674368000
```

Doing something for each alternative takes a correspondingly large amount of time. In fact, factorial algorithms exceed the number of particles in the universe with very small inputs. The factorial of 500 is greater than ten raised to the *thousandth* power!

```
use Math::BigInt;
sub factorial {
    my $n = shift;
    my $s = 1;
    $s *= $n-- while $n > 0;
    return $s;
}
print factorial(Math::BigInt->new("500"));
```
+1220136... (1035 digits total)

The two solutions that follow differ in the order of the permutations they return.

The solution in Example 4-3 uses a classic list permutation algorithm used by Lisp hackers. It's relatively straightforward but makes unnecessary copies. It's also hard-wired to do nothing but print out its permutations.

Example 4-3. tsc-permute

```
#!/usr/bin/perl -n
# tsc_permute: permute each word of input
permute([split], []);
sub permute {
    my @items = @{ $_[0] };
    my @perms = @{ $_[1] };
```

Example 4-3. tsc-permute (continued)

```
        unless (@items) {
            print "@perms\n";
        } else {
            my (@newitems,@newperms,$i);
            foreach $i (0 .. $#items) {
                @newitems = @items;
                @newperms = @perms;
                unshift(@newperms, splice(@newitems, $i, 1));
                permute( \@newitems, \@newperms);
            }
        }
    }
```

The solution in Example 4-4, provided by Mark-Jason Dominus, is faster (by around 25%) and more elegant. Rather than precalculate all permutations, his code generates the *n*th particular permutation. It is elegant in two ways. First, it avoids recursion except to calculate the factorial, which the permutation algorithm proper does not use. Second, it generates a permutation of integers rather than permute the actual data set.

He also uses a time-saving technique called *memoizing*. The idea is that a function that always returns a particular answer when called with a particular argument memorizes that answer. That way, the next time it's called with the same argument, no further calculations are required. The `factorial` function uses a private array `@fact` to remember previously calculated factorial values as described in Recipe 10.3. This technique is so useful that there's a standard module that will handle the value caching for you. If you just had a regular factorial function that didn't have its own caching, you could add caching to the existing function this way:

```
use Memoize;
memoize("factorial");
```

You call n2perm with two arguments: the permutation number to generate (from 0 to factorial(N), where N is the size of your array) and the subscript of the array's last element. The n2perm function calculates directions for the permutation in the n2pat subroutine. Then it converts those directions into a permutation of integers in the pat2perm subroutine. The directions are a list like (0 2 0 1 0), which means: "Splice out the 0th element, then the second element from the remaining list, then the 0th element, then the first, then the 0th."

Example 4-4. mjd-permute

```
#!/usr/bin/perl -w
# mjd_permute: permute each word of input
use strict;
sub factorial($);    # forward reference to declare prototype

while (<>) {
    my @data = split;
    my $num_permutations = factorial(scalar @data);
    for (my $i=0; $i < $num_permutations; $i++) {
```

Example 4-4. mjd-permute (continued)

```perl
        my @permutation = @data[n2perm($i, $#data)];
        print "@permutation\n";
    }
}

# Utility function: factorial with memoizing
BEGIN {
  my @fact = (1);
  sub factorial($) {
      my $n = shift;
      return $fact[$n] if defined $fact[$n];
      $fact[$n] = $n * factorial($n - 1);
  }
}

# n2pat($N, $len) : produce the $N-th pattern of length $len
sub n2pat {
    my $i   = 1;
    my $N   = shift;
    my $len = shift;
    my @pat;
    while ($i <= $len + 1) {   # Should really be just while ($N) { ...
        push @pat, $N % $i;
        $N = int($N/$i);
        $i++;
    }
    return @pat;
}

# pat2perm(@pat) : turn pattern returned by n2pat() into
# permutation of integers.  XXX: splice is already O(N)
sub pat2perm {
    my @pat    = @_;
    my @source = (0 .. $#pat);
    my @perm;
    push @perm, splice(@source, (pop @pat), 1) while @pat;
    return @perm;
}

# n2perm($N, $len) : generate the Nth permutation of $len objects
sub n2perm {
    pat2perm(n2pat(@_));
}
```

See Also

unshift and splice in *perlfunc*(1) or Chapter 29 of *Programming Perl*; the sections discussing closures in *perlsub*(1) and *perlref*(1) and Chapter 8 of *Programming Perl*; Recipe 2.6; Recipe 10.3

CHAPTER 5

Hashes

*Doing linear scans over an associative array is like
trying to club someone to death with a loaded Uzi.*
—Larry Wall

5.0 Introduction

People and parts of computer programs interact in all sorts of ways. Single scalar variables are like hermits, living a solitary existence whose only meaning comes from within the individual. Arrays are like cults, where multitudes marshal themselves under the name of a charismatic leader. In the middle lies the comfortable, intimate ground of the one-to-one relationship that is the hash. (Older documentation for Perl often called hashes *associative arrays*, but that's a mouthful. Other languages that support similar constructs sometimes use different terms for them; you may hear about *hash tables*, *tables*, *dictionaries*, *mappings*, or even *alists*, depending on the language.)

Unfortunately, this isn't a relationship of equals. The relationship encoded in a hash is that of the genitive case or the possessive, like the word "of" in English, or like "'s". We could encode that the boss *of* Nat is Tim. Hashes only give convenient ways to access values for Nat's boss; you can't ask whose boss Tim is. Finding the answer to that question is a recipe in this chapter.

Fortunately, hashes have their own special benefits, just like relationships. Hashes are a built-in data type in Perl. Their use reduces many complex algorithms to simple variable accesses. They are also fast and convenient to build indices and quick lookup tables.

Only use the % when referring to the hash as a whole, such as %boss. When referring to the value associated with a particular key, that's a single scalar value, so a $ is called for—just as when referring to one element of an array, you also use a $. This means that "the boss of Nat" would be written as $boss{"Nat"}. We can assign "Tim" to that:

```
$boss{"Nat"} = "Tim";
```

It's time to put a name to these notions. The relationship embodied in a hash is a good thing to use for its name. In the previous example you see a dollar sign, which might surprise you since this is a hash, not a scalar. But we're setting a single scalar value in that hash, so use a dollar sign. Where a lone scalar has $ as its type identifier and an entire array has @, an entire hash has %.

A regular array uses integers for indices, but the indices of a hash are always strings. Its values may be any arbitrary scalar values, including references. With references as values, you can create hashes that hold not merely strings or numbers, but also arrays, other hashes, or objects. (Or rather, references to arrays, hashes, or objects.)

An entire hash can be initialized with a list, where elements of the list are key and value pairs:

```
%age = ( "Nat",   30,
         "Jules", 31,
         "Josh",  23 );
```

This is equivalent to:

```
$age{"Nat"}   = 30;
$age{"Jules"} = 31;
$age{"Josh"}  = 23;
```

To make it easier to read and write hash initializations, the => operator, sometimes known as a *comma arrow*, was created. Mostly it behaves like a better-looking comma. For example, you can write a hash initialization this way:

```
%food_color = (
                "Apple"  => "red",
                "Banana" => "yellow",
                "Lemon"  => "yellow",
                "Carrot" => "orange"
              );
```

(This particular hash is used in many examples in this chapter.) This initialization is also an example of *hash-list equivalence*—hashes behave in some ways as though they were lists of key-value pairs. We'll use this in a number of recipes, including the merging and inverting recipes.

Unlike a regular comma, the comma arrow has a special property: it quotes any word preceding it, which means you can safely omit the quotes and improve legibility. Single-word hash keys are also automatically quoted when they occur inside braces, which means you can write $hash{somekey} instead of $hash{"somekey"}. You could rewrite the preceding initialization of %food_color as:

```
%food_color = (
                Apple  => "red",
                Banana => "yellow",
                Lemon  => "yellow",
                Carrot => "orange"
              );
```

One important issue to be aware of regarding hashes is that their elements are stored in an internal order convenient for efficient retrieval. This means that no matter what order you insert your data, it will come out in an unpredictable disorder.

See Also

The *perldata*(1) manpage; the two sections on "Hashes" in the first and second chapters of *Programming Perl*

5.1   Adding an Element to a Hash

Problem

You need to add an entry to a hash.

Solution

Simply assign to the hash key:

```
$HASH{$KEY} = $VALUE;
```

Discussion

Putting something into a hash is straightforward. In languages that don't provide the hash as an intrinsic data type, you have to worry about overflows, resizing, and collisions in your hash table. In Perl, all that is taken care of for you with a simple assignment. If that entry was already occupied (had a previous value), memory for that value is automatically freed, just as when assigning to a simple scalar.

```
# %food_color defined per the introduction
$food_color{Raspberry} = "pink";
print "Known foods:\n";
foreach $food (keys %food_color) {
    print "$food\n";
}

Known foods:
Banana
Apple
Raspberry
Carrot
Lemon
```

If you don't want to overwrite an existing value, but somehow have one key reference multiple values, see Recipes 5.8 and 11.2.

See Also

The "List Value Constructors" section of *perldata*(1); the "List Values and Arrays" section of Chapter 2 of *Programming Perl*; Recipe 5.2

5.2   Testing for the Presence of a Key in a Hash

Problem

You need to know whether a hash has a particular key, regardless of whatever value may be associated with that key.

Solution

Use the exists function.

```
# does %HASH have a value for $KEY ?
if (exists($HASH{$KEY})) {
    # it exists
} else {
    # it doesn't
}
```

Discussion

This code uses exists to check whether a key is in the %food_color hash:

```
# %food_color per the introduction
foreach $name ("Banana", "Martini") {
    if (exists $food_color{$name}) {
        print "$name is a food.\n";
    } else {
        print "$name is a drink.\n";
    }
}
```

Banana is a food.
Martini is a drink.

The exists function tests whether a key is *in* the hash. It doesn't test whether the value corresponding to that key is defined, nor whether the value is true or false. We may be splitting hairs, but problems caused by confusing existence, definedness, and truth can multiply like rabbits. Take this code:

```
%age = ( );
$age{"Toddler"}  = 3;
$age{"Unborn"}   = 0;
$age{"Phantasm"} = undef;

foreach $thing ("Toddler", "Unborn", "Phantasm", "Relic") {
    print "$thing: ";
```

```
    print "Exists "  if exists  $age{$thing};
    print "Defined " if defined $age{$thing};
    print "True "    if         $age{$thing};
    print "\n";
}
```

Toddler: Exists Defined True
Unborn: Exists Defined
Phantasm: Exists
Relic:

$age{"Toddler"} passes the existence, definedness, and truth tests. It exists because we gave "Toddler" a value in the hash; it's defined because that value isn't undef; and it's true because the value isn't one of Perl's false values.

$age{"Unborn"} passes only the existence and definedness tests. It exists because we gave "Unborn" a value in the hash, and it's defined because that value isn't undef. It isn't *true*, however, because 0 is one of Perl's false values.

$age{"Phantasm"} passes only the existence test. It exists because we gave "Phantasm" a value in the hash. But because that value was undef, it doesn't pass the definedness test. Because undef is also one of Perl's false values, it doesn't pass the truth test either.

$age{"Relic"} passes none of the tests. We didn't put a value for "Relic" into the hash, so the existence test fails. Because we didn't put a value in, $age{"Relic"} is undef whenever we try to access it. We know from "Phantasm" that undef fails the definedness and truth tests.

Sometimes it's useful to store undef in a hash. This indicates "I've seen this key, but it didn't have a meaningful value associated with it." Take, for instance, a program to look up file sizes given a list of files as input. This version tries to skip files we've seen before, but it doesn't skip zero-length files, and it doesn't skip files that we've seen before but don't exist.

```
%size = ( );
while (<>) {
    chomp;
    next if $size{$_};              # WRONG attempt to skip
    $size{$_} = -s $_;
}
```

If we change the incorrect line to call exists, we also skip files that couldn't be statted, instead of repeatedly trying (and failing) to look them up:

```
next if exists $size{$_};
```

See Also

The exists and defined functions in *perlfunc*(1) and Chapter 29 of *Programming Perl*; the discussion of truth in the "Scalar Values" section of *perldata*(1), and the "Boolean Context" section of Chapter 2 of *Programming Perl*

5.3 Creating a Hash with Immutable Keys or Values

Problem

You'd like to have a hash whose keys or values can't be altered once set.

Solution

Use the appropriate functions from the standard Hash::Util module.

```
use Hash::Util qw{ lock_keys   unlock_keys
                   lock_value unlock_value
                   lock_hash   unlock_hash  };
```

To restrict access to keys already in the hash, so no new keys can be introduced:

```
lock_keys(%hash);                # restrict to current keys
lock_keys(%hash, @klist);        # restrict to keys from @klist
```

To forbid deletion of the key or modification of its value:

```
lock_value(%hash, $key);
```

To make all keys and their values read-only:

```
lock_hash(%hash);
```

Discussion

Suppose you're using a hash to implement a record (or an object) with some predetermined set of keys, such as `"NAME"`, `"RANK"`, and `"SERNO"`. You'd like to consider it an error to access any keys besides the ones initially in the hash, such as `"ANME"`, a typo. Because Perl always creates hash elements on demand, this wouldn't be caught the way it would if you misspelled a variable name while under the use `strict` pragma.

The Hash::Util module's `lock_keys` function takes care of this for you. Once a hash is marked as having locked keys, you can't use any other keys than those. The keys need not yet be in the hash, and they may still be deleted if they are. But no new keys may be used.

Access to the values in those locked keys is not restricted by `lock_keys`. However, you may use the `lock_value` function to render a value in a hash read-only. That hash can also have its keys locked, but doesn't need to if the goal is just to have one or more values marked read-only.

If you want to lock down the entire hash, thereby restricting both its keys and its values, the `lock_hash` function will do.

See Also

The documentation for the Hash::Util module

5.4 Deleting from a Hash

Problem

You want to remove an entry from a hash so that it doesn't show up with keys, values, or each. If you were using a hash to associate salaries with employees, and an employee resigned, you'd want to remove their entry from the hash.

Solution

Use the delete function:

```
# remove $KEY and its value from %HASH
delete($HASH{$KEY});
```

Discussion

Sometimes people mistakenly try to use undef to remove an entry from a hash. undef $hash{$key} and $hash{$key} = undef both make %hash have an entry with key $key and value undef.

The delete function is the only way to remove a specific entry from a hash. Once you've deleted a key, it no longer shows up in a keys list or an each iteration, and exists will return false for that key.

This demonstrates the difference between undef and delete:

```
# %food_color as per Introduction
sub print_foods {
    my @foods = keys %food_color;
    my $food;

    print "Keys: @foods\n";
    print "Values: ";

    foreach $food (@foods) {
        my $color = $food_color{$food};

        if (defined $color) {
            print "$color ";
        } else {
            print "(undef) ";
        }
    }
    print "\n";
}
```

```
print "Initially:\n";
print_foods();

print "\nWith Banana undef\n";
undef $food_color{"Banana"};
print_foods();

print "\nWith Banana deleted\n";
delete $food_color{"Banana"};
print_foods();
```

Initially:
Keys: Banana Apple Carrot Lemon
Values: yellow red orange yellow

With Banana undef
Keys: Banana Apple Carrot Lemon
Values: (undef) red orange yellow

With Banana deleted
Keys: Apple Carrot Lemon
Values: red orange yellow

As you see, if we set $food_color{"Banana"} to undef, "Banana" still shows up as a key in the hash. The entry is still there; we only succeeded in making the value undef. On the other hand, delete actually removed it from the hash—"Banana" is no longer in the list returned by keys.

delete can also take a hash slice, deleting all listed keys at once:

```
delete @food_color{"Banana", "Apple", "Cabbage"};
```

See Also

The delete and keys functions in *perlfunc*(1) and in Chapter 29 of *Programming Perl*; we use keys in Recipe 5.5

5.5   Traversing a Hash

Problem

You want to perform an action on each entry (i.e., each key-value pair) in a hash.

Solution

Use each with a while loop:

```
while(($key, $value) = each(%HASH)) {
    # do something with $key and $value
}
```

Or use keys with a foreach loop, unless the hash is potentially very large:

```
foreach $key (keys %HASH) {
    $value = $HASH{$key};
    # do something with $key and $value
}
```

Discussion

Here's a simple example, iterating through the %food_color hash from the introduction:

```
# %food_color per the introduction
while(($food, $color) = each(%food_color)) {
    print "$food is $color.\n";
}
```
Banana is yellow.
Apple is red.
Carrot is orange.
Lemon is yellow.

```
foreach $food (keys %food_color) {
    my $color = $food_color{$food};
    print "$food is $color.\n";
}
```
Banana is yellow.
Apple is red.
Carrot is orange.
Lemon is yellow.

We didn't really need the $color variable in the foreach example, because we use it only once. Instead, we could have written:

```
print "$food is $food_color{$food}.\n"
```

Every time each is called on the same hash, it returns the "next" key-value pair. We say "next" because the pairs are returned in the order the underlying lookup structure imposes on them, which appears to be no order at all. When each runs out of hash elements, it returns the empty list ( ), whose assignment tests false and terminates the while loop.

The foreach example uses keys, which constructs an entire list containing every key from the hash before the loop even begins executing. The advantage to using each is that it gets the keys and values one pair at a time. If the hash contains many keys, not having to preconstruct a complete list of them can save substantial memory. The each function, however, doesn't let you control the order in which pairs are processed.

Using foreach and keys to loop over the list lets you impose an order. For instance, if we wanted to print the food names in alphabetical order:

```
foreach $food (sort keys %food_color) {
    print "$food is $food_color{$food}.\n";
}
```
Apple is red.
Banana is yellow.

Carrot is orange.
Lemon is yellow.

This is a common use of foreach. We use keys to obtain a list of keys in the hash, and then we use foreach to iterate over them. The danger is that if the hash contains a large number of elements, the list returned by keys will use a lot of memory. The trade-off lies between memory use and the ability to process the entries in a particular order. We cover sorting in more detail in Recipe 5.10.

Because keys, values, and each all share the same internal data structures, be careful about mixing calls to these functions or prematurely exiting an each loop. Each time you call keys or values, the current location for each is reset. This code loops forever, printing the first key returned by each:

```
while ( ($k,$v) = each %food_color ) {
    print "Processing $k\n";
    keys %food_color;                    # goes back to the start of %food_color
}
```

Modifying a hash while looping over it with each or foreach is, in general, fraught with danger. The each function can behave differently with tied and untied hashes when you add or delete keys from a hash. A foreach loops over a pregenerated list of keys, so once the loop starts, foreach can't know whether you've added or deleted keys. Keys added in the body of the loop aren't automatically appended to the list of keys to loop over, nor are keys deleted by the body of the loop deleted from this list.

Example 5-1 reads a mailbox file and reports the number of messages from each person. It uses the From: line to determine the sender. (It isn't clever in this respect, but we're showing hash manipulation, not mail-file processing.) Supply the mailbox filename as a command-line argument, or use a "-" to indicate you're piping the mailbox to the program. (When Perl opens a file named "-" for reading using fewer than three arguments to open, this means to use the current standard input.)

Example 5-1. countfrom

```
#!/usr/bin/perl
# countfrom - count number of messages from each sender
$filename = $ARGV[0] || "-";          # "-" means standard input
open(FILE, "< $filename")                       or die "Can't open $filename : $!";
while(<FILE>) {
    if (/^From: (.*)/) { $from{$1}++ }
}
foreach $person (sort keys %from) {
    print "$person: $from{$person}\n";
}
```

See Also

The each and keys functions in *perlfunc*(1) and in Chapter 29 of *Programming Perl*; we talk about for and foreach in Recipe 4.6

5.6   Printing a Hash

Problem

You want to print a hash, but neither print "%hash" nor print %hash does what you want; the first is a literal, while the second just has the keys and values all scrunched together.

Solution

One of several approaches is to iterate over every key-value pair in the hash using Recipe 5.5 and print them:

```
while ( ($k,$v) = each %hash ) {
    print "$k => $v\n";
}
```

Or use map to generate a list of strings:

```
print map { "$_ => $hash{$_}\n" } keys %hash;
```

Or use the interpolation trick from Recipe 1.15 to interpolate the hash as a list:

```
print "@{[ %hash ]}\n";
```

Or use a temporary array variable to hold the hash, and then print that:

```
{
    my @temp = %hash;
    print "@temp";
}
```

Discussion

The methods differ in the degree that their output is customizable (in order and formatting) and in their efficiency.

The first method, iterating over the hash, is flexible and space-efficient. You can format the output as you like it, and it requires only two scalar variables: the current key and value. You can print the hash in key order (at the cost of building a list of sorted keys) if you use a foreach loop:

```
foreach $k (sort keys %hash) {
    print "$k => $hash{$k}\n";
}
```

The map function is just as flexible. You can still process the list in any order by sorting the keys. You can customize the output to your heart's content. But it builds up a list of strings like "KEY =>VALUE\n" to pass to print.

The last two methods are interpolation tricks. By treating the hash as a list, you can't predict or control the output order of key-value pairs. Furthermore, the output will consist of a list of keys and values, each separated by whatever string that $" happens to hold. You can't put newlines between pairs or "=>" within them, as we could with the other methods.

Another solution is to print the hash in a list context after temporarily localizing the $, variable to a space.

```
{
    local $, = " ";
    print %hash;
}
```

This is like the solution of copying to an array and then doing double-quote interpolation on that array, except it doesn't duplicate the contents of the hash twice more than you need (i.e., once for the array, then again for the string).

The Dumpvalue module, described in Recipe 11.11, can provide for pretty printed output displays, plus much more. For example:

```
use Dumpvalue;
$dumper = Dumpvalue->new;
$dumper->dumpValue(\%food_color);
'Apple' => 'red'
'Banana' => 'yellow'
'Carrot' => 'orange'
'Lemon' => 'yellow'
```

See Also

The $" and $, variables in *perlvar*(1) and in the "Per-Filehandle Variables" section of Chapter 28 of *Programming Perl*; the foreach, map, keys, sort, and each functions in *perlfunc*(1) and Chapter 29 of *Programming Perl*; we give a technique for interpolating into strings in Recipe 1.15; we discuss the techniques for hash traversal in Recipe 5.5

5.7 Retrieving from a Hash in Insertion Order

Problem

The keys and each functions traverse the hash elements in a strange order, and you want them in the order in which you inserted them.

Solution

Use the Tie::IxHash module.

```
use Tie::IxHash;
tie %HASH, "Tie::IxHash";
# manipulate %HASH
@keys = keys %HASH;        # @keys is in insertion order
```

Discussion

Tie::IxHash makes keys, each, and values return the hash elements in the order they were added. This often removes the need to preprocess the hash keys with a complex sort comparison or maintain a distinct array containing the keys in the order they were inserted into the hash.

Tie::IxHash also provides an object-oriented interface to splice, push, pop, shift, unshift, keys, values, and delete, among others.

Here's an example, showing both keys and each:

```
# initialize
use Tie::IxHash;

tie %food_color, "Tie::IxHash";
$food_color{"Banana"} = "Yellow";
$food_color{"Apple"}  = "Green";
$food_color{"Lemon"}  = "Yellow";

print "In insertion order, the foods are:\n";
foreach $food (keys %food_color) {
    print "  $food\n";
}

print "Still in insertion order, the foods' colors are:\n";
while (( $food, $color ) = each %food_color ) {
    print "$food is colored $color.\n";
}

In insertion order, the foods are:
  Banana
  Apple
  Lemon
Still in insertion order, the foods' colors are:
Banana is colored Yellow.
Apple is colored Green.
Lemon is colored Yellow.
```

See Also

The documentation for the CPAN module Tie::IxHash; Recipe 13.5

5.8   Hashes with Multiple Values per Key

Problem

You want to store more than one value for each key.

Solution

Store an array reference in $hash{$key}, then put the values into the referenced array.

Discussion

You can store only scalar values in a hash. References, however, are scalars. This solves the problem of storing multiple values for one key by making $hash{$key} a reference to an array containing values for $key. The normal hash operations—insertion, deletion, iteration, and testing for existence—can now be written in terms of array operations like push, splice, and foreach.

This code shows simple insertion into the hash. It processes the output of *who*(1) on Unix machines and outputs a terse listing of users and the ttys they're logged in on:

```perl
%ttys = ( );

open(WHO, "who|")                        or die "can't open who: $!";
while (<WHO>) {
    ($user, $tty) = split;
    push( @{$ttys{$user}}, $tty );
}

foreach $user (sort keys %ttys) {
    print "$user: @{$ttys{$user}}\n";
}
```

The heart of the code is the push line, the multivalued version of $ttys{$user} = $tty. The first time through, that hash value is undefined, so Perl automatically allocates a new anonymous hash and stores its reference in that value so that the push can succeed. This is called *autovivification*, and is explained more in Chapter 11.

We interpolate all the tty names in the print line with @{$ttys{$user}}. We'd loop over the anonymous array if, for instance, we wanted to print the owner of each tty:

```perl
foreach $user (sort keys %ttys) {
    print "$user: ", scalar( @{$ttys{$user}} ), " ttys.\n";
    foreach $tty (sort @{$ttys{$user}}) {
        @stat = stat("/dev/$tty");
        $user = @stat ? ( getpwuid($stat[4]) )[0] : "(not available)";
        print "\t$tty (owned by $user)\n";
    }
}
```

The exists function can have two meanings: "Is there at least one value for this key?" and "Does this value exist for this key?" Implementing the second approach requires searching the array for the value. The delete function and the first sense of exists are interrelated: if we can guarantee that no anonymous array is ever empty, we can use the built-in exists. We ensure that no anonymous array is ever empty by checking for that after deleting an element.

```
sub multihash_delete {
    my ($hash, $key, $value) = @_;
    my $i;

    return unless ref( $hash->{$key} );
    for ($i = 0; $i < @{ $hash->{$key} }; $i++) {
        if ($hash->{$key}->[$i] eq $value) {
            splice( @{$hash->{$key}}, $i, 1);
            last;
        }
    }

    delete $hash->{$key} unless @{$hash->{$key}};
}
```

An alternative approach to multivalued hashes is given in Chapter 13, implemented as tied normal hashes.

See Also

The splice, delete, push, foreach, and exists functions in *perlfunc*(1) and Chapter 29 of *Programming Perl*; Recipe 11.1; we cover ties in Recipe 13.15

5.9 Inverting a Hash

Problem

Hashes map keys to values. You have a hash and a value whose corresponding key you want to find.

Solution

Use reverse to create an inverted hash whose values are the original hash's keys and vice versa.

```
# %LOOKUP maps keys to values
%REVERSE = reverse %LOOKUP;
```

Discussion

This technique uses the list equivalence of hashes mentioned in the introduction. In list context, reverse treats %LOOKUP as a list and reverses the order of its elements. The significant property of a hash treated as a list is that the list elements come in associated pairs: the first element is the key; the second, the value. When you reverse such a list, the first element is now the value, and the second the key. Treating *this* list as a hash results in a hash whose values are the keys of the original hash and vice versa.

Here's an example:

```
%surname = ( "Mickey" => "Mantle", "Babe" => "Ruth" );
%first_name = reverse %surname;
print $first_name{"Mantle"}, "\n";
```
Mickey

When we treat %surname as a list, it becomes:

```
("Mickey", "Mantle", "Babe", "Ruth")
```

(or maybe ("Babe", "Ruth", "Mickey", "Mantle") because we can't predict the order). Reversing this list gives us:

```
("Ruth", "Babe", "Mantle", "Mickey")
```

When we treat this list as a hash, it becomes:

```
("Ruth" => "Babe", "Mantle" => "Mickey")
```

Now instead of turning first names into surnames, it turns surnames into first names.

Example 5-2 is a program called foodfind. If you give it a food name, it'll tell you the color of that food. If you give it a color, it'll tell you a food of that color.

Example 5-2. foodfind

```perl
#!/usr/bin/perl -w
# foodfind - find match for food or color
$given = shift @ARGV or die "usage: foodfind food_or_color\n";
%color = (
            "Apple"   => "red",
            "Banana"  => "yellow",
            "Lemon"   => "yellow",
            "Carrot"  => "orange"
         );
%food = reverse %color;
if (exists $color{$given}) {
    print "$given is a food with color $color{$given}.\n";
}
if (exists $food{$given}) {
    print "$food{$given} is a food with color $given.\n";
}
```

If two keys in the original hash have the same value (as "Lemon" and "Banana" do in the color example), then the inverted hash will only have one (which is dependent on the hashing order, and you shouldn't try to predict it). This is because hashes have, by Perl definition, unique keys.

If you want to invert a hash with non-unique values, you must use the techniques shown in Recipe 5.8. That is, build up a hash whose values are a list of keys in the original hash:

```perl
# %food_color as per the introduction
while (($food,$color) = each(%food_color)) {
    push(@{$foods_with_color{$color}}, $food);
}
```

```
print "@{$foods_with_color{yellow}} were yellow foods.\n";
```
Banana Lemon were yellow foods.

This also lets us change the foodfind program to handle colors represented by more than one food. For instance, foodfind yellow reports bananas and lemons.

If any values in the original hash were references instead of strings or numbers, the inverted hash poses a problem because references don't work well as hash keys—unless you use the Tie::RefHash module described in Recipe 5.13.

See Also

The reverse function in *perlfunc*(1) and in Chapter 29 of *Programming Perl*; Recipe 13.15

5.10 Sorting a Hash

Problem

You need to work with the elements of a hash in a particular order.

Solution

Use keys to get a list of keys, then sort them based on the ordering you want:

```
# %hash is the hash to sort
@keys = sort { criterion() } (keys %hash);
foreach $key (@keys) {
    $value = $hash{$key};
    # do something with $key, $value
}
```

Discussion

Even though you can't directly maintain a hash in a specific order (unless you use the Tie::IxHash module mentioned in Recipe 5.7), you can access its entries in any order.

This technique offers many variations on the same basic mechanism: you extract the keys, reorder them using the sort function, and then process the entries in the new order. All the sorting tricks shown in Chapter 4 can be used here. Let's look at some applications.

The following code simply uses sort to order the keys alphabetically:

```
foreach $food (sort keys %food_color) {
    print "$food is $food_color{$food}.\n";
}
```

This sorts the keys by their associated values:

```
foreach $food (sort { $food_color{$a} cmp $food_color{$b} }
                keys %food_color)
{
    print "$food is $food_color{$food}.\n";
}
```

This sorts by length of the values:

```
@foods = sort {
          length($food_color{$a}) <=> length($food_color{$b})
          } keys %food_color;
foreach $food (@foods) {
    print "$food is $food_color{$food}.\n";
}
```

See Also

The sort and keys functions in *perlfunc*(1) and in Chapter 29 of *Programming Perl*; Recipe 5.7; we discuss sorting lists in Recipe 4.16

5.11   Merging Hashes

Problem

You need to make a new hash with the entries of two existing hashes.

Solution

Treat them as lists, and join them as you would lists.

```
%merged = (%A, %B);
```

To save memory, loop over the hashes' elements and build a new hash that way:

```
%merged = ();
while ( ($k,$v) = each(%A) ) {
    $merged{$k} = $v;
}
while ( ($k,$v) = each(%B) ) {
    $merged{$k} = $v;
}
```

Discussion

The first method, like the earlier recipe on inverting a hash, uses the hash-list equivalence explained in the introduction. (%A, %B) evaluates to a list of paired keys and values. When we assign it to %merged, Perl turns that list of pairs back into a hash.

Here's an example of that technique:

```
# %food_color as per the introduction
%drink_color = ( Galliano  => "yellow",
```

```
                    "Mai Tai" => "blue" );

    %ingested_color = (%drink_color, %food_color);
```

Keys in both input hashes appear just once in the output hash. If a food and a drink shared the same name, for instance, then the last one seen by the first merging technique would be the one that showed up in the resultant hash.

This style of direct assignment, as in the first example, is easier to read and write, but requires a lot of memory if the hashes are large. That's because Perl has to unroll both hashes into a temporary list before the assignment to the merged hash is done. Step-by-step merging using each, as in the second technique, spares you that cost and lets you decide what to do with duplicate keys.

The first example could be rewritten to use the each technique:

```
    # %food_color per the introduction, then
    %drink_color = ( Galliano  => "yellow",
                     "Mai Tai" => "blue" );

    %substance_color = ( );
    while (($k, $v) = each %food_color) {
        $substance_color{$k} = $v;
    }
    while (($k, $v) = each %drink_color) {
        $substance_color{$k} = $v;
    }
```

That technique duplicated the while and assignment code. Here's a sneaky way to get around that:

```
    foreach $substanceref ( \%food_color, \%drink_color ) {
        while (($k, $v) = each %$substanceref) {
            $substance_color{$k} = $v;
        }
    }
```

If we're merging hashes with duplicates, we can insert our own code to decide what to do with those duplicates:

```
    foreach $substanceref ( \%food_color, \%drink_color ) {
        while (($k, $v) = each %$substanceref) {
            if (exists $substance_color{$k}) {
                print "Warning: $k seen twice.  Using the first definition.\n";
                next;
            }
            $substance_color{$k} = $v;
        }
    }
```

In the special case of appending one hash to another, we can use the hash slice notation to give an elegant shorthand:

```
    @all_colors{keys %new_colors} = values %new_colors;
```

This requires enough memory for lists of the keys and values of %new_colors. As with the first technique, the memory requirement might make this technique infeasible when such lists would be large.

See Also

This is a variation on Recipe 4.10; the each function in *perlfunc*(1) and in Chapter 29 of *Programming Perl*

5.12   Finding Common or Different Keys in Two Hashes

Problem

You need to find keys in one hash that are or are not present in another hash.

Solution

Use keys to loop through the keys of one hash, checking whether each key is also in the other hash.

Find common keys

```
my @common = ( );
foreach (keys %hash1) {
        push(@common, $_) if exists $hash2{$_};
}
# @common now contains common keys
```

Find keys from one hash that aren't in both

```
my @this_not_that = ( );
foreach (keys %hash1) {
        push(@this_not_that, $_) unless exists $hash2{$_};
}
```

Discussion

Because we're finding common or different keys of the hashes, we can apply our earlier array recipes for finding common or different elements to arrays of the hashes' keys. For an explanation, see Recipe 4.9.

This code uses the difference technique to find non-citrus foods:

```
# %food_color per the introduction

# %citrus_color is a hash mapping citrus food name to its color.
%citrus_color = ( Lemon  => "yellow",
```

```
                    Orange => "orange",
                    Lime   => "green" );

    # build up a list of non-citrus foods
    @non_citrus = ( );

    foreach (keys %food_color) {
        push (@non_citrus, $_) unless $citrus_color{$_};
    }
```

See Also

The "Hashes" section of Chapter 2 of *Programming Perl*; the each function in *perlfunc*(1) and in Chapter 29 of *Programming Perl*

5.13   Hashing References

Problem

When you use keys on a hash whose keys are references, the references that keys returns no longer work. This situation often arises when you want to cross-reference two different hashes.

Solution

Use Tie::RefHash:

```
    use Tie::RefHash;
    tie %hash, "Tie::RefHash";
    # you may now use references as the keys to %hash
```

Discussion

Hash keys are automatically "stringified," that is, treated as though they appeared between double quotes. With numbers or strings, nothing is lost. This isn't so with references, though.

Stringified references look like these:

```
    Class::Somewhere=HASH(0x72048)
    ARRAY(0x72048)
```

A stringified reference can't be dereferenced, because it is just a string and no longer a reference. This means you can't use references as the keys to a hash without losing their "magic."

Hand-rolled solutions to this problem involve maintaining a distinct hash whose keys are stringified references and whose values are the actual references. This is what Tie::RefHash does. We'll use IO objects for filehandles here to show you that even such strange references can index a hash tied with Tie::RefHash.

Here's an example:

```
use Tie::RefHash;
use IO::File;

tie %name, "Tie::RefHash";
foreach $filename ("/etc/termcap", "/vmunix", "/bin/cat") {
    $fh = IO::File->new("< $filename") or next;
    $name{$fh} = $filename;
}
print "open files: ", join(", ", values %name), "\n";
foreach $file (keys %name) {
    seek($file, 0, 2);       # seek to the end
    printf("%s is %d bytes long.\n", $name{$file}, tell($file));
}
```

If you're storing objects as the keys to a hash, though, you almost always should be storing a unique attribute of the object (e.g., name or ID number) instead.

See Also

The documentation for the standard Tie::RefHash module; the "Warning" section of *perlref*(1)

5.14   Presizing a Hash

Problem

You want to preallocate memory for a hash to speed up your program so Perl won't have to incrementally allocate memory each time a new entry is added to the hash. Often you know the final size of a hash before you start building it up, and it's possible to use this information to speed up your program.

Solution

Assign the number of key-value pairs your hash will have to keys %HASH.

```
# presize %hash to $num
keys(%hash) = $num;
```

Discussion

This feature may or may not improve your performance. Perl already shares keys between hashes, so if you already have a hash with "Apple" as a key, Perl won't need to allocate memory for another copy of "Apple" when you add an entry whose key is "Apple" to another hash.

```
# will have 512 users in %users
keys(%users) = 512;
```

Perl's internal data structures require the number of keys to be a power of 2. If we had said:

```
keys(%users) = 1000;
```

Perl would have internally allocated 1024 "buckets" for the hash. Keys and buckets aren't always one to one. You get the best performance when they are, but the distribution of keys to buckets is dependent on your keys and Perl's (immutable) hash algorithm.

See Also

The keys function in *perlfunc*(1) and Chapter 29 of *Programming Perl*; Recipe 4.3

5.15   Finding the Most Common Anything

Problem

You have an aggregate data structure, such as an array or a hash. You want to know how often each element in the array (or value in the hash) occurs. For instance, if your array contains web server transactions, you might want to find the most commonly requested file. If your hash maps usernames to number of logins, you want to find the most common number of logins.

Solution

Use a hash to count how many times each element, key, or value appears:

```
%count = ( );
foreach $element (@ARRAY) {
    $count{$element}++;
}
```

Discussion

Any time you want to count how often different things appear, you should probably be using a hash. The foreach adds one to $count{$element} for every occurrence of $element.

See Also

Recipes 4.7 and 4.8

5.16 Representing Relationships Between Data

Problem

You want to represent relationships between elements of data—for instance, the *mother of* relationship in a family tree or *parent process* for a process table. This is closely related to representing tables in relational databases (tables represent relationships between information) and to representing computer science graph structures (edges represent relationships between nodes).

Solution

Use a hash to represent the relationship.

Discussion

Here's part of the family tree from the Bible:

```
%father = ( 'Cain'       => 'Adam',
            'Abel'       => 'Adam',
            'Seth'       => 'Adam',
            'Enoch'      => 'Cain',
            'Irad'       => 'Enoch',
            'Mehujael'   => 'Irad',
            'Methusael'  => 'Mehujael',
            'Lamech'     => 'Methusael',
            'Jabal'      => 'Lamech',
            'Jubal'      => 'Lamech',
            'Tubalcain'  => 'Lamech',
            'Enos'       => 'Seth' );
```

This lets us, for instance, easily trace a person's lineage:

```
while (<>) {
    chomp;
    do {
        print "$_ ";            # print the current name
        $_ = $father{$_};       # set $_ to $_'s father
    } while defined;            # until we run out of fathers
    print "\n";
}
```

We can already ask questions like "Who begat Seth?" by checking the %father hash. By inverting this hash, we invert the relationship. This lets us use Recipe 5.9 to answer questions like "Whom did Lamech beget?"

```
while ( ($k,$v) = each %father ) {
    push( @{ $children{$v} }, $k );
}

$" = ', ';                      # separate output with commas
```

```
while (<>) {
    chomp;
    if ($children{$_}) {
        @children = @{$children{$_}};
    } else {
        @children = "nobody";
    }
    print "$_ begat @children.\n";
}
```

Hashes can also represent relationships such as the C language #includes. A includes B if A contains #include B. This code builds the hash (it doesn't look for files in /usr/include as it should, but that's a minor change):

```
foreach $file (@files) {
    local *FH;
    unless (open(FH, " < $file")) {
        warn "Couldn't read $file: $!; skipping.\n";
        next;
    }

    while (<FH>) {
        next unless /^\s*#\s*include\s*<([^>]+)>/;
        push(@{$includes{$1}}, $file);
    }
    close FH;
}
```

This shows which files with include statements are not included in other files:

```
@include_free = ();                    # list of files that don't include others
@uniq{map { @$_ } values %includes} = undef;
foreach $file (sort keys %uniq) {
        push( @include_free , $file ) unless $includes{$file};
}
```

The values of %includes are anonymous arrays because a single file can (and often does) include more than one other file. We use map to build up a big list of the included files and remove duplicates using a hash.

See Also

Recipe 4.7; the more complex data structures in Recipes 11.9 through 11.14

5.17   Program: dutree

The *dutree* program, shown in Example 5-3, turns the output of *du*:

```
% du pcb
19      pcb/fix
20      pcb/rev/maybe/yes
10      pcb/rev/maybe/not
705     pcb/rev/maybe
54      pcb/rev/web
```

```
1371    pcb/rev
3       pcb/pending/mine
1016    pcb/pending
2412    pcb
```

into sorted, indented output:

```
2412 pcb
    |   1371 rev
    |      |    705 maybe
    |      |       |    675 .
    |      |       |     20 yes
    |      |       |     10 not
    |      |    612 .
    |      |     54 web
    |   1016 pending
    |      |        1013 .
    |      |           3 mine
    |     19 fix
    |      6 .
```

The arguments you give *dutree* are passed through to *du*. That way you could call *dutree* in any of these ways, or maybe more if your *du* supports other options:

```
% dutree
% dutree /usr
% dutree -a
% dutree -a /bin
```

The %Dirsize hash maintains the mapping of names to sizes. For example, $Dirsize{"pcb"} contains 2412 in this sample run. We'll use that hash both for output and for sorting each directory's subdirectories by size.

%Kids is more interesting. For any given path *PATH*, $Kids{*PATH*} contains a (reference to an) array of names of subdirectories of this one. The "pcb" entry contains a reference to an anonymous array containing "fix", "rev", and "pending". The "rev" entry contains "maybe" and "web". The "maybe" entry contains "yes" and "not", which do not have their own entries because they are end nodes in the tree.

The output function is passed the start of the tree—the last line read in from the output of *du*. First it prints that directory and its size. Then the function sorts the directory's children (if any) so that those with the most disk usage float to the top. Finally, output calls itself, recursing on each child in order. The extra arguments are used in formatting.

This program is inherently recursive because the filesystem is recursive. However, its data structure is not recursive; at least, not the way a circular linked list is. Each value is an array of further keys to process. The recursion resides in the processing, not in the storage.

Example 5-3. dutree

```
#!/usr/bin/perl -w
# dutree - print sorted indented rendition of du output
```

Example 5-3. dutree (continued)

```perl
use strict;
my %Dirsize;
my %Kids;
getdots(my $topdir = input());
output($topdir);
# run du, read in input, save sizes and kids
# return last directory (file?) read
sub input {
    my($size, $name, $parent);
    @ARGV = ("du @ARGV |");          # prep the arguments
    while (<>) {                      # magic open is our friend
        ($size, $name) = split;
        $Dirsize{$name} = $size;
        ($parent = $name) =~ s#/[^/]+$##;   # dirname
        push @{ $Kids{$parent} }, $name unless eof;
    }
    return $name;
}
# figure out how much is taken up in each directory
# that isn't stored in subdirectories.  add a new
# fake kid called "." containing that much.
sub getdots {
    my $root = $_[0];
    my($size, $cursize);
    $size = $cursize = $Dirsize{$root};
    if ($Kids{$root}) {
        for my $kid (@{ $Kids{$root} }) {
            $cursize -= $Dirsize{$kid};
            getdots($kid);
        }
    }
    if ($size != $cursize) {
        my $dot = "$root/.";
        $Dirsize{$dot} = $cursize;
        push @{ $Kids{$root} }, $dot;
    }
}
# recursively output everything,
# passing padding and number width in as well
# on recursive calls
sub output {
    my($root, $prefix, $width) = (shift, shift || '', shift || 0);
    my $path;
    ($path = $root) =~ s#.*/##;       # basename
    my $size = $Dirsize{$root};
    my $line = sprintf("%${width}d %s", $size, $path);
    print $prefix, $line, "\n";
    for ($prefix .= $line) {          # build up more output
        s/\d /| /;
        s/[^|]/ /g;
    }
    if ($Kids{$root}) {               # not a bachelor node
```

Example 5-3. dutree (continued)

```
        my @Kids = @{ $Kids{$root} };
        @Kids = sort { $Dirsize{$b} <=> $Dirsize{$a} } @Kids;
        $Dirsize{$Kids[0]} =~ /(\d+)/;
        my $width = length $1;
        for my $kid (@Kids) { output($kid, $prefix, $width) }
    }
}
```

Before Perl supported hashes of arrays directly, Herculean efforts were required to emulate these higher order constructs. Some folks used repeated calls to split and join, but these were exceedingly slow.

Example 5-4 is a version of *dutree* from those days of Perl antiquity. Because we didn't have proper array references, we had to usurp the Perl symbol table itself. This program created variables on the fly with bizarre names. Can you find which hash this program is using?

The @{"pcb"} array contains "pcb/fix", "pcb/rev", and "pcb/pending". The @{"pcb/rev"} array contains "pcb/rev/maybe" and "pcb/rev/web". The @{"pcb/rev/maybe"} array contains "pcb/rev/yes" and "pcb/rev/not".

When you assign something like "pcb/fix" to *kid, it promotes the string on the righthand side to a typeglob. This makes @kid an alias for @{"pcb/fix"}—among other things. It would also alias &kid to &{"pcb/fix"}, and so on.

If that isn't interesting enough, consider how the local is using dynamic scoping of global variables to avoid passing in extra arguments. Check out what's happening with the $width variable in the output routine.

Example 5-4. dutree-orig

```
#!/usr/bin/perl
# dutree_orig: the old version pre-perl5 (early 90s)
@lines = `du @ARGV`;
chop(@lines);
&input($top = pop @lines);
&output($top);
exit;
sub input {
    local($root, *kid, $him) = @_[0,0];
    while (@lines && &childof($root, $lines[$#lines])) {
        &input($him = pop(@lines));
        push(@kid, $him);
    }
    if (@kid) {
        local($mysize) = ($root =~ /^(\d+)/);
        for (@kid) { $mysize -= (/^(\d+)/)[0]; }
        push(@kid, "$mysize .") if $size != $mysize;
    }
    @kid = &sizesort(*kid);
}
sub output {
```

Example 5-4. dutree-orig (continued)

```
    local($root, *kid, $prefix) = @_[0,0,1];
    local($size, $path) = split(' ', $root);
    $path =~ s!.*/!!;
    $line = sprintf("%${width}d %s", $size, $path);
    print $prefix, $line, "\n";
    $prefix .= $line;
    $prefix =~ s/\d /| /;
    $prefix =~ s/[^|]/ /g;
    local($width) = $kid[0] =~ /(\d+)/ && length("$1");
    for (@kid) { &output($_, $prefix); };
  }
  sub sizesort {
    local(*list, @index) = shift;
    sub bynum { $index[$b] <=> $index[$a]; }
    for (@list) { push(@index, /(\d+)/); }
    @list[sort bynum 0..$#list];
  }
  sub childof {
    local(@pair) = @_;
    for (@pair) { s/^\d+\s+//g; s/$/\//; }
    index($pair[1], $pair[0]) >= 0;
  }
```

The answer to the question posed earlier—"Which hash is the old *dutree* using?"—is %main::, that is, the Perl symbol table itself. Needless to say, this program will never run under use strict. We're happy to report that the updated version runs three times as fast as the old one. That's because the old one keeps looking up variables in the symbol table, and the new one doesn't have to. It's also because we avoid all that slow splitting of the space used and the directory name. But we thought we'd show you the old version because it is instructive, too.

## CHAPTER 6

Pattern Matching

[Art is] pattern informed by sensibility.
—Sir Herbert Read, *The Meaning of Art*

6.0 Introduction

Most modern programming languages offer primitive pattern-matching tools, usually through an extra library. In contrast, Perl's patterns are integrated directly into the language core. Perl's pattern matching boasts features not found elsewhere, features that encourage a whole different way of looking at data. Just as chess players see patterns in the board positions that their pieces control, Perl adepts look at data in terms of patterns. These patterns, expressed in the intensely symbolic notation of regular expressions,* provide access to powerful algorithms normally available only to scholars of computer science.

"If this pattern matching thing is so powerful and so fantastic," you may be asking, "why don't you have a hundred different recipes on regular expressions in this chapter?" Regular expressions are the natural solution to many problems involving numbers, strings, dates, web documents, mail addresses, and almost everything else in this book; we use pattern matching over 100 times in other chapters. This chapter mostly presents recipes in which pattern matching forms part of the questions, not just part of the answers.

Perl's extensive and integrated support for regular expressions means that you not only have features available that you won't find in any other language, but you have new ways of using them, too. Programmers new to Perl often look for functions like these:

```
match( $string, $pattern );
subst( $string, $pattern, $replacement );
```

---

* Technically, Perl's patterns far exceed the capabilities of mere *regular expressions* as that term is formally used in computing theory.

but matching and substituting are such common tasks that they merit their own notation:

```
$meadow =~ m/sheep/;   # True if $meadow contains "sheep"
$meadow !~ m/sheep/;   # True if $meadow doesn't contain "sheep"
$meadow =~ s/old/new/; # Replace "old" with "new" in $meadow
```

Pattern matching isn't like direct string comparison, even at its simplest level; it's more like string searching with mutant wildcards on steroids. Without anchors, the position where the match occurs can float freely throughout the string. Any of the following lines would also be matched by the expression $meadow =~ /ovine/, giving false positives when looking for lost sheep:

```
Fine bovines demand fine toreadors.
Muskoxen are a polar ovibovine species.
Grooviness went out of fashion decades ago.
```

Sometimes they're right in front of you but they still don't match:

```
Ovines are found typically in oviaries.
```

The problem is that while you are probably thinking in some human language, the pattern-matching engine most assuredly is not. When the engine is presented with the pattern /ovine/ and a string to match against, it searches the string for an "o" that is immediately followed by a "v", then by an "i", then by an "n", and then finally by an "e". What comes before or after that sequence doesn't matter. Additionally, those letters are matched case-sensitively. That's why it didn't find "Ovines", since that string starts with a capital letter.

As you find your patterns matching some strings you don't want them to match and not matching other strings that you do want them to match, you start embellishing. When looking for nothing but sheep, you probably want to match a pattern more like this:

```
if ($meadow =~ /\bovines?\b/i) { print "Here be sheep!" }
```

Don't be tricked by the phantom cow lurking in that string—that's not a bovine. It's an ovine with a \b in front, which matches at a word boundary only.* The s? indicates an optional "s" so we can find one or more ovines. The trailing /i makes the whole pattern match case-insensitive.

As you see, certain character sequences have special meaning to the pattern-matching engine, often standing in for several possible literal characters. These so-called metacharacters let you do such things as restrict the pattern to the start or end of the string, give alternatives for parts of a pattern, allow repetition and wildcarding, and remember part of the matching substring for use later in the pattern or in code.

Learning the syntax of pattern matching isn't as daunting as it might appear. Sure, there are a lot of symbols, but each has a reason for existing. Regular expressions

---

* For Perl's idea of what defines a "word."

aren't random jumbles of punctuation—they're carefully thought-out jumbles of punctuation! If you forget one, you can always look it up. Summary tables are included in *Programming Perl*, *Learning Perl*, *Mastering Regular Expressions*, and the *perlre*(1) and *perlop*(1) manpages included with every Perl installation.

The Tricky Bits

Much trickier than the syntax of regular expressions is their sneaky semantics. The three aspects of pattern-matching behavior that seem to cause folks the most trouble are greed, eagerness, and backtracking—and also how these three interact with each other.

Greed is the principle that if a standard quantifier (such as *) can match a varying number of times, it matches as long a substring as it can. This is explained in Recipe 6.15.

Eagerness is the notion that the leftmost match wins. The engine is eager to return you a match as quickly as possible, sometimes even before you are expecting it. Consider the match "Fred" =~ /x*/. If asked to explain this in plain language, you might say "Does the string "Fred" contain any x's?" If so, you might be surprised to learn that it seems to. That's because /x*/ doesn't truly mean "any x's," unless your idea of "any" includes nothing at all. Formally, it means *zero or more* of them, and here zero sufficed for the eager matcher.

A more illustrative example of eagerness would be the following:

```
$string = "good food";
$string =~ s/o*/e/;
```

Can you guess which of the following is in $string after that substitution?

good food
geod food
geed food
geed feed
ged food
ged fed
egood food

The correct answer is the last one, because the earliest point at which zero or more occurrences of "o" could be found was right at the beginning of the string. Surprised? Regular expressions can do that to you if you're unfamiliar with their semantics.

Here's another example of where greed takes a back seat to eagerness:

```
$ echo longest | perl -ne 'print "$&\n" if /long|longer|longest/'
long
```

That's because Perl uses what's called a traditional NFA,* a non-deterministic finite automaton. This kind of matching engine is not guaranteed to return the longest *overall* match, just the first match. You might think of Perl's greed as being left-to-right directed, not globally greedy.

NFAs can be slow, but significant performance gains can be made by rewriting the patterns to exploit how the particular NFA implementation runs. This is a major part of Jeffrey Friedl's book, *Mastering Regular Expressions*.

The last and most powerful of the three tricky bits in pattern matching is backtracking. For a pattern to match, the entire regular expression must match, not just part of it. So if the beginning of a pattern containing a quantifier succeeds in a way that causes later parts in the pattern to fail, the matching engine backs up and tries to find another match for the beginning part—that's why it's called backtracking. It means that the engine is going to try different possibilities, systematically investigating alternate matches until it finds one that works. In some pattern-matching implementations, the engine keeps backtracking in case other submatches make the overall match longer. Perl's matcher doesn't do that; as soon as one possibility works, it uses that—until and unless something later in the pattern fails, forcing a backtrack to retry another possible way of matching. This is discussed in Recipe 6.16.

Pattern-Matching Modifiers

Pattern-matching modifiers are a lot easier to list and learn than the different metacharacters. Table 6-1 contains a brief summary of them.

Table 6-1. Pattern-matching modifiers and their meanings

Modifier	Meaning
/i	Ignore alphabetic case
/x	Ignore most whitespace in pattern and permit comments
/g	Global—match/substitute as often as possible
/gc	Don't reset search position on failed match
/s	Let . match newline
/m	Let ^ and $ match next to embedded \n
/o	Compile pattern once only
/e	Righthand side of an s/// is code whose result is used as the replacement value
/ee	Righthand side of an s/// is a string that's eval'd twice; the final result then used as the replacement value

/i and /g are the most commonly used modifiers. The pattern /ram/i matches "ram", "RAM", "Ram", and so forth. Backreferences are checked case-insensitively if this

---

* As opposed to a POSIX-style NFA. See *Mastering Regular Expressions* for the differences.

modifier is on; see Recipe 6.16 for an example. This case-insensitivity can be made aware of the user's current locale settings if the use locale pragma has been invoked.

The /g modifier is used with s/// to replace every non-overlapping match, not just the first one. /g is also used with m// in loops to find (but not replace) every matching occurrence:

```
while (m/(\d+)/g) {
    print "Found number $1\n";
}
```

Used on m// in list context, /g pulls out all matches:

```
@numbers = m/(\d+)/g;
```

That finds only non-overlapping matches. You have to be much sneakier to get overlapping ones by making a zero-width look-ahead with the (?=...) construct. Because it's zero-width, the match engine hasn't advanced at all. Within the look-ahead, capturing parentheses are used to grab the thing anyway. Although we've saved something, Perl notices we haven't made any forward progress on the /g, so it bumps us forward one character position.

This shows the difference:

```
$digits = "123456789";
@nonlap = $digits =~ /(\d\d\d)/g;
@yeslap = $digits =~ /(?=(\d\d\d))/g;
print "Non-overlapping: @nonlap\n";
print "Overlapping:     @yeslap\n";
Non-overlapping:  123 456 789
Overlapping:      123 234 345 456 567 678 789
```

The /s and /m modifiers are useful when matching strings with embedded newlines. /s makes dot match "\n", something it doesn't normally do; it also makes the match ignore the value of the old, deprecated $* variable. /m makes ^ and $ match after and before "\n", respectively. They are useful with paragraph slurping mode as explained in the Introduction to Chapter 8, and in Recipe 6.6.

The /e modifier is used on replacements so that the righthand part is run as code and its return value is used as the replacement string. s/(\d+)/sprintf("%#x", $1)/ge converts all numbers into hex, changing, for example, 2581 into 0xb23.

Because different countries have different ideas of what constitutes an alphabet, the POSIX standard provides systems (and thus programs) with a standard way of representing alphabets, character set ordering, and so on. Perl gives you access to some of these through the use locale pragma; see the perllocale manpage for more information. When use locale is in effect, the \w character class includes accented and other exotic characters. The case-changing \u, \U, \l, and \L (and the corresponding uc, ucfirst, etc. functions) escapes also respect use locale, so σ will be turned into Σ with \u if the locale says it should. (This only matters in 8-bit encodings, such as ISO

8859-7 for the Greek character set. If those characters had been in Unicode, case translation would always apply, irrespective of current locale setting.)

Special Variables

Perl sets special variables as the result of certain matches: $1, $2, $3, and so on *ad infinitum* are set when a pattern contains capturing parentheses within parts of the pattern. Each open parenthesis as you read left to right in the pattern begins filling a new, numbered variable. The variable $+ contains the contents of the last backreference of the last successful match. This helps distinguish which of several alternate matches was found (for example, if /(x.*y)|(y.*z)/ matches, $+ contains whichever of $1 or $2 were filled). $& contains the complete text matched in the last successful pattern match. $` and $´ are the strings before and after the successful match, respectively:

```
$string = "And little lambs eat ivy";
$string =~ /l[^s]*s/;
print "($`) ($&) ($´)\n";
(And ) (little lambs) ( eat ivy)
```

$`, $&, and $´ are tempting, but dangerous. Their very presence anywhere in a program slows down every pattern match because the engine must populate these variables for every match. This is true even if you use one of these variables only once, or, for that matter, if you never use them at all, only mention them. Using $& is no longer so expensive as the other two.

A cheaper approach is to use the substr function in conjunction with the built-in array variables @- and @+, first introduced in Perl v5.6. These represent the starting and ending positions of the last submatches, respectively. The Nth elements of these two arrays hold the beginning and ending offset of the Nth submatch. So $-[1] is the offset where $1 begins, and $+[1] is the offset where it ends; $-[2] is the offset where $2 begins, and $+[2] is the offset where it ends; and so on. $-[0] is the offset of the beginning of the entire match, and $+[0] the offset of the end of the entire match. (When we say "offset of the end," we mean the offset to the first character *following* the end of whatever matched, so that we can subtract beginning offsets from end offsets and arrive at the length.)

After a match against some variable $string, the following equivalencies hold true:

```
Variable    Equivalent
--------    ----------
$`          substr($string, 0,     $-[0])
$&          substr($string, $-[0], $+[0] - $-[0])
$´          substr($string, $+[0])
$1          substr($string, $-[1], $+[1] - $-[1])
$2          substr($string, $-[2], $+[2] - $-[2])
$3          substr($string, $-[3], $+[3] - $-[3])
```

And so on and so forth.

To learn far more about regular expressions than you ever thought existed, check out *Mastering Regular Expressions*, written by Jeffrey Friedl (O'Reilly). This book is dedicated to explaining regular expressions from a practical perspective. Not only does it cover general regular expressions and Perl specials, it also compares and contrasts these with patterns in other programming languages.

6.1   Copying and Substituting Simultaneously

Problem

You're tired of using two separate statements with redundant information, one to copy and another to substitute.

Solution

Instead of:

```
$dst = $src;
$dst =~ s/this/that/;
```

use:

```
($dst = $src) =~ s/this/that/;
```

Discussion

Sometimes you wish you could run a search and replace on a copy of a string, but you don't care to write this in two separate steps. You don't have to, because you can apply the regex operation to the result of the copy operation.

For example:

```
# strip to basename
($progname = $0)        =~ s!^.*/!!;

# Make All Words Title-Cased
($capword  = $word)     =~ s/(\w+)/\u\L$1/g;

# /usr/man/man3/foo.1 changes to /usr/man/cat3/foo.1
($catpage  = $manpage)  =~ s/man(?=\d)/cat/;
```

You can even use this technique on an entire array:

```
@bindirs = qw( /usr/bin /bin /usr/local/bin );
for (@libdirs = @bindirs) { s/bin/lib/ }
print "@libdirs\n";
/usr/lib /lib /usr/local/lib
```

Because of precedence, parentheses are required when combining an assignment if you wish to change the result in the leftmost variable. The result of a substitution is its success: either "" for failure, or an integer number of times the substitution was done. Contrast this with the preceding examples where the parentheses surround the assignment itself. For example:

```
($a =  $b) =~ s/x/y/g;      # 1: copy $b and then change $a
 $a = ($b =~ s/x/y/g);      # 2: change $b, count goes in $a
 $a =  $b  =~ s/x/y/g;      # 3: same as 2
```

See Also

The "Variables" section of Chapter 2 of *Programming Perl*, and the "Assignment Operators" section of *perlop*(1) and Chapter 3 of *Programming Perl*

6.2   Matching Letters

Problem

You want to see whether a string contains only alphabetic characters.

Solution

The obvious character class for matching regular letters isn't good enough in the general case:

```
if ($var =~ /^[A-Za-z]+$/) {
    # it is purely alphabetic
}
```

because it doesn't pay attention to letters with diacritics or characters from other writing systems. The best solution is to use Unicode properties:

```
if ($var =~ /^\p{Alphabetic}+$/) {   # or just /^\pL+$/
    print "var is purely alphabetic\n";
}
```

On older releases of Perl that don't support Unicode, your only real option was to use either a negated character class:

```
if ($var =~ /^[^\W\d_]+$/) {
    print "var is purely alphabetic\n";
}
```

or, if supported, POSIX character classes:

```
if ($var =~ /^[[:alpha:]]+$/) {
    print "var is purely alphabetic\n";
}
```

But these don't work for non-ASCII letters unless you use locale and the system you're running on actually *supports* POSIX locales.

Discussion

Apart from Unicode properties or POSIX character classes, Perl can't directly express "something alphabetic" independent of locale, so we have to be more clever. The \w regular expression notation matches one alphabetic, numeric, or underscore character—hereafter known as an "alphanumunder" for short. Therefore, \W is one character that is not one of those. The negated character class [^\W\d_] specifies a character that must be neither a non-alphanumunder, a digit, nor an underscore. That leaves nothing but alphabetics, which is what we were looking for.

Here's how you'd use this in a program:

```
use locale;
use POSIX 'locale_h';

# the following locale string might be different on your system
unless (setlocale(LC_ALL, "fr_CA.ISO8859-1")) {
    die "couldn't set locale to French Canadian\n";
}

while (<DATA>) {
    chomp;
    if (/^[^\W\d_]+$/) {
        print "$_: alphabetic\n";
    } else {
        print "$_: line noise\n";
    }
}

__END__
silly
façade
coöperate
niño
Renée
Molière
hæmoglobin
naïve
tschüß
random!stuff#here
```

POSIX character classes help a little here; available ones are alpha, alnum, ascii, blank, cntrl, digit, graph, lower, print, punct, space, upper, word, and xdigit. These are valid only within a square-bracketed character class specification:

```
$phone =~ /\b[:digit:]{3}[[:space:][:punct:]]?[:digit:]{4}\b/;      # WRONG
$phone =~ /\b[[:digit:]]{3}[[:space:][:punct:]]?[[:digit:]]{4}\b/; # RIGHT
```

It would be easier to use properties instead, because they don't have to occur only within other square brackets:

```
$phone =~ /\b\p{Number}{3}[\p{Space}\p{Punctuation}]?\p{Number}{4}\b/;
$phone =~ /\b\pN{3}[\pS\pP]?\pN{4}\b/;   # abbreviated form
```

Match any one character with Unicode property *prop* using \p{*prop*}; to match any character lacking that property, use \P{*prop*} or [^\p{*prop*}]. The relevant property when looking for alphabetics is *Alphabetic*, which can be abbreviated as simply *Letter* or even just *L*. Other relevant properties include *UppercaseLetter*, *LowercaseLetter*, and *TitlecaseLetter*; their short forms are *Lu*, *Ll*, and *Lt*, respectively.

See Also

The treatment of locales in Perl in *perllocale*(1); your system's *locale*(3) manpage; we discuss locales in greater depth in Recipe 6.12; the "Perl and the POSIX Locale" section of Chapter 7 of *Mastering Regular Expressions*; also much of that book's Chapter 3

6.3   Matching Words

Problem

You want to pick out words from a string.

Solution

Think hard about what you want a word to be and what separates one word from the next, and then write a regular expression that encodes your decisions. For example:

```
/\S+/                   # as many non-whitespace characters as possible
/[A-Za-z'-]+/           # as many letters, apostrophes, and hyphens
```

Discussion

Because words vary between applications, languages, and input streams, Perl does not have built-in definitions of words. You must make them from character classes and quantifiers yourself, as we did previously. The second pattern is an attempt to recognize "shepherd's" and "sheep-shearing" each as single words.

Most approaches have limitations because of the vagaries of written language. For instance, although the second pattern successfully identifies "spank'd" and "counter-clockwise" as words, it also pulls the "rd" out of "23rd Psalm". To be more precise when pulling words out from a string, specify the characters surrounding the word. Normally, this should be a word boundary, not whitespace:

```
/\b([A-Za-z]+)\b/       # usually best
/\s([A-Za-z]+)\s/       # fails at ends or w/ punctuation
```

Although Perl provides \w, which matches a character that is part of a valid Perl identifier, Perl identifiers are rarely what you think of as words, since we mean a string of alphanumerics and underscores, but not colons or quotes. Because it's defined in terms of \w, \b may surprise you if you expect to match an English word boundary (or, even worse, a Mongolian word boundary).

\b and \B can still be useful. For example, /\Bis\B/ matches the string "is" within a word only, not at the edges. And while "thistle" would be found, "vis-à-vis" wouldn't.

See Also

The treatment of \b, \w, and \s in *perlre*(1) and Chapter 5 of *Programming Perl*; the words-related patterns in Recipe 6.23

6.4 Commenting Regular Expressions

Problem

You want to make your complex regular expressions understandable and maintainable.

Solution

You have several techniques at your disposal: electing alternate delimiters to avoid so many backslashes, placing comments outside the pattern or inside it using the /x modifier, and building up patterns piecemeal in named variables.

Discussion

The piece of sample code in Example 6-1 uses the first couple techniques, and its initial comment describes the overall intent of the regular expression. For simple patterns, this may be all that is needed. More complex patterns, as in the example, require more documentation.

Example 6-1. resname

```
#!/usr/bin/perl -p
# resname - change all "foo.bar.com" style names in the input stream
# into "foo.bar.com [204.148.40.9]" (or whatever) instead
use Socket;                 # load inet_addr
s{
    (                       # capture the hostname in $1
        (?:                 # these parens for grouping only
            (?! [-_] )      # lookahead for neither underscore nor dash
            [\w-] +         # hostname component
            \.              # and the domain dot
        ) +                 # now repeat that whole thing a bunch of times
        [A-Za-z]            # next must be a letter
        [\w-] +             # now trailing domain part
    )                       # end of $1 capture
}{                          # replace with this:
    "$1 " .                 # the original bit, plus a space
        ( ($addr = gethostbyname($1))   # if we get an addr
            ? "[" . inet_ntoa($addr) . "]" #       format it
```

Example 6-1. resname (continued)

```
            : "[???]"                        # else mark dubious
        )
    }gex;              # /g for global
                       # /e for execute
                       # /x for nice formatting
```

For aesthetics, the example uses alternate delimiters. When you split your match or substitution over multiple lines, using matching braces aids readability. A more common use of alternate delimiters is for patterns and replacements that themselves contain slashes, such as in s/\/\//\/..\//g. Alternate delimiters, as in s!//!/../!g or s{//}{/../}g, avoid escaping the non-delimiting slashes with backslashes, again improving legibility.

The /x pattern modifier makes Perl ignore whitespace in the pattern (outside a character class) and treat # characters and their following text as comments. The /e modifier changes the replacement portion from a string into code to run. Since it's code, you can put regular comments there, too.

To include literal whitespace or # characters in a pattern to which you've applied /x, escape them with a backslash:

```
    s/               # replace
      \#             #    a pound sign
      (\w+)          #    the variable name
      \#             #    another pound sign
    /${$1}/xg;       # with the value of the global variable
```

Remember that comments should explain what you're doing and why, not merely restate the code. Using "$i++ # add one to i" is apt to lose points in your programming course or at least get you talked about in substellar terms by your coworkers.

The last technique for rendering patterns more legible (and thus, more maintainable) is to place each semantic unit into a variable given an appropriate name. We use single quotes instead of doubles so backslashes don't get lost.

```
    $optional_sign     = '[-+]?';
    $mandatory_digits  = '\d+';
    $decimal_point     = '\.?';
    $optional_digits   = '\d*';

    $number = $optional_sign
            . $mandatory_digits
            . $decimal_point
            . $optional_digits;
```

Then use $number in further patterns:

```
    if (/($number)/) {      # parse out one
        $found = $1;
    }

    @allnums = /$number/g;  # parse all out
```

```
unless (/^$number$/) {  # any extra?
    print "need a number, just a number\n";
}
```

We can even combine all of these techniques:

```
# check for line of whitespace-separated numbers
m{
    ^ \s *                  # optional leading whitespace
    $number                 # at least one number
    (?:                     # begin optional cluster
        \s +                # must have some separator
        $number             # more the next one
    ) *                     # repeat at will
    \s * $                  # optional trailing whitespace
}x
```

which is certainly a lot better than writing:

```
/^\s*[-+]?\d+\.?\d*(?:\s+[-+]?\d+\.?\d*)*\s*/
```

Patterns that you put in variables should probably not contain capturing parentheses or backreferences, since a capture in one variable could change the numbering of those in others.

Clustering parentheses—that is, /(?:...)/ instead of /(...)/—though, are fine. Not only are they fine, they're necessary if you want to apply a quantifier to the whole variable. For example:

```
$number = "(?:"
        . $optional_sign
        . $mandatory_digits
        . $decimal_point
        . $optional_digits
        . ")";
```

Now you can say /$number+/ and have the plus apply to the whole number group. Without the grouping, the plus would have shown up right after the last star, which would have been illegal.

One more trick with clustering parentheses is that you can embed a modifier switch that applies only to that cluster. For example:

```
$hex_digit = '(?i:[0-9a-z])';
$hdr_line  = '(?m:[^:]*:.*)';
```

The qr// construct does this automatically using cluster parentheses, enabling any modifiers you specified and disabling any you didn't for that cluster:

```
$hex_digit = qr/[0-9a-z]/i;
$hdr_line  = qr/^[^:]*:.*/m;

print "hex digit is: $hex_digit\n";
print "hdr line is: $hdr_line\n";
```

```
hex digit is: (?i-xsm:[0-9a-z])
hdr line is: (?m-xis:^[^:]*:.*)
```

It's probably a good idea to use qr// in the first place:

```
$optional_sign      = qr/[-+]?/;
$mandatory_digits   = qr/\d+/;
$decimal_point      = qr/\.?/;
$optional_digits    = qr/\d*/;

$number = qr{
                $optional_sign
                $mandatory_digits
                $decimal_point
                $optional_digits
        }x;
```

Although the output can be a bit odd to read:

```
print "Number is $number\n";
```

```
Number is (?x-ism:
                (?-xism:[-+]?)
                (?-xism:\d+)
                (?-xism:\.?)
                (?-xism:\d*)
        )
```

See Also

The /x modifier in *perlre*(1) and Chapter 5 of *Programming Perl*; the "Comments Within a Regular Expression" section of Chapter 7 of *Mastering Regular Expressions*

6.5   Finding the Nth Occurrence of a Match

Problem

You want to find the Nth match in a string, not just the first one. For example, you'd like to find the word preceding the third occurrence of "fish":

```
One fish two fish red fish blue fish
```

Solution

Use the /g modifier in a while loop, keeping count of matches:

```
$WANT = 3;
$count = 0;
while (/(\w+)\s+fish\b/gi) {
    if (++$count == $WANT) {
        print "The third fish is a $1 one.\n";
        # Warning: don't `last' out of this loop
```

```
        }
    }
```
The third fish is a red one.

Or use a repetition count and repeated pattern like this:

```
/(?:\w+\s+fish\s+){2}(\w+)\s+fish/i;
```

Discussion

As explained in this chapter's Introduction, using the /g modifier in scalar context creates something of a *progressive match*, useful in while loops. This is commonly used to count the number of times a pattern matches in a string:

```
# simple way with while loop
$count = 0;
while ($string =~ /PAT/g) {
    $count++;                    # or whatever you'd like to do here
}

# same thing with trailing while
$count = 0;
$count++ while $string =~ /PAT/g;

# or with for loop
for ($count = 0; $string =~ /PAT/g; $count++) { }

# Similar, but this time count overlapping matches
$count++ while $string =~ /(?=PAT)/g;
```

To find the Nth match, it's easiest to keep your own counter. When you reach the appropriate N, do whatever you care to. A similar technique could be used to find every Nth match by checking for multiples of N using the modulus operator. For example, (++$count % 3) = = 0 would be used to find every third match.

If this is too much bother, you can always extract all matches and then hunt for the ones you'd like.

```
$pond  = 'One fish two fish red fish blue fish';

# using a temporary
@colors = ($pond =~ /(\w+)\s+fish\b/gi);     # get all matches
$color  = $colors[2];                         # then the one we want

# or without a temporary array
$color = ( $pond =~ /(\w+)\s+fish\b/gi )[2];  # just grab element 3

print "The third fish in the pond is $color.\n";
```
The third fish in the pond is red.

To find all even-numbered fish:

```
$count = 0;
$_ = 'One fish two fish red fish blue fish';
```

```
@evens = grep { $count++ % 2 == 0 } /(\w+)\s+fish\b/gi;
print "Even numbered fish are @evens.\n";
```
Even numbered fish are two blue.

For substitution, the replacement value should be a code expression that returns the proper string. Make sure to return the original as a replacement string for cases you aren't interested in changing. Here we fish out the fourth specimen and turn it into a snack:

```
$count = 0;
s{
    \b                      # makes next \w more efficient
    ( \w+ )                 # this is what we'll be changing
    (
      \s+ fish \b
    )
}{
    if (++$count == 4) {
        "sushi" . $2;
    } else {
        $1   . $2;
    }
}gex;
```
One fish two fish red fish sushi fish

Picking out the last match instead of the first one is a fairly common task. The easiest way is to skip the beginning part greedily. After `/.*\b(\w+)\s+fish\b/s`, for example, the `$1` variable has the last fish.

Another way to get arbitrary counts is to make a global match in list context to produce all hits, then extract the desired element of that list:

```
$pond = 'One fish two fish red fish blue fish swim here.';
$color = ( $pond =~ /\b(\w+)\s+fish\b/gi )[-1];
print "Last fish is $color.\n";
```
Last fish is blue.

To express this same notion of finding the last match in a single pattern without `/g`, use the negative lookahead assertion `(?!THING)`. When you want the last match of arbitrary pattern P, you find P followed by any amount of not P through the end of the string. The general construct is `P(?!.*P)*`, which can be broken up for legibility:

```
m{
    P                   # find some pattern P
    (?!                 # mustn't be able to find
        .*              # something
        P               # and P
    )
}xs
```

That leaves us with this approach for selecting the last fish:

```
$pond = 'One fish two fish red fish blue fish swim here.';
if ($pond =~ m{
                \b  ( \w+) \s+ fish \b
```

```
                (?! .* \b fish \b )
            }six )
{
    print "Last fish is $1.\n";
} else {
    print "Failed!\n";
}
```
Last fish is blue.

This approach has the advantage that it can fit in just one pattern, which makes it suitable for similar situations as shown in Recipe 6.18. It has its disadvantages, though. It's obviously much harder to read and understand, although once you learn the formula, it's not too bad. However, it also runs more slowly—around half as fast on the data set tested here.

See Also

The behavior of m//g in scalar context is given in the "Regexp Quote-like Operators" section of *perlop*(1), and in the "Pattern Matching Operators" section of Chapter 5 of *Programming Perl*; zero-width positive lookahead assertions are shown in the "Regular Expressions" section of *perlre*(1), and in the "Fancy Patterns" section of Chapter 5 of *Programming Perl*

6.6   Matching Within Multiple Lines

Problem

You want to use regular expressions on a string containing more than one logical line, but the special characters . (any character but newline), ^ (start of string), and $ (end of string) don't seem to work for you. This might happen if you're reading in multiline records or the whole file at once.

Solution

Use /m, /s, or both as pattern modifiers. /s allows . to match a newline (normally it doesn't). If the target string has more than one line in it, /foo.*bar/s could match a "foo" on one line and a "bar" on a following line. This doesn't affect dots in character classes like [#%.], since they are literal periods anyway.

The /m modifier allows ^ and $ to match immediately after and before an embedded newline, respectively. /^=head[1-7]/m would match that pattern not just at the beginning of the record, but anywhere right after a newline as well.

Discussion

A common, brute-force approach to parsing documents where newlines are not significant is to read the file one paragraph at a time (or sometimes even the entire file as one string) and then extract tokens one by one. If the pattern involves dot, such as .+ or .*?, and must match across newlines, you need to do something special to make dot match a newline; ordinarily, it does not. When you've read more than one line into a string, you'll probably prefer to have ^ and $ match beginning- and end-of-line, not just beginning- and end-of-string.

The difference between /m and /s is important: /m allows ^ and $ to match next to an embedded newline, whereas /s allows . to match newlines. You can even use them together—they're not mutually exclusive.

Example 6-2 creates a simplistic filter to strip HTML tags out of each file in @ARGV and then send those results to STDOUT. First we undefine the record separator so each read operation fetches one entire file. (There could be more than one file, because @ARGV could have several arguments in it. If so, each readline would fetch the entire contents of one file.) Then we strip out instances of beginning and ending angle brackets, plus anything in between them. We can't use just .* for two reasons: first, it would match closing angle brackets, and second, the dot wouldn't cross newline boundaries. Using .*? in conjunction with /s solves these problems.

Example 6-2. killtags

```
#!/usr/bin/perl
# killtags - very bad html tag killer
undef $/;              # each read is whole file
while (<>) {           # get one whole file at a time
    s/<.*?>//gs;       # strip tags (terribly)
    print;             # print file to STDOUT
}
```

Because this is just a single character, it would be much faster to use s/<[^>]*>//gs, but that's still a naïve approach: it doesn't correctly handle tags inside HTML comments or angle brackets in quotes (<IMG SRC="here.gif" ALT="<<Ooh la la!>>">). Recipe 20.6 explains how to avoid these problems.

Example 6-3 takes a plain text document and looks for lines at the start of paragraphs that look like "Chapter 20: Better Living Through Chemisery". It wraps these with an appropriate HTML level-one header. Because the pattern is relatively complex, we use the /x modifier so we can embed whitespace and comments.

Example 6-3. headerfy

```
#!/usr/bin/perl
# headerfy: change certain chapter headers to html
$/ = '';
while (<> ) {                  # fetch a paragraph
    s{
```

Example 6-3. headerfy (continued)

```
        \A                  # start of record
        (                   # capture in $1
            Chapter         # text string
            \s+             # mandatory whitespace
            \d+             # decimal number
            \s*             # optional whitespace
            :               # a real colon
            . *             # anything not a newline till end of line
        )
    }{<H1>$1</H1>}gx;
    print;
}
```

Here it is as a one-liner from the command line for those of you for whom the extended comments just get in the way of understanding:

```
% perl -00pe 's{\A(Chapter\s+\d+\s*:.*)}{<H1>$1</H1>}gx' datafile
```

This problem is interesting because we need to be able to specify start-of-record and end-of-line in the same pattern. We could normally use ^ for start-of-record, but we need $ to indicate not only end-of-record, but end-of-line as well. We add the /m modifier, which changes ^ and $. Instead of using ^ to match beginning-of-record, we use \A instead. We're not using it here, but in case you're interested, the version of $ that always matches end-of-record with an optional newline, even in the presence of /m, is \Z. To match the real end without the optional newline, use \z.

The following example demonstrates using /s and /m together. That's because we want ^ to match the beginning of any line in the paragraph; we also want dot to match a newline. The predefined variable $. represents the record number of the file-handle most recently read from using readline(FH) or <FH>. The predefined variable $ARGV is the name of the file that's automatically opened by implicit <ARGV> processing.

```
$/ = '';                # paragraph read mode
while (<ARGV>) {
    while (/^START(.*?)^END/sm) {   # /s makes . span line boundaries
                                     # /m makes ^ match near newlines
        print "chunk $. in $ARGV has <<$1>>\n";
    }
}
```

If you're already committed to the /m modifier, use \A and \Z for the old meanings of ^ and $, respectively. But what if you've used the /s modifier and want the original meaning of dot? You use [^\n].

Finally, although $ and \Z can match one before the end of a string if that last character is a newline, \z matches only at the very end of the string. We can use lookaheads to define the other two as shortcuts involving \z:

$ without /m	(?=\n)?\z
$ with /m	(?=\n)|\z
\Z always	(?=\n)?\z

See Also

The $/ variable in *perlvar*(1) and in the "Per-Filehandle Variables" section of Chapter 28 of *Programming Perl*; the /s and /m modifiers in *perlre*(1) and "The Fine Print" section of Chapter 2 of *Programming Perl*; the "Anchors and Other Zero-Width Assertions" section in Chapter 3 of *Mastering Regular Expressions*; we talk more about the special variable $/ in Chapter 8

6.7 Reading Records with a Separator

Problem

You want to read records separated by a pattern, but Perl doesn't allow its input record separator variable to be a regular expression.

Many problems, most obviously those involving parsing complex file formats, become simpler when you can extract records separated by different strings.

Solution

Read the whole file and use split:

```
undef $/;
@chunks = split(/pattern/, <FILEHANDLE>);
```

Discussion

Perl's official record separator, the $/ variable, must be a fixed string, not a pattern. To sidestep this limitation, undefine the input record separator entirely so that the next readline operation reads the rest of the file. This is sometimes called *slurp mode*, because it slurps in the whole file as one big string. Then split that huge string using the record separating pattern as the first argument.

Here's an example where the input stream is a text file that includes lines consisting of ".Se", ".Ch", and ".Ss", which are special codes in the *troff* macro set that this book was developed under. These strings are the separators, and we want to find text that falls between them.

```
# .Ch, .Se and .Ss divide chunks of STDIN
{
    local $/ = undef;
    @chunks = split(/^\.(Ch|Se|Ss)$/m, <>);
}
print "I read ", scalar(@chunks), " chunks.\n";
```

We create a localized version of $/ so its previous value is restored once the block finishes. By using split with parentheses in the pattern, captured separators are also returned. This way data elements in the return list alternate with elements containing "Se", "Ch", or "Ss".

If you don't want separators returned, but still need parentheses, use non-capturing parentheses in the pattern: /^\.(?:Ch|Se|Ss)$/m.

To split *before* a pattern but include the pattern in the return, use a lookahead assertion: /^(?=\.(?:Ch|Se|Ss))/m. That way each chunk except the first starts with the pattern.

Be aware that this uses a lot of memory when the file is large. However, with today's machines and typical text files, this is less often an issue now than it once was. Just don't try it on a 200 MB logfile unless you have plenty of virtual memory for swapping out to disk! Even if you do have enough swap space, you'll likely end up thrashing.

See Also

The $/ variable in *perlvar*(1) and in the "Per-Filehandle Variables" section of Chapter 28 of *Programming Perl*; the split function in *perlfunc*(1) and Chapter 29 of *Programming Perl*; we talk more about the special variable $/ in Chapter 8.

6.8   Extracting a Range of Lines

Problem

You want to extract all lines from a starting pattern through an ending pattern or from a starting line number up to an ending line number.

A common example of this is extracting the first 10 lines of a file (line numbers 1 to 10) or just the body of a mail message (everything past the blank line).

Solution

Use the operators .. or ... with patterns or line numbers.

The .. operator will test the right operand on the same iteration that the left operand flips the operator into the true state.

```
while (<>) {
    if (/BEGIN PATTERN/ .. /END PATTERN/) {
        # line falls between BEGIN and END in the
        # text, inclusive.
    }
}

while (<>) {
    if (FIRST_LINE_NUM .. LAST_LINE_NUM) {
        # operate only between first and last line, inclusive.
    }
}
```

But the ... operator waits until the next iteration to check the right operand.

```
while (<>) {
    if (/BEGIN PATTERN/ ... /END PATTERN/) {
        # line is between BEGIN and END on different lines
    }
}

while (<>) {
    if (FIRST_LINE_NUM ... LAST_LINE_NUM) {
        # operate only between first and last line, not inclusive
    }
}
```

Discussion

The range operators, .. and ..., are probably the least understood of Perl's myriad operators. They were designed to allow easy extraction of ranges of lines without forcing the programmer to retain explicit state information. Used in scalar context, such as in the test of if and while statements, these operators return a true or false value that's partially dependent on what they last returned. The expression left_operand .. right_operand returns false until left_operand is true, but once that test has been met, it stops evaluating left_operand and keeps returning true until right_operand becomes true, after which it restarts the cycle. Put another way, the first operand turns on the construct as soon as it returns a true value, whereas the second one turns it off as soon as *it* returns true.

The two operands are completely arbitrary. You could write mytestfunc1( ) .. mytestfunc2( ), although this is rarely seen. Instead, the range operators are usually used with either line numbers as operands (the first example), patterns as operands (the second example), or both.

```
# command-line to print lines 15 through 17 inclusive (see below)
perl -ne 'print if 15 .. 17' datafile

# print all <XMP> .. </XMP> displays from HTML doc
while (<>) {
    print if m#<XMP>#i .. m#</XMP>#i;
}

# same, but as shell command
% perl -ne 'print if m#<XMP>#i .. m#</XMP>#i' document.html
```

If either operand is a numeric literal, the range operators implicitly compare against the $. variable ($NR or $INPUT_LINE_NUMBER if you use English). Be careful with implicit line number comparisons here. You must specify literal numbers in your code, not variables containing line numbers. That means you simply say 3 .. 5 in a conditional, but not $n .. $m where $n and $m are 3 and 5 respectively. For that, be more explicit by testing the $. variable directly.

```
perl -ne 'BEGIN { $top=3; $bottom=5 }  print if $top .. $bottom' /etc/passwd
        # WRONG
perl -ne 'BEGIN { $top=3; $bottom=5 }
```

```
        print if $. == $top .. $. ==     $bottom' /etc/passwd     # RIGHT
perl -ne 'print if 3 .. 5' /etc/passwd  # also RIGHT
```

The difference between .. and ... is their behavior when both operands become true on the same iteration. Consider these two cases:

```
print if /begin/ .. /end/;
print if /begin/ ... /end/;
```

Given the line "You may not end ere you begin", both versions of the previous range operator return true. But the code using .. won't print any further lines. That's because .. tests both conditions on the same line once the first test matches, and the second test tells it that it's reached the end of its region. On the other hand, ... continues until the *next* line that matches /end/ because it never tries to test both operands on the same line.

You may mix and match conditions of different sorts, as in:

```
while (<>) {
    $in_header =   1  .. /^$/;
    $in_body   = /^$/ .. eof();
}
```

The first assignment sets $in_header to be true from the first input line until after the blank line separating the header, such as from a mail message, a USENET news posting, or even an HTTP header. (Technically, an HTTP header should have linefeeds and carriage returns as network line terminators, but in practice, servers are liberal in what they accept.) The second assignment sets $in_body to true as soon as the first blank line is encountered, up through end-of-file. Because range operators do not retest their initial condition, any further blank lines, like those between paragraphs, won't be noticed.

Here's an example. It reads files containing mail messages and prints addresses it finds in headers. Each address is printed only once. The extent of the header is from a line beginning with a "From:" up through the first blank line. If we're not within that range, go on to the next line. This isn't an RFC-822 notion of an address, but it is easy to write.

```
%seen = ();
while (<>) {
    next unless /^From:?\s/i .. /^$/;
    while (/([^<>(),;\s]+\@[^<>(),;\s]+)/g) {
        print "$1\n" unless $seen{$1}++;
    }
}
```

See Also

The .. and ... operators in the "Range Operator" sections of *perlop*(1) and Chapter 3 of *Programming Perl*; the entry for $NR in *perlvar*(1) and the "Per-Filehandle Variables" section of Chapter 28 of *Programming Perl*

6.9 Matching Shell Globs as Regular Expressions

Problem

You want to allow users to specify matches using traditional shell wildcards, not full Perl regular expressions. Wildcards are easier to type than full regular expressions for simple cases.

Solution

Use the following subroutine to convert four shell wildcard characters into their equivalent regular expression; all other characters are quoted to render them literals.

```
sub glob2pat {
    my $globstr = shift;
    my %patmap = (
        '*' => '.*',
        '?' => '.',
        '[' => '[',
        ']' => ']',
    );
    $globstr =~ s{(.)} { $patmap{$1} || "\Q$1" }ge;
    return '^' . $globstr . '$';
}
```

Discussion

A Perl regex pattern is not the same as a shell wildcard pattern. The shell's *.* is not a valid regular expression. Its meaning as a pattern would be /^.*\..*$/s, which is admittedly much less fun to type.

The function given in the Solution makes these conversions for you, following the standard wildcard rules used by the glob built-in. Table 6-2 shows equivalent wildcard patterns in the shell and in Perl.

Table 6-2. Shell globs and equivalent Perl wildcard patterns

Shell	Perl
list.?	^list\..$
project.*	^project\..*$
*old	^.*old$
type*.[ch]	^type.*\.[ch]$
.	^.*\..*$
*	^.*$

The function returns a string, not a regex object, because the latter would lock in (and out) any modifier flags, such as /i, but we'd rather delay that decision until later.

Shell wildcard rules are different from those of a regular expression. The entire pattern is implicitly anchored at the ends; a question mark maps into any character; an asterisk is any amount of anything; and brackets are character ranges. Everything else is a literal.

Most shells do more than simple one-directory globbing. For instance, */* means "all files (including directory files) in all subdirectories of the current directory." Also, shells usually don't expand wildcards to include files with names beginning with a period; you usually have to put that leading period into your glob pattern explicitly. Our glob2pat function doesn't do these things—if you need them, use the File::KGlob module from CPAN.

See Also

Your system manpages for the various shells, such as *csh*(1), *tcsh*(1), *sh*(1), *ksh*(1), and *bash*(1); the glob function in *perlfunc*(1) and Chapter 29 of *Programming Perl*; the documentation for the CPAN module Glob::DosGlob; the "I/O Operators" section of *perlop*(1); we talk more about globbing in Recipe 9.6

6.10   Speeding Up Interpolated Matches

Problem

You want your function or program to take one or more regular expressions as arguments, but doing so seems to run slower than using literals.

Solution

To overcome this bottleneck, if you have only one pattern whose value won't change during the entire run of a program, store it in a string and use /$pattern/o:

```
while ($line = <>) {
    if ($line =~ /$pattern/o) {
        # do something
    }
}
```

However, that won't work for more than one pattern. Precompile the pattern strings using the qr// operator, then match each result against each of the targets:

```
@pats = map { qr/$_/ } @strings;
while ($line = <>) {
    for $pat (@pats) {
        if ($line =~ /$pat/) {
```

```
            # do something;
        }
    }
}
```

Discussion

When Perl compiles a program, it converts patterns into an internal form. This conversion occurs at compile time for patterns without variables, but at runtime for those that do. Interpolating variables into patterns, as in /$pattern/, can slow your program down—sometimes substantially. This is particularly noticeable when $pattern changes often.

The /o modifier locks in the values from variables interpolated into the pattern. That is, variables are interpolated only once: the first time the match is run. Because Perl ignores any later changes to those variables, make sure to use it only on unchanging variables.

Using /o on patterns without interpolated variables doesn't hurt, but it also doesn't help. The /o modifier is also of no help when you have an unknown number of regular expressions and need to check one or more strings against all of these patterns, since you need to vary the patterns' contents. Nor is it of any use when the interpolated variable is a function argument, since each call to the function gives the variable a new value.

Example 6-4 is an example of the slow but straightforward technique for matching many patterns against many lines. The array @popstates contains the standard two-letter abbreviations for some of the places in the heartland of North America where we normally refer to soft drinks as *pop* (*soda* to us means either plain soda water or else handmade delicacies from the soda fountain at the corner drugstore, preferably with ice cream). The goal is to print any line of input that contains any of those places, matching them at word boundaries only. It doesn't use /o, because the variable that holds the pattern keeps changing.

Example 6-4. popgrep1

```perl
#!/usr/bin/perl
# popgrep1 - grep for abbreviations of places that say "pop"
# version 1: slow but obvious way
@popstates = qw(CO ON MI WI MN);
LINE: while (defined($line = <>)) {
    for $state (@popstates) {
        if ($line =~ /\b$state\b/) {  # this is  s l o o o w
            print; next LINE;
        }
    }
}
```

Such a direct, obvious, brute-force approach is also distressingly slow, because Perl has to recompile all patterns with each line of input. A better solution is the qr// operator (used in Example 6-5), which first appeared in v5.6 and offers a way to step around this bottleneck. The qr// operator quotes and possibly compiles its string argument, returning a scalar to use in later pattern matches. If that scalar is used by itself in the interpolated match, Perl uses the cached compiled form and so avoids recompiling the pattern.

Example 6-5. popgrep2

```
#!/usr/bin/perl
# popgrep2 - grep for abbreviations of places that say "pop"
# version 2: fast way using qr//
@popstates = qw(CO ON MI WI MN);
@poppats = map { qr/\b$_\b/ } @popstates;
LINE: while (defined($line = <>)) {
    for $pat (@poppats) {
        if ($line =~ /$pat/) {           # this is fast
            print; next LINE;
        }
    }
}
```

Print the array @poppats and you'll see strings like this:

```
(?-xism:\bCO\b)
(?-xism:\bON\b)
(?-xism:\bMI\b)
(?-xism:\bWI\b)
(?-xism:\bMN\b)
```

Those are used for the stringified print value of the qr// operator, or to build up a larger pattern if the result is interpolated into a larger string. But also associated with each is a cached, compiled version of that string as a pattern, and this is what Perl uses when the interpolation into a match or substitution operator contains nothing else.

See Also

The qr// operator in *perlop*(1) and in the section on "The qr// quote regex operator" in Chapter 5 of *Programming Perl*

6.11 Testing for a Valid Pattern

Problem

You want to let users enter their own patterns, but an invalid one would abort your program the first time you tried to use it.

Solution

Test the pattern in an eval { } construct first, matching against some dummy string. If $@ is not set, no exception occurred, so you know the pattern successfully compiled as a valid regular expression. Here is a loop that continues prompting until the user supplies a valid pattern:

```
do {
    print "Pattern? ";
    chomp($pat = <>);
    eval { "" =~ /$pat/ };
    warn "INVALID PATTERN $@" if $@;
} while $@;
```

Here's a standalone subroutine that verifies whether a pattern is valid:

```
sub is_valid_pattern {
    my $pat = shift;
    eval { "" =~ /$pat/ };
    return $@ ? 0 : 1;
}
```

Another way to write that is like this:

```
sub is_valid_pattern {
    my $pat = shift;
    return eval { "" =~ /$pat/; 1 } || 0;
}
```

This version doesn't need to use $@, because if the pattern match executes without exception, the next statement with just a 1 is reached and returned. Otherwise it's skipped, so just a 0 is returned.

Discussion

There's no limit to the number of invalid, uncompilable patterns. The user could mistakenly enter "<I\s*[^">", "*** GET RICH ***", or "+5-i". If you blindly use the proffered pattern in your program, it raises an exception, normally a fatal event.

The tiny program in Example 6-6 demonstrates this.

Example 6-6. paragrep

```
#!/usr/bin/perl
# paragrep - trivial paragraph grepper
die "usage: $0 pat [files]\n" unless @ARGV;
$/ = '';
$pat = shift;
eval { "" =~ /$pat/; 1 }      or die "$0: Bad pattern $pat: $@\n";
while (<>) {
    print "$ARGV $.: $_" if /$pat/o;
}
```

That /o means to interpolate variables once only, even if their contents later change.

You could encapsulate this in a function call that returns 1 if the block completes and 0 if not, as shown in the Solution. The simpler eval "/$pat/" would also work to trap the exception, but has two other problems. One is that any slashes (or whatever your chosen pattern delimiter is) in the string the user entered would raise an exception. More importantly, it would open a drastic security hole that you almost certainly want to avoid. Strings like this could ruin your day:

```
$pat = "You lose @{[ system('rm -rf *')]} big here";
```

If you don't want to let the user provide a real pattern, you can always metaquote the string first:

```
$safe_pat = quotemeta($pat);
something( ) if /$safe_pat/;
```

Or, even easier, use:

```
something( ) if /\Q$pat/;
```

But if you're going to do that, why are you using pattern matching at all? In that case, a simple use of index would be enough. But sometimes you want a literal part and a regex part, such as:

```
something( ) if /^\s*\Q$pat\E\s*$/;
```

Letting the user supply a real pattern gives them power enough for many interesting and useful operations. This is a good thing. You just have to be slightly careful. Suppose they wanted to enter a case-insensitive pattern, but you didn't provide the program with an option like *grep*'s **-i** option. By permitting full patterns, the user can enter an embedded /i modifier as (?i), as in /(?i)stuff/.

What happens if the interpolated pattern expands to nothing? If $pat is the empty string, what does /$pat/ match—that is, what does a blank // match? It doesn't match the start of all possible strings. Surprisingly, matching the null pattern exhibits the dubiously useful semantics of reusing the previous *successfully* matched pattern. In practice, this is hard to make good use of in Perl.

See Also

The eval function in *perlfunc*(1) and in Chapter 29 of *Programming Perl*; Recipe 10.12

6.12 Honoring Locale Settings in Regular Expressions

Problem

You want to translate case when in a different locale, or you want to make \w match letters with diacritics, such as *José* or *déjà vu*.

For example, let's say you're given half a gigabyte of text written in German and told to index it. You want to extract words (with \w+) and convert them to lowercase (with lc or \L), but the normal versions of \w and lc neither match the German words nor change the case of accented letters.

Solution

Perl's regular-expression and text-manipulation routines have hooks to the POSIX locale setting. Under the use locale pragma, accented characters are taken care of—assuming a reasonable LC_CTYPE specification and system support for the same.

```
use locale;
```

Discussion

By default, \w+ and case-mapping functions operate on upper- and lowercase letters, digits, and underscores. This works only for the simplest of English words, failing even on many common imports. The use locale directive redefines what a "word character" means.

In Example 6-7 you see the difference in output between having selected the English ("en") locale and the German ("de") one.

Example 6-7. localeg

```
#!/usr/bin/perl -w
# localeg - demonstrate locale effects
use locale;
use POSIX 'locale_h';
$name = "andreas k\xF6nig";
@locale{qw(German English)} = qw(de_DE.ISO_8859-1 us-ascii);
setlocale(LC_CTYPE, $locale{English})
  or die "Invalid locale $locale{English}";
@english_names = ( );
while ($name =~ /\b(\w+)\b/g) {
        push(@english_names, ucfirst($1));
}
setlocale(LC_CTYPE, $locale{German})
  or die "Invalid locale $locale{German}";
@german_names = ( );
while ($name =~ /\b(\w+)\b/g) {
        push(@german_names, ucfirst($1));
}
print "English names: @english_names\n";
print "German names:  @german_names\n";
English names: Andreas K Nig
German names:  Andreas König
```

This approach relies on POSIX locale support for 8-bit character encodings, which your system may or may not provide. Even if your system does claim to provide

POSIX locale support, the standard does not specify the locale names. As you might guess, portability of this approach is not assured. If your data is already in Unicode, you don't need POSIX locales for this to work.

See Also

The treatment of \b, \w, and \s in *perlre*(1) and in the "Classic Perl Character Class Shortcuts" section of Chapter 5 of *Programming Perl*; the treatment of locales in Perl in *perllocale*(1); your system's *locale*(3) manpage; we discuss locales in greater depth in Recipe 6.2; the "POSIX—An Attempt at Standardization" section of Chapter 3 of *Mastering Regular Expressions*

6.13   Approximate Matching

Problem

You want to match fuzzily, that is, allowing for a margin of error, where the string doesn't *quite* match the pattern. Whenever you want to be forgiving of misspellings in user input, you want fuzzy matching.

Solution

Use the String::Approx module, available from CPAN:

```
use String::Approx qw(amatch);

if (amatch("PATTERN", @list)) {
    # matched
}

@matches = amatch("PATTERN", @list);
```

Discussion

String::Approx calculates the difference between the pattern and each string in the list. If less than a certain number—by default, 10 percent of the pattern length—of one-character insertions, deletions, or substitutions are required to make the string fit the pattern, it still matches. In scalar context, amatch returns the number of successful matches. In list context, it returns the strings matched.

```
use String::Approx qw(amatch);
open(DICT, "/usr/dict/words")           or die "Can't open dict: $!";
while(<DICT>) {
    print if amatch("balast");
}
```

```
ballast
balustrade
blast
blastula
sandblast
```

Options passed to amatch control case-sensitivity and the permitted number of insertions, deletions, or substitutions. These are fully described in the String::Approx documentation.

The module's matching function seems to run between 10 and 40 times slower than Perl's built-in pattern matching. So use String::Approx only if you're after a fuzziness in your matching that Perl's patterns can't provide.

See Also

The documentation for the CPAN module String::Approx; Recipe 1.22

6.14 Matching from Where the Last Pattern Left Off

Problem

You want to match again in the same string, starting from where the last match left off. This is a useful approach to take when repeatedly extracting data in chunks from a string.

Solution

Use a combination of the /g and /c match modifiers, the \G pattern anchor, and the pos function.

Discussion

The /g modifier on a pattern match makes the matching engine keep track of the position in the string where it finished matching. If the next match also uses /g on that string, the engine starts looking for a match from this remembered position. This lets you, for example, use a while loop to progressively extract repeated occurrences of a match. Here we find all non-negative integers:

```
while (/(\d+)/g) {
    print "Found number $1\n";
}
```

Within a pattern, \G means the end of the previous match. For example, if you had a number stored in a string with leading blanks, you could change each leading blank into the digit zero this way:

```perl
$n = "    49 here";
$n =~ s/\G /0/g;
print $n;
```
00049 here

You can also make good use of \G in a while loop. Here we use \G to parse a comma-separated list of numbers (e.g., "3,4,5,9,120"):

```perl
while (/\G,?(\d+)/g) {
    print "Found number $1\n";
}
```

By default, when your match fails (when we run out of numbers in the examples, for instance) the remembered position is reset to the start. If you don't want this to happen, perhaps because you want to continue matching from that position but with a different pattern, use the modifier /c with /g:

```perl
$_ = "The year 1752 lost 10 days on the 3rd of September";

while (/(\d+)/gc) {
    print "Found number $1\n";
}
# the /c above left pos at end of final match

if (/\G(\S+)/g) {
    print "Found $1 right after the last number.\n";
}
```

Found number 1752
Found number 10
Found number 3
Found rd after the last number.

Successive patterns can use /g on a string, which remembers the ending position of the last successful match. That position is associated with the scalar matched against, not with the pattern. It's reset if the string is modified.

The position of the last successful match can be directly inspected or altered with the pos function, whose argument is the string whose position you want to get or set. Assign to the function to set the position.

```perl
$a = "Didst thou think that the eyes of the White Tower were blind?";
$a =~ /(\w{5,})/g;
print "Got $1, position in \$a is ", pos($a), "\n";
```
Got Didst, position in $a is 5

```perl
pos($a) = 30;
$a =~ /(\w{5,})/g;
print "Got $1, position in \$a now ", pos($a), "\n";
```
Got White, position in $a now 43

Without an argument, pos operates on $_:

```perl
$_ = "Nay, I have seen more than thou knowest, Grey Fool.";
/(\w{5,})/g;
```

```
print "Got $1, position in \$_ is ", pos, "\n";
pos = 42;
/\b(\w+)/g;
print "Next full word after position 42 is $1\n";
```

Got knowest, position in $_ is 39
Next full word after position 42 is Fool

See Also

The /g and /c modifiers are discussed in *perlre*(1) and the "The m// Operator (Matching)" section of Chapter 5 of *Programming Perl*

6.15   Greedy and Non-Greedy Matches

Problem

You have a pattern with a greedy quantifier like *, +, ?, or { }, and you want to stop it from being greedy.

A classic example is the naïve substitution to remove tags from HTML. Although it looks appealing, s#<TT>.*</TT>##gsi deletes everything from the first open TT tag through the last closing one. This would turn "Even <TT>vi</TT> can edit <TT> troff</TT> effectively." into "Even effectively", completely changing the meaning of the sentence!

Solution

Replace the offending greedy quantifier with the corresponding non-greedy version. That is, change *, +, ?, and { } into *?, +?, ??, and { }?, respectively.

Discussion

Perl has two sets of quantifiers: the *maximal* ones—*, +, ?, and { }—and the *minimal* ones—*?, +?, ??, and { }?. Less formally, these two sorts of quantifiers are often referred to as *greedy* and *non-greedy* (or sometimes *lazy*), respectively. For instance, given the string "Perl is a Swiss Army Chainsaw!", the pattern /(r.*s)/ matches "rl is a Swiss Army Chains", whereas /(r.*?s)/ matches "rl is".

With maximal quantifiers, when you ask to match a variable number of times, such as zero or more times for * or one or more times for +, the matching engine prefers the "or more" portion of that description. Thus /foo.*bar/ matches the first "foo" through the last "bar" in the string, rather than only through the next "bar" as some might expect. That's because the greedy .* first expands to the rest of the string, but since that wouldn't leave any characters for "bar" to match, the engine backs up one character at a time until it finds "bar".

To make any repetition operator match minimally instead of maximally, add an extra ?. So *? still matches zero or more times, but rather than match as much as it can, the way * would, it matches as little as it can.

```
# greedy pattern
s/<.*>//gs;                 # try to remove tags, very badly

# nongreedy pattern
s/<.*?>//gs;                # try to remove tags, better (but still rather badly)
```

This approach doesn't remove tags from all possible HTML correctly, because a single regular expression is seldom an acceptable replacement for a real parser. See Recipe 20.6 for the right way.

Minimal matching isn't all it's cracked up to be. Don't fall into the trap of thinking that including the partial pattern BEGIN.*?END in a pattern amidst other elements will always match the shortest amount of text between occurrences of BEGIN and END. Consider the pattern /BEGIN(.*?)END/. If matched against the string "BEGIN and BEGIN and END", $1 would contain "and BEGIN and". This is probably not what you want.

Imagine trying to pull out everything between bold-italic pairs:

```
<b><i>this</i> and <i>that</i> are important</b> Oh, <b><i>me too!</i></b>
```

A pattern to find only text *between* bold-italic HTML pairs, that is, text that doesn't include them, might appear to be:

```
m{ <b><i>(.*?)</i></b> }sx
```

You might be surprised to learn that the pattern doesn't find such pairs. Many people incorrectly understand this as matching a "" sequence, then anything up to a "" sequence, leaving the intervening text in $1. While it often works out that way due to the input data, that's *not* what it says. There's nothing in that pattern that says .*? can't match "" again (and again and again) before it comes to "". If the intention were to extract only stuff between "" and its *corresponding* "", with no other bold-italic tags in between, that pattern would be incorrect.

If the string in question is just one character, and if what follows the minimal match is not a literal character, a negated class is remarkably more efficient than a minimal match, as in /X([^X]*)X/. But the general way to say "match BEGIN, then not BEGIN, then END" for any arbitrary values of BEGIN and END would be as follows (this also stores the intervening part in $1):

```
/BEGIN((?:(?!BEGIN).)*)END/s
```

or, more legibly:

```
{
  BEGIN                 # locate initial portion
  (                     # save this group into $1
     (?:                # non-capturing group
        (?! BEGIN)      # assert: can't be at another BEGIN
```

```
                .              # now match any one character
        ) *                    # entire group 0 or more
    )                          # end $1 group
    END                        # locate final portion
  }sx
```

However, this might not be what you're after, either. The greedy star quantifier means that the non-BEGIN portion in $1 will be maximized, giving fence posts of the last BEGIN through not the first END, but the last one. So if your string were:

```
$_ = "BEGIN1 BEGIN2 BEGIN3 3END 2END 1END";
```

$1 would contain "3 3END 2END 1". Making the quantifier a minimal matching one:

```
/BEGIN((?:(?!BEGIN).)*?)END/s
```

puts "3 3" in $1 for you. Now add another lookahead negation, (?!END), next to the existing one. Written out with plenty of whitespace, we now have:

```
  m{
      BEGIN            # locate initial portion
      (                # save this group into $1
        (?:            # non-capturing group
           (?! BEGIN  )   # can't be at a BEGIN
           (?! END    )   # also can't be at an END
                .          # finally, match any one char
        ) *            # repeat entire group ad libitum
      )                # end $1 capture
      END
  }sx
```

Instead of adding another lookahead, another possibility is to use alternation within the existing one: (?!BEGIN|END). Applying this approach to the HTML-matching code, we end up with something like:

```
  m{ <b><i>(  (?: (?!</b>|</i>). )*  ) </i></b> }sx
```

or perhaps:

```
  m{ <b><i>(  (?: (?!</[ib]>). )*  ) </i></b> }sx
```

Jeffrey Friedl points out that this quick-and-dirty method isn't particularly efficient. He suggests crafting a more elaborate pattern when speed matters, such as:

```
  m{
      <b><i>
      [^<]*  # stuff not possibly bad, and not possibly the end.
      (?:
   # at this point, we can have '<' if not part of something bad
        (?! </?[ib]> )   # what we can't have
        <                # okay, so match the '<'
        [^<]*            # and continue with more safe stuff
      ) *
      </i> </b>
  }sx
```

This is a variation on Jeffrey's unrolling-the-loop technique, described in Chapter 6 of *Mastering Regular Expressions*, Second Edition.

See Also

The non-greedy quantifiers in the "Regular Expressions" section of *perlre*(1) and in Chapter 5 of *Programming Perl*

6.16 Detecting Doubled Words

Problem

You want to check for doubled words in a document.

Solution

Use backreferences in your pattern.

Discussion

Parentheses in a pattern make the matching engine remember what text that portion of the pattern matched. Later in the pattern, refer to the actual string that matched with \1 (indicating the string matched by the first set of parentheses), \2 (for the string matched by the second set of parentheses), and so on. Don't use $1 within a regex, because it would be a variable interpolated before the match began. The pattern /([A-Z])\1/ matches a capital letter followed not just by any capital letter, but by whichever one was just matched (i.e., captured by the first set of parentheses in that pattern).

The next sample code reads its input files by paragraph, with the definition of *paragraph* following Perl's notion of a paragraph—a chunk of text terminated by two or more contiguous newlines. Within each paragraph, the code finds all doubled words. It ignores case and can match across newlines.

Here we use /x to embed whitespace and comments to improve readability. The /i permits both instances of "is" in the sentence "Is is this ok?" to match, even though they differ in case. We use /g in a while loop to keep finding doubled words until we run out of text.

```
$/ = '';                    # paragrep mode
while (<>) {
    while ( m{
                \b          # start at a word boundary (begin letters)
                (\S+)       # find chunk of non-whitespace
                \b          # until another word boundary (end letters)
                (
```

```
                \s+        # separated by some whitespace
                \1         # and that very same chunk again
                \b         # until another word boundary
            ) +            # one or more sets of those
        }xig
    )
    {
        print "dup word '$1' at paragraph $.\n";
    }
}
```

That code finds the duplicated *test* in the following paragraph:

```
This is a test
test of the doubled word finder.
```

Word boundary anchors surrounding \S+ are often a bad idea because they do something you might not be expecting. That's because word boundaries in Perl are defined as transitions between alphanumunders (that's a \w) and either the edge of the string or a non-alphanumunder. Surrounding \S+ with \b subtly changes \S+ from its normal meaning of one or more non-whitespace characters to a stretch of non-whitespace whose first and last character must be an alphanumunder.

Sometimes, though, this might be just what you're looking for. Consider the string:

```
$string = q("I can't see this," she remarked.);

@a = $string =~ /\b\S+\b/g;
@b = $string =~ /\S+/g;
```

The elements of @a are now:

```
0  I
1  can't
2  see
3  this
4  she
5  remarked
```

but those of @b are:

```
0  "I
1  can't
2  see
3  this,"
4  she
5  remarked.
```

Here's another interesting demonstration of backreferences. Imagine two words in which the end of the first word is the same as the start of the next one, such as "nobody" and "bodysnatcher". You'd like to find that overlapping part and come up with "nobodysnatcher". This is a variant on the doubled word problem.

Conventional character-by-character processing the way a C programmer would write it would take a great deal of tricky code. But with a backtracking pattern matcher, it just takes one simple pattern match.

```
$a = 'nobody';
$b = 'bodysnatcher';
if ("$a $b" =~ /^(\w+)(\w+) \2(\w+)$/) {
    print "$2 overlaps in $1-$2-$3\n";
}
```
body overlaps in no-body-snatcher

You might think that $1 would first grab up all of "nobody" due to greediness. It does—for a while. But once it's done so, there aren't any more characters to put in $2. So the engine backs up, and $1 begrudgingly gives up one character to $2. The space character matches successfully, but then sees \2, which currently holds a lone "y". The next character in the string is not a "y", but a "b". This makes the engine back up, eventually forcing $1 to surrender enough to $2 that the pattern can match some string, a space, and then that same string again.

That won't quite work out if the overlap is itself the product of a doubling, as in "rococo" and "cocoon". The preceding algorithm would have decided that the overlapping string, $2, must be just "co" rather than "coco". But we don't want a "rocococoon"; we want a "rococoon". Adding a minimal matching quantifier to the $1 part gives the much better pattern:

```
/^(\w+?)(\w+) \2(\w+)$/,
```

which solves this problem.

Backtracking is more powerful than you might imagine. Example 6-8 offers another take on the prime factorization problem from Chapter 1.

Example 6-8. prime-pattern
```
#!/usr/bin/perl
# prime_pattern -- find prime factors of argument using pattern matching
for ($N = ('o' x shift); $N =~ /^(oo+?)\1+$/; $N =~ s/$1/o/g) {
    print length($1), " ";
}
print length ($N), "\n";
```

Although not practical, this approach marvelously demonstrates the power of backtracking.

Here's another example. Using a brilliant insight first illustrated by Doug McIlroy (or so says Andrew Hume), you can find solutions to Diophantine equations of order one with regular expressions. Consider the equation $12x + 15y + 16z = 281$. Can you think of possible values for x, y, and z? Perl can!

```
# solve for 12x + 15y + 16z = 281, maximizing x
if (($X, $Y, $Z)  =
    (('o' x 281)  =~ /^(o*)\1{11}(o*)\2{14}(o*)\3{15}$/))
{
    ($x, $y, $z) = (length($X), length($Y), length($Z));
    print "One solution is: x=$x; y=$y; z=$z.\n";
} else {
```

```
            print "No solution.\n";
        }
One solution is: x=17; y=3; z=2.
```

Because the first o* was greedy, *x* was allowed to grow as large as it could. Changing one or more * quantifiers to *?, +, or +? can produce different solutions.

```
('o' x 281)  =~ /^(o+)\1{11}(o+)\2{14}(o+)\3{15}$/
One solution is: x=17; y=3; z=2
('o' x 281)  =~ /^(o*?)\1{11}(o*)\2{14}(o*)\3{15}$/
One solution is: x=0; y=7; z=11.
('o' x 281)  =~ /^(o+?)\1{11}(o*)\2{14}(o*)\3{15}$/
One solution is: x=1; y=3; z=14.
```

An important lesson to be learned from these amazing feats of mathematical prowess by a lowly pattern matcher is that a pattern-matching engine, particularly a backtracking one, very much wants to give you an answer, and it will work phenomenally hard to do so. But solving a regular expression with backreferences can take time exponentially proportional to the length of the input to complete. For all but trivial inputs, such algorithms make continental drift seem brisk.

See Also

The explanation of backreferences in the "Regular Expressions" section of *perlre*(1), and in "The Little Engine That /Could(n't)?/" section of Chapter 5 of *Programming Perl*; the "The Doubled-Word Thing" section in Chapter 2 of *Mastering Regular Expressions*

6.17 Matching Nested Patterns

Problem

You want to match a nested set of enclosing delimiters, such as the arguments to a function call.

Solution

Use match-time pattern interpolation, recursively:

```
my $np;
$np = qr{
            \(
            (?:
                (?> [^()]+ )    # Non-capture group w/o backtracking
             |
                (??{ $np })     # Group with matching parens
            )*
            \)
        }x;
```

Or use the Text::Balanced module's extract_bracketed function.

Discussion

The $(??{ *CODE* }) construct runs the code and interpolates the string that the code returns right back into the pattern. A simple, non-recursive example that matches palindromes demonstrates this:

```
if ($word =~ /^(\w+)\w?(??{reverse $1})$/ ) {
    print "$word is a palindrome.\n";
}
```

Consider a word like "reviver", which this pattern correctly reports as a palindrome. The $1 variable contains "rev" partway through the match. The optional word character following catches the "i". Then the code reverse $1 runs and produces "ver", and that result is interpolated into the pattern.

For matching something balanced, you need to recurse, which is a bit tricker. A compiled pattern that uses (??{ *CODE* }) can refer to itself. The pattern given in the Solution matches a set of nested parentheses, however deep they may go. Given the value of $np in that pattern, you could use it like this to match a function call:

```
$text = "myfunfun(1,(2*(3+4)),5)";
$funpat = qr/\w+$np/;    # $np as above
$text =~ /^$funpat$/;    # Matches!
```

You'll find many CPAN modules that help with matching (parsing) nested strings. The Regexp::Common module supplies canned patterns that match many of the tricker strings. For example:

```
use Regexp::Common;
$text = "myfunfun(1,(2*(3+4)),5)";
if ($text =~ /(\w+\s*$RE{balanced}{-parens=>'()'})/o) {
  print "Got function call: $1\n";
}
```

Other patterns provided by that module match numbers in various notations and quote-delimited strings:

```
$RE{num}{int}
$RE{num}{real}
$RE{num}{real}{'-base=2'}{'-sep=,'}{'-group=3'}
$RE{quoted}
$RE{delimited}{-delim=>'/'}
```

The standard (as of v5.8) Text::Balanced module provides a general solution to this problem.

```
use Text::Balanced qw/extract_bracketed/;
$text = "myfunfun(1,(2*(3+4)),5)";
if (($before, $found, $after) = extract_bracketed($text, "(")) {
    print "answer is $found\n";
} else {
    print "FAILED\n";
}
```

See Also

The section on "Match-time pattern interpolation" in Chapter 5 of *Programming Perl*; the documentation for the Regexp::Common CPAN module and the standard Text::Balanced module

6.18 Expressing AND, OR, and NOT in a Single Pattern

Problem

You have an existing program that accepts a pattern as an argument or as input. It doesn't allow you to add extra logic, like case-insensitive options, ANDs, or NOTs. So you need to write a single pattern that matches either of two different patterns (the "or" case) or both of two patterns (the "and" case), or that reverses the sense of the match ("not").

This situation arises often in configuration files, web forms, or command-line arguments. Imagine there's a program that does this:

```
chomp($pattern = <CONFIG_FH>);
if ( $data =~ /$pattern/ ) { ..... }
```

As the maintainer of CONFIG_FH, you need to convey Booleans through to the program using one configuration parameter.

Solution

True if either /ALPHA/ or /BETA/ matches, like /ALPHA/ || /BETA/:

```
/ALPHA|BETA/
/(?:ALPHA)|(?:BETA)/  # works no matter what in both
```

True if both /ALPHA/ and /BETA/ match, but may overlap, meaning "BETALPHA" should be okay, like /ALPHA/ && /BETA/:

```
/^(?=.*ALPHA)BETA/s
```

True if both /ALPHA/ and /BETA/ match, but may not overlap, meaning that "BETALPHA" should fail:

```
/ALPHA.*BETA|BETA.*ALPHA/s
```

True if pattern /PAT/ does not match, like $var !~ /PAT/:

```
/^(?:(?!PAT).)*$/s
```

True if pattern BAD does not match, but pattern GOOD does:

```
/(?=^(?:(?!BAD).)*$)GOOD/s
```

(You can't actually count on being able to place the /s modifier there after the trailing slash, but we'll show how to include it in the pattern itself at the end of the Discussion.)

Discussion

When in a normal program you want to know whether something *doesn't* match, use one of:

```
        if (!($string =~ /pattern/)) { something() }   # ugly
        if (  $string !~ /pattern/)  { something() }   # preferred
    unless (  $string =~ /pattern/)  { something() }   # sometimes clearer
```

To see whether both patterns match, use:

```
    if ($string =~ /pat1/ && $string =~ /pat2/ ) { something() }
```

To see whether either of two patterns matches:

```
    if ($string =~ /pat1/ || $string =~ /pat2/ ) { something() }
```

Instead of trying to do it all within a single pattern, it's often more efficient and clearer to use Perl's normal Boolean connectives to combine regular expressions. However, imagine a trivially short *minigrep* program that reads its single pattern as an argument, as shown in Example 6-9.

Example 6-9. minigrep

```
#!/usr/bin/perl
# minigrep - trivial grep
$pat = shift;
while (<>) {
    print if /$pat/o;
}
```

To tell *minigrep* that some pattern must not match, or that it has to match both subpatterns in any order, you're at an impasse. The program isn't built to accept multiple patterns. How can you do it using one pattern? This need comes up in programs reading patterns from configuration files.

The OR case is pretty easy, since the | metacharacter provides for alternation. The AND and NOT cases, however, are more complex.

For AND, you have to distinguish between overlapping and non-overlapping needs. If, for example, you want to see whether a string matches both "bell" and "lab" and allow overlapping, the word "labelled" should be matched. But if you don't want to count overlaps, it shouldn't be matched. The overlapping case uses a lookahead assertion:

```
"labelled" =~ /^(?=.*bell)lab/s
```

Remember: in a normal program, you don't have to go through these contortions. Simply say:

```
$string =~ /bell/ && $string =~ /lab/
```

To unravel this, we'll spell it out using /x and comments. Here's the long version:

```
if ($murray_hill =~ m{
                ^          # start of string
              (?=          # zero-width lookahead
                .*         # any amount of intervening stuff
                bell       # the desired bell string
              )            # rewind, since we were only looking
                lab        # and the lab part
            }sx )          # /s means . can match newline
{
    print "Looks like Bell Labs might be in Murray Hill!\n";
}
```

We didn't use .*? to end early, because minimal matching is more expensive than maximal matching. It's more efficient to use .* over .*?, given random input where the occurrence of matches at the front or the end of the string is completely unpredictable. Of course, sometimes choosing between .* and .*? may depend on correctness rather than efficiency, but not here.

To handle the non-overlapping case, you need two parts separated by an OR. The first branch is THIS followed by THAT; the second is the other way around:

```
"labelled" =~ /(?:^.*bell.*lab)|(?:^.*lab.*bell)/
```

or in long form:

```
$brand = "labelled";
if ($brand =~ m{
          (?:              # non-capturing grouper
              bell         # look for a bell
              .*?          # followed by any amount of anything
              lab          # look for a lab
          )                # end grouper
        |                  # otherwise, try the other direction
          (?:              # non-capturing grouper
              lab          # look for a lab
              .*?          # followed by any amount of anything
              bell         # followed by a bell
          )                # end grouper
        }sx )              # /s means . can match newline
{
    print "Our brand has bell and lab separate.\n";
}
```

Neither of those patterns matches the test data of "labelled", since there "bell" and "lab" *do* overlap.

These patterns aren't necessarily efficient. $murray_hill =~ /bell/ && $murray_hill =~ /lab/ scans the string at most twice, but the pattern-matching engine's only option is to try to find a "lab" for each occurrence of "bell" with (?=^.*?bell)(?=^.*?lab), leading to quadratic worst-case running times.

If you followed those examples, the NOT case should be a breeze. The general form looks like this:

```
$map =~ /^(?:(?!waldo).)*$/s
```

Spelled out in long form, this yields:

```
if ($map =~ m{
            ^                   # start of string
            (?:                 # clustering grouper
                (?!             # look ahead negation
                    waldo       # is he ahead of us now?
                )               # if so, the negation failed
                .               # any character (cuzza /s)
            ) *                 # repeat that grouping 0 or more
            $                   # through the end of the string
    }sx )                       # /s means . can match newline
{
    print "There's no waldo here!\n";
}
```

How would you combine AND, OR, and NOT? It's not a pretty picture, and in a regular program, you'd almost never do this. But you have little choice when you're reading from a config file or pulling in arguments from the command line, because you specify only one pattern. You just have to combine what we've learned so far. Carefully.

Let's say you wanted to run the Unix *w* program and find out whether user tchrist were logged on anywhere but a terminal whose name began with ttyp; that is, tchrist must match, but ttyp must not.

Here's sample input from *w*:

```
 7:15am  up 206 days, 13:30,  4 users,  load average: 1.04, 1.07, 1.04
USER     TTY     FROM            LOGIN@  IDLE   JCPU   PCPU  WHAT
tchrist  tty1                    5:16pm 36days 24:43   0.03s xinit
tchrist  tty2                    5:19pm  6days  0.43s  0.43s -tcsh
tchrist  ttyp0   chthon          7:58am  3days 23.44s  0.44s -tcsh
gnat     ttyS4   coprolith       2:01pm 13:36m  0.30s  0.30s -tcsh
```

Here's how to do that using the *minigrep* program previously outlined or with the *tcgrep* program from the end of this chapter:

```
% w | minigrep '(?!.*ttyp)tchrist'
```

Decoding that pattern:

```
m{
    (?!                     # zero-width look-ahead assertion
        .*                  # any amount of anything (faster than .*?)
        ttyp                # the string you don't want to find
    )                       # end look-ahead negation; rewind to start
```

```
    tchrist            # now try to find Tom
}x
```

Of course, this example is contrived: any sane person would call the standard *grep* program twice, once with a **-v** option to select only non-matches.

```
% w | grep tchrist | grep -v ttyp
```

The point is that Boolean conjunctions and negations *can* be coded up in one single pattern. You should comment this kind of thing, though, having pity on those who come after you—before they do.

One last thing: how would you embed that /s in a pattern passed to a program from the command line? The same way as you would a /i modifier: by using (?i) in the pattern. The /s and /m modifiers can be painlessly included in a pattern as well, using (?s) or (?m). These can even cluster, as in (?smi). That would make these two reasonably interchangeable:

```
% grep -i 'pattern' files
% minigrep '(?i)pattern' files
```

When you turn on a modifier that way, it remains on for the entire pattern. An alternative notation restricts the scope of the modifier. Use a clustering parenthesis set, (?:...), and place the modifiers between the question mark and the colon. Printing out a qr// quoted regex demonstrates how to do this:

```
% perl -le 'print qr/pattern/i'
(?i-xsm:pattern)
```

Modifiers placed before a minus are enabled for just that pattern; those placed after the minus are disabled for that pattern.

See Also

Lookahead assertions are shown in the "Regular Expressions" section of *perlre* (1), and in the "Lookaround Assertions" section of Chapter 5 of *Programming Perl*; your system's *grep*(1) and *w*(1) manpages; we talk about configuration files in Recipe 8.16

6.19 Matching a Valid Mail Address

Problem

You want to find a pattern to verify the validity of a supplied mail address.

Solution

Because you cannot do real-time validation of deliverable mail addresses, no single, succinct pattern will solve this problem. You must pick from several available compromise approaches.

Discussion

Our best advice for verifying a person's mail address is to have them enter their address twice, just as you would when changing a password. This usually weeds out typos. If both entries match, send mail to that address with a personal message such as:

```
Dear someuser@host.com,

Please confirm the mail address you gave us on Sun Jun 29
10:29:01 MDT 2003 by replying to this message.  Include the
string "Rumpelstiltskin" in that reply, but spelled in reverse;
that is, start with "Nik...".  Once this is done, your confirmed
address will be entered into our records.
```

If you get back a message where they've followed your directions, you can be reasonably assured that it's real.

A related strategy that's less open to forgery is to give them a personal identification number (PIN). Record the address and PIN (preferably a random one) for later processing. In the mail you send, ask them to include the PIN in their reply. In case your email bounces, or the message is included via a vacation script, ask them to mail back the PIN slightly altered, such as with the characters reversed, one added or subtracted to each digit, etc.

Most common patterns used for address verification or validation fail in various and sometimes subtle ways. For example, the address this&that@somewhere.com is valid and quite possibly deliverable, but most patterns that allegedly match valid mail addresses fail to let that one pass.

```
1 while $addr =~ s/\(([^()]*\)//g;
```

You *could* use the 6598-byte pattern given on the last page of the first edition of *Mastering Regular Expressions* to test for RFC conformance, but even that monster isn't perfect, for three reasons.

First, not all RFC-valid addresses are deliverable. For example, foo@foo.foo.foo.foo is valid in form, but in practice is not deliverable. Some people try to do DNS lookups for MX records, even trying to connect to the host handling that address's mail to check if it's valid at that site. This is a poor approach because most sites can't do a direct connect to any other site, and even if they could, mail-receiving sites increasingly either ignore the SMTP VRFY command or fib about its answer.

Second, some RFC-invalid addresses, in practice, are perfectly deliverable. For example, a lone postmaster is almost certainly deliverable, but doesn't pass RFC 822 muster: it doesn't have an @ in it.

Finally and most importantly, just because the address happens to be valid and deliverable doesn't mean that it's the right one. president@whitehouse.gov, for example, is valid by the RFC and deliverable. But it's unlikely in the extreme that that would be the mail address of the person submitting information to your CGI script.

The Email::Valid CPAN module makes a valiant (albeit provably imperfect) attempt at doing this correctly. It jumps through many hoops, including the RFC 822 regular expression from *Mastering Regular Expressions*, DNS MX record lookup, and stop lists for naughty words and famous people. But this is still a weak approach. The approach suggested at the beginning of the Discussion is easier to implement and less prone to error.

See Also

The "Matching an Email Address" section of Chapter 7 of the first edition *Mastering Regular Expressions*; Recipe 18.16

6.20 Matching Abbreviations

Problem

Suppose you had a list of commands, such as "send", "abort", "list", and "edit". The user types one in, but you don't want to make them type out the whole thing.

Solution

Use the following technique if all strings start with different characters, or to arrange matches so one takes precedence over another, as "SEND" has precedence over "STOP" here:

```
chomp($answer = <>);
if    ("SEND" =~ /^\Q$answer/i) { print "Action is send\n"  }
elsif ("STOP" =~ /^\Q$answer/i) { print "Action is stop\n"  }
elsif ("ABORT" =~ /^\Q$answer/i) { print "Action is abort\n" }
elsif ("LIST" =~ /^\Q$answer/i) { print "Action is list\n"  }
elsif ("EDIT" =~ /^\Q$answer/i) { print "Action is edit\n"  }
```

Or use the Text::Abbrev module:

```
use Text::Abbrev;
$href = abbrev qw(send abort list edit);
for (print "Action: "; <>; print "Action: ") {
    chomp;
    my $action = $href->{ lc($_) };
    print "Action is $action\n";
}
```

Discussion

The first technique exchanges the typical operand order of a match. Normally you have a variable on the left side of the match and a known pattern on the right side. We might try to decide which action the user wanted us to take by saying

$answer =~ /^ABORT/i, which is true if $answer begins with the string "ABORT". It matches regardless of whether $answer has anything after "ABORT", so "ABORT LATER" would still match. Handling abbreviations generally requires quite a bit of ugliness: $answer =~ /^A(B(O(R(T)?)?)?)?$/i.

Compare the classic variable =~ /pattern/ with "ABORT" =~ /^\Q$answer/i. The \Q escapes characters that would otherwise be treated specially: that way your program won't blow up if the user enters an invalid pattern. When the user enters something like "ab", the expanded match becomes "ABORT" =~ /^ab/i after variable substitution and metaquoting. This matches.

The standard Text::Abbrev module takes a different approach. You supply a list of words, and the abbrev( ) function returns a reference to a hash whose keys are all unambiguous abbreviations and whose values are the fully expanded strings. So if $href were created as in the Solution example, $href->{"a"} would return the string "abort".

This technique is commonly used to call a function based on the name of the string the user types in. Although it's possible to implement this using symbolic references, as in:

```
$name = 'send';
&$name($message);
$name->($message);    # alternate, simpler syntax
```

that's scary because it lets the user run any function whose name they know (or can guess), not just those we want to make available to them. It also runs afoul of that pesky use strict 'refs' pragma.

Here's a partial program that creates a hash in which the key is the command name and the value is a reference to the function to call for that command:

```
# assumes that &invoke_editor, &deliver_message,
# $file and $PAGER are defined somewhere else.
use Text::Abbrev;
my($href, %actions, $errors);
%actions = (
    "edit"  => \&invoke_editor,
    "send"  => \&deliver_message,
    "list"  => sub { system($PAGER, $file) },
    "abort" => sub {
                    print "See ya!\n";
                    exit;
               },
    ""      => sub {
                    print "Unknown command: $cmd\n";
                    $errors++;
               },
);

$href = abbrev(keys %actions);
for (print "Action: "; my $choice = <>; print "Action: ") {
```

```
        $choice =~ s/^\s+//;        # trim leading  white space
        $choice =~ s/\s+$//;        # trim trailing white space
        next unless $choice;
        $actions->{ $href->{ lc($choice) } }->();
    }
```

If you're not into long expressions or need practice typing, that last statement could
have been written:

```
    $abbreviation = lc($_);
    $expansion    = $href->{$abbreviation};
    $coderef      = $actions->{$expansion};
    $coderef->();
```

See Also

The documentation for the standard Text::Abbrev module; interpolation is
explained in the "Scalar Value Constructors" section of *perldata*(1), and in the
"String Literals" section of Chapter 2 of *Programming Perl*

6.21 Program: urlify

This program puts HTML links around URLs in files. It doesn't work on all possible
URLs, but does hit the most common ones. It tries to avoid including end-of-sen-
tence punctuation in the marked-up URL.

It is a typical Perl filter, so it can be fed input from a pipe:

```
    % gunzip -c ~/mail/archive.gz | urlify > archive.urlified
```

or by supplying files on the command line:

```
    % urlify ~/mail/*.inbox > ~/allmail.urlified
```

The program is shown in Example 6-10.

Example 6-10. urlify

```
#!/usr/bin/perl
# urlify - wrap HTML links around URL-like constructs
$protos = '(http|telnet|gopher|file|wais|ftp)';
$ltrs  = '\w';
$gunk  = ';/#~:.?+=&%@!\-';
$punc  = '.:?\-';
$any   = "${ltrs}${gunk}${punc}";
while (<>) {
    s{
      \b                      # start at word boundary
      (                       # begin $1  {
       $protos    :           # need resource and a colon
       [$any] +?              # followed by on or more
                              #  of any valid character, but
                              #  be conservative and take only
                              #  what you need to....
```

Example 6-10. urlify (continued)

```
        )                        # end   $1  }
        (?=                      # look-ahead non-consumptive assertion
        [$punc]*                 # either 0 or more punctuation
        [^$any]                  #   followed by a non-url char
        |                        # or else
        $                        #   then end of the string
      )
    }{<A HREF="$1">$1</A>}igox;
    print;
}
```

6.22 Program: tcgrep

This program is a Perl rewrite of the Unix *grep* program. Although it runs slower than C versions (especially the GNU *grep*s), it offers many more features.

The first and perhaps most important feature is that it runs anywhere Perl does. Other enhancements are that it can ignore anything that's not a plain text file, automatically expand compressed or *gzip*ped files, recurse down directories, search complete paragraphs or user-defined records, look in younger files before older ones, and add underlining or highlighting of matches. It also supports the **-c** option to indicate a count of matching records, as well as **-C** for a count of matching patterns when there could be more than one per record.

This program uses *gzcat* or *zcat* to decompress compressed files, so this feature is unavailable on systems without these programs and systems that can't run external programs (such as old Macs).

Run the program with no arguments for a usage message (see the usage subroutine in the following code). The following example recursively and case-insensitively greps every file in *~/mail* for mail messages from someone called "kate", reporting filenames that contained matches:

```
% tcgrep -ril '^From: .*kate' ~/mail
```

The program is shown in Example 6-11.

Example 6-11. tcgrep

```
#!/usr/bin/perl -w
# tcgrep: tom christiansen's rewrite of grep
# v1.0: Thu Sep 30 16:24:43 MDT 1993
# v1.1: Fri Oct  1 08:33:43 MDT 1993
# v1.2: Fri Jul 26 13:37:02 CDT 1996
# v1.3: Sat Aug 30 14:21:47 CDT 1997
# v1.4: Mon May 18 16:17:48 EDT 1998
use strict;
                              # globals
our ($Me, $Errors, $Grand_Total, $Mult, %Compress, $Matches);
my ($matcher, $opt);          # matcher - anon. sub to check for matches
                              # opt - ref to hash w/ command-line options
```

Example 6-11. tcgrep (continued)

```perl
    init();                         # initialize globals
    ($opt, $matcher) = parse_args(); # get command line options and patterns
    matchfile($opt, $matcher, @ARGV); # process files
    exit(2) if $Errors;
    exit(0) if $Grand_Total;
    exit(1);
    ##################################
    sub init {
        ($Me = $0) =~ s!.*/!!;       # get basename of program, "tcgrep"
        $Errors = $Grand_Total = 0;  # initialize global counters
        $Mult = "";                  # flag for multiple files in @ARGV
        $| = 1;                      # autoflush output
        %Compress = (                # file extensions and program names
            z  => 'gzcat',           # for uncompressing
            gz => 'gzcat',
            Z  => 'zcat',
        );
    }
    ##################################
    sub usage {
            die << EOF
    usage: $Me [flags] [files]
    Standard grep options:
            i    case insensitive
            n    number lines
            c    give count of lines matching
            C    ditto, but >1 match per line possible
            w    word boundaries only
            s    silent mode
            x    exact matches only
            v    invert search sense (lines that DON'T match)
            h    hide filenames
            e    expression (for exprs beginning with -)
            f    file with expressions
            l    list filenames matching
    Specials:
            1    1 match per file
            H    highlight matches
            u    underline matches
            r    recursive on directories or dot if none
            t    process directories in 'ls -t' order
            p    paragraph mode (default: line mode)
            P    ditto, but specify separator, e.g. -P '%%\\n'
            a    all files, not just plain text files
            q    quiet about failed file and dir opens
            T    trace files as opened
    May use a TCGREP environment variable to set default options.
    EOF
    }
    ##################################
    sub parse_args {
        use Getopt::Std;
        my ($optstring, $zeros, $nulls, %opt, $pattern, @patterns, $match_code);
```

Example 6-11. tcgrep (continued)

```perl
my ($SO, $SE);
if (my $opts = $ENV{TCGREP}) {    # get envariable TCGREP
    $opts =~ s/^([^\-])/-$1/;     # add leading - if missing
    unshift(@ARGV, $opts);        # add TCGREP opt string to @ARGV
}
$optstring = "incCwsxvhe:f:l1HurtpP:aqT";
$zeros = 'inCwxvhelut';       # options to init to 0
$nulls = 'pP';                # options to init to ""
@opt{ split //, $zeros } = ( 0 )  x length($zeros);
@opt{ split //, $nulls } = ( '' ) x length($nulls);
getopts($optstring, \%opt)              or usage();
# handle option "-f patfile", for list of patterns
if ($opt{f}) {
    open(PATFILE, $opt{f})          or die "$Me: Can't open '$opt{f}': $!";
    # make sure each pattern in file is valid
    while ($pattern = <PATFILE>) {
        chomp $pattern;
        eval { 'foo' =~ /$pattern/, 1 } or
            die "$Me: $opt{f}:$.: bad pattern: $@";
        push @patterns, $pattern;
    }
    close PATFILE;
}
else {                              # make sure pattern is valid
    $pattern = $opt{e} || shift(@ARGV) || usage();
    eval { 'foo' =~ /$pattern/; 1 } or
        die "$Me: bad pattern: $@";
    @patterns = ($pattern);
}
# option -H is for highlight, option -u is for underline
if ($opt{H} || $opt{u}) {
    my $term = $ENV{TERM} || 'vt100';
    my $terminal;
    # eval{} only to trap potential exceptions in function calls
    eval {                    # try to look up escapes for stand-out
        require POSIX;        # or underline via Term::Cap
        use Term::Cap;
        my $termios = POSIX::Termios->new();
        $termios->getattr;
        my $ospeed = $termios->getospeed;
        $terminal = Tgetent Term::Cap { TERM=>undef, OSPEED=>$ospeed }
    };
    unless ($@) {             # if successful, get escapes for either
        local $^W = 0;        # stand-out (-H) or underlined (-u)
        ($SO, $SE) = $opt{H}
            ? ($terminal->Tputs('so'), $terminal->Tputs('se'))
            : ($terminal->Tputs('us'), $terminal->Tputs('ue'));
    }
    else {                    # if use of Term::Cap fails,
        ($SO, $SE) = $opt{H}  # use tput command to get escapes
            ? (`tput -T $term smso`, `tput -T $term rmso`)
            : (`tput -T $term smul`, `tput -T $term rmul`)
    }
```

Example 6-11. tcgrep (continued)

```
}
# option -i makes all pattern case insensitive
if ($opt{i}) {
    @patterns = map {"(?i)$_"} @patterns;
}
# option -p or -P is paragraph mode, so add /m
if ($opt{p} || $opt{P}) {
    @patterns = map {"(?m)$_"} @patterns;
}
# option -p is standard paragraph mode
$opt{p}    && ($/ = '');
# option -p is user-defined paragraph mode
$opt{P}    && ($/ = eval(qq("$opt{P}")));      # for -P '%%\n'
# option -w is at word boundary only (XXX: is this always optimal?)
$opt{w}    && (@patterns = map {'\b' . $_ . '\b'} @patterns);
# option -x is for whole lines only
$opt{'x'} && (@patterns = map {"^$_\$"} @patterns);
# determine whether to emit file name in front of each match
if (@ARGV) {
    $Mult = 1 if ($opt{r} || (@ARGV > 1) || -d $ARGV[0]) && !$opt{h};
}
# if just listing filenames, stop after first match
$opt{1}    += $opt{l};                    # that's a one and an ell
# this way only need look for -H
$opt{H}    += $opt{u};
# if we're doing a complete count, where doing some counting
$opt{c}    += $opt{C};
# if we're counting, keep track of status
$opt{'s'} += $opt{c};
# stop at first match if checking status but not counting
$opt{1}    += $opt{'s'} && !$opt{c};      # that's a one
# default args are cwd if recursive, stdin otherwise
@ARGV = ($opt{r} ? '.' : '-') unless @ARGV;
# we're recursive even w/o -r if all args are directories
$opt{r} = 1 if !$opt{r} && grep(-d, @ARGV) == @ARGV;
######
# now the hard part: build of the matching function as text to eval
#
$match_code  = '';
$match_code .= 'study;' if @patterns > 5; # might speed things up a bit
foreach (@patterns) { s(/)(\\/)g }
# add the stand-out and end-stand-out sequences for highlight mode
if ($opt{H}) {
    foreach $pattern (@patterns) {
        $match_code .= "\$Matches += s/($pattern)/${SO}\$1${SE}/g;";
    }
}
# option -v means to count a line if it *doesn't* match
elsif ($opt{v}) {
    foreach $pattern (@patterns) {
        $match_code .= "\$Matches += !/$pattern/;";
    }
}
```

Example 6-11. tcgrep (continued)

```perl
        # do full count, multiple hits per line
        elsif ($opt{C}) {
            foreach $pattern (@patterns) {
                $match_code .= "\$Matches++ while /$pattern/g;";
            }
        }
        else {
            foreach $pattern (@patterns) {
                $match_code .= "\$Matches++ if /$pattern/;";
            }
        }
        # now compile as a closure, and grab function pointer
        $matcher = eval "sub { $match_code }";
        die if $@;
        return (\%opt, $matcher);
}
##################################
sub matchfile {
    $opt = shift;                   # reference to option hash
    $matcher = shift;               # reference to matching sub
    my ($file, @list, $total, $name);
    local($_);
    $total = 0;
FILE: while (defined ($file = shift(@_))) {
        if (-d $file) {
            if (-l $file && @ARGV != 1) {
                warn "$Me: \"$file\" is a symlink to a directory\n"
                    if $opt->{T};
                next FILE;
            }
            if (!$opt->{r}) {
                warn "$Me: \"$file\" is a directory, but no -r given\n"
                    if $opt->{T};
                next FILE;
            }
            unless (opendir(DIR, $file)) {
                unless ($opt->{'q'}) {
                    warn "$Me: can't opendir $file: $!\n";
                    $Errors++;
                }
                next FILE;
            }
            @list = ();
            for (readdir(DIR)) {                    # skip cwd and parent dir
                push(@list, "$file/$_") unless /^\.{1,2}$/;
            }
            closedir(DIR);
            # option -t is sort by age, youngest first
            # use algorithm from Recipe 4.XXX, Sorting a List by Computable Field
            if ($opt->{t}) {
                @list = map  { $_->[0] }
                        sort { $a->[1] <=> $b->[1] }
                        map  { [ $_, -M $_ ] } @list;
```

Example 6-11. tcgrep (continued)

```perl
        }
        else {
            @list = sort @list;
        }
        matchfile($opt, $matcher, @list);    # process files
        next FILE;
    }
    # avoid annoying situation of grep wanting to read from keyboard
    # but user not realizing this
    if ($file eq '-') {
        warn "$Me: reading from stdin\n" if -t STDIN && !$opt->{'q'};
        $name = '<STDIN>';
    }
    else {
        $name = $file;
        unless (-e $file) {
            warn qq($Me: file "$file" does not exist\n) unless $opt->{'q'};
            $Errors++;
            next FILE;
        }
        unless (-f $file || $opt->{a}) {
            warn qq($Me: skipping non-plain file "$file"\n) if $opt->{T};
            next FILE;
        }
        # could use File::Spec instead
        my ($ext) = $file =~ /\.([^.]+)$/;
        # check whether it's an extension whose contents we know
        # how to convert to plain text via a filter program
        if (defined($ext) && exists($Compress{$ext})) {
            $file = "$Compress{$ext} < $file |";
        }
        elsif (! (-T $file   || $opt->{a})) {
            warn qq($Me: skipping binary file "$file"\n) if $opt->{T};
            next FILE;
        }
    }
    warn "$Me: checking $file\n" if $opt->{T};
    unless (open(FILE, $file)) {
        unless ($opt->{'q'}) {
            warn "$Me: $file: $!\n";
            $Errors++;
        }
        next FILE;
    }
    $total = 0;
    $Matches = 0;
LINE: while (<FILE>) {
        $Matches = 0;
        #############
        &{$matcher}();          # do it! (check for matches)
        #############
        next LINE unless $Matches;
```

Example 6-11. tcgrep (continued)

```
                $total += $Matches;
                if ($opt->{p} || $opt->{P}) {
                  s/\n{2,}$/\n/ if $opt->{p};
                  chomp        if $opt->{P};
                }
                print("$name\n"), next FILE if $opt->{l};
                # The following commented out block is the
                # expanded/legible version of the statement
                # that immediately follows it.  This is one
                # of the few times we sacrifice readability
                # for execution speed: we carefully arrange
                # that print() be called just once, not four times,
                # and we don't resort to a braced block either.
                # (note that $Mult must be "" not 0 for this to work)
                ########
                ## unless ($opt->{'s'}) {
                ##    print "$name:"                 if $Mult;
                ##    print "$.:"                    if $opt{n};
                ##    print;
                ##    print (('-' x 20) . "\n")      if $opt->{p} || $opt->{P};
                ## }
                ########
                $opt->{'s'} || print $Mult && "$name:",
                    $opt->{n} ? "$.:" : "",
                    $_,
                    ($opt->{p} || $opt->{P}) && ('-' x 20) . "\n";
                next FILE if $opt->{l};                 # that's a one
            }
        }
        continue {
            # again, next block equivalent to line following
            #######
            ## if ($opt->{c}) {
            ##        print $name if $Mult;
            ##        print "$total\n";
            ## }
            #######
            print $Mult && "$name:", "$total\n" if $opt->{c};
        }
        $Grand_Total += $total;
    }
```

6.23   Regular Expression Grab Bag

We have found these regular expressions useful or interesting:

Swap first two words

```
        s/(\S+)(\s+)(\S+)/$3$2$1/
```

Keyword = Value

```
        m/^(\w+)\s*=\s*(.*?)\s*$/              # keyword is $1, value is $2
```

Line of at least 80 characters

```
m/.{80,}/
length( ) >= 80        # ok, not a regex
```

MM/DD/YY HH:MM:SS

```
m|(\d+)/(\d+)/(\d+) (\d+):(\d+):(\d+)|
```

Changing directories

```
s(/usr/bin)(/usr/local/bin)g
```

Expanding %7E (hex) escapes

```
s/%([0-9A-Fa-f][0-9A-Fa-f])/chr(hex($1))/ge
```

Deleting C comments (imperfectly)

```
s{
    /*                      # Match the opening delimiter
    .*?                     # Match a minimal number of characters
    */                      # Match the closing delimiter
}{ }gsx;
```

Removing leading and trailing whitespace

```
s/^\s+//;
s/\s+$//;
```

Turning \ followed by n into a real newline

```
s/\\n/\n/g;
```

Removing package portion of fully qualified symbols

```
s/^.*:://
```

Dotted quads (most IP addresses)

```
# XXX: fails on legal IPs 127.1 and 2130706433.
m{
        ^  ( \d | [01]?\d\d | 2[0-4]\d | 25[0-5] )
        \. ( \d | [01]?\d\d | 2[0-4]\d | 25[0-5] )
        \. ( \d | [01]?\d\d | 2[0-4]\d | 25[0-5] )
        \. ( \d | [01]?\d\d | 2[0-4]\d | 25[0-5] )
        $
}x
```

Removing leading path from filename

```
s{^.*/}{ }
```

Extracting columns setting from TERMCAP

```
$cols = ( ($ENV{TERMCAP} || " ") =~ m/:co#(\d+):/ ) ? $1 : 80;
```

Removing directory components from program name and arguments

```
($name = " $0 @ARGV") =~ s{ /\S+/}{ }g;
```

Checking your operating system

```
die "This isn't Linux" unless $^O =~ m/linux/i;
```

Joining continuation lines in multiline string

```
s/\n\s+/ /g
```

Extracting all numbers from a string

```
@nums = m/(\d+\.?\d*|\.\d+)/g;
```

Finding all-caps words

```
@capwords = m/(\b\p{ Upper-case Letter }+\b)/g;
```

Finding all-lowercase words

```
@lowords = m/(\b\p{ Lower-case Letter }+\b)/g;
```

Finding initial-caps word

```
@icwords = m{
    ( \b
        [\p{ Upper-case Letter }\p{ Title-case Letter }]
        \p{ Lower-case Letter } *
    \b )
}gx;
```

Finding links in simple HTML

```
@links = m/<A[^>]+?HREF\s*=\s*["'"']?([^'" >]+?)['"']?\s*>/ig;
```

Finding middle initial in $_

```
$initial = /^\S+\s+(\S)\S*\s+\S/ ? $1 : "";
```

Changing double vertical prime pairs to curly quotes

```
s/"([^"]*)"/``$1''/g                          # old way

# next is unicode only
s/"([^"]*)"/\x{201C}\x{201C}$1\x{201D}\x{201D}/g
```

Extracting sentences (double spaces required between each)

```
{ local $/ = "";
    while (<>) {
        s/\n/ /g;
        s/ {3,}/ /g;
        push @sentences, m/(\S.*?[!?.])(?= {2}|\Z)/g;
    }
}
```

YYYY-MM-DD

```
m/\b(\d{4})-(\d\d)-(\d\d)\b/            # YYYY in $1, MM in $2, DD in $3
```

North American telephone numbers

```
m/ ^
        (?:
        1 \s (?: \d\d\d \s)?          # 1, or 1 and area code
        |                             # ... or ...
        \(\d\d\d\) \s                 # area code with parens
        |                             # ... or ...
        (?: \+\d\d?\d? \s)?           # optional +country code
        \d\d\d ([\s\-])               # and area code
        )
        \d\d\d (\s|\1)                # prefix (and area code separator)
        \d\d\d\d                      # exchange
        $
    /x
```

Exclamations

```
m/\boh\s+my\s+gh?o(d(dess(es)?|s?)|odness|sh)\b/i
```

Extracting lines regardless of line terminator

```
push(@lines, $1) while $input =~ s{
    ^                                 # gobble from front

    (
```

```
              .                        # begin $1: any single char (/s)
         ?*                          # but minimally matching even none
      )

     (?:                               # make capturing if saving terminators
          \x0D \x0A             # CRLF
      |   \x0A            # LF
      |   \x0D            # CR
      |   \x0C            # FF
   # (see http://www.unicode.org/reports/tr13/tr13-9.html)
      |   \x{2028}              # Unicode LS
      |   \x{2029}              # Unicode PS
     )
   }{ }sx;                   # consumes $input
```

Or use split:

```
   @lines = split m{
     (?:                               # make capturing if saving terminators
          \x0D \x0A             # CRLF
      |   \x0A            # LF
      |   \x0D            # CR
      |   \x0C            # FF
   # (see http://www.unicode.org/reports/tr13/tr13-9.html)
      |   \x{2028}              # Unicode LS
      |   \x{2029}              # Unicode PS
     )
   }x, $input;
```

## CHAPTER 7

File Access

I the heir of all ages, in the foremost files of time.
—Alfred, Lord Tennyson, *Locksley Hall*

7.0 Introduction

Nothing is more central to data processing than the file. As with everything else in Perl, easy things are easy and hard things are possible. Common tasks (opening files, reading data, writing data) use simple I/O functions and operators, whereas fancier functions do hard things like non-blocking I/O and file locking.

This chapter deals with the mechanics of file *access*: opening a file, telling subroutines which files to work with, locking files, and so on. Chapter 8 deals with techniques for working with the *contents* of a file: reading, writing, shuffling lines, and other operations you can do once you have access to the file.

Here's Perl code for printing all lines from the file */usr/local/widgets/data* that contain the word "blue":

```
open(INPUT, "<", "/acme/widgets/data")
    or die "Couldn't open /acme/widgets/data for reading: $!\n";
while (<INPUT>) {
    print if /blue/;
}
close(INPUT);
```

Getting a Handle on the File

Central to file access in Perl is the *filehandle*, like INPUT in the previous code example. Filehandles are symbols inside your Perl program that you associate with an external file, usually using the open function. Whenever your program performs an input or output operation, it provides that operation with an internal filehandle, not an external filename. It's the job of open to make that association, and of close to break it. Actually, any of several functions can be used to open files, and handles can refer to entities beyond mere files on disk; see Recipe 7.1 for details.

While users think of open files in terms of those files' names, Perl programs do so using their filehandles. But as far as the operating system itself is concerned, an open file is nothing more than a *file descriptor*, which is a small, non-negative integer. The fileno function divulges the system file descriptor of its filehandle argument. Filehandles are enough for most file operations, but for when they aren't, Recipe 7.9 turns a system file descriptor into a filehandle you can use from Perl.

Like the names for labels, subroutines, and packages, those for filehandles are unadorned symbols like INPUT, not variables like $input. However, with a few syntactic restrictions, Perl also accepts in lieu of a named filehandle a scalar expression that evaluates to a filehandle—or to something that passes for a filehandle, such as a typeglob, a reference to a typeglob, or an IO object. Typically, this entails storing the filehandle's typeglob in a scalar variable and then using that variable as an indirect filehandle. Code written this way can be simpler than code using named filehandles, because now that you're working with regular variables instead of names, certain untidy and unobvious issues involving quoting, scoping, and packages all become clearer.

As of the v5.6 release, Perl can be coaxed into implicitly initializing variables used as indirect filehandles. If you supply a function expecting to initialize a filehandle (like open) with an undefined scalar, that function automatically allocates an anonymous typeglob and stores its reference into the previously undefined variable—a tongue-twisting description normally abbreviated to something more along the lines of, "Perl autovivifies filehandles passed to open as undefined scalars."

```
my $input;                              # new lexical starts out undef
open($input, "<", "/acme/widgets/data")
    or die "Couldn't open /acme/widgets/data for reading: $!\n";
while (<$input>) {
    print if /blue/;
}
close($input);                          # also occurs when $input GC'd
```

For more about references and their autovivification, see Chapter 11. That chapter deals more with customary data references, though, than it does with exotics like the typeglob references seen here.

Having open autovivify a filehandle is only one of several ways to get indirect filehandles. We show different ways of loading up variables with named filehandles and several esoteric equivalents for later use as indirect filehandles in Recipe 7.5.

Some recipes in this chapter use filehandles along with the standard IO::Handle module, and sometimes with the IO::File module. Object constructors from these classes return new objects for use as indirect filehandles anywhere a regular handle would go, such as with built-ins like print, readline, close, <FH>, etc. You can likewise invoke any IO::Handle method on your regular, unblessed filehandles. This includes autovivified handles and even named ones like INPUT or STDIN, although none of these has been blessed as an object.

Method invocation syntax is visually noisier than the equivalent Perl function call, and incurs some performance penalty compared with a function call (where an equivalent function exists). We generally restrict our method use to those providing functionality that would otherwise be difficult or impossible to achieve in pure Perl without resorting to modules.

For example, the blocking method sets or disables blocking on a filehandle, a pleasant alternative to the Fcntl wizardry that at least one of the authors and probably most of the readership would prefer not having to know. This forms the basis of Recipe 7.20.

Most methods are in the IO::Handle class, which IO::File inherits from, and can even be applied directly to filehandles that aren't objects. They need only be something that Perl will accept as a filehandle. For example:

```
STDIN->blocking(0);                 # invoke on named handle
open($fh, "<", $filename) or die;   # first autovivify handle, then...
$fh->blocking(0);                   # invoke on unblessed typeglob ref
```

Like most names in Perl, including those of subroutines and global variables, named filehandles reside in packages. That way, two packages can have filehandles of the same name. When unqualified by package, a named filehandle has a full name that starts with the current package. Writing INPUT is really main::INPUT in the main package, but it's SomeMod::INPUT if you're in a hypothetical SomeMod package.

The built-in filehandles STDIN, STDOUT, and STDERR are special. If they are left unqualified, the main package rather than the current one is used. This is the same exception to normal rules for finding the full name that occurs with built-in variables like @ARGV and %ENV, a topic discussed in the Introduction to Chapter 12.

Unlike named filehandles, which are global symbols within the package, autovivified filehandles implicitly allocated by Perl are anonymous (i.e., nameless) and have no package of their own. More interestingly, they are also like other references in being subject to automatic garbage collection. When a variable holding them goes out of scope and no other copies or references to that variable or its value have been saved away somewhere more lasting, the garbage collection system kicks in, and Perl implicitly closes the handle for you (if you haven't yet done so yourself). This is important in large or long-running programs, because the operating system imposes a limit on how many underlying file descriptors any process can have open—and usually also on how many descriptors can be open across the entire system.

In other words, just as real system memory is a finite resource that you can exhaust if you don't carefully clean up after yourself, the same is true of system file descriptors. If you keep opening new filehandles forever without ever closing them, you'll eventually run out, at which point your program will die if you're lucky or careful, and malfunction if you're not. The implicit close during garbage collection of autoallocated filehandles spares you the headaches that can result from less than perfect bookkeeping.

For example, these two functions both autovivify filehandles into distinct lexical variables of the same name:

```
sub versive {
    open(my $fh, "<", $SOURCE)
        or die "can't open $SOURCE: $!";
    return $fh;
}

sub apparent {
    open(my $fh, ">", $TARGET)
        or die "can't open $TARGET: $!";
    return $fh;
}

my($from, to) = ( versive(), apparent() );
```

Normally, the handles in $fh would be closed implicitly when each function returns. But since both functions return those values, the handles will stay open a while longer. They remain open until explicitly closed, or until the $from and $to variables and any copies you make all go out of scope—at which point Perl dutifully tidies up by closing them if they've been left open.

For buffered handles with internal buffers containing unwritten data, a more valuable benefit shows up. Because a flush precedes a close, this guarantees that all data finally makes it to where you thought it was going in the first place.* For global filehandle names, this implicit flush and close takes place on final program exit, but it is not forgotten.†

Standard Filehandles

Every program starts with three standard filehandles already open: STDIN, STDOUT, and STDERR. STDIN, typically pronounced *standard in*, represents the default source for data flowing *into* a program. STDOUT, typically pronounced *standard out*, represents the default destination for data flowing *out* from a program. Unless otherwise redirected, standard input will be read directly from your keyboard, and standard output will be written directly to your screen.

One need not be so direct about matters, however. Here we tell the shell to redirect your program's standard input to *datafile* and its standard output to *resultsfile*, all before your program even starts:

---

* Or at least tries to; currently, no error is reported if the implicit write syscall should fail at this stage, which might occur if, for example, the filesystem the open file was on has run out of space.
† Unless you exit by way of an uncaught signal, either by execing another program or by calling POSIX::_exit().

```
% program < datafile > resultsfile
```

Suppose something goes wrong in your program that you need to report. If your standard output has been redirected, the person running your program probably wouldn't notice a message that appeared in this output. These are the precise circumstances for which STDERR, typically pronounced *standard error*, was devised. Like STDOUT, STDERR is initially directed to your screen, but if you redirect STDOUT to a file or pipe, STDERR's destination remains unchanged. That way you always have a standard way to get warnings or errors through to where they're likely to do some good.

Unlike STDERR for STDOUT, for STDIN there's no preopened filehandle for times when STDIN has been redirected. That's because this need arises much less frequently than does the need for a coherent and reliable diagnostic stream. Rarely, your program may need to ask something of whoever ran it and read their response, even in the face of redirection. The *more*(1) and *less*(1) programs do this, for example, because their STDINs are often pipes from other programs whose long output you want to see a page at a time. On Unix systems, open the special file */dev/tty*, which represents the controlling device for this login session. The open fails if the program has no controlling tty, which is the system's way of reporting that there's no one for your program to communicate with.

This arrangement makes it easy to plug the output from one program into the input of the next, and so on down the line.

```
% first | second | third
```

That means to apply the first program to the input of the second, and the output of the second as the input of the third. You might not realize it at first, but this is the same logic as seen when stacking function calls like *third(second(first()))*, although the shell's pipeline is a bit easier to read because the transformations proceed from left to right instead of from inside the expression to outside.

Under the uniform I/O interface of standard input and output, each program can be independently developed, tested, updated, and executed without risk of one program interfering with another, but they will still easily interoperate. They act as tools or parts used to build larger constructs, or as separate stages in a larger manufacturing process. Like having a huge stock of ready-made, interchangeable parts on hand, they can be reliably assembled into larger sequences of arbitrary length and complexity. If the larger sequences (call them scripts) are given names by being placed into executable scripts indistinguishable from the store-bought parts, they can then go on to take part in still larger sequences as though they were basic tools themselves.

An environment where every data-transformation program does one thing well and where data flows from one program to the next through redirectable standard input and output streams is one that strongly encourages a level of power, flexibility, and reliability in software design that could not be achieved otherwise. This, in a nutshell, is the so-called tool-and-filter philosophy that underlies the design of not only the Unix shell but the entire operating system. Although problem domains do exist where this model breaks down—and Perl owes its very existence to plugging one of several infelicities the model forces on you—it is a model that has nevertheless demonstrated its fundamental soundness and scalability for nearly 30 years.

I/O Operations

Perl's most common operations for file interaction are open, print, <FH> to read a record, and close. Perl's I/O functions are documented in Chapter 29 of *Programming Perl*, and in the *perlfunc*(1) and *perlopentut*(1) manpages. The next chapter details I/O operations like <FH>, print, seek, and tell. This chapter focuses on open and how you access the data, rather than what you do with the data.

Arguably the most important I/O function is open. You typically pass it two or three arguments: the filehandle, a string containing the access mode indicating how to open the file (for reading, writing, appending, etc.), and a string containing the filename. If two arguments are passed, the second contains both the access mode and the filename jammed together. We use this conflation of mode and path to good effect in Recipe 7.14.

To open */tmp/log* for writing and to associate it with the filehandle LOGFILE, say:

```
open(LOGFILE, "> /tmp/log")     or die "Can't write /tmp/log: $!";
```

The three most common access modes are < for reading, > for overwriting, and >> for appending. The open function is discussed in more detail in Recipe 7.1. Access modes can also include I/O layers like :raw and :encoding(iso-8859-1). Later in this Introduction we discuss I/O layers to control buffering, deferring until Chapter 8 the use of I/O layers to convert the contents of files as they're read.

When opening a file or making virtually any other system call,* checking the return value is indispensable. Not every open succeeds; not every file is readable; not every piece of data you print reaches its destination. Most programmers check open, seek, tell, and close in robust programs. You might want to check other functions, too.

If a function is documented to return an error under such and such conditions, and you don't check for these conditions, then this will certainly come back to haunt you someday. The Perl documentation lists return values from all functions and operators. Pay special attention to the glyph-like annotations in Chapter 29 of *Programming Perl* that are listed on the righthand side next to each function call entry—they tell you at a glance which variables are set on error and which conditions trigger exceptions.

---

* The term *system call* denotes a call into your operating system kernel. It is unrelated to the C and Perl function that's actually named system. We'll therefore often call these *syscalls*, after the C and Perl function of that name.

Typically, a function that's a true system call fails by returning undef, except for wait, waitpid, and syscall, which all return -1 on failure. You can find the system error message as a string and its corresponding numeric code in the $! variable. This is often used in die or warn messages.

The most common input operation in Perl is <FH>, the line input operator. Instead of sitting *in* the middle of its operands the way *in*fix operators are, the line input operator *sur*rounds its filehandle operand, making it more of a *circ*umfix operator, like parentheses. It's also known as the angle operator because of the left- and right-angle brackets that compose it, or as the readline function, since that's the underlying Perl core function that it calls.

A record is normally a line, but you can change the record terminator, as detailed in Chapter 8. If FH is omitted, it defaults to the special filehandle, ARGV. When you read from this handle, Perl opens and reads in succession data from those filenames listed in @ARGV, or from STDIN if @ARGV is empty. Customary and curious uses of this are described in Recipe 7.14.

At one abstraction level, files are simply streams of octets; that is, of eight-bit bytes. Of course, hardware may impose other organizations, such as blocks and sectors for files on disk or individual IP packets for a TCP connection on a network, but the operating system thankfully hides such low-level details from you.

At a higher abstraction level, files are a stream of logical characters independent of any particular underlying physical representation. Because Perl programs most often deal with text strings containing characters, this is the default set by open when accessing filehandles. See the Introduction to Chapter 8 or Recipe 8.11 for how and when to change that default.

Each filehandle has a numeric value associated with it, typically called its seek offset, representing the position at which the next I/O operation will occur. If you're thinking of files as octet streams, it's how many octets you are from the beginning of the file, with the starting offset represented by 0. This position is implicitly updated whenever you read or write non-zero-length data on a handle. It can also be updated explicitly with the seek function.

Text files are a slightly higher level of abstraction than octet streams. The number of octets need not be identical to the number of characters. Unless you take special action, Perl's filehandles are logical streams of characters, not physical streams of octets. The only time those two numbers (characters and octets) are the same in text files is when each character read or written fits comfortably in one octet (because all code points are below 256), and when no special processing for end of line (such as conversion between "\cJ\cM" and "\n") occurs. Only then do logical character position and physical byte position work out to be the same.

This is the sort of file you have with ASCII or Latin1 text files under Unix, where no fundamental distinction exists between text and binary files, which significantly simplifies programming. Unfortunately, 7-bit ASCII text is no longer prevalent, and even

8-bit encodings of ISO 8859-*n* are quickly giving way to multibyte-encoded Unicode text.

In other words, because encoding layers such as ":utf8" and translation layers such as ":crlf" can change the number of bytes transferred between your program and the outside world, you cannot sum up how many characters you've transferred to infer your current file position in bytes. As explained in Chapter 1, characters are not bytes—at least, not necessarily and not dependably. Instead, you must use the tell function to retrieve your current file position. For the same reason, only values returned from tell (and the number 0) are guaranteed to be suitable for passing to seek.

In Recipe 7.17, we read the entire contents of a file opened in update mode into memory, change our internal copy, and then seek back to the beginning of that file to write those modifications out again, thereby overwriting what we started with.

When you no longer have use for a filehandle, close it. The close function takes a single filehandle and returns true if the filehandle could be successfully flushed and closed, and returns false otherwise. You don't need to explicitly close every filehandle. When you open a filehandle that's already open, Perl implicitly closes it first. When your program exits, any open filehandles also get closed.

These implicit closes are for convenience, not stability, because they don't tell you whether the syscall succeeded or failed. Not all closes succeed, and even a close on a read-only file can fail. For instance, you could lose access to the device because of a network outage. It's even more important to check the close if the file was opened for writing; otherwise, you wouldn't notice if the filesystem filled up.

```
close(FH)          or die "FH didn't close: $!";
```

Closing filehandles as soon as you're done with them can also aid portability to non-Unix platforms, because some have problems in areas such as reopening a file before closing it and renaming or removing a file while it's still open. These operations pose no problem to POSIX systems, but others are less accommodating.

The paranoid programmer even checks the close on standard output stream at the program's end, lest STDOUT had been redirected from the command line and the output filesystem filled up. Admittedly, your runtime system should take care of this for you, but it doesn't.

Checking standard error, though, is more problematic. After all, if STDERR fails to close, what are you planning to do about it? Well, you could determine why the close failed to see whether there's anything you might do to correct the situation. You could even load up the Sys::Syslog module and call syslog( ), which is what system daemons do, since they don't otherwise have access to a good STDERR stream.

STDOUT is the default filehandle used by the print, printf, and write functions if no filehandle argument is passed. Change this default with select, which takes the new default output filehandle and returns the previous one. The new output filehandle must have already been opened before calling select:

```perl
$old_fh = select(LOGFILE);              # switch to LOGFILE for output
print "Countdown initiated ...\n";
select($old_fh);                        # return to original output
print "You have 30 seconds to reach minimum safety distance.\n";
```

Some of Perl's special variables change the behavior of the currently selected output filehandle. Most important is $|, which controls output buffering for each filehandle. Flushing output buffers is explained in Recipe 7.19.

Perl has functions for buffered and unbuffered I/O. Although there are some exceptions (see the following table), you shouldn't mix calls to buffered and unbuffered I/O functions. That's because buffered functions may keep data in their buffers that the unbuffered functions can't know about. The following table shows the two sets of functions you should not mix. Functions on a particular row are only loosely associated; for instance, sysread doesn't have the same semantics as <FH>, but they are on the same row because they both read from a filehandle. Repositioning is addressed in Chapter 8, but we also use it in Recipe 7.17.

Action	Buffered	Unbuffered
input	<FH>, readline	sysread
output	print	syswrite
repositioning	seek, tell	sysseek

As of Perl v5.8 there is a way to mix these functions: I/O layers. You can't turn on buffering for the unbuffered functions, but you can turn off buffering for the unbuffered ones. Perl now lets you select the implementation of I/O you wish to use. One possible choice is :unix, which makes Perl use unbuffered syscalls rather than your stdio library or Perl's portable reimplementation of stdio called perlio. Enable the unbuffered I/O layer when you open the file with:

```perl
open(FH, "<:unix", $filename)  or die;
```

Having opened the handle with the unbuffered layer, you can now mix calls to Perl's buffered and unbuffered I/O functions with impunity because with that I/O layer, in reality there are no buffered I/O functions. When you print, Perl is then really using the equivalent of syswrite. More information can be found in Recipe 7.19.

7.1 Opening a File

Problem

You want to read or write a file from Perl.

Solution

Use open with two arguments for convenience or with three arguments for precision. Use sysopen for access to low-level features.

The open function takes arguments specifying the internal filehandle to open, the external filename, and some indication of how to open it (the access mode). Called with only two arguments, the second comprises both path and mode:

```
open(SOURCE, "< $path")
    or die "Couldn't open $path for reading: $!\n";

open(SINK, "> $path")
    or die "Couldn't open $path for writing: $!\n";
```

When called with three (or more) arguments, the mode is split out from the path, lest there be any ambiguity between one and the other:

```
open(SOURCE, "<", $path)
    or die "Couldn't open $path for reading: $!\n";

open(SINK, ">", $path)
    or die "Couldn't open $path for writing: $!\n";
```

The sysopen function takes either three or four arguments: filehandle, filename, file-access flags, plus an optional permissions value. The flags argument is a number constructed from constants provided by the Fcntl module:

```
use Fcntl;

sysopen(SOURCE, $path, O_RDONLY)
    or die "Couldn't open $path for reading: $!\n";

sysopen(SINK, $path, O_WRONLY, 0600)
    or die "Couldn't open $path for writing: $!\n";
```

If you pass open or sysopen a scalar variable that's undefined, Perl fills in that variable with a new, anonymous filehandle.

```
open(my $fh, "<", $path)
    or die "Couldn't open $path for reading: $!\n";
```

Discussion

All input and output goes through filehandles, regardless of whether filehandles are mentioned. Filehandles aren't exclusively connected to regular files in the filesystem—they're also used to communicate with other programs (see Chapter 16) and for network communication (see Chapter 17). The open function can also be used to manipulate file descriptors, as discussed in Recipe 7.9.

The open function quickly and conveniently solves the problem of associating a filehandle with a file. It permits a shorthand for common access modes (reading, writing, reading and writing, appending) passed in with the filename. It doesn't let you control the permissions that files are created with or even whether files are created. For this level of control, you need sysopen, which uses constants provided by the Fcntl module to control individual settings like read, write, create, and truncate.

Most programmers meet open long before they meet sysopen. Table 7-1 shows how open file-access modes (the "Filename" column) correspond to sysopen constants ("O_ flags") and to the *fopen*(3) strings that IO::File->new can take ("Char"). "Read" and "Write" indicate that the filehandle may be read from or written to. "Append" means no matter where you are in the file, output goes to the end of the file (on most systems). "Create" indicates whether the open statement creates a file if one having the given name doesn't already exist. "Trunc" indicates open will clobber any existing data if the file already exists.

Table 7-1. File-access modes

Filename	Read	Write	Append	Create	Trunc	O_flags	Char
< *file*	yes	no	no	no	no	RDONLY	"r"
> *file*	no	yes	no	yes	yes	WRONLY TRUNC CREAT	"w"
>> *file*	no	yes	yes	yes	no	WRONLY APPEND CREAT	"a"
+< *file*	yes	yes	no	no	no	RDWR	"r+"
+> *file*	yes	yes	no	yes	yes	RDWR TRUNC CREAT	"w+"
+>> *file*	yes	yes	yes	yes	no	RDWR APPEND CREAT	"a+"

Here's a tip: you almost never want to use +> or +>>. The first clobbers your file before you can read it, and the second one can be confusing. Although you can read from anywhere with +>>, many systems jump to the end of the file when you write.

The sysopen function takes either three or four arguments:

```
sysopen(FILEHANDLE, $name, $flags)          or die "Can't open $name : $!";
sysopen(FILEHANDLE, $name, $flags, $perms) or die "Can't open $name : $!";
```

$name is the name of the file, without any < or + funny business. $flags is a number, formed by ORing together separate values for O_CREAT, O_WRONLY, O_TRUNC, etc. Availability of particular O_* constants depends on your operating system, so consult the online documentation for this (usually *open*(2), but not always), or look in */usr/include/fcntl.h*. Common ones are:

O_RDONLY	Read only
O_WRONLY	Write only
O_RDWR	Read and write
O_CREAT	Create the file if it doesn't exist
O_EXCL	Fail if the file already exists
O_APPEND	Append to the file
O_TRUNC	Truncate the file
O_NONBLOCK	Non-blocking access

Less common O_* flags sometimes available include O_SHLOCK, O_EXLOCK, O_BINARY, O_NOCTTY, and O_SYNC. Consult your *open*(2) manpage or its local equivalent for details.

If you omit the $perms argument to sysopen, Perl uses the octal value 0666. These permissions values need to be in octal and are modified by your process's current umask. A umask value is a number representing disabled permissions bits—if your umask were 027 (group can't write; others can't read, write, or execute), then passing sysopen 0666 would create a file with mode 0640 (mathematically, 0666 & ~027 is 0640).

If umask seems confusing, here's some advice: supply a creation mode of 0666 for regular files and one of 0777 for directories and executable files. This gives users a choice: if they want protected files, they can choose process umasks of 022, 027, or even the particularly antisocial mask of 077. Programs should rarely if ever make policy decisions better left to the user. One exception, though, is files that should be kept private: mail files, web browser cookies, *.rhosts* files, and so on. In short, seldom if ever use 0644 as argument to sysopen because that takes away the user's option to have a more permissive umask.

Here are examples of open and sysopen in action.

To open for reading:

```
open(FH, "<", $path)                              or die $!;
sysopen(FH, $path, O_RDONLY)                      or die $!;
```

To open for writing, create a new file if needed, or else truncate an old one:

```
open(FH, ">", $path)                              or die $!;
sysopen(FH, $path, O_WRONLY|O_TRUNC|O_CREAT)      or die $!;
sysopen(FH, $path, O_WRONLY|O_TRUNC|O_CREAT, 0600) or die $!;
```

To open for writing, create a new file, but that file must not previously exist:

```
sysopen(FH, $path, O_WRONLY|O_EXCL|O_CREAT)       or die $!;
sysopen(FH, $path, O_WRONLY|O_EXCL|O_CREAT, 0600) or die $!;
```

To open for appending, creating it if necessary:

```
open(FH, ">>", $path)                             or die $!;
sysopen(FH, $path, O_WRONLY|O_APPEND|O_CREAT)     or die $!;
sysopen(FH, $path, O_WRONLY|O_APPEND|O_CREAT, 0600) or die $!;
```

To open for appending, where the file must exist:

```
sysopen(FH, $path, O_WRONLY|O_APPEND)             or die $!;
```

To open for update, where the file must exist:

```
open(FH, "+<", $path)                             or die $!;
sysopen(FH, $path, O_RDWR)                        or die $!;
```

To open for update, but create a new file if necessary:

```
sysopen(FH, $path, O_RDWR|O_CREAT)                or die $!;
sysopen(FH, $path, O_RDWR|O_CREAT, 0600)          or die $!;
```

To open for update, where the file must not exist:

```
sysopen(FH, $path, O_RDWR|O_EXCL|O_CREAT)          or die $!;
sysopen(FH, $path, O_RDWR|O_EXCL|O_CREAT, 0600)    or die $!;
```

We use a creation mask of 0600 here only to show how to create a private file. The argument is normally omitted.

See Also

The open, sysopen, and umask functions in *perlfunc*(1) and Chapter 29 of *Programming Perl*; the *perlopentut*(1) manpage; the documentation for the standard IO::File and Fcntl modules (also in Chapter 32 of *Programming Perl*); your system's *open*(2), *fopen*(3), and *umask*(2) manpages; Recipe 7.2; Recipe 9.11

7.2   Opening Files with Unusual Filenames

Problem

You want to open a file with a funny filename, such as "-", or one that starts with <, >, or |; has leading or trailing whitespace; or ends with |. You don't want these to trigger open's do-what-I-mean behavior, since in this case, that's *not* what you mean.

Solution

When open is called with three arguments, not two, place the mode in the second argument:

```
open(HANDLE, "<", $filename)          or die "cannot open $filename : $!\n";
```

Or simply use sysopen:

```
sysopen(HANDLE, $filename, O_RDONLY)   or die "cannot open $filename: $!\n";
```

Discussion

When open is called with three arguments, the access mode and the filename are kept separate. But when called with only two arguments, open has to extract the access mode and the filename from a single string. If your filename begins with the same characters used to specify an access mode, open could easily do something unexpected. Imagine the following code:

```
$filename = shift @ARGV;
open(INPUT, $filename)          or die "Couldn't open $filename : $!\n";
```

If the user gave ">/etc/passwd" as the filename on the command line, this code would attempt to open */etc/passwd* for writing. We can try to give an explicit mode, say for writing:

```
open(OUTPUT, ">$filename")
    or die "Couldn't open $filename for writing: $!\n";
```

but even this would let the user give a filename of ">data", and the code would append to the file data instead of erasing the old contents.

The easiest solution is to pass three arguments to open, where the second argument is the mode and the third the path. Now there can be neither confusion nor subterfuge.

```
open(OUTPUT, ">", $filename)
    or die "Couldn't open $filename for writing: $!\n";
```

Another solution is sysopen, which also takes the mode and filename as distinct arguments:

```
use Fcntl;                       # for file constants

sysopen(OUTPUT, $filename, O_WRONLY|O_TRUNC)
    or die "Can't open $filename for writing: $!\n";
```

This special way that open interprets filenames, sometimes referred to as *magic open*, is a matter of convenience—and usually a good thing. You don't have to worry about a space or two between the access mode and the path. You never have to use the special case of "-" to mean standard input or output. If you write a filter and use a simple open, users can pass "gzip -dc bible.gz|" as a filename, and your filter will automatically run the decoding program.

It's only those programs that run under special privilege that should worry about security with open. When designing programs that will be run on someone else's behalf, such as setuid programs or CGI scripts, the prudent programmer always considers whether the user can supply their own filename and thereby cajole what would otherwise appear to be a normal open used for simple reading into overwriting a file or even running another program. Perl's **-T** command-line flag to enable taint-checking would take care of this.

In versions of Perl without three-argument open (those before v5.6.0), one had little recourse but to resort to the following sort of chicanery to cope with filenames with leading or trailing whitespace:

```
$file =~ s#^(\s)#./$1#;
open(OUTPUT, "> $file\0")
        or die "Couldn't open $file for OUTPUT : $!\n";
```

The substitution protects initial whitespace (this cannot occur in fully specified filenames like "/etc/passwd", but only in relative filenames like ">passwd"). The NUL byte (ASCII 0, "\0") isn't considered part of the filename by open, but it does prevent trailing whitespace from being ignored.

See Also

The open and sysopen functions in *perlfunc*(1) and Chapter 29 of *Programming Perl*; Recipe 7.1; Recipe 7.14; Recipe 16.2; Recipe 19.4; Recipe 19.5

7.3   Expanding Tildes in Filenames

Problem

You want to open filenames like *~username/blah* or *~/.mailrc*, but open doesn't inter-pret the tilde to mean a home directory.

Solution

Either use the glob function:

```
open(FH, glob("~joebob/somefile")) || die "Couldn't open file: $!";
```

or expand the filename manually with a substitution:

```
$filename =~ s{ ^ ~ ( [^/]* ) }
            { $1
                ? (getpwnam($1))[7]
                : ( $ENV{HOME} || $ENV{LOGDIR}
                    || (getpwuid($<))[7]
                  )
}ex;
```

Discussion

There is a useful convention, begun with the Unix *csh* shell and propagated widely by web addresses of the form *http://www.example.com/~user/*, that ~ in a filename represents a user's home directory. Thus:

```
~               # current user's home directory
~/blah          # file blah in current user's home directory
~user           # a particular user's home directory
~user/blah      # file blah in a particular user's home directory
```

Unfortunately, Perl's open function does not expand wildcards, including tildes. As of the v5.6 release, Perl internally uses the File::Glob module when you use the glob operator. So all you need to do is glob the result first.

```
open(MAILRC, "<", "~/.mailrc")          # WRONG: tilde is a shell thing
    or die "can't open ~/.mailrc: $!";

open(MAILRC, "<", glob("~/.mailrc"))    # so expand tilde first
    or die "can't open ~/.mailrc: $!";
```

The alternative solution, the substitution, uses /e to evaluate the replacement as Perl code. If a username follows the tilde, it's stored in $1, which getpwnam uses to extract the user's home directory out of the return list. This directory becomes the replacement string. If the tilde was not followed by a username, substitute in either the current HOME environment variable or the LOGDIR one. If neither of those is valid, look up the effective user ID's home directory.

You *could* spell glob('~gnat') as <~gnat>, but that would look too much like a read from a filehandle, so don't do that.

See Also

The glob and getpwnam functions in *perlfunc*(1) and Chapter 29 of *Programming Perl*; your system's *getpwnam*(2) manpage; Recipe 9.6

7.4 Making Perl Report Filenames in Error Messages

Problem

Your program works with files, but Perl's errors and warnings only report the last used filehandle, not the name of the file.

Solution

Use the filename as the filehandle:

```
open($path, "<", $path)
    or die "Couldn't open $path for reading : $!\n";
```

Discussion

Ordinarily, error messages say:

> *Argument "3\n" isn't numeric in multiply at tallyweb line 16, <LOG> chunk 17.*

The filehandle LOG doesn't help much because you don't know which file the handle was connected to. By using the filename itself as indirect filehandle, Perl produces more informative errors and warnings:

> *Argument "3\n" isn't numeric in multiply at tallyweb*
> *line 16, </usr/local/data/mylog3.dat> chunk 17.*

Unfortunately, this doesn't work with strict refs turned on because the variable $path doesn't really have a filehandle in it, only a string that sometimes behaves like one. The chunk number mentioned in warnings and error messages is the current value of the $. variable.

See Also

Recipe 7.1; the open function in *perlfunc*(1) and Chapter 29 of *Programming Perl*

7.5 Storing Filehandles into Variables

Problem

You want to use a filehandle like a normal variable so you can pass it to or return it from a function, store it in a data structure, and so on.

Solution

The easiest way to get a filehandle into a variable is to have open put it there for you:

```
open(my $fh, "<", $filename)      or die "$0: can't open $filename: $!";
```

To store named filehandles into a variable or pass them into or out of a function, use typeglob notation (*FH):

```
$variable = *FILEHANDLE;          # save in variable
subroutine(*FILEHANDLE);          # or pass directly

sub subroutine {
    my $fh = shift;
    print $fh "Hello, filehandle!\n";
}
```

Discussion

If you pass an undefined scalar variable as the first argument to open, Perl allocates an anonymous typeglob and stores a reference to that typeglob in that scalar, effectively creating filehandles on demand. Like all other references, autovivified filehandles are subject to garbage collection, so this code doesn't leak a filehandle:

```
{
    open(my $fh, "< /etc/motd") or die;
    local $/;          # slurp mode
    $text = <$fh>;
}
```

When Perl reaches the end of the block, $fh goes out of scope. As explained earlier in the Introduction, because that variable contained the last reference to the anonymous filehandle created by open, the variable is garbage collected and the filehandle implicitly closed.

Autovivified filehandles, being anonymous and already held in variables, don't help you to understand how to pass named filehandles as function parameters or store them in variables, including elements of arrays or hashes. By named filehandles, we mean those of the form FH, including all predefined handles, such as STDIN and ARGV. So let's look at what FH is and how to extract a scalar value from it to use for all of those things.

Named filehandles used in:

```
print STDERR "stuff\n";
$input = <STDIN>;
open(TTY, "+<", "/dev/tty");
if (eof(ARGV)) { .... }
```

are names, not variables. They're like subroutines in that way. This makes them inconvenient to pass around or store into data structures. Assuming you follow the prudent advice to compile all your code under use strict by default, normally you can't get away with this:

```
$fh = SOMEHANDLE;
somefunc(SOMEHANDLE);
```

because, absent declarations to the contrary, SOMEHANDLE is in both of these cases an unquoted string, which is forbidden by use strict. Even if you aren't using strict subs, you'll get into trouble if you try to pass your handle into a subroutine that was compiled under strict refs or in a different package than the calling code was compiled in.

The four named handles (STDERR, STDIN, TTY, and ARGV) we showed earlier didn't require special handling, but not because they are built-ins themselves; TTY, in fact, is not. Rather, they were okay because the built-in operations using them as arguments are all prototyped to take a filehandle argument.

So you must do one of two things. You could use a prototype for the function as explained in Recipe 7.6. Otherwise, you must use something that Perl will accept in lieu of a filehandle name. Acceptable substitutes include strings, typeglobs, references to typeglobs, and an I/O object, all of which may be stored into variables or passed into a function for later use as indirect filehandles.

```
somefunc(   SOMEHANDLE    );     # only w/ somefunc(*) proto
somefunc(   "SOMEHANDLE"  );     # an quoted string
somefunc(   *SOMEHANDLE   );     # a typeglob
somefunc(   \*SOMEHANDLE  );     # ref to a typeglob
somefunc(   *SOMEHANDLE{IO} );   # an I/O object
```

Using a quoted string for the named handle has potential problems, as already explained, although this can work if the code is careful enough (again, see the next recipe). Better to use typeglob notation, either directly using *SOMEHANDLE or by reference using *SOMEHANDLE:

```
somefunc(*SOMEHANDLE);
$fh = *SOMEHANDLE;  # or indirectly via a variable
somefunc($fh);

print $fh "data\n";
```

Typeglob notation spares you quoting or qualifying the handle name. It may help to conceptualize the asterisk as the type symbol for a filehandle. Like the little colored balls from high school chemistry that stood for atomic particles, it's not really true, but it is a convenient mental shorthand. By the time you understand where this model breaks down, you won't need it anymore.

If you assign any of the four alternate forms for named filehandles into a scalar variable, you can use that variable as an indirect filehandle wherever you would use a named filehandle.

However, complex expressions and subscripts into hashes or arrays cannot be used directly with built-ins like print, printf, or the line input operator. These are syntactically illegal and won't even compile:

```
@fd = (*STDIN, *STDOUT, *STDERR);
print $fd[1] "Type it: ";                    # WRONG
$got = <$fd[0]>                              # WRONG
print $fd[2] "What was that: $got";          # WRONG
```

With print and printf, you can get around this by using a block, returning an expression where you would place the filehandle:

```
print  { $fd[1] } "funny stuff\n";
printf { $fd[1] } "Pity the poor %x.\n", 3_735_928_559;
Pity the poor deadbeef.
```

That block is a proper block in all senses, so you can put more complicated code there. This sends the message out to one of two places:

```
$ok = -x "/bin/cat";
print { $ok ? $fd[1] : $fd[2]  } "cat stat $ok\n";
print { $fd[ 1 + ($ok || 0) ]  } "cat stat $ok\n";
```

This is so-called "indirect object" notation, discussed at length in Chapter 13. This restriction against using anything but simple scalar variables in the indirect object slot holds true for any sort of object. As with user-created objects, infix arrow notation avoids syntactic snafus here. If you have the IO::Handle module loaded, or anything that inherits from it, use an expression that produces the filehandle as though it were a proper object to invoke methods from that class:

```
$fd[1]->print("funny stuff\n");
($ok ? $fd[1] : $fd[2])->print("cat stat $ok\n");
```

This approach of treating print and printf like object methods calls won't work for the line input operator. Assuming you've been storing typeglobs in your structure as we did previously, the built-in readline function reads records just as <FH> does. Given the preceding initialization of @fd, this would work:

```
$got = readline($fd[0]);
```

or, with IO::Handle available, you can use the getline method:

```
$got = $fd[0]->getline( );
```

IO::Handle doesn't replace the readline function using just one method—it uses two, one per context. If you prefer readline's context-dependent behavior, you could always do this, adding something to the class on the fly:

```
sub IO::Handle::readline {
    my $fh = shift;
    if (wantarray) {
        return $fh->getlines();
    } else {
        return $fh->getline();
    }
}
```

See Also

The open function in *perlfunc*(1) and in Chapter 29 of *Programming Perl*; Recipe 7.1; the documentation with the standard IO::Handle module (also in Chapter 32 of *Programming Perl*); and the "Typeglobs and Filehandles" sections of Chapter 2 of *Programming Perl*

7.6 Writing a Subroutine That Takes Filehandles as Built-ins Do

Problem

You can pass a bareword filehandle to Perl functions like eof, and you'd like to write similar subroutines of your own.

Solution

Use the Symbol module's qualify_to_ref in conjunction with a * prototype on the subroutine:

```
use Symbol qw(qualify_to_ref);

sub my_eof (*) {
  my $handle = shift;
  $handle = qualify_to_ref($handle, caller());
  # use $handle
}
```

Discussion

The * prototype tells Perl that the function expects a bareword filehandle as its argument. This lets you call the function like so:

```
my_eof(HANDLE);
```

This works even when use `strict 'subs'` is in effect. The function receives a string as its argument, though. To safely use the argument as a filehandle, you need the Symbol module to turn it into a reference to a typeglob. And since typeglob refs can be used wherever you'd use named filehandles, store that reference in a scalar variable and use the variable as an indirect filehandle within your subroutine.

If you pass in a filehandle that is already a reference to a typeglob, like those autovivified by open, Perl and `qualify_to_ref` still do the right thing:

```
open(my $fh, "<", $filename) or die;
my_eof($fh);
```

This technique is used in Recipe 7.23.

See Also

The documentation for the standard module Symbol (also in Chapter 32 of *Programming Perl*); the "Prototypes" section in the *perlsub*(1) manpage (also in Chapter 6 of *Programming Perl*); Recipe 7.23

7.7   Caching Open Output Filehandles

Problem

You need more output files open simultaneously than your system allows.

Solution

Use the standard FileCache module:

```
use FileCache;
cacheout ($path);          # each time you use a filehandle
print $path "output";
```

Discussion

FileCache's cacheout function lets you work with more output files than your operating system lets you have open at any one time. If you use it to open an existing file that FileCache is seeing for the first time, the file is truncated to length zero, no questions asked. However, in its opening and closing of files in the background, cacheout tracks files it has opened before and does not overwrite them, but appends to them instead. This does not create directories for you, so if you give it */usr/local/dates/ merino.ewe* to open but the directory */usr/local/dates* doesn't exist, cacheout will die.

The cacheout function checks the value of the C-level constant NOFILE from the standard system include file *sys/param.h* to determine how many concurrently open files are allowed on your system. This value can be incorrect on some systems and even missing on a few (for instance, on those where the maximum number of open file descriptors is a process resource limit that can be set with the *limit* or *ulimit* commands). If cacheout can't get a value for NOFILE, set $FileCache::cacheout_maxopen to be four less than the correct value, or choose a reasonable number by trial and error.

Example 7-1 splits an *xferlog* file (created by most FTP servers nowadays) into separate files, each named after the authenticated user. Fields in *xferlog* files are space-separated, with the fourth field from the last holding the authenticated username.

Example 7-1. splitwulog

```perl
#!/usr/bin/perl
# splitwulog - split wuftpd log by authenticated user
use FileCache;
$outdir = "/var/log/ftp/by-user";
while (<>) {
    unless (defined ($user = (split)[-4])) {
        warn "Invalid line: $.\n";
        next;
    }
    $path = "$outdir/$user";
    cacheout $path;
    print $path $_;



}
```

See Also

Documentation for the standard FileCache module (also in Chapter 32 of *Programming Perl*); the open function in *perlfunc*(1) and in Chapter 29 of *Programming Perl*

7.8   Printing to Many Filehandles Simultaneously

Problem

You need to output the same data to several different filehandles.

Solution

If you want to do it without forking, write a foreach loop that iterates across the filehandles:

```perl
foreach $filehandle (@FILEHANDLES) {
    print $filehandle $stuff_to_print;
}
```

If you don't mind forking, open a filehandle that's a pipe to a *tee* program:

```
open(MANY, "| tee file1 file2 file3 > /dev/null")    or die $!;
print MANY "data\n"                                  or die $!;
close(MANY)                                           or die $!;
```

If you don't have a *tee* program handy, use the IO::Tee module from CPAN:

```
use IO::Tee;
$tee = IO::Tee->new(@FILEHANDLES);
print $tee $stuff_to_print;
```

Discussion

A filehandle sends output to one file or program only. To duplicate output to several places, you must call print multiple times or make a filehandle connected to a program like *tee*, which distributes its input elsewhere. If you use the first option, it's probably easiest to put the filehandles in a list or array and loop through them (see Recipe 7.5):

```
for $fh (*FH1, *FH2, *FH3)      { print $fh "whatever\n" }
```

However, if your system supports the *tee*(1) program, or if you've installed the Perl version from Recipe 8.25, you may open a pipe to *tee* and let it do the work of copying the file to several places. Remember that *tee* normally also copies its output to STDOUT, so you must redirect *tee*'s standard output to */dev/null* if you don't want an extra copy:

```
open (FH, "| tee file1 file2 file3 >/dev/null");
print FH "whatever\n";
```

You could even redirect your own STDOUT to the *tee* process, and then you're able to use a regular print directly:

```
# make STDOUT go to three files, plus original STDOUT
open (STDOUT, "| tee file1 file2 file3") or die "Teeing off: $!\n";
print "whatever\n"                       or die "Writing: $!\n";
close(STDOUT)                            or die "Closing: $!\n";
```

The IO::Tee module from CPAN gives you a single filehandle (an object of the IO::Tee class) that you can write to. The object prints to many different filehandles whatever you print to it. Pass destination filehandles to the constructor:

```
use IO::Tee;

$t = IO::Tee->new(*FH1, *FH2, *FH3);
print $t "Hello, world\n";
print $t "Goodbye, universe\n";
```

In addition to print, you can do any I/O operation you like to an IO::Tee filehandle. For example, if you close $t in the preceding example, the close will return true if FH1, FH2, and FH3 were all successfully closed.

See Also

The print function in *perlfunc*(1) and in Chapter 29 of *Programming Perl*; the "Typeglobs and Filehandles" sections of Chapter 2 of *Programming Perl*; the documentation for the CPAN module IO::Tee; we use this technique in Recipe 8.25 and Recipe 13.15

7.9 Opening and Closing File Descriptors by Number

Problem

You know which file descriptors you'd like to do I/O on, but Perl requires filehandles, not descriptor numbers.

Solution

To open the file descriptor, supply open with "<&=" or "<&" as the part of the file access mode, combined with a directional arrow:

```
open(FH, "<&=", $FDNUM)      # open FH to the descriptor itself
open(FH, "<&",  $FDNUM);     # open FH to a copy of the descriptor
```

Or use the IO::Handle module's new_from_fd class method:

```
use IO::Handle;
$fh = IO::Handle->new_from_fd($FDNUM, "r");
```

To close a file descriptor by number, either use the POSIX::close function or open it first as shown previously.

Discussion

Occasionally you have a file descriptor but no filehandle. Perl's I/O system uses filehandles instead of file descriptors, so you have to make a new filehandle from an already open file descriptor. The "<&", ">&", and "+<&" access modes to open do this for reading, writing, and updating, respectively. Adding an equals sign to these—making them "<&=", ">&=", and "+<&="—is more parsimonious of file descriptors and nearly always what you want. That's because the underlying implementation of Perl's open statement uses only a C-level *fdopen*(3) function from the C library, not a *dup2*(2) syscall that calls the kernel.

The new_from_fd IO::Handle object method is equivalent to:

```
use IO::Handle;

$fh = new IO::Handle;
$fh->fdopen($FDNUM, "r");              # open fd 3 for reading
```

Here's how you'd open file descriptors that the MH mail system feeds its child processes. It identifies them in the environment variable `MHCONTEXTFD`:

```
$fd = $ENV{MHCONTEXTFD};
open(MHCONTEXT, "<&=", $fd)    or die "couldn't fdopen $fd: $!";
# after processing
close(MHCONTEXT)               or die "couldn't close context file: $!";
```

Closing a file descriptor by number is even rarer. If you've already opened a filehandle for the file descriptor you want to close, simply use Perl's `close` function on the filehandle. If you don't have a filehandle for that file descriptor, the `POSIX::close` function closes a file descriptor by number:

```
use POSIX;

POSIX::close(3);               # close fd 3
```

See Also

The open function in *perlfunc*(1) and in Chapter 29 of *Programming Perl*; the documentation for the standard POSIX and IO::Handle modules (also in Chapter 32 of *Programming Perl*); your system's *fdopen*(3) manpages

7.10   Copying Filehandles

Problem

You want a copy of a filehandle.

Solution

To create an alias for a named filehandle, say:

```
*ALIAS = *ORIGINAL;
```

Use open with the & file access mode to create an independent copy of the file descriptor for that filehandle:

```
open(OUTCOPY, ">&STDOUT")     or die "Couldn't dup STDOUT: $!";
open(INCOPY,  "<&STDIN")      or die "Couldn't dup STDIN : $!";
```

Use open with the &= mode to create an alias for that filehandle or file descriptor:

```
open(OUTALIAS, ">&=STDOUT")   or die "Couldn't alias STDOUT: $!";
open(INALIAS,  "<&=STDIN")    or die "Couldn't alias STDIN : $!";
open(BYNUMBER, ">&=5")        or die "Couldn't alias file descriptor 5: $!";
```

With other types of filehandles (typeglobs, objects), use the same technique with a three-argument open:

```
open(my $copy, "<&",  $original) or die "Couldn't alias original: $!";
open(my $copy, "<&=", $original) or die "Couldn't alias original: $!";
```

Discussion

If you create an alias for a filehandle with typeglobs, only one Perl I/O object is still being accessed. If you close one of these aliased filehandles, the I/O object is closed. Any further attempt to use a copy of that filehandle fails, silently by default or, if you have warnings enabled, with the warning "print on closed filehandle". When alternating access through aliased filehandles, writes work as you'd expect because there are no duplicated stdio data structures to get out of sync.

If you create a copy of a file descriptor with open(COPY, ">&HANDLE"), you're really calling the *dup*(2) syscall. You get two independent file descriptors whose file position, locks, and flags are shared, but which have independent stdio buffers. Closing one filehandle doesn't affect its copy. Simultaneously accessing the file through both filehandles is a recipe for disaster. Instead, this technique is normally used to save and restore STDOUT and STDERR:

```
# take copies of the file descriptors
open(OLDOUT, ">&STDOUT");
open(OLDERR, ">&STDERR");

# redirect stdout and stderr
open(STDOUT, "> /tmp/program.out")  or die "Can't redirect stdout: $!";
open(STDERR, ">&STDOUT")            or die "Can't dup stdout: $!";

# run the program
system($joe_random_program);

# close the redirected filehandles
close(STDOUT)                       or die "Can't close STDOUT: $!";
close(STDERR)                       or die "Can't close STDERR: $!";

# restore stdout and stderr
open(STDERR, ">&OLDERR")            or die "Can't restore stderr: $!";
open(STDOUT, ">&OLDOUT")            or die "Can't restore stdout: $!";

# avoid leaks by closing the independent copies
close(OLDOUT)                       or die "Can't close OLDOUT: $!";
close(OLDERR)                       or die "Can't close OLDERR: $!";
```

If you create an alias for a file descriptor using open(ALIAS, ">&=HANDLE"), you're really calling the *fdopen*(3) function from the stdio library or its equivalent. You get a single file descriptor with two stdio buffers accessed through two filehandles. Closing one filehandle closes the file descriptor of any aliases, but not their filehandles—if you tried to print to a filehandle whose alias had been closed, Perl wouldn't give a "print on closed filehandle" warning, even though the print failed. In short, accessing the file through both filehandles is also a recipe for disaster. This is really used only to open a file descriptor by number. See Recipe 7.9 for more information on this.

See Also

The open function in *perlfunc*(1) and in Chapter 29 of *Programming Perl*; your system's *dup*(2) manpage

7.11 Creating Temporary Files

Problem

You need to create a temporary file and have it deleted automatically when your program exits. For instance, if you needed a temporary configuration file to feed a program you're about to launch, you'd need a name for that file so you could pass that filename along to the utility program. In other cases, you may want a temporary file to write to and read from, but don't need a filename for it.

Solution

Use the `tempfile` function from the File::Temp module:

```
use File::Temp qw(tempfile);
$fh = tempfile( );  # just the handle
```

perhaps in conjunction with a temporary directory:

```
use File::Temp qw(tempfile);
$dir = tempdir( CLEANUP => 1 );
# or specify a directory
use File::Temp qw(tempfile);
($fh, $filename) = tempfile( DIR => $dir );

$template = "myprogtempXXXXXX"; # trailing Xs are changed
($fh, $filename) = tempfile( $template, DIR => $dir);
($fh, $filename) = tempfile( $template, SUFFIX => ".data");
```

Discussion

The File::Temp module's functions are the best way to make temporary files. For one thing, they're extremely easy to use. For another, they're more portable than direct calls to the operating system. But perhaps of greatest importance is the care they take in security matters both various and subtle, especially those involving race conditions.

Although this module provides a handful of slightly different functions for creating a temporary file, most are there simply to support legacy interfaces; few users will need more than the basic `tempfile( )` function. This function safely and atomically creates and opens a brand new, empty file in read-write mode. In scalar context, it returns a filehandle to that temporary file; in list context, it returns the handle and pathname of the temporary file:

```
use File::Temp qw(tempfile);

# just the handle
```

```
$fh = tempfile();

# handle and filename
($fh, $filename) = tempfile();
```

The `tempfile` function optionally accepts an argument containing a template and then named arguments in pairs. Named arguments specify such things as the directory to use instead of the current directory, that a specific file extension should be used, and on systems that support such a thing, whether the tempfile should be immediately unlinked before its handle is returned. (Files whose names have already been deleted from the filesystem are especially difficult for the guys with the black hats to find.) Any trailing X characters in the template are replaced by random characters in the final filename. You might use this feature if you need a temporary file with a specific extension.

```
($fh, $filename) = tempfile(DIR => $dir);
($fh, $filename) = tempfile($template);
($fh, $filename) = tempfile($template, DIR => $dir);
($fh, $filename) = tempfile($template, SUFFIX => ".dat");
($fh, $filename) = tempfile($template, UNLINK => 1);
```

Unless you specify `OPEN => 0`, the temporary file will be deleted automatically when your program finally exits or the file is closed.

In recent releases, Perl's open function offers a simple way to create temporary files whose names you cannot know. Explicitly pass undef as the filename to open:

```
open(my $fh, "+>", undef)
    or die "$0: can't create temporary file: $!\n";
```

See Also

The documentation for the standard File::Temp modules (also in Chapter 32 of *Programming Perl*); the open function in *perlfunc*(1) and in Chapter 29 of *Programming Perl*; Recipe 7.9

7.12   Storing a File Inside Your Program Text

Problem

You have data that you want to bundle with your program and treat as though it were in a file, but you don't want it to be in a different file.

Solution

Use the __DATA__ or __END__ tokens after your program code to mark the start of a data block, which can be read inside your program or module from the DATA filehandle.

Use __DATA__ within a module:

```
while ( <DATA> ) {
    # process the line
}
__DATA__
# your data goes here
```

Similarly, use __END__ within the main program file:

```
while (<main::DATA>) {
    # process the line
}
__END__
# your data goes here
```

Discussion

The __DATA__ and __END__ symbols tell the Perl compiler there's nothing more for it to do in the current file. They represent the logical end for code in a module or a program before the physical end-of-file.

Text after __DATA__ or __END__ can be read through the per-package DATA filehandle. For example, take the hypothetical module Primes. Text after __DATA__ in *Primes.pm* can be read from the Primes::DATA filehandle.

__END__ behaves as a synonym for __DATA__ in the main package. Any text occurring after an __END__ token in a module is completely inaccessible.

This lets you write self-contained programs instead of keeping data in separate files. Often this is used for documentation. Sometimes it's configuration data or old test data that the program was originally developed with, left lying about should it ever be needed again.

Another trick is to use DATA to find out the current program's or module's size or last modification date. On most systems, the $0 variable will contain the full pathname to your running script. On systems where $0 is not correct, you could try the DATA filehandle instead. This can be used to pull in the size, modification date, etc. Put a special token __DATA__ at the end of the file (and maybe a warning not to delete it), and the DATA filehandle is available to the script itself.

```
use POSIX qw(strftime);

$raw_time = (stat(DATA))[9];
$size     = -s DATA;
$kilosize = int($size / 1024) . "k";

print "<P>Script size is $kilosize\n";
print strftime("<P>Last script update: %c (%Z)\n", localtime($raw_time));

__DATA__
DO NOT REMOVE THE PRECEDING LINE.

Everything else in this file will be ignored.
```

If you want to store more than one file in your program, see Recipe 7.13.

See Also

The "Scalar Value Constructors" section of *perldata*(1), and the "Other Literal Tokens" section of Chapter 2 of *Programming Perl*; Recipe 7.13

7.13 Storing Multiple Files in the DATA Area

Problem

You've figured out how to use __END__ or __DATA__ to store a virtual file in your source code, but you now want multiple virtual files in one source file.

Solution

Use the Inline::Files module from CPAN. Carefully.

```
use Inline::Files;

while (<SETUP>) {
  # ...
}

while (<EXECUTION>) {
  # ...
}

__SETUP__
everything for the SETUP filehandle goes here
__EXECUTION__
everything for the EXECUTION filehandle goes here
```

Discussion

One limitation with the __DATA__ setup is that you can have only one embedded data file per physical file. The CPAN module Inline::Files cleverly circumvents this restriction by providing logical embedded files. It's used like this:

```
use Inline::Files;

#
#  All your code for the file goes here first, then...
#

__ALPHA__
This is the data in the first virtual file, ALPHA.

__BETA__
```

```
This is the data in the next virtual file, BETA.

__OMEGA__
This is the data in yet another virtual file, OMEGA.

__ALPHA__
This is more data in the second part of virtual file, ALPHA.
```

The code is expected to read from filehandles whose names correspond to the double-underbarred symbols: here ALPHA, BETA, and OMEGA. You may have more than one section by the same name in the same program, and differently named sections needn't be read in any particular order. These handles work much like the ARGV handle does. For one thing, they're implicitly opened on first usage. For example, using the following code in the designated spot in the preceding code example:

```
while (<OMEGA>) {
    print "omega data: $_";
}

while (<ALPHA>) {
    print "alpha data: $_";
}
```

would produce this:

```
omega data: This is the data in yet another virtual file, OMEGA.
omega data:
alpha data: This is the data in the first virtual file, ALPHA.
alpha data:
alpha data: This is more data in the second part of virtual file, ALPHA.
alpha data:
```

Also like the ARGV handle, while reading from a particular handle, the list of available virtual files is in the array by that name, and the currently opened virtual file is in the scalar by that name. There's also a hash by that name that holds various bits of status information about that set of virtual files, including the current file, line number, and byte offset. If we used the Perl debugger on this program and dumped out the variables, it might show this:

```
DB2> \$ALPHA, \@ALPHA, \%ALPHA
0   SCALAR(0x362e34)
    -> '/home/tchrist/inline-demo(00000000000000000291)'
1   ARRAY(0x362e40)
    0  '/home/tchrist/inline-demo(00000000000000000291)'
    1  '/home/tchrist/inline-demo(00000000000000000476)'
2   HASH(0x362edc)
    'file' => undef
    'line' => undef
    'offset' => undef
    'writable' => 1
```

What's that last line telling us? It tells whether that virtual file is writable. By default, if your script is writable, then so too are the virtual files, and they are opened in read-write mode! Yes, that means you can update them yourself, including even adding new virtual files to your source code simply by running that code. There is absolutely no limit to the mischief or grief that can ensue from this: catastrophes are easy to come by as you accidentally obliterate your painstakingly won data. We therefore implore you to back everything up first. The module itself supports an automatic mechanism for this:

```
use Inline::Files -backup;
```

which saves the original in a file with a ".bak" appended to it. You may also specify an explicit backup file:

```
use Inline::Files -backup => "/tmp/safety_net";
```

See Also

The documentation for the CPAN module Inline::Files; Recipe 7.12

7.14 Writing a Unix-Style Filter Program

Problem

You want to write a program that takes a list of filenames on the command line and reads from STDIN if no filenames were given. You'd like the user to be able to give the file "-" to indicate STDIN or "someprogram |" to indicate the output of another program. You might want your program to modify the files in place or to produce output based on its input.

Solution

Read lines with <>:

```
while (<>) {
    # do something with the line
}
```

Discussion

When you say:

```
while (<>) {
    # ...
}
```

Perl translates this into:[*]

```
unshift(@ARGV, "-") unless @ARGV;
while ($ARGV = shift @ARGV) {
```

---

[*] Except that the code written here won't work, because ARGV has internal magic.

```
        unless (open(ARGV, $ARGV)) {
            warn "Can't open $ARGV: $!\n";
            next;
        }
        while (defined($_ = <ARGV>)) {
            # ...
        }
    }
```

You can access ARGV and $ARGV inside the loop to read more from the filehandle or to find the filename currently being processed. Let's look at how this works.

Behavior

If the user supplies no arguments, Perl sets @ARGV to a single string, "-". This is short-hand for STDIN when opened for reading and STDOUT when opened for writing. It's also what lets the user of your program specify "-" as a filename on the command line to read from STDIN.

Next, the file-processing loop removes one argument at a time from @ARGV and copies the filename into the global variable $ARGV. If the file cannot be opened, Perl goes on to the next one. Otherwise, it processes a line at a time. When the file runs out, the loop goes back and opens the next one, repeating the process until @ARGV is exhausted.

The open statement didn't say open(ARGV, "<", $ARGV). There's no extra less-than sign supplied. This allows for interesting effects, like passing the string "gzip -dc file.gz |" as an argument, to make your program read the output of the command "gzip -dc file.gz". See Recipe 16.6 for more about this use of magic open.

You can change @ARGV before or inside the loop. Let's say you don't want the default behavior of reading from STDIN if there aren't any arguments—you want it to default to all C or C++ source and header files. Insert this line before you start processing <ARGV>:

```
    @ARGV = glob("*.[Cch]") unless @ARGV;
```

Process options before the loop, either with one of the Getopt libraries described in Chapter 15 or manually:

```
    # arg demo 1: Process optional -c flag
    if (@ARGV && $ARGV[0] eq "-c") {
        $chop_first++;
        shift;
    }

    # arg demo 2: Process optional -NUMBER flag
    if (@ARGV && $ARGV[0] =~ /^-(\d+)$/) {
        $columns = $1;
        shift;
    }
```

```
# arg demo 3: Process clustering -a, -i, -n, or -u flags
while (@ARGV && $ARGV[0] =~ /^-(.+)/ && (shift, ($_ = $1), 1)) {
    next if /^$/;
    s/a// && (++$append,       redo);
    die "usage: $0 [-ainu] [filenames] ...\n";
}
```

Other than its implicit looping over command-line arguments, <> is not special. The special variables controlling I/O still apply; see Chapter 8 for more on them. You can set $/ to set the line terminator, and $. contains the current line (record) number. If you undefine $/, you don't get the concatenated contents of all files at once; you get one complete file each time:

```
undef $/;
while (<>) {
    # $_ now has the complete contents of
    # the file whose name is in $ARGV
}
```

If you localize $/, the old value is automatically restored when the enclosing block exits:

```
{       # create block for local
    local $/;           # record separator now undef
    while (<>) {
        # do something; called functions still have
        # undeffed version of $/
    }
}                               # $/ restored here
```

Because processing <ARGV> never explicitly closes filehandles, the record number in $. is not reset. If you don't like that, you can explicitly close the file yourself to reset $.:

```
while (<>) {
    print "$ARGV:$.:$_";
    close ARGV if eof;
}
```

The eof function defaults to checking the end-of-file status of the last file read. Since the last handle read was ARGV, eof reports whether we're at the end of the current file. If so, we close it and reset the $. variable. On the other hand, the special notation eof( ) with parentheses but no argument checks if we've reached the end of all files in the <ARGV> processing.

Command-line options

Perl has command-line options, -n, -p, -a, and -i, to make writing filters and one-liners easier.

The -n option adds the while (<>) loop around your program text. It's normally used for filters like *grep* or programs that summarize the data they read. The program is shown in Example 7-2.

Example 7-2. findlogin1

```
#!/usr/bin/perl
# findlogin1 - print all lines containing the string "login"
while (<>) {# loop over files on command line
    print if /login/;
}
```

The program in Example 7-2 could be written as shown in Example 7-3.

Example 7-3. findlogin2

```
#!/usr/bin/perl -n
# findlogin2 - print all lines containing the string "login"
print if /login/;
```

You can combine the **-n** and **-e** options to run Perl code from the command line:

```
% perl -ne 'print if /login/'
```

The **-p** option is like **-n** but adds a print right before the end of the loop. It's normally used for programs that translate their input, such as the program shown in Example 7-4.

Example 7-4. lowercase1

```
#!/usr/bin/perl
# lowercase - turn all lines into lowercase
while (<>) {                    # loop over lines on command line
    s/(\p{Letter})/\l$1/g;      # change all letters to lowercase
    print;
}
```

The program in Example 7-4 could be written as shown in Example 7-5.

Example 7-5. lowercase2

```
#!/usr/bin/perl -p
# lowercase - turn all lines into lowercase
s/(\p{Letter})/\l$1/g;# change all letters to lowercase
```

Or it could be written from the command line as:

```
% perl -pe 's/(\p{Letter})/\l$1/g'
```

While using **-n** or **-p** for implicit input looping, the special label LINE: is silently created for the whole input loop. That means that from an inner loop, you can skip to the following input record by using next LINE (which is like *awk*'s next statement), or go on to the next file by closing ARGV (which is like *awk*'s nextfile statement). This is shown in Example 7-6.

Example 7-6. countchunks

```
#!/usr/bin/perl -n
# countchunks - count how many words are used.
```

Example 7-6. countchunks (continued)

```
# skip comments, and bail on file if __END__
# or __DATA__ seen.
for (split /\W+/) {
    next LINE if /^#/;
    close ARGV if /__(DATA|END)__/;
    $chunks++;
}
END { print "Found $chunks chunks\n" }
```

The *tcsh* keeps a *.history* file in a format such that every other line contains a commented out timestamp in Epoch seconds:

```
#+0894382237
less /etc/motd
#+0894382239
vi ~/.exrc
#+0894382242
date
#+0894382242
who
#+0894382288
telnet home
```

A simple one-liner can render that legible:

```
% perl -pe 's/^#\+(\d+)\n/localtime($1) . " "/e'
Tue May  5 09:30:37 1998    less /etc/motd
Tue May  5 09:30:39 1998    vi ~/.exrc
Tue May  5 09:30:42 1998    date
Tue May  5 09:30:42 1998    who
Tue May  5 09:31:28 1998    telnet home
```

The **-i** option changes each file on the command line. It is described in Recipe 7.16, and is normally used in conjunction with **-p**.

See Also

perlrun(1), and the "Switches" section of Chapter 19 of *Programming Perl*; Recipe 7.16; Recipe 16.6

7.15   Modifying a File in Place with a Temporary File

Problem

You need to update a file in place, and you can use a temporary file.

Solution

Read from the original file, write changes to a temporary file, and then rename the temporary back to the original:

```
open(OLD, "<", $old)          or die "can't open $old: $!";
open(NEW, ">", $new)          or die "can't open $new: $!";
while (<OLD>) {
    # change $_, then...
    print NEW $_              or die "can't write $new: $!";
}
close(OLD)                     or die "can't close $old: $!";
close(NEW)                     or die "can't close $new: $!";
rename($old, "$old.orig")     or die "can't rename $old to $old.orig: $!";
rename($new, $old)            or die "can't rename $new to $old: $!";
```

This is the best way to update a file "in place."

Discussion

This technique uses little memory compared to the approach that doesn't use a temporary file. It has the added advantages of giving you a backup file and being easier and safer to program.

You can make the same changes to the file using this technique that you can with the version that uses no temporary file. For instance, to insert lines at line 20, say:

```
while (<OLD>) {
    if ($. == 20) {
        print NEW "Extra line 1\n";
        print NEW "Extra line 2\n";
    }
    print NEW $_;
}
```

To delete lines 20 through 30, say:

```
while (<OLD>) {
    next if 20 .. 30;
    print NEW $_;
}
```

Note that rename won't work across filesystems, so you should create your temporary file in the same directory as the file being modified.

The truly paranoid programmer would lock the file during the update. The tricky part is that you have to open the file for writing without destroying its contents before you can get a lock to modify it. Recipe 7.18 shows how to do this.

See Also

Recipe 7.1; Recipe 7.16; Recipe 7.17; Recipe 7.18

7.16 Modifying a File in Place with the -i Switch

Problem

You need to modify a file in place from the command line, and you're too lazy* for the file manipulation of Recipe 7.15.

Solution

Use the **-i** and **-p** switches to Perl. Write your program on the command line:

```
% perl -i.orig -p -e 'FILTER COMMAND' file1 file2 file3 ...
```

or use the switches in programs:

```
#!/usr/bin/perl -i.orig -p
# filter commands go here
```

Discussion

The **-i** command-line switch modifies each file in place. It creates a temporary file as in the previous recipe, but Perl takes care of the tedious file manipulation for you. Use it with **-p** (explained in Recipe 7.14) to turn:

```
while (<>) {
    if ($ARGV ne $oldargv) {            # are we at the next file?
        rename($ARGV, $ARGV . ".orig");
        open(ARGVOUT, ">", $ARGV);      # plus error check
        select(ARGVOUT);
        $oldargv = $ARGV;
    }
    s/DATE/localtime/e;
}
continue{
    print;
}
select (STDOUT);                        # restore default output
```

into:

```
% perl -pi.orig -e 's/DATE/localtime/e'
```

The **-i** switch takes care of making a backup (say -i instead of -i.orig to discard the original file contents instead of backing them up), and **-p** makes Perl loop over filenames given on the command line (or STDIN if no files were given).

The preceding one-liner would turn a file containing the following:

```
Dear Sir/Madam/Ravenous Beast,
    As of DATE, our records show your account
```

---

* Lazy-as-virtue, not lazy-as-sin.

```
is overdue.  Please settle by the end of the month.
Yours in cheerful usury,
    --A. Moneylender
```

into:

```
Dear Sir/Madam/Ravenous Beast,
    As of Sat Apr 25 12:28:33 1998, our records show your account
is overdue.  Please settle by the end of the month.
Yours in cheerful usury,
    --A. Moneylender
```

This switch makes in-place translators a lot easier to write and to read. For instance, this changes isolated instances of "hisvar" to "hervar" in all C, C++, and *yacc* files:

```
% perl -i.old -pe 's{\bhisvar\b}{hervar}g' *.[Cchy]
```

Turn on and off the **-i** behavior with the special variable $^I. Set @ARGV, and then use <> as you would with **-i** on the command line:

```
# set up to iterate over the *.c files in the current directory,
# editing in place and saving the old file with a .orig extension
local $^I   = ".orig";              # emulate  -i.orig
local @ARGV = glob("*.c");          # initialize list of files
while (<>) {
    if ($. == 1) {
        print "This line should appear at the top of each file\n";
    }
    s/\b(p)earl\b/${1}erl/ig;       # Correct typos, preserving case
    print;
} continue {close ARGV if eof}
```

Beware that creating a backup file under a particular name when that name already exists clobbers the version previously backed up.

See Also

perlrun(1), and the "Switches" section of Chapter 19 of *Programming Perl*; the $^I and $. variables in *perlvar*(1), and in Chapter 28 of *Programming Perl*; the .. operator in the "Range Operator" sections of *perlop*(1) and Chapter 3 of *Programming Perl*

7.17 Modifying a File in Place Without a Temporary File

Problem

You need to insert, delete, or change one or more lines in a file, and you don't want to (or can't) use a temporary file.

Solution

Open the file in update mode ("+<"), read the whole file into an array of lines, change the array, then rewrite the file and truncate it to its current seek pointer.

```
open(FH, "+<", $FILE)              or die "Opening: $!";
@ARRAY = <FH>;
# change ARRAY here
seek(FH,0,0)                       or die "Seeking: $!";
print FH @ARRAY                    or die "Printing: $!";
truncate(FH,tell(FH))             or die "Truncating: $!";
close(FH)                          or die "Closing: $!";
```

Discussion

As explained in this chapter's Introduction, the operating system treats files as unstructured streams of bytes. This makes it impossible to insert, modify, or change bits of the file in place. (Except for the special case of fixed-record-length files, discussed in Recipe 8.13.) You can use a temporary file to hold the changed output, or you can read the entire file into memory, change it, and write it back out again.

Reading everything into memory is fine for small files, but doesn't scale well. Trying it on your 800 MB web server log files will either deplete your virtual memory or thrash your machine's VM system. For small files, though, this works:

```
open(F, "+<", $infile)     or die "can't read $infile: $!";
$out = "";
while (<F>) {
    s/DATE/localtime/eg;
    $out .= $_;
}
seek(F, 0, 0)              or die "can't seek to start of $infile: $!";
print F $out              or die "can't print to $infile: $!";
truncate(F, tell(F))      or die "can't truncate $infile: $!";
close(F)                  or die "can't close $infile: $!";
```

For other examples of things you can do in-place, look at the recipes in Chapter 8.

This approach is only for the truly determined. It's harder to write, takes more memory (potentially a *lot* more), doesn't keep a backup file, and may confuse other processes trying to read from the file you're updating. For most purposes, therefore, we suggest it's probably not worth it.

Remember to lock if you're paranoid, careful, or both.

See Also

The seek, truncate, open, and sysopen functions in *perlfunc*(1) and in Chapter 29 of *Programming Perl*; Recipe 7.15; Recipe 7.16; Recipe 7.18

7.18   Locking a File

Problem

Many processes need to update the same file simultaneously.

Solution

Have all processes honor advisory locking by using flock:

```
use Fcntl qw(:flock);              # for the LOCK_* constants
open(FH, "+<", $path)              or die "can't open $path: $!";
flock(FH, LOCK_EX)                 or die "can't flock $path: $!";
# update file, then...
close(FH)                          or die "can't close $path: $!";
```

Discussion

Operating systems vary greatly in the type and reliability of locking techniques available. Perl tries hard to give you something that works, even if your operating system uses its own underlying technique. The flock function takes two arguments: a filehandle and a number representing what to do with the lock on that filehandle. The numbers are normally represented by names, such as LOCK_EX, which you can get from the Fcntl or IO::File modules.

Locks come in two varieties: shared (LOCK_SH) and exclusive (LOCK_EX). Despite what you might infer by "exclusive," processes aren't required to obey locks on files. Another way of saying this is that flock implements *advisory locking*. It allows processes to let the operating system suspend would-be writers of a file until any readers are finished with it.

Flocking files is like putting up a stoplight at an intersection. It works only if people pay attention to whether the light is red or green—or yellow for a shared lock. The red light doesn't stop traffic; it merely signals that traffic should stop. A desperate, ignorant, or rude person will still go flying through the intersection no matter what the light says. Likewise, flock only blocks out other flockers—not all processes trying to do I/O. Unless everyone is polite, accidents can (and will) happen.

The polite process customarily indicates its intent to read from the file by requesting a LOCK_SH. Many processes can have simultaneous shared locks on the file because they (presumably) won't be changing the data. If a process intends to write to the file, it should request an exclusive lock via LOCK_EX. The operating system then suspends the requesting process until all other processes have released their locks, at which point it grants the lock to the suspended process and unblocks it. You are guaranteed that no other process will be able to successfully run flock(FH, LOCK_EX) on the same file while you hold the lock.

(This is almost—but not quite—like saying there can be only one exclusive lock on the file. Forked children inherit not only their parents' open files, but, on some systems, also any locks held. That means if you hold an exclusive lock and fork without execing, your child might also have that same exclusive lock on the file!)

The flock function is therefore by default a blocking operation. You can also acquire a lock without wedging your process by using the LOCK_NB flag when you request a lock. This lets you warn the user that there may be a wait until other processes with locks are done:

```
unless (flock(FH, LOCK_EX|LOCK_NB)) {
    warn "can't immediately write-lock the file ($!), blocking ...";
    unless (flock(FH, LOCK_EX)) {
        die "can't get write-lock on numfile: $!";
    }
}
```

If you use LOCK_NB and are refused a LOCK_SH, then you know that someone else has a LOCK_EX and is updating the file. If you are refused a LOCK_EX, then someone holds either a LOCK_SH or a LOCK_EX, so you shouldn't try to update the file.

Locks dissolve when the file is closed, which may not be until your process exits. If you lock or unlock the file, Perl automatically flushes its buffers for you.

Here's how you increment a number in a file, using flock:

```
use Fcntl qw(:DEFAULT :flock);

sysopen(FH, "numfile", O_RDWR|O_CREAT)
                                or die "can't open numfile: $!";
flock(FH, LOCK_EX)              or die "can't write-lock numfile: $!";
# Now we have acquired the lock, it's safe for I/O
$num = <FH> || 0;               # DO NOT USE "or" THERE!!
seek(FH, 0, 0)                  or die "can't rewind numfile : $!";
truncate(FH, 0)                 or die "can't truncate numfile: $!";
print FH $num+1, "\n"           or die "can't write numfile: $!";
close(FH)                       or die "can't close numfile: $!";
```

Closing the filehandle flushes the buffers and unlocks the file. The truncate function is discussed in Chapter 8.

File locking is not as easy as you might think—or wish. Because locks are advisory, if one process uses locking and another doesn't, all bets are off. Never use the existence of a file as a locking indication because there exists a race condition between the test for the existence of the file and its creation. Furthermore, because file locking is an intrinsically stateful concept, it doesn't get along well with the stateless model embraced by network filesystems such as NFS. Although some vendors claim that fcntl addresses such matters, practical experience suggests otherwise. The CPAN module File::NFSLock uses a clever scheme to obtain and release locks on files over NFS, which is different from the flock system.

Don't confuse Perl's flock with the SysV function lockf. Unlike lockf, flock locks entire files at once. Perl doesn't support lockf directly, although the CPAN module File::Lock does offer its functionality if your operating system has lockf. The only way in pure Perl to lock a portion of a file is to use the fcntl function, as demonstrated in the *lockarea* program at the end of this chapter.

See Also

The flock and fcntl functions in *perlfunc*(1) and in Chapter 29 of *Programming Perl*; the documentation for the standard Fcntl and DB_File modules (also in Chapter 32 of *Programming Perl*); the documentation for the CPAN modules File::Lock and File::NFSLock; Recipe 7.24; Recipe 7.25

7.19   Flushing Output

Problem

When printing to a filehandle, output doesn't appear immediately. This is a problem in CGI scripts running on some programmer-hostile web servers where, if the web server sees warnings from Perl before it sees the (buffered) output of your script, it sends the browser an uninformative 500 Server Error. These buffering problems also arise with concurrent access to files by multiple programs and when talking with devices or sockets.

Solution

Disable buffering by setting the per-filehandle variable $| to a true value, customarily 1:

```
$old_fh = select(OUTPUT_HANDLE);
$| = 1;
select($old_fh);
```

Or, if you don't mind the expense of loading an IO module, disable buffering by invoking the autoflush method:

```
use IO::Handle;
OUTPUT_HANDLE->autoflush(1);
```

This works with indirect filehandles as well:

```
use IO::Handle;
$fh->autoflush(1);
```

Discussion

In most stdio implementations, buffering varies with the type of output device. Disk files are block buffered, often with a buffer size of more than 2K. Pipes and sockets are often buffered with a buffer size between $\frac{1}{2}$ K and 2K. Serial devices, including terminals, modems, mice, and joysticks, are normally line-buffered; stdio sends the entire line out only when it gets the newline.

Perl's print function does not directly support truly unbuffered output, i.e., a physical write for each individual character. Instead, it supports *command buffering*, in which one physical write is made after every separate output command. This isn't as hard on your system as no buffering at all, and it still gets the output where you want it, when you want it.

Control output buffering through the $| special variable. Enable command buffering on output handles by setting it to a true value. This does not affect input handles at all; see Recipes 15.6 and 15.8 for unbuffered input. Set this variable to a false value to use default stdio buffering. Example 7-7 illustrates the difference.

Example 7-7. seeme

```
#!/usr/bin/perl -w
# seeme - demo stdio output buffering
$| = (@ARGV > 0);        # command buffered if arguments given
print "Now you don't see it...";
sleep 2;
print "now you do\n";
```

If you call this program with no arguments, STDOUT is not command buffered. Your terminal (console, window, telnet session, whatever) doesn't receive output until the entire line is completed, so you see nothing for two seconds and then get the full line "Now you don't see it ... now you do". If you call the program with at least one argument, STDOUT is command buffered. That means you first see "Now you don't see it...", and then after two seconds you finally see "now you do".

The dubious quest for increasingly compact code has led programmers to use the return value of select, the filehandle that *was* currently selected, as part of the second select:

```
select((select(OUTPUT_HANDLE), $| = 1)[0]);
```

There's another way. The IO::Handle module and any modules that inherit from that class provide three methods for flushing: flush, autoflush, and printflush. All are invoked on filehandles, either as literals or as variables containing a filehandle or reasonable facsimile.

The flush method causes all unwritten output in the buffer to be written out, returning true on failure and false on success. The printflush method is a print followed by a one-time flush. The autoflush method is syntactic sugar for the convoluted antics just shown. It sets the command-buffering property on that filehandle (or clears it if passed an explicit false value), and returns the previous value for that property on that handle. For example:

```
use FileHandle;

STDERR->autoflush;              # already unbuffered in stdio
$filehandle->autoflush(0);
```

If you're willing to accept the oddities of indirect object notation covered in Chapter 13, you can even write something reasonably close to English:

```
use IO::Handle;
# assume REMOTE_CONN is an interactive socket handle,
# but DISK_FILE is a handle to a regular file.
autoflush REMOTE_CONN  1;          # unbuffer for clarity
autoflush DISK_FILE    0;          # buffer this for speed
```

This avoids the bizarre select business and makes your code much more readable. Unfortunately, your program takes longer to compile because now you're including the IO::Handle module, so dozens of files need to be opened and thousands and thousands of lines must first be read and compiled. For short and simple applications, you might as well learn to manipulate $| directly, and you'll be happy. But for larger applications that already use a class derived from the IO::Handle class, you've already paid the price for the ticket, so you might as well see the show.

To ensure that your output gets where you want it, when you want it, buffer flushing is important. It's particularly important with sockets, pipes, and devices, because you may be trying to do interactive I/O with these—more so, even, because you can't assume line buffering. Consider the program in Example 7-8.

Example 7-8. getpcomidx

```
#!/usr/bin/perl -w
# getpcomidx - fetch www.perl.com's index.html document
use IO::Socket;
$sock = new IO::Socket::INET (PeerAddr => "www.perl.com",
                              PeerPort => "http(80)");
die "Couldn't create socket: $@" unless $sock;
# the library doesn't support $! setting; it uses $@
$sock->autoflush(1);
# Mac *must* have \015\012\015\012 instead of \n\n here.
# It's a good idea for others, too, as that's the spec,
# but implementations are encouraged to accept "\cJ\cJ" too,
# and as far as we've seen, they do.
$sock->print("GET /index.html http/1.1\n\n");
$document = join("", $sock->getlines());
print "DOC IS: $document\n";
```

If you're running at least v5.8 Perl, you can use the new I/O layers mechanism to force unbuffered output. This is available through the :unix layer. If the handle is already open, you can do this:

```
binmode(STDOUT, ":unix")
    || die "can't binmode STDOUT to :unix: $!";
```

or you can specify the I/O layer when initially calling open:

```
open(TTY, ">:unix", "/dev/tty")
    || die "can't open /dev/tty: $!";
print TTY "54321";
sleep 2;
print TTY "\n";
```

There's no way to control input buffering using the sorts of flushing discussed so far. For that, you need to see Recipes 15.6 and 15.8.

See Also

The $| entry in *perlvar*(1), and Chapter 28 of *Programming Perl*; the documentation for the standard FileHandle and IO::Handle modules (also in Chapter 32 of *Programming Perl*); the select function in *perlfunc*(1) and in Chapter 29 of *Programming Perl*; Recipes 15.6 and 15.8

7.20 Doing Non-Blocking I/O

Problem

You want to read from or write to a filehandle without the system blocking your process until the program, file, socket, or device at the other end is ready. This is desired less often of regular files than of special files.

Solution

Open the file with sysopen, specifying the O_NONBLOCK option:

```
use Fcntl;
sysopen(MODEM, "/dev/cua0", O_NONBLOCK|O_RDWR)
    or die "Can't open modem: $!\n";
```

If you already have an open filehandle, invoke the blocking method from IO::Handle with an argument of 0:

```
use IO::Handle;
MODEM->blocking(0);  # assume MODEM already opened
```

Or use the low-level fcntl function:

```
use Fcntl;

$flags = "";
fcntl(HANDLE, F_GETFL, $flags)
    or die "Couldn't get flags for HANDLE : $!\n";
$flags |= O_NONBLOCK;
fcntl(HANDLE, F_SETFL, $flags)
    or die "Couldn't set flags for HANDLE: $!\n";
```

Discussion

On a disk file, when no more data can be read because you're at the end of the file, the input operation returns immediately. But suppose the filehandle in question were the user's keyboard or a network connection. In those cases, simply because there's no data there right now doesn't mean there never will be, so the input function normally doesn't return until it gets data. Sometimes, though, you don't want to wait; you want to grab whatever's there and carry on with whatever you were doing.

Once a filehandle has been set for non-blocking I/O, the `sysread` or `syswrite` calls that would otherwise block will instead return undef and set `$!` to EAGAIN:

```
use Errno;

$rv = syswrite(HANDLE, $buffer, length $buffer);
if (!defined($rv) && $!{EAGAIN}) {
    # would block
} elsif ($rv != length $buffer) {
    # incomplete write
} else {
    # successfully wrote
}

$rv = sysread(HANDLE, $buffer, $BUFSIZ);
if (!defined($rv) && $!{EAGAIN}) {
    # would block
} else {
    # successfully read $rv bytes from HANDLE
}
```

The O_NONBLOCK constant is part of the POSIX standard, so most machines should support it. We use the Errno module to test for the error EAGAIN. Testing `$!{EAGAIN}` is the same as testing whether `$!` == EAGAIN.

See Also

The sysopen and fcntl functions in *perlfunc*(1) and in Chapter 29 of *Programming Perl*; the documentation for the standard Errno and IO::Handle modules (also in Chapter 32 of *Programming Perl*); your system's *open*(2) and *fcntl*(2) manpages; Recipe 7.22; Recipe 7.21

7.21 Determining the Number of Unread Bytes

Problem

You want to know how many unread bytes are available for reading from a filehandle.

Solution

Use the FIONREAD ioctl call:

```
$size = pack("L", 0);
ioctl(FH, $FIONREAD, $size)     or die "Couldn't call ioctl: $!\n";
$size = unpack("L", $size);

# $size bytes can be read
```

Make sure the input filehandle is unbuffered (because you've used an I/O layer like :unix on it), or use only sysread.

Discussion

The Perl ioctl function is a direct interface to the operating system's *ioctl*(2) system call. If your system doesn't have the FIONREAD request or the *ioctl*(2) call, you can't use this recipe. FIONREAD and the other *ioctl*(2) requests are numeric values normally found lurking in C include files.

Perl's *h2ph* tool tries to convert C include files to Perl code, which can be required. FIONREAD ends up defined as a function in the *sys/ioctl.ph* file:

```
require "sys/ioctl.ph";

$size = pack("L", 0);
ioctl(FH, FIONREAD(), $size)     or die "Couldn't call ioctl: $!\n";
$size = unpack("L", $size);
```

If *h2ph* wasn't installed or doesn't work for you, you can manually *grep* the include files:

```
% grep FIONREAD /usr/include/*/*
/usr/include/asm/ioctls.h:#define FIONREAD     0x541B
```

If you install Inline::C from CPAN, you can write a C subroutine to obtain the constant for you:

```
use Inline C;

$FIONREAD = get_FIONREAD();
# ...

__END__
__C__
#include <sys/ioctl.h>

int get_FIONREAD() {
  return FIONREAD;
}
```

If all else fails, write a small C program using the editor of champions:

```
% cat > fionread.c
#include <sys/ioctl.h>
```

```
main( ) {
    printf("%#08x\n", FIONREAD);
}
^D
% cc -o fionread fionread.c
% ./fionread
0x4004667f
```

Then hardcode it, leaving porting as an exercise to your successor.

```
$FIONREAD = 0x4004667f;          # XXX: opsys dependent

$size = pack("L", 0);
ioctl(FH, $FIONREAD, $size)       or die "Couldn't call ioctl: $!\n";
$size = unpack("L", $size);
```

FIONREAD requires a filehandle connected to a stream, which means sockets, pipes, and tty devices all work, but regular files don't.

If this is too much system programming for you, try to think outside the problem. Read from the filehandle in non-blocking mode (see Recipe 7.20). Then, if you manage to read something, that's how much was there waiting to be read. If you couldn't read anything, you know there was nothing to be read. This might get you in trouble with other users (or other processes) who are using the same system, though— because it uses busy-wait I/O, it's a drain on system resources.

See Also

Recipe 7.20; your system's *ioctl*(2) manpage; the ioctl function in *perlfunc*(1) and in Chapter 29 of *Programming Perl*; the documentation for the Inline::C module from CPAN

7.22 Reading from Many Filehandles Without Blocking

Problem

You want to learn whether input is available to be read, rather than blocking until there's input the way <FH> does. This is useful when reading from pipes, sockets, devices, and other programs.

Solution

Use select with a timeout value of 0 seconds if you're comfortable with manipulating bit-vectors representing file descriptor sets:

```
$rin = "";
# repeat next line for all filehandles to poll
```

```
vec($rin, fileno(FH1), 1) = 1;
vec($rin, fileno(FH2), 1) = 1;
vec($rin, fileno(FH3), 1) = 1;

$nfound = select($rout=$rin, undef, undef, 0);
if ($nfound) {
    # input waiting on one or more of those 3 filehandles
    if (vec($rout,fileno(FH1),1)) {
        # do something with FH1
    }
    if (vec($rout,fileno(FH2),1)) {
        # do something with FH2
    }
    if (vec($rout,fileno(FH3),1)) {
        # do something with FH3
    }
}
```

The IO::Select module provides an abstraction layer to hide bit-vector operations:

```
use IO::Select;

$select = IO::Select->new( );
# repeat next line for all filehandles to poll
$select->add(*FILEHANDLE);
if (@ready = $select->can_read(0)) {
    # input waiting on the filehandles in @ready
}
```

Discussion

The select function is really two functions in one. If you call it with one argument, you change the current default output filehandle (see Recipe 7.19). If you call it with four arguments, it tells you which filehandles have input waiting or are ready to receive output. This recipe deals only with four-argument select.

The first three arguments to select are strings containing bit-vectors. Each bit-vector represents a set of file descriptors to inspect for pending input, pending output, and pending expedited data (like out-of-band or urgent data on a socket), respectively. The final argument is the timeout—how long select should spend waiting for status to change. A timeout value of 0 indicates a poll. Timeout can also be a floating-point number of seconds, or undef to wait (block) until status changes:

```
$rin = "";
vec($rin, fileno(FILEHANDLE), 1) = 1;
$nfound = select($rin, undef, undef, 0);    # just check
if ($nfound) {
    # read ten bytes from FILEHANDLE
    sysread(HANDLE, $data, 10);
    print "I read $data";
}
```

The IO::Select module hides the bit-vectors from you. IO::Select->new( ) returns a new object on which you invoke the add method to add one or more filehandles to the set. Once you've added the filehandles you are interested in, invoke can_read, can_write, or has_exception. These methods return a list of filehandles that you can safely read from or write to, or that have unread exceptional data (TCP out-of-band data, for example).

If you want to read an entire line of data, you can't use the readline function or the <FH> line input operator (unless you use an unbuffered I/O layer). Otherwise, you'll mix a buffered I/O function with a check that ignores those buffers in user space and cares only about what's buffered in kernel space. This is a big no-no. For details on this and directions for calling sysread on whatever is available on a socket or pipe and then returning immediately, see Recipe 7.23. If you're trying to do non-blocking reads on a terminal line (that is, on a keyboard or other serial line device), see Recipes 15.6 and 15.8.

See Also

The select function in *perlfunc*(1) and in Chapter 29 of *Programming Perl*; the documentation for the standard module IO::Select (also in Chapter 32 of *Programming Perl*); Recipe 7.20; Recipe 7.23

7.23   Reading an Entire Line Without Blocking

Problem

You need to read a line of data from a handle that select says is ready for reading, but you can't use Perl's normal <FH> operation (readline) in conjunction with select because <FH> may buffer extra data and select doesn't know about those buffers.

Solution

Use the following sysreadline function, like this:

```
$line = sysreadline(SOME_HANDLE);
```

In case only a partial line has been sent, include a number of seconds to wait:

```
$line = sysreadline(SOME_HANDLE, TIMEOUT);
```

Here's the function to do that:

```
use IO::Handle;
use IO::Select;
use Symbol qw(qualify_to_ref);

sub sysreadline(*;$) {
    my($handle, $timeout) = @_;
```

```perl
    $handle = qualify_to_ref($handle, caller());
    my $infinitely_patient = (@_ == 1 || $timeout < 0);
    my $start_time = time();
    my $selector = IO::Select->new();
    $selector->add($handle);
    my $line = "";
SLEEP:
    until (at_eol($line)) {
        unless ($infinitely_patient) {
            return $line if time() > ($start_time + $timeout);
        }
        # sleep only 1 second before checking again
        next SLEEP unless $selector->can_read(1.0);
INPUT_READY:
        while ($selector->can_read(0.0)) {
            my $was_blocking = $handle->blocking(0);
CHAR:       while (sysread($handle, my $nextbyte, 1)) {
                $line .= $nextbyte;
                last CHAR if $nextbyte eq "\n";
            }
            $handle->blocking($was_blocking);
            # if incomplete line, keep trying
            next SLEEP unless at_eol($line);
            last INPUT_READY;
        }
    }
    return $line;
}
sub at_eol($) { $_[0] =~ /\n\z/ }
```

Discussion

As described in Recipe 7.22, to determine whether the operating system has data on a particular handle for your process to read, you can use either Perl's built-in select function or the can_read method from the standard IO::Select module.

Although you can reasonably use functions like sysread and recv to get data, you can't use the buffered functions like readline (that is, <FH>), read, or getc. Also, even the unbuffered input functions might still block. If someone connects and sends a character but never sends a newline, your program will block in a <FH>, which expects its input to end in a newline—or in whatever you've assigned to the $/ variable.

We circumvent this by setting the handle to non-blocking mode and then reading in characters until we find "\n". This removes the need for the blocking <FH> call. The sysreadline function in the Solution takes an optional second argument so you don't have to wait forever in case you get a partial line and nothing more.

A far more serious issue is that select reports only whether the operating system's low-level file descriptor is available for I/O. It's not reliable in the general case to mix calls to four-argument select with calls to any of the buffered I/O functions listed in this chapter's Introduction (read, <FH>, seek, tell, etc.). Instead, you must use sysread—and sysseek if you want to reposition the filehandle within the file.

The reason is that select's response does not reflect any user-level buffering in your own process's address space once the kernel has transferred the data. But the <FH>—really Perl's readline( ) function—still uses your underlying buffered I/O system. If two lines were waiting, select would report true only once. You'd read the first line and leave the second one in the buffer. But the next call to select would block because, as far as the kernel is concerned, it's already given you all of the data it had. That second line, now hidden from your kernel, sits unread in an input buffer that's solely in user space.

See Also

The sysread function in *perlfunc*(1) and in Chapter 29 of *Programming Perl*; the documentation for the standard modules Symbol, IO::Handle, and IO::Select (also in Chapter 32 of *Programming Perl*); Recipe 7.22

7.24 Program: netlock

When locking files, we recommend that you use flock when possible. However, on some systems, flock's locking strategy is not reliable. For example, perhaps the person who built Perl on your system configured flock to use a version of file locking that didn't even try to work over the Net, or you're on the increasingly rare system where no flock emulation exists at all.

The following program and module provide a basic implementation of a file locking mechanism. Unlike a normal flock, with this module you lock file *names*, not file descriptors.

Thus, you can use it to lock directories, domain sockets, and other non-regular files. You can even lock files that don't exist yet. It uses a directory created at the same level in the directory structure as the locked file, so you must be able to write to the enclosing directory of the file you wish to lock. A sentinel file within the lock directory contains the owner of the lock. This is also useful with Recipe 7.15 because you can lock the filename even though the file that has that name changes.

The nflock function takes one or two arguments. The first is the pathname to lock; the second is the optional amount of time to wait for the lock. The function returns true if the lock is granted, returns false if the timeout expired, and raises an exception should various improbable events occur, such as being unable to write the directory.

Set the $File::LockDir::Debug variable to true to make the module emit messages if it stalls waiting for a lock. If you forget to free a lock and try to exit the program, the module will remove them for you. This won't happen if your program is sent a signal it doesn't trap.

Example 7-9 shows a driver program to demonstrate the File::LockDir module.

Example 7-9. drivelock

```perl
#!/usr/bin/perl -w
# drivelock - demo File::LockDir module
use strict;
use File::LockDir;
$SIG{INT} = sub { die "outta here\n" };
$File::LockDir::Debug = 1;
my $path = shift                              or die "usage: $0 <path>\n";
unless (nflock($path, 2)) {
    die "couldn't lock $path in 2 seconds\n";
}
sleep 100;
nunflock($path);
```

The module itself is shown in Example 7-10. For more on building your own modules, see Chapter 12.

Example 7-10. File::LockDir

```perl
package File::LockDir;
# module to provide very basic filename-level
# locks.  No fancy systems calls.  In theory,
# directory info is sync'd over NFS.  Not
# stress tested.
use strict;
use Exporter;
our (@ISA, @EXPORT);
@ISA      = qw(Exporter);
@EXPORT   = qw(nflock nunflock);
our ($Debug, $Check);
$Debug  ||= 0;   # may be predefined
$Check  ||= 5;   # may be predefined
use Cwd;
use Fcntl;
use Sys::Hostname;
use File::Basename;
use File::stat;
use Carp;
my %Locked_Files = ();
# usage: nflock(FILE; NAPTILL)
sub nflock($;$) {
    my $pathname = shift;
    my $naptime  = shift || 0;
    my $lockname = name2lock($pathname);
    my $whosegot = "$lockname/owner";
    my $start    = time();
    my $missed   = 0;
    my $owner;
    # if locking what I've already locked, return
    if ($Locked_Files{$pathname}) {
        carp "$pathname already locked";
```

Example 7-10. File::LockDir (continued)

```
        return 1
    }
    if (!-w dirname($pathname)) {
        croak "can't write to directory of $pathname";
    }
    while (1) {
        last if mkdir($lockname, 0777);
        confess "can't get $lockname: $!" if $missed++ > 10
                        && !-d $lockname;
        if ($Debug) {{
            open($owner, "< $whosegot") || last; # exit "if"!
            my $lockee = <$owner>;
            chomp($lockee);
            printf STDERR "%s $0\[$$]: lock on %s held by %s\n",
                scalar(localtime), $pathname, $lockee;
            close $owner;
        }}
        sleep $Check;
        return if $naptime && time > $start+$naptime;
    }
    sysopen($owner, $whosegot, O_WRONLY|O_CREAT|O_EXCL)
            or croak "can't create $whosegot: $!";
    printf $owner "$0\[$$] on %s since %s\n",
            hostname( ), scalar(localtime);
    close($owner)
            or croak "close $whosegot: $!";
    $Locked_Files{$pathname}++;
    return 1;
}
# free the locked file
sub nunflock($) {
    my $pathname = shift;
    my $lockname = name2lock($pathname);
    my $whosegot = "$lockname/owner";
    unlink($whosegot);
    carp "releasing lock on $lockname" if $Debug;
    delete $Locked_Files{$pathname};
    return rmdir($lockname);
}
# helper function
sub name2lock($) {
    my $pathname = shift;
    my $dir  = dirname($pathname);
    my $file = basename($pathname);
    $dir = getcwd( ) if $dir eq ".";
    my $lockname = "$dir/$file.LOCKDIR";
    return $lockname;
}
# anything forgotten?
END {
    for my $pathname (keys %Locked_Files) {
        my $lockname = name2lock($pathname);
```

Example 7-10. File::LockDir (continued)

```
        my $whosegot = "$lockname/owner";
        carp "releasing forgotten $lockname";
        unlink($whosegot);
        rmdir($lockname);
    }
  }
  1;
```

7.25 Program: lockarea

Perl's flock function only locks complete files, not regions of the file. Although fcntl supports locking of a file's regions, this is difficult to access from Perl, largely because no one has written an XS module that portably packs up the necessary structure.

The program in Example 7-11 implements *fcntl*, but only for the three architectures it already knows about: SunOS, BSD, and Linux. If you're running something else, you'll have to figure out the layout of the flock structure. We did this by eyeballing the C-language *sys/fcntl.h* #include file—and running the *c2ph* program to figure out alignment and typing. This program, while included with Perl, only works on systems with a strong Berkeley heritage, like those listed above. As with Unix—or Perl itself—you don't *have* to use *c2ph*, but it sure makes life easier if you can.

The struct_flock function in the *lockarea* program packs and unpacks in the proper format for the current architectures by consulting the $^O variable, which contains your current operating system name. There is no struct_flock function declaration. It's just aliased to the architecture-specific version. Function aliasing is discussed in Recipe 10.14.

The *lockarea* program opens a temporary file, clobbering any existing contents and writing a screenful (80 by 23) of blanks. Each line is the same length.

The program then forks one or more times and lets the child processes try to update the file at the same time. The first argument, *N*, is the number of times to fork to produce 2 ** N processes. So *lockarea 1* makes two children, *lockarea 2* makes four, *lockarea 3* makes eight, *lockarea 4* makes sixteen, etc. The more kids, the more contention for the locks.

Each process picks a random line in the file, locks that line only, and then updates it. It writes its process ID into the line, prepended with a count of how many times the line has been updated:

```
    4: 18584 was just here
```

If the line was already locked, then when the lock is finally granted, that line is updated with a message telling which process was in the way of this process:

```
    29: 24652 ZAPPED 24656
```

A fun demo is to run the *lockarea* program in the background and the *rep* program from Chapter 15, watching the file change. Think of it as a video game for systems programmers.

```
% lockarea 5 &
% rep -1 'cat /tmp/lkscreen'
```

When you interrupt the original parent, usually with Ctrl-C or by sending it a SIGINT from the command line, it kills all of its children by sending its entire process group a signal.

Example 7-11. lockarea

```perl
#!/usr/bin/perl -w
    # lockarea - demo record locking with fcntl

    use strict;

    my $FORKS = shift || 1;
    my $SLEEP = shift || 1;

    use Fcntl;
    use POSIX qw(:unistd_h);
    use Errno;

    my $COLS = 80;
    my $ROWS = 23;

    # when's the last time you saw *this* mode used correctly?
    open(FH, "+> /tmp/lkscreen")            or  die $!;

    select(FH);
    $| = 1;
    select STDOUT;

    # clear screen
    for (1 .. $ROWS) {
        print FH " " x $COLS, "\n";
    }

    my $progenitor = $$;
    fork() while $FORKS-- > 0;

    print "hello from $$\n";

    if ($progenitor == $$) {
        $SIG{INT} = \&infanticide;
    } else {
        $SIG{INT} = sub { die "goodbye from $$" };
    }

    while (1) {
        my $line_num = int rand($ROWS);
```

Example 7-11. lockarea (continued)

```perl
    my $line;
    my $n;

    # move to line
    seek(FH, $n = $line_num * ($COLS+1), SEEK_SET)              or next;

    # get lock
    my $place = tell(FH);
    my $him;
    next unless defined($him = lockplace(*FH, $place, $COLS));

    # read line
    read(FH, $line, $COLS) == $COLS                            or next;
    my $count = ($line =~ /(\d+)/) ? $1 : 0;
    $count++;

    # update line
    seek(FH, $place, 0)                                        or die $!;
    my $update = sprintf($him
                    ? "%6d: %d ZAPPED %d"
                    : "%6d: %d was just here",
                 $count, $$, $him);
    my $start = int(rand($COLS - length($update)));
    die "XXX" if $start + length($update) > $COLS;
    printf FH "%*.*s\n", -$COLS, $COLS, " " x $start . $update;

    # release lock and go to sleep
    unlockplace(*FH, $place, $COLS);
    sleep $SLEEP if $SLEEP;
}
die "NOT REACHED";                              # just in case

# lock($handle, $offset, $timeout) - get an fcntl lock
    sub lockplace {
    my ($fh, $start, $till) = @_;
    ##print "$$: Locking $start, $till\n";
    my $lock = struct_flock(F_WRLCK, SEEK_SET, $start, $till, 0);
    my $blocker = 0;
    unless (fcntl($fh, F_SETLK, $lock)) {
        die "F_SETLK $$ @_: $!" unless $!{EAGAIN} || $!{EDEADLK};
        fcntl($fh, F_GETLK, $lock)         or die "F_GETLK $$ @_: $!";
        $blocker = (struct_flock($lock))[-1];
        ##print "lock $$ @_: waiting for $blocker\n";
        $lock = struct_flock(F_WRLCK, SEEK_SET, $start, $till, 0);
        unless (fcntl($fh, F_SETLKW, $lock)) {
            warn "F_SETLKW $$ @_: $!\n";
            return;  # undef
        }
    }
    return $blocker;
    }
```

Example 7-11. lockarea (continued)

```
# unlock($handle, $offset, $timeout) - release an fcntl lock
sub unlockplace {
    my ($fh, $start, $till) = @_;
    ##print "$$: Unlocking $start, $till\n";
    my $lock = struct_flock(F_UNLCK, SEEK_SET, $start, $till, 0);
    fcntl($fh, F_SETLK, $lock) or die "F_UNLCK $$ @_: $!";
}

# OS-dependent flock structures

# Linux struct flock
#    short l_type;
#    short l_whence;
#    off_t l_start;
#    off_t l_len;
#    pid_t l_pid;
BEGIN {
    # c2ph says: typedef='s2 l2 i', sizeof=16
    my $FLOCK_STRUCT = "s s l l i";

    sub linux_flock {
        if (wantarray) {
            my ($type, $whence, $start, $len, $pid) =
                unpack($FLOCK_STRUCT, $_[0]);
            return ($type, $whence, $start, $len, $pid);
        } else {
            my ($type, $whence, $start, $len, $pid) = @_;
            return pack($FLOCK_STRUCT,
                    $type, $whence, $start, $len, $pid);
        }
    }

}

# SunOS struct flock:
#    short   l_type;         /* F_RDLCK, F_WRLCK, or F_UNLCK */
#    short   l_whence;       /* flag to choose starting offset */
#    long    l_start;        /* relative offset, in bytes */
#    long    l_len;          /* length, in bytes; 0 means lock to EOF */
#    short   l_pid;          /* returned with F_GETLK */
#    short   l_xxx;          /* reserved for future use */
BEGIN {
    # c2ph says: typedef='s2 l2 s2', sizeof=16
    my $FLOCK_STRUCT = "s s l l s s";

    sub sunos_flock {
        if (wantarray) {
            my ($type, $whence, $start, $len, $pid, $xxx) =
                unpack($FLOCK_STRUCT, $_[0]);
            return ($type, $whence, $start, $len, $pid);
        } else {
```

Example 7-11. lockarea (continued)

```perl
                my ($type, $whence, $start, $len, $pid) = @_;
                return pack($FLOCK_STRUCT,
                        $type, $whence, $start, $len, $pid, 0);
            }
        }

    }

    # (Free)BSD struct flock:
    #   off_t   l_start;       /* starting offset */
    #   off_t   l_len;         /* len = 0 means until end-of-file */
    #   pid_t   l_pid;         /* lock owner */
    #   short   l_type;        /* lock type: read/write, etc. */
    #   short   l_whence;      /* type of l_start */
    BEGIN {
        # c2ph says: typedef="q2 i s2", size=24
        my $FLOCK_STRUCT = "ll ll i s s";   # XXX: q is ll

        sub bsd_flock {
            if (wantarray) {
                my ($xxstart, $start, $xxlen, $len, $pid, $type, $whence) =
                    unpack($FLOCK_STRUCT, $_[0]);
                return ($type, $whence, $start, $len, $pid);
            } else {
                my ($type, $whence, $start, $len, $pid) = @_;
                my ($xxstart, $xxlen) = (0,0);
                return pack($FLOCK_STRUCT,
                    $xxstart, $start, $xxlen, $len, $pid, $type, $whence);
            }
        }
    }

    # alias the fcntl structure at compile time
    BEGIN {
        for ($^O) {
            *struct_flock =              do                              {

                            /bsd/   &&  \&bsd_flock
                                    ||
                        /linux/     &&      \&linux_flock
                                    ||
                      /sunos/       &&        \&sunos_flock
                                    ||
                    die "unknown operating system $^O, bailing out";
            };
        }
    }

    # install signal handler for children
    BEGIN {
        my $called = 0;
```

Example 7-11. lockarea (continued)

```perl
        sub infanticide {
            exit if $called++;
            print "$$: Time to die, kiddies.\n" if $$ == $progenitor;
            my $job = getpgrp( );
            $SIG{INT} = "IGNORE";
            kill -2, $job if $job;  # killpg(SIGINT, job)
            1 while wait > 0;
            print "$$: My turn\n" if $$ == $progenitor;
            exit;
        }

    }

    END { &infanticide }
```

CHAPTER 8

File Contents

The most brilliant decision in all of Unix was the
choice of a single character for the newline sequence.
—Mike O'Dell, only half jokingly

8.0 Introduction

Before the Unix Revolution, every kind of data source and destination was inherently different. Getting two programs merely to understand each other required heavy wizardry and the occasional sacrifice of a virgin stack of punch cards to an itinerant mainframe repairman. This computational Tower of Babel made programmers dream of quitting the field to take up a less painful hobby, like autoflagellation.

These days, such cruel and unusual programming is largely behind us. Modern operating systems work hard to provide the illusion that I/O devices, network connections, process control information, other programs, the system console, and even users' terminals are all abstract streams of bytes called *files*. This lets you easily write programs that don't care where their input came from or where their output goes.

Because programs read and write streams of simple text, every program can communicate with every other program. It is difficult to overstate the power and elegance of this approach. No longer dependent upon troglodyte gnomes with secret tomes of JCL (or COM) incantations, users can now create custom tools from smaller ones by using simple command-line I/O redirection, pipelines, and backticks.

Basic Operations

Treating files as unstructured byte streams necessarily governs what you can do with them. You can read and write sequential, fixed-size blocks of data at any location in the file, increasing its size if you write past the current end. Perl uses an I/O library that emulates C's *stdio*(3) to implement reading and writing of variable-length records like lines, paragraphs, and words.

What can't you do to an unstructured file? Because you can't insert or delete bytes anywhere but at end-of-file, you can't easily change the length of, insert, or delete records. An exception is the last record, which you can delete by truncating the file to the end of the previous record. For other modifications, you need to use a temporary file or work with a copy of the file in memory. If you need to do this a lot, a database system may be a better solution than a raw file (see Chapter 14). Standard with Perl as of v5.8 is the Tie::File module, which offers an array interface to files of records. We use it in Recipe 8.4.

The most common files are text files, and the most common operations on text files are reading and writing lines. Use the line-input operator, <FH> (or the internal function implementing it, readline), to read lines, and use print to write them. These functions can also read or write any record that has a specific record separator. Lines are simply variable-length records that end in "\n".

The <FH> operator returns undef on error or when end of the file is reached, so use it in loops like this:

```
while (defined ($line = <DATAFILE>)) {
    chomp $line;
    $size = length($line);
    print "$size\n";                 # output size of line
}
```

Because this operation is extremely common in Perl programs that process lines of text, and that's an awful lot to type, Perl conveniently provides some shorter aliases for it. If all shortcuts are taken, this notation might be too abstract for the uninitiated to guess what it's really doing. But it's an idiom you'll see thousands of times in Perl, so you'll soon get used to it. Here are increasingly shortened forms, where the first line is the completely spelled-out version:

```
while (defined ($line = <DATAFILE>))     { ... }
while ($line = <DATAFILE>)               { ... }
while (<DATAFILE>)                       { ... }
```

In the second line, the explicit defined test needed for detecting end-of-file is omitted. To make everyone's life easier, you're safe to skip that defined test, because when the Perl compiler detects this situation, it helpfully puts one there for you to guarantee your program's correctness in odd cases. This implicit addition of a defined occurs on all while tests that do nothing but assign to one scalar variable the result of calling readline, readdir, or readlink. As <FH> is just shorthand for readline(FH), it also counts.

We're not quite done shortening up yet. As the third line shows, you can also omit the variable assignment completely, leaving just the line input operator in the while test. When you do that here in a while test, it doesn't simply discard the line it just read as it would anywhere else. Instead, it reads lines into the special global variable $_. Because so many other operations in Perl also default to $_, this is more useful than it might initially appear.

```
while (<DATAFILE>) {
    chomp;
    print length(), "\n";              # output size of line
}
```

In scalar context, <FH> reads just the next line, but in list context, it reads all remaining lines:

```
@lines = <DATAFILE>;
```

Each time <FH> reads a record from a filehandle, it increments the special variable $. (the "current input record number"). This variable is reset only when close is called explicitly, which means that it's not reset when you reopen an already opened filehandle.

Another special variable is $/, the input record separator. It is set to "\n" by default. You can set it to any string you like; for instance, "\0" to read null-terminated records. Read entire paragraphs by setting $/ to the empty string, "". This is almost like setting $/ to "\n\n", in that empty lines function as record separators. However, "" treats two or more consecutive empty lines as a single record separator, whereas "\n\n" returns empty records when more than two consecutive empty lines are read. Undefine $/ to read the rest of the file as one scalar:

```
undef $/;
$whole_file = <FILE>;                 # "slurp" mode
```

The **-0** option to Perl lets you set $/ from the command line:

```
% perl -040 -e '$word = <>; print "First word is $word\n";'
```

The digits after **-0** are the octal value of the single character to which $/ is to be set. If you specify an illegal value (e.g., with **-0777**), Perl will set $/ to undef. If you specify **-00**, Perl will set $/ to "". The limit of a single octal value means you can't set $/ to a multibyte string; for instance, "%%\n" to read *fortune* files. Instead, you must use a BEGIN block:

```
% perl -ne 'BEGIN { $/="%%\n" } chomp; print if /Unix/i' fortune.dat
```

Use print to write a line or any other data. The print function writes its arguments one after another and doesn't automatically add a line or record terminator by default.

```
print HANDLE "One", "two", "three"; # "Onetwothree"
print "Baa baa black sheep.\n";      # Sent to default output handle
```

There is no comma between the filehandle and the data to print. If you put a comma in there, Perl gives the error message "No comma allowed after filehandle". The default output handle is STDOUT. Change it with the select function. (See the Introduction to Chapter 7.)

Newlines

All systems use the virtual "\n" to represent a line terminator, called a *newline*. There is no such thing as a newline character; it is a platform-independent way of saying "whatever your string library uses to represent a line terminator." On Unix, VMS, and Windows, this line terminator in strings is "\cJ" (the Ctrl-J character). Versions of the old Macintosh operating system before Mac OS X used "\cM". As a Unix variant, Mac OS X uses "\cJ".

Operating systems also vary in how they store newlines in files. Unix also uses "\cJ" for this. On Windows, though, lines in a text file end in "\cM\cJ". If your I/O library knows you are reading or writing a text file, it will automatically translate between the string line terminator and the file line terminator. So on Windows, you could read four bytes ("Hi\cM\cJ") from disk and end up with three in memory ("Hi\cJ" where "\cJ" is the physical representation of the newline character). This is never a problem on Unix, as no translation needs to happen between the disk's newline ("\cJ") and the string's newline ("\cJ").

Terminals, of course, are a different kettle of fish. Except when you're in raw mode (as in system("stty raw")), the Enter key generates a "\cM" (carriage return) character. This is then translated by the terminal driver into a "\n" for your program. When you print a line to a terminal, the terminal driver notices the "\n" newline character (whatever it might be on your platform) and turns it into the "\cM\cJ" (carriage return, line feed) sequence that moves the cursor to the start of the line and down one line.

Even network protocols have their own expectations. Most protocols prefer to receive and send "\cM\cJ" as the line terminator, but many servers also accept merely a "\cJ". This varies between protocols and servers, so check the documentation closely!

The important notion here is that if the I/O library thinks you are working with a text file, it may be translating sequences of bytes for you. This is a problem in two situations: when your file is not text (e.g., you're reading a JPEG file) and when your file is text but not in a byte-oriented ASCII-like encoding (e.g., UTF-8 or any of the other encodings the world uses to represent their characters). As if this weren't bad enough, some systems (again, MS-DOS is an example) use a particular byte sequence in a text file to indicate end-of-file. An I/O library that knows about text files on such a platform will indicate EOF when that byte sequence is read.

Recipe 8.11 shows how to disable any translation that your I/O library might be doing.

I/O Layers

With v5.8, Perl I/O operations are no longer simply wrappers on top of stdio. Perl now has a flexible system (I/O layers) that transparently filters multiple encodings of external data. In Chapter 7 we met the :unix layer, which implements unbuffered I/O. There are also layers for using your platform's stdio (:stdio) and Perl's portable stdio implementation (:perlio), both of which buffer input and output. In this chapter, these implementation layers don't interest us as much as the encoding layers built on top of them.

The :crlf layer converts a carriage return and line feed (CRLF, "\cM\cJ") to "\n" when reading from a file, and converts "\n" to CRLF when writing. The opposite of :crlf is :raw, which makes it safe to read or write binary data from the filehandle. You can specify that a filehandle contains UTF-8 data with :utf8, or specify an encoding with :encoding(...). You can even write your own filter in Perl that processes data being read before your program gets it, or processes data being written before it is sent to the device.

It's worth emphasizing: to disable :crlf, specify the :raw layer. The :bytes layer is sometimes misunderstood to be the opposite of :crlf, but they do completely different things. The former refers to the UTF-8ness of strings, and the latter to the behind-the-scenes conversion of carriage returns and line feeds.

You may specify I/O layers when you open the file:

```
open($fh, "<:raw:utf8", $filename);          # read UTF-8 from the file
open($fh, "<:encoding(shiftjis)", $filename); # shiftjis japanese encoding
open(FH,  "+<:crlf", $filename);             # convert between CRLF and \n
```

Or you may use binmode to change the layers of an existing handle:

```
binmode($fh, ":raw:utf8");
binmode($fh, ":raw:encoding(shiftjis)");
binmode(FH,  "<:raw:crlf");
```

Because binmode pushes onto the stack of I/O layers, and the facility for removing layers is still evolving, you should always specify a complete set of layers by making the first layer be :raw as follows:

```
binmode(HANDLE, ":raw");                      # binary-safe
binmode(HANDLE);                              # same as :raw
binmode(HANDLE, ":raw :utf8");                # read/write UTF-8
binmode(HANDLE, ":raw :encoding(shiftjis)"); # read/write shiftjis
```

Recipes 8.18, 8.19, and 8.20 show how to manipulate I/O layers.

Advanced Operations

Use the read function to read a fixed-length record. It takes three arguments: a filehandle, a scalar variable, and the number of characters to read. It returns undef if an error occurred or else returns the number of characters read.

```
$rv = read(HANDLE, $buffer, 4096)
        or die "Couldn't read from HANDLE : $!\n";
# $rv is the number of bytes read,
# $buffer holds the data read
```

To write a fixed-length record, just use print.

The truncate function changes the length (in bytes) of a file, which can be specified as a filehandle or as a filename. It returns true if the file was successfully truncated, false otherwise:

```
truncate(HANDLE, $length)          or die "Couldn't truncate: $!\n";
truncate("/tmp/$$.pid", $length)   or die "Couldn't truncate: $!\n";
```

Each filehandle keeps track of where it is in the file. Reads and writes occur from this point, unless you've specified the O_APPEND flag (see Recipe 7.1). Fetch the file position for a filehandle with tell, and set it with seek. Because the library rewrites data to preserve the illusion that "\n" is the line terminator, and also because you might be using characters with code points above 255 and therefore requiring a multibyte encoding, you cannot portably seek to offsets calculated simply by counting characters. Unless you can guarantee your file uses one byte per character, seek only to offsets returned by tell.

```
$pos = tell(DATAFILE);
print "I'm $pos bytes from the start of DATAFILE.\n";
```

The seek function takes three arguments: the filehandle, the offset (in bytes) to go to, and a numeric argument indicating how to interpret the offset. 0 indicates an offset from the start of the file (like the value returned by tell); 1, an offset from the current location (a negative number means move backward in the file, a positive number means move forward); and 2, an offset from end-of-file.

```
seek(LOGFILE, 0, 2)      or die "Couldn't seek to the end: $!\n";
seek(DATAFILE, $pos, 0)  or die "Couldn't seek to $pos: $!\n";
seek(OUT, -20, 1)        or die "Couldn't seek back 20 bytes: $!\n";
```

So far we've been describing buffered I/O. That is, readline or <FH>, print, read, seek, and tell are all operations that use buffering for speed and efficiency. This is their default behavior, although if you've specified an unbuffered I/O layer for that handle, they won't be buffered. Perl also provides an alternate set of I/O operations guaranteed to be unbuffered no matter what I/O layer is associated with the handle. These are sysread, syswrite, and sysseek, all discussed in Chapter 7.

The sysread and syswrite functions are different in appearance from their <FH> and print counterparts. Both take a filehandle to act on: a scalar variable to either read into or write out from, and the number of characters to transfer. (With binary data, this is the number of bytes, not characters.) They also accept an optional fourth argument, the offset from the start of the scalar variable at which to start reading or writing:

```
$written = syswrite(DATAFILE, $mystring, length($mystring));
die "syswrite failed: $!\n" unless $written == length($mystring);
$read = sysread(INFILE, $block, 256, 5);
warn "only read $read bytes, not 256" if 256 != $read;
```

The syswrite call sends the contents of $mystring to DATAFILE. The sysread call reads 256 characters from INFILE and stores 5 characters into $block, leaving intact the 5 characters it skipped. Both sysread and syswrite return the number of characters transferred, which could be different than the amount of data you were attempting to transfer. Maybe the file didn't have as much data as you thought, so you got a short read. Maybe the filesystem that the file lives on filled up. Maybe your process was interrupted partway through the write. Stdio takes care of finishing the transfer in cases of interruption, but if you use raw sysread and syswrite calls, you must finish up yourself. See Recipe 9.3 for an example.

The sysseek function doubles as an unbuffered replacement for both seek and tell. It takes the same arguments as seek, but it returns the new position on success and undef on error. To find the current position within the file:

```
$pos = sysseek(HANDLE, 0, 1);        # don't change position
die "Couldn't sysseek: $!\n" unless defined $pos;
```

These are the basic operations available to you. The art and craft of programming lies in using these basic operations to solve complex problems such as finding the number of lines in a file, reversing lines in a file, randomly selecting a line from a file, building an index for a file, and so on.

8.1 Reading Lines with Continuation Characters

Problem

You have a file with long lines split over two or more lines, with backslashes to indicate that a continuation line follows. You want to rejoin those split lines. Makefiles, shell scripts, and many other scripting or configuration languages let you break a long line into several shorter ones in this fashion.

Solution

Build up the complete lines one at a time until reaching one without a backslash:

```
while (defined($line = <FH>) ) {
    chomp $line;
    if ($line =~ s/\\$//) {
        $line .= <FH>;
        redo unless eof(FH);
    }
    # process full record in $line here
}
```

Discussion

Here's an example input file:

```
DISTFILES = $(DIST_COMMON) $(SOURCES) $(HEADERS) \
        $(TEXINFOS) $(INFOS) $(MANS) $(DATA)
DEP_DISTFILES = $(DIST_COMMON) $(SOURCES) $(HEADERS) \
        $(TEXINFOS) $(INFO_DEPS) $(MANS) $(DATA) \
        $(EXTRA_DIST)
```

You'd like to process that file a record at a time with the escaped newlines ignored. The first record would then be the first two lines, the second record the next three lines, etc.

Here's how the algorithm works. The while loop reads lines one at a time. The substitution operator s/// tries to remove a trailing backslash. If the substitution fails, we've found a line without a backslash at the end. Otherwise, read another record, concatenate it onto the accumulating $line variable, and use redo to jump back to just inside the opening brace of the while loop. This lands us back on the chomp.

A frequent problem with files intended to be in this format arises when unnoticed spaces or tabs follow the backslash before the newline. The substitution that found continuation lines would be more forgiving if written this way:

```
if ($line =~ s/\\\s*$//) {
    # as before
}
```

Unfortunately, even if your program is forgiving, surely others will not be. Remember to be liberal in what you accept, but conservative in what you produce.

See Also

The chomp function in *perlfunc*(1) and in Chapter 29 of *Programming Perl*; the redo keyword in the "Loop Control" sections of *perlsyn*(1) and Chapter 4 of *Programming Perl*

8.2 Counting Lines (or Paragraphs or Records) in a File

Problem

You need to compute the number of lines in a file.

Solution

Many systems have a *wc* program to count lines in a file:

```
$count = `wc -l < $file`;
die "wc failed: $?" if $?;
chomp($count);
```

You could also open the file and read line-by-line until the end, counting lines as you go:

```
open(FILE, "<", $file) or die "can't open $file: $!";
$count++ while <FILE>;
# $count now holds the number of lines read
```

Here's the fastest solution, assuming your line terminator really *is* "\n":

```
$count += tr/\n/\n/ while sysread(FILE, $_, 2 ** 20);
```

Discussion

Although you can use -s $file to determine the file size in bytes, you generally cannot use it to derive a line count. See the Introduction in Chapter 9 for more on -s.

If you can't or don't want to call another program to do your dirty work, you can emulate *wc* by opening up and reading the file yourself:

```
open(FILE, "<", $file) or die "can't open $file: $!";
$count++ while <FILE>;
# $count now holds the number of lines read
```

Another way of writing this is:

```
open(FILE, "<", $file) or die "can't open $file: $!";
for ($count=0; <FILE>; $count++) { }
```

If you're not reading from any other files, you don't need the $count variable in this case. The special variable $. holds the number of lines read since a filehandle was last explicitly closed:

```
1 while <FILE>;
$count = $.;
```

This reads in all records in the file, then discards them.

To count paragraphs, set the global input record separator variable $/ to the empty string ("") before reading to make the input operator (<FH>) read a paragraph at a time.

```
$/ = "";                 # enable paragraph mode for all reads
open(FILE, "<", $file) or die "can't open $file: $!";
1 while <FILE>;
$para_count = $.;
```

The sysread solution reads the file a megabyte at a time. Once end-of-file is reached, sysread returns 0. This ends the loop, as does undef, which would indicate an error. The tr operation doesn't really substitute \n for \n in the string; it's an old idiom for counting occurrences of a character in a string.

See Also

The tr operator in *perlop*(1) and Chapter 5 of *Programming Perl*; your system's *wc*(1) manpage; the $/ entry in *perlvar*(1), and in the "Special Variables in Alphabetical Order" section of Chapter 28 of *Programming Perl*; the Introduction to Chapter 9

8.3 Processing Every Word in a File

Problem

You need to do something to every word in a file, similar to the foreach function of *csh*.

Solution

Either split each line on whitespace:

```
while (<>) {
    for $chunk (split) {
        # do something with $chunk
    }
}
```

or use the m//g operator to pull out one chunk at a time:

```
while (<>) {
    while ( /(\w[\w'-]*)/g ) {
        # do something with $1
    }
}
```

Discussion

Decide what you mean by "word." Sometimes you want anything but whitespace, sometimes you want only program identifiers, and sometimes you want English words. Your definition governs which regular expression to use.

The preceding two approaches work differently. Patterns are used in the first approach to decide what is *not* a word. In the second, they're used to decide what *is* a word.

With these techniques, it's easy to make a word frequency counter. Use a hash to store how many times each word has been seen:

```
# Make a word frequency count
%seen = ();
while (<>) {
    while ( /(\w[\w'-]*)/g ) {
        $seen{lc $1}++;
    }
}
```

```
# output hash in a descending numeric sort of its values
foreach $word ( sort { $seen{$b} <=> $seen{$a} } keys %seen) {
    printf "%5d %s\n", $seen{$word}, $word;
}
```

To make the example program count line frequency instead of word frequency, omit the second while loop and use $seen{lc $_}++ instead:

```
# Line frequency count
%seen = ( );
while (<>) {
    $seen{lc $_}++;
}
foreach $line ( sort { $seen{$b} <=> $seen{$a} } keys %seen ) {
    printf "%5d %s", $seen{$line}, $line;
}
```

Odd things that may need to be considered as words include "M.I.T.", "Micro$oft", "o'clock", "49ers", "street-wise", "and/or", "&", "c/o", "St.", "Tschüß", and "Niño". Bear this in mind when you choose a pattern to match. The last two require you to place a use locale in your program and then use \w for a word character in the current locale, or else use the Unicode letter property if you have Unicode text:

```
/(\p{Letter}[\p{Letter}'-]*)/
```

See Also

perlre(1); the split function in perlfunc(1) and in Chapter 29 of Programming Perl; Recipe 6.3; Recipe 6.23

8.4 Reading a File Backward by Line or Paragraph

Problem

You want to process each line or paragraph of a text file in reverse.

Solution

Read all lines into an array, then process that array from the end to the start:

```
@lines = <FILE>;
while ($line = pop @lines) {
    # do something with $line
}
```

Or store an array of lines in reverse order:

```
@lines = reverse <FILE>;
foreach $line (@lines) {
```

```
    # do something with $line
}
```

Or use the Tie::File module (standard as of v5.8):

```
use Tie::File;
tie(@lines, "Tie::File", $FILENAME, mode => 0)
    or die "Can't tie $FILENAME: $!";
$max_lines = $#lines;
for ($i = $max_lines; $i; $i--) {
    # do something with $lines[$i], eg line number them:
    printf "%5d  %s\n", $i+1, $lines[$i],
}
```

Discussion

The limitations of file access mentioned in this chapter's Introduction prevent read-ing a line at a time starting from the end. You must read the lines into memory, then process them in reverse order. This requires at least as much available memory as the size of the file, unless you use tricks like Tie::File does.

The first technique moves through the array of lines in reverse order. This *destruc-tively* processes the array, popping an element off the end of the array each time through the loop. We could do it non-destructively with:

```
for ($i = $#lines; $i != -1; $i--) {
    $line = $lines[$i];
}
```

The second approach generates an array of lines already in reverse order. This array can then be processed non-destructively. We get the reversed lines because the assignment to @lines confers list context on the return from reverse, and reverse confers list context on its argument of <FILE>, which returns a list of all lines in the file.

These approaches are easily extended to paragraphs just by changing $/:

```
# this enclosing block keeps local $/ temporary
{
    local $/ = "";
    @paragraphs = reverse <FILE>;
}

foreach $paragraph (@paragraphs) {
    # do something
}
```

The Tie::File module lets you treat the file as an array of lines. The solution then becomes simply iterating through the array a line at a time from the end back to the start. It's much slower than reading everything into memory and reversing it, but works on files too big to fit into memory all at once. Be careful, though: Tie::File will rewrite the file if you change the contents of the tied @lines, so don't do that. In our example, assigning @lines = reverse(@lines) would reverse the file on disk! By opening the file with mode O_RDONLY (0), you can avoid that possibility. The default mode is O_RDWR | O_CREAT. Also, Tie::File cannot emulate the paragraph semantics of setting $/ to the empty string ("").

See Also

The reverse function in *perlfunc*(1) and in Chapter 29 of *Programming Perl*; the $/ entry in *perlvar*(1), and in Chapter 28 of *Programming Perl*; the documentation for the standard Tie::File module; Recipe 4.11; Recipe 1.7

8.5 Trailing a Growing File

Problem

You want to read from a continually growing file, but the read fails when you reach the current end-of-file.

Solution

Read until end-of-file. Sleep, clear the EOF flag, and read some more. Repeat until interrupted. To clear the EOF flag, either use seek:

```
for (;;) {
    while (<FH>) { .... }
    sleep $SOMETIME;
    seek(FH, 0, 1);
}
```

or use the IO::Handle module's clearerr method:

```
use IO::Handle;

for (;;) {
    while (<FH>) { .... }
    sleep $SOMETIME;
    FH->clearerr();
}
```

Discussion

When you read until end-of-file, an internal flag is set that prevents further reading. The most direct way to clear this flag is the clearerr method, if supported: it's in the IO::Handle modules.

```
$naptime = 1;

use IO::Handle;
open (LOGFILE, "/tmp/logfile") or die "can't open /tmp/logfile: $!";
```

```
for (;;) {
    while (<LOGFILE>) { print }      # or appropriate processing
    sleep $naptime;
    LOGFILE->clearerr();             # clear stdio error flag
}
```

Because Perl v5.8 ships with its own stdio implementation, that simple approach should almost always work. On the rare system where it doesn't work, you may need to use seek. The seek code given in the Solution tries to move zero bytes from the current position, which nearly always works. It doesn't change the current position, but it should clear the end-of-file condition on the handle so that the next <LOGFILE> operation picks up new data.

If that still doesn't work, perhaps because it relies on features of your I/O implementation, you may need to use the following seek code, which remembers the old file position explicitly and returns there directly.

```
for (;;) {
    for ($curpos = tell(LOGFILE); <LOGFILE>; $curpos = tell(LOGFILE)) {
        # process $_ here
    }
    sleep $naptime;
    seek(LOGFILE, $curpos, 0);  # seek to where we had been
}
```

On some kinds of filesystems, the file could be removed while you are reading it. If so, there's probably little reason to continue checking whether it grows. To make the program exit in that case, stat the handle and make sure its link count (the third field in the return list) hasn't gone to 0:

```
exit if (stat(LOGFILE))[3] == 0
```

If you're using the File::stat module, you could write that more readably as:

```
use File::stat;
exit if stat(*LOGFILE)->nlink == 0;
```

The CPAN module File::Tail lets you tie a filehandle so that the read operation blocks at the end of the file until more data is available:

```
use File::Tail;

tie *FH, "File::Tail", (name => $FILENAME);
while (<FH>) {
  # do something with line read
}
```

The <FH> operator in this case never returns undef to indicate end-of-file.

See Also

The seek and tell functions in *perlfunc*(1) and in Chapter 29 of *Programming Perl*; your system's *tail*(1) and *stdio*(3) manpages; the documentation for the standard

File::stat module (also in Chapter 32 of *Programming Perl*); the documentation for the CPAN module File::Tail

8.6   Picking a Random Line from a File

Problem

You want to return a random line from a file.

Solution

Use rand and $. (the current line number) to decide which line to print:

```
srand;
rand($.) < 1 && ($line = $_) while <>;
# $line is the random line
```

Discussion

This is a beautiful example of a solution that may not be obvious. We read every line in the file but don't have to store them all in memory. This is great for large files. Each line has a 1 in N (where N is the number of lines read so far) chance of being selected.

Here's a replacement for *fortune* using this algorithm:

```
$/ = "%%\n";
@ARGV = ("/usr/share/games/fortunes") unless @ARGV;
srand;
rand($.) < 1 && ($adage = $_) while <>;
print $adage;
```

If you know line offsets (for instance, you've created an index) and the number of lines, you can randomly select a line and jump to its offset in the file, but you usually don't have such an index.

Here's a more rigorous explanation of how the algorithm works. The function call rand ($.) picks a random number between 0 and the current line number. Therefore, you have a one in N chance, that is, $\frac{1}{N}$, of keeping the Nth line. Therefore you've a 100% chance of keeping the first line, a 50% chance of keeping the second, a 33% chance of keeping the third, and so on. The question is whether this is fair for all N, where N is any positive integer.

First, some concrete examples, then abstract ones.

Obviously, a file with one line (N=1) is fair: you always keep the first line because $\frac{1}{1}$ = 100%, making it fair for files of 1 line. For a file with two lines, N=2. You always keep the first line; then when reaching the second line, you have a 50% chance of keeping it. Thus, both lines have an equal chance of being selected, which shows that N=2 is fair. For a file with three lines, N=3. You have a one-third chance, 33%, of keeping that third line. That leaves a two-thirds chance of retaining one of the first two out of the three lines. But we've already shown that for those first two lines there's a 50-50 chance of selecting either one. 50 percent of two-thirds is one-third. Thus, you have a one-third chance of selecting each of the three lines of the file.

In the general case, a file of N+1 lines will choose the last line $\frac{1}{N+1}$ times and one of the previous N lines $\frac{N}{N+1}$ times. Dividing $\frac{N}{N+1}$ by N leaves us with $\frac{1}{N+1}$ for each the first N lines in our N+1 line file, and also $\frac{1}{N+1}$ for line number N+1. The algorithm is therefore fair for all N, where N is a positive integer.

We've managed to fairly choose a random line from a file with speed directly proportional to the size of the file, but using no more memory than it takes to hold the longest line, even in the worst case.

See Also

The `$.` entry in *perlvar*(1) and in Chapter 28 of *Programming Perl*; Recipe 2.6; Recipe 2.7

8.7 Randomizing All Lines

Problem

You want to copy a file and randomly reorder its lines.

Solution

Read all lines into an array, shuffle the array using List::Util's `shuffle` function, and write the shuffled lines back out:

```
use List::Util qw(shuffle);

while (<INPUT>) {
    push(@lines, $_);
}
@lines = shuffle(@lines);
foreach (@reordered) {
    print OUTPUT $_;
}
```

Discussion

The easiest approach is to read all lines into memory and shuffle them there. Because you don't know where lines start in the file, you can't just shuffle a list of line numbers and then extract lines in the order they'll appear in the shuffled file. Even if you *did* know the byte offsets of the start of each line, it would probably still be slower because you'd be seeking around in the file instead of sequentially reading it from start to finish.

If you have a version of Perl older than v5.8, you can download the List::Util module from CPAN.

See Also

The documentation for the standard List::Util module; Recipe 2.6; Recipe 2.7; Recipe 4.18

8.8   Reading a Particular Line in a File

Problem

You want to extract a single line from a file.

Solution

The simplest solution is to read the lines until you get to the one you want:

```
# looking for line number $DESIRED_LINE_NUMBER
$. = 0;
do { $LINE = <HANDLE> } until $. == $DESIRED_LINE_NUMBER || eof;
```

If you are going to be doing this a lot and the file fits into memory, read the file into an array:

```
@lines = <HANDLE>;
$LINE = $lines[$DESIRED_LINE_NUMBER];
```

The standard (as of v5.8) Tie::File ties an array to a file, one line per array element:

```
use Tie::File;
use Fcntl;

tie(@lines, Tie::File, $FILE, mode => O_RDWR)
  or die "Cannot tie file $FILE: $!\n";
$line = $lines[$sought - 1];
```

If you have the DB_File module, its DB_RECNO access method ties an array to a file, one line per array element:

```
use DB_File;
use Fcntl;

$tie = tie(@lines, DB_File, $FILE, O_RDWR, 0666, $DB_RECNO) or die
    "Cannot open file $FILE: $!\n";
# extract it
$line = $lines[$sought - 1];
```

Discussion

Each strategy has different features, useful in different circumstances. The linear access approach is easy to write and best for short files. The Tie::File module gives good performance, regardless of the size of the file or which line you're reading (and is pure Perl, so doesn't require any external libraries). The DB_File mechanism has some initial overhead, but later accesses are faster than with linear access, so use it for long files that are accessed more than once and are accessed out of order.

It is important to know whether you're counting lines from 0 or 1. The $. variable is 1 after the first line is read, so count from 1 when using linear access. The index mechanism uses many offsets, so count from 0. Tie::File and DB_File treat the file's records as an array indexed from 0, so count lines from 0.

Here are three different implementations of the same program, *print_line*. The program takes two arguments: a filename and a line number to extract.

The version in Example 8-1 simply reads lines until it finds the one it's looking for.

Example 8-1. print_line-v1

```
#!/usr/bin/perl -w
# print_line-v1 - linear style

@ARGV == 2 or die "usage: print_line FILENAME LINE_NUMBER\n";

($filename, $line_number) = @ARGV;
open(INFILE, "<", $filename)
  or die "Can't open $filename for reading: $!\n";
while (<INFILE>) {
    $line = $_;
    last if $. == $line_number;
}
if ($. != $line_number) {
    die "Didn't find line $line_number in $filename\n";
}
print;
```

The Tie::File version is shown in Example 8-2.

Example 8-2. print_line-v2

```
#!/usr/bin/perl -w
# print_line-v2 - Tie::File style
use Tie::File;
use Fcntl;
@ARGV == 2 or die "usage: print_line FILENAME LINE_NUMBER\n";
($filename, $line_number) = @ARGV;
tie @lines, Tie::File, $filename, mode => O_RDWR
    or die "Can't open $filename for reading: $!\n";
if (@lines > $line_number) {
    die "Didn't find line $line_number in $filename\n";
```

Example 8-2. print_line-v2 (continued)

```
}
print "$lines[$line_number-1]\n";
```

The DB_File version in Example 8-3 follows the same logic as Tie::File.

Example 8-3. print_line-v3

```
#!/usr/bin/perl -w
# print_line-v3 - DB_File style
use DB_File;
use Fcntl;

@ARGV == 2 or die "usage: print_line FILENAME LINE_NUMBER\n";
($filename, $line_number) = @ARGV;
$tie = tie(@lines, DB_File, $filename, O_RDWR, 0666, $DB_RECNO)
    or die "Cannot open file $filename: $!\n";

unless ($line_number < $tie->length) {
    die "Didn't find line $line_number in $filename\n"
}

print $lines[$line_number-1];                     # easy, eh?
```

If you will be retrieving lines by number often and the file doesn't fit into memory, build a byte-address index to let you seek directly to the start of the line using the techniques in Recipe 8.27.

See Also

The documentation for the standard Tie::File and DB_File modules (also in Chapter 32 of *Programming Perl*); the tie function in *perlfunc*(1) and in Chapter 29 of *Programming Perl*; the entry on $. in *perlvar*(1) and in Chapter 28 of *Programming Perl*; Recipe 8.27

8.9 Processing Variable-Length Text Fields

Problem

You want to extract variable-length fields from your input.

Solution

Use split with a pattern matching the field separators.

```
# given $RECORD with field separated by a pattern,
# extract a list of fields
@FIELDS = split(/PATTERN/, $RECORD);
```

Discussion

The split function takes up to three arguments: PATTERN, EXPRESSION, and LIMIT. The LIMIT parameter is the maximum number of fields to split into. (If the input contains more fields, they are returned unsplit in the final list element.) If LIMIT is omitted, all fields (except any final empty ones) are returned. EXPRESSION gives the string value to split. If EXPRESSION is omitted, $_ is split. PATTERN is a pattern matching the field separator. If PATTERN is omitted, contiguous stretches of whitespace are used as the field separator and leading empty fields are silently discarded.

If your input field separator isn't a fixed string, you might want split to return the field separators as well as the data by using parentheses in PATTERN to save the field separators. For instance:

```
split(/([+-])/, "3+5-2");
```

returns the values:

```
(3, "+", 5, "-", 2)
```

To split colon-separated records in the style of the */etc/passwd* file, use:

```
@fields = split(/:/, $RECORD);
```

The classic application of split is whitespace-separated records:

```
@fields = split(/\s+/, $RECORD);
```

If $RECORD started with whitespace, this last use of split would have put an empty string into the first element of @fields because split would consider the record to have an initial empty field. If you didn't want this, you could use this special form of split:

```
@fields = split(" ", $RECORD);
```

This behaves like split with a pattern of /\s+/, but ignores leading whitespace.

When the record separator can appear in the record, you have a problem. The usual solution is to escape occurrences of the record separator in records by prefixing them with a backslash. See Recipe 1.18.

See Also

The split function in *perlfunc*(1) and in Chapter 29 of *Programming Perl*; Recipe 1.18

8.10   Removing the Last Line of a File

Problem

You'd like to remove the last line from a file.

Solution

Use the standard (as of v5.8) Tie::File module and delete the last element from the
tied array:

```
use Tie::File;

tie @lines, Tie::File, $file        or die "can't update $file: $!";
delete $lines[-1];
```

Discussion

The Tie::File solution is the most efficient solution, at least for large files, because it
doesn't have to read through the entire file to find the last line and doesn't read the
entire file into memory. It is, however, considerably slower for small files than code
you could implement yourself by hand. That doesn't mean you shouldn't use Tie::
File; it just means you've optimized for programmer time instead of for computer
time.

If you don't have Tie::File and can't install it from CPAN, read the file a line at a
time and keep track of the byte address of the last line you've seen. When you've
exhausted the file, truncate to the last address you saved:

```
open (FH, "+<", $file)              or die "can't update $file: $!";
while (<FH>) {
    $addr = tell(FH) unless eof(FH);
}
truncate(FH, $addr)                 or die "can't truncate $file: $!";
```

Remembering the offset is more efficient than reading the whole file into memory
because it holds only one given line at a time. Although you still have to grope your
way through the whole file, you can use this technique on files larger than available
memory.

See Also

The documentation for the standard Tie::File module; the truncate and tell functions in *perlfunc*(1) and in Chapter 29 of *Programming Perl*; your system's *open*(2)
and *fopen*(3) manpages; Recipe 8.18

8.11 Processing Binary Files

Problem

You want to read 8-bit binary data as 8-bit binary data, i.e., neither as characters in a
particular encoding nor as a text file with any newline or end-of-file conversions that
your I/O library might want to do.

Solution

Use the `binmode` function on the filehandle:

```
binmode(HANDLE);
```

Discussion

The `binmode` function lets you specify new I/O layers for a filehandle. The default layer to specify is `:raw`, which removes any layers that would interfere with binary data. The Solution is thus equivalent to:

```
binmode(HANDLE, ":raw");
```

except that explicitly specifying `:raw` only works on Perl 5.8 and later. The one-argument form of `binmode` works on all versions of Perl.

Because Perl makes `:crlf` the default if you are on an operating system that needs it, you should rarely (if ever) need to specify `:crlf` in your program. Furthermore, it's generally not wise to add or remove the `:crlf` layer once you've begun reading from the file, as there may be data already read into buffers that you can't unread. You can, however, safely change the `:encoding(...)` layer midstream (when parsing XML, for example).

You should get into the habit of calling `binmode` when you open a binary file. This will make your program portable to systems that might (un)helpfully translate bytes in your binary file into something unusable.

You may specify the I/O layers when you open a filehandle, rather than using `binmode` after the fact:

```
open(FH, "< :raw", $filename);      # binary mode
```

Specify the default set of layers for all subsequently opened input and output filehandles with the open pragma:

```
use open IN => ":raw";      # binary files
```

See Also

The *PerlIO*(3) manpage; the open and binmode functions in *perlfunc*(1) and in Chapter 29 of *Programming Perl*; your system's *open*(2) and *fopen*(3) manpages

8.12 Using Random-Access I/O

Problem

You have to read a binary record from the middle of a large file but don't want to read a record at a time to get there.

Solution

Once you know the record's size, multiply it by the record number to get the byte address, and then seek to that byte address and read the record:

```
$ADDRESS = $RECSIZE * $RECNO;
seek(FH, $ADDRESS, 0) or die "seek:$!";
read(FH, $BUFFER, $RECSIZE);
```

Discussion

The Solution assumes the first record has a RECNO of 0. If you're counting from one, use:

```
$ADDRESS = $RECSIZE * ($RECNO-1);
```

This is best applied to binary data. Applying it to text files assumes you have a constant character width and constant line length. This rules out most Unicode encodings, any kind of Windows text file, and any text file where lines can have different lengths.

See Also

The seek function in *perlfunc*(1) and in Chapter 29 of *Programming Perl*; Recipe 8.13

8.13   Updating a Random-Access File

Problem

You want to read an old record from a binary file, change its values, and write back the record.

Solution

After reading the old record, pack up the updated values, seek to the previous address, and write it back.

```
use Fcntl;                          # for SEEK_SET and SEEK_CUR

$ADDRESS = $RECSIZE * $RECNO;
seek(FH, $ADDRESS, SEEK_SET)        or die "Seeking: $!";
read(FH, $BUFFER, $RECSIZE) == $RECSIZE
                                    or die "Reading: $!";
@FIELDS = unpack($FORMAT, $BUFFER);
# update fields, then
$BUFFER = pack($FORMAT, @FIELDS);
seek(FH, -$RECSIZE, SEEK_CUR)       or die "Seeking: $!";
print FH $BUFFER;
close FH                            or die "Closing: $!";
```

Discussion

You don't have to use anything fancier than print in Perl to output a record. Remember that the opposite of read is not write but print, although oddly enough, the opposite of sysread *is* syswrite.

The example program shown in Example 8-4, *weekearly*, takes one argument: the user whose record you want to backdate by a week. (Of course, in practice, you wouldn't really want to (nor be able to!) mess with the system accounting files.) This program requires write access to the file to be updated, since it opens the file in update mode. After fetching and altering the record, it packs it up again, skips backward in the file one record, and writes it out.

Example 8-4. weekearly

```perl
#!/usr/bin/perl -w
# weekearly -- set someone's login date back a week
use User::pwent;
use IO::Seekable;

$typedef = "L A12 A16";        # linux fmt; sunos is "L A8 A16"
$sizeof  = length(pack($typedef, ()));
$user    = shift(@ARGV) || $ENV{USER} || $ENV{LOGNAME};

$address = getpwnam($user)->uid * $sizeof;

open (LASTLOG, "+<:raw", "/var/log/lastlog")
    or die "can't update /var/log/lastlog: $!";
seek(LASTLOG, $address, SEEK_SET)
    or die "seek failed: $!";
read(LASTLOG, $buffer, $sizeof) == $sizeof
    or die "read failed: $!";

($time, $line, $host) = unpack($typedef, $buffer);
$time  -= 24 * 7 * 60 * 60;        # back-date a week
$buffer = pack($typedef, $time, $line, $time);

seek(LASTLOG, -$sizeof, SEEK_CUR)   # backup one record
    or die "seek failed: $!";
print LASTLOG $record;

close(LASTLOG)
    or die "close failed: $!";
```

See Also

The *PerlIO*(3) manpage; the open, seek, read, pack, and unpack functions in the *perlfunc*(1) and in Chapter 29 of *Programming Perl*; Recipe 8.12; Recipe 8.14

8.14   Reading a String from a Binary File

Problem

You want to read a NUL-terminated string from a file, starting at a particular address.

Solution

Ensure you're working with a binary file, set $/ to an ASCII NUL, and read the string with <>:

```
binmode(FH);                    # binary mode
$old_rs = $/;                   # save old $/
$/ = "\0";                      # ASCII 0: NUL
seek(FH, $addr, SEEK_SET)       or die "Seek error: $!\n";
$string = <FH>;                 # read string
chomp $string;                  # remove NUL
$/ = $old_rs;                   # restore old $/
```

You can use local to save and restore $/:

```
{
    local $/ = "\0";
    # ...
}                               # $/ is automatically restored
```

Discussion

The example program shown in Example 8-5, *bgets*, accepts a filename and one or more byte addresses as arguments. Decimal, octal, or hexadecimal addresses may be specified. For each address, the program reads and prints the null- or EOF-terminated string at that position.

Example 8-5. bgets

```
#!/usr/bin/perl -w
# bgets - get a string from an address in a binary file
use IO::Seekable;
use open IO => ":raw";              # binary mode on all opened handles
($file, @addrs) = @ARGV             or die "usage: $0 file addr ...";
open(FH, $file)                     or die "cannot open $file: $!";
$/ = "\000";
foreach $addr (@addrs) {
    $addr = oct $addr if $addr =~ /^0/;
    seek(FH, $addr, SEEK_SET)
        or die "can't seek to $addr in $file: $!";
    printf qq{%#x %#o %d "%s"\n}, $addr, $addr, $addr, scalar <>;
}
```

Example 8-6 is a simple implementation of the Unix *strings* program.

Example 8-6. strings

```
#!/usr/bin/perl -w
# strings - pull strings out of a binary file
$/ = "\0";
use open IO => ":raw";
while (<>) {
    while (/([\040-\176\s]{4,})/g) {
        print $1, "\n";
    }
}
```

See Also

The *PerlIO*(3) manpage; the seek, getc, and ord functions in *perlfunc*(1) and in Chapter 29 of *Programming Perl*; the discussion of qq// in the "Quote and Quote-Like Operators" section of the *perlop*(1) manpage, and in the "Pick Your Own Quotes" section of Chapter 2 of *Programming Perl*

8.15   Reading Fixed-Length Records

Problem

You want to read a file whose records have a fixed length.

Solution

Use read and unpack:

```
# $RECORDSIZE is the length of a record, in bytes.
# $TEMPLATE is the unpack template for the record
# FILE is the file to read from
# @FIELDS is an array, one element per field

until ( eof(FILE) ) {
    read(FILE, $record, $RECORDSIZE) == $RECORDSIZE
        or die "short read\n";
    @FIELDS = unpack($TEMPLATE, $record);
}
```

Discussion

Because the file in question is not a text file, you can't use <FH> or IO::Handle's getline method to read records. Instead, you must simply read a particular number of bytes into a variable. This variable contains one record's data, which you decode using unpack with the appropriate format.

For binary data, the catch is determining that format. When reading data written by a C program, this can mean peeking at C include files or manpages describing the structure layout, and this requires knowledge of C. It also requires that you become unnaturally chummy with your C compiler, because otherwise it's hard to predict field padding and alignment (such as the x2 in the format used in Recipe 8.24). If you're lucky enough to be on a Berkeley Unix system or a system supporting *gcc*, then you may be able to use the *c2ph* tool distributed with Perl to cajole your C compiler into helping you with this.

The *tailwtmp* program at the end of this chapter uses the format described in *utmp*(5) under Linux, and works on its */var/log/wtmp* and */var/run/utmp* files. Once you commit to working in binary format, machine dependencies creep in fast. It probably won't work unaltered on your system, but the procedure is still illustrative. Here is the relevant layout from the C include file on Linux:

```
#define UT_LINESIZE         12
#define UT_NAMESIZE         8
#define UT_HOSTSIZE         16

struct utmp {                       /* here are the pack template codes */
    short ut_type;                  /* s for short, must be padded      */
    pid_t ut_pid;                   /* i for integer                    */
    char ut_line[UT_LINESIZE];      /* A12 for 12-char string           */
    char ut_id[2];                  /* A2, but need x2 for alignment     */
    time_t ut_time;                 /* l for long                       */
    char ut_user[UT_NAMESIZE];      /* A8 for 8-char string             */
    char ut_host[UT_HOSTSIZE];      /* A16 for 16-char string           */
    long ut_addr;                   /* l for long                       */
};
```

Once you figure out the binary layout, feed that (in this case, "s x2 i A12 A2 x2 l A8 A16 l") to pack with an empty field list to determine the record's size. Remember to check the return value of read to make sure you got the number of bytes you asked for.

If your records are text strings, use the "a" or "A" unpack templates.

Fixed-length records are useful in that the *n*th record begins at byte offset SIZE * (*n*-1) in the file, where SIZE is the size of a single record. See the indexing code in Recipe 8.8 for an example.

See Also

The unpack, pack, and read functions in *perlfunc*(1) and in Chapter 29 of *Programming Perl*; Recipe 1.1

8.16 Reading Configuration Files

Problem

You want to allow users of your program to change its behavior through configuration files.

Solution

Either process a file in trivial VAR=VALUE format, setting a hash key-value pair for each setting:

```
while (<CONFIG>) {
    chomp;                    # no newline
    s/#.*//;                  # no comments
    s/^\s+//;                 # no leading white
    s/\s+$//;                 # no trailing white
    next unless length;       # anything left?
    my ($var, $value) = split(/\s*=\s*/, $_, 2);
    $User_Preferences{$var} = $value;
}
```

or better yet, treat the config file as full Perl code:

```
do "$ENV{HOME}/.progrc";
```

Discussion

The first solution lets you read config files in a trivial format like this (comments and empty lines are allowed):

```
# set class C net
NETMASK = 255.255.255.0
MTU     = 296

DEVICE  = cua1
RATE    = 115200
MODE    = adaptive
```

After you're done, you can pull in a setting by using something like $User_ Preferences{"RATE"} to find the value 115200. If you wanted the config file to set the global variable by that name, instead of assigning to the hash, use this:

```
no strict "refs";
$$var = $value;
```

and the $RATE variable would contain 115200.

The second solution uses do to pull in raw Perl code directly. When used with an expression instead of a block, do interprets the expression as a filename. This is nearly identical to using require, but without risk of taking a fatal exception. In the second format, the config file would look like:

```
# set class C net
$NETMASK = "255.255.255.0";
$MTU     = 0x128;
# Brent, please turn on the modem
$DEVICE  = "cua1";
$RATE    = 115_200;
$MODE    = "adaptive";
```

If you don't see the point of having extra punctuation and live code, consider this: you can have all of Perl at your disposal. You can now add arbitrary logic and tests to your simple assignments:

```
if ($DEVICE =~ /1$/) {
    $RATE = 28_800;
} else {
    $RATE = 115_200;
}
```

Many programs support system and personal configuration files. If you want the user's choices to override the system ones, load the user file second:

```
$APPDFLT = "/usr/local/share/myprog";

do "$APPDFLT/sysconfig.pl";
do "$ENV{HOME}/.myprogrc";
```

If you want to ignore the system config file when the user has his own, test the return value of the do.

```
do "$APPDFLT/sysconfig.pl"
    or
do "$ENV{HOME}/.myprogrc";
```

You might wonder what package those files are compiled in. They will be in the same package that do itself was compiled into. Typically you'll direct users to set particular variables, which, being unqualified globals, will end up in the current package. If you'd prefer unqualified variables go into a particular package, do this:

```
{ package Settings; do "$ENV{HOME}/.myprogrc" }
```

As with a file read using require or use, those read using do count as a separate and unrelated lexical scope. That means the configuration file can't access its caller's lexical (my) variables, nor can the caller find any such variables that might have been set in the file. It also means that the user's code isn't held accountable to a lexically scoped pragma like use strict or use warnings, which may be in effect in the caller.

If you don't want clean partitioning of variable visibility, you can get the config file's code executed in your own lexical scope. If you have a cat program or its technical equivalent handy, you could write yourself a hand-rolled do:

```
eval `cat $ENV{HOME}/.myprogrc`;
```

We've never actually seen anyone (except Larry Wall himself) use that approach in production code.

For one thing, do is a lot easier to type. Also, it respects the @INC path, which is normally searched if a full path is not specified, but, unlike using a require, no implicit error checking happens under do. This means you don't have to wrap it in an eval to catch exceptions that would otherwise cause your program to die, because do already functions as an eval.

You can still check for errors on your own if you'd like:

```
$file = "someprog.pl";
unless ($return = do $file) {
    warn "couldn't parse $file: $@"        if $@;
    warn "couldn't do $file: $!"           unless defined $return;
    warn "couldn't run $file"              unless $return;
}
```

This is much simpler for the programmer to source in code than it would be to invent and then parse a complicated, new syntax. It's also much easier on the users than forcing them to learn the syntax rules of yet another configuration file. Even better, you give the user access to a powerful algorithmic programming language.

One reasonable concern is security. How do you know that the file hasn't been tampered with by someone other than the user? The traditional approach here is to do nothing, trusting the directory and file permissions. Nine times out of ten, this is also the right approach. Most projects just aren't worth being that paranoid over. For those that are, see the next recipe.

See Also

The eval and require functions in *perlfunc*(1) and in Chapter 29 of *Programming Perl*; Recipe 8.17

8.17   Testing a File for Trustworthiness

Problem

You want to read from a file, perhaps because it has configuration information. You want to use the file only if it can't be written to (or perhaps not even be read from) by anyone else than its owner.

Solution

Use the stat function to retrieve ownership and file permissions information. You can use the built-in version, which returns a list:

```
( $dev, $ino, $mode, $nlink,
  $uid, $gid, $rdev, $size,
  $atime, $mtime, $ctime,
  $blksize, $blocks )        = stat($filename)
      or die "no $filename: $!";

$mode &= 07777;                # discard file type info
```

Or you can use the by-name interface:

```
use File::stat;

$info = stat($filename)       or die "no $filename: $!";
```

```
if ($info->uid == 0) {
    print "Superuser owns $filename\n";
}
if ($info->atime > $info->mtime) {
    print "$filename has been read since it was written.\n";
}
```

Discussion

Usually you trust users to set file permissions as they wish. If they want others to read their files, or even to write to them, that's their business. Applications such as editors, mailers, and shells are often more discerning, though, refusing to evaluate code in configuration files if anyone but the owner can write to them. This helps avoid Trojan horse attacks. Security-minded programs such as *ftp* and *ssh* may even reject config files that can be read by anyone but their owner.

If the file is writable by someone other than the owner or is owned by someone other than the current user or the superuser, it shouldn't be trusted. To figure out file ownership and permissions, the stat function is used. The following function returns true if the file is deemed safe and false otherwise. If the stat fails, undef is returned.

```
use File::stat;

sub is_safe {
    my $path = shift;
    my $info = stat($path);
    return unless $info;

    # owner neither superuser nor me
    # the real uid is stored in the $< variable
    if (($info->uid != 0) && ($info->uid != $<)) {
        return 0;
    }

    # check whether group or other can write file.
    # use 066 to detect either reading or writing
    if ($info->mode & 022) {   # someone else can write this
        return 0 unless -d _;  # non-directories aren't safe
            # but directories with the sticky bit (01000) are
        return 0 unless $info->mode & 01000;
    }
    return 1;
}
```

A directory is considered safe even if others can write to it, provided its mode 01000 (owner delete only) bit is set.

Careful programmers also ensure that no enclosing directory is writable. This is due to systems with the "chown giveaway" problem in which any user can give away a file they own to make it owned by someone else. The following function handles that by using the is_safe function to check every enclosing directory up to the root if it detects that you have the chown problem, for which it queries the POSIX::sysconf. If you don't have an unrestricted version of chown, the is_verysafe subroutine just calls is_safe. If you do have the problem, it walks up the filesystem tree until it reaches the root.

```
use Cwd;
use POSIX qw(sysconf _PC_CHOWN_RESTRICTED);
sub is_verysafe {
    my $path = shift;
    return is_safe($path) if sysconf(_PC_CHOWN_RESTRICTED);
    $path = getcwd() . "/" . $path if $path !~ m{^/};
    do {
        return unless is_safe($path);
        $path =~ s#([^/]+|/)$##;                 # dirname
        $path =~ s#/$## if length($path) > 1;    # last slash
    } while length $path;

    return 1;
}
```

To use this in a program, try something like this:

```
$file = "$ENV{HOME}/.myprogrc";
readconfig($file) if is_safe($file);
```

This has potential for a race condition, because it's presumed that the hypothetical readconfig function will open the file. Between the time when is_safe checks the file's stats and when readconfig opens it, something wicked could theoretically occur. To avoid this, pass is_safe the already open filehandle, which is set up to handle this:

```
$file = "$ENV{HOME}/.myprogrc";
if (open(FILE, "<", $file)) {
    readconfig(*FILE) if is_safe(*FILE);
}
```

You would still have to arrange for readconfig to accept a filehandle instead of a filename, though.

See Also

The stat function in *perlfunc*(1) and in Chapter 29 of *Programming Perl*; documentation for the standard POSIX and File::stat modules; Recipe 8.16

8.18 Treating a File as an Array

Problem

Your file contains a list of lines or records, and you'd like to be able to use Perl's powerful array operations to access and manipulate the file.

Solution

Use the Tie::File module, standard with v5.8 of Perl:

```
use Tie::File;
use Fcntl;

tie @data, Tie::File, $FILENAME or die "Can't tie to $filename : $!\n";
# use array operations on @data to work with the file
```

Discussion

The Tie::File module makes a file appear to be an array, one record per element. You can then fetch and assign to elements of the array, use array functions like push and splice, use negative indices, or reverse it, and in every instance you're really working with the data on disk.

If you don't specify how Tie::File should open the file, it is opened for read and write access and created if it doesn't exist. To specify a particular access mode (see Recipe 7.1), pass the Fcntl mode with the mode parameter when you tie. For example:

```
use Fcntl;
tie(@data, Tie::File, $filename, mode => O_RDONLY)
   or die "Can't open $filename for reading: $!\n";
```

When you alter the array, the file is rewritten on disk. For example, if you change the length of an element, all records later in the file must be copied to make the change. Take this code:

```
foreach (@data) {
   s/Perl Cookbook/Perl Cookbook (2nd edition)/g;
}
```

That's close because you change the length of record 0, forcing a copy of records 1..N. Then you change the length of record 1, forcing a copy of records 2..N. It's better to defer the update until all changes have been made and then have Tie::File update the file in one single write. To do this, call a method on the object behind the tied array:

```
(tied @data)->defer;                   # defer updates
foreach (@data) {
   s/Perl Cookbook/Perl Cookbook (2nd edition)/g;
}
(tied @data)->flush;
```

Exactly how much rewriting to defer is governed by how much memory you let Tie:: File use, because the only way to keep track of changes without updating the file is to store those changes in memory. The Tie::File manpage shows how to change options for memory use.

See Also

Recipe 8.4; Recipe 8.8; Recipe 8.10

8.19 Setting the Default I/O Layers

Problem

You want to ensure all files opened by your program use a particular set of I/O layers. For example, you know that every file will contain UTF-8 data.

Solution

Use the open pragma:

```
use open IO => ":raw:utf8";
```

Discussion

You can easily specify I/O layers when you open a filehandle directly, but that doesn't help you when the filehandle is opened by someone else's code (possibly even the Perl core). The open pragma lets you specify a default set of layers for every open that doesn't specify its own layers.

The open module also offers separate IN and OUT control for input and output handles. For example, to read bytes and emit UTF-8:

```
use open "IN" => ":bytes", "OUT" => ":utf8";
```

The :std option tells open to apply the input and output layers to STDIN and STDOUT/STDERR. For example, the following code makes input handles read Greek (ISO 8859-7) and output handles write in the UTF-8 Unicode encoding. Then it applies the same layers to STDIN, STDOUT, and STDERR:

```
use open "IN" => ":encoding(Greek)",    # reading Greek
         "OUT" => ":utf8",              # writing 8-bit data in Unicode UTF-8,
         ":std";                        # STDIN is Greek,
```

See Also

The documentation for the standard open pragma; Recipes 8.12 and 8.19

8.20 Reading or Writing Unicode from a Filehandle

Problem

You have a file containing text in a particular encoding and when you read data from that into a Perl string, Perl treats it as a series of 8-bit bytes. You'd like to work with characters instead of bytes because your encoding characters can take more than one byte. Also, if Perl doesn't know about your encoding, it may fail to identify certain characters as letters. Similarly, you may want to output text in a particular encoding.

Solution

Use I/O layers to tell Perl that data from that filehandle is in a particular encoding.

```
open(my $ifh, "<:encoding(ENCODING_NAME)", $filename);
open(my $ofh, ">:encoding(ENCODING_NAME)", $filename);
```

Discussion

Perl's text manipulation functions handle UTF-8 strings just as well as they do 8-bit data—they just need to know what type of data they're working with. Each string in Perl is internally marked as either UTF-8 or 8-bit data. The encoding(...) layer converts data between variable external encodings and the internal UTF-8 within Perl. This is done by way of the Encode module.

In the section on "Unicode Support in Perl" back in the Introduction to Chapter 1, we explained how under Unicode, every different character had a different code point (i.e., a different number) associated with it. Assigning all characters unique code points solves many problems. No longer does the same number, like 0xC4, represent one character under one character repertoire (e.g., a LATIN CAPITAL LETTER A WITH DIAERESIS under ISO-8859-1) and a different character in another repertoire (e.g., a GREEK CAPITAL LETTER DELTA under ISO-8859-7).

This neatly solves many problems, but still leaves one important issue: the precise format used in memory or disk for each code point. If most code points fit in 8 bits, it would seem wasteful to use, say, a full 32 bits for each character. But if every character is the same size as every other character, the code is easier to write and may be faster to execute.

This has given rise to different encoding systems for storing Unicode, each offering distinct advantages. Fixed-width encodings fit every code point into the same number of bits, which simplifies programming but at the expense of some wasted space. Variable-width encodings use only as much space as each code point requires, which saves space but complicates programming.

One further complication is combined characters, which may look like single letters on paper but in code require multiple code points. When you see a capital A with two dots above it (a diaeresis) on your screen, it may not even be character U+00C4. As explained in Recipe 1.8, Unicode supports the idea of combining characters, where you start with a base character and add non-spacing marks to it. U+0308 is a "COMBINING DIAERESIS", so you could use a capital A (U+0041) followed by U+0308, or A\x{308} to produce the same output.

The following table shows the old ISO 8859-1 way of writing a capital A with a diaeresis, in which the logical character code and the physical byte layout enjoyed an identical representation, and the new way under Unicode. We'll include both ways of writing that character: one precomposed in one code point and the other using two code points to create a combined character.

	Old way	New way		
	Ä	A	Ä	Ä
Character(s)	0xC4	U+0041	U+00C4	U+0041 U+0308
Character repertoire	ISO 8859-1	Unicode	Unicode	Unicode
Character code(s)	0xC4	0x0041	0x00C4	0x0041 0x0308
Encoding	—	UTF-8	UTF-8	UTF-8
Byte(s)	0xC4	0x41	0xC3 0x84	0x41 0xCC 0x88

The internal format used by Perl is UTF-8, a variable-width encoding system. One reason for this choice is that legacy ASCII requires no conversion for UTF-8, looking in memory exactly as it did before—just one byte per character. Character U+0041 is just 0x41 in memory. Legacy data sets don't increase in size, and even those using Western character sets like ISO 8859-n grow only slightly, since in practice you still have a favorable ratio of regular ASCII characters to 8-bit accented characters.

Just because Perl uses UTF-8 internally doesn't preclude using other formats externally. Perl automatically converts all data between UTF-8 and whatever encoding you've specified for that handle. The Encode module is used implicitly when you specify an I/O layer of the form ":encoding(....)". For example:

```
binmode(FH, ":encoding(UTF-16BE)")
    or die "can't binmode to utf-16be: $!";
```

or directly in the open:

```
open(FH, "< :encoding(UTF-32)", $pathname)
    or die "can't open $pathname: $!";
```

Here's a comparison of actual byte layouts of those two sequences, both representing a capital A with diaeresis, under several other popular formats:

	U+00C4	U+0041 U+0308
UTF-8	c3 84	41 cc 88
UTF-16BE	00 c4	00 41 03 08
UTF-16LE	c4 00	41 00 08 03
UTF-16	fe ff 00 c4	fe ff 00 41 03 08
UTF-32LE	c4 00 00 00	41 00 00 00 08 03 00 00
UTF-32BE	00 00 00 c4	00 00 00 41 00 00 03 08
UTF-32	00 00 fe ff 00 00 00 c4	00 00 fe ff 00 00 00 41 00 00 03 08

This can chew up memory quickly. It's also complicated by the fact that some computers are big-endian, others little-endian. So fixed-width encoding formats that don't specify their endian-ness require a special byte-ordering sequence ("FF EF" versus "EF FF"), usually needed only at the start of the stream.

If you're reading or writing UTF-8 data, use the :utf8 layer. Because Perl natively uses UTF-8, the :utf8 layer bypasses the Encode module for performance.

The Encode module understands many aliases for encodings, so ascii, US-ascii, and ISO-646-US are synonymous. Read the Encode::Supported manpage for a list of available encodings. Perl supports not only standard Unicode names but vendor-specific names, too; for example, iso-8859-1 is cp850 on DOS, cp1252 on Windows, MacRoman on a Mac, and hp-roman8 on NeXTstep. The Encode module recognizes all of these as names for the same encoding.

See Also

The documentation for the standard Encode module; the Encode::Supported manpage; Recipes 8.12 and 8.19

8.21 Converting Microsoft Text Files into Unicode

Problem

You have a text file written on a Microsoft computer that looks like garbage when displayed. How do you fix this?

Solution

Set the encoding layer appropriately when reading to convert this into Unicode:

```
binmode(IFH, ":encoding(cp1252)")
    || die "can't binmode to cp1252 encoding: $!";
```

Discussion

Suppose someone sends you a file in cp1252 format, Microsoft's default in-house 8-bit character set. Files in this format can be annoying to read—while they might claim to be Latin1, they are not, and if you look at them with Latin1 fonts loaded, you'll get garbage on your screen. A simple solution is as follows:

```
open(MSMESS, "< :crlf :encoding(cp1252)", $inputfile)
    || die "can't open $inputfile: $!";
```

Now data read from that handle will be automatically converted into Unicode when you read it in. It will also be processed in CRLF mode, which is needed on systems that don't use that sequence to indicate end of line.

You probably won't be able to write out this text as Latin1. That's because cp1252 includes characters that don't exist in Latin1. You'll have to leave it in Unicode, and displaying Unicode properly may not be as easy as you wish, because finding tools to work with Unicode is something of a quest in its own right. Most web browsers support ISO 10646 fonts; that is, Unicode fonts (see *http://www.cl.cam.ac.uk/~mgk25/ucs-fonts.html*). Whether your text editor does is a different matter, although both *emacs* and *vi* (actually, *vim*, not *nvi*) have mechanisms for handling Unicode. The authors used the following *xterm*(1) command to look at text:

```
xterm -n unicode -u8 -fn -misc-fixed-medium-r-normal--20-200-75-75-c-100-iso10646-1
```

But many open questions still exist, such as cutting and pasting of Unicode data between windows.

The *www.unicode.org* site has help for finding and installing suitable tools for a variety of platforms, including both Unix and Microsoft systems.

You'll also need to tell Perl it's alright to emit Unicode. If you don't, you'll get a warning about a "Wide character in print" every time you try. Assuming you're running in an *xterm* like the one shown previously (or its equivalent for your system) that has Unicode fonts available, you could just do this:

```
binmode(STDOUT, ":utf8");
```

But that requires the rest of your program to emit Unicode, which might not be convenient. When writing new programs specifically designed for this, though, it might not be too much trouble.

As of v5.8.1, Perl offers a couple of other means of getting this effect. The **-C** command-line switch controls some Unicode features related to your runtime environment. This way you can set those features on a per-command basis without having to edit the source code.

The **-C** switch can be followed by either a number or a list of option letters. Some available letters, their numeric values, and effects are as follows:

Letter	Number	Meaning
I	1	STDIN is assumed to be in UTF-8
O	2	STDOUT will be in UTF-8
E	4	STDERR will be in UTF-8
S	7	I + O + E
i	8	UTF-8 is the default PerlIO layer for input streams
o	16	UTF-8 is the default PerlIO layer for output streams
D	24	i + o
A	32	the @ARGV elements are expected to be strings encoded in UTF-8

You may use letters or numbers. If you use numbers, you have to add them up. For example, **-COE** and **-C6** are synonyms of UTF-8 on both STDOUT and STDERR.

One last approach is to use the PERL_UNICODE environment variable. If set, it contains the same value as you would use with **-C**. For example, with the *xterm* that has Unicode fonts loaded, you could do this in a POSIX shell:

```
sh% export PERL_UNICODE=6
```

or this in the *csh*:

```
csh% setenv PERL_UNICODE 6
```

The advantage of using the environment variable is that you don't have to edit the source code as the pragma would require, and you don't even need to change the command invocation as setting **-C** would require.

See Also

The *perlrun*(1), *encoding*(3), *PerlIO*(3), and *Encode*(3) manpages

8.22 Comparing the Contents of Two Files

Problem

You have two files and want to see whether they're the same or different.

Solution

Use the standard File::Compare module with filenames, typeglobs, or any indirect filehandles:

```
use File::Compare;

if (compare($FILENAME_1, $FILENAME_2) == 0) {
  # they're equal
}

if (compare(*FH1, *FH2) == 0) {
  # they're equal
}

if (compare($fh1, $fh2) == 0) {
  # they're equal
}
```

Discussion

The File::Compare module (standard as of v5.8 and available on CPAN if you have an earlier version of Perl) compares two files for equality. The compare function, exported by default, returns 0 when the files are equal, 1 when they differ, and -1 when any error occurs during reading.

To compare more than two filehandles, simply loop, comparing two at a time:

```
# ensure all filehandles in @fh hold the same data
foreach $fh (@fh[1..$#fh]) {
  if (compare($fh[0], $fh)) {
    # $fh differs
  }
}
```

If you want details of exactly how two files differ, use the Text::Diff module from CPAN:

```
use Text::Diff;

$diff = diff(*FH1, *FH2);
$diff = diff($FILENAME_1, $FILENAME_2, { STYLE => "Context" });
```

In addition to filehandles, diff can also take filenames, strings, and even arrays of records. Pass a hash of options as the third argument. The STYLE option controls the type of output returned; it can be "Unified" (the default), "Context", or "OldStyle". You can even write your own class for custom diff formats.

The value returned by diff is a string similar to the output of the *diff*(1) program. This string is in valid diff format, suitable for feeding into *patch*(1). Although Text::Diff will not always produce the same output as GNU *diff*, byte for byte, its diffs are nevertheless correct.

See Also

The documentation for the standard File::Compare module; the documentation for the CPAN module Text::Diff; the *diff*(1) and *patch*(1) manpages.

8.23 Pretending a String Is a File

Problem

You have data in string, but would like to treat it as a file. For example, you have a subroutine that expects a filehandle as an argument, but you would like that subroutine to work directly on the data in your string instead. Additionally, you don't want to write the data to a temporary file.

Solution

Use the scalar I/O in Perl v5.8:

```
open($fh, "+<", \$string);   # read and write contents of $string
```

Discussion

Perl's I/O layers include support for input and output from a scalar. When you read a record with <$fh>, you are reading the next line from $string. When you write a record with print, you change $string. You can pass $fh to a function that expects a filehandle, and that subroutine need never know that it's really working with data in a string.

Perl respects the various access modes in open for strings, so you can specify that the strings be opened as read-only, with truncation, in append mode, and so on:

```
open($fh, "<",  \$string);   # read only
open($fh, ">",  \$string);   # write only, discard original contents
open($fh, "+>", \$string);   # read and write, discard original contents
open($fh, "+<", \$string);   # read and write, preserve original contents
```

These handles behave in all respects like regular filehandles, so all I/O functions work, such as seek, truncate, sysread, and friends.

See Also

The open function in *perlfunc*(1) and in Chapter 29 of *Programming Perl*; Recipes 8.12 and 8.19

8.24 Program: tailwtmp

Every time a user logs into or out of a Unix system, a record is added to the *wtmp* file. You can't use the normal *tail* program on it, because the file is in binary format. The *tailwtmp* program in Example 8-7 knows the format of the binary file and shows every new record as it appears. You'll have to adjust the pack format for your own system.

Example 8-7. tailwtmp

```
#!/usr/bin/perl -w
# tailwtmp - watch for logins and logouts;
# uses linux utmp structure, from utmp(5)
$typedef = "s x2 i A12 A4 l A8 A16 l";
$sizeof = length pack($typedef, () );
use IO::File;
open(WTMP, "< :raw", "/var/log/wtmp") or die "can't open /var/log/wtmp: $!";
seek(WTMP, 0, SEEK_END);
for (;;) {
        while (read(WTMP, $buffer, $sizeof) == $sizeof) {
        ($type, $pid,  $line, $id, $time, $user, $host, $addr)
            = unpack($typedef, $buffer);
        next unless $user && ord($user) && $time;
        printf "%1d %-8s %-12s %2s %-24s %-16s %5d %08x\n",
            $type,$user,$line,$id,scalar(localtime($time)),
            $host,$pid,$addr;
```

Example 8-7. tailwtmp (continued)

```
    }
    for ($size = -s WTMP; $size == -s WTMP; sleep 1) { }
    WTMP->clearerr( );
}
```

8.25   Program: tctee

Not all systems support the classic *tee* program for splitting output pipes to multiple destinations. This command sends the output from *someprog* to */tmp/output* and to the mail pipe beyond:

```
% someprog | tee /tmp/output | Mail -s "check this" user@host.org
```

This program helps not only users who aren't on Unix systems and don't have a regular *tee*; it also helps those who are, because it offers features not found on other versions of *tee*.

The four flag arguments are **-i** to ignore interrupts, **-a** to append to output files, **-u** for unbuffered output, and **-n** to omit copying the output on to standard out.

Because this program uses Perl's magic open, you can specify pipes as well as files.

```
% someprog | tctee f1 "|cat -n" f2 ">>f3"
```

That sends the output from *someprog* to the files *f1* and *f2*, appends it to *f3*, sends a copy to the program *cat -n*, and also produces the stream on standard output.

The program in Example 8-8 is one of many venerable Perl programs written nearly a decade ago that still runs perfectly well. If written from scratch now, we'd probably use strict, warnings, and ten to thirty thousand lines of modules. But if it ain't broke…

Example 8-8. tctee

```
#!/usr/bin/perl
# tctee - clone that groks process tees
# perl3 compatible, or better.

while ($ARGV[0] =~ /^-(.+)/ && (shift, ($_ = $1), 1)) {
    next if /^$/;
    s/i// && (++$ignore_ints, redo);
    s/a// && (++$append,      redo);
    s/u// && (++$unbuffer,    redo);
    s/n// && (++$nostdout,    redo);
    die "usage $0 [-aiun] [filenames] ...\n";
}

if ($ignore_ints) {
    for $sig ("INT", "TERM", "HUP", "QUIT") { $SIG{$sig} = "IGNORE"; }
}
```

Example 8-8. tctee (continued)

```
$SIG{"PIPE"} = "PLUMBER";
$mode = $append ? ">>" : ">";
$fh = "FH000";

unless ($nostdout) {
    %fh = ("STDOUT", "standard output"); # always go to stdout
}

$| = 1 if $unbuffer;

for (@ARGV) {
    if (!open($fh, (/^[^>|]/ && $mode) . $_)) {
        warn "$0: cannot open $_: $!\n"; # like sun's; i prefer die
        $status++;
        next;
    }
    select((select($fh), $| = 1)[0]) if $unbuffer;
    $fh{$fh++} = $_;
}

while (<STDIN>) {
    for $fh (keys %fh) {
        print $fh $_;
    }
}

for $fh (keys %fh) {
    next if close($fh) || !defined $fh{$fh};
    warn "$0: couldnt close $fh{$fh}: $!\n";
    $status++;
}

exit $status;

sub PLUMBER {
    warn "$0: pipe to \"$fh{$fh}\" broke!\n";
    $status++;
    delete $fh{$fh};
}
```

8.26 Program: laston

When you log in to a Unix system, it tells you when you last logged in. That information is stored in a binary file called *lastlog*. Each user has their own record; UID 8 is at record 8, UID 239 at record 239, and so on. To find out when a given user last logged in, convert their login name to a number, seek to their record in that file, read, and unpack. Doing so with shell tools is hard, but with the *laston* program, it's easy. Here's an example:

```
% laston gnat
gnat  UID 314 at Mon May 25 08:32:52 2003 on ttyp0 from below.perl.com
```

The program in Example 8-9 is much newer than the *tctee* program in Example 8-8, but it's less portable. It uses the Linux binary layout of the *lastlog* file. You'll have to change this for other systems.

Example 8-9. laston

```perl
#!/usr/bin/perl -w
# laston - find out when given user last logged on
use User::pwent;
use IO::Seekable qw(SEEK_SET);

open (LASTLOG, "< :raw", "/var/log/lastlog")
    or die "can't open /var/log/lastlog: $!";

$typedef = "L A12 A16";  # linux fmt; sunos is "L A8 A16"
$sizeof  = length(pack($typedef, ()));

for $user (@ARGV) {
    $U = ($user =~ /^\d+$/) ? getpwuid($user) : getpwnam($user);
    unless ($U) { warn "no such uid $user\n"; next; }
    seek(LASTLOG, $U->uid * $sizeof, SEEK_SET) or die "seek failed: $!";
    read(LASTLOG, $buffer, $sizeof) == $sizeof        or next;
    ($time, $line, $host) = unpack($typedef, $buffer);
    printf "%-8s UID %5d %s%s%s\n", $U->name, $U->uid,
            $time ? ("at " . localtime($time)) : "never logged in",
            $line && " on $line",
            $host && " from $host";



}
```

8.27   Program: Flat File Indexes

It sometimes happens that you need to jump directly to a particular line number in a file, but the lines vary in length, so you can't use Recipe 8.12. Although you could start at the beginning of the file and read every line, this is inefficient if you're making multiple queries.

The solution is to build an index of fixed-width records, one per line. Each record contains the offset in the data file of the corresponding line. The subroutine in Example 8-10 takes the data file and a filehandle to send the index to. It reads a record at a time and prints the current offset in the file to the index, packed into a big-ending unsigned 32-bit integer; see the documentation for the pack function in *perlfunc*(1) for alternative storage types.

Example 8-10. build_index

```
# usage: build_index(*DATA_HANDLE, *INDEX_HANDLE)
sub build_index {
    my $data_file  = shift;
    my $index_file = shift;
    my $offset     = 0;

    while (<$data_file>) {
        print $index_file pack("N", $offset);
        $offset = tell($data_file);
    }
}
```

Once you have an index, it becomes easy to read a particular line from the data file. Jump to that record in the index, read the offset, and jump to that position in the data file. The next line you read will be the one you want. Example 8-11 returns the line, given the line number and the index and data file handles.

Example 8-11. line_with_index

```
# usage: line_with_index(*DATA_HANDLE, *INDEX_HANDLE, $LINE_NUMBER)
# returns line or undef if LINE_NUMBER was out of range
sub line_with_index {
    my $data_file   = shift;
    my $index_file  = shift;
    my $line_number = shift;
    my $size;                  # size of an index entry
    my $i_offset;              # offset into the index of the entry
    my $entry;                 # index entry
    my $d_offset;              # offset into the data file
    $size = length(pack("N", 0));
    $i_offset = $size * ($line_number-1);
    seek($index_file, $i_offset, 0) or return;
    read($index_file, $entry, $size);
    $d_offset = unpack("N", $entry);
    seek($data_file, $d_offset, 0);
    return scalar(<$data_file>);
}
```

To use these subroutines, just say:

```
open($fh,  "<", $file)       or die "Can't open $file for reading: $!\n";
open($index, "+>", $file.idx)
    or die "Can't open $file.idx for read/write: $!\n";
build_index($fh, $index);
$line = line_with_index($file, $index, $seeking);
```

The next step is to cache the index file between runs of the program, so you're not building it each time. This is shown in Example 8.12. Then add locking for concurrent access, and check time stamps on the files to see whether a change to the data file has made an old index file out of date.

Example 8-12. cache_line_index

```perl
#!/usr/bin/perl -w
# cache_line_index - index style
# build_index and line_with_index from above
@ARGV == 2 or
    die "usage: print_line FILENAME LINE_NUMBER";

($filename, $line_number) = @ARGV;
open(my $orig, "<", $filename)
        or die "Can't open $filename for reading: $!";

# open the index and build it if necessary
# there's a race condition here: two copies of this
# program can notice there's no index for the file and
# try to build one.  This would be easily solved with
# locking
$indexname = "$filename.index";
sysopen(my $idx, $indexname, O_CREAT|O_RDWR)
          or die "Can't open $indexname for read/write: $!";
build_index($orig, $idx) if -z $indexname;  # XXX: race unless lock

$line = line_with_index($orig, $idx, $line_number);
die "Didn't find line $line_number in $filename" unless defined $line;
print $line;
```

## CHAPTER 9

Directories

*Unix has its weak points, but its file system
is not one of them.*
—Chris Torek

9.0   Introduction

To fully understand directories, you need to be acquainted with the underlying mechanics. The following explanation is slanted toward the Unix filesystem, for whose syscalls and behavior Perl's directory access routines were designed, but it is applicable to some degree to most other platforms.

A filesystem consists of two parts: a set of data blocks where the contents of files and directories are kept, and an index to those blocks. Each entity in the filesystem has an entry in the index, be it a plain file, a directory, a link, or a special file like those in */dev*. Each entry in the index is called an *inode* (short for *index node*). Since the index is a flat index, inodes are addressed by number.

A directory is a specially formatted file, whose inode entry marks it as a directory. A directory's data blocks contain a set of pairs. Each pair consists of the name of something in that directory and the inode number of that thing. The data blocks for */usr/bin* might contain:

Name	Inode
bc	17
du	29
nvi	8
pine	55
vi	8

Every directory is like this, even the root directory (*/*). To read the file */usr/bin/vi*, the operating system reads the inode for */*, reads its data blocks to find the entry for */usr*, reads */usr*'s inode, reads its data block to find */usr/bin*, reads */usr/bin*'s inode, reads its data block to find */usr/bin/vi*, reads */usr/bin/vi*'s inode, and then reads the data from its data block.

The name in a directory entry isn't fully qualified. The file */usr/bin/vi* has an entry with the name *vi* in the */usr/bin* directory. If you open the directory */usr/bin* and read entries one by one, you get filenames like *patch*, *rlogin*, and *vi* instead of fully qualified names like */usr/bin/patch*, */usr/bin/rlogin*, and */usr/bin/vi*.

The inode has more than a pointer to the data blocks. Each inode also contains the type of thing it represents (directory, plain file, etc.), the size of the thing, a set of permissions bits, owner and group information, the time the thing was last modified, the number of directory entries that point to this inode, and so on.

Some operations on files change the contents of the file's data blocks; others change just the inode. For instance, appending to or truncating a file updates its inode by changing the size field. Other operations change the directory entry that points to the file's inode. Changing a file's name changes only the directory entry; it updates neither the file's data nor its inode.

Three fields in the inode structure contain the last access, change, and modification times: `atime`, `ctime`, and `mtime`. The `atime` field is updated each time the pointer to the file's data blocks is followed and the file's data is read. The `mtime` field is updated each time the file's data changes. The `ctime` field is updated each time the file's inode changes. The `ctime` is *not* creation time; there is no way under standard Unix to find a file's creation time.

Reading a file changes its `atime` only. Changing a file's name doesn't change `atime`, `ctime`, or `mtime`, because the directory entry changed (it *does* change the `atime` and `mtime` of the directory the file is in, though). Truncating a file doesn't change its `atime` (because we haven't read; we've just changed the size field in its directory entry), but it does change its `ctime` because we changed its size field and its `mtime` because we changed its contents (even though we didn't follow the pointer to do so).

We can access the inode of a file or directory by calling the built-in function `stat` on its name. For instance, to get the inode for */usr/bin/vi*, say:

```
@entry = stat("/usr/bin/vi") or die "Couldn't stat /usr/bin/vi : $!";
```

To get the inode for the directory */usr/bin*, say:

```
@entry = stat("/usr/bin")    or die "Couldn't stat /usr/bin : $!";
```

You can stat filehandles, too:

```
@entry = stat(INFILE)        or die "Couldn't stat INFILE : $!";
```

The `stat` function returns a list of the values of the fields in the directory entry. If it couldn't get this information (for instance, if the file doesn't exist), it returns an empty list. It's this empty list we test for using the or `die` construct. Be careful of using `|| die` because that throws the expression into scalar context, in which case stat only reports whether it worked. It doesn't return the list of values. The under-score (_) cache referred to later will still be updated, though.

The values returned by stat are listed in Table 9-1.

Table 9-1. Stat return values

Element	Abbreviation	Description
0	dev	Device number of filesystem
1	ino	Inode number (the "pointer" field)
2	mode	File mode (type and permissions)
3	nlink	Number of (hard) links to the file
4	uid	Numeric user ID of file's owner
5	gid	Numeric group ID of file's owner
6	rdev	The device identifier (special files only)
7	size	Total size of file, in bytes
8	atime	Last access time, in seconds, since the Epoch
9	mtime	Last modify time, in seconds, since the Epoch
10	ctime	Inode change time, in seconds, since the Epoch
11	blksize	Preferred block size for filesystem I/O
12	blocks	Actual number of blocks allocated

The standard File::stat module provides a named interface to these values. It over-rides the stat function, so instead of returning the preceding array, it returns an object with a method for each attribute:

```
use File::stat;

$inode = stat("/usr/bin/vi");
$ctime = $inode->ctime;
$size  = $inode->size;
```

In addition, Perl provides operators that call stat and return one value only (see Table 9-2). These are collectively referred to as the -X operators because they all take the form of a dash followed by a single character. They're modeled on the shell's *test* operators.

Table 9-2 . File test operators

-X	Stat field	Meaning
-r	mode	File is readable by effective UID/GID
-w	mode	File is writable by effective UID/GID
-x	mode	File is executable by effective UID/GID
-o	mode	File is owned by effective UID

Table 9-2 . File test operators (continued)

-X	Stat field	Meaning
-R	mode	File is readable by real UID/GID
-W	mode	File is writable by real UID/GID
-X	mode	File is executable by real UID/GID
-O	mode	File is owned by real UID
-e		File exists
-z	size	File has zero size
-s	size	File has nonzero size (returns size)
-f	mode,rdev	File is a plain file
-d	mode,rdev	File is a directory
-l	mode	File is a symbolic link
-p	mode	File is a named pipe (FIFO)
-S	mode	File is a socket
-b	rdev	File is a block special file
-c	rdev	File is a character special file
-t	rdev	Filehandle is opened to a tty
-u	mode	File has setuid bit set
-g	mode	File has setgid bit set
-k	mode	File has sticky bit set
-T	N/A	File is a text file
-B	N/A	File is a binary file (opposite of -T)
-M	mtime	Age of file in days when script started
-A	atime	Same for access time
-C	ctime	Same for inode change time (not creation)

The stat and the -X operators cache the values that the *stat*(2) syscall returned. If you then call stat or a -X operator with the special filehandle _ (a single underscore), it won't call *stat* again but will instead return information from its cache. This lets you test many properties of a single file without calling *stat*(2) many times or introducing a race condition:

```
open(F, "<", $filename )
    or die "Opening $filename: $!\n";
unless (-s F && -T _) {
```

```
        die "$filename doesn't have text in it.\n";
    }
```

The stat call just returns the information in one inode, though. How do we list the directory contents? For that, Perl provides opendir, readdir, and closedir:

```
opendir(DIRHANDLE, "/usr/bin") or die "couldn't open /usr/bin : $!";
while ( defined ($filename = readdir(DIRHANDLE)) ) {
    print "Inside /usr/bin is something called $filename\n";
}
closedir(DIRHANDLE);
```

These directory-reading functions are designed to look like the file open and close functions. Where open takes a filehandle, though, opendir takes a directory handle. They may look the same to you (the same bare word), but they occupy different namespaces. Therefore, you could open(BIN, "/a/file") and opendir(BIN, "/a/dir"), and Perl won't get confused. You might, but Perl won't. Because filehandles and directory handles are different, you can't use the <> operator to read from a directory handle (<> calls readline on the filehandle).

Similar to what happens with open and the other functions that initialize filehandles, you can supply opendir an undefined scalar variable where the directory handle is expected. If the function succeeds, Perl initializes that variable with a reference to a new, anonymous directory handle.

```
opendir(my $dh, "/usr/bin") or die;
while (defined ($filename = readdir($dh))) {
  # ...
}
closedir($dh);
```

Just like any other autovivified reference, when this one is no longer used (for example, when it goes out of scope and no other references to it are held), Perl automatically deallocates it. And just as close is implicitly called on filehandles autovivified through open at that point, directory handles autovivified through opendir have closedir called on them, too.

Filenames in a directory aren't necessarily stored alphabetically. For an alphabetical list of files, read the entries and sort them yourself.

The separation of directory information from inode information can create some odd situations. Operations that update the directory—such as linking, unlinking, or renaming a file—all require write permission only on the directory, not on the file. This is because the name of a file is actually something the directory calls that file, not a property inherent to the file itself. Only directories hold names of files; files are ignorant of their own names. Only operations that change information in the file data itself demand write permission on the file. Lastly, operations that alter the file's permissions or other metadata are restricted to the file's owner or the superuser. This can lead to the interesting situation of being able to delete (i.e., unlink from its directory) a file you can't read, or write to a file you can't delete.

Although these situations may make the filesystem structure seem odd at first, they're actually the source of much of Unix's power. Links, two filenames that refer to the same file, are now extremely simple. The two directory entries just list the same inode number. The inode structure includes a count of the number of directory entries referring to the file (nlink in the values returned by stat). This lets the operating system store and maintain only one copy of the modification times, size, and other file attributes. When one directory entry is unlinked, data blocks are deleted only if the directory entry was the last one that referred to the file's inode—and no processes still have the file open. You can unlink an open file, but its disk space won't be released until the last close.

Links come in two forms. The kind described previously, where two directory entries list the same inode number (like *vi* and *nvi* in the earlier table), are called *hard links*. The operating system cannot tell the first directory entry of a file (the one created when the file was created) from any subsequent hard links to it. The other kind, *soft* or *symbolic links*, are very different. A soft link is a special type of file whose data block stores the filename the file is linked to. Soft links have a different mode value, indicating they're not regular files. The operating system, when asked to open a soft link, instead opens the filename contained in the data block.

Executive Summary

Filenames are kept in a directory, separate from the size, protections, and other metadata kept in an inode.

The stat function returns the inode information (metadata).

opendir, readdir, and friends provide access to filenames in a directory through a *directory handle*.

Directory handles look like filehandles, but they are not the same. In particular, you can't use <> on directory handles.

Permissions on a directory determine whether you can read and write the list of filenames. Permissions on a file determine whether you can change the file's metadata or contents.

Three different times are stored in an inode. None of them is the file's creation time.

9.1   Getting and Setting Timestamps

Problem

You need to retrieve or alter when a file was last modified (written or changed) or accessed (read).

Solution

Use stat to get those times and utime to set them. Both functions are built into Perl:

```
($READTIME, $WRITETIME) = (stat($filename))[8,9];

utime($NEWREADTIME, $NEWWRITETIME, $filename);
```

Discussion

As explained in the Introduction, three different times are associated with an inode in the traditional Unix filesystem. Of these, any user can set the atime and mtime with utime, assuming the user has write access to the parent directory of the file. There is effectively no way to change the ctime. This example shows how to call utime:

```
$SECONDS_PER_DAY = 60 * 60 * 24;
($atime, $mtime) = (stat($file))[8,9];
$atime -= 7 * $SECONDS_PER_DAY;
$mtime -= 7 * $SECONDS_PER_DAY;

utime($atime, $mtime, $file)
    or die "couldn't backdate $file by a week w/ utime: $!";
```

You must call utime with both atime and mtime values. If you want to change only one, you must call stat first to get the other:

```
$mtime = (stat $file)[9];
utime(time, $mtime, $file);
```

This is easier to understand if you use File::stat:

```
use File::stat;
utime(time, stat($file)->mtime, $file);
```

Use utime to make it appear as though you never touched a file at all (beyond its ctime being updated). For example, to edit a file, use the program in Example 9-1.

Example 9-1. uvi

```
#!/usr/bin/perl -w
# uvi - vi a file without changing its access times

$file = shift or die "usage: uvi filename\n";
($atime, $mtime) = (stat($file))[8,9];
system($ENV{EDITOR} || "vi", $file);
utime($atime, $mtime, $file)
    or die "couldn't restore $file to orig times: $!";
```

See Also

The stat and utime functions in *perlfunc*(1) and in Chapter 29 of *Programming Perl*; the standard File::stat module (also in Chapter 32 of *Programming Perl*); your system's *utime*(3) manpage

9.2   Deleting a File

Problem

You want to delete a file. Perl's delete function isn't what you want.

Solution

Use Perl's unlink function:

```
unlink($FILENAME)                        or die "Can't delete $FILENAME: $!\n";
unlink(@FILENAMES) == @FILENAMES     or die "Couldn't unlink all of @FILENAMES: $!\n";
```

Discussion

The unlink function takes its name from the Unix syscall. Perl's unlink takes a list of filenames and returns the number of filenames successfully deleted. This return value can then be tested with || or or:

```
unlink($file) or die "Can't unlink $file: $!";
```

unlink doesn't report which filenames it couldn't delete, only how many it deleted. Here's one way to test for successful deletion of many files and report the number deleted:

```
unless (($count = unlink(@filelist)) == @filelist) {
    warn "could only delete $count of "
            . (@filelist) . " files";
}
```

A foreach over @filelist would permit individual error messages.

Under Unix, deleting a file from a directory requires write access to the directory,* not to the file, because it's the directory you're changing. Under some circumstances, you could remove a file you couldn't write to or write to a file you couldn't remove.

If you delete a file that some process still has open, the operating system removes the directory entry but doesn't free up data blocks until all processes have closed the file. This is how the tmpfile function in File::Temp works (see Recipe 7.11).

See Also

The unlink function in *perlfunc*(1) and in Chapter 29 of *Programming Perl*; your system's *unlink*(2) manpage; Recipe 7.11

---

* Unless the sticky bit, mode 01000, is turned on for the directory, which further restricts deletions to be by the file's owner only. Shared directories such as */tmp* are usually mode 01777 for security reasons.

9.3 Copying or Moving a File

Problem

You need to copy a file, but Perl has no built-in copy function.

Solution

Use the copy function from the standard File::Copy module:

```
use File::Copy;
copy($oldfile, $newfile);
```

You can do it by hand:

```
open(IN,  "<", $oldfile)                    or die "can't open $oldfile: $!";
open(OUT, ">", $newfile)                    or die "can't open $newfile: $!";

$blksize = (stat IN)[11] || 16384;          # preferred block size?
while (1) {
    $len = sysread IN, $buf, $blksize;
    if (!defined $len) {
        next if $! =~ /^Interrupted/;       # ^Z and fg on EINTR
        die "System read error: $!\n";
    }
    last unless $len;

    $offset = 0;
    while ($len) {          # Handle partial writes.
        defined($written = syswrite OUT, $buf, $len, $offset)
            or die "System write error: $!\n";
        $len    -= $written;
        $offset += $written;
    };
}

close(IN);
close(OUT);
```

or you can call your system's copy program:

```
system("cp $oldfile $newfile");       # unix
system("copy $oldfile $newfile");     # dos, vms
```

Discussion

The File::Copy module provides copy and move functions. These are more convenient than resorting to low-level I/O calls and more portable than calling system. This version of move works across file-system boundaries; the standard Perl built-in rename (usually) does not.

```
use File::Copy;

copy("datafile.dat", "datafile.bak")
```

```
        or die "copy failed: $!";

    move("datafile.dat", "datafile.new")
        or die "move failed: $!";
```

Because these functions return only a simple success status, you can't easily tell which file prevented the copy or move from working. Copying the files manually lets you pinpoint which files didn't copy, but it fills your program with complex sysreads and syswrites.

See Also

Documentation for the standard File::Copy module (also in Chapter 32 of *Programming Perl*); the rename, read, and syswrite functions in *perlfunc*(1) and in Chapter 29 of *Programming Perl*

9.4   Recognizing Two Names for the Same File

Problem

You want to determine whether two filenames in a list correspond to the same file on disk (because of hard and soft links, two filenames can refer to a single file). You might do this to make sure that you don't change a file you've already worked with.

Solution

Maintain a hash, keyed by the device and inode number of the files you've seen. The values are the names of the files:

```
%seen = ();

sub do_my_thing {
    my $filename = shift;
    my ($dev, $ino) = stat $filename;

    unless ($seen{$dev, $ino}++) {
        # do something with $filename because we haven't
        # seen it before
    }
}
```

Discussion

A key in %seen is made by combining the device number ($dev) and inode number ($ino) of each file. Files that are the same will have the same device and inode numbers, so they will have the same key.

If you want to maintain a list of all files of the same name, instead of counting the number of times seen, save the name of the file in an anonymous array.

```
foreach $filename (@files) {
    ($dev, $ino) = stat $filename;
    push( @{ $seen{$dev,$ino} }, $filename);
}

foreach $devino (sort keys %seen) {
    ($dev, $ino) = split(/$;/o, $devino);
    if (@{$seen{$devino}} > 1) {
        # @{$seen{$devino}} is a list of filenames for the same file
    }
}
```

The $; variable contains the separator string using the old multidimensional associative array emulation syntax, $hash{$x,$y,$z}. It's still a one-dimensional hash, but it has composite keys. The key is really join($; => $x, $y, $z). The split separates them again. Although you'd normally just use a real multilevel hash directly, here there's no need, and it's cheaper not to.

See Also

The $; ($SUBSEP) variable in *perlvar*(1), and in the "Special Variables" section of Chapter 28 of *Programming Perl*; the stat function in *perlfunc*(1) and in Chapter 29 of *Programming Perl*; Chapter 5

9.5   Processing All Files in a Directory

Problem

You want to do something to each file in a particular directory.

Solution

Use opendir to open the directory and readdir to retrieve every filename:

```
opendir(DIR, $dirname) or die "can't opendir $dirname: $!";
while (defined($file = readdir(DIR))) {
    # do something with "$dirname/$file"
}
closedir(DIR);
```

Discussion

The opendir, readdir, and closedir functions operate on directories as open, <>, and close operate on files. Both use handles, but the directory handles used by opendir and friends are different from the filehandles used by open and friends. In particular, you can't use <> on a directory handle.

In scalar context, readdir returns the next filename in the directory until it reaches the end of the directory, when it returns undef. In list context it returns the rest of the filenames in the directory or an empty list if there were no files left. As explained in this chapter's Introduction, the filenames returned by readdir do not include the directory name. When you work with the filenames returned by readdir, you must either move to the right directory first or prepend the directory to the filename.

This shows one way of prepending:

```
$dir = "/usr/local/bin";
print "Text files in $dir are:\n";
opendir(BIN, $dir) or die "Can't open $dir: $!";
while( $file = readdir BIN) {
    print "$file\n" if -T "$dir/$file";
}
closedir(BIN);
```

The readdir function will return the special directories "." (the directory itself) and ".." (the parent of the directory). Most people skip those files with code like:

```
while ( defined ($file = readdir BIN) ) {
    next if $file =~ /^\.\.?$/;      # skip . and ..
    # ...
}
```

Like filehandles, bareword directory handles are per-package constructs. You can use the local *DIRHANDLE syntax to get a new bareword directory handle. Alternatively, pass an undefined scalar as the first argument to opendir and Perl will put a new indirect directory handle into that scalar:

```
opendir my $dh, $directory or die;
while (defined ($filename = readdir($dh))) {
  # ...
}
closedir $dh;
```

Or, finally, you can use DirHandle to get an object-oriented view of a directory handle. The following code uses DirHandle and produces a sorted list of plain files that aren't dotfiles (that is, their names don't begin with a "."):

```
use DirHandle;

sub plainfiles {
   my $dir = shift;
   my $dh = DirHandle->new($dir)    or die "can't opendir $dir: $!";
   return sort                      # sort pathnames
        grep {    -f    }           # choose only "plain" files
        map  { "$dir/$_" }          # create full paths
        grep { !/^\./  }            # filter out dot files
        $dh->read();                # read all entries
}
```

DirHandle's read method behaves just like readdir, returning all remaining filenames. The bottom grep returns only those that don't begin with a period. The map turns the filenames returned by read into fully qualified filenames, and the top grep filters out directories, links, etc. The resulting list is then sorted and returned.

In addition to readdir, there's also rewinddir (to move the directory handle back to the start of the filename list), seekdir (to move to a specific offset in the list), and telldir (to find out how far from the start of the list you are).

See Also

The closedir, opendir, readdir, rewinddir, seekdir, and telldir functions in *perlfunc*(1) and in Chapter 29 of *Programming Perl*; documentation for the standard DirHandle module (also in Chapter 32 of *Programming Perl*)

9.6   Globbing, or Getting a List of Filenames Matching a Pattern

Problem

You want to get a list of filenames similar to those produced by MS-DOS's *.* and Unix's *.h. This is called *globbing*, and the filename wildcard expression is called a *glob*, or occasionally a *fileglob* to distinguish it from a *typeglob*.

Solution

Perl provides globbing with the semantics of the Unix C shell through the glob keyword and <>:

```
@list = <*.c>;
@list = glob("*.c");
```

You can also use readdir to extract the filenames manually:

```
opendir(DIR, $path);
@files = grep { /\.c$/ } readdir(DIR);
closedir(DIR);
```

Discussion

In versions of Perl before v5.6, Perl's built-in glob and <WILDCARD> notation (not to be confused with <FILEHANDLE>) ran an external program (often the *csh* shell) to get the list of filenames. This led to globbing being tarred with security and performance concerns. As of v5.6, Perl uses the File::Glob module to glob files, which solves the security and performance problems of the old implementation. Globs have C shell semantics on non-Unix systems to encourage portability. In particular, glob syntax isn't regular expression syntax—glob uses ? to mean "any single character" and * to mean "zero or more characters," so glob("f?o*") matches flo and flood but not fo.

For complex rules about which filenames you want, roll your own selection mechanism using readdir and regular expressions.

At its simplest, an opendir solution uses grep to filter the list returned by readdir:

```
@files = grep { /\.[ch]$/i } readdir(DH);
```

As always, the filenames returned don't include the directory. When you use the filename, prepend the directory name to get the full pathname:

```
opendir(DH, $dir)         or die "Couldn't open $dir for reading: $!";

@files = ();
while( defined ($file = readdir(DH)) ) {
    next unless /\.[ch]$/i;

    my $filename = "$dir/$file";
    push(@files, $filename) if -T $filename;
}
```

The following example combines directory reading and filtering with the efficient sorting technique from Recipe 4.16. It sets @dirs to a sorted list of the subdirectories in a directory whose names are all numeric:

```
@dirs = map  { $_->[1] }          # extract pathnames
        sort { $a->[0] <=> $b->[0] }   # sort names numeric
        grep { -d $_->[1] }            # path is a dir
        map  { [ $_, "$path/$_" ] }    # form (name, path)
        grep { /^\d+$/ }               # just numerics
        readdir(DIR);                  # all files
```

Recipe 4.16 explains how to read these strange-looking constructs. As always, formatting and documenting your code can make it much easier to read and understand.

See Also

The opendir, readdir, closedir, grep, map, and sort functions in *perlfunc*(1) and in Chapter 29 of *Programming Perl*; documentation for the standard DirHandle module (also in Chapter 32 of *Programming Perl*); the "I/O Operators" section of *perlop*(1), and the "Filename Globbing Operator" section of Chapter 2 of *Programming Perl*; we talk more about globbing in Recipe 6.9; Recipe 9.5

9.7   Processing All Files in a Directory Recursively

Problem

You want to do something to each file and subdirectory in a particular directory.

Solution

Use the standard File::Find module.

```
use File::Find;
sub process_file {
    # do whatever;
}
find(\&process_file, @DIRLIST);
```

Discussion

File::Find provides a convenient way to process a directory recursively. It does the directory scans and recursion for you. All you do is pass find a code reference and a list of directories. For each file in those directories, recursively, find calls your function.

Before calling your function, find by default changes to the directory being visited, whose path relative to the starting directory is stored in the $File::Find::dir variable. $_ is set to the basename of the file being visited, and the full path of that file can be found in $File::Find::name. Your code can set $File::Find::prune to true to tell find not to descend into the directory just seen.

This simple example demonstrates File::Find. We give find an anonymous subroutine that prints the name of each file visited and adds a / to the names of directories:

```
@ARGV = qw(.) unless @ARGV;
use File::Find;
find sub { print $File::Find::name, -d && "/", "\n" }, @ARGV;
```

The **-d** file test operator returns the empty string '' if it fails, making the && return that, too. But if **-d** succeeds, the && returns "/", which is then printed.

The following program prints the total bytes occupied by everything in a directory, including subdirectories. It gives find an anonymous subroutine to keep a running sum of the sizes of each file it visits. That includes all inode types, including the sizes of directories and symbolic links, not just regular files. Once the find function returns, the accumulated sum is displayed.

```
use File::Find;
@ARGV = (".") unless @ARGV;
my $sum = 0;
find sub { $sum += -s }, @ARGV;
print "@ARGV contains $sum bytes\n";
```

This code finds the largest single file within a set of directories:

```
use File::Find;
@ARGV = (".") unless @ARGV;
my ($saved_size, $saved_name) = (-1, "");
sub biggest {
    return unless -f && -s _ > $saved_size;
    $saved_size = -s _;
    $saved_name = $File::Find::name;
}
```

```
find(\&biggest, @ARGV);
print "Biggest file $saved_name in @ARGV is $saved_size bytes long.\n";
```

We use $saved_size and $saved_name to keep track of the name and the size of the largest file visited. If we find a file bigger than the largest seen so far, we replace the saved name and size with the current ones. When the find finishes, the largest file and its size are printed out, rather verbosely. A more general tool would probably just print the filename, its size, or both. This time we used a named function rather than an anonymous one because the function was getting big.

It's simple to change this to find the most recently changed file:

```
use File::Find;
@ARGV = (".") unless @ARGV;
my ($age, $name);
sub youngest {
    return if defined $age && $age > (stat($_))[9];
    $age = (stat(_))[9];
    $name = $File::Find::name;
}
find(\&youngest, @ARGV);
print "$name " . scalar(localtime($age)) . "\n";
```

The File::Find module doesn't export its $name variable, so always refer to it by its fully qualified name. Example 9-2 is more a demonstration of namespace munging than of recursive directory traversal, although it does find all directories. It makes $name in our current package an alias for the one in File::Find, which is essentially how Exporter works. Then it declares its own version of find with a prototype so it can be called like grep or map.

Example 9-2. fdirs

```
#!/usr/bin/perl -lw
# fdirs - find all directories
@ARGV = qw(.) unless @ARGV;
use File::Find ();
sub find(&@) { &File::Find::find }
*name = *File::Find::name;
find { print $name if -d } @ARGV;
```

Our own find only calls the find in File::Find, which we were careful not to import by specifying an ( ) empty list in the use statement. Rather than write this:

```
find sub { print $File::Find::name if -d }, @ARGV;
```

we can write the more pleasant:

```
find { print $name if -d } @ARGV;
```

See Also

The documentation for the standard File::Find and Exporter modules (also in Chapter 32 of *Programming Perl*); your system's *find*(1) manpage; Recipe 9.6

9.8   Removing a Directory and Its Contents

Problem

You want to remove a directory tree recursively without using rm -r.

Solution

Use the finddepth function from File::Find, shown in Example 9-3.

Example 9-3. rmtree1

```
#!/usr/bin/perl
# rmtree1 - remove whole directory trees like rm -r
use File::Find;
die "usage: $0 dir ..\n" unless @ARGV;
find {
    bydepth   => 1,
    no_chdir  => 1,
    wanted    => sub {
        if (!-l && -d _) {
            rmdir     or warn "couldn't rmdir directory $_: $!";
        } else {
            unlink    or warn "couldn't unlink file $_: $!";
        }
    }
} => @ARGV;
```

Or use rmtree from File::Path, as shown in Example 9-4.

Example 9-4. rmtree2

```
#!/usr/bin/perl
# rmtree2 - remove whole directory trees like rm -r
use File::Path;
die "usage: $0 dir ..\n" unless @ARGV;
foreach $dir (@ARGV) {
    rmtree($dir);
}
```

 These programs remove an entire directory tree. Use with extreme caution!

Discussion

The File::Find module supports an alternate interface in which find's first argument is a hash reference containing options and their settings. The bydepth option is the same as calling finddepth instead of find. This is guaranteed to visit all files beneath a directory before the directory itself, just what we need to remove a directory and its contents. The no_chdir option stops find from descending into directories during processing; under this option, $_ is the same as $File::Find::name. Finally, the wanted option takes a code reference, our old wanted( ) function.

We use two different functions, rmdir and unlink; both default to $_ if no argument is provided. The unlink function deletes only files, and rmdir deletes only *empty* directories. We need to use finddepth or the bydepth option to make sure we've first removed the directory's contents before we rmdir the directory itself.

We first check that the file isn't a symbolic link before determining whether it's a directory, because -d returns true for both a real directory and a symbolic link to a directory. stat, lstat, and file test operators like -d all use the syscall *stat*(2), which returns the file meta-information stored in the file's inode. These functions and operators cache that information in the special underscore (_) filehandle. This permits tests on the same file while avoiding redundant syscalls that would return the same information, slowly.

According to POSIX, if the directory is either the root directory (the mount point for the filesystems or the result of a *chroot*(2) syscall) or the current working directory of any process, it is unspecified whether the rmdir syscall succeeds, or whether it fails and sets errno ($! in Perl) to EBUSY ("Device busy"). Many systems tolerate the latter condition, but few the former.

See Also

The unlink, rmdir, lstat, and stat functions in *perlfunc*(1) and in Chapter 29 of *Programming Perl*; the documentation for the standard File::Find module (also in Chapter 32 of *Programming Perl*); your system's *rm*(1) and *stat*(2) manpages; the -X section of *perlfunc*(1), and the "Named Unary and File Test Operators" section of Chapter 3 of *Programming Perl*

9.9   Renaming Files

Problem

You have many files whose names you want to change.

Solution

Use a foreach loop and the rename function:

```
foreach $file (@NAMES) {
    my $newname = $file;
    # change $newname
    rename($file, $newname) or
        warn "Couldn't rename $file to $newname: $!\n";
}
```

Discussion

This is straightforward. rename takes two arguments. The first is the filename to change, and the second is its new name. Perl's rename is a frontend to the operating system's rename syscall, which typically won't rename files across filesystem boundaries.

A small change turns this into a generic rename script, such as the one by Larry Wall shown in Example 9-5.

Example 9-5. rename

```
#!/usr/bin/perl -w
# rename - Larry's filename fixer
$op = shift or die "Usage: rename expr [files]\n";
chomp(@ARGV = <STDIN>) unless @ARGV;
for (@ARGV) {
    $was = $_;
    eval $op;
    die $@ if $@;
    rename($was,$_) unless $was eq $_;
}
```

This script's first argument is Perl code that alters the filename (stored in $_) to reflect how you want the file renamed. It can do this because it uses an eval to do the hard work. It also skips rename calls when the filename is untouched. This lets you simply use wildcards like rename EXPR * instead of making long lists of filenames.

Here are five examples of calling the *rename* program from the shell:

```
% rename 's/\.orig$//'  *.orig
% rename "tr/A-Z/a-z/ unless /^Make/"  *
% rename '$_ .= ".bad"'  *.f
% rename 'print "$_: "; s/foo/bar/ if <STDIN> =~ /^y/i'  *
% find /tmp -name "*~" -print | rename 's/^(.+)~$/.#$1/'
```

The first shell command removes a trailing ".orig" from each filename.

The second converts uppercase to lowercase. Because a translation is used rather than the lc function, this conversion won't be locale-aware. To fix that, you'd have to write:

```
% rename 'use locale; $_ = lc($_) unless /^Make/' *
```

The third appends ".bad" to each Fortran file ending in ".f", something many of us have wanted to do for a long time.

The fourth prompts the user for the change. Each file's name is printed to standard output and a response read from standard input. If the user types something starting with a "y" or "Y", any "foo" in the filename is changed to "bar".

The fifth uses *find* to locate files in /tmp that end with a tilde. It renames these so that instead of ending with a tilde, they start with a dot and a pound sign. In effect, this switches between two common conventions for backup files.

The *rename* script exemplifies the powerful Unix tool-and-filter philosophy. Even though we could have created a dedicated command for lowercase conversion, it's nearly as easy to write a flexible, reusable tool by embedding an eval. By reading filenames from standard input, we don't have to build in the recursive directory walk. Instead, we just use *find*, which performs this function well. There's no reason to recreate the wheel, although using File::Find we could have.

See Also

The rename function in *perlfunc*(1) and in Chapter 29 of *Programming Perl*; your system's *mv*(1) and *rename*(2) manpages; the documentation for the standard File::Find module (also in Chapter 32 of *Programming Perl*)

9.10 Splitting a Filename into Its Component Parts

Problem

You want to extract a filename, its enclosing directory, or the extension(s) from a string that contains a full pathname.

Solution

Use routines from the standard File::Basename module.

```
use File::Basename;

$base = basename($path);
$dir  = dirname($path);
($base, $dir, $ext) = fileparse($path);
```

Discussion

The standard File::Basename module contains routines to split up a filename. dirname and basename supply the directory and filename portions, respectively:

```
$path = "/usr/lib/libc.a";
$file = basename($path);
$dir  = dirname($path);

print "dir is $dir, file is $file\n";
# dir is /usr/lib, file is libc.a
```

The fileparse function can extract the extension. Pass fileparse the path to decipher and a regular expression that matches the extension. You must supply a pattern because an extension isn't necessarily dot-separated. Consider ".tar.gz": is the extension ".tar", ".gz", or ".tar.gz"? By specifying the pattern, you control which you get.

```
$path = "/usr/lib/libc.a";
($name,$dir,$ext) = fileparse($path,'\..*');

print "dir is $dir, name is $name, extension is $ext\n";
# dir is /usr/lib/, name is libc, extension is .a
```

By default, these routines parse pathnames using your operating system's normal conventions for directory separators by consulting the $^O ($OSNAME) variable, which holds a string identifying the platform you're running on. That value was determined when Perl was built and installed. You can change the default by calling the fileparse_set_fstype routine. This alters the behavior of subsequent calls to the File::Basename functions:

```
fileparse_set_fstype("MacOS");
$path = "Hard%20Drive:System%20Folder:README.txt";
($name,$dir,$ext) = fileparse($path,'\..*');

print "dir is $dir, name is $name, extension is $ext\n";
# dir is Hard%20Drive:System%20Folder, name is README, extension is .txt
```

To pull out just the extension, you might use this:

```
sub extension {
    my $path = shift;
    my $ext = (fileparse($path,'\..*'))[2];
    $ext =~ s/^\.//;
    return $ext;
}
```

When called on a file like *source.c.bak*, this returns an extension of "c.bak", not just "bak". If you want ".bak" returned, use '\.[^.]*' as the second argument to fileparse (this will, of course, leave the filename as source.c).

When passed a pathname with a trailing directory separator, such as "lib/", fileparse considers the directory name to be "lib/", whereas dirname considers it to be ".".

See Also

The documentation for the standard File::Basename module (also in Chapter 32 of *Programming Perl*); the entry for $^O ($OSNAME) in *perlvar*(1), and in the "Special Variables in Alphabetical Order" section of Chapter 28 of *Programming Perl*

9.11 Working with Symbolic File Permissions Instead of Octal Values

Problem

You want to print, inspect, or change permissions on a file or directory, but you don't want to specify the permissions in octal (e.g., 0644, 0755). You want to print permissions as *ls*(1) shows them (e.g., -rwx-r-xr-x) and specify permissions changes in the way that *chmod*(1) does (e.g., g-w to remove write access for the group).

Solution

Use the CPAN module Stat::lsMode to convert numeric permissions to a string:

```
use Stat::lsMode;

$lsmode = file_mode($pathname);
```

Use the CPAN module File::chmod to manipulate symbolic permissions:

```
use File::chmod;

chmod("g=rw,o=-w", @files);    # group can read/write, others can't write
chmod("-rwxr-xr--", @files);   # ls-style permissions
```

Discussion

The Stat::lsMode module provides functions for generating *ls*-style permissions strings. The file_mode function takes a pathname and returns a permissions string. This string is false if the pathname doesn't exist or Perl can't *stat* it. If all goes well, you get a string like "drwxr-x---" for a directory or "-rwxr-x----" for a file. For more fine-grained control, Stat::lsMode offers format_mode, which takes a numeric permissions value and returns the 10-character *ls*-style string.

Notice the leading d and - in those strings. This indicates the type of file whose permissions you're inspecting: - means regular file, d means directory, l means symbolic link, and so on. The format_perms function from Stat::lsMode does the same job as format_mode, but it returns a nine-character string, which does not have the type indicator. For example:

```
use Stat::lsMode;
print file_mode("/etc"), "\n";
print format_mode((stat "/etc")[2]), "\n";
drwxr-xr-x
r-xr-xr-x
```

The File::chmod module gives you a chmod that accepts these nine-character permissions strings:

```
use File::chmod;
chmod("rwxr-xr-x", @files);
```

These strings are three clusters of three characters. The three clusters represent what the user, group, and others can do to the file (respectively). The three characters represent *reading*, *writing*, and *executing*, with a dash (-) in a column indicating the corresponding permission is denied to the group. So in "rwxrw-r--", the owner can read, write, and execute; users in the same group as the file can read and write but not execute; and everyone else can only read.

You can specify relative changes to the permissions for a particular file; for example, g-w removes write permission from the group. The first letter(s) indicates whose permissions are being changed (*u*ser, *g*roup, *o*ther, or a combination). Then comes a + or - to indicate adding or removing permissions, or = to indicate you're specifying the complete set of permissions. Then you specify some or all of rwx. You can join these with commas to form relative permissions; for example, g-w,o+x (remove write from group, add execute to other). If you omit the u, g, or o, then the change applies to everyone.

Here are some valid permissions changes and what they do:

```
u=                  remove all permissions for the user
g=r                 group can only read
g+wx                group can also write and execute
g=rwx,o=rx          group can do all, other can only read and execute
=rwx                everybody can do everything
```

So you can now say:

```
chmod("u=", @files);  # remove all permissions for the user on @files
chmod("g=r", @files);
chmod("g+wx", @files);
chmod("g=rwx,o-rx", @files);
chmod("=rwx", @files);
```

File::chmod also provides functions for seeing what the new permission would be without actually making the change. See the File::chmod documentation for more details.

See Also

The documentation for the CPAN modules File::chmod and Stat::lsMode; the chmod and stat functions in *perlfunc*(1)

9.12   Program: symirror

The program in Example 9-6 recursively duplicates a directory tree, making a shadow forest full of symlinks pointing back at the real files.

Example 9-6. symirror

```perl
#!/usr/bin/perl
# symirror - build spectral forest of symlinks

use warnings;
use strict;

use Cwd         qw(realpath);
use File::Find  qw(find);

die "usage: $0 realdir mirrordir" unless @ARGV == 2;

our $SRC = realpath $ARGV[0];
our $DST = realpath $ARGV[1];

my $oldmask = umask 077;        # in case was insanely uncreatable
chdir $SRC                      or die "can't chdir $SRC: $!";
unless (-d $DST) {
    mkdir($DST, 0700)           or die "can't mkdir $DST: $!";
}
find {
    wanted      => \&shadow,
    postprocess => \&fixmode,
} => ".";
umask $oldmask;

sub shadow {
    (my $name = $File::Find::name) =~ s!^\./!!;     # correct name
    return if $name eq ".";
    if (-d) { # make a real dir; we'll copy mode later
        mkdir("$DST/$name", 0700)
                        or die "can't mkdir $DST/$name: $!";
    } else {   # all else gets symlinked
        symlink("$SRC/$name", "$DST/$name")
                        or die "can't symlink $SRC/$name to $DST/$name: $!";
    }
}

sub fixmode {
    my $dir = $File::Find::dir;
    my $mode = (stat("$SRC/$dir"))[2] & 07777;
    chmod($mode, "$DST/$dir")
        or die "can't set mode on $DST/$dir: $!";
}
```

9.13 Program: lst

Have you ever wondered what the newest or biggest files within a directory are? The standard *ls* program has options for listing out directories sorted in time order (the **-t** flag) and for recursing into subdirectories (the **-R** flag). However, it pauses at each directory to display the sorted contents of just that directory. It doesn't descend through all subdirectories first and then sort everything it found.

The following *lst* program does that. Here's an example using its **-l** flag to get a long listing:

```
% lst -l /etc
12695 0600    1    root    wheel      512 Fri May 29 10:42:41 1998
      /etc/ssh_random_seed
12640 0644    1    root    wheel    10104 Mon May 25  7:39:19 1998
      /etc/ld.so.cache
12626 0664    1    root    wheel    12288 Sun May 24 19:23:08 1998
      /etc/psdevtab
12304 0644    1    root    root       237 Sun May 24 13:59:33 1998
      /etc/exports
12309 0644    1    root    root      3386 Sun May 24 13:24:33 1998
      /etc/inetd.conf
12399 0644    1    root    root     30205 Sun May 24 10:08:37 1998
      /etc/sendmail.cf
18774 0644    1    gnat    perldoc   2199 Sun May 24  9:35:57 1998
      /etc/X11/XMetroconfig
12636 0644    1    root    wheel      290 Sun May 24  9:05:40 1998
      /etc/mtab
12627 0640    1    root    root         0 Sun May 24  8:24:31 1998
      /etc/wtmplock
12310 0644    1    root    tchrist     65 Sun May 24  8:23:04 1998
      /etc/issue
....
```

/etc/X11/XMetroconfig showed up in the middle of the listing for */etc* because it wasn't just for */etc*, but for everything within that directory, recursively.

Other supported options include sorting on read time instead of write time using **-u** and sorting on size rather than time with **-s**. The **-i** flag takes the list of filenames from standard input instead of recursing with find. That way, if you already had a list of filenames, you could feed them to *lst* for sorting.

The program is shown in Example 9-7.

Example 9-7. lst

```
#!/usr/bin/perl
# lst - list sorted directory contents (depth first)

use Getopt::Std;
use File::Find;
use File::stat;
```

Example 9-7. lst (continued)

```perl
use User::pwent;
use User::grent;

getopts("lusrcmi")                               or die << DEATH;
Usage: $0 [-mucsril] [dirs ...]
  or    $0 -i [-mucsrl] < filelist

Input format:
    -i  read pathnames from stdin
Output format:
    -l  long listing
Sort on:
    -m  use mtime (modify time) [DEFAULT]
    -u  use atime (access time)
    -c  use ctime (inode change time)
    -s  use size for sorting
Ordering:
    -r  reverse sort
NB: You may only use select one sorting option at a time.
DEATH

unless ($opt_i || @ARGV) { @ARGV = (".") }

if ($opt_c + $opt_u + $opt_s + $opt_m > 1) {
    die "can only sort on one time or size";
}

$IDX = "mtime";
$IDX = "atime" if $opt_u;
$IDX = "ctime" if $opt_c;
$IDX = "size"  if $opt_s;

$TIME_IDX = $opt_s ? "mtime" : $IDX;

*name = *File::Find::name;  # forcibly import that variable

# the $opt_i flag tricks wanted into taking
# its filenames from ARGV instead of being
# called from find.

if ($opt_i) {
    *name = *_;  # $name now alias for $_
    while (<>) { chomp; &wanted; }   # ok, not stdin really
} else {
    find(\&wanted, @ARGV);
}

# sort the files by their cached times, youngest first
@skeys = sort { $time{$b} <=> $time{$a} } keys %time;

# but flip the order if -r was supplied on command line
@skeys = reverse @skeys if $opt_r;
```

Example 9-7. lst (continued)

```perl
for (@skeys) {
    unless ($opt_l) {   # emulate ls -l, except for permissions
        print "$_\n";
        next;
    }
    $now = localtime $stat{$_}->$TIME_IDX( );
    printf "%6d %04o %6d %8s %8s %8d %s %s\n",
            $stat{$_}->ino( ),
            $stat{$_}->mode( ) & 07777,
            $stat{$_}->nlink( ),
            user($stat{$_}->uid( )),
            group($stat{$_}->gid( )),
            $stat{$_}->size( ),
            $now, $_;
}

# get stat info on the file, saving the desired
# sort criterion (mtime, atime, ctime, or size)
# in the %time hash indexed by filename.
# if they want a long list, we have to save the
# entire stat object in %stat.  yes, this is a
# hash of objects
sub wanted {
    my $sb = stat($_);   # XXX: should be stat or lstat?
    return unless $sb;
    $time{$name} = $sb->$IDX( );   # indirect method call
    $stat{$name} = $sb if $opt_l;
}

# cache user number to name conversions; don't worry
# about the apparently extra call, as the system caches the
# last one called all by itself
sub user {
    my $uid = shift;
    $user{$uid} = getpwuid($uid) ? getpwuid($uid)->name : "#$uid"
        unless defined $user{$uid};
    return $user{$uid};
}

# cache group number to name conversions; ditto on unworryness
sub group {
    my $gid = shift;
    $group{$gid} = getgrgid($gid) ? getgrgid($gid)->name : "#$gid"
        unless defined $group{$gid};
    return $group{$gid};
```

## CHAPTER 10

Subroutines

Composing mortals with immortal fire.
—W. H. Auden, "Three Songs for St Cecilia's Day"

10.0 Introduction

To avoid the dangerous practice of copying and pasting code, larger programs reuse chunks of code as subroutines and functions. We'll use the terms *subroutine* and *function* interchangeably because Perl doesn't distinguish between the two. Even object-oriented methods are just subroutines that are called using a special syntax, described in Chapter 13.

A subroutine is declared with the sub keyword. Here's a simple subroutine definition:

```
sub hello {
    $greeted++;            # global variable
    print "hi there!\n";
}
```

The typical way of calling that subroutine is:

```
hello();                   # call subroutine hello with no arguments/parameters
```

Because Perl compiles your program before executing it, it doesn't matter where subroutines are declared. Definitions don't have to be in the same file as your main program. They can be pulled in from other files using the do, require, or use operators, as described in Chapter 12. They can even be created on the fly using eval or AUTO-LOAD, or generated using closures, which can act as function templates.

If you are familiar with other programming languages, several characteristics of Perl's functions may surprise you if you're unprepared for them. Most recipes in this chapter illustrate how to be aware of—and to take advantage of—these properties.

- Perl functions have no formal, named parameters, but this is not necessarily a bad thing. See Recipes 10.1 and 10.7.

- All variables are global unless declared otherwise. See Recipes 10.2, 10.3, and 10.13 for details.

- Passing or returning more than one array or hash normally causes them to lose their separate identities. See Recipes 10.5, 10.8, 10.9, and 10.11 to avoid this.

- A function can know in which context it was called, how many arguments it was called with, and even which other function called it. See Recipes 10.4 and 10.6 to find out how.

- Perl's undef value can be used to signal an error return from the function because no valid string, number, or reference ever has that value. Recipe 10.10 covers subtle pitfalls with undef you should avoid, and Recipe 10.12 shows how to deal with other catastrophic conditions.

- Perl supports interesting operations on functions that you might not see in other languages, such as anonymous functions, creating functions on the fly, and calling them indirectly using function pointers. See Recipes 10.14 and 10.16 for these esoteric topics.

- Calling a function as $x = &func; does not supply any arguments, but rather provides direct access to its caller's @_ array! If you omit the ampersand and use either func( ) or func, then a new and empty @_ is provided instead.

- Historically, Perl hasn't provided a construct like C's switch or the shell's case for multiway branching. The switch function shown in Recipe 10.17 takes care of that for you.

10.1 Accessing Subroutine Arguments

Problem

You have written a function that takes arguments supplied by its caller, and you need to access those arguments.

Solution

The special array @_ holds the values passed in as the function's arguments. Thus, the first argument to the function is in $_[0], the second in $_[1], and so on. The number of arguments is simply scalar(@_).

For example:

```
sub hypotenuse {
    return sqrt( ($_[0] ** 2) + ($_[1] ** 2) );
}

$diag = hypotenuse(3,4);  # $diag is 5
```

Most subroutines start by copying arguments into named private variables for safer and more convenient access:

```
sub hypotenuse {
    my ($side1, $side2) = @_;
    return sqrt( ($side1 ** 2) + ($side2 ** 2) );
}
```

Discussion

It's been said that programming has only three nice numbers: zero, one, and however many you please. Perl's subroutine mechanism was designed to facilitate writing functions with as many—or as few—elements in the parameter and return lists as you wish. All incoming parameters appear as separate scalar values in the special array @_, which is automatically local to each function (see Recipe 10.13). To return a value or values from a subroutine, use the return statement with arguments. If there is no return statement, the return value is the result of the last evaluated expression.

Here are some sample calls to the hypotenuse function defined in the Solution:

```
print hypotenuse(3, 4), "\n";                    # prints 5

@a = (3, 4);
print hypotenuse(@a), "\n";                       # prints 5
```

If you look at the arguments used in the second call to hypotenuse, it might appear that only one argument was passed: the array @a. This isn't what happens—the elements of @a are copied into the @_ array separately. Similarly, if you called a function with (@a, @b), you'd be giving it all arguments from both arrays. This is the same principle of flattened lists at work as in:

```
@both = (@men, @women);
```

The scalars in @_ are implicit aliases for the ones passed in, not copies. That means changing the elements of @_ in a subroutine changes the values in the subroutine's caller. This is a holdover from before Perl had proper references.

You can write functions that leave their arguments intact by copying the arguments to private variables like this:

```
@nums = (1.4, 3.5, 6.7);
@ints = int_all(@nums);        # @nums unchanged
sub int_all {
    my @retlist = @_;          # make safe copy for return
    for my $n (@retlist) { $n = int($n) }
    return @retlist;
}
```

You can also write functions that change their caller's variables:

```
@nums = (1.4, 3.5, 6.7);
trunc_em(@nums);               # @nums now (1,3,6)
sub trunc_em {
    for (@_) { $_ = int($_) }  # truncate each argument
}
```

Don't pass constants as arguments to a function that intends to modify those arguments; for example, don't call trunc_em(1.4, 3.5, 6.7). If you do, you'll get a runtime exception to the effect of Modification of a read-only value attempted at ....

The built-in functions chop and chomp are like that; they modify their caller's variables and return something else entirely. Beginning Perl programmers who notice regular functions that all return some new value—including int, uc, and readline—without modifying those functions' arguments sometimes incorrectly infer that chop and chomp work similarly. This leads them to write code like:

```
$line = chomp(<>);                # WRONG

$removed_chars = chop($line);     # RIGHT
$removed_count = chomp($line);    # RIGHT
```

until they get the hang of how this pair really works. Given the vast potential for confusion, you might want to think twice before modifying @_ in your own subroutines, especially if you also intend to provide a distinct return value.

See Also

Chapter 6 of *Programming Perl* and *perlsub*(1)

10.2   Making Variables Private to a Function

Problem

Your subroutine needs temporary variables. You shouldn't use global variables, because another subroutine might also use the same variables.

Solution

Use my to declare a variable private to a region of your program:

```
sub somefunc {
    my $variable;                      # $variable is invisible outside somefunc()
    my ($another, @an_array, %a_hash); # declaring many variables at once

    # ...
}
```

Discussion

The my operator confines a variable to a particular region of code in which it can be used and accessed. Outside that region, it can't be accessed. This region is called its *scope*.

Variables declared with my have *lexical scope*, meaning that they exist only within a specific textual region of code. For instance, the scope of $variable in the Solution is the function it was defined in, somefunc. The variable is created when somefunc is entered, and it is destroyed when the function returns. The variable can be accessed only from inside the function, not from outside.

A lexical scope is usually a block of code with braces around it, such as those defining the body of the somefunc subroutine or those marking the code blocks of if, while, for, foreach, and eval. An entire source file and the string argument to eval are each a lexical scope;* think of them as blocks with invisible braces delimiting their confines. Because a lexical scope is most often found as a brace-delimited block, when discussing lexical variables we sometimes say that they are visible only in their *block*, but what we really mean is that they're visible only in their *scope*.

The code that can legally access a my variable is determined statically at compile time and never changes, and so lexical scoping is sometimes referred to as *static scoping*, especially when in contrast to *dynamic scoping*, a topic we'll cover in Recipe 10.13.

You can combine a my declaration with an assignment. Use parentheses when defining more than one variable:

```perl
my ($name, $age) = @ARGV;
my $start        = fetch_time();
```

These lexical variables behave as you would expect of a local variable. Nested blocks can see lexicals declared in enclosing, outer blocks, but not in unrelated blocks:

```perl
my ($a, $b) = @pair;
my $c = fetch_time();

sub check_x {
    my $x = $_[0];
    my $y = "whatever";
    run_check();
    if ($condition) {
        print "got $x\n";
    }
}
```

In the preceding code, the if block inside the function can access the private $x variable. However, the run_check function called from within that scope cannot access $x or $y, because run_check was presumably defined in another scope. However, check_x can access $a, $b, or $c from the outer scope because the function was defined in the same scope as those three variables.

Don't nest definitions of named subroutines. If you do, they won't get the right bindings of the lexical variables. Recipe 10.16 shows how to cope with this restriction.

---

* Although not of the same sort: the eval scope is a nested scope, just like a nested block, but the file scope is unrelated to any other.

When a lexical variable goes out of scope, its storage is freed unless a reference to the variable still exists, as with @arguments in the following code:

```perl
sub save_array {
    my @arguments = @_;
    push(our @Global_Array, \@arguments);
}
```

This code creates a new array each time save_array is called, so you don't have to worry that it'll reuse the same array each time the function is called.

Perl's garbage collection system knows not to deallocate things until they're no longer used. This is why you can return a reference to a private variable without leaking memory.

See Also

The section on "Scoped Declarations" in Chapter 4 of *Programming Perl* and the section on "Private Variables via my( )" in *perlsub*(1)

10.3   Creating Persistent Private Variables

Problem

You want a variable to retain its value between calls to a subroutine but not be visible outside that routine. For instance, you'd like your function to keep track of how many times it was called.

Solution

Wrap the function in another block, then declare my variables in that block's scope rather than in the function's:

```perl
{
    my $variable;
    sub mysub {
        # ... accessing $variable
    }
}
```

If the variables require initialization, make that block an INIT so the variable is guaranteed to be set before the main program starts running:

```perl
INIT {
    my $variable = 1;                    # initial value
    sub othersub {
      # ... accessing $variable
    }
}
```

Discussion

Unlike local* variables in C or C++, Perl's lexical variables don't necessarily get recycled just because their scope has exited. If something more permanent is still aware of the lexical, it will stick around. In this code, mysub uses $variable, so Perl doesn't reclaim the variable when the block around the definition of mysub ends.

Here's how to write a counter:

```
{
    my $counter;
    sub next_counter { return ++$counter }
}
```

Each time next_counter is called, it increments and returns the $counter variable. The first time next_counter is called, $counter is undefined, so it behaves as though it were 0 for the ++. The variable is not part of next_counter's scope, but rather part of the block surrounding it. No code from outside can change $counter except by calling next_counter.

Generally, you should use an INIT for the extra scope. Otherwise, you could call the function before its variables were initialized.

```
INIT {
    my $counter = 42;
    sub next_counter { return ++$counter }
    sub prev_counter { return --$counter }
}
```

This technique creates the Perl equivalent of C's static variables. Actually, it's a little better: rather than being limited to just one function, both functions share their private variable.

See Also

The sections on "Closures" in Chapter 8 of *Programming Perl* and on "Avante-Garde Compiler, Retro Interpreter" in Chapter 18 of *Programming Perl*; the section on "Private Variables via my()" in *perlsub*(1); the section on "Package Constructors and Destructors" in *perlmod*(1); Recipe 11.4

10.4 Determining Current Function Name

Problem

You want to determine the name of the currently running function. This is useful for creating error messages that don't need to be changed if you copy and paste the subroutine code.

---

* Technically speaking, *auto* variables.

Solution

Use the caller function:

```
$this_function = (caller(0))[3];
```

Discussion

Code can always determine the current source line number via the special symbol __LINE__, the current file via __FILE__, and the current package via __PACKAGE__. But no such symbol for the current subroutine name exists, let alone the name for the subroutine that called this one.

The built-in function caller handles all of these. In scalar context it returns the calling function's package name, but in list context it returns much more. You can also pass it a number indicating how many frames (nested subroutine calls) back you'd like information about: 0 is your own function, 1 is your caller, and so on.

Here's the full syntax, where $i is how far back you're interested in:

```
($package, $filename, $line, $subr, $has_args, $wantarray
#   0          1          2      3        4           5
 $evaltext, $is_require, $hints, $bitmask
#   6          7            8        9
)= caller($i);
```

Here's what each of those return values means:

$package
: The package in which the code was compiled.

$filename
: The name of the file in which the code was compiled, reporting -e if launched from that command-line switch, or - if the script was read from standard input.

$line
: The line number from which that frame was called.

$subr
: The name of that frame's function, including its package. Closures are indicated by names like main::__ANON__, which are not callable. In an eval, it contains (eval).

$has_args
: Whether the function had its own @_ variable set up. It may be that there are no arguments, even if true. The only way for this to be false is if the function was called using the &fn notation instead of fn( ) or &fn( ).

$wantarray
: The value the wantarray function would return for that stack frame; either true, false but defined, or else undefined. This tells whether the function was called in list, scalar, or void context (respectively).

`$evaltext`

> The text of the current eval *STRING*, if any.

`$is_require`

> Whether the code is currently being loaded by a do, require, or use.

`$hints, $bitmask`

> These both contain pragmatic hints that the caller was compiled with. Consider them to be for internal use only by Perl itself.

Rather than using `caller` directly as in the Solution, you might want to write functions instead:

```
$me  = whoami();
$him = whowasi();

sub whoami  { (caller(1))[3] }
sub whowasi { (caller(2))[3] }
```

These use arguments of 1 and 2 for parent and grandparent functions because the call to whoami or whowasi would itself be frame number 0.

See Also

The `wantarray` and `caller` functions in Chapter 29 of *Programming Perl* and in *perlfunc*(1); Recipe 10.6

10.5   Passing Arrays and Hashes by Reference

Problem

You want to pass a function more than one array or hash and have each remain distinct. For example, you want to put the algorithm from Recipe 4.8 into a subroutine. This subroutine must then be called with two arrays that remain distinct.

Solution

Pass arrays and hashes by reference, using the backslash operator:

```
array_diff( \@array1, \@array2 );
```

Discussion

See Chapter 11 for more about manipulation of references. Here's a subroutine that expects array references, along with code to call it correctly:

```
@a = (1, 2);
@b = (5, 8);
@c = add_vecpair( \@a, \@b );
```

```
    print "@c\n";
    6 10

    sub add_vecpair {                    # assumes both vectors the same length
        my ($x, $y) = @_;                # copy in the array references
        my @result;

        for (my $i=0; $i < @$x; $i++) {
            $result[$i] = $x->[$i] + $y->[$i];
        }

        return @result;
    }
```

A potential problem with this function is that it doesn't verify the number and types of arguments passed into it. You could check explicitly this way:

```
    unless (@_ == 2 && ref($x) eq 'ARRAY' && ref($y) eq 'ARRAY') {
        die "usage: add_vecpair ARRAYREF1 ARRAYREF2";
    }
```

If all you plan to do is die on error (see Recipe 10.12), you can sometimes omit this check, since dereferencing the wrong kind of reference triggers an exception anyway. However, good defensive programming style encourages argument validation for all functions.

See Also

The sections on "Passing References" and on "Prototypes" in Chapter 6 of *Programming Perl* and on "Pass by Reference" in *perlsub*(1); Recipe 10.11; Chapter 11; Chapter 8 of *Programming Perl*

10.6   Detecting Return Context

Problem

You want to know in which context your function was called. This lets one function do different things, depending on how its return value or values are used, just like many of Perl's built-in functions.

Solution

Use the wantarray( ) function, which has three possible return values, depending on how the current function was called:

```
    if (wantarray( )) {
        # list context
    }
    elsif (defined wantarray( )) {
        # scalar context
```

```
}
else {
    # void context
}
```

Discussion

Many built-in functions act differently when called in scalar context than they do
when called in list context. A user-defined function can learn which context it was
called in by checking wantarray. List context is indicated by a true return value. If
wantarray returns a value that is false but defined, then the function's return value
will be used in scalar context. If wantarray returns undef, your function isn't being
asked to provide any value at all.

```
if (wantarray( )) {
    print "In list context\n";
    return @many_things;
} elsif (defined wantarray( )) {
    print "In scalar context\n";
    return $one_thing;
} else {
    print "In void context\n";
    return;  # nothing
}

mysub( );                       # void context

$a = mysub( );                  # scalar context
if (mysub( )) {  }              # scalar context

@a = mysub( );                  # list context
print mysub( );                 # list context
```

See Also

The return and wantarray functions in Chapter 29 of *Programming Perl* and in
perlfunc(1)

10.7   Passing by Named Parameter

Problem

You want to make a function with many parameters that are easy to call so that programmers remember what the arguments do, rather than having to memorize their
order.

Solution

Name each parameter in the call:

```
thefunc(INCREMENT => "20s", START => "+5m", FINISH => "+30m");
thefunc(START => "+5m", FINISH => "+30m");
thefunc(FINISH => "+30m");
thefunc(START => "+5m", INCREMENT => "15s");
```

Then in the subroutine, create a hash loaded up with default values plus the array of named pairs.

```
sub thefunc {
    my %args = (
        INCREMENT   => '10s',
        FINISH      => 0,
        START       => 0,
        @_,             # argument pair list goes here
    );
    if ($args{INCREMENT}  =~ /m$/ ) { ... }
}
```

Discussion

Functions whose arguments require a particular order work well for short argument lists, but as the number of parameters increases, it's awkward to make some optional or have default values. You can only leave out trailing arguments, never initial ones.

A more flexible approach allows the caller to supply arguments using name-value pairs. The first element of each pair is the argument name; the second, its value. This makes for self-documenting code because you can see the parameters' intended meanings without having to read the full function definition. Even better, programmers using your function no longer have to remember argument order, and they can leave unspecified any extraneous, unused arguments.

This works by having the function declare a private hash variable to hold the default parameter values. Put the current arguments, @_, after the default values, so the actual arguments override the defaults because of the order of the values in the assignment.

A common variation on this is to preface the parameter name with a hyphen, intended to evoke the feel of command-line parameters:

```
thefunc(-START => "+5m", -INCREMENT => "15s");
```

Ordinarily the hyphen isn't part of a bareword, but the Perl tokenizer makes an exception for the => operator to permit this style of function argument.

See Also

Chapter 4

10.8   Skipping Selected Return Values

Problem

You have a function that returns many values, but you only care about some of them. The stat function is a classic example: you often want only one value from its long return list (mode, for instance).

Solution

Either assign to a list that has undef in some positions:

```
($a, undef, $c) = func();
```

or else take a slice of the return list, selecting only what you want:

```
($a, $c) = (func())[0,2];
```

Discussion

Using dummy temporary variables is wasteful; plus it feels artificial and awkward:

```
($dev,$ino,$DUMMY,$DUMMY,$uid) = stat($filename);
```

A nicer style is to use undef instead of dummy variables to discard a value:

```
($dev,$ino,undef,undef,$uid)   = stat($filename);
```

Or you can take a slice, picking up just the values you care about:

```
($dev,$ino,$uid,$gid)   = (stat($filename))[0,1,4,5];
```

If you want to put an expression into list context and discard all of its return values (calling it simply for side effects), you can assign this to the empty list:

```
() = some_function();
```

This last strategy is rather like a list version of the scalar operator—it calls the function in list context, even in a place it wouldn't otherwise do so. You can get just a count of return values this way:

```
$count = () = some_function();
```

or you can call it in list context and make sure it returns some non-zero number of items (which you immediately discard) like this:

```
if (() = some_function()) { .... }
```

If you hadn't assigned to the empty list, the Boolean context of the if test would have called the function in scalar context.

See Also

The section on "List Values and Arrays" in Chapter 2 of *Programming Perl* and *perlsub*(1); Recipe 3.1

10.9   Returning More Than One Array or Hash

Problem

You want a function to return more than one array or hash, but the return list flattens into just one long list of scalars.

Solution

Return references to the hashes or arrays:

```
($array_ref, $hash_ref) = somefunc();

sub somefunc {
    my @array;
    my %hash;

    # ...

    return ( \@array, \%hash );
}
```

Discussion

Just as all arguments collapse into one flat list of scalars, return values do, too. Functions that want to return multiple, distinct arrays or hashes need to return those by reference, and the caller must be prepared to receive references. If a function wants to return three separate hashes, for example, it should use one of the following:

```
sub fn {
    .....
    return (\%a, \%b, \%c); # or
    return \(%a,  %b,  %c); # same thing
}
```

The caller must expect a list of hash references returned by the function. It cannot just assign to three hashes.

```
(%h0, %h1, %h2)  = fn();     # WRONG!
@array_of_hashes = fn();     # eg: $array_of_hashes[2]{"keystring"}
($r0, $r1, $r2)  = fn();     # eg: $r2->{"keystring"}
```

See Also

The general discussions on references in Chapter 11, and in Chapter 8 of *Programming Perl*; Recipe 10.5

10.10 Returning Failure

Problem

You want to return a value indicating that your function failed.

Solution

Use a bare `return` statement without any argument, which returns `undef` in scalar context and the empty list ( ) in list context.

```
return;
```

Discussion

A return without an argument means:

```
sub empty_retval {
    return ( wantarray ? () : undef );
}
```

You can't use just `return undef`, because in list context you will get a list of one value: `undef`. If your caller says:

```
if (@a = yourfunc()) { ... }
```

then the "error" condition will be perceived as true because `@a` will be assigned `(undef)` and then evaluated in scalar context. This yields 1, the number of elements assigned to `@a`, which is true. You could use the `wantarray` function to see what context you were called in, but a bare `return` is a clear and tidy solution that always works:

```
unless ($a = sfunc()) { die "sfunc failed" }
unless (@a = afunc()) { die "afunc failed" }
unless (%a = hfunc()) { die "hfunc failed" }
```

Some of Perl's built-in functions have a peculiar return value. Both `fcntl` and `ioctl` have the curious habit of returning the string "0 but true" in some circumstances. (This magic string is conveniently exempt from nagging warnings about improper numerical conversions.) This has the advantage of letting you write code like this:

```
ioctl(....) or die "can't ioctl: $!";
```

That way, code doesn't have to check for a defined zero as distinct from the undefined value, as it would for the `read` or `glob` functions. "0 but true" is zero when used numerically. It's rare that this kind of return value is needed. A more common (and spectacular) way to indicate failure in a function is to raise an exception, as described in Recipe 10.12.

See Also

The undef, wantarray, and return functions in Chapter 29 of *Programming Perl* and in *perlfunc*(1); Recipe 10.12

10.11 Prototyping Functions

Problem

You want to use function prototypes so the compiler can check your argument types.

Solution

Perl has something of a prototype facility, but it isn't what you're thinking. Perl's function prototypes are more like a context coercion used to write functions that behave like some Perl built-ins, such as push and pop.

Discussion

Manually checking the validity of a function's arguments can't happen until runtime. If you make sure the function is declared before it is used, you can tickle the compiler into using a very limited form of prototype checking. But don't confuse Perl's function prototypes with those found in any other language.

A Perl function prototype is zero or more spaces, backslashes, or type characters enclosed in parentheses after the subroutine definition or name. A backslashed type symbol means that the argument is passed by reference, and the argument in that position must start with that type character.

A prototype can impose context on the prototyped function's arguments. This is done when Perl compiles your program. But this does not always mean that Perl checks the number or type of arguments; since a scalar prototype is like inserting a scalar in front of just one argument, sometimes an implicit conversion occurs instead. For example, if Perl sees func(3, 5) for a function prototyped as sub func ($), it will stop with a compile-time error. But if it sees func(@array) with the same prototype, it will merely put @array into scalar context instead of complaining that you passed an array, but it wanted a scalar.

This is so important that it bears repeating: don't use Perl prototypes expecting the compiler to check type and number of arguments for you. It does a little bit of that, sometimes, but mostly it's about helping you type less, and sometimes to emulate the calling and parsing conventions of built-in functions.

Omitting parentheses

Ordinarily your subroutines take a list of arguments, and you can omit parentheses on the function call if the compiler has already seen a declaration or definition for that function:

```
@results = reverse myfunc 3, 5;
```

Without prototypes, this is the same as:

```
@results = reverse(myfunc(3, 5));
```

Without parentheses, Perl puts the righthand side of the subroutine call into list context. You can use prototypes to change this behavior. Here is a function that's prototyped to take just one argument:

```
sub myfunc($);
@results = reverse myfunc 3, 5;
```

Now this is the same as:

```
@results = reverse(myfunc(3), 5);
```

Notice how the scalar prototype has altered the Perl parser! It grabs only the next thing it sees, leaving what remains for whatever other function is looking for arguments.

A void prototype like:

```
sub myfunc( );
```

will also alter the parser, causing no arguments to be passed to the function. This works just like the time built-in.

That means that in the absence of parentheses, *you cannot know what is going on* by casual inspection. Things that look the same can quietly behave completely differently from one another. Consider these declarations and assignments:

```
sub fn0( );
sub fn1($);
sub fnN(@);

$x = fn0 + 42;
$x = fn1 + 42;

$y = fnN fn1 + 42, fn0 + 42;
$y = fnN fn0 + 42, fn1 + 42;

$z = fn1 fn1 + 42, fn1 + 42;
$z = fnN fnN + 42, fnN + 42;
```

Astonishingly enough, those are parsed by the Perl compiler as though they'd been written this way:

```
$x = fn0( ) + 42;
$x = fn1(42);
```

```
$y = fnN(fn1(42), fn0( ) + 42);
$y = fnN(fn0( ) + 42, fn1(42));

$z = fn1(fn1(42)), fn1(42);
$z = fnN(fnN(42, fnN(42)));
```

Without first looking closely at the prototypes and then thinking really hard about how Perl's parser works, you'd never be able to predict that. Maintainability would suffer horribly.

This is one strong argument for using more parentheses than might be demanded by purely precedential concerns (or, alternatively, this is an argument for avoiding prototypes).

Mimicking built-ins

The other common use of prototypes is to give the convenient pass-without-flattening behavior of built-in functions like push and shift. When you call push as push(@array, 1, 2, 3) the function gets a *reference* to @array instead of the actual array. This is accomplished by backslashing the @ character in the prototype:

```
sub mypush (\@@) {
   my $array_ref = shift;
   my @remainder = @_;

   # ...
}
```

The \@ in the prototype says "require the first argument to begin with an @ character, and pass it by reference." The second @ says "the rest of the arguments are a (possibly empty) list." A backslash in a prototype requires that the argument actually begin with the literal type character, which can sometimes be annoying. You can't even use the conditional ?: construct to pick which array to pass:

```
mypush( $x > 10 ? @a : @b, 3, 5 );        # WRONG
```

Instead, you must play games with references:

```
mypush( @{ $x > 10 ? \@a : \@b }, 3, 5 );   # RIGHT (but ugly)
```

Here's an hpush function that works like push, but on hashes. It uses a list of key-value pairs to add to an existing hash, overwriting any previous values associated with those keys.

```
sub hpush(\%@) {
    my $href = shift;
    while ( my ($k, $v) = splice(@_, 0, 2) ) {
        $href->{$k} = $v;
    }
}
hpush(%pieces, "queen" => 9, "rook" => 5);
```

You may also backslash several argument types simultaneously by using the \[ ] notation:

```
sub mytie ( \[$@%&*] $; @ )
```

That function accepts any of the five types and passes it by reference, followed by one mandatory scalar context argument and optional trailing list of remaining arguments.

You can discover a particular function's prototype using the prototype built-in function. For example, calling prototype("hpush") given the previous definition would return the string "\%@". You can even find out a built-in's prototype this way—if it has one, that is. Not all core built-ins can be emulated. For those that can, the prototype function returns what their built-in prototype is. Since you can always call a core built-in function like int as CORE::int, built-ins are deemed to reside in package CORE. For example:

```
for $func (qw/int reverse keys push open print/) {
    printf "Prototype for %s is %s\n", $func,
        prototype("CORE::$func") || "UNAVAILABLE";
}

Prototype for int is ;$
Prototype for reverse is @
Prototype for keys is \%
Prototype for push is \@@
Prototype for open is *;$@
Prototype for print is UNAVAILABLE
```

See Also

The prototype function in *perlfunc*(1); the section on "Prototypes" in Chapter 6 of *Programming Perl* and in *perlsub*(1); Recipe 10.5

10.12 Handling Exceptions

Problem

How do you safely call a function that might raise an exception? How do you create a function that raises an exception?

Solution

Sometimes you encounter a problem so exceptional that merely returning an error isn't strong enough, because the caller could unintentionally ignore the error. Use die STRING from your function to trigger an exception:

```
die "some message";        # raise exception
```

The caller can wrap the function call in an eval to intercept that exception, then consult the special variable $@ to see what happened:

```
eval { func() };
if ($@) {
    warn "func raised an exception: $@";
}
```

Discussion

Raising exceptions is not a facility to be used lightly. Most functions should return an error using a bare return statement. Wrapping every call in an exception trap is tedious and unsightly, removing the appeal of using exceptions in the first place.

But, on rare occasions, failure in a function should cause the entire program to abort. Rather than calling the irrecoverable exit function, you should call die instead, which at least gives the programmer the chance to cope. If no exception handler has been installed via eval, then the program aborts at that point.

To detect this, wrap the call to the function with a block eval. The $@ variable will be set to the offending exception if one occurred; otherwise, it will be false.

```
eval { $val = func() };
warn "func blew up: $@" if $@;
```

Any eval catches all exceptions, not just specific ones. Usually you should propagate unexpected exceptions to an enclosing handler. For example, suppose your function raised an exception containing the string "Full moon!". You could safely trap that exception while letting others through by inspecting the $@ variable. Calling die without an argument uses the contents of $@ to construct a new exception string.

```
eval { $val = func() };
if ($@ && $@ !~ /Full moon!/) {
    die;    # re-raise unknown errors
}
```

If the function is part of a module, consider using the Carp module and call croak or confess instead of die. The only difference between die and croak is that with croak, the error appears to be from the caller's perspective, not the module's. The confess function, on the other hand, creates a full stack backtrace of who called whom and with what arguments.

Another intriguing possibility is for the function to detect that its return value is being completely ignored because the function was called in a void context. If that were returning an error indication would be useless, so raise an exception instead.

```
if (defined wantarray()) {
        return;
} else {
    die "pay attention to my error!";
}
```

Of course, just because it's not voided doesn't mean the return value is being dealt with appropriately. But if it is voided, it's certainly not being checked.

There are CPAN modules that offer alternative ways of handling exceptions. The Error module offers try, catch, and throw notation instead of eval and die:

```
use Error ':try';
try {
    something();
}
catch Error::Database with {
    my $e = shift;
    warn "Problem in " . $e->{'-database'} . " (caught)\n";
};
```

Error offers try, catch ... with, except, otherwise, and finally blocks for maximum flexibility in error handling. The Exception::Class module from CPAN lets you create classes of exceptions and objects to represent specific exceptions. The two modules can be combined so that you can catch these exception objects.

See Also

The $@ ($EVAL_ERROR) variable in Chapter 28 of *Programming Perl* and *perlvar*(1); the die and eval functions in Chapter 29 of *Programming Perl* and *perlfunc*(1); the documentation for the CPAN modules Error and Exception::Class; Recipe 10.15; Recipe 12.2; Recipe 16.21

10.13 Saving Global Values

Problem

You need to temporarily save away the value of a global variable.

Solution

Use the local operator to save a previous global value, automatically restoring it when the current block exits:

```
our $age = 18;          # declare and set global variable
if (CONDITION) {
    local $age = 23;
    func();             # sees temporary value of 23
} # Perl restores the old value at block exit
```

Discussion

Despite its name, Perl's local operator does not create a local variable. That's what my does. Instead, local merely preserves an existing value for the duration of its enclosing block. Hindsight shows that if local had been called *save_value* instead, much confusion could have been avoided.

Three places where you *must* use local instead of my are:

1. You need to give a global variable a temporary value, especially $_.
2. You need to create a local file or directory handle or a local function.
3. You want to temporarily change just one element of an array or hash.

Using local( ) for temporary values for globals

The first situation is more apt to happen with predefined, built-in variables than with user variables. Often these are variables that Perl consults for hints for its high-level operations. In particular, any function that uses $_, implicitly or explicitly, should certainly have a local $_. This is annoyingly easy to forget to do. See Recipe 13.15 for one solution to this.

Another common target for local is the $/ variable, a global that implicitly affects the behavior of the readline operator used in <FH> operations.

```
$para = get_paragraph(*FH);          # pass filehandle glob
$para = get_paragraph(*FH);          # pass filehandle by glob reference
$para = get_paragraph(*FH{IO});      # pass filehandle by IO reference
sub get_paragraph {
    my $fh = shift;
    local $/ = '';
    my $paragraph = <$fh>;
    chomp($paragraph);
    return $paragraph;
}
```

Using local( ) for local handles

The second situation used to arise whenever you needed a local filehandle or directory handle—or more rarely, a local function.

```
$contents = get_motd( );
sub get_motd {
    local *MOTD;
    open(MOTD, "/etc/motd")         or die "can't open motd: $!";
    local $/ = undef;  # slurp full file;
    local $_ = <MOTD>;
    close (MOTD);
    return $_;
}
```

If you wanted to return the open filehandle, you'd use:

```
return *MOTD;
```

However, in modern releases of Perl, you would make use of the filehandle autovivification property:

```
$contents = get_motd( );
sub get_motd {
    my $motd;  # this will be filled in by the next line
    open($motd, "/etc/motd")         or die "can't open motd: $!";
    local $/ = undef;  # slurp full file;
    return scalar <$motd>;
}
```

When the function returns, the anonymous filehandle is automatically closed for you. However, if you'd chosen to return $motd, then it wouldn't be. This is explained more fully in the Introduction to Chapter 7.

Using local( ) on parts of aggregates

The third situation is exceedingly rare, except for one common case. Because the local operator is really a "save value" operator, you can use it to save off just one element of an array or hash, even if that array or hash is itself a lexical!

```
my @nums = (0 .. 5);
sub first {
    local $nums[3] = 3.14159;
    second( );
}
sub second {
    print "@nums\n";
}
second( );
0 1 2 3 4 5
first( );
0 1 2 3.14159 4 5
```

The only common use for this kind of thing is for temporary signal handlers.

```
sub first {
    local $SIG{INT} = 'IGNORE';
    second( );
}
```

Now while second is running, interrupt signals are ignored. When first returns, the previous value of $SIG{INT} is automatically restored.

Although a lot of old code uses local, it's definitely something to steer clear of when it can be avoided. Because local still manipulates the values of global variables, not local variables, you'll run afoul of use strict unless you declared the globals using our or the older use vars.

The local operator produces *dynamic scoping* or *runtime scoping*. This is in contrast with the other kind of scoping Perl supports, which is much more easily understood. That's the kind of scoping that my provides, known as *lexical scoping*, or sometimes as *static* or *compile-time scoping*.

With dynamic scoping, a variable is accessible if it's found in the current scope—or in the scope of any frames (blocks) in its entire subroutine call stack, as determined at runtime. Any functions called have full access to dynamic variables, because they're still globals, just ones with temporary values. Only lexical variables are safe from such tampering.

Old code that says:

```
sub func {
    local($x, $y) = @_;
    #....
}
```

can almost always be replaced without ill effect by the following:

```
sub func {
    my($x, $y) = @_;
    #....
}
```

The only case where code can't be so upgraded is when it relies on dynamic scoping. That would happen if one function called another, and the latter relied upon access to the former's temporary versions of the global variables $x and $y. Code that handles global variables and expects strange action at a distance instead of using proper parameters is fragile at best. Good programmers avoid this kind of thing like the plague. (The solution is to explicitly pass values as parameters, rather than storing them in shared global variables.)

If you come across old code that uses:

```
&func(*Global_Array);
sub func {
    local(*aliased_array) = shift;
    for (@aliased_array) { .... }
}
```

this should probably be changed into something like this:

```
func(\@Global_Array);
sub func {
    my $array_ref  = shift;
    for (@$array_ref) { .... }
}
```

They're using the old pass-the-typeglob strategy devised before Perl supported proper references. It's not a pretty thing.

See Also

The local, my, and our functions in Chapter 29 of *Programming Perl* and *perlfunc*(1); Chapter 6 of *Programming Perl*; the section on "Scoped Declarations" in Chapter 4 of *Programming Perl*; the sections on "Private Variables via my()" and "Temporary Values via local()" in *perlsub*(1); Recipe 10.2; Recipe 10.16

10.14 Redefining a Function

Problem

You want to temporarily or permanently redefine a function, but functions can't be assigned to.

Solution

To redefine a function, assign a new code reference to the typeglob of the name of that function. Use local if you want this redefinition to be temporary.

```
undef &grow;                    # silence -w complaints of redefinition
*grow = \&expand;
grow( );                        # calls expand( )

{
    local *grow = \&shrink;     # only until this block exists
    grow( );                    # calls shrink( )
}
```

Discussion

Unlike a variable (but like named filehandles, directory handles, and formats), a named function cannot be directly assigned to. It's just a name and doesn't vary. You can manipulate it almost as though it were a variable, because you can directly manipulate the runtime symbol table using typeglobs like *foo to produce interesting aliasing effects.

Assigning a reference to a typeglob changes what is accessed the next time a symbol of the referent's type is needed. This is what the Exporter does when you import a function or variable from one package into another. Since this is direct manipulation of the package symbol table, it works only on package variables (globals), not lexicals.

```
*one::var = \%two::Table;   # make %one::var alias for %two::Table
*one::big = \&two::small;   # make &one::big alias for &two::small
```

A typeglob is one of those things you can only use local on, not my. If you do use local, the aliasing effect is then limited to the duration of the current block.

```
local *fred = \&barney;     # temporarily alias &fred to &barney
```

If the value assigned to a typeglob is not a reference but itself another typeglob, then *all* types by that name are aliased. The types aliased in a full typeglob assignment are scalar, array, hash, function, filehandle, directory handle, and format. That means that assigning *Top = *Bottom would make the current package variable $Top an alias for $Bottom, @Top for @Bottom, %Top for %Bottom, and &Top for &Bottom. It would even alias the corresponding file and directory handles and formats! You probably don't want to do this.

Use assignments to typeglobs together with closures to clone a bunch of similar functions cheaply and easily. Imagine you wanted a function for HTML generation to help with colors. For example:

```
$string = red("careful here");
print $string;
<FONT COLOR='red'>careful here</FONT>
```

You could write the red function this way:

```
sub red { "<FONT COLOR='red'>@_</FONT>" }
```

If you need more colors, you could do something like this:

```
sub color_font {
    my $color = shift;
    return "<FONT COLOR='$color'>@_</FONT>";
}
sub red    { color_font("red", @_)    }
sub green  { color_font("green", @_)  }
sub blue   { color_font("blue", @_)   }
sub purple { color_font("purple", @_) }
# etc
```

The similar nature of these functions suggests that there may be a way to factor out the common bit. To do this, use an assignment to an indirect typeglob. If you're running with the highly recommended use strict pragma, you must first disable strict "refs" for that block.

```
@colors = qw(red blue green yellow orange purple violet);
for my $name (@colors) {
    no strict 'refs';
    *$name = sub { "<FONT COLOR='$name'>@_</FONT>" };
}
```

These functions all seem independent, but the real code was compiled only once. This technique saves on compile time and memory use. To create a proper closure, any variables in the anonymous subroutine *must* be lexicals. That's the reason for the my on the loop iteration variable.

This is one of the few places where giving a prototype to a closure is sensible. If you wanted to impose scalar context on the arguments of these functions (probably not a wise idea), you could have written it this way instead:

```
*$name = sub ($) { "<FONT COLOR='$name'>$_[0]</FONT>" };
```

However, since prototype checking happens at compile time, the preceding assignment happens too late to be useful. So, put the whole loop of assignments within a BEGIN block, forcing it to occur during compilation. You really want to use a BEGIN here, not an INIT, because you're doing something that you want the compiler itself to notice right away, not something for the interpreter to do just before your program runs.

See Also

The sections on "Symbol Tables" in Chapter 10 of *Programming Perl* and in *perlmod*(1); the sections on "Closures" and "Symbol Table References" in Chapter 8 of *Programming Perl*; the discussion of closures in *perlref*(1); Recipe 10.11; Recipe 11.4

10.15 Trapping Undefined Function Calls with AUTOLOAD

Problem

You want to intercept calls to undefined functions so you can handle them gracefully.

Solution

Declare a function called AUTOLOAD for the package whose undefined function calls you'd like to trap. While running, that package's $AUTOLOAD variable contains the name of the undefined function being called.

Discussion

Another strategy for creating similar functions is to use a proxy function. If you call an undefined function, instead of automatically raising an exception, you can trap the call. If the function's package has a function named AUTOLOAD, then this function is called in its place, with the special package global $AUTOLOAD set to the package-qualified function name. The AUTOLOAD subroutine can then do whatever that function would do.

```
sub AUTOLOAD {
    my $color = our $AUTOLOAD;
    $color =~ s/.*:://;
    return "<FONT COLOR='$color'>@_</FONT>";
}
#note: sub chartreuse isn't defined.
print chartreuse("stuff");
```

When the nonexistent main::chartreuse function is called, rather than raising an exception, main::AUTOLOAD is called with the same arguments as you passed chartreuse. The package variable $AUTOLOAD would contain the string main::chartreuse because that's the function it's proxying.

The technique using typeglob assignments shown in Recipe 10.14 is faster and more flexible than using AUTOLOAD. It's faster because you don't have to run the copy and substitute. It's more flexible because it lets you do this:

```
{
    local *yellow = \&violet;
```

```
    local (*red, *green) = (\&green, \&red);
    print_stuff();
}
```

While `print_stuff( )` is running, including from within any functions it calls, anything printed in yellow will come out violet, and the red and green texts will
exchange colors.

Aliasing subroutines like this won't handle calls to undefined subroutines. AUTOLOAD
does.

See Also

The section on "Autoloading" in Chapter 10 of *Programming Perl* and in *perlsub*(1);
the documentation for the standard modules AutoLoader and AutoSplit; Recipe 10.
12; Recipe 12.11; Recipe 13.12

10.16 Nesting Subroutines

Problem

You want subroutines to nest, such that one subroutine is visible and callable only
from another. When you try the obvious approach of nesting sub FOO { sub BAR { } ... },
Perl gives warnings about variables that will not stay shared.

Solution

Instead of making the inner functions normal subroutines, make them closures and
temporarily assign their references to the typeglob of the right name to create a localized function.

Discussion

If you use nested subroutines in other programming languages with their own private variables, you'll have to work at it a bit in Perl. The intuitive coding of this kind
of thing gives the warning "will not stay shared." For example, this won't work:

```
sub outer {
    my $x = $_[0] + 35;
    sub inner { return $x * 19 }    # WRONG
    return $x + inner();
}
```

The following is a workaround:

```
sub outer {
    my $x = $_[0] + 35;
    local *inner = sub { return $x * 19 };
    return $x + inner();
}
```

Now inner( ) can be called only from within outer( ) because of the temporary assignments of the closure. Once called, it has normal access to the lexical variable $x from the scope of outer( ).

This essentially creates a function local to another function, something not directly supported in Perl; however, the programming isn't always clear.

See Also

The sections on "Symbol Tables" in Chapter 10 in *Programming Perl* and in *perlmod*(1); the sections on "Closures" and "Symbol Table References" in Chapter 8 of *Programming Perl* and the discussion of closures in *perlref*(1); Recipe 10.13; Recipe 11.4

10.17 Writing a Switch Statement

Problem

You want to write a multiway branch statement, much as you can in C using its switch statement or in the shell using case—but Perl seems to support neither.

Solution

Use the Switch module, standard as of the v5.8 release of Perl.

```
use Switch;
switch ($value) {
    case 17        { print "number 17"      }
    case "snipe"   { print "a snipe"        }
    case /[a-f]+/i { print "pattern matched" }
    case [1..10,42] { print "in the list"    }
    case (@array)  { print "in the array"   }
    case (%hash)   { print "in the hash"    }
    else           { print "no case applies" }
}
```

Discussion

The Switch module extends Perl's basic syntax by providing a powerful and flexible switch construct. In fact, it's *so* powerful and flexible that instead of a complete description of how it works, we'll instead provide examples of some common uses. For the full story, make sure to consult the documentation that accompanies the module.

A switch takes an argument and a mandatory block, within which can occur any number of cases. Each of those cases also takes an argument and a mandatory block. The arguments to each case can vary in type, allowing (among many other things) any or all of string, numeric, or regex comparisons against the switch's value. When the case is an array or hash (or reference to the same), the case matches if the switch value corresponds to any of the array elements or hash keys. If no case matches, a trailing else block will be executed.

Unlike certain languages' multiway branching constructs, here once a valid case is found and its block executed, control transfers out of the enclosing switch. In other words, there's no implied fall-through behavior the way there is in C. This is considered desirable because even the best of programmers will occasionally forget about fall-through.

However, this is Perl, so you can have your cake and eat it, too. Just use a next from within a switch to transfer control to the next case. Consider:

```
%traits = (pride => 2, sloth => 3, hope => 14);
switch (%traits) {
    case "impatience"                   { print "Hurry up!\n";       next }
    case ["laziness","sloth"]           { print "Maybe tomorrow!\n"; next }
    case ["hubris","pride"]             { print "Mine's best!\n";    next }
    case ["greed","cupidity","avarice"] { print "More more more!";   next }
}
```

Maybe tomorrow!
Mine's best!

Because each case has a next, it doesn't just do the first one it finds, but goes on for further tests. The next can be conditional, too, allowing for conditional fall through.

You might have noticed something else interesting about that previous example: the argument to the switch wasn't a scalar; it was the %traits hash. It turns out that you can switch on other things than scalars. In fact, both case and switch accept nearly any kind of argument. The behavior varies depending on the particular combination. Here, the strings from each of those cases are taken as keys to index into the hash we're switching on.

If you find yourself preferring fall-through as the default, you can have that, too:

```
use Switch 'fallthrough';
%traits = (pride => 2, sloth => 3, hope => 14);
switch (%traits) {
    case "impatience"                   { print "Hurry up!\n"       }
    case ["laziness","sloth"]           { print "Maybe tomorrow!\n" }
    case ["hubris","pride"]             { print "Mine's best!\n"    }
    case ["greed","cupidity","avarice"] { print "More more more!"   }
}
```

One area where a bunch of cascading ifs would still seem to excel is when each test involves a different expression, and those expressions are more complex than a simple string, numeric, or pattern comparison. For example:

```
if    ($n % 2 == 0) { print "two "   }
elsif ($n % 3 == 0) { print "three " }
elsif ($n % 5 == 0) { print "five "  }
elsif ($n % 7 == 0) { print "seven " }
```

Or if you want more than one test to be able to apply, you can do this with fall-through behavior:

```
if ($n % 2 == 0) { print "two "   }
if ($n % 3 == 0) { print "three " }
if ($n % 5 == 0) { print "five "  }
if ($n % 7 == 0) { print "seven " }
```

Perl's switch can handle this too, but you have to be a bit more careful. For a case item to be an arbitrary expression, wrap that expression in a subroutine. That subroutine is called with the switch argument as the subroutine's argument. If the subroutine returns a true value, then the case is satisfied.

```
use Switch 'fallthrough';
$n = 30;
print "Factors of $n include: ";
switch ($n) {
    case sub{$_[0] % 2 == 0} { print "two "   }
    case sub{$_[0] % 3 == 0} { print "three " }
    case sub{$_[0] % 5 == 0} { print "five "  }
    case sub{$_[0] % 7 == 0} { print "seven " }
}
```

That's pretty cumbersome to write—and to read—but with a little bit of highly magical syntactic sugar, even that clumsiness goes away. If you import the __ subroutine (yes, that really is a double underscore), you can use that in an expression as the case target, and the __ will represent the value being switched on. For example:

```
use Switch qw( __  fallthrough );
$n = 30;
print "Factors of $n include: ";
switch ($n) {
    case __ % 2 == 0 { print "two "   }
    case __ % 3 == 0 { print "three " }
    case __ % 5 == 0 { print "five "  }
    case __ % 7 == 0 { print "seven " }
}
print "\n";
```

Due to the way that __ is implemented, some restrictions on its use apply. The main one is that your expression can't use && or || in it.

Here's one final trick with switch. This time, instead of having a scalar in the switch and subroutines in the cases, let's do it the other way around. You can switch on a subroutine reference; each case value will be passed into that subroutine, and if the sub returns a true value, then the case is deemed to have matched and its code block executed. That makes the factor example read:

```
use Switch qw(fallthrough);
$n = 30;
print "Factors of $n include: ";
switch (sub {$n % $_[0] == 0} ) {
    case 2 { print "two "   }
    case 3 { print "three " }
```

```
        case 5 { print "five " }
        case 7 { print "seven " }
    }
```

This is probably the most aesthetically pleasing way of writing it, since there's no longer duplicate code on each line.

 The Switch module uses a facility called source filters to emulate behavior anticipated in Perl6 (whenever that might be). This has been known to cause mysterious compilation errors if you use constructs in your code you were warned against. You should therefore pay very close attention to the section on "Dependencies, Bugs, and Limitations" in the Switch manpage.

See Also

The documentation for the Switch module; the *perlsyn*(1) manpage's section on "Basic BLOCKs and Switch Statements"; the section on "Case Statements" in Chapter 4 of *Programming Perl*

10.18 Program: Sorting Your Mail

The program in Example 10-1 sorts a mailbox by subject by reading input a paragraph at a time, looking for one with a "From" at the start of a line. When it finds one, it searches for the subject, strips it of any "Re: " marks, and stores its lowercased version in the @sub array. Meanwhile, the messages themselves are stored in a corresponding @msgs array. The $msgno variable keeps track of the message number.

Example 10-1. bysub1

```
#!/usr/bin/perl
# bysub1 - simple sort by subject
my(@msgs, @sub);
my $msgno = -1;
$/ = '';                        # paragraph reads
while (<>) {
    if (/^From/m) {
        /^Subject:\s*(?:Re:\s*)*(.*)/mi;
        $sub[++$msgno] = lc($1) || '';
    }
    $msgs[$msgno] .= $_;
}
for my $i (sort { $sub[$a] cmp $sub[$b] || $a <=> $b } (0 .. $#msgs)) {
    print $msgs[$i];
}
```

That sort is only sorting array indices. If the subjects are the same, cmp returns 0, so the second part of the || is taken, which compares the message numbers in the order they originally appeared.

If sort were fed a list like (0,1,2,3), that list would get sorted into a different permutation, perhaps (2,1,3,0). We iterate across them with a for loop to print out each message.

Example 10-2 shows how an *awk* programmer might code this program, using the -00 switch to read paragraphs instead of lines.

Example 10-2. bysub2

```
#!/usr/bin/perl -n00
# bysub2 - awkish sort-by-subject
INIT { $msgno = -1 }
$sub[++$msgno] = (/^Subject:\s*(?:Re:\s*)*(.*)/mi)[0] if /^From/m;
$msg[$msgno] .= $_;
END { print @msg[ sort { $sub[$a] cmp $sub[$b] || $a <=> $b } (0 .. $#msg) ] }
```

Perl programmers have used parallel arrays like this since Perl 1. Keeping each message in a hash is a more elegant solution, though. We'll sort on each field in the hash, by making an anonymous hash as described in Chapter 11.

Example 10-3 is a program similar in spirit to Example 10-1 and Example 10-2.

Example 10-3. bysub3

```
#!/usr/bin/perl -00
# bysub3 - sort by subject using hash records
use strict;
my @msgs = ();
while (<>) {
    push @msgs, {
        SUBJECT => /^Subject:\s*(?:Re:\s*)*(.*)/mi,
        NUMBER  => scalar @msgs,    # which msgno this is
        TEXT    => '',
    } if /^From/m;
    $msgs[-1]{TEXT} .= $_;
}

for my $msg (sort {
                    $a->{SUBJECT} cmp $b->{SUBJECT}
                                ||
                    $a->{NUMBER}  <=> $b->{NUMBER}
                } @msgs
            )
{
    print $msg->{TEXT};
}
```

Once you have real hashes, adding further sorting criteria is simple. A common way to sort a folder is subject major, date minor order. The hard part is figuring out how to parse and compare dates. Date::Manip does this, returning a string you can compare; however, the *datesort* program in Example 10-4, which uses Date::Manip, runs more than 10 times slower than the previous one. Parsing dates in unpredictable formats is extremely slow.

Example 10-4. datesort

```perl
#!/usr/bin/perl -00
# datesort - sort mbox by subject then date
use strict;
use Date::Manip;
my @msgs = ();
while (<>) {
    next unless /^From/m;
    my $date = '';
    if (/^Date:\s*(.*)/m) {
        ($date = $1) =~ s/\s+\(.*//;  # library hates (MST)
        $date = ParseDate($date);
    }
    push @msgs, {
        SUBJECT => /^Subject:\s*(?:Re:\s*)*(.*)/mi,
        DATE    => $date,
        NUMBER  => scalar @msgs,
        TEXT    => '',
    };
} continue {
    $msgs[-1]{TEXT} .= $_;
}

for my $msg (sort {
                    $a->{SUBJECT} cmp $b->{SUBJECT}
                                  ||
                    $a->{DATE}    cmp $b->{DATE}
                                  ||
                    $a->{NUMBER}  <=> $b->{NUMBER}

                   } @msgs
            )
{
    print $msg->{TEXT};
}
```

Example 10-4 is written to draw attention to the continue block. When a loop's end is reached, either because it fell through to that point or got there from a next, the whole continue block is executed. It corresponds to the third portion of a three-part for loop, except that the continue block isn't restricted to an expression. It's a full block, with separate statements.

See Also

The sort function in Chapter 29 of *Programming Perl* and in *perlfunc*(1); the discussion of the $/ ($RS, $INPUT_RECORD_SEPARATOR) variable in Chapter 28 of *Programming Perl*, in *perlvar*(1), and in the Introduction to Chapter 8; Recipe 3.7; Recipe 4.16; Recipe 5.10; Recipe 11.9

## CHAPTER 11

References and Records

With as little a web as this will I ensnare
as great a fly as Cassio.
—Shakespeare, *Othello, Act II, scene i*

11.0 Introduction

Perl provides three fundamental data types: scalars, arrays, and hashes. It's certainly possible to write many programs without complex records, but most programs need something more sophisticated than simple variables and lists.

Perl's three built-in types combine with references to produce arbitrarily complex and powerful data structures. Selecting the proper data structure and algorithm can make the difference between an elegant program that does its job quickly and an ungainly concoction that's glacially slow to execute and consumes system resources voraciously.

The first part of this chapter shows how to create and use plain references. The second part shows how to create higher-order data structures out of references.

References

To grasp the concept of references, you must first understand how Perl stores values in variables. Each defined variable has associated with it a name and the address of a chunk of memory. This idea of storing addresses is fundamental to references because a reference is a value that holds the location of another value. The scalar value that contains the memory address is called a *reference*. Whatever value lives at that memory address is called its *referent*. See Figure 11-1.

The referent could be any built-in type (scalar, array, hash, ref, code, or glob) or a user-defined type based on one of the built-ins.

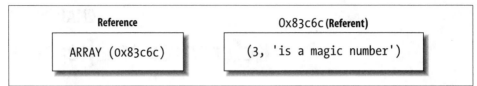

Figure 11-1. Reference and referent

Referents in Perl are *typed*. This means, for example, that you can't treat a reference to an array as though it were a reference to a hash. Attempting to do so raises a runtime exception. No mechanism for type casting exists in Perl. This is considered a feature.

So far, it may look as though a reference were little more than a raw address with strong typing. But it's far more than that. Perl takes care of automatic memory allocation and deallocation (garbage collection) for references, just as it does for everything else. Every chunk of memory in Perl has a *reference count* associated with it, representing how many places know about that referent. The memory used by a referent is not returned to the process's free pool until its reference count reaches zero. This ensures that you never have a reference that isn't valid—no more core dumps and general protection faults from mismanaged pointers as in C.

Freed memory is returned to Perl for later use, but few operating systems reclaim it and decrease the process's memory footprint. This is because most memory allocators use a stack, and if you free up memory in the middle of the stack, the operating system can't take it back without moving the rest of the allocated memory around. That would destroy the integrity of your pointers and blow XS code out of the water.

To follow a reference to its referent, preface the reference with the appropriate type symbol for the data you're accessing. For instance, if $sref is a reference to a scalar, you can say:

```
print $$sref;    # prints the scalar value that the reference $sref refers to
$$sref = 3;      # assigns to $sref's referent
```

To access one element of an array or hash whose reference you have, use the infix pointer-arrow notation, as in `$rv->[37]` or `$rv->{"wilma"}`. Besides dereferencing array references and hash references, the arrow is also used to call an indirect function through its reference, as in `$code_ref->("arg1", "arg2")`; this is discussed in Recipe 11.4. If you're using an object, use an arrow to call a method, `$object->methodname("arg1", "arg2")`, as shown in Chapter 13.

Perl's syntax rules make dereferencing complex expressions tricky—it falls into the category of "hard things that should be possible." Mixing right associative and left associative operators doesn't work out well. For example, `$$x[4]` is the same as `$x->[4]`; that is, it treats $x as a reference to an array and then extracts element number four from that. This could also have been written `${$x}[4]`. If you really meant "take the fifth element of @x and dereference it as a scalar reference," then you need to use `${$x[4]}`. Avoid putting two type signs ($@%&) side-by-side, unless it's simple and unambiguous like `%hash = %$hashref`.

In the simple cases using $$sref in the previous example, you could have written:

```
print ${$sref};              # prints the scalar $sref refers to
${$sref} = 3;                # assigns to $sref's referent
```

For safety, some programmers use this notation exclusively.

When passed a reference, the ref function returns a string describing its referent. (It returns false if passed a non-reference.) This string is usually one of SCALAR, ARRAY, HASH, or CODE, although the other built-in types of GLOB, REF, IO, Regexp, and LVALUE also occasionally appear. If you call ref on a non-reference, it returns an empty string. If you call ref on an object (a reference whose referent has been blessed), it returns the class the object was blessed into: CGI, IO::Socket, or even ACME::Widget.

Create references in Perl by using a backslash on things already there, or dynamically allocate new things using the [ ], { }, and sub { } composers. The backslash operator is simple to use: put it before whatever you want a reference to. For instance, if you want a reference to the contents of @array, just say:

```
$aref = \@array;
```

You can even create references to constant values; future attempts to change the value of the referent cause a runtime exception:

```
$pi = \3.14159;
$$pi = 4;               # runtime error
```

Anonymous Data

Using a backslash to produce references to existing, named variables is simple enough for implementing pass-by-reference semantics in subroutine calls, but for creating complex data structures on the fly, it quickly becomes cumbersome. You don't want to be bogged down by having to invent a unique name for each subsection of the large, complex data structure. Instead, you allocate new, nameless arrays and hashes (or scalars or functions) on demand, growing your structure dynamically.

Explicitly create anonymous arrays and hashes with the [ ] and { } composers. This notation allocates a new array or hash, initializes it with any data values listed between the pair of square or curly brackets, and returns a reference to the newly allocated aggregate:

```
$aref = [ 3, 4, 5 ];                         # new anonymous array
$href = { "How" => "Now", "Brown" => "Cow" };     # new anonymous hash
```

Perl also implicitly creates anonymous data types through *autovivification*. This occurs when you indirectly store data through a variable that's currently undefined; that is, you treat that variable as though it holds the reference type appropriate for that operation. When you do so, Perl allocates the needed array or hash and stores its reference in the previously undefined variable.

```
undef $aref;
@$aref = (1, 2, 3);
print $aref;
ARRAY(0x80c04f0)
```

See how we went from an undefined variable to one with an array reference in it
without explicitly assigning that reference? Perl filled in the reference for us. This
property lets code like the following work correctly, even as the first statement in
your program, all without declarations or allocations:

```
$a[4][23][53][21] = "fred";
print $a[4][23][53][21];
fred
print $a[4][23][53];
ARRAY(0x81e2494)
print $a[4][23];
ARRAY(0x81e0748)
print $a[4];
ARRAY(0x822cd40)
```

Table 11-1 shows mechanisms for producing references to both named and anonymous scalars, arrays, hashes, functions, and typeglobs. (See the discussion of filehandle autovivification in the Introduction to Chapter 7 for a discussion of anonymous
filehandles.)

Table 11-1. Syntax for named and anonymous values

Reference to	Named	Anonymous
Scalar	\$scalar	\do{my $anon}
Array	\@array	[LIST]
Hash	\%hash	{ LIST }
Code	\&function	sub { CODE }
Glob	*symbol	open(my $handle, ...);$handle

Figures 11-2 and 11-3 illustrate the differences between named and anonymous values. Figure 11-2 shows named values, and Figure 11-3 shows anonymous ones.

In other words, saying $a = \$b makes $$a and $b the *same piece of memory*. If you say
$$a = 3, then $b is set to 3, even though you only mentioned $a by name, not $b.

All references evaluate to true when used in Boolean context. That way a subroutine
that normally returns a reference can indicate an error by returning undef.

```
sub cite {
  my (%record, $errcount);
    ...
    return $errcount ? undef : %record;
}

$op_cit = cite($ibid)      or die "couldn't make a reference";
```

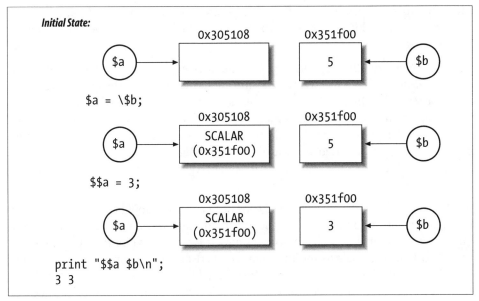

Figure 11-2. Named values

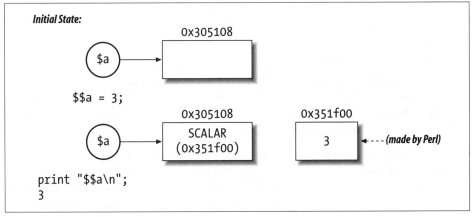

Figure 11-3. Anonymous values

Without an argument, undef produces an undefined value. But passed a variable or function as its argument, the undef operator renders that variable or function undefined when subsequently tested with the defined function. However, this does not necessarily free memory, call object destructors, etc. It just decrements its referent's reference count by one.

```
my ($a, $b) = ("Thing1", "Thing2");
$a = \$b;
undef $b;
```

Memory isn't freed yet, because you can still reach "Thing2" indirectly using its reference in $a. "Thing1", however, is completely gone, having been recycled as soon as $a was assigned \$b.

Although memory allocation in Perl is sometimes explicit and sometimes implicit, memory *deallocation* is nearly always implicit. You don't routinely have cause to undefine variables. Just let lexical variables (those declared with my) evaporate when their scope terminates; the next time you enter that scope, those variables will be new again. For global variables (those declared with our, fully-qualified by their package name, or imported from a different package) that you want reset, it normally suffices to assign the empty list to an aggregate variable or a false value to a scalar one.

It has been said that there exist two opposing schools of thought regarding memory management in programming. One school holds that memory management is too important a task to be left to the programming language, while the other judges it too important to be left to the programmer. Perl falls solidly in the second camp, since if you never have to remember to free something, you can never forget to do so. As a rule, you need rarely concern yourself with freeing any dynamically allocated storage in Perl,[*] because memory management—garbage collection, if you would—is fully automatic. Recipes 11.15 and 13.13, however, illustrate exceptions to this rule.

Records

The predominant use of references in Perl is to circumvent the restriction that arrays and hashes may hold scalars only. References are scalars, so to make an array of arrays, make an array of array *references*. Similarly, hashes of hashes are implemented as hashes of hash references, arrays of hashes as arrays of hash references, hashes of arrays as hashes of array references, and so on.

Once you have these complex structures, you can use them to implement records. A record is a single logical unit comprising various different attributes. For instance, a name, an address, and a birthday might compose a record representing a person. C calls such things *structs*, and Pascal calls them *RECORDs*. Perl doesn't have a particular name for these because you can implement this notion in different ways.

The most common technique in Perl is to treat a hash as a record, where the keys of the hash are the record's field names and the values of the hash are those fields' values.

For instance, we might create a "person" record like this:

```
$person = { "Name"     => "Leonhard Euler",
            "Address"  => "1729 Ramanujan Lane\nMathworld, PI 31416",
            "Birthday" => 0x5bb5580,
          };
```

---

[*] External subroutines compiled in C notwithstanding.

Because $person is a scalar, it can be stored in an array or hash element, thus creating groups of people. Now apply the array and hash techniques from Chapters 4 and 5 to sort the sets, merge hashes, pick a random record, and so on.

The attributes of a record, including the "person" record, are always scalars. You can certainly use numbers as readily as strings there, but that's no great trick. The real power play happens when you use even more references for values in the record. "Birthday", for instance, might be stored as an anonymous array with three elements: day, month, and year. You could then say $person->{"Birthday"}->[0] to access just the day field. Or a date might be represented as a hash record, which would then lend itself to access such as $person->{"Birthday"}->{"day"}. Adding references to your collection of skills makes possible many more complex and useful programming strategies.

At this point, we've conceptually moved beyond simple records. We're now creating elaborate data structures that represent complicated relationships between the data they hold. Although we *can* use these to implement traditional data structures like linked lists, recipes in the second half of this chapter don't deal specifically with any particular structure. Instead, they give generic techniques for loading, printing, copying, and saving generic data structures. The final program example demonstrates creating binary trees.

See Also

Chapters 8 and 9 of *Programming Perl*; *perlref*(1), *perlreftut*(1), *perllol*(1), and *perldsc*(1)

11.1 Taking References to Arrays

Problem

You need to manipulate an array by reference.

Solution

To get a reference to an array:

```
$aref              = \@array;
$anon_array        = [1, 3, 5, 7, 9];
$anon_copy         = [ @array ];
@$implicit_creation = (2, 4, 6, 8, 10);
```

To deference an array reference, precede it with an at sign (@):

```
push(@$anon_array, 11);
```

Or use a pointer arrow plus a bracketed subscript for a particular element:

```
$two = $implicit_creation->[0];
```

To get the last index number by reference, or the number of items in that referenced array:

```
$last_idx  = $#$aref;
$num_items = @$aref;
```

Or defensively embracing and forcing context:

```
$last_idx  = $#{ $aref };
$num_items = scalar @{ $aref };
```

Discussion

Here are array references in action:

```
# check whether $someref contains a simple array reference
if (ref($someref) ne "ARRAY") {
    die "Expected an array reference, not $someref\n";
}

print "@{$array_ref}\n";        # print original data

@order = sort @{ $array_ref };  # sort it

push @{ $array_ref }, $item;     # append new element to orig array
```

If you can't decide whether to use a reference to a named array or to create a new one, here's a simplistic guideline that will prove right more often than not. Only take a reference to an existing array to return the reference out of scope, thereby creating an anonymous array, or to pass the array by reference to a function. For virtually all other cases, use [@array] to create a new array reference with a copy of the old values.

Automatic reference counting and the backslash operator make a powerful combination:

```
sub array_ref {
    my @array;
    return \@array;
}

$aref1 = array_ref();
$aref2 = array_ref();
```

Each time array_ref is called, the function allocates a new piece of memory for @array. If we hadn't returned a reference to @array, its memory would have been freed when its block, the subroutine, ended. But here a reference to @array is still accessible, so Perl doesn't free that storage, and we wind up with a reference to a piece of memory no longer accessible through the symbol table. Such a piece of memory is called *anonymous* because it has no name associated with it.

To access a particular element of the array referenced by $aref, you could write $$aref[4], but $aref->[4] is the same thing, and clearer.

```
print $array_ref->[$N];          # access item in position N (best)
print $$array_ref[$N];           # same, but confusing
print ${$array_ref}[$N];         # same, but still confusing, and ugly to boot
```

If you have an array reference, you can only access a slice of the referenced array in this way:

```
@$pie[3..5];                     # array slice, but a little confusing to read
@{$pie}[3..5];                   # array slice, easier (?) to read
```

Array slices, even when accessed through array references, are assignable. In the next line, the array dereference happens first, then the slice:

```
@{$pie}[3..5] = ("blackberry", "blueberry", "pumpkin");
```

An array slice is just syntactic sugar for a list of individual array elements. Because you can't take a reference to a list, you can't take a reference to an array slice:

```
$sliceref = \@{$pie}[3..5];      # WRONG!
```

To iterate through the entire array, loop with foreach or for:

```
foreach $item ( @{$array_ref} ) {
    # $item has data
}

for ($idx = 0; $idx <= $#{ $array_ref }; $idx++) {
    # $array_ref->[$idx] has data
}
```

See Also

Chapters 8 and 9 of *Programming Perl*; *perlref*(1), *perlreftut*(1), and *perllol*(1); Recipe 2.13; Recipe 4.6

11.2   Making Hashes of Arrays

Problem

For each key in a hash, only one scalar value is allowed, but you'd like to use one key to store and retrieve multiple values. That is, you'd like the value to produce a list.

Solution

Use references to arrays as the hash values. Use push to append:

```
push(@{ $hash{"KEYNAME"} }, "new value");
```

Then, dereference the value as an array reference when printing out the hash:

```
foreach $string (keys %hash) {
    print "$string: @{$hash{$string}}\n";
}
```

Discussion

You can only store scalar values in a hash. References, however, are scalars. This solves the problem of storing multiple values for one key by making $hash{$key} a reference to an array containing the values for $key. Normal hash operations acting on individual scalar values (insertion, deletion, iteration, and testing for existence) are now written with array operations acting on lists of values (like push, splice, and foreach).

Here's how to give a key many values:

```
$hash{"a key"} = [ 3, 4, 5 ];        # anonymous array
```

Once you have a key with many values, here's how to use them:

```
@values = @{ $hash{"a key"} };
```

To append a new value to the array of values associated with a particular key, use push:

```
push @{ $hash{"a key"} }, $value;
```

One common application of such data structures is inverting a hash that may have several keys with the same associated value. When inverted, you end up with a hash that has many values for the same key. This is addressed in Recipe 5.9.

Be warned that this:

```
@residents = @{ $phone2name{$number} };
```

causes a runtime exception under use strict because you're dereferencing an undefined reference where autovivification won't occur. You must do this instead:

```
@residents = exists( $phone2name{$number} )
                    ? @{ $phone2name{$number} }
                    : ();
```

See Also

The section on "Hashes of Arrays" in Chapter 9 of *Programming Perl* and in *perldsc*(1); the section on "Symbolic References" in Chapter 8 of *Programming Perl*; Recipe 5.9; the example "Tie Example: Make a Hash That Always Appends" in Recipe 13.15

11.3   Taking References to Hashes

Problem

You need to manipulate a hash by reference. This might be because it was passed into a function that way or because it's part of a larger data structure.

Solution

To get a hash reference:

```
$href = \%hash;
$anon_hash = { "key1" => "value1", "key2" => "value2", ... };
$anon_hash_copy = { %hash };
```

To dereference a hash reference:

```
%hash  = %$href;
$value = $href->{$key};
@slice = @$href{$key1, $key2, $key3};  # note: no arrow!
@keys  = keys %$href;
```

To check whether something is a hash reference:

```
if (ref($someref) ne "HASH") {
    die "Expected a hash reference, not $someref\n";
}
```

Discussion

This example prints out all keys and values from two predefined hashes:

```
foreach $href ( \%ENV, \%INC ) {        # OR: for $href ( \(%ENV,%INC) ) {
    foreach $key ( keys %$href ) {
        print "$key => $href->{$key}\n";
    }
}
```

Access slices of hashes by reference as you'd access slices of arrays by reference. For example:

```
@values = @$hash_ref{"key1", "key2", "key3"};

for $val (@$hash_ref{"key1", "key2", "key3"}) {
    $val += 7;   # add 7 to each value in hash slice
}
```

See Also

The Introduction in Chapter 5; Chapter 8 of *Programming Perl*; *perlref*(1); Recipe 11.9

11.4   Taking References to Functions

Problem

You need to manipulate a subroutine by reference. This might happen if you need to create a signal handler, a Tk callback, or a hash of function pointers.

Solution

To get a code reference:

```
$cref = \&func;
$cref = sub { ... };
```

To call a code reference:

```
@returned = $cref->(@arguments);
@returned = &$cref(@arguments);
```

Discussion

If the name of a function is func, you can produce a reference to it by prefixing its name with \&. You can also dynamically allocate anonymous functions using the sub { } notation. These code references can be stored just like any other reference.

It is possible to store the name of a function in a variable, such as:

```
$funcname = "thefunc";
&$funcname();
```

but that's not a very good solution for several reasons. First, it uses symbolic references, not real (hard) references, and so is forbidden under the use strict "refs" pragma. Symbolic references to variables are usually a bad idea, since they can't access lexical variables, only globals, and aren't reference counted. Second, as written it doesn't include package information, so if executed in a different package, it would try to call the wrong function. Finally, in the odd case that the function were redefined at some point, the symbolic reference would get whatever the current definition for the function was, whereas the hard reference would still access the old definition.

Instead of placing the name of the function in the variable, use the backslash operator to create a reference to the function. This is the normal way to store a function in a variable or pass along to another function. You can mix and match references to named functions with references to unnamed ones:

```
my %commands = (
    "happy" => \&joy,
    "sad"   => \&sullen,
    "done"  => sub { die "See ya!" },
    "mad"   => \&angry,
);

print "How are you? ";
chomp($string = <STDIN>);
if ($commands{$string}) {
    $commands{$string}->();
} else {
    print "No such command: $string\n";
}
```

If you create an anonymous function that refers to a lexical (my) variable from an enclosing scope, reference counting ensures that the lexical variable is never deallocated so long as that function reference exists:

```
sub counter_maker {
    my $start = 0;
    return sub {                    # this is a closure
        return $start++;            # lexical from enclosing scope
    };
}

$counter = counter_maker();

for ($i = 0; $i < 5; $i ++) {
    print &$counter, "\n";
}
```

Even though counter_maker has ended and $start gone out of scope, Perl doesn't free the variable, because the anonymous subroutine referenced by $counter still has a reference to $start. If we call counter_maker again, it'll return another, different anonymous subroutine reference that uses a *different* $start:

```
$counter1 = counter_maker();
$counter2 = counter_maker();

for ($i = 0; $i < 5; $i ++) {
    print &$counter1, "\n";
}

print &$counter1, " ", &$counter2, "\n";

0
1
2
3
4
5 0
```

Closures are often used in callback routines. In graphical and other event-based programming, you associate code with a keypress, mouse click, window expose event, etc. The code will be called much later, probably from an entirely different scope. Variables mentioned in the closure must be available when it's finally called. To work properly, such variables must be lexicals, not globals.

Another use for closures is *function generators*, functions that create and return brand-new functions. The counter_maker function is one example. Here's another simple one:

```
sub timestamp {
    my $start_time = time();
    return sub { return time() - $start_time };
}
$early = timestamp();
sleep 20;
$later = timestamp();
```

```
sleep 10;
printf "It's been %d seconds since early.\n", $early->();
printf "It's been %d seconds since later.\n", $later->();
It's been 30 seconds since early.
It's been 10 seconds since later.
```

Each call to timestamp generates and returns a brand-new function. The timestamp function creates a lexical called $start_time that contains the current clock time (in epoch seconds). Every time that closure is called, it returns how many seconds have elapsed since it was created by subtracting its starting time from the current time.

See Also

The section on "Closures" in Chapter 8 of *Programming Perl* and the discussion on closures in *perlref*(1); Recipe 10.11; Recipe 11.4

11.5   Taking References to Scalars

Problem

You want to create and manipulate a reference to a scalar value.

Solution

To create a reference to a scalar variable, use the backslash operator:

```
$scalar_ref = \$scalar;        # get reference to named scalar
```

To create a reference to an anonymous scalar value (a value that isn't in a variable), assign to a dereferenced undefined variable:

```
undef $anon_scalar_ref;
$$anon_scalar_ref = 15;
```

This creates a reference to a constant scalar:

```
$anon_scalar_ref = \15;
```

Use ${...} to dereference:

```
print ${ $scalar_ref };        # dereference it
${ $scalar_ref } .= "string"; # alter referent's value
```

Discussion

If you want to create many new anonymous scalars, use a subroutine that returns a reference to a lexical variable out of scope, as explained in this chapter's Introduction:

```
sub new_anon_scalar {
    my $temp;
    return \$temp;
}
```

Dereference a scalar reference by prefacing it with $ to get at its contents:

```
$sref = new_anon_scalar();
$$sref = 3;
print "Three = $$sref\n";
@array_of_srefs = ( new_anon_scalar(), new_anon_scalar() );
${ $array[0] } = 6.02e23;
${ $array[1] } = "avocado";
print "\@array contains: ", join(", ", map { $$_ } @array ), "\n";
```

Notice we put braces around $array[0] and $array[1]. If we tried to say $$array[0], the tight binding of dereferencing would turn it into $array->[0]. It would treat $array as an array reference and return the element at index zero.

Here are other examples where it is safe to omit the braces:

```
$var     = `uptime`;      # $var holds text
$vref    = \$var;         # $vref "points to" $var
if ($$vref =~ /load/) {}  # look at $var, indirectly
chomp $$vref;             # alter $var, indirectly
```

As mentioned in the Introduction, you may use the ref built-in to inspect a reference for its referent's type. Calling ref on a scalar reference returns the string "SCALAR":

```
# check whether $someref contains a simple scalar reference
if (ref($someref) ne "SCALAR") {
    die "Expected a scalar reference, not $someref\n";
}
```

See Also

Chapters 8 and 9 of *Programming Perl* and *perlref*(1)

11.6 Creating Arrays of Scalar References

Problem

You want to create and manipulate an array of references to scalars. This arises when you pass variables by reference to a function so the function can change their values.

Solution

To create an array, either backslash each scalar in the list to store in the array:

```
@array_of_scalar_refs = ( \$a, \$b );
```

or simply backslash the entire list, taking advantage of the backslash operator's distributive property:

```
@array_of_scalar_refs = \( $a, $b );
```

To get or set the value of an element of the list, use ${ ... }:

```
${ $array_of_scalar_refs[1] } = 12;        # $b = 12
```

Discussion

In the following examples, @array is a simple array containing references to scalars (an array of references is not a reference to an array). To access the original data indirectly, braces are mandatory.

```
($a, $b, $c, $d) = (1 .. 4);        # initialize
@array = (\$a, \$b, \$c, \$d);      # refs to each scalar
@array = \( $a,  $b,  $c,  $d);     # same thing!
@array = map { \my $anon } 0 .. 3;  # allocate 4 anon scalar refs

${ $array[2] } += 9;                # $c now 12

${ $array[ $#array ] } *= 5;        # $d now 20
${ $array[-1] }        *= 5;        # same; $d now 100

$tmp    = $array[-1];               # using temporary
$$tmp *= 5;                         # $d now 500
```

The two assignments to @array are equivalent—the backslash operator is distributive across a list. So preceding a list (including a slice or a function's return list, but not an array) with a backslash is the same as applying a backslash to everything in that list. The ensuing code changes the values of the variables whose references were stored in the array.

Here's how to deal with such an array without explicit indexing:

```
use Math::Trig qw(pi);              # load the constant pi
foreach $sref (@array) {            # prepare to change $a,$b,$c,$d
    ($$sref **= 3) *= (4/3 * pi);   # replace with spherical volumes
}
```

This code uses the formula for deriving the volume of a sphere:

$$Volume = \frac{4}{3}\pi r^3$$

The $sref loop index variable is each reference in @array, and $$sref is the number itself, that is, the original variables $a, $b, $c, and $d. Changing $$sref in the loop changes those variables as well. First we replace $$sref with its cube, then multiply the resulting value by 4/3π. This takes advantage of the fact that assignment in Perl returns an lvalue, letting you chain assignment operators together as we've done using the **= and *= assignment operators.

Actually, anonymous scalars are pretty useless, given that a scalar value fits in the same space as a scalar reference. That's why there's no explicit composer. Scalar references exist only to allow aliasing—which can be done in other ways.

See Also

The section on "Assignment Operators" in Chapter 3 of *Programming Perl* and in *perlop*(1); the section on "Other Tricks You Can Do with Hard References" in Chapter 8 of *Programming Perl*

11.7   Using Closures Instead of Objects

Problem

You want records with private state, behavior, and identity, but you don't want to learn object-oriented programming to accomplish this.

Solution

Write a function that returns (by reference) a hash of code references. These code references are closures created in the same scope, so when they execute, they'll share bindings to the same private variables.

Discussion

Because a closure is a binding of code and data, it can implement what might be thought of as an object.

Here's an example that creates and returns a hash of anonymous functions. mkcounter takes an argument of a seed counter and returns a reference to a hash of code references that you can use to manipulate the counter indirectly.

```
$c1 = mkcounter(20);
$c2 = mkcounter(77);

printf "next c1: %d\n", $c1->{NEXT}->( );   # 21
printf "next c2: %d\n", $c2->{NEXT}->( );   # 78
printf "next c1: %d\n", $c1->{NEXT}->( );   # 22
printf "last c1: %d\n", $c1->{PREV}->( );   # 21
printf "old  c2: %d\n", $c2->{RESET}->( );  # 77
```

The code values in the hash references in $c1 and $c2 maintain their own separate state. Here's how to set that up:

```
sub mkcounter {
    my $count  = shift;
    my $start  = $count;
    my $bundle = {
        "NEXT"   => sub { return ++$count  },
        "PREV"   => sub { return --$count  },
        "GET"    => sub { return $count    },
        "SET"    => sub { $count = shift   },
        "BUMP"   => sub { $count += shift  },
```

```
        "RESET"  => sub { $count = $start  },
    };
    $bundle->{"LAST"} = $bundle->{"PREV"};
    return $bundle;
}
```

Because the lexical variables used by the closures in the $bundle hash reference are returned by the function, they are not deallocated. The next time mkcounter is called, the closures get a different set of variable bindings for the same code. Because no one outside those closures can access these two variables, this assures true privacy.

The assignment right before the return makes both "PREV" and "LAST" values point to the same closure. Depending on your object-oriented background, you might think of these as being two different messages, both implemented using the same method.

The bundle we return is not an object in that it has no obvious inheritance and polymorphism. (Yet.) But it certainly does have state, behavior, and identity, as well as encapsulation.

See Also

The section on "Closures" in Chapter 8 of *Programming Perl* and the discussion on closures in *perlref*(1); Recipe 11.4; Recipe 11.9; Chapter 13

11.8   Creating References to Methods

Problem

You want to store a reference to a method.

Solution

Create a closure that makes the proper method call on the appropriate object.

Discussion

When you ask for a reference to a method, you're asking for more than just a raw function pointer. You also need to record which object the method needs to be called upon as the object contains the data the method will work with. The best way to do this is using a closure. Assuming $obj is lexically scoped, you can say:

```
$mref = sub { $obj->meth(@_) };
# later...
$mref->("args", "go", "here");
```

Even when $obj goes out of scope, the closure stored in $mref has captured it. Later when it's called indirectly, the correct object is used for the method call.

Be aware that the notation:

```
$sref = \$obj->meth;
```

doesn't do what you probably expected. It first calls the method on that object and gives you either a reference to the return value or a reference to the last of the return values if the method returns a list.

The can method from the UNIVERSAL base class, while appealing, is also unlikely to produce what you want.

```
$cref = $obj->can("meth");
```

This produces a code ref to the appropriate method (should one be found), but one that carries no object information. Think of it as a raw function pointer. The information about the object is lost. That's why you need a closure to capture both the object state as well as the method to call.

See Also

The discussion on methods in the Introduction to Chapter 13; the section on "Closures" in Chapter 8 of *Programming Perl*; Recipe 11.7; Recipe 13.8

11.9 Constructing Records

Problem

You want to create a record data type.

Solution

Use a reference to an anonymous hash.

Discussion

Suppose you wanted to create a data type that contained various data fields. The easiest way is to use an anonymous hash. For example, here's how to initialize and use that record:

```
$record = {
    NAME   => "Jason",
    EMPNO  => 132,
    TITLE  => "deputy peon",
    AGE    => 23,
    SALARY => 37_000,
    PALS   => [ "Norbert", "Rhys", "Phineas"],
};
```

```
printf "I am %s, and my pals are %s.\n",
    $record->{NAME},
    join(", ", @{$record->{PALS}});
```

Just having one of these records isn't much fun—you'd like to build larger structures. For example, you might want to create a %byname hash that you could initialize and use this way:

```
# store record
$byname{ $record->{NAME} } = $record;

# later on, look up by name
if ($rp = $byname{"Aron"}) {        # false if missing
    printf "Aron is employee %d.\n", $rp->{EMPNO};
}

# give jason a new pal
push @{$byname{"Jason"}->{PALS}}, "Theodore";
printf "Jason now has %d pals\n", scalar @{$byname{"Jason"}->{PALS}};
```

That makes %byname a hash of hashes because its values are hash references. Looking up employees by name would be easy using such a structure. If we find a value in the hash, we store a reference to the record in a temporary variable, $rp, which we then use to get any field we want.

We can use our existing hash tools to manipulate %byname. For instance, we could use the each iterator to loop through it in an arbitrary order:

```
# Go through all records
while (($name, $record) = each %byname) {
    printf "%s is employee number %d\n", $name, $record->{EMPNO};
}
```

What about looking employees up by employee number? Just build and use another data structure, an array of hashes called @employees. If your employee numbers aren't consecutive (for instance, they jump from 1 to 159997) an array would be a bad choice. Instead, you should use a hash mapping employee number to record. For consecutive employee numbers, use an array:

```
# store record
$employees[ $record->{EMPNO} ] = $record;

# lookup by id
if ($rp = $employee[132]) {
    printf "employee number 132 is %s\n", $rp->{NAME};
}
```

With a data structure like this, updating a record in one place effectively updates it everywhere. For example, this gives Jason a 3.5% raise:

```
$byname{"Jason"}->{SALARY} *= 1.035;
```

This change is reflected in all views of these records. Remember that $byname{"Jason"} and $employees[132] both refer to the same record because the references they contain refer to the same anonymous hash.

How would you select all records matching a particular criterion? This is what grep is for. Here's how to get everyone with "peon" in their titles or all 27-year-olds:

```
@peons   = grep { $_->{TITLE} =~ /peon/i } @employees;
@tsevens = grep { $_->{AGE}   == 27 }      @employees;
```

Each element of @peons and @tsevens is itself a reference to a record, making them arrays of hashes, like @employees.

Here's how to print all records sorted in a particular order, say by age:

```
# Go through all records
foreach $rp (sort { $a->{AGE} <=> $b->{AGE} } values %byname) {
    printf "%s is age %d.\n", $rp->{NAME}, $rp->{AGE};
    # or with a hash slice on the reference
    printf "%s is employee number %d.\n", @$rp{"NAME","EMPNO"};
}
```

Rather than take time to sort them by age, you could create another view of these records, @byage. Each element in this array, $byage[27] for instance, would be an array of all records with that age. In effect, this is an array of arrays of hashes. Build it this way:

```
# use @byage, an array of arrays of records
push @{ $byage[ $record->{AGE} ] }, $record;
```

Then you could find them all this way:

```
for ($age = 0; $age <= $#byage; $age++) {
    next unless $byage[$age];
    print "Age $age: ";
    foreach $rp (@{$byage[$age]}) {
        print $rp->{NAME}, " ";
    }
    print "\n";
}
```

A similar approach is to use map to avoid the foreach loop:

```
for ($age = 0; $age <= $#byage; $age++) {
    next unless $byage[$age];
    printf "Age %d: %s\n", $age,
        join(", ", map {$_->{NAME}} @{$byage[$age]});

}
```

See Also

Recipe 4.14; Recipe 11.3

11.10 Reading and Writing Hash Records to Text Files

Problem

You want to read or write hash records stored in text files.

Solution

Use a simple file format with one field per line:

```
FieldName: Value
```

and separate records with blank lines.

Discussion

If you have an array of records that you'd like to store into and retrieve from a text file, you can use a simple format based on mail headers. The format's simplicity requires that the keys have neither colons nor newlines, and the values not have newlines.

This code writes them out:

```
foreach $record (@Array_of_Records) {
    for $key (sort keys %$record) {
        print "$key: $record->{$key}\n";
    }
    print "\n";
}
```

Reading them in is easy, too.

```
$/ = "";                # paragraph read mode
while (<>) {
    my @fields = split /^([^:]+):\s*/m;
    shift @fields;       # for leading null field
    push(@Array_of_Records, { map /(.*)/, @fields });
}
```

The split acts upon $_, its default second argument, which contains a full paragraph. The pattern looks for start of line (not just start of record, thanks to the /m) followed by one or more non-colons, followed by a colon and optional whitespace. When split's pattern contains parentheses, these are returned along with the values. The return values placed in @fields are in key-value order, with a leading null field we shift off. The braces in the call to push produce a reference to a new anonymous hash, which we copy @fields into. Since that array was stored in order of the needed key-value pairing, this makes for well-ordered hash contents.

All you're doing is reading and writing a plain text file, so you can use related recipes for additional components. You could use Recipe 7.18 to ensure that you have clean, concurrent access; Recipe 1.18 to store colons and newlines in keys and values; and Recipe 11.3 to store more complex structures.

If you are willing to sacrifice the elegance of a plain textfile for a quick, random-access database of records, use a DBM file, as described in Recipe 11.14.

See Also

The split function in *perlfunc*(1) and Chapter 29 of *Programming Perl*; Recipe 11.9; Recipe 11.13; Recipe 11.14

11.11 Printing Data Structures

Problem

You want to print out a data structure.

Solution

If the output's legibility and layout are important, write your own custom printing routine.

If you are in the Perl debugger, use the x command:

```
DB<1> $reference = [ { "foo" => "bar" }, 3, sub { print "hello, world\n" } ];
DB<2> x $reference
  0  ARRAY(0x1d033c)
     0  HASH(0x7b390)
        'foo' = 'bar'
     1  3
     2  CODE(0x21e3e4)
        -> &main::__ANON__[(eval 15)[/usr/local/...perl5db.pl:17]:2]
        in (eval 15)[/usr/local/.../perl5db.pl:17]:2-2
```

From within your own programs, use the Dumper function from the standard module Data::Dumper:

```
use Data::Dumper;
print Dumper($reference);
```

Or if you'd like output formatted in the same style as the Debugger uses:

```
use Dumpvalue;
Dumpvalue->new->dumpValue($reference);
```

Discussion

Sometimes you'll want to make a dedicated function for your data structure that delivers a particular output format, but often this is overkill. If you're running under the Perl debugger, the x and X commands provide nice pretty-printing. The x command is more useful because it works on both global and lexical variables, whereas X works only on globals. Pass x a reference to the data structure you want to print.

```
DB<3> x @INC
0  ARRAY(0x807d0a8)
   0  '/home/tchrist/perllib'
   1  '/usr/lib/perl5/i686-linux/5.00403'
   2  '/usr/lib/perl5'
   3  '/usr/lib/perl5/site_perl/i686-linux'
   4  '/usr/lib/perl5/site_perl'
   5  '.'
```

The standard Dumpvalue module provides the Debugger's output formatting using an object-oriented interface. Here's an example:

```
use Dumpvalue;
Dumpvalue->new->dumpvars("main", "INC");

@INC = (
   0  '/usr/local/lib/perl5/5.8.1/OpenBSD.i386-openbsd'
   1  '/usr/local/lib/perl5/5.8.1'
   2  '/usr/local/lib/perl5/site_perl/5.8.1/OpenBSD.i386-openbsd'
   3  '/usr/local/lib/perl5/site_perl/5.8.1'
   4  '/usr/local/lib/perl5/site_perl/5.8.0/OpenBSD.i386-openbsd'
   5  '/usr/local/lib/perl5/site_perl/5.8.0'
   6  '/usr/local/lib/perl5/site_perl'
   7  '.'
)
%INC = (
   'Dumpvalue.pm' = '/usr/local/lib/perl5/5.8.1/Dumpvalue.pm'>
   'strict.pm' = '/usr/local/lib/perl5/5.8.1/strict.pm'>
)
```

which is like using the V main INC command in the Debugger. All the output formatting options from the Debugger are available from Dumpvalue. Just pass Dumpvalue-> new option pairs:

```
$dobj = Dumpvalue->new(option1 => value1, option2 => value2);
```

Options available as of v5.8.1 include arrayDepth, hashDepth, compactDump, veryCompact, globPrint, dumpDBFiles, dumpPackages, dumpReused, tick, quoteHighBit, printUndef, usageOnly, unctrl, subdump, bareStringify, quoteHighBit, and stopDbSignal.

The Data::Dumper module, also included in the standard Perl distribution, has a different approach. It provides a Dumper function that takes a list of references and returns a string with a printable (and evalable) form of those references.

```
use Data::Dumper; print Dumper(\@INC);
$VAR1 = [
'/usr/local/lib/perl5/5.8.1/OpenBSD.i386-openbsd',
'/usr/local/lib/perl5/5.8.1',
'/usr/local/lib/perl5/site_perl/5.8.1/OpenBSD.i386-openbsd',
'/usr/local/lib/perl5/site_perl/5.8.1',
'/usr/local/lib/perl5/site_perl/5.8.0/OpenBSD.i386-openbsd',
```

```
    '/usr/local/lib/perl5/site_perl/5.8.0',
    '/usr/local/lib/perl5/site_perl', '.'
  ];
```

Data::Dumper supports a variety of output formats. Check its documentation for details. Particularly useful is the option to decompile Perl code:

```
use Data::Dumper;
$Data::Dumper::Deparse = 1;
$a = sub { print "hello, world\n" };
print Dumper($a);
$VAR1 = sub {
                print 'hello, world';
            };
```

See Also

The documentation for Data::Dumper; Chapter 20 of *Programming Perl* or *perldebug*(1)

11.12 Copying Data Structures

Problem

You need to copy a complex data structure.

Solution

Use the dclone function from the standard Storable module:

```
use Storable;

$r2 = dclone($r1);
```

Discussion

Two types of "copy" are sometimes confused. A *surface copy* (also known as *shallow copy*) simply copies references without creating copies of the data behind them:

```
@original = ( \@a, \@b, \@c );
@surface = @original;
```

A *deep copy* creates an entirely new structure with no overlapping references. This copies references to one layer deep:

```
@deep = map { [ @$_ ] } @original;
```

If @a, @b, and @c themselves contain references, the preceding map is no longer adequate. Writing your own code to deep-copy structures is laborious and rapidly becomes tiresome.

The Storable module provides a function called dclone that recursively copies its argument:

```
use Storable qw(dclone);
$r2 = dclone($r1);
```

This only works on references or blessed objects of type SCALAR, ARRAY, HASH, or CODE;* references of type GLOB, IO, and the more esoteric types are not supported. The safeFreeze function from the FreezeThaw module supports even these types when used in the same address space by using a reference cache that could interfere with garbage collection and object destructors under some circumstances.

Because dclone takes and returns references, you must add extra punctuation if you have a hash or arrays to copy:

```
%newhash = %{ dclone(\%oldhash) };
```

See Also

The documentation for the standard Storable and Data::Dumper modules, and for the FreezeThaw CPAN module.

11.13 Storing Data Structures to Disk

Problem

You want to save your large, complex data structure to disk so you don't have to reconstruct it from scratch each time your program runs.

Solution

Use the Storable module's store and retrieve functions:

```
use Storable;
store(\%hash, "filename");

# later on...
$href = retrieve("filename");        # by ref
%hash = %{ retrieve("filename") };   # direct to hash
```

Discussion

The Storable module uses C functions and a binary format to walk Perl's internal data structures and lay out its data. It's more efficient than a pure Perl and string-based approach, but it's also more fragile.

---

* Believe it or not, it's true. Storable can even serialize closures. See its manpage for how to unthaw these using a Safe compartment.

The store and retrieve functions expect binary data using the machine's own byte-ordering. This means files created with these functions cannot be shared across different architectures. nstore does the same job store does, but keeps data in canonical (network) byte order, at a slight speed cost:

```
use Storable qw(nstore);
nstore(\%hash, "filename");
# later ...
$href = retrieve("filename");
```

No matter whether store or nstore was used, you need to call the same retrieve routine to restore the objects in memory. The producer must commit to portability, but the consumer doesn't have to. Code need only be changed in one place when the producer has a change of heart; the code thus offers a consistent interface for the consumer, who does not need to know or care.

The store and nstore functions don't lock the files they work on. If you're worried about concurrent access, open the file yourself, lock it using Recipe 7.18, and then use store_fd or its slower but machine-independent version nstore_fd.

Here's code to save a hash to a file, with locking. We don't open with the O_TRUNC flag because we have to wait to get the lock before we can clobber the file.

```
use Storable qw(nstore_fd);
use Fcntl qw(:DEFAULT :flock);
sysopen(DF, "/tmp/datafile", O_RDWR|O_CREAT, 0666)
        or die "can't open /tmp/datafile: $!";
flock(DF, LOCK_EX)                  or die "can't lock /tmp/datafile: $!";
nstore_fd(\%hash, *DF)
    or die "can't store hash\n";
truncate(DF, tell(DF));
close(DF);
```

Here's code to restore that hash from a file, with locking:

```
use Storable qw(retrieve_fd);
use Fcntl qw(:DEFAULT :flock);
open(DF, " < /tmp/datafile")    or die "can't open /tmp/datafile: $!";
flock(DF, LOCK_SH)              or die "can't lock /tmp/datafile: $!";
$href = retrieve_fd(*DF);
close(DF);
```

With care, you can pass large data objects efficiently between processes using this strategy, since a filehandle connected to a pipe or socket is still a byte stream, just like a plain file.

Unlike the various DBM bindings, Storable does not restrict you to using only hashes (or arrays, with DB_File). Arbitrary data structures, including objects, can be stored to disk. The whole structure must be read in or written out in its entirety.

See Also

The section on "Remote Procedure Calls (RPC)" in Chapter 13 of *Advanced Perl Programming*, by Sriram Srinivasan (O'Reilly); Recipe 11.14

11.14 Transparently Persistent Data Structures

Problem

You have a complex data structure that you want to persist outside your program.

Solution

Use MLDBM and either (preferably) DB_File or else GDBM_File:

```
use MLDBM qw(DB_File);
use Fcntl;

tie(%hash, "MLDBM", "testfile.db", O_CREAT|O_RDWR, 0666)
    or die "can't open tie to testfile.db: $!";

# ... act on %hash

untie %hash;
```

Discussion

A hash with 100,000 items in it would undoubtably take considerable time to build. Storing this to disk, either slowly by hand or quickly with Storable, is still an expensive operation in memory and computation.

The DBM modules solve this by tying hashes to disk database files. Rather than reading the whole structure in at once, they only pull in what they need, when they need it. To the user, it looks like a hash that persists across program invocations.

Unfortunately, the values in this persistent hash must be plain strings. You cannot readily use a database file as a backing store for a hash of hashes, a hash of arrays, and so on—just for a hash of strings.

However, the MLDBM module from CPAN allows you to store references in a database. It uses Data::Dumper to stringify these references for external storage:

```
use MLDBM qw(DB_File);
use Fcntl;
tie(%hash, "MLDBM", "testfile.db", O_CREAT|O_RDWR, 0666)
    or die "can't open tie to testfile.db: $!";
```

Now you can use %hash to fetch or store complex records from disk. The only drawback is that you can't access the references piecemeal. You have to pull in the reference from the database, work with it, and then store it back.

```
# this doesn't work!
$hash{"some key"}[4] = "fred";

# RIGHT
$aref = $hash{"some key"};
$aref->[4] = "fred";
$hash{"some key"} = $aref;
```

See Also

Recipe 11.13

11.15 Coping with Circular Data Structures Using Weak References

Problem

You have an inherently self-referential data structure, so Perl's reference-based gar-bage collection system won't notice when that structure is no longer being used. You want to prevent your program from leaking memory.

Solution

Convert all internal references within the data structure into weak references so they don't increment the reference count.

Description

Perl's memory management system relies on an underlying reference count to know when to reclaim memory. In practice, this works fairly well except for one particular situation: when a variable directly or indirectly points at itself. Consider:

```
{
    my ($a, $b);
    ($a, $b) = \($b, $a);   # same as (\$b, \$a);
}
```

The two underlying scalars that $a and $b represent each start out with a reference count of one apiece in the first line of the block. In the second line, those scalars are each initialized to contain a reference to the other variable; $a points to $b and vice versa. Saving a reference increments the underlying reference count on the scalars, so now both refcounts are set to two. As the block exits and those lexical variables become unreachable (by name), both refcounts are decremented by one, leaving one in each—forever. Since the refcounts can never reach zero, memory used by those two underlying scalars will never be reclaimed. You'll leak two scalars every time that block executes; if it's a loop or a subroutine, you could eventually run out of memory.

The standard Devel::Peek module's Dump function shows you underlying reference counts, plus a whole lot more. This code:

```
use Devel::Peek;
$a = 42;
$b = \$a;
Dump $a;
```

produces this output:

```
SV = IV(0xd7cc4) at 0xd72b8
  REFCNT = 2
  FLAGS = (IOK,pIOK)
  IV = 42
```

The important thing to notice there is that the refcount is two. That's because the scalar can be reached two ways: once via the variable named $a, and then again through dereferencing $b using $$b.

You can produce the same condition, even without using another variable:

```
{ my $a; $a = \$a; }
```

This most often occurs when creating a data structure whose elements contain references that directly or indirectly point back to the initial element. Imagine a circular linked list—a ring data structure.

```
$ring = {
    VALUE => undef,
    NEXT  => undef,
    PREV  => undef,
};
$ring->{NEXT} = $ring;
$ring->{PREV} = $ring;
```

The underlying hash has an underlying refcount of three, and undeffing $ring or letting it go out of scope will decrement that count only by one, resulting in a whole hash full of memory irrecoverable by Perl.

To address this situation, Perl introduced in its v5.6 release the concept of *weak references*. A weak reference is just like any other regular reference (meaning a "hard" reference, not a "symbolic" one) except for two critical properties: it no longer contributes to the reference count on its referent, and when its referent is garbage collected, the weak reference itself becomes undefined. These properties make weak references perfect for data structures that hold internal references to themselves. That way those internal references do not count toward the structure's reference count, but external ones still do.

Although Perl supported weak references starting in v5.6, there was no standard weaken( ) function to access them from Perl itself in the standard release. You had to go to CPAN to pull in the WeakRef module. Beginning in v5.8.1, the weaken( )

function is included standard with the Scalar::Util module. That module also provides an is_weak( ) function that reports whether its reference argument has been weakened.

Here's how you would apply weak references to the ring example just given:

```
use Scalar::Util qw(weaken);

$ring = {
    VALUE => undef,
    NEXT  => undef,
    PREV  => undef,
};
$ring->{NEXT} = $ring;
$ring->{PREV} = $ring;
weaken($ring->{NEXT});
weaken($ring->{PREV});
```

In Recipe 13.13, we show how to create a circular-linked list data structure that won't leak memory by employing an elaborate trick using a dummy head node and an object-oriented device called a destructor. With weak references, the code becomes much simpler. Here's the same algorithm as that recipe uses, but here using weak references to address the memory-leak issue.

```
use Scalar::Util qw(weaken);

my $COUNT = 1000;
for (1..20) {
    my $ring = node(100_000 + $_);
    for my $value (1 .. $COUNT) {
        insert_value($ring, $value);
    }
}

# return a node
sub node($) {
    my ($init_value) = @_;
    my $node  = { VALUE => $init_value };
    $node->{NEXT} = $node->{PREV} = $node;
    weaken($node->{NEXT});
    weaken($node->{PREV});
    return $node;
}

# $node = search_ring($ring, $value) : find $value in the ring
# structure in $node
sub search_ring {
    my ($ring, $value) = @_;
    my $node = $ring->{NEXT};
    while ($node != $ring && $node->{VALUE} != $value) {
        $node = $node->{NEXT};
    }
    return $node;
}
```

```
# insert_value( $ring, $value ) : insert $value into the ring structure
sub insert_value {
    my ($ring, $value) = @_;
    my $node = { VALUE => $value };
    weaken($node->{NEXT} = $ring->{NEXT});
    weaken($ring->{NEXT}->{PREV} = $node);
    weaken($ring->{NEXT} = $node);
    weaken($node->{PREV} = $ring);
    ++$ring->{COUNT};
}

# delete_value( $ring, $value ) : delete a node from the ring
# structure by value
sub delete_value {
  my ($ring, $value) = @_;
  my $node = search_ring($ring, $value);
  return if $node == $ring;
  $ring->delete_node($node);
}

# delete a node from the ring structure
sub delete_node {
  my ($ring, $node) = @_;
  weaken($node->{PREV}->{NEXT} = $node->{NEXT});
  weaken($node->{NEXT}->{PREV} = $node->{PREV});
  --$ring->{COUNT};
}
```

Every time we store a reference to part of the data structure within that same structure, we weaken the reference so it doesn't count toward the reference count. Otherwise our program's in-core memory footprint would have grown terrifically. You can
watch that happen by adding:

```
system("ps v$$");
```

within the loop on systems that support the *ps*(1) program. All it takes to trigger the
leak is not weakening any of the four assignments in the insert_value function just
shown.

See Also

The algorithms in this recipe derive in part from pages 206–207 of *Introduction to
Algorithms*, by Cormen, Leiserson, and Rivest (MIT Press/McGraw-Hill). See also
Recipe 13.13; the section on "Garbage Collection, Circular References, and Weak
References" in Chapter 8 of *Programming Perl*; the documentation for the standard
Devel::Peek and Scalar::Util modules

11.16 Program: Outlines

Outlines are a simple (and thus popular) way of structuring data. The hierarchy of
detail implied by an outline maps naturally to our top-down way of thinking about

---

the world. The only problem is that it's not obvious how to represent outlined data as a Perl data structure.

Take, for example, this simple outline of some musical genres:

```
Alternative
.Punk
..Emo
..Folk Punk
.Goth
..Goth Rock
..Glam Goth
Country
.Old Time
.Bluegrass
.Big Hats
Rock
.80s
..Big Hair
..New Wave
.60s
..British
..American
```

Here we use a period to indicate a subgroup. There are many different formats in which that outline could be output. For example, you might write the genres out in full:

```
Alternative
Alternative - Punk
Alternative - Punk - Emo
Alternative - Punk - Folk Punk
Alternative - Goth
...
```

You might number the sections:

```
1 Alternative
1.1 Punk
1.1.1 Emo
1.1.2 Folk Punk
1.2 Goth
...
```

or alphabetize:

```
Alternative
Alternative - Goth
Alternative - Goth - Glam Goth
Alternative - Goth - Goth Rock
Alternative - Punk
Alternative - Punk - Emo
...
```

or show inheritance:

```
Alternative
Punk - Alternative
```

```
Emo - Punk - Alternative
Folk Punk - Punk - Alternative
Goth - Alternative
Goth Rock - Goth - Alternative
...
```

These transformations are all much easier than it might seem. The trick is to represent the levels of the hierarchy as elements in an array. For example, you'd represent the third entry in the sample outline as:

```
@array = ("Alternative", "Goth", "Glam Goth");
```

Now reformatting the entry is trivial. There's an elegant way to parse the input file to get this array representation:

```
while (<FH>) {
    chomp;
    $tag[$in = s/\G\.//g] = $_;
    # do something with @tag[0..$in]
}
```

The substitution deletes leading periods from the current entry, returning how many it deleted. This number indicates the indentation level of the current entry.

Alphabetizing is now simple using the Unix sort program:

```
$ISA = "-";
open(STDOUT, "|sort -b -t'$ISA' -df");
while (<DATA>) {
    chomp;
    $tag[$in = s/\G\.//g] = $_;
    print join(" $ISA ", @tag[0 .. $in]);
}
close STDOUT;
__END__
Alternative
.Punk
..Emo
..Folk Punk
.Goth
```

Numbering the outline is equally simple:

```
while (<DATA>) {
    chomp;
    $count[$in = s/\G\.//g]++;
    delete @count[($in+1) .. $#count];
    print join(".", @count), " $_";
}
__END__
Alternative
.Punk
..Emo
..Folk Punk
.Goth
..Goth Rock
```

Notice that renumbering is our only application where we've deleted elements from the array. This is because we're not keeping names of hierarchy levels in the array; now we're keeping counts. When we go up a level (e.g., from three levels down to a new second-level heading), we reset the counter on the old level.

11.17 Program: Binary Trees

Because Perl's built-in data types are already powerful, high-level, dynamic data types in their own right, most code can use what's already provided. If you just want quick lookups, you nearly always want to use a simple hash. As Larry has said, "The trick is to use Perl's strengths rather than its weaknesses."

However, hashes provide no inherent ordering. To traverse the hash in a particular order, you must first extract its keys and then sort them. If you find yourself doing so many times, performance will suffer, but probably not enough to justify the time required to craft a fancy algorithm.

A tree structure provides ordered traversals. How do you write a tree in Perl? First, you grab one of your favorite textbooks on data structures; the authors recommend Cormen et al., as mentioned in Other Books in the Preface. Using an anonymous hash to represent each node in the tree, translate the algorithms in the book into Perl. This is usually much more straightforward than you would imagine.

The program code in Example 11-1 demonstrates an ordered binary tree implementation using anonymous hashes. Each node has three fields: a left child, a right child, and a value. The crucial property of an ordered binary tree is that at every node, all left children have values that are less than the current node value, and all right children have values that are greater.

The main program does three things. First, it creates a tree with 20 random nodes. Then it shows the in-order, pre-order, and post-order traversals of that tree. Finally, it allows the user to enter a key and reports whether that key is in the tree.

The insert function takes advantage of Perl's implicit pass-by-reference behavior on scalars to initialize an empty tree when asked to insert into an empty node. The assignment of the new node back to $_[0] alters the value in its caller.

Although this data structure takes much more memory than a simple hash and the lookups are slower, the ordered traversals themselves are faster.

A B-Tree is not a binary tree; it is a more flexible tree structure normally maintained on disk. DB_File has a BTREE interface (see *DB_File*(3)), and Mark-Jason Dominus has an excellent article on B-Trees in *The Perl Journal*, Volume 2, Issue 4, Winter 1997, pp. 35-42.

If you want to learn more about binary trees, *Introduction to Algorithms*, by Cormen, Leiserson, and Rivest, and *Algorithms in C*, by Robert Sedgewick, both cover the basic material. But for a treatment of that material cast in native Perl, no book can compare with *Mastering Algorithms with Perl*, by Orwant, Hietaniemi, and MacDonald.

The program is shown in Example 11-1.

Example 11-1. bintree

```perl
#!/usr/bin/perl -w
# bintree - binary tree demo program
use strict;
my($root, $n);
# first generate 20 random inserts
while ($n++ < 20) { insert($root, int(rand(1000)))}
# now dump out the tree all three ways
print "Pre order:  ";  pre_order($root);  print "\n";
print "In order:   ";  in_order($root);   print "\n";
print "Post order: ";  post_order($root); print "\n";
# prompt until EOF
for (print "Search? "; <>; print "Search? ") {
    chomp;
    my $found = search($root, $_);
    if ($found) { print "Found $_ at $found, $found->{VALUE}\n" }
    else        { print "No $_ in tree\n" }
}
exit;

#######################################
# insert given value into proper point of
# provided tree.  If no tree provided,
# use implicit pass by reference aspect of @_
# to fill one in for our caller.
sub insert {
    my($tree, $value) = @_;
    unless ($tree) {
        $tree = {};                        # allocate new node
        $tree->{VALUE}  = $value;
        $tree->{LEFT}   = undef;
        $tree->{RIGHT}  = undef;
        $_[0] = $tree;                            # $_[0] is reference param!
        return;
    }
    if    ($tree->{VALUE} > $value) { insert($tree->{LEFT},  $value) }
    elsif ($tree->{VALUE} < $value) { insert($tree->{RIGHT}, $value) }
    else                            { warn "dup insert of $value\n"  }
                                     # XXX: no dups
}
# recurse on left child,
# then show current value,
# then recurse on right child.
sub in_order {
    my($tree) = @_;
    return unless $tree;
    in_order($tree->{LEFT});
    print $tree->{VALUE}, " ";
    in_order($tree->{RIGHT});
}
```

Example 11-1. bintree (continued)

```perl
# show current value,
# then recurse on left child,
# then recurse on right child.
sub pre_order {
    my($tree) = @_;
    return unless $tree;
    print $tree->{VALUE}, " ";
    pre_order($tree->{LEFT});
    pre_order($tree->{RIGHT});
}
# recurse on left child,
# then recurse on right child,
# then show current value.
sub post_order {
    my($tree) = @_;
    return unless $tree;
    post_order($tree->{LEFT});
    post_order($tree->{RIGHT});
    print $tree->{VALUE}, " ";
}
# find out whether provided value is in the tree.
# if so, return the node at which the value was found.
# cut down search time by only looking in the correct
# branch, based on current value.
sub search {
    my($tree, $value) = @_;
    return unless $tree;
    if ($tree->{VALUE} == $value) {
        return $tree;
    }
    search($tree->{ ($value < $tree->{VALUE}) ? "LEFT" : "RIGHT"}, $value)
}
```

## CHAPTER 12

Packages, Libraries, and Modules

Like all those possessing a library, Aurelian was aware
that he was guilty of not knowing his in its entirety.
—Jorge Luis Borges, *The Theologians*

12.0 Introduction

Imagine that you have two separate programs, both of which work fine by themselves, and you decide to make a third program that combines the best features from the first two. You copy both programs into a new file or cut and paste selected pieces. You find that the two programs had variables and functions with the same names that should remain separate. For example, both might have an init function or a global $count variable. When merged into one program, these separate parts would interfere with each other.

The solution to this problem is *packages*. Perl uses packages to partition the global namespace. The package is the basis for both traditional modules and object-oriented classes. Just as directories contain files, packages contain identifiers. Every global identifier (variables, functions, file and directory handles, and formats) has two parts: its package name and the identifier proper. These two pieces are separated from one another with a double colon. For example, the variable $CGI::needs_binmode is a global variable named $needs_binmode, which resides in package CGI.

Where the filesystem uses slashes to separate the directory from the filename, Perl uses a double colon. $Names::startup is the variable named $startup in the package Names, whereas $Dates::startup is the $startup variable in package Dates. Saying $startup by itself without a package name means the global variable $startup in the current package. (This assumes that no lexical $startup variable is currently visible. Lexical variables are explained in Chapter 10.) When looking at an unqualified variable name, a lexical takes precedence over a global. Lexicals live in scopes; globals live in packages. If you really want the global instead, you need to fully qualify it.

package is a compile-time declaration that sets the default package prefix for unqualified global identifiers, much as chdir sets the default directory prefix for relative pathnames. This effect lasts until the end of the current scope (a brace-enclosed block, file, or eval). The effect is also terminated by any subsequent package statement in the same scope. (See the following code.) All programs are in package main until they use a package statement to change this.

```
package Alpha;
$name = "first";

package Omega;
$name = "last";

package main;
print "Alpha is $Alpha::name, Omega is $Omega::name.\n";
Alpha is first, Omega is last.
```

Unlike user-defined identifiers, built-in variables with punctuation names (like $_ and $.) and the identifiers STDIN, STDOUT, STDERR, ARGV, ARGVOUT, ENV, INC, and SIG are all forced to be in package main when unqualified. That way things like STDIN, @ARGV, %ENV, and $_ are always the same no matter what package you're in; for example, @ARGV always means @main::ARGV, even if you've used package to change the default package. A fully qualified @ElseWhere::ARGV would not, and carries no special built-in meaning. Make sure to localize $_ if you use it in your module.

Modules

The unit of software reuse in Perl is the *module*, a file containing related functions designed to be used by programs and other modules. Every module has a public interface, a set of variables and functions that outsiders are encouraged to use. From inside the module, the interface is defined by initializing certain package variables that the standard Exporter module looks at. From outside the module, the interface is accessed by importing symbols as a side effect of the use statement. The public interface of a Perl module is whatever is documented to be public. When we talk about modules in this chapter, and traditional modules in general, we mean those that use the Exporter.

The require and use statements load a module into your program, although their semantics vary slightly. require loads modules at runtime, with a check to avoid the redundant loading of a given module. use is like require, with two added properties: compile-time loading and automatic importing.

Modules included with use are processed at compile time, but require processing happens at runtime. This is important because if a module needed by a program is missing, the program won't even start because the use fails during compilation of your script. Another advantage of compile-time use over runtime require is that function prototypes in the module's subroutines become visible to the compiler. This matters because only the compiler cares about prototypes, not the interpreter. (Then again, we don't usually recommend prototypes except for replacing built-in commands, which do have them.)

use is suitable for giving hints to the compiler because of its compile-time behavior. A *pragma* is a special module that acts as a directive to the compiler to alter how Perl compiles your code. A pragma's name is always all lowercase, so when writing a regular module instead of a pragma, choose a name that starts with a capital letter. Pragmas supported by the v5.8.1 release of Perl include attributes, autouse, base, bigint, bignum, bigrat, bytes, charnames, constant, diagnostics, fields, filetest, if, integer, less, locale, open, overload, sigtrap, sort, strict, subs, utf8, vars, vmsish, and warnings. Each has its own manpage.

The other difference between require and use is that use performs an implicit *import* on the included module's package. Importing a function or variable from one package to another is a form of aliasing; that is, it makes two different names for the same underlying thing. It's like linking files from another directory into your current one by the command *ln /somedir/somefile*. Once it's linked in, you no longer have to use the full pathname to access the file. Likewise, an imported symbol no longer needs to be fully qualified by package name (or declared with our or the older use vars if a variable, or with use subs if a subroutine). You can use imported variables as though they were part of your package. If you imported $English::OUTPUT_AUTOFLUSH in the current package, you could refer to it as $OUTPUT_AUTOFLUSH.

The required file extension for a Perl module is .pm. The module named FileHandle would be stored in the file *FileHandle.pm*. The full path to the file depends on your include path, which is stored in the global @INC variable. Recipe 12.8 shows how to manipulate this array for your own purposes.

If the module name itself contains any double colons, these are translated into your system's directory separator. That means that the File::Find module resides in the file *File/Find.pm* under most filesystems. For example:

```
require "FileHandle.pm";        # runtime load
require FileHandle;             # ".pm" assumed; same as previous
use FileHandle;                 # compile-time load

require "Cards/Poker.pm";       # runtime load
require Cards::Poker;           # ".pm" assumed; same as previous
use Cards::Poker;               # compile-time load
```

Import/Export Regulations

The following is a typical setup for a hypothetical module named Cards::Poker that demonstrates how to manage its exports. The code goes in the file named *Poker.pm* within the directory *Cards*; that is, *Cards/Poker.pm*. (See Recipe 12.8 for where the *Cards* directory should reside.) Here's that file, with line numbers included for reference:

```
1    package Cards::Poker;
2    use Exporter;
3    @ISA = ("Exporter");
4    @EXPORT = qw(&shuffle @card_deck);
5    @card_deck = ();                    # initialize package global
6    sub shuffle { }                     # fill-in definition later
7    1;                                  # don't forget this
```

Line 1 declares the package that the module will put its global variables and functions in. Typically, a module first switches to a particular package so that it has its own place for global variables and functions, one that won't conflict with that of another program. This package name *must* be written exactly as in the corresponding use statement when the module is loaded.

Don't say package Poker just because the basename of your file is *Poker.pm*. Rather, say package Cards::Poker because your users will say use Cards::Poker. This common problem is hard to debug. If you don't make the package names specified by the package and use statements identical, you won't see a problem until you try to call imported functions or access imported variables, which will be mysteriously missing.

Line 2 loads in the Exporter module, which manages your module's public interface as described later. Line 3 initializes the special, per-package array @ISA to contain the word "Exporter". When a user says use Cards::Poker, Perl implicitly calls a special method, Cards::Poker->import(). You don't have an import method in your package, but that's okay, because the Exporter package does, and you're *inheriting* from it because of the assignment to @ISA (*is a*). Perl looks at the package's @ISA for resolution of undefined methods. Inheritance is a topic of Chapter 13. You may ignore it for now—so long as you put code like that in lines 2 and 3 into each module you write.

Line 4 assigns the list ('&shuffle', '@card_deck') to the special, per-package array @EXPORT. When someone imports this module, variables and functions listed in that array are aliased into the caller's own package. That way they don't have to call the function Cards::Poker::shuffle(23) after the import. They can just write shuffle(23) instead. This won't happen if they load Cards::Poker with require Cards::Poker; only a use imports.

Lines 5 and 6 set up the package global variables and functions to be exported. (We presume you'll actually flesh out their initializations and definitions more than in these examples.) You're free to add other variables and functions to your module, including ones you don't put in the public interface via @EXPORT. See Recipe 12.1 for more about using the Exporter.

Finally, line 7 is a simple 1, indicating the overall return value of the module. If the last evaluated expression in the module doesn't produce a true value, an exception will be raised. Trapping this is the topic of Recipe 12.2.

Packages group and organize global identifiers. They have nothing to do with privacy. Code compiled in package Church can freely examine and alter variables in package State. Package variables are always global and are used for sharing. But that's okay, because a module is more than just a package; it's also a file, and files count as their own scope. So if you want privacy, use lexical variables instead of globals. This is the topic of Recipe 12.4.

Other Kinds of Library Files

A library is a collection of loosely related functions designed to be used by other programs. It lacks the rigorous semantics of a Perl module. The file extension .pl indicates that it's a Perl library file. Examples include *syslog.pl* and *abbrev.pl*. These are included with the standard release for compatibility with prehistoric scripts written under Perl v4 or below.

Perl libraries—or in fact, any arbitrary file with Perl code in it—can be loaded in using do "file.pl" or with require "file.pl". The latter is preferred in most situations, because unlike do, require does implicit error checking. It raises an exception if the file can't be found in your @INC path, doesn't compile, or if it doesn't return a true value when any initialization code is run (the last part is what the 1 was for earlier). Another advantage of require is that it keeps track of which files have already been loaded in the global hash %INC. It doesn't reload the file if %INC indicates that the file has already been read.

Libraries work well when used by a program, but problems arise when libraries use one another. Consequently, simple Perl libraries have been rendered mostly obsolete, replaced by the more modern modules. But some programs still use libraries, usually loading them in with require instead of do.

Other file extensions are occasionally seen in Perl. A .ph is used for C header files that have been translated into Perl libraries using the *h2ph* tool, as discussed in Recipe 12.17. A .xs indicates an augmented C source file, possibly created by the *h2xs* tool, which will be compiled by the *xsubpp* tool and your C compiler into native machine code. This process of creating mixed-language modules is discussed in Recipe 12.18.

So far we've talked only about traditional modules, which export their interface by allowing the caller direct access to particular subroutines and variables. Most modules fall into this category. But some problems—and some programmers—lend themselves to more intricately designed modules: those involving objects. An object-oriented module seldom uses the import-export mechanism at all. Instead, it provides an object-oriented interface full of constructors, destructors, methods, inheritance, and operator overloading. This is the subject of Chapter 13.

Not Reinventing the Wheel

CPAN, the Comprehensive Perl Archive Network, is a gigantic repository of nearly everything about Perl you could imagine, including source, documentation, alternate ports, and above all, modules—some 4,500 of them as of spring of 2003. Before you write a new module, check with CPAN to see whether one already exists that does what you need. Even if one doesn't, something close enough might give you ideas.

CPAN is a replicated archive, currently mirrored on nearly 250 sites. Access CPAN via *http://www.cpan.org/*. If you just want to poke around, you can manually browse through the directories there. There are many indices, including listings of just new modules and of all modules organized by name, author, or category.

A convenient alternative to picking through thousands of modules is the search engine available at *http://search.cpan.org/*. You can search for modules by their name or author, but the facility for grepping through all registered modules' documentation is often more useful. That way you don't have download and install a module just to see what it's supposed to do.

See Also

Chapters 10, 11, and 22 of *Programming Perl*; *perlmod*(1)

12.1 Defining a Module's Interface

Problem

You want the standard Exporter module to define the external interface to your module.

Solution

In module file *YourModule.pm*, place the following code. Fill in the ellipses as explained in the Discussion section.

```
package YourModule;
use strict;
our (@ISA, @EXPORT, @EXPORT_OK, %EXPORT_TAGS, $VERSION);

use Exporter;
$VERSION = 1.00;            # Or higher
@ISA = qw(Exporter);

@EXPORT      = qw(...);     # Symbols to autoexport (:DEFAULT tag)
@EXPORT_OK   = qw(...);     # Symbols to export on request
%EXPORT_TAGS = (            # Define names for sets of symbols
    TAG1 => [...],
    TAG2 => [...],
    ...
);

#########################
# your code goes here
```

```
#########################

1;                               # this should be your last line
```

In other files where you want to use YourModule, choose one of these lines:

```
use YourModule;                  # Import default symbols into my package
use YourModule qw(...);          # Import listed symbols into my package
use YourModule ();               # Do not import any symbols
use YourModule qw(:TAG1);        # Import whole tag set
```

Discussion

The standard Exporter module handles the module's external interface. Although you could define your own import method for your package, almost no one does this.

When someone says use YourModule, this does a require "YourModule.pm" statement followed a YourModule->import( ) method call, both during compile time. The import method inherited from the Exporter package looks for global variables in your package to govern its behavior. Because they must be package globals, we've declared them with our to satisfy use strict. These variables are:

$VERSION

When a module is loaded, a minimal required version number can be supplied. If the version isn't at least this high, the use will raise an exception.

```
use YourModule 1.86;           # If $VERSION < 1.86, fail
```

@EXPORT

This array contains a list of functions and variables that will be exported into the caller's own namespace so they can be accessed without being fully qualified. Typically, a qw( ) list is used.

```
@EXPORT = qw(&F1 &F2 @List);
@EXPORT = qw( F1  F2 @List);          # same thing
```

With the simple use YourModule call the function &F1 can be called as F1( ) rather than YourModule::F1( ), and the array can be accessed as @List instead of @YourModule::List. The ampersand is optional in front of an exported function specification.

To load the module at compile time but request that no symbols be exported, use the special form use Your Module ( ), using empty parentheses for the import list.

@EXPORT_OK

This array contains symbols that can be imported if they're specifically asked for. If the array were loaded this way:

```
@EXPORT_OK = qw(Op_Func %Table);
```

then the user could load the module like so:

```
use YourModule qw(Op_Func %Table F1);
```

and import only the Op_Func function, the %Table hash, and the F1 function. The F1 function was listed in the @EXPORT array. Notice that this does not automatically import F2 or @List, even though they're in @EXPORT. To get everything in @EXPORT plus extras from @EXPORT_OK, use the special :DEFAULT tag, such as:

```
use YourModule qw(:DEFAULT %Table);
```

%EXPORT_TAGS

This hash is used by large modules like CGI or POSIX to create higher-level groupings of related import symbols. Its values are references to arrays of symbol names, all of which must be in either @EXPORT or @EXPORT_OK. Here's a sample initialization:

```
%EXPORT_TAGS = (
        Functions => [ qw(F1 F2 Op_Func) ],
        Variables => [ qw(@List %Table)  ],
    );
```

An import symbol with a leading colon means to import a whole group of symbols. Here's an example:

```
use YourModule qw(:Functions %Table);
```

That pulls in all symbols from:

```
@{ $YourModule::EXPORT_TAGS{Functions} },
```

that is, it pulls in the F1, F2, and Op_Func functions and then the %Table hash.

Although you don't list it in %EXPORT_TAGS, the implicit tag :DEFAULT automatically means everything in @EXPORT.

You don't have to have all those variables defined in your module. You just need the ones that you expect people to be able to use.

See Also

The "Creating Modules" section of Chapter 11 of *Programming Perl*; the documentation for the standard Exporter module, also found in Chapter 32 of *Programming Perl*; Recipe 12.8; Recipe 12.22

12.2 Trapping Errors in require or use

Problem

You need to load in a module that might not be present on your system. This normally results in a fatal exception. You want to detect and trap these failures.

Solution

Wrap the require or use in an eval, and wrap the eval in a BEGIN block:

```
# no import
BEGIN {
    unless (eval "require $mod; 1") {
        warn "couldn't require $mod: $@";
```

```
        }
    }

    # imports into current package
    BEGIN {
        unless (eval "use $mod; 1") {
            warn "couldn't use $mod: $@";
        }
    }
}
```

Discussion

You usually want a program to fail if it tries to load a module that is missing or doesn't compile. Sometimes, though, you'd like to recover from that error, perhaps trying an alternative module instead. As with any other exception, you insulate yourself from compilation errors with an eval.

You don't want to use eval { BLOCK }, because this traps only runtime exceptions, and use is a compile-time event. Instead, you must use eval "string" to catch compile-time problems as well. Remember, require on a bareword has a slightly different meaning than require on a variable. It adds a ".pm" and translates double-colons into your operating system's path separators, canonically / (as in URLs), but sometimes \, :, or even . on some systems.

If you need to try several modules in succession, stopping at the first one that works, you could do something like this:

```
    BEGIN {
        my($found, @DBs, $mod);
        $found = 0;
        @DBs = qw(Giant::Eenie Giant::Meanie Mouse::Mynie Moe);
        for $mod (@DBs) {
            if (eval "require $mod") {
                $mod->import();          # if needed
                $found = 1;
                last;
            }
        }
        die "None of @DBs loaded" unless $found;
    }
```

We wrap the eval in a BEGIN block to ensure the module-loading happens at compile time instead of runtime.

See Also

The eval, die, use, and require functions in Chapter 32 of *Programming Perl* and in *perlfunc*(1); Recipe 10.12; Recipe 12.3

12.3 Delaying use Until Runtime

Problem

You have a module that you don't need to load each time the program runs, or whose inclusion you wish to delay until after the program starts up.

Solution

Either break up the use into its separate require and import components, or else employ the use autouse pragma.

Discussion

Programs that check their arguments and abort with a usage message on error have no reason to load modules they never use. This delays the inevitable and annoys users. But those use statements happen during compilation, not execution, as explained in the Introduction.

Here, an effective strategy is to place argument checking in a BEGIN block before loading the modules. The following is the start of a program that checks to make sure it was called with exactly two arguments, which must be whole numbers, before going on to load the modules it will need:

```
BEGIN {
    unless (@ARGV == 2 && (2 == grep {/^\d+$/} @ARGV)) {
        die "usage: $0 num1 num2\n";
    }
}
use Some::Module;
use More::Modules;
```

A related situation arises in programs that don't always use the same set of modules every time they're run. For example, the *factors* program from Chapter 2 needs the infinite precision arithmetic library only when the **-b** command-line flag is supplied. A use statement would be pointless within a conditional because it's evaluated at compile time, long before the if can be checked. So we use a require instead:

```
if ($opt_b) {
    require Math::BigInt;
}
```

Because Math::BigInt is an object-oriented module instead of a traditional one, no import was needed. If you have an import list, specify it with a qw( ) construct as you would with use. For example, rather than this:

```
use Fcntl qw(O_EXCL O_CREAT O_RDWR);
```

you might say this instead:

```
require Fcntl;
Fcntl->import(qw(O_EXCL O_CREAT O_RDWR));
```

Delaying the import until runtime means that the rest of your program is not subject to any imported semantic changes that the compiler would have seen if you'd used a use. In particular, subroutine prototypes and the overriding of built-in functions are not seen in time.

You might want to encapsulate this delayed loading in a subroutine. The following deceptively simple approach does not work:

```
sub load_module {
    require $_[0];    #WRONG
    import  $_[0];    #WRONG
}
```

It fails for subtle reasons. Imagine calling require with an argument of "Math::BigFloat". If that's a bareword, the double colon is converted into your operating system's path separator and a trailing .pm is added. But as a simple variable, it's a literal filename. Worse, Perl doesn't have a built-in import function. Instead, there's a class method named import that we're using the dubious indirect object syntax on. As with indirect filehandles, you can use indirect objects only on a plain scalar variable, a bareword, or a block returning the object, not an expression or one element from an array or hash.

A better implementation might look more like:

```
load_module("Fcntl", qw(O_EXCL O_CREAT O_RDWR));

sub load_module {
    eval "require $_[0]";
    die if $@;
    $_[0]->import(@_[1 .. $#_]);
}
```

But this still isn't perfectly correct in the general case. It really shouldn't import those symbols into its own package. It should put them into its caller's package. We could account for this, but the whole procedure is getting increasingly messy.

Occasionally, the condition can be reasonably evaluated before runtime, perhaps because it uses only built-in, predefined variables, or because you've arranged to initialize the variables used in the conditional expression at compile time with a BEGIN block. If so, the if pragma comes in handy. The syntax is:

```
use CONDITION, MODULE;
use CONDITION, MODULE => ARGUMENTS;
```

As in:

```
use if $^O =~ /bsd/i, BSD::Resource;
use if $] >= 5.006_01, File::Temp => qw/tempfile tempdir/;
```

A convenient alternative is the use autouse pragma. This directive can save time on infrequently loaded functions by delaying their loading until they're actually used:

```
use autouse Fcntl => qw( O_EXCL() O_CREAT() O_RDWR() );
```

We put parentheses after O_EXCL, O_CREAT, and O_RDWR when we autoused them but not when we used them or imported them. The autouse pragma doesn't just take function names; it can also take a prototype for the function. The Fcntl constants are prototyped to take no arguments, so we can use them as barewords in our program without use strict kvetching.

Remember, too, that use strict's checks take place at compile time. If we use Fcntl, the prototypes in the Fcntl module are compiled and we can use the constants without parentheses. If we require or wrap the use in an eval, as we did earlier, we prevent the compiler from reading the prototypes, so we can't use the Fcntl constants without parentheses.

Read the autouse pragma's online documentation to learn its various caveats and provisos.

See Also

Recipe 12.2; the discussion on the import method in the documentation for the standard Exporter module, also found in Chapter 32 of *Programming Perl*; the documentation for the standard use autouse pragma

12.4   Making Variables Private to a Module

Problem

You want to make a variable private to a package.

Solution

You can't. But you can make them private to the file that the module sits in, which usually suffices.

Discussion

Remember that a package is just a way of grouping variables and functions together, conferring no privacy. Anything in a package is by definition global and accessible from anywhere. Packages only group; they don't hide.

For privacy, only lexical variables will do. A module is implemented in a *Module.pm* file, with all its globals in the package named Module. Because that whole file is by definition a scope and lexicals are private to a scope, creating file-scoped lexicals is effectively the same thing as a module-private variable.

If you alternate packages within a scope, though, you may be surprised that the scope's lexicals are still visible throughout that scope. That's because a package statement only sets a different prefix for a global identifier; it does not end the current scope, not does it begin a new one.

```
package Alpha;
my $aa = 10;
    $x = "azure";

package Beta;
my $bb = 20;
    $x = "blue";

package main;
print "$aa, $bb, $x, $Alpha::x, $Beta::x\n";
10, 20, , azure, blue
```

Was that the output you expected? The two lexicals, $aa and $bb, are still in scope because we haven't left the current block, file, or eval. You might think of globals and lexicals as existing in separate dimensions, forever unrelated to each other. Package statements have nothing to do with lexicals. By setting the current prefix, the first global variable $x is really $Alpha::x, whereas the second $x is now $Beta::x because of the intervening package statement changing the default prefix. Package identifiers, if fully qualified, can be accessed from anywhere, as we've done in the print statement.

So, packages can't have privacy—but modules can because they're in a file, which is always its own scope. Here's a simple module, placed in the file *Flipper.pm*, that exports two functions, flip_words and flip_boundary. The module provides code to reverse words in a line, and to change the definition of a word boundary.

```
# Flipper.pm
package Flipper;
use strict;

require Exporter;
use vars qw(@ISA @EXPORT $VERSION);
@ISA     = qw(Exporter);
@EXPORT  = qw(flip_words flip_boundary);
$VERSION = 1.0;

my $Separatrix = " ";  # default to blank; must precede functions

sub flip_boundary {
    my $prev_sep = $Separatrix;
    if (@_) { $Separatrix = $_[0] }
    return $prev_sep;
}
sub flip_words {
    my $line  = $_[0];
    my @words = split($Separatrix, $line);
```

```
        return join($Separatrix, reverse @words);
    }
    1;
```

This module sets three package variables needed by the Exporter and also initializes a lexical variable at file level called $Separatrix. Again, this variable is private to the file, not to the package. All code beneath its declaration in the same scope (or nested within that scope, as are the functions' blocks) can see $Separatrix perfectly. Even though they aren't exported, global variables could be accessed using the fully qualified name, as in $Flipper::VERSION.

A scope's lexicals cannot be examined or tinkered with from outside that scope, which in this case is the entire file below their point of declaration. You cannot fully qualify lexicals or export them either; only globals can be exported. If someone outside the module needs to look at or change the file's lexicals, they must ask the module itself. That's where the flip_boundary function comes into play, allowing indirect access to the module's private parts.

This module would work the same even if its $Separatrix variable were a package global rather than a file lexical. Someone from the outside could theoretically play with it without the module realizing this. On the other hand, if they really want to that badly, perhaps you should let them do so. Peppering your module with file-scoped lexicals is not necessary. You already have your own namespace (Flipper, in this case) where you can store any identifier you want. That's what it's there for, after all. Good Perl programming style nearly always avoids fully qualified identifiers.

Speaking of style, the case of identifiers used in the Flipper module was not random. Following the Perl style guide, identifiers in all capitals are reserved for those with special meaning to Perl itself. Functions and local variables are all lowercase. The module's persistent variables (either file lexicals or package globals) are capitalized. Identifiers with multiple words have each word separated by an underscore to make them easier to read. We advise against using mixed capitals without underscores—you wouldn't like reading this book without spaces, either.

See Also

The discussion on file-scoped lexicals in *perlmod*(1); the "Scoped Declarations" section in Chapter 4 of *Programming Perl*; the section on "Programming with Style" in Chapter 24 of *Programming Perl* or *perlstyle*(1); Recipe 10.2; Recipe 10.3

12.5 Making Functions Private to a Module

Problem

You want to make a function private to a package.

Solution

You can't. But you can make a private variable and store a reference to an anonymous function in it.

```
# this is the file SomeModule.pm
package Some_Module;

my $secret_function = sub {
    # your code here
};

sub regular_function {
    # now call your "private" function via the code ref
    $secret_function->(ARG1, ARG2);
}
```

Discussion

Even a function that isn't exported can still be accessed by anyone, anywhere if they qualify that function's name with its package. That's because function names are always in the package symbol table, which is globally accessible.

By creating a lexical variable at the file scope, code in that module file below the point of declaration has full access to that variable. Code in other files will not, because those scopes are unrelated. The subroutine created via sub { .... } is anonymous, so there's no name in the symbol table for anyone outside to find. Not even other code in the module can call the function by name, since it doesn't have one, but that code *can* use the lexical variable to dereference the code reference indirectly.

```
$secret_function->(ARGS);              # infix deref form
&$secret_function(ARGS);               # prefix deref form
```

Curiously, if you really wanted to, you could give this anonymous function a temporary name. Using the technique outlined in Recipe 10.16, assign the code reference to a localized typeglob, like this:

```
sub module_function {
    local *secret = $secret_function;
    Other_Package::func1();
    secret(ARG1, ARG2);
    Yet_Another_Package::func2();
}
```

Now for the duration of module_function, your previously secret function can be called using a direct function call; no indirection required. However, code outside the module can also find that function. In the example, it doesn't matter whether func1 and func2 are in the module's file scope, because you've made a temporary symbol table entry through which they could get at your secret function. Therefore, if Other_Package::func1 turned around and called Some_Module::secret, it could find it—but only if func1 were called from the module_function in the example. If it were called from some other point, there wouldn't be any secret function in the Some_ Module package symbol table, so the attempted function call would fail.

This slightly peculiar behavior, where temporaries' values and visibility depend upon who called whom at runtime, is called *dynamic scoping*. This is the nature of the local keyword. You can see why we don't usually suggest using it.

See Also

Recipe 12.4; the section on "Dynamically Scoped Variables: local" in Chapter 4 of *Programming Perl*; the section on "Symbol Tables" in Chapter 10 of *Programming Perl*

12.6 Determining the Caller's Package

Problem

You need to find out the current or calling package.

Solution

To find the current package:

```
$this_pack = __PACKAGE__;
```

To find the caller's package:

```
$that_pack = caller();
```

Discussion

The __PACKAGE__ symbol returns the package that the code is currently being compiled into. This doesn't interpolate into double-quoted strings:

```
print "I am in package __PACKAGE__\n";          # WRONG!
I am in package __PACKAGE__
```

Needing to figure out the caller's package arose more often in older code that received as input a string of code to be evaluated, or a filehandle, format, or directory handle name. Consider a call to a hypothetical runit function:

```
package Alpha;
runit('$line = <TEMP>');

package Beta;
sub runit {
    my $codestr = shift;
    eval $codestr;
    die if $@;
}
```

Because runit was compiled in a different package than was currently executing, when the eval runs, it acts as though it were passed $Beta::line and Beta::TEMP. The old workaround was to include your caller's package first:

```
package Beta;
sub runit {
    my $codestr = shift;
    my $hispack = caller;
    eval "package $hispack; $codestr";
    die if $@;
}
```

That approach works only when $line is a global variable. If it's lexical, that won't help at all. Instead, arrange for runit to accept a reference to a subroutine:

```
package Alpha;
runit( sub { $line = <TEMP> } );

package Beta;
sub runit {
    my $coderef = shift;
    &$coderef( );
}
```

This not only works with lexicals, but has the added benefit of checking the code's syntax at compile time, which is a major win.

If all that's being passed in is a filehandle, it's more portable to use the Symbol:: qualify function. This function takes a name and package to qualify the name into. If the name needs qualification, it fixes it; otherwise, it's left alone. But that's considerably less efficient than a * prototype.

Here's an example that reads and returns *n* lines from a filehandle. The function qualifies the handle before working with it.

```
open (FH, "<", "/etc/termcap")        or die "can't open /etc/termcap: $!";
($a, $b, $c) = nreadline(3, "FH");

use Symbol ( );
use Carp;
sub nreadline {
    my ($count, $handle) = @_;
    my(@retlist,$line);

    croak "count must be > 0" unless $count > 0;
    $handle = Symbol::qualify($handle, (caller( ))[0]);
    croak "need open filehandle" unless defined fileno($handle);

    push(@retlist, $line) while defined($line = <$handle>) && $count--;
    return @retlist;
}
```

If everyone who called your nreadline function passed the filehandle as a typeglob *FH, as a glob reference *FH, or using FileHandle or IO::Handle objects, you wouldn't need to do this. It's only the possibility of a bare "FH" string that requires qualification.

See Also

The documentation for the standard Symbol module, also found in Chapter 32 of *Programming Perl*; the descriptions of the special symbols __FILE__, __LINE__, and __PACKAGE__ in *perldata*(1); Recipe 12.14; Recipe 7.6

12.7 Automating Module Cleanup

Problem

You need to create module setup code and cleanup code that gets called automatically, without user intervention.

Solution

For setup code, put executable statements outside subroutine definitions in the module file. For cleanup code, use an END subroutine in that module.

Discussion

In some languages, the programmer must remember to call module initialization code before accessing any of that module's regular functions. Similarly, when the program is done, the programmer may have to call module-specific finalization code.

Not so in Perl. For per-module initialization code, executable statements outside of any subroutines in your module suffice. When the module is loaded in, that code runs right then and there. The user never has to remember to do this, because it's done automatically.

Now, why would you want automatic cleanup code? It depends on the module. You might want to write a shutdown message to a logfile, tell a database server to commit any pending state, refresh a screen, or return the tty to its original state.

Suppose you want a module to log quietly whenever a program using it starts up or finishes. Add code in an END subroutine to run after your program finishes:

```
$Logfile = "/tmp/mylog" unless defined $Logfile;
open(LF, ">>", $Logfile)
    or die "can't append to $Logfile: $!";
select(((select(LF), $|=1))[0]);  # unbuffer LF
logmsg("startup");

sub logmsg {
    my $now = scalar gmtime;
    print LF "$0 $$ $now: @_\n"
        or die "write to $Logfile failed: $!";
}
```

```
END {
    logmsg("shutdown");
    close(LF)
        or die "close $Logfile failed: $!";
}
```

The first part of code, outside any subroutine declaration, is executed at module load time. The module user doesn't have to do anything special to make this happen. Someone might be unpleasantly surprised, however, if the file couldn't be accessed, since the die would make the use or require fail.

END routines work like exit handlers, such as trap 0 in the shell, atexit in C programming, or global destructors or finalizers in object-oriented languages. All of the ENDs in a program are run in the opposite order that they were loaded; that is, last seen, first run. These get called whether the program finishes through normal process termination by implicitly reaching the end of your main program, through an explicit call to the exit function, or via an uncaught exception such as die or a mistake involving division by zero.

Uncaught signals are a different matter, however. Death by signal does not run your exit handlers. The following pragma takes care of them:

```
use sigtrap qw(die normal-signals error-signals);
```

That causes all normal signals and error signals to make your program expire via the die mechanism, effectively converting a signal into an exception and thus permitting your END handlers to run.

You can get fancier, too:

```
use sigtrap qw(
    die         untrapped normal-signals
    stack-trace any       error-signals
);
```

That says to die only on an untrapped normal signal, but for error signals, to produce a stack trace before dying—like the confess function from the Carp module.

END also isn't called when a process polymorphs itself via the exec function because you are still in the same process, just a different program. All normal process attributes remain, like process ID and parent PID, user and group IDs, umask, current directory, environment variables, resource limits and accumulated statistics, and open file descriptors (however, see the $^F variable in *perlvar*(1) or *Programming Perl*). If it didn't work this way, exit handlers would execute redundantly in programs manually managing their fork and exec calls. This would not be good.

See Also

The standard use sigtrap pragma, also in Chapter 31 of *Programming Perl*; Chapter 18 of *Programming Perl* and the section on "Package Constructors and Destructors" in *perlmod*(1); the $^F ($SYSTEM_FD_MAX) variable in Chapter 28 of *Programming Perl*

---

and in *perldata*(1); the fork and exec functions in Chapter 29 of *Programming Perl* and in *perlmod*(1)

12.8 Keeping Your Own Module Directory

Problem

You don't want to install your own personal modules in the standard per-system extension library.

Solution

You have several choices: use Perl's **-I** command line switch; set your PERL5LIB environment variable; or employ the use lib pragma, possibly in conjunction with the FindBin module.

Discussion

The @INC array contains a list of directories to consult when do, require, or use pulls in code from another file. You can print these out easily from the command line:

```
% perl -e 'printf "%d %s\n", $i++, $_ for @INC'
0 /usr/local/lib/perl5/5.8.0/OpenBSD.i386-openbsd
1 /usr/local/lib/perl5/5.8.0
2 /usr/local/lib/perl5/site_perl/5.8.0/OpenBSD.i386-openbsd
3 /usr/local/lib/perl5/site_perl/5.8.0
4 /usr/local/lib/perl5/site_perl/5.6.0
5 /usr/local/lib/perl5/site_perl/5.00554
6 /usr/local/lib/perl5/site_perl/5.005
7 /usr/local/lib/perl5/site_perl
8 .
```

The first two directories, elements 0 and 1 of @INC, are respectively the standard architecture-dependent and architecture-independent directories, which all standard libraries, modules, and pragmas will go into. You have two of them because some modules contain information or formatting that makes sense only on that particular architecture. For example, the Config module contains information that cannot be shared across several architectures, so it goes in the 0th array element. Modules that include compiled C components, such as *Socket.so*, are also placed there. Most modules, however, go in the platform-independent directory in the 1st element.

The next pair, elements 2 and 3, fulfills roles analogous to elements 0 and 1, but on a site-specific basis. Suppose you have a module that didn't come with Perl, such as one from CPAN or that you wrote yourself. When you or (more likely) your system administrator installs this module, its components go into one of the site-specific directories. You are encouraged to use these for any modules that your entire site should be able to access conveniently.

In this particular configuration, elements 4–7 are there so that Perl can find any site-specific modules installed under a previous release of Perl. Such directories can be automatically added to @INC when you configure, build, and install a newer Perl release, making it easier to upgrade.

The last standard component, "." (your current working directory), is useful only when developing and testing your software, not when deploying it. If your modules are in the same directory that you last chdired to, you're fine. If you're anywhere else, it doesn't work.

So sometimes none of the @INC directories work out. Maybe you have your own personal modules. Perhaps your project group has particular modules that are relevant only to that project. In these cases, you need to augment the standard @INC search.

The first approach involves a command-line flag, **-Idirlist**. The *dirlist* is a colon-separated[*] list of one or more directories, which are prepended to the front of the @INC array. This works well for simple command lines, and thus can be used on a per-command basis, such as when you call a quick one-liner from a shell script.

This technique should not be used in the #! (pound-bang) line. First, it's not much fun to modify each program. More importantly, some older operating systems have bugs related to how long that line can be, typically 32 characters, including the #! part. That means if you have a very long path, such as #!/opt/languages/free/extrabits/perl, you may get the mysterious "Command not found" error. Perl does its best to rescan the line manually, but this is still too dicey to rely on.

Often, a better solution is to set the PERL5LIB environment variable. This can be done in your shell start-up file. Or, your system administrator may want to do so in a systemwide start-up file so all users can benefit. For example, suppose you have all your own modules in a directory called *~/perllib*. You would place one of the following lines in your shell start-up file, depending on which shell you use:

```
# syntax for sh, bash, ksh, or zsh
$ export PERL5LIB=$HOME/perllib

# syntax for csh or tcsh
% setenv PERL5LIB ~/perllib
```

Probably the most convenient solution from your users' perspective is for you to add a use lib pragma near the top of your script. That way users of the program need take no special action to run that program. Imagine a hypothetical project called Spectre whose programs rely on its own set of libraries. Those programs could have a statement like this at their start:

```
use lib "/projects/spectre/lib";
```

What happens when you don't know the exact path to the library? Perhaps you've installed the whole project in an arbitrary path. You *could* create an elaborate

---

[*] Comma-separated on Mac OS 9.

installation procedure to dynamically update the script, but even if you did, paths would still be frozen at installation time. If someone moved the files later, the libraries wouldn't be found.

The FindBin module conveniently solves this problem. This module tries to determine the full path to the executing script's enclosing directory, setting an importable package variable called $Bin to that directory. Typical usage is to look for modules either in the same directory as the program or in a *lib* directory at the same level.

To demonstrate the first case, suppose you have a program called */wherever/spectre/ myprog* that needs to look in */wherever/spectre* for its modules, but you don't want that path hardcoded.

```
use FindBin;
use lib $FindBin::Bin;
```

The second case would apply if your program lives in */wherever/spectre/bin/myprog* but needs to look at */wherever/spectre/lib* for its modules.

```
use FindBin qw($Bin);
use lib "$Bin/../lib";
```

See Also

The documentation for the standard use lib pragma (also in Chapter 31 of *Programming Perl*) and the standard FindBin module; the discussion of the PERL5LIB environment in *perl*(1) and the "Environmental Variables" section of Chapter 19 of *Programming Perl*; your shell's syntax for setting environment variables

12.9   Preparing a Module for Distribution

Problem

You want to prepare your module in standard distribution format so you can easily send your module to a friend. Better yet, you plan to contribute your module to CPAN so everyone can use it.

Solution

It's best to start with Perl's standard *h2xs* tool. Let's say you want to make a Planets module or an Astronomy::Orbits module. You'd type:

```
% h2xs -XA -n Planets
% h2xs -XA -n Astronomy::Orbits
```

These commands make subdirectories called *./Planets/* and *./Astronomy/Orbits/*, respectively, where you will find all the components you need to get you started. The **-n** flag names the module you want to make, **-X** suppresses creation of XS (external subroutine) components, and **-A** means the module won't use the AutoLoader.

Discussion

Writing modules is easy—once you know how. Writing a proper module is like filling out a legal contract: it's full of places to initial, sign, and date exactly right. If you miss any, it's not valid. Instead of hiring a contract lawyer, you can get a quick start on writing modules using the *h2xs* program. This tool gives you a skeletal module file with the right parts filled in, and it also gives you the other files needed to correctly install your module and its documentation or to bundle up for contributing to CPAN or sending off to a friend.

h2xs is something of a misnomer because XS is Perl's external subroutine interface for linking with C or C++. But the *h2xs* tool is also extremely convenient for preparing a distribution even when you aren't using the XS interface.

Let's look at the module file that *h2xs* has made. Because the module is called Astronomy::Orbits, the user specifies not use Orbits but rather use Astronomy:: Orbits. Therefore an extra *Astronomy* subdirectory is made, under which an *Orbits* subdirectory is placed. Here is the first and perhaps most important line of *Orbit.pm*:

```
package Astronomy::Orbits;
```

This sets the package—the default prefix—on all global identifiers (variables, functions, filehandles, etc.) in the file. Therefore a variable like @ISA is really the global variable @Astronomy::Orbits::ISA.

As we said in the Introduction, you must not make the mistake of saying package Orbits because it's in the file *Orbits.pm*. The package statement in the module must be exactly match the target of the use or require statement, which means the leading directory portion needs to be there and the characters' case must be the same. Furthermore, it must be installed in an *Astronomy* subdirectory. The *h2xs* command will set this all up properly, including the installation rule in the Makefile. But if you're doing this by hand, you must keep this in mind. See Recipe 12.1 for that.

If you plan to use autoloading, described in Recipe 12.11, omit the **-A** flag to *h2xs*, which produces lines like this:

```
require Exporter;
require AutoLoader;
@ISA = qw(Exporter AutoLoader);
```

If your module is bilingual in Perl and C as described in Recipe 12.18, omit the **-X** flag to *h2xs* to produce lines like this:

```
require Exporter;
require DynaLoader;
@ISA = qw(Exporter DynaLoader);
```

Following this is the Exporter's variables as explained in Recipe 12.1. If you're writing an object-oriented module as described in Chapter 13, you probably won't use the Exporter at all.

That's all there is for setup. Now, write your module code. When you're ready to ship it off, use the make dist directive from your shell to bundle it all up into a tar archive for easy distribution. (The name of the *make* program may vary from system to system.)

```
% perl Makefile.PL
% make dist
```

This will leave you with a file whose name is something like *Astronomy-Orbits-1.03.tar.Z*.

To register as a CPAN developer, check out *http://pause.cpan.org*.

See Also

http://www.cpan.org to find a mirror near you and directions for submission; *h2xs*(1); the documentation for the standard Exporter, AutoLoader, AutoSplit, and ExtUtils::MakeMaker modules, also found in Chapter 32 of *Programming Perl*

12.10 Speeding Module Loading with SelfLoader

Problem

You'd like to load a very large module quickly.

Solution

Use the SelfLoader module:

```
require Exporter;
require SelfLoader;
@ISA = qw(Exporter SelfLoader);
#
# other initialization or declarations here
#
__DATA__
sub abc { .... }
sub def { .... }
```

Discussion

When you load a module using require or use, the entire module file must be read and compiled (into internal parse trees, not into byte code or native machine code) right then. For very large modules, this annoying delay is unnecessary if you need only a few functions from a particular file.

To address this problem, the SelfLoader module delays compilation of each subroutine until that subroutine is actually called. SelfLoader is easy to use: just place your module's subroutines underneath the __DATA__ marker so the compiler will ignore them, use a require to pull in the SelfLoader, and include SelfLoader in the module's @ISA array. That's all there is to it. When your module is loaded, the SelfLoader creates stub functions for all routines below __DATA__. The first time a function gets called, the stub replaces itself by first compiling the real function and then calling it.

There is one significant restriction on modules that employ the SelfLoader (or the AutoLoader for that matter, described in Recipe 12.11). SelfLoaded or AutoLoaded subroutines have no access to lexical variables in the file whose __DATA__ block they are in because they are compiled via eval in an imported AUTOLOAD block. Such dynamically generated subroutines are therefore compiled in the scope of Self-Loader's or AutoLoader's AUTOLOAD.

Whether the SelfLoader helps or hinders performance depends on how many subroutines the module has, how large they are, and whether they are all called over the lifetime of the program or not.

You should initially develop and test your module without SelfLoader. Commenting out the __DATA__ line will take care of that, making those functions visible to the compiler.

See Also

The documentation for the standard module SelfLoader; Recipe 12.11

12.11 Speeding Up Module Loading
with Autoloader

Problem

You want to use the AutoLoader module.

Solution

The easiest solution is to use the *h2xs* facility to create a directory and all the files you need. Here we assume you have your own directory, *~/perllib/*, which contains your personal library modules.

```
% h2xs -Xn Sample
% cd Sample
% perl Makefile.PL LIB=~/perllib
% (edit Sample.pm)
% make install
```

Discussion

The AutoLoader addresses the same performance issues as the SelfLoader. It also provides stub functions that get replaced by real ones the first time they're called. But instead of looking for functions all in the same file, hidden below a __DATA__ marker, the AutoLoader expects to find the real definition for each function in its own file. If your *Sample.pm* module had two functions, foo and bar, then the AutoLoader would expect to find them in *Sample/auto/foo.al* and *Sample/auto/bar.al*, respectively. Modules employing the AutoLoader load faster than those using the SelfLoader, but at the cost of extra files, disk space, and complexity.

This setup sounds complicated. If you were doing it manually, it probably would be. Fortunately, *h2xs* helps out tremendously here. Besides creating a module directory with templates for your *Sample.pm* file and other files you need, it also generates a Makefile that uses the AutoSplit module to break your module's functions into little files, one function per file. The make install rule installs these so they will be found automatically. All you have to do is put the module functions down below an __END__ line (rather than a __DATA__ line as in SelfLoader) that *h2xs* already created.

As with the SelfLoader, it's easier to develop and test your module without the Auto-Loader. Just comment out the __END__ line while developing it.

The same restrictions about invisibility of file lexicals that apply to modules using the SelfLoader also apply when using the AutoLoader, so using file lexicals to maintain private state doesn't work. If state is becoming that complex and significant an issue, consider writing an object module instead of a traditional one.

See Also

The documentation for the standard module AutoLoader; *h2xs*(1); Recipe 12.10

12.12 Overriding Built-in Functions

Problem

You want to replace a standard, built-in function with your own version.

Solution

Import that function from another module into your own namespace.

Discussion

Suppose you want to give a function of your own the same name as one of Perl's core built-ins. If you write:

```
sub time { "it's howdy doody time" }
print time( );
```

then you won't get your function called—you'll still get Perl's original, built-in version. You could use an explicit ampersand to call the function:

```
print &time();
```

because that always gets your function, never the built-in. But then you forego any prototype checking and context coercion on the function's arguments. However, there *is* a way to override that.

Many (but not all) of Perl's built-in functions may be overridden. This is not something to be attempted lightly, but it is possible. You might do this, for example, if you are running on a platform that doesn't support the function that you'd like to emulate. Or, you might want to add your own wrapper around the built-in.

Not all reserved words have the same status. Those that return a negative number in the C-language keyword( ) function in the *toke.c* file in your Perl source kit may be overridden. Keywords that cannot be overridden as of v5.8.1 are defined, delete, do, else, elsif, eval, exists, for, foreach, format, glob, goto, grep, if, last, local, m, map, my, next, no, our, package, pos, print, printf, prototype, q, qq, qr, qw, qx, redo, require, return, s, scalar, sort, split, study, sub, tie, tied, tr, undef, unless, untie, until, use, while, and y. The rest can.

A standard Perl module that overrides a built-in is Cwd, which can overload chdir. Others are the by-name versions of functions that return lists: File::stat, Net::hostent, Net::netent, Net::protoent, Net::servent, Time::gmtime, Time::localtime, Time::tm, User::grent, and User::pwent. These modules all override built-in functions like stat or getpwnam to return an object that can be accessed using a name, like getpwnam("daemon")->dir. To do this, they have to override the original, list-returning versions of those functions.

Overriding may be done uniquely by importing the function from another package. This import only takes effect in the importing package, not in all possible packages. It's not enough simply to predeclare the function. You have to import it. This is a guard against accidentally redefining built-ins.

Let's say that you'd like to replace the built-in time function, whose return value is in integer seconds, with one that returns a floating-point number instead. You could make a Time::HiRes module with an optionally exported time function as follows:

```
package Time::HiRes;
use strict;
require Exporter;
use vars qw(@ISA @EXPORT_OK);
@ISA = qw(Exporter);
@EXPORT_OK = qw(time);

sub time() { ..... }   # TBA
```

Then the user who wants to use this augmented version of time would say something like:

```
use Time::HiRes qw(time);
$start = time();
1 while print time() - $start, "\n";
```

This code assumes that your system has a function you can stick in the "TBA" definition shown previously. It just so happens, however, that you don't have to figure that part out, because the Time::HiRes module (which is included standard with the Perl distribution) does indeed behave as we've outlined it here. You can import its time() function to get the one that is fancier than the core built-in, just as we did here.

If you don't want to take the trouble to create a full module file, set up its exports, and all the rest of the rigamarole, there's a shortcut approach via the subs pragma. It works like this:

```
use subs qw(time);
sub time { "it's howdy doody time" }
print time();
```

Now you'd get your own function, even without the ampersand.

Even when you override a built-in by importing a function, that built-in is always still accessible if you fully qualify it using the (pseudo)package named CORE. Thus, even if you imported time() from FineTime, overriding the built-in, that original built-in can be called as CORE::time().

For overriding of methods and operators, see Chapter 13.

See Also

The section on "Overriding Built-in Functions" in Chapter 11 of *Programming Perl* and in *perlsub*(1); Recipe 10.11

12.13 Overriding a Built-in Function in All Packages

Problem

You want to change the definition of a core built-in function within your entire program, not just the current package.

Solution

Manually import, via direct symbol-table manipulation, the function into the CORE::GLOBAL pseudopackage.

```
*CORE::GLOBAL::int = \&myown_int;
```

Discussion

The technique demonstrated in the previous recipe only overrides a built-in in a particular package. It doesn't change everything for your whole program, no matter what package that function is called from. To do so would risk changing the behavior of code from modules you didn't write, and which were therefore not prepared for the change.

It has been said that Unix was not designed to stop you from doing stupid things, because that would also stop you from doing clever things. So, too, with Perl. Just because overriding a function in all packages at once might seem, well, imprudent doesn't mean a clever person won't someday find a marvelous use for such a facility.

For example, let's suppose that you've decided that the core int function's behavior of integer truncation, also known as rounding toward zero, is so annoying to your program that you want to provide an alternative by the same name. This would do it:

```perl
package Math::Rounding;
use warnings;
use Carp;
use Exporter;
our @EXPORT = qw(int);
our @ISA    = qw(Exporter);

sub int(;$) {
    my $arg = @_ ? shift : $_;
    use warnings FATAL => "numeric";  # promote to die()ing
    my $result = eval { sprintf("%.0f", $arg) };
    if ($@) {
        die if $@ !~ /isn't numeric/;
        $@ =~ s/ in sprintf.*/ in replacement int/s;
        croak $@;
    } else {
        return $result;
    }
}
```

Your replacement version uses sprintf( ) to round to the closest integer. It also raises an exception if passed a non-numeric string. A program could access this function either by saying:

```perl
use Math::Rounding ();
$y = Math::Rounding::int($x);
```

or by importing the function and overriding the built-in:

```perl
use Math::Rounding qw(int);
$y = int($x);
```

However, that only manages to replace the built-in for the current package. To replace it in all packages, at some point during compile time you'll have to execute a line of code like this:

```perl
*CORE::GLOBAL::int = \&Math::Rounding::int;
```

The standard File::Glob module allows you to change Perl's core glob operator using special import tags:

```
## override the core glob, forcing case sensitivity
use File::Glob qw(:globally :case);
my @sources = <*.{c,h,y}>

## override the core glob forcing case insensitivity
use File::Glob qw(:globally :nocase);
my @sources = <*.{c,h,y}>
```

The module does this with its own version of import that detects those tags and makes the necessary assignments. You could do this, too. That way, this:

```
use Math::Rounding qw(-global int);
```

would make Perl use your replacement version for all calls to int from any package anywhere in your program. Here's a replacement import function that handles this:

```
sub import {
    if (@_ && $_[1] =~ /^-/) {
        if ($_[1] ne "-global") {
            croak "unknown import pragma";
        }
        splice(@_, 1, 1);              # discard "-global"
        no warnings "once";     # suppress "used only once" warnings
        *CORE::GLOBAL::int = \&int;
    } else {
        die;
    }
    __PACKAGE__ -> export_to_level(1, @_);
}
```

The assignment happens only if the first thing to import is "-global". The last line in our import function uses part of the Exporter module's internal API to handle any normal import.

See Also

Recipe 12.12; the section on "Overriding Built-in Functions" in Chapter 11 of *Programming Perl* and in *perlsub*(1); the documentation for the standard BSD::Glob module, as well as its source code

12.14 Reporting Errors and Warnings Like Built-ins

Problem

You want to generate errors and warnings in your modules, but when you use warn or die, the user sees your own filename and line number. You'd like your functions to act like built-ins and report messages from the perspective of the user's code, not your own.

Solution

The standard Carp module provides functions to do this. Use carp instead of warn. Use croak (for a short message) and confess (for a long message) instead of die.

Discussion

Like built-ins, some of your module's functions generate warnings or errors if all doesn't go well. Think about sqrt: when you pass it a negative number (and you haven't used the Math::Complex module), an exception is raised, producing a message such as "Can't take sqrt of -3 at /tmp/negroot line 17", where */tmp/negroot* is the name of your own program. But if you write your own function that dies, perhaps like this:

```
sub even_only {
    my $n = shift;
    die "$n is not even" if $n & 1;  # one way to test
    #....
}
```

then the message will say it's coming from the file your even_only function was itself compiled in, rather than from the file the user was in when they called your function. That's where the Carp module comes in handy. Instead of using die, use croak instead:

```
use Carp;
sub even_only {
    my $n = shift;
    croak "$n is not even" if $n % 2;  # here's another
    #....
}
```

If you just want to complain about something, but have the message report where in the user's code the problem occurred, call carp instead of warn. For example:

```
use Carp;
sub even_only {
    my $n = shift;
    if ($n & 1) {           # test whether odd number
        carp "$n is not even, continuing";
        ++$n;
    }
    #....
}
```

Many built-ins emit warnings only when the **-w** command-line switch has been used. The $^W variable (which is not meant to be a control character but rather a ^ followed by a W) reflects whether that switch was used. You could choose to grouse only if the user asked for complaints:

```
carp "$n is not even, continuing" if $^W;
```

The Carp module provides a third function: confess. This works just like croak, except that it provides a full stack backtrace as it dies, reporting who called whom and with what arguments.

If you're only interested in the error message from carp, croak, and friends, the longmess and shortmess functions offer those:

```
use Carp;
$self->transplant_organ() or
    $self->error( Carp::longmess("Unable to transplant organ") );
```

See Also

The warn and die functions in Chapter 29 of *Programming Perl* and in *perlfunc*(1); the documentation for the standard Carp module, also in Chapter 32 of *Programming Perl*; Recipe 19.2; the discussion on __WARN__ and __DIE__ in the %SIG entry of Chapter 28 of *Programming Perl*, in *perlvar*(1), and in Recipe 16.15

12.15 Customizing Warnings

Problem

You would like your module to respect its caller's settings for lexical warnings, but you can't inspect the predefined $^W* variable to determine those settings.

Solution

Your module should use this pragma:

```
use warnings::register;
```

Then from inside your module, use the warnings::enabled function from that module as described in the Discussion to check whether the caller has warnings enabled. This works for both the old-style, global warnings and for lexical warnings set via the use warnings pragma.

Discussion

Perl's **-w** command-line flag, mirrored by the global $^W variable, suffers from several problems. For one thing, it's an all-or-nothing affair, so if you turn it on for the program, module code included by that program—including code you may not have written—is also affected by it. For another, it's at best cumbersome to control com-

---

* That's $WARNING if you've used English.

pile-time warnings with it, forcing you to resort to convoluted BEGIN blocks. Finally, suppose you were interested in numeric warnings but not any other sort; you'd have to write a $SIG{__WARN__} handler to sift through all warnings to find those you did or did not want to see.

Lexical warnings, first introduced in Perl v5.6, address all this and more. By lexical, we mean that their effects are constrained to the lexical scope in which use warnings or no warnings occurs. Lexical warnings pay no attention to the **-w** command-line switch. Now when you turn warnings on in one scope, such as the main program's file scope, that doesn't enable warnings in modules you load. You can also selectively enable or disable individual categories of warnings. For example:

```
use warnings qw(numeric uninitialized);

use warnings qw(all);
no warnings qw(syntax);
```

The warnings::register pragma permits a module to check the warnings preferences of its caller's lexical scope. The pragma also creates a new warning category, taken from the name of the current package. These user-defined warning categories are easily distinguishable from the built-in warning categories because a module's package always starts (or *should* always start) with an uppercase letter. This way lowercase warning categories, like lowercase module names, are reserved to Perl itself.

Built-in warnings categories are organized into several groups. The all category means all built-in warnings categories, including subcategories such as unsafe, io, syntax, etc. (see Figure 12-1). The syntax category comprises particular warnings categories, such as ambiguous, precedence, and deprecated. These can be added and subtracted at will, but order matters:

```
use warnings;              # turn on all warnings
no  warnings "syntax";     # turn off the syntax group
use warnings "deprecated"; # but turn back on deprecated warnings
```

Back to your module. Suppose you write a module called Whiskey. The *Whiskey.pm* file begins this way:

```
package Whiskey;
use warnings::register;
```

Now code using that module does this:

```
use Whiskey;
use warnings qw(Whiskey);
```

It's important to load the module before asking to use warnings for that module. Otherwise, the Whiskey warning category hasn't been registered yet, and you'll raise an exception if you try to use it as a warnings category.

Here's a whimsical Whiskey module:

```
package Whiskey;

use strict;
```

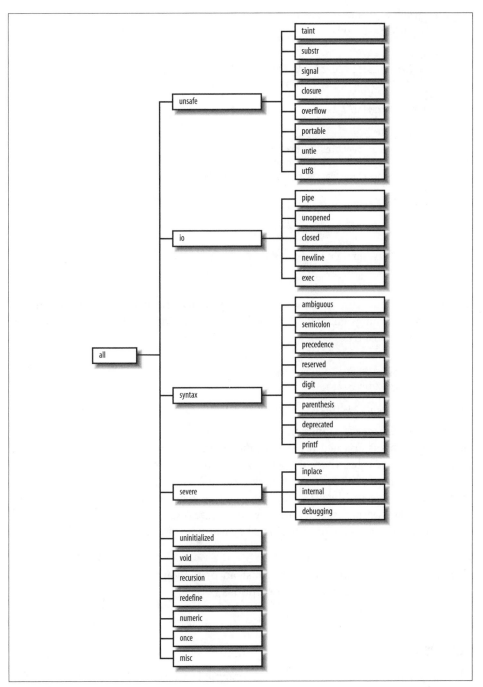

Figure 12-1. Warnings categories

```
use warnings;  # for our own code, not our caller
use warnings::register;

sub drink {
    if (warnings::enabled() && (localtime())[2] < 12) {
        warnings:warn("Sun not yet over the yardarm");
    }
    print "Merry!\n";
}
sub quaff {
    if (warnings::enabled("deprecated")) {
        warnings::warn("deprecated",
            "quaffing deprecated in favor of chugging");
    }
    &drink;
}
# chuggers care not of the hour
sub chug {
    print "Very merry\n";
}
1;
```

The Whiskey::drink function uses the warnings::enabled function to check whether its caller has warnings enabled. Any of these in the caller's scope is enough to make that function return true:

```
use warnings;
use warnings qw(all);  # means same as previous
use warnings qw(Whiskey);
```

The function will also return true if global warnings are enabled using **-w** or $^W.

In the Whiskey::quaff function, a specific category of warnings is checked: deprecated. This is enabled if all warnings have been selected, if the syntax warnings have been selected (because deprecated warnings are considered a subcategory of syntax warnings, which is a subcategory of all warnings), or if deprecated warnings have been specifically selected. It will not be enabled just because the caller has enabled Whiskey warnings. Any category you create is considered a subcategory of all, but not of anything else. Check for Whiskey warnings using:

```
warnings::enabled("Whiskey")
```

The warnings::warn function is used instead of the warn built-in, in case Whiskey warnings have been promoted into exceptions:

```
use warnings FATAL => "Whiskey";
```

See Also

The documentation on the use warnings pragma in Chapter 31 of *Programming Perl* and *perllexwarn*(1)

12.16 Referring to Packages Indirectly

Problem

You want to refer to a variable or function in a package unknown until runtime, but syntax like $packname::$varname is illegal.

Solution

Use symbolic references:

```
{
    no strict "refs";
    $val  = ${ $packname . "::" . $varname };
    @vals = @{ $packname . "::" . $aryname };
    &{ $packname . "::" . $funcname }("args");
    ($packname . "::" . $funcname) -> ("args");
}
```

Discussion

A package declaration has meaning at compile time. If you don't know the name of the package or variable until runtime, you'll have to resort to symbolic references for direct access to the package symbol table. Assuming you normally run with use strict in effect, you must disable part of it to use symbolic references. Once you've used the no strict "refs" directive in that block, build up a string with the fully qualified name of the variable or function you're interested in. Then dereference this name as though it were a proper Perl reference.

During the prehistoric eras (before Perl 5), programmers were forced to use an eval for this kind of thing:

```
eval "package $packname; \$'$val = \$$varname"; # set $main'val
die if $@;
```

As you see, this approach makes quoting difficult. It's also comparatively slow. Fortunately, you never need to do this just to access variables indirectly by name. Symbolic references are a necessary compromise.

Similarly, eval could be used to define functions on the fly. Suppose you wanted to be able to get the base 2 or base 10 logs of numbers:

```
printf "log2  of 100 is %.2f\n", log2(100);
printf "log10 of 100 is %.2f\n", log10(100);
```

Perl has only the natural log function. Here's how one could use eval to create these functions at runtime. Here we'll create functions named log2 up through log999:

```
$packname = "main";
for ($i = 2; $i < 1000; $i++) {
    $logN = log($i);
```

```
eval "sub ${packname}::log$i { log(shift) / $logN }";
die if $@;
}
```

Here, at least, you don't need to do that. The following code does the same thing, but instead of compiling a new function 998 times, we compile it only once, as a closure. Then we use symbolic dereferencing of the symbol table to assign the same subroutine reference to many function names:

```
$packname = "main";
for ($i = 2; $i < 1000; $i++) {
    my $logN = log($i);
    no strict "refs";
    *{"${packname}::log$i"} = sub { log(shift) / $logN };
}
```

When you assign a reference to a typeglob, you create an alias for just the referent type of that name. That's how the Exporter does its job. The first line in the next code sample manually imports the function name Colors::blue into the current package. The second makes the main::blue function an alias for the Colors::azure function.

```
*blue      = \&Colors::blue;
*main::blue = \&Colors::azure;
```

Given the flexibility of typeglob assignments and symbolic references, a full-blown eval "STRING" is nearly always unnecessary for these sorts of indirect namespace manipulation, the last resort of the desperate programmer. The only thing worse would be if it weren't available at all.

See Also

The section on "Symbolic References" in Chapter 8 of *Programming Perl* and in the start of *perlsub*(1); Recipe 11.4

12.17 Using h2ph to Translate C #include Files

Problem

Someone gave you code that generates the bizarre error message:

```
Can't locate sys/syscall.ph in @INC (did you run h2ph?)
(@INC contains: /usr/lib/perl5/i686-linux/5.00404 /usr/lib/perl5
/usr/lib/perl5/site_perl/i686-linux /usr/lib/perl5/site_perl .)
at some_program line 7.
```

You want to know what it means and how to fix it.

Solution

Get your system administrator to do this, running as the superuser:

```
% cd /usr/include; h2ph sys/syscall.h
```

However, most include files require other include files, which means you should probably just translate them all:

```
% cd /usr/include; h2ph *.h */*.h
```

If that reports too many filenames or misses some that are more deeply nested, try this instead:

```
% cd /usr/include; find . -name "*.h" -print | xargs h2ph
```

Discussion

A file whose name ends in .ph has been created by the *h2ph* tool, which translates C preprocessor directives from C #include files into Perl. The goal is to allow Perl code to access the same constants as C code. *h2xs* is a better approach in most cases because it provides compiled C code for your modules, not Perl code simulating C code. However, using *h2xs* requires a lot more programming savvy (at least, for accessing C code) than *h2ph* does.

When *h2ph*'s translation process works, it's wonderful. When it doesn't, you're probably out of luck. As system architectures and include files become more complex, *h2ph* fails more frequently. If you're lucky, the constants you need are already in the Fcntl, Socket, or POSIX modules. The POSIX module implements constants from *sys/file.h*, *sys/errno.h*, and *sys/wait.h*, among others. It also allows fancy tty handling, as described in Recipe 15.8.

So what can you do with these .ph files? Here are a few examples. The first uses the pessimally non-portable syscall function to access your operating system's gettimeofday syscall. This implements the FineTime module described in Recipe 12.12.

```
# file FineTime.pm
package main;
require "sys/syscall.ph";
die "No SYS_gettimeofday in sys/syscall.ph"
    unless defined &SYS_gettimeofday;

package FineTime;
use strict;
require Exporter;
use vars qw(@ISA @EXPORT_OK);
@ISA = qw(Exporter);
@EXPORT_OK = qw(time);

sub time( ) {
    my $tv = pack("LL", ( ));  # presize buffer to two longs
    syscall(&main::SYS_gettimeofday, $tv, undef) >= 0
        or die "gettimeofday: $!";
    my($seconds, $microseconds) = unpack("LL", $tv);
    return $seconds + ($microseconds / 1_000_000);
}

1;
```

If you are forced to require an old-style *.pl* or *.ph* file, do so from the main package (package main in the preceding code). These old libraries always put their symbols in the current package, and main serves as a reasonable rendezvous point. To use a symbol, use its fully qualified name, as we did with main::SYS_gettimeofday.

The *sys/ioctl.ph* file, if you can get it to build on your system, is the gateway to your system's idiosyncratic I/O functions through the ioctl function. One such function is the TIOCSTI ioctl, shown in Example 12-1. That abbreviation stands for "terminal I/O control, simulate terminal input." On systems that implement this function, it will push one character into your device stream so that the next time any process reads from that device, it gets the character you put there.

Example 12-1. jam

```
#!/usr/bin/perl -w
# jam - stuff characters down STDIN's throat
require "sys/ioctl.ph";
die "no TIOCSTI" unless defined &TIOCSTI;
sub jam {
    local $SIG{TTOU} = "IGNORE"; # "Stopped for tty output"
    local *TTY;  # make local filehandle
    open(TTY, "+<", "/dev/tty")              or die "no tty: $!";
    for (split(//, $_[0])) {
        ioctl(TTY, &TIOCSTI, $_)             or die "bad TIOCSTI: $!";
    }
    close(TTY);
}
jam("@ARGV\n");
```

Since *sys/ioctl.h* translation is so dodgy, you'll probably have to run this C program to get your TIOCSTI value:

```
% cat > tio.c << EOF && cc tio.c && a.out
#include <sys/ioctl.h>
main() { printf("%#08x\n", TIOCSTI); }
EOF
0x005412
```

Another popular use for ioctl is for figuring out your current window size in rows and columns, and maybe even in pixels. This is shown in Example 12-2.

Example 12-2. winsz

```
#!/usr/bin/perl
# winsz - find x and y for chars and pixels
require "sys/ioctl.ph";
die "no TIOCGWINSZ " unless defined &TIOCGWINSZ;
open(TTY, "+<", "/dev/tty")                  or die "No tty: $!";
unless (ioctl(TTY, &TIOCGWINSZ, $winsize="")) {
    die sprintf "$0: ioctl TIOCGWINSZ (%08x: $!)\n", &TIOCGWINSZ;
}
($row, $col, $xpixel, $ypixel) = unpack("S4", $winsize);
print "(row,col) = ($row,$col)";
```

Example 12-2. winsz (continued)

```
print "  (xpixel,ypixel) = ($xpixel,$ypixel)" if $xpixel || $ypixel;
print "\n";
```

As you see, as soon as you start playing with *.ph* files, unpacking binary data, and calling syscall and ioctl, you need to know about the C APIs that Perl normally hides. The only other thing that requires this much C knowledge is using the XS interface. Some suggest you should resist the temptation to descend into such unportable convolutions. Others feel that the demands put upon the trenchworkers are such that they must be forgiven these desperate measures.

Fortunately, less fragile mechanisms are increasingly available. CPAN modules for most of these functions now exist, which should theoretically prove more robust than sourcing *.ph* files.

See Also

h2ph(1); the instructions on running *h2ph* in the *INSTALL* file from the Perl source distribution; the syscall and ioctl functions in Chapter 29 of *Programming Perl* and in *perlmod*(1); Recipe 12.18

12.18 Using h2xs to Make a Module with C Code

Problem

You'd like to access your system's unique C functions from Perl.

Solution

Use the *h2xs* tool to generate the necessary template files, fill the files in appropriately, and then type:

```
% perl Makefile.PL
% make
```

Discussion

A Perl module need not be written solely in Perl. As with any other module, first pick a module name and use *h2xs* on it. We'll make a FineTime::time function with the same semantics as in the previous recipe, but this time around, we'll implement it using real C.

First, we run the following command:

```
% h2xs -cn FineTime
```

If we had a *.h* file with function prototype declarations, we could include that, but because we're writing this one from scratch, we'll use the **-c** switch to omit building code to translate any #define symbols. The **-n** switch says to create a module directory named *FineTime/*, which will have the following files:

Manifest	List of files in the distribution
Changes	Change log
Makefile.PL	A meta-makefile
FineTime.pm	The Perl parts
FineTime.xs	The soon-to-be C parts
test.pl	A test driver

Before we can type make, we'll have to generate a *Makefile* based on our system's configuration using the *Makefile.PL* template. Here's how to do that:

```
% perl Makefile.PL
```

If the XS code calls library code that isn't in the normal set of libraries Perl links from, add one more line to *Makefile.PL* first. For example, if we wanted to link against the *librpm.a* library, which lives in the */usr/redhat/lib* directory, we'd change the line of *Makefile.PL* that reads:

```
"LIBS"      => [""],   # e.g., "-lm"
```

so that it says:

```
"LIBS"      => ["-L/usr/redhat/lib -lrpm"],
```

If the module is to be installed somewhere other than the local *site_lib* directory, specify that on the command line:

```
% perl Makefile.PL LIB=~/perllib
```

Finally, edit the *FineTime.pm* and *FineTime.xs* files. In the first case, most of the work has been done for us. We just set up the export list with the function to be exported. This time we put it in @EXPORT_OK so that if the user wants the function, they must ask for it by name. Here's *FineTime.pm*:

```
package FineTime;
use strict;
use vars qw($VERSION @ISA @EXPORT_OK);
require Exporter;
require DynaLoader;
@ISA = qw(Exporter DynaLoader);
@EXPORT_OK = qw(time);
$VERSION = "0.01";
bootstrap FineTime $VERSION;
1;
```

The *make* process automatically translates *FineTime.xs* into a *FineTime.c* file and eventually into a shared library, probably called *FineTime.so* on most platforms. The utility that does this translation is *xsubpp*, which is described in its own manpage and *perlxstut*(1). The build will call *xsubpp* automatically.

Besides a strong C background, you also need to understand the C-to-Perl interface, called XS (external subroutine). The details and nuances of XS are beyond the scope of this book. The automatically generated *FineTime.xs* had the Perl-specific include files in it, as well as the MODULE declaration. We've added some extra includes and written the code for the new `time` function. Although this doesn't look entirely like C, it will, once *xsubpp* is done with it.

Here's the *FineTime.xs* we used:

```
#include <unistd.h>
#include <sys/time.h>
#include "EXTERN.h"
#include "perl.h"
#include "XSUB.h"

MODULE = FineTime          PACKAGE = FineTime

double
time()
    CODE:
        struct timeval tv;
        gettimeofday(&tv,0);
        RETVAL = tv.tv_sec + ((double) tv.tv_usec) / 1000000;
    OUTPUT:
        RETVAL
```

Defining a function by the same name as one from the standard C library won't cause a problem when it's compiled, because that's not its real name. That's just what Perl calls it. The C linker will see it as `XS_FineTime_time`, so no conflict exists.

Here's what happened with make install (with some edits):

```
% make install
mkdir ./blib/lib/auto/FineTime
cp FineTime.pm ./blib/lib/FineTime.pm
/usr/local/bin/perl -I/usr/lib/perl5/i686-linux/5.00403  -I/usr/lib/perl5
/usr/lib/perl5/ExtUtils/xsubpp -typemap
        /usr/lib/perl5/ExtUtils/typemap FineTime.xs
FineTime.tc && mv FineTime.tc FineTime.c && cc -c -Dbool=char -DHAS_BOOL
    -O2 -DVERSION=\"0.01\" -DXS_VERSION=\"0.01\" -fpic
    -I/usr/lib/perl5/i686-linux/5.00403/CORE  FineTime.c
Running Mkbootstrap for FineTime ()
chmod 644 FineTime.bs
LD_RUN_PATH="" cc -o blib/arch/auto/FineTime/FineTime.so
    -shared -L/usr/local/lib FineTime.o
chmod 755 blib/arch/auto/FineTime/FineTime.so
cp FineTime.bs ./blib/arch/auto/FineTime/FineTime.bs
chmod 644 blib/arch/auto/FineTime/FineTime.bs
Installing /home/tchrist/perllib/i686-linux/./auto/FineTime/FineTime.so
Installing /home/tchrist/perllib/i686-linux/./auto/FineTime/FineTime.bs
Installing /home/tchrist/perllib/./FineTime.pm
Writing /home/tchrist/perllib/i686-linux/auto/FineTime/.packlist
Appending installation info to /home/tchrist/perllib/i686-linux/perllocal.pod
```

Once this is all done, we'll be able to type something like this into the shell:

```
% perl -I ~/perllib -MFineTime=time -le "1 while print time()" | head
888177070.090978
```

```
888177070.09132
888177070.091389
888177070.091453
888177070.091515
888177070.091577
888177070.091639
888177070.0917
888177070.091763
888177070.091864
```

See Also

Chapters 18 through 20 in *Advanced Perl Programming*; *perlxstut*(1) and *perlxs*(1) to learn how to call C from Perl; *perlcall*(1) and *perlguts*(1) to understand the internal Perl API, also the "Extending Perl" section of Chapter 21 of *Programming Perl*; *perlembed*(1) to learn how to call Perl from C, also the "Embedding Perl" section of Chapter 21 of *Programming Perl*; the documentation for the standard ExtUtils:: MakeMaker module, *h2ph*(1) and *xsubpp*(1); *http://www.cpan.org/authors/Dean_Roehrich/*, which contains Dean's comprehensive XS cookbook that includes directions on interfacing with C++

12.19 Writing Extensions in C with Inline::C

Problem

You'd like to write functions in C that you can call from Perl. You may already have tried XS and found it harmful to your mental health.

Solution

Use the Inline::C module available from CPAN:

```
use Inline C;
$answer = somefunc(20, 4);
print "$answer\n";                    # prints 80
__END__
__C__
double somefunc(int a, int b) {   /* Inline knows most basic C types */
  double answer = a * b;
  return answer;
}
```

Discussion

Inline::C was created as an alternative to the XS system for building C extension modules. Rather than jumping through all the hoopla of *h2xs* and the format of an *.xs* file, Inline::C lets you embed C code into your Perl program. There are also Inline modules for Python, Ruby, and Java, among other languages.

By default, your C source is in the __END__ or __DATA__ section of your program after a __C__ token. This permits multiple Inlined language blocks in a single file. If you want, use a here document when you load Inline:

```
use Inline C <<'END_OF_C';
double somefunc(int a, int b) {   /* Inline knows most basic C types */
  double answer = a * b;
  return answer;
}
END_OF_C
```

Inline::C scans the source code for ANSI-style function definitions. When it finds a function definition it knows how to deal with, it creates a Perl wrapper for the function. Inline can automatically translate the basic C data types (double, int, char *, etc.) by using the *typemap* that comes with Perl. A typemap shows Perl how to convert between C values and Perl data types, and you can install your own if you need to use more complex data structures than the basic typemap supports.

You can link against external libraries, parse header files as *h2xs* does, pass and return multiple values, handle objects, and more. See the *Inline::C-Cookbook* manpage that comes with the Inline::C module for more details.

See Also

The documentation with the Inline::C module from CPAN; the *Inline::C-Cookbook* manpage

12.20 Documenting Your Module with Pod

Problem

You need to document your module, but don't know what format to use.

Solution

Embed your documentation in the your module file using pod format.

Discussion

Pod stands for *plain old documentation*. It's documentation embedded in your program using a very simple markup format. Programmers are notorious for writing the code first and the documentation never, so pod was designed to make writing documentation so easy that anyone can and will do so. Sometimes this even works.

When Perl is parsing your source code, a line starting with an equals sign (where a new statement is expected) says to ignore all text until it finds a line beginning with =cut, after which it will start parsing code again. This lets you mix code and documentation throughout your Perl program or module file. Since it's mostly plain text, type in your documentation as literal text, or nearly so. The translators try to be clever and make output-specific decisions so the programmer doesn't have to specifically format variable names, function calls, etc.

Perl ships with several translators that filter generic pod format into specific output styles. These include *pod2man* to change your pods into *troff* for use with the *man* program or for phototypesetting and printing; *pod2html* for creating web pages (which works even on non-Unix systems); and *pod2text* for plain ASCII. Other translators, such as *pod2ipf*, *pod2fm*, *pod2texi*, *pod2latex*, and *pod2ps*, may also be available or can be found on CPAN.

Many books are written using proprietary word processors with limited scripting capabilities. Not this one! It was written in pod format using common text editors (*vi* for Tom, *emacs* for Nat). The final book was produced by converting the pod source files to FrameMaker.

Although formally documented in *perlpod*(1), pod is probably easiest to learn by reading existing module files. If you started making your module using *h2xs*, then you already have the sample pods right there. The *Makefile* knows to convert these into *man* format and install those manpages so others can read them. Alternatively, the *perldoc* program can translate pods on the fly using *pod2text*.

Indented paragraphs will be left verbatim. Other paragraphs will be reformatted to fit the page. Only two kinds of markups are used in pod: paragraphs beginning with an equals sign and one or more words, and interior sequences starting with a single letter followed by text enclosed in angle brackets. Paragraph tags are for headers, list enumeration, and per-translator escapes. Angle bracket sequences are mainly used for font changes, such as selecting bold, italic, or constant-width fonts. Here's an example of an =head2 pod directive and various bracket escapes for font changes:

```
=head2 Discussion

If we had a I<.h> file with function prototype declarations, we
could include that, but since we're writing this one from scratch,
we'll use the B<-c> flag to omit building code to translate any
#define symbols.  The B<-n> flag says to create a module directory
named I<FineTime/>, which will have the following files.
```

The =for escape introduces specific code that is only *for* a particular output filter. This book, for example, written mostly in pod, includes calls to the standard *troff* tools *eqn*, *tbl*, and *pic*. Here's an example of embedded *eqn*. Only translators that produce *troff* will heed this paragraph.

```
=for troff
.EQ
log sub n (x) = { {log sub e (x)} over {log sub e (n)} }
.EN
```

Pod can also create multiline comments. In C, the sequence /* .... */ can comment out many lines of text all at once—there's no need to put a marker on each line.

Since Perl ignores pod directives, use these for block commenting. The trick is to find a directive that the pod filters ignore. You could specify that a block is "for later" or "for nobody":

```
=for later
next if 1 .. ?^$?;
s/^(.)/>$1/;
s/(.{73})........*/$1
<SNIP>/;

=cut back to perl
```

or you could use a =begin and =end pair:

```
=begin comment

if (!open(FILE, "<", $file)) {
    unless ($opt_q) {
        warn "$me: $file: $!\n";
        $Errors++;
    }
    next FILE;
}

$total = 0;
$matches = 0;

=end comment
```

See Also

The section on "PODs: Embedded Documentation" in *perlsyn*(1), as well as *perlpod*(1), *pod2man*(1), *pod2html*(1), and *pod2text*(1); Chapter 26 of *Programming Perl*

12.21 Building and Installing a CPAN Module

Problem

You want to install a module file that you downloaded from CPAN over the Net or obtained from a CD.

Solution

Type the following commands into your shell. It will build and install Version 4.54 of the Some::Module package.

```
% gunzip Some-Module-4.54.tar.gz
% tar xf Some-Module-4.54.tar
% cd Some-Module-4.54
```

```
% perl Makefile.PL
% make
% make test
% make install
```

Discussion

Like most programs on the Net, Perl modules are available in source kits stored as *tar* archives in GNU zip format.* If *tar* warns of "Directory checksum errors", then you downloaded the binary file in text format, mutilating it.

You'll probably have to become a privileged user with adequate permissions to install the module in the system directories. Standard modules are installed in a directory like */usr/lib/perl5*, whereas third-party modules are installed in */usr/lib/perl5/site_ perl*.

Here's a sample run, showing the installation of the MD5 module:

```
% gunzip MD5-1.7.tar.gz
% tar xf MD5-1.7.tar
% cd MD5-1.7
% perl Makefile.PL
Checking if your kit is complete...
Looks good
Writing Makefile for MD5
% make
mkdir ./blib
mkdir ./blib/lib
cp MD5.pm ./blib/lib/MD5.pm
AutoSplitting MD5 (./blib/lib/auto/MD5)
/usr/bin/perl -I/usr/local/lib/perl5/i386 ...
...
cp MD5.bs ./blib/arch/auto/MD5/MD5.bs
chmod 644 ./blib/arch/auto/MD5/MD5.bsmkdir ./blib/man3
Manifying ./blib/man3/MD5.3
% make test
PERL_DL_NONLAZY=1 /usr/bin/perl -I./blib/arch -I./blib/lib
-I/usr/local/lib/perl5/i386-freebsd/5.00404 -I/usr/local/lib/perl5 test.pl
1..14
ok 1
ok 2
...
ok 13
ok 14
% sudo make install
Password:
Installing /usr/local/lib/perl5/site_perl/i386-freebsd/./auto/MD5/
    MD5.so
```

---

* This is not the same as the zip format common on Windows machines, but newer version of Windows *winzip* will read it. Prior to Perl 5.005, you'll need the standard port of Perl for Win32, not the ActiveState port, to build CPAN modules. Free versions of *tar* and *gnutar* are also available for Microsoft systems.

```
Installing /usr/local/lib/perl5/site_perl/i386-freebsd/./auto/MD5/
    MD5.bs
Installing /usr/local/lib/perl5/site_perl/./auto/MD5/autosplit.ix
Installing /usr/local/lib/perl5/site_perl/./MD5.pm
Installing /usr/local/lib/perl5/man/man3/./MD5.3
Writing /usr/local/lib/perl5/site_perl/i386-freebsd/auto/MD5/.packlist
Appending installation info to /usr/local/lib/perl5/i386-freebsd/
5.00404/perllocal.pod
```

If your system manager isn't around or can't be prevailed upon to run the installation, don't worry. When you use Perl to generate the Makefile from template *Makefile.PL*, you can specify alternate installation directories.

```
# if you just want the modules installed in your own directory
% perl Makefile.PL LIB=~/lib

# if you have your own complete distribution
% perl Makefile.PL PREFIX=~/perl5-private
```

An even simpler approach is to use the CPAN module from the command line, because it can search for, download, and install the module you need. Suppose you wanted to find the CPAN module Getopt::Declare. All you'd have to do is type:

```
% perl -MCPAN -e "install Getopt::Declare"
```

The first time you use the CPAN module, it will ask you some configuration questions. It saves these away so that when you use it in the future, it won't need to ask you those questions again.

The CPAN module also supports an interactive command shell. This can be used to search for modules whose precise names you're uncertain of, check which CPAN modules have newer versions than you have installed, install bundles of related modules, and various other useful commands.

Here's an example run of the interactive shell.

```
% perl -MCPAN -e shell

cpan shell -- CPAN exploration and modules installation (v1.70)
ReadLine support enabled

cpan> h

Display Information
  command  argument           description
  a,b,d,m  WORD or /REGEXP/   about authors, bundles, distributions, modules
  i        WORD or /REGEXP/   about anything of above
  r        NONE               reinstall recommendations
  ls       AUTHOR             about files in the author's directory

Download, Test, Make, Install...
  get                         download
  make                        make (implies get)
```

```
test     MODULES,        make test (implies make)
install  DISTS, BUNDLES  make install (implies test)
clean                    make clean
look                     open subshell in these dists' directories
readme                   display these dists' README files

Other
h,?          display this menu     ! perl-code  eval a perl command
o conf [opt] set and query options q            quit the cpan shell
reload cpan  load CPAN.pm again    reload index  load newer indices
autobundle   Snapshot              force cmd    unconditionally do cmd

cpan> i /inflect/
CPAN: Storable loaded ok
Going to read /home/tchrist/.cpan/Metadata
  Database was generated on Mon, 07 Apr 2003 22:42:33 GMT
Distribution    D/DC/DCONWAY/Lingua-EN-Inflect-1.88.tar.gz
Module          Lingua::EN::Inflect (D/DC/DCONWAY/Lingua-EN-Inflect-1.88.tar.gz)
2 items found

cpan> install Lingua::EN::Inflect
[build and install output deleted]

cpan> quit
```

The CPAN module is slowly being phased out in favor of CPANPLUS, a module
with similar functionality that is built for flexibility as well as power. The CPAN-
PLUS text interface is similar to that of the CPAN module, but it also offers a GUI
and programmer interfaces, which can access a lot of functionality that the CPAN
module hides.

See Also

The documentation for the standard ExtUtils::MakeMaker module; the INSTALL
file in the Perl source distribution for information on building a statically linked *perl*
binary

12.22 Example: Module Template

Following is the skeleton of a module. If you want to write a module of your own,
you can copy this and customize it.

```
package Some::Module;  # must live in Some/Module.pm

use strict;

require Exporter;

# set the version for version checking
our $VERSION   = 0.01;
```

```
our @ISA         = qw(Exporter);
our @EXPORT      = qw(&func1 &func2 &func4);
our %EXPORT_TAGS = ( );      # eg: TAG => [ qw!name1 name2! ],

# your exported package globals go here,
# as well as any optionally exported functions
our @EXPORT_OK   = qw($Var1 %Hashit &func3);

use vars qw($Var1 %Hashit);
# non-exported package globals go here
our(@more, $stuff);

# initialize package globals, first exported ones
$Var1   = "";
%Hashit = ( );

# then the others (which are still accessible as $Some::Module::stuff)
$stuff  = "";
@more   = ( );

# all file-scoped lexicals must be created before
# the functions below that use them.

# file-private lexicals go here
my $priv_var    = "";
my %secret_hash = ( );

# here's a file-private function as a closure,
# callable as &$priv_func.
my $priv_func = sub {
    # stuff goes here.
};

# make all your functions, whether exported or not;
# remember to put something interesting in the { } stubs
sub func1       { .... }    # no prototype
sub func2()     { .... }    # proto'd void
sub func3($$)   { .... }    # proto'd to 2 scalars

# this one isn't auto-exported, but could be called!
sub func4(\%)   { .... }    # proto'd to 1 hash ref

END { }        # module cleanup code here (global destructor)

1;
```

12.23 Program: Finding Versions and Descriptions of Installed Modules

Perl comes with many modules included standard. Even more can be found on CPAN. The following program prints out the names, versions, and descriptions of all modules installed on your system. It uses standard modules like File::Find and includes several techniques described in this chapter.

To run it, type:

```
% pmdesc
```

It prints a list of modules and their descriptions:

```
FileHandle (2.00) - supply object methods for filehandles
IO::File (1.06021) - supply object methods for filehandles
IO::Select (1.10) - OO interface to the select system call
IO::Socket (1.1603) - Object interface to socket communications
...
```

With the **-v** flag, *pmdesc* provides the names of the directories the files are in:

```
% pmdesc -v

<<<Modules from /usr/lib/perl5/i686-linux/5.00404>>>

FileHandle (2.00) - supply object methods for filehandles
    ...
```

The **-w** flag warns if a module doesn't come with a pod description, and **-s** sorts the module list within each directory.

The program is given in Example 12-3.

Example 12-3. pmdesc

```perl
#!/usr/bin/perl -w
# pmdesc - describe pm files
# tchrist@perl.com

use strict;
use File::Find      qw(find);
use Getopt::Std     qw(getopts);
use Carp;

use vars (
    q!$opt_v!,              # give debug info
    q!$opt_w!,              # warn about missing descs on modules
    q!$opt_a!,              # include relative paths
    q!$opt_s!,              # sort output within each directory
);

$| = 1;

getopts("wvas")            or die "bad usage";

@ARGV = @INC unless @ARGV;

# Globals.  wish I didn't really have to do this.
use vars (
    q!$Start_Dir!,         # The top directory find was called with
```

Example 12-3. pmdesc (continued)

```perl
        q!%Future!,             # topdirs find will handle later
);

my $Module;

# install an output filter to sort my module list, if wanted.
if ($opt_s) {
    if (open(ME, "-|")) {
        $/ = "";
        while (<ME>) {
            chomp;
            print join("\n", sort split /\n/), "\n";
        }
        exit;
    }
}

MAIN: {
    my %visited;
    my ($dev,$ino);

    @Future{@ARGV} = (1) x @ARGV;

    foreach $Start_Dir (@ARGV) {
        delete $Future{$Start_Dir};

        print "\n << Modules from $Start_Dir>>\n\n"
            if $opt_v;

        next unless ($dev,$ino) = stat($Start_Dir);
        next if $visited{$dev,$ino}++;
        next unless $opt_a || $Start_Dir =~ m!^/!;

        find(\&wanted, $Start_Dir);
    }
    exit;
}

# calculate module name from file and directory
sub modname {
    local $_ = $File::Find::name;

    if (index($_, $Start_Dir . "/") == 0) {
        substr($_, 0, 1+length($Start_Dir)) = "";
    }

    s { /              }    {::}gx;
    s { \.p(m|od)$      }    { }x;

    return $_;
}
```

Example 12-3. pmdesc (continued)

```
# decide if this is a module we want
sub wanted {
    if ( $Future{$File::Find::name} ) {
        warn "\t(Skipping $File::Find::name, qui venit in futuro.)\n"
            if 0 and $opt_v;
        $File::Find::prune = 1;
        return;
    }
    return unless /\.pm$/ && -f;
    $Module = &modname;
    # skip obnoxious modules
    if ($Module =~ /^CPAN(\Z|::)/) {
        warn("$Module -- skipping because it misbehaves\n");
        return;
    }

    my    $file = $_;

    unless (open(POD, "<", $file)) {
        warn "\tcannot open $file: $!";
            # if $opt_w;
        return 0;
    }

    $: = " -:";

    local $/ = "";
    local $_;
    while (<POD>) {
        if (/=head\d\s+NAME/) {
            chomp($_ = <POD>);
            s/^.*?-\s+//s;
            s/\n/ /g;
            #write;
            my $v;
            if (defined ($v = getversion($Module))) {
                print "$Module ($v) ";
            } else {
                print "$Module ";
            }
            print "- $_\n";
            return 1;
        }
    }

    warn "\t(MISSING DESC FOR $File::Find::name)\n"
        if $opt_w;

    return 0;
}

# run Perl to load the module and print its version number, redirecting
```

Example 12-3. pmdesc (continued)

```
# errors to /dev/null
sub getversion {
    my $mod = shift;

    my $vers = `$^X -m$mod -e 'print \$${mod}::VERSION' 2>/dev/null`;
    $vers =~ s/^\s*(.*?)\s*$/$1/; # remove stray whitespace
    return ($vers || undef);
}

format = ^<<<<<<<<<<<<<<<<<<<~~^<<<<<<<<<<<<<<<<<<<<<<<<<<<<<<<<<<<<<<<<<<<<<<<<<<<<<
$Module,          $_
.
```

This can also be accomplished through the backend programmer interface in the CPANPLUS module, if you have it installed. This program displays information on all available modules (the **-X** option is to silence any warnings about invalid paths or version numbers):

```
#!/usr/bin/perl -X

use CPANPLUS::Backend;
use Data::Dumper;

$cp = CPANPLUS::Backend->new;
$installed = $cp->installed->rv;            # fetch list of installed mods

foreach my $module (sort keys %$installed) {
  # get the module's information
  $info = $cp->details(modules => [$module])->rv->{$module};
  # display the fields we care about
  printf("%-35.35s %44.44s\n", $module, $info->{Description});
}
```

When run, it outputs a table like this:

```
Algorithm::Cluster            Perl extension for the C clustering library
Algorithm::NaiveBayes                                         None given
AnyDBM_File                   Uses first available *_File module above
Apache                              Interface to the Apache server API
Apache::AuthDBI                                               None given
Apache::Connection                 Inteface to Apache conn_rec struct
```

## CHAPTER 13

Classes, Objects, and Ties

All the world over, I will back
the masses against the classes.
—William E. Gladstone
  Speech at Liverpool, 28 June 1886

13.0 Introduction

Although Perl was not initially conceived of as an object-oriented language, within a few years of its initial release, complete support for object-oriented programming had been added. As usual, Perl doesn't try to enforce one true style, but embraces many. This helps more people do their job the way they want to do it.

You don't have to use objects to write programs, unlike Java, where programs are instances of objects. If you want to, though, you can write Perl programs that use nearly every weapon in the object-oriented arsenal. Perl supports classes and objects, single and multiple inheritance, instance methods and class methods, access to overridden methods, constructors and destructors, operator overloading, proxy methods through autoloading, delegation, a rooted hierarchy for all objects, and two levels of garbage collection.

You can use as many or as few object-oriented techniques as you want and need. Ties are the only part of Perl where you must use object orientation. And even then, only the module implementor need be aware of this; the casual user gets to remain blissfully unaware of the internal mechanics. Ties, discussed in Recipe 13.15, let you transparently intercept access to a variable. For example, you can use ties to create hashes that support lookups by key or value instead of just by key.

Under the Hood

If you ask 10 people what object orientation is, you'll get 10 different answers. People bandy about terms like abstraction and encapsulation, trying to isolate the basic units of object-oriented programming languages and give them big names to write papers and books about. Not all object-oriented languages offer the same features, yet they are still deemed object-oriented. This, of course, produces more papers and books.

We follow the nomenclature used in Perl's documentation, the *perlobj*(1) manpage, and Chapter 12 of *Programming Perl*. An *object* is a variable that belongs to a *class*. *Methods* are functions associated with a class. In Perl, a class is a package—and usually a module. An object is a reference to something associated with a class.

Once associated with a class, something is said to be *blessed* into that class. There's nothing ecclesiastical or spooky going on here. Blessing merely associates a referent with a class, and this is done with the bless function, which takes one or two arguments. The first is a reference to the thing you want associated with the class; the second is the package with which to make that association.

```
$object = {};                        # hash reference
bless($object, "Data::Encoder");     # bless $object into Data::Encoder class
bless($object);                      # bless $object into current package
```

The class name is the package name (Data::Encoder in this example). Because classes are modules (usually), the code for the Data::Encoder class resides in the file *Data/Encoder.pm*. As with traditional modules, the directory structure is purely for convenience; it implies nothing about inheritance, variable sharing, or anything else. Unlike a traditional module, though, an object module seldom if ever uses the Exporter. Access should be through methods only, not imported functions or variables.

Once an object has been blessed, calling the ref function on its reference returns the name of its class instead of the fundamental type of referent:

```
$obj = [3,5];
print ref($obj), " ", $obj->[1], "\n";
bless($obj, "Human::Cannibal");
print ref($obj), " ", $obj->[1], "\n";
```

ARRAY 5
Human::Cannibal 5

As you can see, you can still dereference a reference once it has been blessed. Most frequently, objects are implemented as blessed hash references. You can use any kind of reference you want, but hash references are the most flexible because they allow arbitrarily named data fields in an object.

```
$obj->{Stomach} = "Empty";   # directly accessing an object's contents
$obj->{NAME}    = "Thag";
# uppercase field name to make it stand out (optional)
```

Although Perl permits it, it's considered poor form for code outside the class to directly access the contents of an object. The point of objects, everyone agrees, is to give you an abstract *something* with mediated access through designated methods. This lets the maintainer of the class change its implementation without needing to change all application code that uses the class.

Methods

The whole purpose for blessing—that is, associating a package with a referent—is so that Perl can determine the package namespace in which to find functions when you invoke methods against an object. To invoke a method, use ->. Here, we invoke the encode( ) method of $object with the argument "data" and store the return value in $encoded:

```
$encoded = $object->encode("data");
```

The lefthand operand of the -> operator is said to be the method's *invocant*. Think of the invocant as the entity on whose behalf the method was called. Methods always involve invocants. Here we have an *object method* because we invoke the method on an object. We can also have *class methods* where the invocant is a string representing the package—meaning, of course, the class.

```
$encoded = Data::Encoder->encode("data");
```

Invoking a method calls the function in the corresponding class, implicitly passing its invocant as the initial argument to that function: a reference for object methods, a string for class methods. It isn't always obvious which of the two invocation types you have, because the invocant could be a variable holding a class name instead of one holding a reference that's been blessed.

```
$class = "Animal::" . ($aquatic ? "Fish" : "Mammal");
$beastie = $class->create();
```

That will sometimes invoke the create method from class Animal::Fish and sometimes invoke the create method from class Animal::Mammal. This might even end up being the same underlying function if those two classes share a common ancestral class. Here you don't know the class until runtime. Recipe 13.8 shows how to invoke a method where the method name isn't determined until runtime.

Most classes provide *constructor* methods, which return new objects. Unlike in some object-oriented languages, constructor methods in Perl are not specially named. In fact, you can name them anything you like. C++ programmers have a penchant for naming their constructors in Perl new. We recommend that you name your constructors whatever makes sense in the context of the problem you're solving. For example, constructors in the Tk extension to Perl are named after the widgets they create. A less common approach is to export a function with the same name as the class; see "Example: Overloaded StrNum Class" in Recipe 13.14 for an example.

A typical constructor used as a class method looks like this:

```
sub new {
    my $class = shift;
    my $self  = {};        # allocate new hash for object
    bless($self, $class);
    return $self;
}
```

Call the constructor with:

```
$object = Classname->new();
```

If there isn't any inheritance or other monkey business working behind the scenes, this is effectively the same as:

```
$object = Classname::new("Classname");
```

The new function's first argument here is the name of the class—hence, the package—to bless the new reference into. A constructor should pass that string as the second argument to bless.

Recipe 13.1 also talks about functions that return blessed references. Constructors don't have to be class methods; it's often useful to have object methods that themselves return new objects, as discussed in Recipes 13.6 and 13.7.

A *destructor* is a subroutine that runs when an object's referent is garbage collected, which happens when its internal reference count becomes zero. Because it is invoked implicitly by Perl, unlike a constructor, you have no choice in naming a destructor. You must name your destructor method DESTROY. This method, if it exists, is invoked on an object immediately prior to memory deallocation. Destructors, described in Recipe 13.2, are optional in Perl.

Some languages syntactically allow the compiler to restrict access to a class's methods. Perl does not—it allows code to invoke any method of an object. The author of a class should clearly document the *public* methods (those that may be used), and the user of a class should avoid undocumented (implicitly *private*) methods.

Perl doesn't distinguish between methods that can be invoked on a class (*class methods*) and methods that can be invoked on an object (*instance methods*). If you want a particular method to be invoked as a class method only, do something like this:

```
use Carp;
sub class_only_method {
    my $class = shift;
    croak "class method invoked on object" if ref $class;
    # more code here
}
```

If you want to allow a particular method to be invoked as an instance method only, do something like this:

```
use Carp;
sub instance_only_method {
    my $self = shift;
    croak "instance method invoked on class" unless ref $self;
    # more code here
}
```

If your code invokes an undefined method on an object, Perl won't complain at compile time, but this will trigger an exception at runtime. Methods are just function calls whose package is determined at runtime. Like all indirect functions, they can have no prototype checking, because that happens at compile time. Even if methods were aware of prototypes, in Perl the compiler never checks the precise types or ranges of arguments to functions. Perl prototypes are used to coerce a function argument's context, not to check ranges. Recipe 10.11 details Perl's peculiar perspective on prototypes.

You can prevent Perl from triggering an exception for undefined methods by using the AUTOLOAD mechanism to catch calls to nonexistent methods. We show an application of this in Recipe 13.12.

Inheritance

Inheritance defines a hierarchy of classes. Calls to methods not defined in a class search this hierarchy for a method of that name. The first method found is used. Inheritance means allowing one class to piggyback on top of another so you don't have to write the same code again and again. This is a form of software reuse, and therefore related to Laziness, the principal virtue of a programmer.

Some languages provide special syntax for inheritance. In Perl, each class (package) can put its list of *superclasses* (parents in the hierarchy) into the package variable @ISA. This list is searched at runtime when a method that is not defined in the object's class is invoked. If the first package listed in @ISA doesn't have the method but that package has its own @ISA, Perl looks first in *that* package's own @ISA, recursively, before going on.

If the inheritance search fails, the same check is run again, this time looking for a method named AUTOLOAD. The lookup sequence for $invocant->meth( ), where $invocant is either a package name or a reference to something blessed into that package, is:

- P::meth
- All packages S in @P::ISA, recursively, for any S::meth( )
- UNIVERSAL::meth
- The P::AUTOLOAD subroutine
- All packages S in @P::ISA, recursively, for any S::AUTOLOAD( )
- The UNIVERSAL::AUTOLOAD subroutine

Most classes have just one item in their @ISA array, a situation called *single inheritance*. Classes with more than one element in @ISA represent *multiple inheritance*. The benefits of multiple inheritance are widely contested, but it is supported by Perl.

Recipe 13.10 talks about the basics of inheritance and designing a class so it can be easily subclassed. In Recipe 13.11, we show how a subclass can invoke overridden methods in its superclasses.

Perl doesn't support inheritance of data values. You could say that Perl supports only interface (method) inheritance, not implementation (data) inheritance. A class usually can, but seldom should, touch another's data directly. This violates the envelope and ruins the abstraction. If you follow the advice in Recipe 13.11, this won't be much of an issue.

A Warning on Indirect Object Notation

The *indirect* notation for method invocations:

```
$lector = new Human::Cannibal;
feed $lector "Zak";
move $lector "New York";
```

is an alternative syntax for:

```
$lector = Human::Cannibal->new( );
$lector->feed("Zak");
$lector->move("New York");
```

This indirect object notation is appealing to English speakers and familiar to C++ programmers, who use new this way. However, it suffers from several tricky problems. One is that the construct follows the same quirky rules as the filehandle slot in print and printf:

```
printf STDERR "stuff here\n";
```

This slot, if filled, is limited to a bare symbol, a block, or a scalar variable name; it can't be just any old scalar expression. This can lead to horribly confusing precedence problems, as in these next two lines:

```
move $obj->{FIELD};          # probably wrong
move $ary[$i];               # probably wrong
```

Surprisingly, those actually parse as:

```
$obj->move->{FIELD};         # Surprise!
$ary->move->[$i];            # Surprise!
```

rather than as you might have expected:

```
$obj->{FIELD}->move( );      # Nope, you wish
$ary[$i]->move;              # Nope, you wish
```

As with printf, you can fix this by wrapping the expression in braces to make it a block:

```
move { $obj->{FIELD} };              # These work
move { $ary[$i] };
```

Furthermore, just like print or printf with a filehandle in the indirect object slot, parentheses are optional, and the method invocation becomes a list operator syntactically. Therefore, if you write:

```
move $obj (3 * $position) + 2;
print STDERR (3 * $position) + 2;
```

that will end up being taken to mean:

```
$obj->move(3 * $position) + 2;
STDERR->print(3 * $position) + 2;
```

So you'd need to put in an extra set of parentheses:

```
move $obj ((3 * $position) + 2);
print STDERR ((3 * $position) + 2);
```

The other problem is that Perl must guess at compile time whether name and move are functions or methods. If you write:

```
$obj = new Game;
```

that could, depending on what's in scope and what the compiler has seen, mean any of the following:

```
$obj = new("Game");
$obj = new(Game());
$obj = "Game"->new();
```

of which only the third is the one you want. In fact, even using the infix arrow operator for method invocation has a potential problem. For example:

```
$obj = Game->new();
```

could end up being interpreted as:

```
$obj = Game()->new();
```

under slightly esoteric circumstances: when there's a function in the current package named Game(). Usually Perl gets it right, but when it doesn't, you get a function call compiled as a method invocation, or vice versa. This can introduce incredibly subtle bugs that are hard to unravel.

The surest way to disambiguate this is to put a double-colon after the package (class) name.

```
$obj = new Game::;          # always "Game"->new()
$obj = Game::->new;         # always "Game"->new()
```

Now it doesn't matter whether there is a function named Game or new visible in the current package; you'll always get the method invocation. When you use a package-quoted class like this, the invocant has the double-colon stripped off again when the method is run, as the comments indicate.

To be honest, you can almost always get away using just the bare class name and omitting the ugly trailing double-colon—provided two things are true. First, there must be no subroutine of the same name as the class. (If you follow the convention that subroutine names like new start with a lowercase letter and class names like Game start with an uppercase letter, this is never a problem.) Second, the class needs to have been loaded with one of:

```
use Game;
require Game;
```

Either of these declarations ensures that Perl knows Game is a module name. This forces any bare name like new before the class name Game to be interpreted as a method invocation, even if you happen to have declared a new subroutine of your own in the current package. People don't generally get into trouble with indirect objects unless they start cramming multiple classes into the same file, in which case Perl might not know that a particular package name was supposed to be a class name. People who name subroutines with names that look like ModuleNames also come to grief eventually.

For more information about this, see the sections on "Syntactic Snafus with Indirect Objects" and "Package-Quoted Classes" in Chapter 12 of *Programming Perl*.

Some Notes on Object Terminology

In the object-oriented world, many words describe only a few concepts. If you've programmed in another object-oriented language, you might like to know how familiar terms and concepts map onto Perl.

For example, it's common to refer to objects as *instances* of a class and those objects' methods *instance methods*. Data fields peculiar to each object are often called *instance data* or *object attributes*, and data fields common to all members of that class are *class data*, *class attributes*, or *static data members*.

Also, *base class*, *generic class*, and *superclass* all describe the same notion (a parent or similar ancestor in the inheritance hierarchy), whereas *derived class*, *specific class*, and *subclass* describe the opposite relationship (a child or descendent in the inheritance hierarchy).

C++ programmers have *static methods*, *virtual methods*, and *instance methods*, but Perl only has *class methods* and *object methods*. Actually, Perl only has methods. It accepts any sort of invocant you choose to employ. Whether a method acts as a class or an object method is determined solely by actual usage. You could call a class method (one expecting a string argument) on an object or an object method (one expecting a reference) on a class, but you shouldn't expect reasonable results if you do.

A C++ programmer thinks about global (class) constructors and destructors. These correspond to module initialization code and per-module END{ } blocks, respectively.

From the C++ perspective, all methods in Perl are virtual. This is why their arguments are never checked for function prototypes as the built-in and user-defined functions can be. Prototypes are checked by the compiler at compile time, and you can't determine until runtime the function called by method invocation.

Philosophical Aside

In its OO programming, Perl gives you a lot of freedom: the ability to do things more than one way (you can bless any data type to make an object), to inspect and modify classes you didn't write (adding functions to their packages), and to use these to write tangled pits of misery—if that's really what you want to do.

Less flexible programming languages are usually more restrictive. Many are fanatically devoted to enforced privacy, compile-time type checking, complex function signatures, and a smorgasbord of other features. Perl doesn't provide these things with objects because it doesn't provide them anywhere else, either. Keep this in mind if you find Perl's object-oriented implementation weird. You only think it's weird because you're used to another language's philosophy. Perl's treatment of OO is perfectly sensible—if you think in Perl. For every problem that you can't solve by writing Perl as though it were Java or C++, there is a native Perl solution that works perfectly. The absolutely paranoid programmer can even have complete privacy: the *perltoot*(1) manpage describes how to bless closures to produce objects that are as private as those in C++ (and more so).

Perl's objects are not wrong; they're differently right.

See Also

The general literature on object-oriented programming rarely refers directly to Perl. The documentation that came with Perl is a good place to begin learning about object-oriented programming, particularly the object tutorials *perltoot*(1) and *perlboot*(1). For a reference, read *perlobj*(1) and Chapter 12 of *Programming Perl*. You might need it when you read *perlbot*(1), which is full of object-oriented tricks.

Damian Conway's *Object Oriented Perl* (Manning) is the best introduction and reference for object-oriented programming in Perl. It's readable, accurate, and comprehensive.

13.1 Constructing an Object

Problem

You want to create a way for your users to generate new objects.

Solution

Make a constructor. In Perl, the constructor method must not only initialize its object, but must also first allocate memory for it, typically using an anonymous hash. C++ constructors, on the other hand, are called with memory already allocated. Some of the object-oriented world would call C++'s constructors *initializers*.

Here's the canonical object constructor in Perl:

```
sub new {
    my $class = shift;
    my $self  = { };
    bless($self, $class);
    return $self;
}
```

This is the equivalent one-liner:

```
sub new { bless( { }, shift ) }
```

Discussion

Any method that allocates and initializes a new object acts as a constructor. The most important thing to remember is that a reference isn't an object until bless has been called on it. The simplest possible constructor, although not particularly useful, is the following:

```
sub new { bless({}) }
```

Let's add some initialization:

```
sub new {
    my $self = { };  # allocate anonymous hash
    bless($self);
    # init two sample attributes/data members/fields
    $self->{START} = time();
    $self->{AGE}   = 0;
    return $self;
}
```

This constructor isn't very useful, because it uses the single-argument form of bless, which always blesses the object into *the current package*. This means it can't be usefully inherited from; objects it constructs will always be blessed into the class that the new function was compiled into. With inheritance, this is not necessarily the class on whose behalf the method was invoked.

To solve this, have the constructor heed its first argument. For a class method, this is the package name. Pass this class name as the second argument to bless:

```
sub new {
    my $classname  = shift;        # What class are we constructing?
    my $self       = {};           # Allocate new memory
    bless($self, $classname);      # Mark it of the right type
    $self->{START} = time();       # init data fields
    $self->{AGE}   = 0;
    return $self;                  # And give it back
}
```

Now the constructor can be correctly inherited by a derived class.

You might also want to separate the memory allocation and blessing step from the instance data initialization step. Simple classes won't need this, but it can sometimes make inheritance easier by separating memory allocation from initialization; see Recipe 13.11.

```
sub new {
    my $classname  = shift;          # What class are we constructing?
    my $self       = { };            # Allocate new memory
    bless($self, $classname);        # Mark it of the right type
    $self->_init(@_);                # Call _init with remaining args
    return $self;
}

# "private" method to initialize fields.  It always sets START to
# the current time, and AGE to 0.  If invoked with arguments, _init
# interprets them as key+value pairs to initialize the object with.
sub _init {
    my $self = shift;
    $self->{START} = time();
    $self->{AGE}   = 0;
    if (@_) {
        my %extra = @_;
        @$self{keys %extra} = values %extra;
    }
}
```

See Also

perltoot(1), *perlboot*(1), and *perlobj*(1); Chapter 12 of *Programming Perl*; Recipe 13.6; Recipe 13.10; Recipe 13.11

13.2   Destroying an Object

Problem

You want to run special code whenever an object is no longer used. This is sometimes needed when the object is an interface to the outside world—or contains circular data structures—and must clean up after itself. You might remove temporary files, break circular links, gracefully disconnect from a socket, or kill a spawned subprocess.

Solution

Create a method named DESTROY. This will be invoked when there are no more references to the object, or else when the program shuts down, whichever comes first. You don't need to do any memory deallocation here, just any finalization code that makes sense for the class.

```
sub DESTROY {
    my $self = shift;
    printf("$self dying at %s\n", scalar localtime);
}
```

Discussion

Every story has a beginning and an end. The beginning of the object's story is its constructor, explicitly invoked when the object comes into existence. The end of its story is the *destructor*, a method implicitly invoked when an object leaves this life. Any per-object clean-up code is placed in the destructor, which must be named DESTROY.

Why can't destructors have arbitrary names? Because although constructors are explicitly called by name, the destructor is not. Destruction happens automatically via Perl's garbage collection (GC) system, which is currently implemented as a quick but lazy reference-based GC system. To know what to call, Perl insists that the destructor be named DESTROY. If more than one object goes out of scope at once, Perl makes no promise about invoking destructors in any particular order.

Why is DESTROY in all caps? Perl on occasion uses purely uppercase function names as a convention to indicate that the function will be automatically called by Perl. Others that are called implicitly include BEGIN, INIT, END, AUTOLOAD, plus all methods used by tied objects (see Recipe 13.15), such as STORE and FETCH.

The user doesn't care when the destructor is invoked. It just happens when it's supposed to. In languages without any form of GC, this is undependable, so the programmer must explicitly invoke the destructor to clean up memory and state, crossing their fingers that it's the right time to do so. This is a terrible state of affairs.

Because of Perl's automatic memory management, an object destructor is rarely needed in Perl. Even when it is, explicit invocation is not only uncalled for, it's downright dangerous. The destructor will be invoked by the run-time system when the object is no longer in use. Most classes don't need a destructor because Perl takes care of simple matters like memory deallocation.

The only situation where Perl's reference-based garbage collection system won't work for you is when there's a circularity in your data structure, such as:

```
$self->{WHATEVER} = $self;
```

In that case, you must delete the self-reference manually if you expect your program not to leak memory. While admittedly error-prone, this is the best we can do right now. Recipes 11.5 and 13.13 provide solutions to this problem using techniques easily generalizable to any data structure. Nonetheless, rest assured that when your program is finished, all objects' destructors are duly invoked. At interpreter shutdown time, a second, more sweeping form of garbage collection is performed. Not even unreachable or circular objects can escape this final destruction. So you are guaranteed that an object *eventually* gets properly destroyed, unless a program never exits.

If you're running Perl embedded in another application, the second GC pass happens more frequently—whenever an interpreter shuts down.

DESTROY is *not* invoked when a program replaces itself with another via exec.

See Also

perltoot(1), *perlboot*(1), and *perlobj*(1); the section "Garbage Collection, Circular References, and Weak References" in Chapter 8 of *Programming Perl*; Recipe 13.11; Recipe 13.13

13.3   Managing Instance Data

Problem

Each data attribute of an object, sometimes named data members or properties, needs its own method for access. How do you write functions that manipulate the object's instance data?

Solution

Either write pairs of get and set methods that affect the appropriate key in the object hash, like this:

```
sub get_name {
    my $self = shift;
    return $self->{NAME};
}

sub set_name {
    my $self      = shift;
    $self->{NAME} = shift;
}
```

or make single methods that do both jobs depending on whether they're passed an argument:

```
sub name {
    my $self = shift;
    if (@_) { $self->{NAME} = shift }
    return $self->{NAME};
}
```

When setting a new value, sometimes it may be useful to return not that new value, but the previous one:

```
# returns previously set value if changing it
sub age {
    my $self = shift;
    my $oldage = $self->{AGE};
    if (@_) { $self->{AGE} = shift }
```

```
        return $oldage;
    }
$previous_age = $obj->age( $obj->age() + $TIME_PASSES );
```

Discussion

Methods are how you implement the public interface to the object. A proper class doesn't encourage anyone to poke around inside its innards. Each data attribute should have a method to update it, retrieve it, or both. If a user writes code like this:

```
$him = Person->new();
$him->{NAME} = "Sylvester";
$him->{AGE}  = 23;
```

then an argument could justifiably be made that they have violated the interface and so deserve whatever they get.

For nominally private data elements, you may omit methods that access them. However, then if—better make that when—you update the implementation, you'll need to scour the class to find where other methods within the class rely upon the particular representation that you're now changing. To be squeaky clean, you could have the class itself go through a mediated, functional interface to access instance data.

This extraordinary care isn't strictly required by the class of its own methods, but from the perspective of code that simply uses your module, it most certainly is. By mandating a strictly functional interface, you are free to alter your internal representation later without fear of breaking user code. The functional interface allows you to run arbitrary range checks and take care of any data reformatting or conversion.

Here's a fancy version of the name method that demonstrates this:

```
use Carp;
sub name {
    my $self = shift;
    return $self->{NAME} unless @_;
    local $_ = shift;
    croak "too many arguments" if @_;
    if ($^W) {
        /[^\s\w'-]/          && carp "funny characters in name";
        /\d/                 && carp "numbers in name";
        /\S+(\s+\S+)+/       || carp "prefer multiword name";
        /\S/                 || carp "name is blank";
    }
    s/(\w+)/\u\L$1/g;        # enforce capitalization
    $self->{NAME} = $_;
}
```

If users, or even other classes through inheritance, had been accessing the "NAME" field directly, you couldn't add this kind of code later. By insisting on only indirect, functional access to all data attributes, you keep your options open.

If you're used to C++ objects, then you're accustomed to being able to get at an object's data members as simple variables from within a method. The Alias module from CPAN provides for this, as well as a good bit more, such as the possibility of private methods that the object can invoke but folks outside the class cannot.

Here's an example of creating a Person using the Alias module. When you update these magical instance variables, you automatically update value fields in the hash. Convenient, eh?

```perl
package Person;

# this is the same as before...
sub new {
    my $that  = shift;
    my $class = ref($that) || $that;
    my $self = {
            NAME  => undef,
            AGE   => undef,
            PEERS => [ ],
    };
    bless($self, $class);
    return $self;
}

use Alias qw(attr);
our ($NAME, $AGE, @PEERS);

sub name {
    my $self = attr shift;
    if (@_) { $NAME = shift; }
    return     $NAME;
};

sub age {
    my $self = attr shift;
    if (@_) { $AGE = shift; }
    return     $AGE;
}

sub peers {
    my $self = attr shift;
    if (@_) { @PEERS = @_; }
    return     @PEERS;
}

sub exclaim {
    my $self = attr shift;
    return sprintf "Hi, I'm %s, age %d, working with %s",
            $NAME, $AGE, join(", ", @PEERS);
}

sub happy_birthday {
    my $self = attr shift;
    return ++$AGE;
}
```

You need to declare the package variables via our because Alias plays with package globals by the same names as the fields. To use globals while use strict is in effect, you have to predeclare them. These variables are localized to the block enclosing the attr invocation, just as though local were used on them. That means that they're still considered global package variables with temporary values.

See Also

perltoot(1), *perlboot*(1), *perlobj*(1), and *perlbot*(1); the section on "Managing Instance Data" in Chapter 12 of *Programming Perl*; the documentation for the Alias module from CPAN; Recipe 13.12

13.4 Managing Class Data

Problem

You need a method invoked on behalf of the whole class, not just on one object. This might be a procedural request, or it might be a global data attribute shared by all instances of the class.

Solution

Instead of expecting a reference as their first argument as object methods do, class methods expect a string containing the name of the class. Class methods access package data, not object data, as in the population method shown here:

```
package Person;

$Body_Count = 0;

sub population { return $Body_Count }

sub new {                              # constructor
    $Body_Count++;
    return bless({}, shift);
}

sub DESTROY { --$Body_Count }          # destructor

# later, the user can say this:
package main;

for (1..10) { push @people, Person->new }
printf "There are %d people alive.\n", Person->population();
```

There are 10 people alive.

Discussion

Normally, each object has its own complete state stored within itself. The value of a data attribute in one object is unrelated to the value that attribute might have in another instance of the same class. For example, setting *her* gender here does nothing to *his* gender, because they are different objects with distinct states:

```
$him = Person->new( );
$him->gender("male");

$her = Person->new( );
$her->gender("female");
```

Imagine a classwide attribute where changing the attribute for one instance changes it for all of them. Just as some programmers prefer capitalized global variables, some prefer uppercase names when the method affects class data instead of instance data. Here's an example of using a class method named Max_Bounds:

```
FixedArray->Max_Bounds(100);                  # set for whole class
$alpha = FixedArray->new( );
printf "Bound on alpha is %d\n", $alpha->Max_Bounds( );
100
$beta = FixedArray->new( );
$beta->Max_Bounds(50);                        # still sets for whole class
printf "Bound on alpha is %d\n", $alpha->Max_Bounds( );
50
```

The implementation is simple:

```
package FixedArray;
$Bounds = 7;  # default
sub new { bless( {}, shift ) }
sub Max_Bounds {
    my $proto  = shift;
    $Bounds    = shift if @_;         # allow updates
    return $Bounds;
}
```

To make the value effectively read-only, simply remove the update possibility, as in:

```
sub Max_Bounds { $Bounds }
```

If you're deeply paranoid, make $Bounds a lexical variable private to the scope of the file containing the class. Then no one could say $FixedArray::Bounds to discover its values. They'd be forced to go through the method interface instead.

Here's a tip to help build scalable classes: store object data on the object's namespace (in the hash), and store class data in the class namespace (package variables or file-scoped lexicals). Only class methods should directly access classwide attributes. Object methods should access only instance data. If the object method needs access to class data, its constructor should store a reference to that data in the object. Here's an example:

```
sub new {
    my $class = shift;
    my $self = bless({ }, $class);
    $self->{Max_Bounds_ref} = \$Bounds;
    return $self;
}
```

See Also

perltoot(1), *perlboot*(1), *perlobj*(1), and *perlbot*(1); the section on "Managing Class Data" in Chapter 12 of *Programming Perl*; Recipe 13.3; the places method in "Example: Overloaded FixNum Class" in Recipe 13.14

13.5 Using Classes as Structs

Problem

You're used to structured data types more complex than Perl's arrays and hashes, such as C's structs and Pascal's records. You've heard that Perl's classes are comparable, but you aren't an object-oriented programmer.

Solution

Use the standard Class::Struct module's struct to declare data structures reminiscent of those in the C programming language:

```
use Class::Struct;          # load struct-building module

struct Person => {          # create a definition for a "Person"
    name    => '$',         #     name field is a scalar
    age     => '$',         #     age field is also a scalar
    peers   => '@',         #     but peers field is an array (reference)
};

my $p = Person->new();      # allocate an empty Person struct

$p->name("Jason Smythe");                       # set its name field
$p->age(13);                                    # set its age field
$p->peers( ["Wilbur", "Ralph", "Fred" ] );      # set its peers field

# or this way:
@{$p->peers} = ("Wilbur", "Ralph", "Fred");

# fetch various values, including the zeroth friend
printf "At age %d, %s's first friend is %s.\n",
    $p->age, $p->name, $p->peers(0);
```

Discussion

The `Class::Struct::struct` function builds struct-like classes on the fly. It creates a class of the name given in the first argument, complete with a constructor named new and per-field accessor methods.

In the structure layout definition, the keys are the names of the fields and the values are the data type. This type can be one of the three base types: `'$'` for scalars, `'@'` for arrays, and `'%'` for hashes. Each accessor method can be invoked without arguments to fetch the current value, or with an argument to set the value. For a field whose type is an array or hash, a zero-argument method invocation returns a reference to the entire array or hash, a one-argument invocation retrieves the value at that subscript,* and a two-argument invocation sets the value at that subscript.

The type can even be the name of another named structure—or any class, for that matter. Because a class constructor doesn't have to be named new, if a component of your class is another object class, you'll have to invoke that named constructor yourself.

```
use Class::Struct;

struct Person => {name => '$',     age  => '$'};
struct Family => {head => 'Person', address => '$', members => '@'};

$folks  = Family->new();

$folks->head($dad = Person->new);
$dad->name("John");
$dad->age(34);

printf("%s's age is %d\n", $folks->head->name, $folks->head->age);
```

You can pass the constructors created by Class::Struct initializer pairs:

```
$dad = Person->new(name => "John", age => 34);
$folks->head($dad);
```

Internally, the class is implemented using a hash, just as most classes are. This makes your code easy to debug and manipulate. Consider the effect of printing out a structure in the debugger, for example. If you use the Perl debugger's **x** command to dump out the $folks object you've just created, you'll notice something interesting:

```
DB<2> x $folks
0   Family=HASH(0xcc360)
     'Family::address' => undef
     'Family::head' => Person=HASH(0x3307e4)
        'Person::age' => 34
        'Person::name' => 'John'
     'Family::members' => ARRAY(0xcc078)
           empty array
```

---

* Unless it's a reference, in which case it uses *that* as the new aggregate, with type checking.

Each hash key contains more than the just the name of the method: that name is prefixed by the package name and a double-colon. This convention guards against two classes in the same inheritance hierarchy using the same slot in the object hash for different purposes. This is a wise practice to follow for your own classes, too. Always use the package name as part of the hash key, and you won't have to worry about conflicting uses in subclasses.

If you'd like to impose more parameter checking on the fields' values, supply your own version for the accessor method to override the default version. Let's say you wanted to make sure the age value contains only digits, and that it falls within reasonably human age requirements. Here's how that function might be coded:

```
sub Person::age {
    use Carp;
    my ($self, $age) = @_;
    if     (@_ > 2) { confess "too many arguments" }
    elsif (@_ == 1) { return $self->{"Person::age"}      }
    elsif (@_ == 2) {
        carp "age `$age' isn't numeric"   if $age !~ /^\d+/;
        carp "age `$age' is unreasonable" if $age > 150;
        $self->{'Person::age'} = $age;
    }
}
```

Using the principles outlined in Recipe 12.15, you can provide warnings only when warnings have been requested using warnings::enabled. Once your module has registered its package as a warnings class with use warnings::register, you can write:

```
if (warnings::enabled("Person") || warnings::enabled("numeric")) {
    carp "age `$age' isn't numeric"   if $age !~ /^\d+/;
    carp "age `$age' is unreasonable" if $age > 150;
}
```

You could even complain when warnings are in force, but raise an exception if the user hadn't asked for warnings. (Don't be confused by the pointer arrow; it's an indirect function call, not a method invocation.)

```
my $gripe = warnings::enabled("Person") ? \&carp : \&croak;
$gripe->("age `$age' isn't numeric")   if $age !~ /^\d+/;
$gripe->("age `$age' is unreasonable") if $age > 150;
```

The Class::Struct module also supports an array representation. Just specify the fields within square brackets instead of curly ones:

```
struct Family => [head => 'Person', address => '$', members => '@'];
```

Empirical evidence suggests that selecting the array representation instead of a hash trims between 10% and 50% off the memory consumption of your objects, and up to 33% of the access time. The cost is less informative debugging information and more mental overhead when writing override functions, such as Person::age shown earlier. Choosing an array representation for the object would make it difficult to use inheritance. That's not an issue here, because C-style structures employ the much more easily understood notion of aggregation instead.

The use `fields` pragma provides the speed and space of arrays with the expressiveness of hashes, and adds compile-time checking of an object's field names.

If all fields are the same type, rather than writing it out this way:

```
struct Card => {
    name    => '$',
    color   => '$',
    cost    => '$',
    type    => '$',
    release => '$',
    text    => '$',
};
```

you could use a `map` to shorten it:

```
struct Card => { map { $_ => '$' } qw(name color cost type release text) };
```

Or, if you're a C programmer who prefers to precede the field name with its type, rather than vice versa, just reverse the order:

```
struct hostent => { reverse qw{
    $ name
    @ aliases
    $ addrtype
    $ length
    @ addr_list
}};
```

You can even make aliases, in the (dubious) spirit of #define, that allow the same field to be accessed under multiple aliases. In C, you can say:

```
#define h_type h_addrtype
#define h_addr h_addr_list[0]
```

In Perl, you might try this:

```
# make (hostent object)->type() same as (hostent object)->addrtype()
*hostent::type = \&hostent::addrtype;

# make (hostenv object)->addr() same as (hostenv object)->addr_list(0)
sub hostent::addr { shift->addr_list(0,@_) }
```

As you see, you can add methods to a class—or functions to a package—simply by declaring a subroutine in the right namespace. You don't have to be in the file defining the class, subclass it, or do anything fancy and complicated. It might be better to subclass it, however:

```
package Extra::hostent;
use Net::hostent;
@ISA = qw(hostent);
sub addr {
shift->addr_list(0,@_) }
1;
```

That one's already available in the standard Net::hostent class, so you needn't bother. Check out that module's source code as a form of inspirational reading. We can't be held responsible for what it inspires you to do, though.

See Also

perltoot(1), *perlboot*(1), *perlobj*(1), and *perlbot*(1); the documentation for the standard Class::Struct module; the source code for the standard Net::hostent module; the documentation for the use fields pragma; the documentation for the Alias module from CPAN; Recipe 13.3

13.6   Cloning Constructors

Problem

You want to write a constructor method that might be invoked on an existing object, and if so, to use that object for default values.

Solution

Start your constructor like this:

```
my $proto  = shift;
my $class  = ref($proto) || $proto;
my $parent = ref($proto) && $proto;
```

The $class variable will contain the class to bless into, and the $parent variable will either be false, or else the object you're cloning.

Discussion

Sometimes you need another object of the same type as the current one. You could do this:

```
$ob1 = SomeClass->new( );
# later on
$ob2 = (ref $ob1)->new( );
```

but that's not very clear. It's clearer to have a single constructor that behaves correctly, regardless of whether its invocant is a class name or an existing object of that class. As a class method, it should return a new object with the default initialization. As an instance method, it should return a new object initialized from the object it was invoked on:

```
$ob1 = Widget->new( );
$ob2 = $ob1->new( );
```

Here's a version of new that takes this into consideration:

```
sub new {
    my $proto  = shift;
    my $class  = ref($proto) || $proto;
    my $parent = ref($proto) && $proto;

    my $self;
    # check whether we're shadowing a new from @ISA
    if (@ISA && $proto->SUPER::can("new") ) {
        $self = $proto->SUPER::new(@_);
    } else {
        $self = {};
        bless ($self, $class);
    }

    $self->{PARENT}  = $parent;
    $self->{START}   = time();   # init data fields
    $self->{AGE}     = 0;

    return $self;
}
```

Initializing doesn't have to mean simply copying values from the parent. If you're writing a linked list or binary tree class, your constructor can return a new object linked into the list or tree, when invoked as an instance method.

See Also

perlobj(1) and Chapter 12 of *Programming Perl*; Recipe 13.1; Recipe 13.10; Recipe 13.13

13.7 Copy Constructors

Problem

You would like to provide users of your class with a copy method, or you would like to copy an object for which no copy method has been provided by the class.

Solution

Use the dclone( ) function from the standard Storable module.

```
use Storable qw(dclone);
use Carp;
sub copy {
    my $self = shift;
    croak "can't copy class $self" unless ref $self;
    my $copy = Storable::dclone($self);
    return $copy;
}
```

Discussion

As described in Recipe 11.12, the Storable module's `dclone` function will recursively copy (virtually) any data structure. It works on objects, too, correctly giving you back new objects that are appropriately blessed. This assumes that the underlying types are SCALAR, ARRAY, HASH, or CODE refs. Things like GLOB and IO refs won't serialize.

Some classes already provide methods to copy their objects; others do not, not so much out of intent as out of neglect. Consider this:

```
sub UNIVERSAL::copy {
    my $self = shift;
    unless (ref $self) {
        require Carp;
        Carp::croak("can't copy class $self");
    }
    require Storable;
    my $copy = Storable::dclone($self);
    return $copy;
}
```

Now all objects can be copied, providing they're of the supported types. Classes that provide their own copy methods are unaffected, but any class that *doesn't* provide its own copy method will pick up this definition. We placed the `require` on Storable within the function call itself so that you load Storable only if you actually plan to use it. Likewise, we placed the one for Carp inside the test that will end up using it. By using `require`, we delay loading until the module is actually needed.

We also avoid use because it would import things into our current package. This could be antisocial. From the previous code snippet, you cannot determine what package you're even in. Just because we've declared a subroutine named copy to be in package UNIVERSAL doesn't mean that the code within that subroutine is in package UNIVERSAL. Rather, it's in whatever package we are currently compiling into.

Some folks would argue that we're being outrageously cavalier by interjecting a function into somebody else's namespace like that—especially into all possible class namespaces, as it's in UNIVERSAL. Cavalier perhaps, but hardly outrageously so; after all, UNIVERSAL is there to be used. It's no holy namespace, sacrosanct against any change. Whether this ends up being a very stupid thing or a very clever thing is not up to Perl to decide, or prevent.

See Also

Recipe 11.12; Recipe 13.9; the documentation for the standard Storable modules; the section on "Inheritance" in the introduction to this chapter; the section on "UNIVERSAL: The Ultimate Ancestor Class" in Chapter 12 of *Programming Perl*

13.8   Invoking Methods Indirectly

Problem

You want to invoke a method by a name that isn't known until runtime.

Solution

Store the method name as a string in a scalar variable and use it where you would use
the real method name to the right of the arrow operator:

```
$methname = "flicker";
$obj->$methname(10);            # invokes $obj->flicker(10);

# invoke three methods on the object, by name
foreach $m ( qw(start run stop) ) {
    $obj->$m();
}
```

Discussion

Sometimes you need to invoke a method whose name you've stored somewhere. You
can't take the address of a method, but you can store its name. If you have a scalar
variable $meth containing the method name, invoke the method on an object
$crystal with $crystal->$meth( ).

```
@methods = qw(name rank serno);
%his_info = map { $_ => $ob->$_() } @methods;

# same as this:

%his_info = (
    'name' => $ob->name(),
    'rank' => $ob->rank(),
    'serno' => $ob->serno(),
);
```

If you're desperate to devise a way to get a method's address, you should try to
rethink your algorithm. For example, instead of incorrectly taking \$ob->method( ),
which simply applies the backslash to that method's return value or values, do this:

```
my $fnref = sub { $ob->method(@_) };
```

Now when it's time to invoke that indirectly, you would use:

```
$fnref->(10, "fred");
```

and have the closure in turn correctly use the original value of $ob (provided $ob was
a lexical variable) that was around when it was created to call:

```
$ob->method(10, "fred");
```

This works even if $ob has gone out of scope. This solution is much cleaner.

When using indirect method invocation, it is permitted to store a subroutine reference in the scalar variable instead of a string representing the method name. No verification that the function represents a valid method.

The code reference returned by the UNIVERSAL can method should probably not be used for indirect method invocation on objects other than the one on which it was called, or at least those of the same class. That's because you have no reason to believe that this will be a valid method when applied to an object of an arbitrary class.

For example, this is highly dubious code:

```
$coderef = $some_object->can("wither");
$other_object->$coderef();   # wither() it even if we shouldn't
```

That is reasonable only when the two objects are of the same, or compatible, classes. If they were not, and the second did not have a wither method, no exception would be raised, unlike here:

```
$some_object->wither();
$other_object->wither();
```

Another interesting possibility is to use the strategy outlined in Recipe 12.5 to implement nominally private methods.

```
my $secret_meth = sub { ... }
sub reg_meth {
    my $self = shift;
    # ... do whatever you want, then
    $self->$secret_meth(@_);
    #
}
```

Because the lexical variable $secret_meth is scoped to the class module's file, code from outside the class cannot access it, and therefore cannot invoke the closure. However, code that is in the module file can see that scalar, so it can use the code reference with $secret_meth to make an indirect method invocation.

When you use a code reference to invoke a method indirectly, Perl doesn't consult a package or its @ISA at all; it just makes the function call and passes in the invocant in the initial slot. That means these two lines are the same:

```
$self->$secret_meth(@_);        # indirect method invocation
$secret_meth->($self, @_)       # indirect function call
```

So if you hadn't shifted the invocant off, but had left it in @_, then you could just make the equivalent dereferenced function call yourself:

```
sub reg_meth {
    # ... do whatever you want, then
    $secret_meth->(@_);
}
```

See Also

perlobj(1); Recipe 11.8

13.9 Determining Subclass Membership

Problem

You want to know whether an object is an instance of a particular class or that class's subclasses. Perhaps you want to decide whether a particular method should be invoked on an arbitrary object.

Solution

Use methods from the special UNIVERSAL class:

```
$obj->isa("HTTP::Message");              # as object method
HTTP::Response->isa("HTTP::Message");    # as class method

if ($obj->can("method_name")) { .... }   # check method validity
```

Discussion

Wouldn't it be convenient if all objects were rooted at some ultimate base class? That way you could give every object common methods without having to add to each @ISA. Well, you can. You don't see it, but Perl pretends there's an extra element at the end of @ISA—the package named UNIVERSAL.

UNIVERSAL has only a few predefined methods, although you are free to add your own. These are built right into your Perl binary, so they don't take extra time to load. Predefined methods include isa, can, and VERSION. All three may be used for both sorts of invocants: classes and objects.

The isa method reports whether its invocant inherits the class name directly or indirectly from the class name supplied as the argument. This saves having to traverse the hierarchy yourself, and is much better than testing with an exact check against the string returned by the ref built-in. You may even supply a basic type that ref might return as an argument, such as SCALAR, ARRAY, HASH, or GLOB.

```
$has_io = $fd->isa("IO::Handle") || $fd->isa("GLOB");
$itza_handle = IO::Socket->isa("IO::Handle");
```

Type checks like this are sometimes frowned upon as being too constraining. If you just want to know if a certain method can be invoked against something, it might be better to just try to invoke the method you're hoping will be there instead of checking for the class.

Another possibility is to use another UNIVERSAL method, can. The can method reports whether its string argument is a valid method for its invocant. In fact, it even returns a function reference for that method:

```
$his_print_method = $obj->can('as_string');
```

Finally, the VERSION method checks whether the invocant class has a package global called $VERSION that's high enough, as in:

```
Some_Module->VERSION(3.0);
$his_vers = $obj->VERSION( );
```

However, we don't usually invoke VERSION ourselves. Remember, in Perl an all-uppercase function name means that the function will be automatically called by Perl in some way. In this case, it happens when you say:

```
use Some_Module 3.0;
```

If you wanted to add version checking to your Person class explained earlier, add this to *Person.pm*:

```
our $VERSION = "1.01";
```

Then, in the user code say use Person 1.01; to make sure that you have at least that version number or higher available. This is not the same as loading in that exact version number; it just has to be at least that high. Lamentably, no mechanism for concurrent installation of multiple versions of a module yet exists.

See Also

The documentation for the standard UNIVERSAL module; the use keyword in *perlfunc*(1) and in Chapter 11 of *Programming Perl*

13.10 Writing an Inheritable Class

Problem

You're not sure whether you've designed your class robustly enough to be inherited.

Solution

Use the "empty subclass test" on your class.

Discussion

Imagine you've implemented a class named Person that supplies a constructor named new, and methods such as age and name. Here's the straightforward implementation:

```
package Person;
sub new {
    my $class = shift;
    my $self  = { };
    return bless $self, $class;
}
sub name {
    my $self = shift;
```

```
        $self->{NAME} = shift if @_;
        return $self->{NAME};
    }
    sub age {
        my $self = shift;
        $self->{AGE} = shift if @_;
        return $self->{AGE};
    }
```

You might use the class in this way:

```
use Person;
my $dude = Person->new( );
$dude->name("Jason");
$dude->age(23);
printf "%s is age %d.\n", $dude->name, $dude->age;
```

Now consider another class, the one named Employee:

```
package Employee;
use Person;
@ISA = ("Person");
1;
```

There's not a lot to that one. All it's doing is loading in class Person and stating that
Employee will inherit any needed methods from Person. Since Employee has no
methods of its own, it will get all of its methods from Person. We rely upon an
Employee to behave just like a Person.

Setting up an empty class like this is called the *empty base class test*; that is, it creates
a derived class that does nothing but inherit from a base class. If the original base
class has been designed properly, then the new derived class can be used as a drop-in
replacement for the old one. This means you should be able to change just the class
name and everything will still work:

```
use Employee;
my $empl = Employee->new( );
$empl->name("Jason");
$empl->age(23);
printf "%s is age %d.\n", $empl->name, $empl->age;
```

By proper design, we mean using only the two-argument form of bless, avoiding any
direct access of class data, and exporting nothing. In the Person::new( ) function
defined previously, we were careful to do these things. We use some package data in
the constructor, but the reference to this is stored on the object itself. Other methods access package data via that reference, so we should be okay.

Why did we say the Person::new *function*—is that not actually a method? A method
is just a function that expects its first argument to be a class name (package) or
object (blessed reference). Person::new is the function that the Person->new method
and the Employee->new method both end up calling. (See Table 13-1.) Although
method invocation looks a lot like a function call, they aren't the same. If you treat
them as the same, very soon you'll be left with nothing but broken programs. First,

the actual underlying calling conventions are different: methods get an extra argument. Second, function calls don't do inheritance, but methods do.

Table 13-1. Mapping methods to functions

Method call	Resulting function call
`Person->new( )`	`Person::new("Person")`
`Employee->new( )`	`Person::new("Employee")`

If you got in the habit of calling:

```
$him = Person::new( );              # WRONG
```

you'd have a subtle problem, because the function wouldn't get an argument of "Person" as it is expecting, and so it couldn't bless into the passed-in class. Still worse, you'd probably want to try to call `Employee::new` also. But there is no such function! It's just an inherited method.

So, don't call a function when you mean to invoke a method.

See Also

perltoot(1), *perlobj*(1), and *perlbot*(1); Chapter 13 of *Programming Perl*; Recipe 13.1; Recipe 13.11

13.11 Accessing Overridden Methods

Problem

Your class's constructor method overrides the constructor of its parent class. You want your constructor to invoke the parent class's constructor.

Solution

Learn about the special pseudoclass, SUPER.

```
sub meth {
    my $self = shift;
    $self->SUPER::meth( );
}
```

Discussion

In languages like C++ where constructors don't actually allocate memory but just initialize the object, all base class constructors are automatically invoked for you. In languages like Java and Perl, you have to invoke them yourself.

To invoke a method in a particular class, the notation $self->SUPER::meth( ) is used. This is an extension of the regular notation that means to begin searching for a method in a particular class. It is valid only from within an overridden method. Here's a comparison of styles:

```
$self->meth();                 # Call wherever first meth is found
$self->Where::meth();          # Start looking in package "Where"
$self->SUPER::meth();          # Call overridden version
```

Simple users of the class should probably restrict themselves to the first line in the previous example. The second is possible, but not suggested for this situation, because we have the special notation shown in the third line, which only works within the overridden method.

An overriding constructor should invoke its SUPER's constructor to allocate and bless the object, limiting itself to instantiating any data fields needed. It makes sense here to separate the object allocation code from the object initialization code for reasons that will become clear a couple paragraphs from now. We'll name it with a leading underscore, a convention indicating a nominally private method. Think of it as a "Do Not Disturb" sign.

```
sub new {
    my $classname  = shift;          # What class are we constructing?
    my $self       = $classname->SUPER::new(@_);
    $self->_init(@_);
    return $self;                     # And give it back
}

sub _init {
    my $self = shift;
    $self->{START}    = time();   # init data fields
    $self->{AGE}      = 0;
    $self->{EXTRA}    = { @_ };   # anything extra
}
```

Both SUPER::new and _init are invoked with any remaining arguments. That way the user might pass other field initializers in, as in:

```
$obj = Widget->new( haircolor => red, freckles => 121 );
```

Whether you store these user parameters in their own extra hash is up to you.

Note that SUPER works only on the *first* overridden method. If your @ISA array has several classes, there could be several. A manual traversal of @ISA is possible, but seldom worth the hassle.

```
my $self = bless {}, $class;
for my $class (@ISA) {
    my $meth = $class . "::_init";
    $self->$meth(@_) if $class->can("_init");
}
```

This fragile code assumes that all superclasses initialize their objects with _init instead of initializing in the constructor. It also assumes that a hash reference is used for the underlying object.

For a slightly more general approach to accessing all overridden methods, save the return value from the can( ) method, which is the code reference to the subroutine that would be invoked through normal method invocation. Then use that reference for indirect method invocation.

```
sub some_method {
    my $self = shift;
    my %seen;
    print "some_method($self): checking all ancestors\n";
    for my $parent (our @ISA) {
        if (my $code = $parent->can("some_method")) {
            $self->$code(@_) unless $seen{$code}++;
        }
    }
}
```

To avoid calling the same subroutine more than once, the %seen hash keeps track of which subroutines have been called. This could happen if several parent classes shared a common ancestor.

Methods that would trigger an AUTOLOAD will not be accurately reported unless that package has declared (but not defined) the subroutines it wishes to have autoloaded.

See Also

The discussion on the SUPER class in *perltoot*(1) and *perlobj*(1), and in the section on "Method Invocation" in Chapter 12 of *Programming Perl*

13.12 Generating Attribute Methods Using AUTOLOAD

Problem

Your object needs accessor methods to set or get its data fields, and you're tired of writing them all out one at a time.

Solution

Carefully use Perl's AUTOLOAD mechanism as something of a proxy method generator so you don't have to create them all yourself each time you want to add a new data field.

Discussion

Perl's AUTOLOAD mechanism intercepts all possible undefined method invocations. To disallow arbitrary data names, we store the list of permitted fields in a hash. The AUTOLOAD method checks for whether the accessed field name is in that hash.

```
package Person;
use strict;
use Carp;
our(%ok_field);

# Authorize four attribute fields
for my $attr ( qw(name age peers parent) ) { $ok_field{$attr}++; }

sub AUTOLOAD {
    my $self = shift;
    my $attr = our $AUTOLOAD;
    $attr =~ s/.*:://;
    return unless $attr =~ /[^A-Z]/;  # skip DESTROY and all-cap methods
    croak "invalid attribute method: ->$attr()" unless $ok_field{$attr};
    $self->{uc $attr} = shift if @_;
    return $self->{uc $attr};
}
sub new {
    my $proto  = shift;
    my $class  = ref($proto) || $proto;
    my $parent = ref($proto) && $proto;
    my $self = { };
    bless($self, $class);
    $self->parent($parent);
    return $self;
}
1;
```

This class supports a constructor method named new, plus four attribute methods: name, age, peers, and parent. Use the module this way:

```
use Person;
my ($dad, $kid);
$dad = Person->new;
$dad->name("Jason");
$dad->age(23);
$kid = $dad->new;
$kid->name("Rachel");
$kid->age(2);
printf "Kid's parent is %s\n", $kid->parent->name;
Kid's parent is Jason
```

This is tricky when producing inheritance trees. Suppose you'd like an Employee class that had every data attribute of the Person class, plus two new ones, like salary and boss. Class Employee can't rely upon an inherited Person::AUTOLOAD to determine what Employee's attribute methods are. So each class would need its own AUTOLOAD function. This would check just that class's known attribute fields, but instead of croaking when incorrectly triggered, it would invoke overridden super-class version.

Here's a version that takes this into consideration:

```
sub AUTOLOAD {
    my $self = shift;
    my $attr = our $AUTOLOAD;
    $attr =~ s/.*:://;
    return if $attr eq "DESTROY";

    if ($ok_field{$attr}) {
        $self->{uc $attr} = shift if @_;
        return $self->{uc $attr};
    } else {
        my $superior = "SUPER::$attr";
        $self->$superior(@_);
    }
}
```

If the attribute isn't in our OK list, we'll pass it up to our superior, hoping that it can cope with it. But you can't inherit this AUTOLOAD; each class has to have its own, because it is unwisely accessing class data directly, not through the object. Even worse, if a class A inherits from two classes B and C, both of which define their own AUTOLOAD, an undefined method invoked on A will hit the AUTOLOAD in only one of the two parent classes.

We could try to cope with these limitations, but AUTOLOAD eventually begins to feel like a kludge piled on a hack piled on a workaround. There are better approaches for the more complex situations.

One further proviso: the UNIVERSAL::can method will not normally report as invokable a method that would only trigger a class's AUTOLOAD. If you prefer that it do so, declare the methods without defining them. For example:

```
sub eat;
sub drink;
sub be_merry;
sub AUTOLOAD  {
    my $self = shift;
    my $funcname = our $AUTOLOAD;
    $funcname =~ s/.*:://;
    ...
}
```

You don't normally need to declare functions to trigger AUTOLOAD. If you had an object of that class:

```
$man->be_merry();
```

the AUTOLOAD would still trigger, even without the declarations. However, you need the declarations to make the can method notice them:

```
$man->be_merry() if $man->can("be_merry");
```

See Also

The examples using AUTOLOAD in *perltoot*(1); Chapter 10 of *Programming Perl*; Recipe 10.15

13.13 Coping with Circular Data Structures Using Objects

Problem

You have an inherently self-referential data structure, so Perl's reference-based garbage collection system won't notice when it's no longer being used. You want to prevent your program from leaking memory.

Solution

Create a non-circular container object that holds a pointer to the self-referential data structure. Define a DESTROY method for the containing object's class that manually breaks the self-referential circularities.

Or use *weak references*, as described in Recipe 11.15.

Discussion

Many interesting data structures include references back to themselves. This can occur in code as simple as this:

```
$node->{NEXT} = $node;
```

As soon as you do that, you've created a circularity that will hide the data structure from Perl's referenced-based garbage collection system. Destructors will eventually be invoked when your program exits, but sometimes you don't want to wait that long.

A circular linked list is similarly self-referential. Each node contains a front pointer, a back pointer, and the node's value. If you implement it with references in Perl, you get a circular set of references and the data structure won't be automatically garbage collected when there are no external references to its nodes.

Making each node an instance of class Ring doesn't solve the problem. What you want is for Perl to clean up this structure as it would any other structure—which it will do if you implement your object as a structure that contains a reference to the real circle. That reference will be stored in the "DUMMY" field:

```
package Ring;

# return an empty ring structure
```

```
sub new {
    my $class = shift;
    my $node  = { };
    $node->{NEXT} = $node->{PREV} = $node;
    my $self  = { DUMMY => $node, COUNT => 0 };
    bless $self, $class;
    return $self;
}
```

It's the nodes contained in the ring that are circular, not the returned ring object itself. That means code like the following won't cause a memory leak:

```
use Ring;

$COUNT = 1000;
for (1 .. 20) {
    my $r = Ring->new( );
    for ($i = 0; $i < $COUNT; $i++) { $r->insert($i) }
}
```

Even though we create 20 rings of 1,000 nodes each, each ring is thrown away before a new one is created. The user of the class need do no more to free the ring's memory than they would to free a string's memory. That is, this all happens automatically, just as it's supposed to.

However, the implementer of the class does have to have a destructor for the ring, one that will manually delete the nodes:

```
# when a Ring is destroyed, destroy the ring structure it contains
sub DESTROY {
    my $ring = shift;
    my $node;
    for ( $node  =  $ring->{DUMMY}->{NEXT};
          $node  !=  $ring->{DUMMY};
          $node  =  $node->{NEXT} )
    {
            $ring->delete_node($node);
    }
    $node->{PREV} = $node->{NEXT} = undef;
}

# delete a node from the ring structure
sub delete_node {
    my ($ring, $node) = @_;
    $node->{PREV}->{NEXT} = $node->{NEXT};
    $node->{NEXT}->{PREV} = $node->{PREV};
    --$ring->{COUNT};
}
```

Here are a few other methods you might like in your Ring class. Notice how the real work lies within the circularity hidden inside the object:

```
# $node = $ring->search( $value ) : find $value in the ring
# structure in $node
sub search {
```

```
    my ($ring, $value) = @_;
    my $node = $ring->{DUMMY}->{NEXT};
    while ($node != $ring->{DUMMY} && $node->{VALUE} != $value) {
        $node = $node->{NEXT};
    }
    return $node;
}

# $ring->insert( $value ) : insert $value into the ring structure
sub insert_value {
    my ($ring, $value) = @_;
    my $node = { VALUE => $value };
    $node->{NEXT} = $ring->{DUMMY}->{NEXT};
    $ring->{DUMMY}->{NEXT}->{PREV} = $node;
    $ring->{DUMMY}->{NEXT} = $node;
    $node->{PREV} = $ring->{DUMMY};
    ++$ring->{COUNT};
}

# $ring->delete_value( $value ) : delete a node from the ring
# structure by value
sub delete_value {
    my ($ring, $value) = @_;
    my $node = $ring->search($value);
    return if $node == $ring->{DUMMY};
    $ring->delete_node($node);
}

1;
```

Here's one for your *fortune* file: Perl's garbage collector abhors a naked circularity.

In Recipe 11.15, we see an alternate implementation for this same code, one that doesn't involve objects at all. Because it uses weak references for the data structure's own references back to itself, Perl's memory management system suffices to clean up the data structure once it's no longer needed. This obviates the need for a destructor, and therefore even allows the data structure to be constructed using simple reference without recourse to classes or objects.

See Also

The algorithms in both this recipe and Recipe 11.15 derive in part from *Introduction to Algorithms*, by Cormen, Leiserson, and Rivest (MIT Press/McGraw-Hill); the section on "Garbage Collection, Circular References, and Weak References" in Chapter 8 of *Programming Perl*; the documentation for the standard Devel::Peek and Scalar:: Util modules

13.14 Overloading Operators

Problem

You want to use familiar operators like == or + on objects from a class you've written, or you want to define the print interpolation value for objects.

Solution

Use the use overload pragma. Here are two of the more commonly overloaded operators:

```
use overload
  '<=>' => \&threeway_compare;

sub threeway_compare {
    my ($s1, $s2) = @_;
    return uc($s1->{NAME}) cmp uc($s2->{NAME});
}

use overload
   '""'  => \&stringify;

sub stringify {
    my $self = shift;
    return sprintf "%s (%05d)",
            ucfirst(lc($self->{NAME})),
            $self->{IDNUM};
}
```

Discussion

When you use built-in types, certain operators apply, like + for addition or . for string concatenation. With the use overload pragma, you can customize these operators so they do something special on your own objects.

This pragma takes a list of operator/function call pairs, such as:

```
package TimeNumber;
use overload          '+' => \&my_plus,
                      '-' => \&my_minus,
                      '*' => \&my_star,
                      '/' => \&my_slash;
```

Those four operators can now be used with objects of class TimeNumber, and the listed functions will be called as method invocations. These functions can do anything you'd like.

Here's a simple example of an overload of + for use with an object that holds hours, minutes, and seconds. It assumes that both operands are of a class that has a new method that can be invoked as an object method, and that the structure names are as shown:

```
sub my_plus {
    my($left, $right) = @_;
    my $answer = $left->new( );
    $answer->{SECONDS} = $left->{SECONDS} + $right->{SECONDS};
    $answer->{MINUTES} = $left->{MINUTES} + $right->{MINUTES};
    $answer->{HOURS}   = $left->{HOURS}   + $right->{HOURS};

    if ($answer->{SECONDS} >= 60) {
        $answer->{SECONDS} %= 60;
        $answer->{MINUTES} ++;
    }

    if ($answer->{MINUTES} >= 60) {
        $answer->{MINUTES} %= 60;
        $answer->{HOURS}   ++;
    }

    return $answer;

}
```

It's probably best to overload numeric operators only when the objects themselves are mirroring some sort of inherently numeric construct, such as complex or infinite precision numbers, vectors, or matrices. Otherwise, the code becomes hard to understand and might lead users to invalid assumptions. Imagine a class that modeled a country. If you can add one country to another, couldn't you subtract one country from another? Applying overloaded mathematical operators for non-mathematical objects rapidly becomes ridiculous.

You may compare objects (and, in fact, any reference) using either == or eq, but this only tells you whether the addresses are the same. (Using == is about 10 times faster than eq though.) Because an object is a higher-level notion than a raw machine address, you often want to define your own notion of what it takes for two of them to be considered equal.

Two operators frequently overloaded even for a non-numeric class are the comparison and string interpolation operators. Both the <=> and the cmp operators can be overloaded, although the former is more prevalent. Once the spaceship operator <=> is defined for an object, you can use ==, !=, <, <=, >, and >= as well. This lets objects be collated. If ordering is not desired, overload only ==. Similarly, an overloaded cmp is used for lt, gt, and other string comparisons if they aren't explicitly overloaded.

The string interpolation operator goes by the unlikely name of "", that is, two double quotes. This operator is triggered whenever a conversion to a string is called for, such as within double or back quotes or when passed to the print function.

Read the documentation on the overload pragma that comes with Perl or Chapter 13 of *Programming Perl*. Perl's operator overloading has some elaborate features, such as string, numeric, and Boolean conversion methods, autogeneration of missing methods, and reversing operands if needed, as in 5 + $a where $a is an object.

Example: Overloaded StrNum Class

Here's a StrNum class that lets you use strings with numeric operators. Yes, we're about to do something we advised against—that is, use numeric operators on non-numeric entities—but programmers from other backgrounds are always expecting + and == to work on strings. This is a simple way to demonstrate operator overloading. We almost certainly wouldn't use this in a time-critical production program due to performance concerns. It's also an interesting illustration of using a constructor of the same name as the class, something that C++ and Python programmers may take some small comfort in.

```
#!/usr/bin/perl
# show_strnum - demo operator overloading
use StrNum;

$x = StrNum("Red"); $y = StrNum("Black");
$z = $x + $y; $r = $z * 3;
print "values are $x, $y, $z, and $r\n";
print "$x is ", $x < $y ? "LT" : "GE", " $y\n";
```

values are Red, Black, RedBlack, and RedBlackRedBlackRedBlack
Red is GE Black

The class is shown in Example 13-1.

Example 13-1. StrNum

```
package StrNum;
use Exporter ();
@ISA = "Exporter";
@EXPORT = qw(StrNum);  # unusual
use overload        (
        '<=>'    => \&spaceship,
        "cmp"    => \&spaceship,
        '""'     => \&stringify,
        "bool"   => \&boolify,
        '0+'     => \&nummify,
        '+'      => \&concat,
        '*'      => \&repeat,
);
# constructor
sub StrNum {
    my ($value) = @_;
    return bless \$value;
}
sub stringify { ${ $_[0] } }
sub nummify   { ${ $_[0] } }
sub boolify   { ${ $_[0] } }
# providing <=> gives us <, ==, etc. for free.
sub spaceship {
```

Example 13-1. StrNum (continued)

```
    my ($s1, $s2, $inverted) = @_;
    return $inverted ? $$s2 cmp $$s1 : $$s1 cmp $$s2;
}
# this uses stringify
sub concat {
    my ($s1, $s2, $inverted) = @_;
    return StrNum($inverted ? ($s2 . $s1) : ($s1 . $s2));
}
# this uses stringify
sub repeat {
    my ($s1, $s2, $inverted) = @_;
    return StrNum($inverted ? ($s2 x $s1) : ($s1 x $s2));
}
1;
```

Example: Overloaded FixNum Class

This class uses operator overloading to control the number of decimal places in output. It still uses full precision for its operations. A places method can be used on the class or a particular object to set the number of places of output to the right of the decimal point.

```
#!/usr/bin/perl
# demo_fixnum - show operator overloading
use FixNum;

FixNum->places(5);

$x = FixNum->new(40);
$y = FixNum->new(12);

print "sum of $x and $y is ", $x + $y, "\n";
print "product of $x and $y is ", $x * $y, "\n";

$z = $x / $y;
printf "$z has %d places\n", $z->places;
$z->places(2) unless $z->places;
print "div of $x by $y is $z\n";
print "square of that is ", $z * $z, "\n";

sum of STRFixNum: 40 and STRFixNum: 12 is STRFixNum: 52
product of STRFixNum: 40 and STRFixNum: 12 is STRFixNum: 480
STRFixNum: 3 has 0 places
div of STRFixNum: 40 by STRFixNum: 12 is STRFixNum: 3.33
square of that is STRFixNum: 11.11
```

The class itself is shown in Example 13-2. It overloads only the addition, multiplication, and division operations for math operators. Other overloaded operators are the spaceship operator (which handles all comparisons), the string-interpolation operator, and the numeric conversion operator. The string interpolation operator is given a distinctive look for debugging purposes.

Example 13-2. FixNum

```perl
package FixNum;
use strict;
my $PLACES = 0;
sub new {
    my $proto  = shift;
    my $class  = ref($proto) || $proto;
    my $parent = ref($proto) && $proto;
    my $v = shift;
    my $self = {
        VALUE  => $v,
        PLACES => undef,
    };
    if ($parent && defined $parent->{PLACES}) {
        $self->{PLACES} = $parent->{PLACES};
    } elsif ($v =~ /(\.\d*)/) {
        $self->{PLACES} = length($1) - 1;
    } else {
        $self->{PLACES} = 0;
    }
    return bless $self, $class;
}
sub places {
    my $proto = shift;
    my $self  = ref($proto) && $proto;
    my $type  = ref($proto) || $proto;
    if (@_) {
        my $places = shift;
        ($self ? $self->{PLACES} : $PLACES) = $places;
    }
    return $self ? $self->{PLACES} : $PLACES;
}
sub _max { $_[0] > $_[1] ? $_[0] : $_[1] }
use overload '+'   => \&add,
             '*'   => \&multiply,
             '/'   => \&divide,
             '<=>' => \&spaceship,
             '""'  => \&as_string,
             '0+'  => \&as_number;
sub add {
    my ($this, $that, $flipped) = @_;
    my $result = $this->new( $this->{VALUE} + $that->{VALUE} );
    $result->places( _max($this->{PLACES}, $that->{PLACES} ));
    return $result;
}
sub multiply {
    my ($this, $that, $flipped) = @_;
    my $result = $this->new( $this->{VALUE} * $that->{VALUE} );
    $result->places( _max($this->{PLACES}, $that->{PLACES} ));
    return $result;
}
sub divide {
    my ($this, $that, $flipped) = @_;
```

Example 13-2. FixNum (continued)

```
    my $result = $this->new( $this->{VALUE} / $that->{VALUE} );
    $result->places( _max($this->{PLACES}, $that->{PLACES} ));
    return $result;
}
sub as_string {
    my $self = shift;
    return sprintf("STR%s: %.*f", ref($self),
        defined($self->{PLACES}) ? $self->{PLACES} : $PLACES,
}
sub as_number {
    my $self = shift;
    return $self->{VALUE};
}
sub spaceship {
    my ($this, $that, $flipped) = @_;
    $this->{VALUE} <=> $that->{VALUE};
}
1;
```

See Also

The documentation for the standard overload, bigint, and bigrat pragmata and the standard Math::BigInt, Math::BigFloat, and Math::Complex modules; also Chapters 13, 31, and 32 of *Programming Perl*

13.15 Creating Magic Variables with tie

Problem

You want to add special processing to a variable or handle.

Solution

Use the tie function to give your ordinary variables object hooks.

Discussion

Anyone who's ever used a DBM file under Perl has already used tied objects. Perhaps the most excellent way of using objects is such that the user need never notice them. With tie, you can bind a variable or handle to a class, after which all access to the tied variable or handle is transparently intercepted by specially named object methods (see Table 13-2).

The most important tie methods are FETCH to intercept read access, STORE to intercept write access, and the constructor, which is one of TIESCALAR, TIEARRAY, TIEHASH, or TIEHANDLE.

Table 13-2. How tied variables are interpreted

User code	Executed code
tie $s, "SomeClass"	SomeClass->TIESCALAR( )
$p = $s	$p = $obj->FETCH( )
$s = 10	$obj->STORE(10)

Where did that $obj come from? The tie triggers an invocation of the class's TIE-SCALAR constructor method. Perl squirrels away the object returned and surreptitiously uses it for later access.

Here's a simple example of a tie class that implements a value ring. Every time the variable is read from, the next value on the ring is displayed. When it's written to, a new value is pushed on the ring. Here's an example:

```
#!/usr/bin/perl
# demo_valuering - show tie class
use ValueRing;
tie $color, "ValueRing", qw(red blue);
print "$color $color $color $color $color $color\n";
red blue red blue red blue

$color = "green";
print "$color $color $color $color $color $color\n";
green red blue green red blue
```

The simple implementation is shown in Example 13-3.

Example 13-3. ValueRing

```
package ValueRing;
# this is the constructor for scalar ties
sub TIESCALAR {
    my ($class, @values) = @_;
    bless \@values, $class;
    return \@values;
}
# this intercepts read accesses
sub FETCH {
    my $self = shift;
    push(@$self, shift(@$self));
    return $self->[-1];
}
# this intercepts write accesses
sub STORE {
    my ($self, $value) = @_;
    unshift @$self, $value;
    return $value;
}
1;
```

This example might not be compelling, but it illustrates how easy it is to write ties of arbitrary complexity. To the user, $color is just a plain old variable, not an object.

All the magic is hidden beneath the tie. You don't have to use a scalar reference just because you're tying a scalar. Here we've used an array reference, but you can use anything you'd like. Usually a hash reference will be used no matter what's being tied because hashes provide the most flexible object representation.

For arrays and hashes, more elaborate operations are possible. Because so many object methods are needed to fully support tied variables (except perhaps for scalars), most users choose to inherit from standard modules that provide base class definitions of customary methods for operations on that variable type. They then selectively override only those whose behaviors they wish to alter.

These four modules are Tie::Scalar, Tie::Array, Tie::Hash, and Tie::Handle. Each module provides two different classes: a bare-bones class by the name of the module itself, as well as a more fleshed out class named Tie::Std*TYPE*, where *TYPE* is one of the four types.

Following are numerous examples of interesting uses of ties.

Tie Example: Outlaw $_

This curious tie class is used to outlaw unlocalized uses of the implicit variable, $_. Instead of pulling it in with use, which implicitly invokes the class's import() method, this one should be loaded with no to call invoke the seldom-used unimport() method. The user says:

```
no UnderScore;
```

Then, all uses of the unlocalized global $_ will raise an exception.

Here's a little test suite for the module:

```
#!/usr/bin/perl
#nounder_demo - show how to ban $_ from your program
no UnderScore;
@tests = (
    "Assignment"  => sub { $_ = "Bad" },
    "Reading"     => sub { print },
    "Matching"    => sub { $x = /badness/ },
    "Chop"        => sub { chop },
    "Filetest"    => sub { -x },
    "Nesting"     => sub { for (1..3) { print } },
);

while ( ($name, $code) = splice(@tests, 0, 2) ) {
    print "Testing $name: ";
    eval { &$code };
    print $@ ? "detected" : "missed!";
    print "\n";
}
```

The result is the following:

```
Testing Assignment: detected
Testing Reading: detected
Testing Matching: detected
Testing Chop: detected
Testing Filetest: detected
Testing Nesting: 123missed!
```

The reason the last one was missed is that it was properly localized by the for loop, so it was considered safe.

The UnderScore module itself is shown in Example 13-4. Notice how small it is. The module itself does the tie in its initialization code.

Example 13-4. UnderScore

```
package UnderScore;
use Carp;
sub TIESCALAR {
    my $class = shift;
    my $dummy;
    return bless \$dummy => $class;
}
sub FETCH { croak "Read access to \$_ forbidden"  }
sub STORE { croak "Write access to \$_ forbidden" }
sub unimport { tie($_, __PACKAGE__) }
sub import { untie $_ }
tie($_, __PACKAGE__) unless tied $_;
1;
```

You can't usefully mix calls to use and no for this class in your program, because they all happen at compile time, not runtime. To renege and let yourself use $_ again, localize it.

Tie Example: Make a Hash That Always Appends

The class shown here produces a hash whose keys accumulate in an array.

```
#!/usr/bin/perl
#appendhash_demo - show magic hash that autoappends
use Tie::AppendHash;
tie %tab, "Tie::AppendHash";

$tab{beer} = "guinness";
$tab{food} = "potatoes";
$tab{food} = "peas";

while (my($k, $v) = each %tab) {
    print "$k => [@$v]\n";
}
```

Here is the result:

```
food => [potatoes peas]
beer => [guinness]
```

To make this class easy, we use the boilerplate hash tying module from the standard distribution, shown in Example 13-5. To do this, we load the Tie::Hash module and then inherit from the Tie::StdHash class. (Yes, those are different names. The file *Tie/Hash.pm* provides both the Tie::Hash and Tie::StdHash classes, which are slightly different.)

Example 13-5. Tie::AppendHash

```
package Tie::AppendHash;
use strict;
use Tie::Hash;
use Carp;
our @ISA = qw(Tie::StdHash);
sub STORE {
    my ($self, $key, $value) = @_;
    push @{$self->{$key}}, $value;
}
1;
```

Tie Example: Case-Insensitive Hash

Here's a fancier hash tie called Tie::Folded. It provides a hash with case-insensitive keys.

```
#!/usr/bin/perl
#folded_demo - demo hash that magically folds case
use Tie::Folded;
tie %tab, "Tie::Folded";

$tab{VILLAIN}  = "big ";
$tab{herOine}  = "red riding hood";
$tab{villain} .= "bad wolf";

while ( my($k, $v) = each %tab ) {
    print "$k is $v\n";
}
```

The following is the output of this demo program:

```
heroine is red riding hood
villain is big bad wolf
```

Because we have to trap more accesses, the class in Example 13-6 is slightly more complicated than the one in Example 13-5.

Example 13-6. Tie::Folded

```
package Tie::Folded;
use strict;
use Tie::Hash;
our @ISA = qw(Tie::StdHash);
sub STORE {
    my ($self, $key, $value) = @_;
```

Example 13-6. Tie::Folded (continued)

```perl
    return $self->{lc $key} = $value;
    }
sub FETCH {
    my ($self, $key) = @_;
    return $self->{lc $key};
}
sub EXISTS {
    my ($self, $key) = @_;
    return exists $self->{lc $key};
}
sub DEFINED {
    my ($self, $key) = @_;
    return defined $self->{lc $key};
}
1;
```

Tie Example: Hash That Allows Lookups by Key or Value

Here is a hash that lets you look up members by key or by value. It does this by having a store method that uses not only the key to store the value, but also uses the
value to store the key.

Normally there could be a problem if the value being stored were a reference, since
you can't normally use a reference as a key. The standard distribution comes with
the Tie::RefHash class that avoids this problem. We'll inherit from it so that we can
also avoid this difficulty.

```perl
#!/usr/bin/perl -w
#revhash_demo - show hash that permits key *or* value lookups
use strict;
use Tie::RevHash;
my %tab;
tie %tab, "Tie::RevHash";
%tab = qw{
    Red         Rojo
    Blue        Azul
    Green       Verde
};
$tab{EVIL} = [ "No way!", "Way!!" ];

while ( my($k, $v) = each %tab ) {
    print ref($k) ? "[@$k]" : $k, " => ",
        ref($v) ? "[@$v]" : $v, "\n";
}
```

When run, *revhash_demo* produces this:

```
[No way! Way!!] => EVIL
EVIL => [No way! Way!!]
Blue => Azul
Green => Verde
Rojo => Red
```

```
Red => Rojo
Azul => Blue
Verde => Green
```

The module is shown in Example 13-7. Notice how small it is!

Example 13-7. Tie::RevHash

```
package Tie::RevHash;
use Tie::RefHash;
our @ISA = qw(Tie::RefHash);
sub STORE {
    my ($self, $key, $value) = @_;
    $self->SUPER::STORE($key, $value);
    $self->SUPER::STORE($value, $key);
}
sub DELETE {
    my ($self, $key) = @_;
    my $value = $self->SUPER::FETCH($key);
    $self->SUPER::DELETE($key);
    $self->SUPER::DELETE($value);
}
1;
```

Tie Example: Handle That Counts Access

Here's an example of tying a filehandle:

```
use Counter;
tie *CH, "Counter";
while (<CH>) {
    print "Got $_\n";
}
```

When run, that program keeps printing Got 1, Got 2, and so on until the universe collapses, you hit an interrupt, or your computer reboots, whichever comes first. Its simple implementation is shown in Example 13-8.

Example 13-8. Counter

```
package Counter;
sub TIEHANDLE {
    my $class = shift;
    my $start = shift;
    return bless \$start => $class;
}
sub READLINE {
    my $self = shift;
    return ++$$self;
}
1;
```

Tie Example: Multiple Sink Filehandles

Finally, here's an example of a tied handle that implements a *tee*-like functionality by twinning standard out and standard error:

```
use Tie::Tee;
tie *TEE, "Tie::Tee", *STDOUT, *STDERR;
print TEE "This line goes both places.\n";
```

Or, more elaborately:

```
#!/usr/bin/perl
# demo_tietee
use Tie::Tee;
use Symbol;

@handles = (*STDOUT);
for $i ( 1 .. 10 ) {
    push(@handles, $handle = gensym( ));
    open($handle, ">/tmp/teetest.$i");
}

tie *TEE, "Tie::Tee", @handles;
print TEE "This lines goes many places.\n";
```

The *Tie/Tee.pm* file is shown in Example 13-9.

Example 13-9. Tie::Tee

```
package Tie::Tee;
sub TIEHANDLE {
    my $class   = shift;
    my $handles = [@_];
    bless $handles, $class;
    return $handles;
}
sub PRINT {
    my $href = shift;
    my $handle;
    my $success = 0;
    foreach $handle (@$href) {
        $success += print $handle @_;
    }
    return $success == @$href;
}
1;
```

See Also

The tie function in *perlfunc*(1); *perltie*(1); Chapter 14 of *Programming Perl*

CHAPTER 14

Database Access

I only ask for information.
—Charles Dickens, *David Copperfield*

14.0 Introduction

Everywhere you find data, you find databases. At the simplest level, every file can be considered a database. At the most complex level, expensive and complex relational database systems handle thousands of transactions per second. In between are countless improvised schemes for fast access to loosely structured data. Perl can work with all of them.

Early in the history of computers, people noticed that flat file databases don't scale to large data sets. Flat files were tamed using fixed-length records or auxiliary indices, but updating became expensive, and previously simple applications bogged down with I/O overhead.

After some head-scratching, clever programmers devised a better solution. As hashes in memory provide more flexible access to data than do arrays, hashes on disk offer more convenient kinds of access than array-like text files. These benefits in access time cost you space, but disk space is cheap these days (or so the reasoning goes).

The DBM library gives Perl programmers a simple, easy-to-use database. You use the same standard operations on hashes bound to DBM files as you do on hashes in memory. In fact, that's how you use DBM databases from Perl. You use tie to associate a hash with a class and a file. Then whenever you access the hash, the class consults or changes the DBM database on disk. The old dbmopen function also did this, but only let you use one DBM implementation in your program, so you couldn't copy from one format to another.

Recipe 14.1 shows how to create a DBM database and gives tips on using it efficiently. Although you can do with DBM files the same things you do with regular hashes, their disk-based nature leads to performance concerns that don't exist with in-memory hashes. Because DBM files are disk-based and can be shared between processors, use a sentinel lock file (see Recipe 7.24) to regulate concurrent access to them.Recipes 14.2 and 14.4 explain these concerns and show how to work around them. DBM files also make possible operations that aren't available using regular hashes. Recipe 14.5 explains two of these things.

Various DBM implementations offer varying features. Table 14-1 shows several possible DBM libraries you can choose from.

Table 14-1. DBM libraries and their features

Feature	NDBM	SDBM	GDBM	DB
Linkage comes with Perl	yes	yes	yes	yes
Source bundled with Perl	no	yes	no	no
Source redistributable	no	yes	gpl[a]	yes
FTPable	no	yes	yes	yes
Easy to build	N/A	yes	yes	ok[b]
Often comes with Unix	yes[c]	no	no[d]	no[d]
Builds okay on Unix	N/A	yes	yes	yes[e]
Builds okay on Windows	N/A	yes	yes	yes[f]
Code size	g	small	big	big[h]
Disk usage	g	small	big	ok
Speed	g	slow	ok	fast
Block size limits	4k	1k[i]	none	none
Byte-order independent	no	no	no	yes
User-defined sort order	no	no	no	yes
Partial key lookups	no	no	no	yes

[a] Using GPLed code in your program places restrictions upon you. See *http://www.gnu.org* for more details.
[b] See the DB_File library method. Requires symbolic links.
[c] On mixed-universe machines, this may be in the BSD compatibility library, which is often shunned.
[d] Except for free Unix ports such as Linux, FreeBSD, OpenBSD, and NetBSD.
[e] Providing you have an ANSI C compiler.
[f] Prior to unification in 5.005, several divergent versions of Perl on Windows systems were widely available, including the standard port build from the normal Perl distribution and several proprietary ports. Like most CPAN modules, DB builds only on the standard port.
[g] Depends on how much your vendor has tweaked it.
[h] Can be reduced if you compile for one access method.
[i] By default, but can be redefined (at the expense of compatibility with older files).

NDBM comes with most BSD-derived machines. GDBM is a GNU DBM implementation. SDBM is part of the X11 distribution and also the standard Perl source distribution. DB refers to the Berkeley DB library. While the others are essentially reimplementations of the original DB library, the Berkeley DB code gives you three different types of database on disk and attempts to solve many of the disk, speed, and size limitations that hinder the other implementations.

Code size refers to the size of the compiled libraries. Disk usage refers to the size of the database files it creates. Block size limits refer to the database's maximum key or value size. Byte-order independence refers to whether the database system relies on hardware byte order or whether it instead creates portable files. A user-defined sort order lets you tell the library in what order to return lists of keys. Partial key lookups let you make approximate searches on the database.

Most Perl programmers prefer the Berkeley DB implementations. Many systems already have this library installed, and Perl can use it. For others, you are advised to fetch and install it from CPAN. It will make your life much easier.

DBM files provide key/value pairs. In relational database terms, you get a database with one table that has only two columns. Recipe 14.6 shows you how to use the MLDBM module from CPAN to store arbitrarily complex data structures in a DBM file.

As good as MLDBM is, it doesn't get around the limitation that you only retrieve rows based on one single column, the hash key. If you need complex queries, the difficulties can be overwhelming. In these cases, consider a separate database management system (DBMS). The DBI project provides modules to work with Oracle, Sybase, mSQL, MySQL, Ingres, and others.

An interesting medium between a full relational database server and a DBM file is the DBD::SQLite module. This provides an SQL interface to a relational database, but without a server process—the module reads and writes the single file that contains all your tables. This gives you the power of SQL and multiple tables without the inconvenience of RDBMS administration. A benefit of manipulating tables from the one process is a considerable gain in speed.

See *http://dbi.perl.org/doc/index.html* and *http://search.cpan.org/modlist/Database_Interfaces*. DBI supports most major and minor databases, including Oracle, ODBC, Sybase, Informix, MySQL, PostgreSQL, and XBase. There are also DBD interfaces to data sources such as SQLite, Excel files, and CSV files.

14.1   Making and Using a DBM File

Problem

You want to create, populate, inspect, or delete values in a DBM database.

Solution

Use tie to open the database and make it accessible through a hash. Then use the hash as you normally would. When you're done, call untie:

```
use DB_File;            # load database module

tie %HASH, "DB_File", $FILENAME            # open database to be accessed
```

```
        or die "Can't open $FILENAME:$!\n";        # through %HASH

    $V = $HASH{$KEY};                               # retrieve from database
    $HASH{$KEY} = $VALUE;                           # put value into database
    if (exists $HASH{$KEY}) {                       # check whether in database
        # ...
    }
    delete $HASH{$KEY};                             # delete from database
    untie %HASH;                                    # close the database
```

Discussion

Accessing a database as a hash is powerful but easy, giving you a persistent hash that sticks around after the program using it has finished running. It's also much faster than loading in a new hash every time; even if the hash has a million entries, your program starts up virtually instantaneously.

The program in Example 14-1 treats the database as though it were a normal hash. You can even call keys or each on it. Likewise, exists and defined are implemented for tied DBM hashes. Unlike a normal hash, a DBM hash does not distinguish between those two functions.

Example 14-1. userstats

```
#!/usr/bin/perl -w
# userstats - generates statistics on who is logged in.
# call with an argument to display totals

use DB_File;

$db = "/tmp/userstats.db";        # where data is kept between runs

tie(%db, 'DB_File', $db)          or die "Can't open DB_File $db : $!\n";

if (@ARGV) {
    if ("@ARGV" eq "ALL") {
        @ARGV = sort keys %db;
    }
    foreach $user (@ARGV) {
        print "$user\t$db{$user}\n";
    }
} else {
    @who = `who`;                             # run who(1)
    if ($?) {
        die "Couldn't run who: $?\n";         # exited abnormally
    }
    # extract username (first thing on the line) and update
    foreach $line (@who) {
        $line =~ /^(\S+)/;
        die "Bad line from who: $line\n" unless $1;
        $db{$1}++;
    }
```

Example 14-1. userstats (continued)

```
}

untie %db;
```

We use *who* to get a list of users logged in. This typically produces output like:

```
gnat    ttyp1   May 29 15:39   (coprolith.frii.com)
```

If the *userstats* program is called without any arguments, it checks who's logged on and updates the database appropriately.

If the program is called with arguments, these are treated as usernames whose information will be presented. The special argument "ALL" sets @ARGV to a sorted list of DBM keys. For large hashes with many keys, this is prohibitively expensive—a better solution would be to use the BTREE bindings of DB_File described in Recipe 14.5.

The old dbmopen function still works. Here's the solution rewritten to use dbmopen and dbmclose:

```
use DB_File;                            # optional; overrides default
dbmopen %HASH, $FILENAME, 0666          # open database, accessed through
%HASH
    or die "Can't open $FILENAME:$!\n";

$V = $HASH{$KEY};                       # retrieve from database
$HASH{$KEY} = $VALUE;                    # put value into database
if (exists $HASH{$KEY}) {               # check whether in database
    # ...
}
delete $HASH{$KEY};                     # remove from database
dbmclose %HASH;                         # close the database
```

See Also

The documentation for the standard modules GDBM_File, NDBM_File, SDBM_File, and DB_File, some of which are in Chapter 32 of *Programming Perl*; *perltie*(1); Chapter 14 of *Programming Perl*; the discussion on the effect of your umask on file creation in Recipe 7.1; Recipe 13.15

14.2   Emptying a DBM File

Problem

You want to clear out a DBM file.

Solution

Open the database and assign ( ) to it. Use tie:

```
use DB_File;

tie(%HASH, "DB_File", $FILENAME)         or die "Can't open FILENAME: $!\n";
%HASH = ( );
untie %HASH;
```

Alternatively, delete the file and reopen:

```
unlink $FILENAME
    or die "Couldn't unlink $FILENAME to empty the database: $!\n";
tie(%HASH => "DB_File", $FILENAME)
    or die "Couldn't create $FILENAME database: $!\n";
```

Discussion

It may be quicker to delete the file and create a new one than to reset it, but doing so opens you up to a race condition that trips up a careless program or makes it vulnerable to an attacker. The attacker could make a link pointing to the file */etc/precious* with the same name as your file between the time when you deleted the file and when you recreated it. When the DBM library opens the file, it clobbers */etc/precious*.

If you delete a DB_File database and recreate it, you'll lose any customizable settings like page size, fill-factor, and so on. This is another good reason to assign the empty list to the tied hash.

See Also

The documentation for the standard DB_File module, also in Chapter 32 of *Programming Perl*; the unlink function in *perlfunc*(1); Recipe 14.1

14.3 Converting Between DBM Files

Problem

You have a file in one DBM format, but another program expects input in a different DBM format.

Solution

Read the keys and values from the initial DBM file and write them to a new file in the different DBM format as in Example 14-2.

Example 14-2. db2gdbm

```
#!/usr/bin/perl -w
# db2gdbm: converts DB to GDBM

use strict;
```

Example 14-2. db2gdbm (continued)

```
use DB_File;
use GDBM_File;

unless (@ARGV == 2) {
    die "usage: db2gdbm infile outfile\n";
}

my ($infile, $outfile) = @ARGV;
my (%db_in, %db_out);

# open the files
tie(%db_in, 'DB_File', $infile)
    or die "Can't tie $infile: $!";
tie(%db_out, 'GDBM_File', $outfile, GDBM_WRCREAT, 0666)
    or die "Can't tie $outfile: $!";

# copy (don't use %db_out = %db_in because it's slow on big databases)
while (my($k, $v) = each %db_in) {
    $db_out{$k} = $v;
}

# these unties happen automatically at program exit
untie %db_in;
untie %db_out;
```

Call the program as:

```
% db2gdbm /tmp/users.db /tmp/users.gdbm
```

Discussion

When multiple types of DBM file are used in the same program, you have to use tie, not the dbmopen interface. That's because with dbmopen you can use only one database format, which is why its use is deprecated.

Copying hashes by simple assignment, as in %new = %old, works on DBM files. However, it loads everything into memory first as a list, which doesn't matter with small hashes, but can be prohibitively expensive in the case of DBM files. For database hashes, use each to iterate through them instead.

See Also

The documentation for the standard modules GDBM_File, NDBM_File, SDBM_File, DB_File, some of which are in Chapter 32 of *Programming Perl*; Recipe 14.1

14.4   Merging DBM Files

Problem

You want to combine two DBM files into a single DBM file with original key-value pairs.

Solution

Either merge the databases by treating their hashes as lists:

```
%OUTPUT = (%INPUT1, %INPUT2);
```

or, more wisely, by iterating over each key-value pair:

```
%OUTPUT = ( );
foreach $href ( \%INPUT1, \%INPUT2 ) {
    while (my($key, $value) = each(%$href)) {
        if (exists $OUTPUT{$key}) {
            # decide which value to use and set $OUTPUT{$key} if necessary
        } else {
            $OUTPUT{$key} = $value;
        }
    }
}
```

Discussion

This straightforward application of Recipe 5.11 comes with the same caveats. Merging hashes by treating them as lists requires that the hashes be preloaded into memory, creating a potentially humongous temporary list. If you're dealing with large hashes, have little virtual memory, or both, then you want to iterate over the keys with each to save memory.

Another difference between these merging techniques is what to do if the same key exists in both input databases. The blind assignment merely overwrites the first value with the second value. The iterative merging technique lets you decide what to do. Possibilities include issuing a warning or error, choosing the first over the second, choosing the second over the first, or concatenating the new value to the old one. If you're using the MLDBM module, you can even store them both, using an array reference to the two values.

See Also

Recipe 5.11; Recipe 14.6

14.5   Sorting Large DBM Files

Problem

You want to process a large dataset you'd like to commit to a DBM file in a particular order.

Solution

Use the DB_File's B-tree bindings and supply a comparison function of your own devising:

```perl
use DB_File;

# specify the Perl sub to do key comparison using the
# exported $DB_BTREE hash reference
$DB_BTREE->{'compare'} = sub {
    my ($key1, $key2) = @_ ;
    "\L$key1" cmp "\L$key2" ;
};

tie(%hash, "DB_File", $filename, O_RDWR|O_CREAT, 0666, $DB_BTREE)
    or die "can't tie $filename: $!";
```

Description

An annoyance of hashes, whether in memory or as DBM files, is that they do not maintain proper ordering. The CPAN module Tie::IxHash can make a regular hash in memory maintain its insertion order, but that doesn't help for DBM databases or arbitrary sorting criteria.

The DB_File module supports a nice solution to this using a B-tree implementation. One advantage of a B-tree over a regular DBM hash is its ordering. When the user defines a comparison function, all calls to keys, values, and each are automatically ordered. For example, Example 14-3 is a program that maintains a hash whose keys will always be sorted case-insensitively.

Example 14-3. sortdemo

```perl
#!/usr/bin/perl
#
sortdemo - show auto dbm sorting
use strict;
use DB_File;

$DB_BTREE->{'compare'} = sub {
    my ($key1, $key2) = @_ ;
    "\L$key1" cmp "\L$key2" ;
};
```

Example 14-3. sortdemo (continued)

```perl
my %hash;
my $filename = '/tmp/sorthash.db';
tie(%hash, "DB_File", $filename, O_RDWR|O_CREAT, 0666, $DB_BTREE)
    or die "can't tie $filename: $!";

my $i = 0;
for my $word (qw(Can't you go camp down by Gibraltar)) {
    $hash{$word} = ++$i;
}

while (my($word, $number) = each %hash) {
    printf "%-12s %d\n", $word, $number;
}
```

By default, the entries in a B-tree DB_File database are stored alphabetically. Here, though, we provide a case-insensitive comparison function, so using each to fetch all the keys would show:

by	*6*
camp	*4*
Can't	*1*
down	*5*
Gibraltar	*7*
go	*3*
you	*2*

This sorting property on hashes is so convenient that it's worth using even without a permanent database. If you pass undef where the filename is expected on the tie, DB_File will create a file in */tmp* and then immediately unlink it, giving an anonymous database:

```perl
tie(%hash, "DB_File", undef, O_RDWR|O_CREAT, 0666, $DB_BTREE)
        or die "can't tie: $!";
```

Remember these two things if you supply a comparison for your BTREE database. One, the new compare function must be specified when you create the database. Two, you cannot change the ordering once the database has been created; you must use the same compare function every time you access the database.

Using BTREE databases under DB_File also permits duplicate or partial keys. See its documentation for examples.

See Also

Recipe 5.7

14.6 Storing Complex Data in a DBM File

Problem

You want values in a DBM file to be something other than scalars. For instance, you use a hash of hashes in your program and want to store them in a DBM file for other programs to access, or you want them to persist across process runs.

Solution

Use the CPAN module MLDBM to store more complex values than strings and numbers.

```
use MLDBM 'DB_File';
tie(%HASH, 'MLDBM', [... other DBM arguments]) or die $!;
```

Specify a particular serializing module with:

```
use MLDBM qw(DB_File Storable);
```

Discussion

MLDBM uses a serializing module like Storable, Data::Dumper, or FreezeThaw (see Recipe 11.4) to convert data structures to and from strings so that they can be stored in a DBM file. It doesn't store references; instead, it stores the data those references refer to:

```
# %hash is a tied hash
$hash{"Tom Christiansen"} = [ "book author", 'tchrist@perl.com' ];
$hash{"Tom Boutell"} = [ "shareware author", 'boutell@boutell.com' ];

# names to compare
$name1 = "Tom Christiansen";
$name2 = "Tom Boutell";

$tom1 = $hash{$name1};        # snag local pointer
$tom2 = $hash{$name2};        # and another

print "Two Toming: $tom1 $tom2\n";
```

Tom Toming: ARRAY(0x73048) ARRAY(0x73e4c)

Each time MLDBM retrieves a data structure from the DBM file, it generates a new copy of that data. To compare data that you retrieve from a MLDBM database, you need to compare the values within the structure:

```
if ($tom1->[0] eq $tom2->[0] &&
    $tom1->[1] eq $tom2->[1]) {
    print "You're having runtime fun with one Tom made two.\n";
} else {
    print "No two Toms are ever alike.\n";
}
```

This is more efficient than:

```
if ($hash{$name1}->[0] eq $hash{$name2}->[0] &&      # INEFFICIENT
    $hash{$name1}->[1] eq $hash{$name2}->[1]) {
    print "You're having runtime fun with one Tom made two.\n";
} else {
    print "No two Toms are ever alike.\n";
}
```

Each time we say $hash{...}, the DBM file is consulted. The inefficient code accesses the database four times, whereas the code using the temporary variables $tom1 and $tom2 only accesses the database twice.

Current limitations of Perl's tie mechanism prevent you from storing or modifying parts of a MLDBM value directly:

```
$hash{"Tom Boutell"}->[0] = "Poet Programmer";      # WRONG
```

Always get, change, and set pieces of the stored structure through a temporary variable:

```
$entry = $hash{"Tom Boutell"};                      # RIGHT
$entry->[0] = "Poet Programmer";
$hash{"Tom Boutell"} = $entry;
```

If MLDBM uses a database with size limits on values, like SDBM, you'll quickly hit those limits. To get around this, use GDBM_File or DB_File, which don't limit the size of keys or values. DB_File is the better choice because it is byte-order neutral, which lets the database be shared between both big- and little-endian architectures.

See Also

The documentation for the standard Data::Dumper and Storable modules; the documentation for the FreezeThaw and MLDBM modules from CPAN; Recipe 11.13; Recipe 14.7

14.7   Persistent Data

Problem

You want your variables to retain their values between calls to your program.

Solution

Use a MLDBM to store the values between calls to your program:

```
use MLDBM "DB_File";

my ($VARIABLE1,$VARIABLE2);
my $Persistent_Store = "/projects/foo/data";
BEGIN {
    my %data;
```

```
        tie(%data, "MLDBM", $Persistent_Store)
            or die "Can't tie to $Persistent_Store : $!";
        $VARIABLE1 = $data{VARIABLE1};
        $VARIABLE2 = $data{VARIABLE2};
        # ...
        untie %data;
    }
    END {
        my %data;
        tie (%data, "MLDBM", $Persistent_Store)
            or die "Can't tie to $Persistent_Store : $!";
        $data{VARIABLE1} = $VARIABLE1;
        $data{VARIABLE2} = $VARIABLE2;
        # ...
        untie %data;
    }
```

Discussion

An important limitation of MLDBM is that you can't add to or alter the structure in
the reference without assignment to a temporary variable. We do this in the sample
program in Example 14-4, assigning to $array_ref before we push. You can't simply
do this:

```
    push(@{$db{$user}}, $duration);
```

For a start, MLDBM doesn't allow it. Also, $db{$user} might not be in the database
(the array reference isn't automatically created as it would be if %db weren't tied to a
DBM file). This is why we test exists $db{$user} when we give $array_ref its initial
value. We're creating the empty array for the case where it doesn't already exist.

Example 14-4. mldbm-demo

```perl
#!/usr/bin/perl -w
# mldbm_demo - show how to use MLDBM with DB_File

use MLDBM "DB_File";

$db = "/tmp/mldbm-array";

tie %db, "MLDBM", $db
  or die "Can't open $db : $!";

while(<DATA>) {
    chomp;
    ($user, $duration) = split(/\s+/, $_);
    $array_ref = exists $db{$user} ? $db{$user} : [ ];
    push(@$array_ref, $duration);
    $db{$user} = $array_ref;
}

foreach $user (sort keys %db) {
```

Example 14-4. mldbm-demo (continued)

```
    print "$user: ";
    $total = 0;
    foreach $duration (@{ $db{$user} }) {
        print "$duration ";
        $total += $duration;
    }
        print "($total)\n";
    }

__END__
gnat        15.3
tchrist     2.5
jules       22.1
tchrist     15.9
gnat        8.7
```

Newer versions of MLDBM allow you to select not just the database module (we recommend DB_File), but also the serialization module (we recommend Storable). Early
versions limited you to Data::Dumper for serializing, which is slower than Storable.
Here's how you use DB_File with Storable:

```
    use MLDBM qw(DB_File Storable);
```

See Also

The documentation for the standard Data::Dumper and Storable modules; the documentation for the FreezeThaw and MLDBM modules from CPAN; Recipe 11.13;
Recipe 14.6

14.8   Saving Query Results to Excel or CSV

Problem

You want to query a relational database and create a file of the results so that another
program or person can use them. The two common formats people want to get data
in are CSV and Excel.

Solution

Use the CPAN module DBIx::Dump to dump the statement handle after the query:

```
    use DBIx::Dump;
    use DBI;

    # ... connect to your database as normal
    $sth = $dbh->prepare("SELECT ...");  # your query here
    $sth->execute();
```

```
$out = DBIx::Dump->new('format' => $FORMAT,    # excel or csv
                       'output' => $FILENAME, # file to save as
                       'sth'    => $sth);
$out->dump();
```

Discussion

The CPAN module DBIx::Dump supports Excel and CSV file formats. It uses the CPAN module Spreadsheet::WriteExcel to write Excel files, and the CPAN module Text::CSV_XS to write CSV files.

The first row in the output files holds the column names. For example:

```
ID,NAME
1,Nat
2,Tom
4,Larry
5,Damian
6,Jon
7,Dan
```

See Also

The documentation for the CPAN modules DBIx::Dump, Spreadsheet::WriteExcel, and Text::CSV_XS; Recipe 14.17

14.9   Executing an SQL Command Using DBI

Problem

You want to send SQL queries to a database system such as Oracle, Sybase, mSQL, or MySQL, and process the results.

Solution

Use the DBI (DataBase Interface) and DBD (DataBase Driver) modules available from CPAN:

```
use DBI;

$dbh = DBI->connect('dbi:driver:database', 'username', 'auth',
          { RaiseError => 1, AutoCommit => 1});

$dbh->do($NON_SELECT_SQL_STATEMENT);

$results = $dbh->selectall_arrayref($SELECT_SQL_STATEMENT);

$sth = $dbh->prepare($SQL_SELECT_STATEMENT);
$sth->execute();
while (@row = $sth->fetchrow_array) {
```

```
  # ...
}

$dbh->disconnect();
```

Discussion

The DBI module abstracts away the different database APIs, offering you a single set of functions for accessing every database. The actual work of connecting to a database, issuing queries, parsing results, etc. is done by a DBD module specific to that database (e.g., DBD::mysql, DBD::Oracle, etc.).

All work with databases via the DBI is done through handles. A handle is simply an object, created by calling DBI->connect. This is attached to a specific database and driver using the DBI->connect call.

The first argument to DBI->connect is a single string with three colon-separated fields. This DSN (Data Source Name) identifies the database you're connecting to. The first field is always dbi (though this is case-insensitive, so DBI will do just as well), and the second is the name of the driver you're going to use (Oracle, mysql, etc.). The rest of the string is passed by the DBI module to the requested driver module (DBD::mysql, for example) where it identifies the database.

The second and third arguments authenticate the user.

The fourth argument is an optional hash reference defining attributes of the connection. PrintError controls whether DBI warns when a DBI method fails (the default is true; setting it to a false value keeps DBI quiet). Setting RaiseError is like PrintError except that die is used instead of warn. AutoCommit controls transactions, and setting it to true says that you don't want to deal with them (see Recipe 14.11).

At the time of this writing, there were DBD modules for all common databases (MySQL, Oracle, PostgreSQL, Informix, DB2, SQLServer), many fringe ones (XBase, SQLite), and several non-databases. For a list, see *http://search.cpan.org/modlist/Database_Interfaces/DBD*.

Here are some sample DSNs:

```
dbi:Oracle:tnsname
dbi:Oracle:host=foo.bar.com;sid=ORCL
dbi:Oracle:host=foo.bar.com;sid=ORCL;port=1521
dbi:mysql:database=foo;host=foo.bar.com;port=3306;mysql_compression=1
dbi:Pg:dbname=foo;host=foo.bar.com;options=-F
```

You can execute simple SQL statements (those that don't return rows of data) with a database handle's do method. This returns Boolean true or false. The quickest way to perform a query that returns rows of data is with the selectall_arrayref and selectall_hashref methods:

```
$rows = $dbh->selectall_arrayref("SELECT isbn,title,author FROM books");
print $row[0][1];           # prints title from first row
```

```
$rows = $dbh->selectall_hashref("SELECT isbn,title,author FROM books", "isbn");
print $rows->{596000278}[2]; # prints "Programming Perl"
```

The database system uses the second and third arguments, the username and password, to authenticate the user.

Sometimes your query will generate many rows of results, but you're only interested in one column. The selectcol_arrayref method is designed for just such a case: it turns a series of one-column rows into a reference to a simple Perl array of values:

```
$books = $dbh->selectcol_arrayref("SELECT title FROM books");
print $books[3]; # prints the title of the fourth book
```

If you don't want to read all results into memory at once, or you want to efficiently reuse queries, use the database handle's prepare method to create a statement handle. Then call the execute method on the statement handle to perform the query, and retrieve rows with a fetch method like fetchrow_array or fetchrow_hashref (which returns a reference to a hash, mapping column name to value). This is used in Recipe 14.12.

If you know your result will return only a single row, use the selectrow_* methods:

```
@row = $dbh->selectrow_array("SELECT title,author FROM books WHERE
isbn='596000278'");
print $row[1];            # prints author of first book returned

$row = $dbh->selectrow_arrayref("SELECT title,author FROM books WHERE
isbn='596000278'");
print $row->[1];          # prints author of first book returned

$row = $dbh->selectrow_hashref("SELECT title,author FROM books WHERE
isbn='596000278'", "title");
print $row->{author};     # prints author of first book returned
```

Statement handles and database handles often correspond to underlying connections to the database, so some care must be taken with them. A connection is automatically cleaned up when its handle goes out of scope. If a database handle goes out of scope while there are active statement handles for that database, though, you will get a warning like this:

```
disconnect(DBI::db=HASH(0x9df84)) invalidates 1 active cursor(s)
        at -e line 1.
```

This indicates that you have not fetched all of the data returned by a SELECT statement. In the few rare cases where this does not indicate a problem, and you don't want to use one of the selectrow_* methods, then the finish method can be used to discard the unfetched data and mark the statement handle as inactive.

The DBI module comes with a FAQ (the *DBI::FAQ*(3) manpage, kept up to date at *http://dbi.perl.org*) and regular documentation (perldoc DBI). The driver for your DBMS also has documentation (*DBD::mysql*(3), for instance). The DBI API is larger than the simple subset we've shown here: it provides diverse ways of fetching results, and it hooks into DBMS-specific features like stored procedures. Consult the driver module's documentation to learn about these.

The program in Example 14-5 creates, populates, and searches a MySQL table of users. It uses the RaiseError attribute so it doesn't have to check the return status of every method call.

Example 14-5. dbusers

```perl
#!/usr/bin/perl -w
# dbusers - manage MySQL user table
use DBI;
use User::pwent;

$dbh = DBI->connect('dbi:mysql:dbname:mysqlserver.domain.com:3306',
                    'user', 'password',
                    { RaiseError => 1, AutoCommit => 1 })

$dbh->do("CREATE TABLE users (uid INT, login CHAR(8))");

$sql_fmt = "INSERT INTO users VALUES( %d, %s )";
while ($user = getpwent) {
    $sql = sprintf($sql_fmt, $user->uid, $dbh->quote($user->name));
    $dbh->do($sql);
}
$rows = $dbh->selectall_arrayref("SELECT uid,login FROM users WHERE uid < 50");
foreach $row (@$rows) {
    print join(", ", map {defined $_ ? $_ : "(null)"} @$row), "\n";
}

$dbh->do("DROP TABLE users");

$dbh->disconnect;
```

See Also

The documentation for the DBI and relevant DBD modules from CPAN; *http://dbi.perl.org/* and *http://search.cpan.org/modlist/Database_Interfaces*; *Programming the Perl DBI*, by Alligator Descartes and Tim Bunce (O'Reilly)

14.10 Escaping Quotes

Problem

You want to put Perl values into queries as literal strings, but you're not sure how your database wants strings to be quoted.

Solution

Use the database handle's quote method:

```
$quoted = $dbh->quote($unquoted);
```

This $quoted value is now suitable for interpolation into queries:

```
$sth->prepare("SELECT id,login FROM People WHERE name = $quoted");
```

Or simply use placeholders in your query and DBI automatically quotes strings for you:

```
$sth->prepare("SELECT id,login FROM People WHERE name = ?");
$sth->execute($unquoted);
```

Discussion

Each database has its own quoting idiosyncrasies, so leave the quoting to the quote method or placeholders rather than trying to roll your own quoting function. Not only is hardcoding quotes into your SQL non-portable, it doesn't take into account the possibility that the strings you're interpolating might have quotes in them. For example, take this:

```
$sth = $dbh->prepare(qq{SELECT id,login FROM People WHERE name="$name"});
```

If $name is Jon "maddog" Orwant, then you are effectively preparing this query, which is invalid SQL:

```
SELECT id,login FROM People WHERE name="Jon "maddog" Orwant"
```

The only strange quoting behavior from quote is this: because the DBI represents NULL values as undef, if you pass undef to quote, it returns NULL without quotes.

See Also

The documentation with the DBI module from CPAN; *http://dbi.perl.org*; *Programming the Perl DBI*

14.11 Dealing with Database Errors

Problem

You want your program to catch and handle database errors, possibly displaying informative error messages.

Solution

The best solution is to enable RaiseError when you connect to the database, then wrap database calls in eval:

```
$dbh = DBI->connect($DSN, $user, $password,
                    { RaiseError => 1 });
eval {
  $dbh->do($SQL);
  $sth = $dbh->prepare($SQL2);
  $sth->execute();
  while (@row = $sth->fetchrow_array) {
    # ...
  }
};
if ($@) {
  # recover here using $DBI::lasth->errstr to get
  # the error message
}
```

Discussion

The logic here is simple: first tell DBI to die if there's a problem with your SQL (otherwise, the database can't do what you wanted it to). Then, wrap the code that might die in eval to catch fatal errors. Next, check $@ (either the error message you would have died with or empty if there was no error) to see whether something went wrong. If it did, somehow deal with the error.

DBI supplies the $DBI::lasth variable, containing the last handle acted on. If something went wrong, that's the handle that caused it. You could use the $@ error message, but that also has the "died at file ... line ..." text from die that you might not want. To discover the SQL statement that died, use $DBI::lasth->{Statement}. If you are using only the one handle, you can call the methods directly on your handle instead of on $DBI::lasth:

```
$msg = $dbh->errstr;
$sql = $dbh->{Statement};
```

An alternative approach is to disable RaiseError and check the return value for each database call. Methods such as do and execute return a true value if successful, so you can say:

```
$dbh->do($SQL) or die $dbh->errstr;
$sth->execute() or die $sth->errstr;
```

The do method returns the number of rows affected, but in such a way that it always returns a true value if successful. (If you're curious how to do this, see the Introduction to Chapter 1 for the gory details of how Perl decides what's true and what's false.)

If you're debugging error catching and error handling, you might want to add the PrintError attribute to your database connection:

```
$dbh = DBI->connect($DSN, $user, $password,
                    { RaiseError => 1, PrintError => 1 });
```

When problems occur on the handle, PrintError issues a warning before RaiseError calls die. So even if you catch the error with eval and it doesn't necessarily kill your program, you still get to see the text of the error message.

See Also

The documentation with the DBI module from CPAN; *http://dbi.perl.org*; *Programming the Perl DBI*; Recipe 14.12

14.12 Repeating Queries Efficiently

Problem

You have a query that you want to execute repeatedly, and you'd like to do it as efficiently as possible. Sometimes you have several queries that are similar, but not quite identical, that you'd like to execute efficiently (for example, you have a loop through an array of names and want to SELECT ... WHERE name=$name).

Solution

Take advantage of the fact that you can repeatedly execute a query that you need prepare only once.

```
$sth = $dbh->prepare($SQL);
# execute query ten times
for ($i=0; $i < 10; $i++) {
  $sth->execute();
  while (@row = $sth->fetchrow_array) {
    # ...
  }
}
```

If you have changing parameters, use the DBI's binding features:

```
$sth = $dbh->prepare('SELECT uid,login FROM People WHERE name = ?');
foreach $person (@names) {
  $sth->execute($person);
  while (@row = $sth->fetchrow_array) {
    # ...
  }
}
```

Discussion

"Prepare once, execute often" is one secret to DBI success. By separating preparation from execution, the database server can parse and optimize queries once and then execute them many times. Most databases can do this even when the queries contain placeholders for values to be filled when the query is executed.

The process of replacing placeholders with actual values is known as binding. The simplest way is to bind when you execute:

```
$sth = $dbh->prepare('SELECT id,login FROM People WHERE middle_initial = ?');
$sth->execute('J');
```

If you have multiple parameters to bind, pass more values to execute:

```
$sth = $dbh->prepare('SELECT * FROM Addresses WHERE House = ?
                      AND Street LIKE ?');
$sth->execute('221b', 'Baker%');
```

You don't have to do the binding and the execution in one step. The bind_param function binds without executing:

```
$sth = $dbh->prepare('SELECT id,login FROM People WHERE middle_initial = ?');
$sth->bind_param(1, 'J');
$sth->execute();
```

The first argument to bind_param is the placeholder number (starting from 1) in the statement:

```
$sth = $dbh->prepare('SELECT * FROM Addresses WHERE House = ?
                      AND Street LIKE ?');
$sth->bind_param(1, '221b');
$sth->bind_param(2, 'Baker');
```

You can give an optional third argument to bind_param that identifies the data type of the value and thus whether to quote it:

```
$sth->bind_param(1, 'J', SQL_CHAR);
```

If you want to use this type argument, you must import the types explicitly or import all of them:

```
use DBI qw(SQL_CHAR SQL_INTEGER);
use DBI qw(:sql_types);
```

List all types with:

```
foreach (@{ $dbi::EXPORT_TAGS{sql_types} }) {
  printf "%s=%d\n", $_, &{"DBI::$_"};
}
```

You do not need to quote the values you pass to bind or to a binding execute. DBI automatically quotes them if they are to be used as strings.

The major limitation to binding is that you often can't use placeholders for table or column names. That is, you can't prepare this query:

```
SELECT ?,? FROM ? WHERE ? = ?
```

Remember, the goal of separate prepare and execute is to let the database server optimize the query. There's precious little information to do any optimization on in that query!

A smaller limitation is that each placeholder can represent only a single scalar value. Consider this query:

```
SELECT id,login FROM People WHERE name IN (?)
```

You can prepare this query without a problem, but you can't bind more than one value to the placeholder.

See Also

The documentation with the DBI module from CPAN; *http://dbi.perl.org*; *Programming the Perl DBI*

14.13 Building Queries Programmatically

Problem

You want to create searches at runtime. For example, you want users of your program to be able to specify combinations of columns and allowable ranges of values.

Solution

Build a list of clauses and join them together to form the SQL WHERE clause:

```
if ($year_min)     { push @clauses, "Year >= $year_min" }
if ($year_max)     { push @clauses, "Year <= $year_max" }
if ($bedrooms_min) { push @clauses, "Beds >= $bedrooms_min" }
if ($bedrooms_max) { push @clauses, "Beds <= $bedrooms_max" }
# ...
$clause = join(" AND ", @clauses);
$sth = $dbh->prepare("SELECT beds,baths FROM Houses WHERE $clause");
```

Discussion

Don't try to build up a string in a loop:

```
$where = '';
foreach $possible (@names) {
  $where .= ' OR Name=' . $dbh->quote($possible);
}
```

That code will end up creating a WHERE clause like:

```
OR Name="Tom" OR Name="Nat" OR Name="Larry" OR Name="Tim"
```

Then you end up having to lop off the leading " OR ". It's much cleaner to use map and never have the extra text at the start:

```
$where = join(" OR ", map { "Name=".$dbh->quote($_) } @names);
```

The map produces a list of strings like:

```
Name="Nat"
Name="Tom"
Name="Larry"
Name="Tim"
```

and then they're joined together with " OR " to create a well-formed clause:

```
Name="Nat" OR Name="Tom" OR Name="Larry" OR Name="Tim"
```

Unfortunately, you cannot use placeholders here:

```
$sth = $dbh->prepare("SELECT id,login FROM People WHERE ?");   # BAD
$sth->bind_param(1, $where);
```

As explained in Recipe 14.12, placeholders can only be used for simple scalar values and not entire clauses. However, there is an elegant solution: construct the clause and the values to be bound in parallel:

```
if ($year_min)     { push @clauses, "Year >= ?"; push @bind, $year_min }
if ($year_max)     { push @clauses, "Year <= ?"; push @bind, $year_max }
if ($bedrooms_min) { push @clauses, "Beds >= ?"; push @bind, $bedrooms_min }
if ($bedrooms_max) { push @clauses, "Beds <= ?"; push @bind, $bedrooms_max }
$clause = join(" AND ", @clauses);
$sth = $dbh->prepare("SELECT id,price FROM Houses WHERE $clause");
$sth->execute(@bind);
```

See Also

The documentation with the DBI module from CPAN; *http://dbi.perl.org*; *Programming the Perl DBI*; Recipe 14.12

14.14 Finding the Number of Rows Returned by a Query

Problem

You want to find out how many rows were returned by a query.

Solution

For operations that aren't queries (such as INSERTs, UPDATEs, and DELETEs), the do method returns the number of rows affected, -1 when it can't determine the right value, or else undef in case of failure.

```
$rows = $dbh->do("DELETE FROM Conference WHERE Language='REBOL'");
if (! defined $rows) {
  # failed, but this is not needed if RaiseError is active
} else {
  print "Deleted $rows rows\n";
}
```

You can't reliably get row counts from queries without either fetching all of the results and then counting them, or writing another query.

Discussion

The easiest way to find out how many rows a query will return is to use the COUNT function in SQL. For example, take this query:

```
SELECT id,name FROM People WHERE Age > 30
```

To find out how many rows it will return, simply issue this query:

```
SELECT COUNT(*) FROM People WHERE Age > 30
```

If the database is so volatile that you're afraid the number of rows will change between the COUNT query and the data-fetching query, your best option is to fetch the data and then count rows yourself.

With some DBD modules, execute returns the number of rows affected. This isn't portable and may change in the future.

See Also

The documentation with the DBI module from CPAN; *http://dbi.perl.org*; *Programming the Perl DBI*

14.15 Using Transactions

Problem

A single change to the database requires several INSERT, UPDATE, or DELETE commands in SQL. For example, you might have to add a person to the People table, add an address to the Address table, and add a link between them to the LivesAt table. The database is in a logically inconsistent state from the first insert until the last completes. If another client queries the database, it will get inconsistent data (e.g., there'll be a Person with no address).

You want to perform the update in such a way that another client never sees an inconsistent database—either all of the changes or none of them should be visible in the database during and after the changes, regardless of any client or server failures during processing.

Solution

Use transactions. The DBI supports these via the commit and rollback methods on a database handle. Use them thus:

```
$dbh->{AutoCommit} = 0; # enable transactions
$dbh->{RaiseError} = 1; # die() if a query has problems

eval {
  # do inserts, updates, deletes, queries here
  $dbh->commit();
};

if ($@) {
  warn "Transaction aborted: $@";
  eval { $dbh->rollback() };    # in case rollback() fails
  # do your application cleanup here
}
```

Discussion

The AutoCommit option controls whether the database commits each change as soon as you issue the command. When AutoCommit is disabled, the database won't update until you call the commit method. If midway through the series of updates you change your mind or an error occurs, the rollback method undoes all pending changes.

You don't have to explicitly set the AutoCommit and RaiseError attributes before each transaction. For convenience, set those attributes in the connect call:

```
$dbh = DBI->connect($dsn, $username, $password,
                    { AutoCommit => 0, RaiseError => 1 });
```

Because RaiseError causes DBI to call die whenever a database operation fails, you break out of the eval if any database operation fails while the eval is in effect (even if from within the eval you call a function that accesses the database).

Always explicitly call commit or rollback to end a transaction. Different databases react differently if you disconnect with an unfinished transaction. Some (for example, Oracle and Ingres) commit the transaction, while some (MySQL, Informix) rollback.

When a database handle commits or rolls back a transaction, many database drivers invalidate any active statement handles from that database handle. For example:

```
$sth = $dbh->prepare(...);
$sth->execute();
eval {
  $dbh->do(...);
  $dbh->commit;
};
if ($@) { eval { $dbh->rollback } }
while (@row = $sth->fetchrow_array) { ... }  # may not work
```

The last line is not guaranteed to work across database handles, as the acts of committing and rolling back may invalidate the statement handle in $sth. The standard solution to this is to create two database handles for the database (by calling connect twice) and use one handle for all SELECT statements.

See Also

The documentation with the DBI module from CPAN; *http://dbi.perl.org*; *Programming the Perl DBI*

14.16 Viewing Data One Page at a Time

Problem

You want to display the contents of a table or the results of a query one page at a time.

Solution

Keep track of which record you're starting with, then use that value to decide how many records to skip before you display a page worth. If your database supports a LIMIT clause that takes a range, use this to avoid transferring unnecessary rows into your program.

Discussion

The example code in this recipe pages through the contents of a table. To page through the results of a query, select the data into a temporary table and page through that.

In desktop applications (e.g., Tk), you can keep track of the current page number yourself. With web applications, the easiest thing to do is to use query parameters in the URL to indicate where you are. For example:

```
/users-report/view?start=1
```

Begin by finding out how many records there are in total:

```
$row = $Dbh->selectrow_arrayref("SELECT COUNT(*) FROM Users");
$count = $row->[0];
```

Find the first record to display by looking at the start parameter, then calculate the last record from that. You need to know the number of records per page, which here we assume is in the $Page_Size variable:

```
$first = param('start') || 1;
$last  = $first + $Page_Size - 1;
$last = $count if $last > $count;    # don't go past the end
```

Now fetch the data into an array and display the records you're interested in:

```
$results = $Dbh->selectall_arrayref('SELECT id,lastname,firstname FROM Users
                                     ORDER BY lastname,firstname,id');

for (my $i=$first; $i <= $last; $i++) {
  my $user = $results->[$i-1];        # result 1 is in row 0
  printf("%d.  %s, %s.<br>\n", $i, $user->[1], $user->[2]);
}
```

That will produce output like:

1. **Brocard, Leon.
**
2. **Cawley, Piers.
**
3. **Christiansen, Tom.
**

The last step is adding next and previous links to move to the next and previous pages (if available):

```
$prev_rec = $first - $Page_Size;
$prev_rec = 1 if $prev_rec < 1;
$prev_link = sprintf('%s/%d', url(-full => 1), $prev_rec);
$next_rec = $last + 1;
$next_link = sprintf('%s/%d', url(-full => 1), $next_rec);

if ($first == 1) {
  print 'Previous';
} else {
  printf('<a href="%s">Previous</a>', $prev_link);
}
print " | ";   # separate "Previous" and "Next"
if ($next_rec < $count) {
  printf('<a href="%s">Next</a>', $next_link);
} else {
  print 'Next';
}
```

This becomes easier if your database lets you specify an offset as part of the LIMIT clause (MySQL and PostgreSQL both do). Instead of transferring all records in the database back to your program, you need transfer only the records you're interested in:

```
$results = $dbh->selectall_arrayref("SELECT id,lastname,firstname FROM Users
                                     ORDER BY lastname,firstname,id
                                     LIMIT " . ($first-1) . ", $Page_Size");

for ($i=0; $i < @$results; $i++) {
  my $user = $results->[$i];
  printf("%d.  %s, %s.<br>", $i+$first, $user->[1], $user->[2]);
}
```

MySQL's LIMIT m,n is written LIMIT n OFFSET m in PostgreSQL.

See Also

The documentation with the DBI and DBIx::Pager modules from CPAN; *http://dbi. perl.org* and *http://www.mysql.com*; *Programming the Perl DBI*; *MySQL Reference Manual*, by Michael "Monty" Widenius, David Axmark, and MySQL AB (O'Reilly)

14.17 Querying a CSV File with SQL

Problem

You want to use SQL to insert, delete, or retrieve data from a comma-separated values (CSV) file.

Solution

Use the DBD::CSV module from CPAN:

```
use DBI;

$dbh = DBI->connect("dbi:CSV:f_dir=/home/gnat/payroll", "", "",
                    { AutoCommit => 1, RaiseError => 1 });

$dbh->do("UPDATE salaries SET salary = salary * 2 WHERE name = 'Nat'");

$sth = $dbh->prepare("SELECT name,salary FROM salaries WHERE name = 'Nat'");
$sth->execute( );
while (@row = $sth->fetchrow_array) {
  # ...
}
$sth->finish( );

$dbh->disconnect( );
```

Discussion

A "table" in CSV terms is a file (the table name becomes the filename). The tables are kept in the directory specified by the f_dir parameter in the connect method call. The DBD::CSV module supports CREATE and DROP to make and destroy tables:

```
$dbh->do("CREATE TABLE salaries (salary FLOAT, name CHAR(20))");
```

Valid column types are: TINYINT, BIGINT, LONGVARBINARY, VARBINARY, BINARY, LONGVARCHAR, CHAR, NUMERIC, DECIMAL, INTEGER, SMALL-INT, FLOAT, REAL, and DOUBLE.

When you access a table, the DBD::CSV module locks the corresponding file with the *flock*(2) syscall. If *flock*(2) isn't supported on the filesystem containing the CSV file, two processes will be able to access the file at the same time, possibly leading to incorrect results or lost data.

If you're reading or writing an Excel CSV file, you need to tell the DBD::CSV module that the value separator is actually a semicolon:

```
$dbh = DBI->connect('dbi:CSV:f_dir=/home/gnat/payroll;csv_sep_char=\;');
```

We need to quote the semicolon to prevent connect from thinking it's separating csv_sep_char= from another connection attribute. We use single quotes rather than double quotes to avoid having to backslash the backslash:

```
$dbh = DBI->connect("dbi:CSV:f_dir=/home/gnat/payroll;csv_sep_char=\\;");
```

See Also

The documentation for the CPAN module DBD::CSV; Recipe 1.20; Recipe 14.8

14.18 Using SQL Without a Database Server

Problem

You want to make complex SQL queries but don't want to maintain a relational database server.

Solution

Use the DBD::SQLite module from CPAN:

```
use DBI;

$dbh = DBI->connect("dbi:SQLite:dbname=/Users/gnat/salaries.sqlt", "", "",
                    { RaiseError => 1, AutoCommit => 1 });

$dbh->do("UPDATE salaries SET salary = 2 * salary WHERE name = 'Nat'");

$sth = $dbh->prepare("SELECT id,deductions FROM salaries WHERE name = 'Nat'");
# ...
```

Discussion

An SQLite database lives in a single file, specified with the dbname parameter in the DBI constructor. Unlike most relational databases, there's no database server here—DBD::SQLite interacts directly with the file. Multiple processes can read from the same database file at the same time (with SELECTs), but only one process can make changes (and other processes are prevented from reading while those changes are being made).

SQLite supports transactions. That is, you can make a number of changes to different tables, but the updates won't be written to the file until you commit them:

```
use DBI;
$dbh = DBI->connect("dbi:SQLite:dbname=/Users/gnat/salaries.sqlt", "", "",
```

```
                    { RaiseError => 1, AutoCommit => 0 });
    eval {
      $dbh->do("INSERT INTO people VALUES (29, 'Nat', 1973)");
      $dbh->do("INSERT INTO people VALUES (30, 'William', 1999)");
      $dbh->do("INSERT INTO father_of VALUES (29, 30)");
      $dbh->commit( );
    };
    if ($@) {
        eval { $dbh->rollback( ) };
        die "Couldn't roll back transaction" if $@;
    }
```

SQLite is a typeless database system. Regardless of the types specified when you created a table, you can put any type (strings, numbers, dates, blobs) into any field. Indeed, you can even create a table without specifying any types:

```
CREATE TABLE people (id, name, birth_year);
```

The only time that data typing comes into play is when comparisons occur, either through WHERE clauses or when the database has to sort values. The database ignores the type of the column and looks only at the type of the specific value being compared. Like Perl, SQLite recognizes only strings and numbers. Two numbers are compared as floating-point values, two strings are compared as strings, and a number is always less than a string when values of two different types are compared.

There is only one case when SQLite looks at the type you declare for a column. To get an automatically incrementing column, such as unique identifiers, specify a field of type "INTEGER PRIMARY KEY":

```
CREATE TABLE people (id INTEGER PRIMARY KEY, name, birth_year);
```

Example 14-6 shows how this is done.

Example 14-6. ipk

```
#!/usr/bin/perl -w
# ipk - demonstrate integer primary keys
use DBI;
use strict;
my $dbh = DBI->connect("dbi:SQLite:ipk.dat", "", "",
{RaiseError => 1, AutoCommit => 1});
# quietly drop the table if it already existed
eval {
  local $dbh->{PrintError} = 0;
  $dbh->do("DROP TABLE names");
};
# (re)create it
$dbh->do("CREATE TABLE names (id INTEGER PRIMARY KEY, name)");
# insert values
foreach my $person (qw(Nat Tom Guido Larry Damian Jon)) {
  $dbh->do("INSERT INTO names VALUES (NULL, '$person')");
}
# remove a middle value
$dbh->do("DELETE FROM names WHERE name='Guido'");
```

Example 14-6. ipk (continued)

```
# add a new value
$dbh->do("INSERT INTO names VALUES (NULL, 'Dan')");
# display contents of the table
my $all = $dbh->selectall_arrayref("SELECT id,name FROM names");
foreach my $row (@$all) {
  my ($id, $word) = @$row;
  print "$word has id $id\n";
}
```

SQLite can hold 8-bit text data, but can't hold an ASCII NUL character (\0). The only workaround is to do your own encoding (for example, URL encoding or Base64) before you store and after you retrieve the data. This is true even of columns declared as BLOBs.

See Also

Recipe 14.9; the documentation for the CPAN module DBD::SQLite; the SQLite home page at *http://www.hwaci.com/sw/sqlite/*

14.19 Program: ggh—Grep Netscape Global History

This program divulges the contents of Netscape's *history.db* file. It can be called with full URLs or with a (single) pattern. If called without arguments, it displays every entry in the history file. The *~/.netscape/history.db* file is used unless the **-database** option is given.

Each output line shows the URL and its access time. The time is converted into localtime representation with **-localtime** (the default) or gmtime representation with **-gmtime**—or left in raw form with **-epochtime**, which is useful for sorting by date.

To specify a pattern to match against, give one single argument without a ://.

To look up one or more URLs, supply them as arguments:

```
% ggh http://www.perl.com/index.html
```

To find out a link you don't quite recall, use a regular expression (a single argument without a :// is a pattern):

```
% ggh perl
```

To find out everyone you've mailed:

```
% ggh mailto:
```

To find out the FAQ sites you've visited, use a snazzy Perl pattern with an embedded /i modifier:

```
% ggh -regexp '(?i)\bfaq\b'
```

If you don't want the internal date converted to localtime, use **-epoch**:

```
% ggh -epoch http://www.perl.com/perl/
```

If you prefer gmtime to localtime, use **-gmtime**:

```
% ggh -gmtime http://www.perl.com/perl/
```

To look at the whole file, give no arguments (but perhaps redirect to a pager):

```
% ggh | less
```

If you want the output sorted by date, use the **-epoch** flag:

```
% ggh -epoch | sort -rn | less
```

If you want it sorted by date into your local time zone format, use a more sophisticated pipeline:

```
% ggh -epoch | sort -rn | perl -pe 's/\d+/localtime $&/e' | less
```

The Netscape release notes claim that they're using NDBM format. This is misleading: they're actually using Berkeley DB format, which is why we require DB_File (not supplied standard with all systems Perl runs on) instead of NDBM_File (which is). The program is shown in Example 14-7.

Example 14-7. ggh

```perl
#!/usr/bin/perl -w
# ggh -- grovel global history in netscape logs
$USAGE = << EO_COMPLAINT;
usage: $0 [-database dbfilename] [-help]
          [-epochtime | -localtime | -gmtime]
          [ [-regexp] pattern] | href ... ]
EO_COMPLAINT

use Getopt::Long;

($opt_database, $opt_epochtime, $opt_localtime,
 $opt_gmtime,   $opt_regexp,    $opt_help,
 $pattern,                                 )      = (0) x 7;

usage() unless GetOptions qw{ database=s
                              regexp=s
                              epochtime localtime gmtime
                              help
                            };

if ($opt_help) { print $USAGE; exit; }

usage("only one of localtime, gmtime, and epochtime allowed")
    if $opt_localtime + $opt_gmtime + $opt_epochtime > 1;

if ( $opt_regexp ) {
    $pattern = $opt_regexp;
} elsif (@ARGV && $ARGV[0] !~ m(://)) {
```

Example 14-7. ggh (continued)

```perl
        $pattern = shift;
    }

    usage("can't mix URLs and explicit patterns")
        if $pattern && @ARGV;

    if ($pattern && !eval { '' =~ /$pattern/; 1 } ) {
        $@ =~ s/ at \w+ line \d+\.//;
        die "$0: bad pattern $@";
    }

    require DB_File; DB_File->import( );  # delay loading until runtime
    $| = 1;                               # feed the hungry PAGERs

    $dotdir  = $ENV{HOME}    || $ENV{LOGNAME};
    $HISTORY = $opt_database || "$dotdir/.netscape/history.db";

    die "no netscape history dbase in $HISTORY: $!" unless -e $HISTORY;
    die "can't dbmopen $HISTORY: $!" unless dbmopen %hist_db, $HISTORY, 0666;

    # the next line is a hack because the C programmers who did this
    # didn't understand strlen vs strlen+1.  jwz told me so. :-)
    $add_nulls   = (ord(substr(each %hist_db, -1)) == 0);

    # XXX: should now do scalar keys to reset but don't
    #       want cost of full traverse, required on tied hashes.
    #    better to close and reopen?

    $nulled_href = "";
    $byte_order  = "V";          # PC people don't grok "N" (network order)

    if (@ARGV) {
        foreach $href (@ARGV) {
            $nulled_href = $href . ($add_nulls && "\0");
            unless ($binary_time = $hist_db{$nulled_href}) {
                warn "$0: No history entry for HREF $href\n";
                next;
            }
            $epoch_secs = unpack($byte_order, $binary_time);
            $stardate   = $opt_epochtime ? $epoch_secs
                                         : $opt_gmtime ? gmtime    $epoch_secs
                                                       : localtime $epoch_secs;
            print "$stardate $href\n";
        }
    } else {
        while ( ($href, $binary_time) = each %hist_db ) {
            chop $href if $add_nulls;
            next unless defined $href && defined $binary_time;
            # gnat reports some binary times are missing
            $binary_time = pack($byte_order, 0) unless $binary_time;
            $epoch_secs = unpack($byte_order, $binary_time);
```

Example 14-7. ggh (continued)

```
        $stardate   = $opt_epochtime ? $epoch_secs
                                 : $opt_gmtime ? gmtime     $epoch_secs
                                              : localtime $epoch_secs;
        print "$stardate $href\n" unless $pattern && $href !~ /$pattern/o;
    }
}

sub usage {
    print STDERR "@_\n" if @_;
    die $USAGE;
}
```

See Also

The Introduction to this chapter; Recipe 6.18 .

## CHAPTER 15

Interactivity

And then the Windows failed—
and then I could not see to see—
—Emily Dickinson
"I heard a Fly buzz—when I died"

15.0 Introduction

Everything we use has a user interface: VCRs, computers, telephones, even books. Our programs have user interfaces: do we have to supply arguments on the command line? Can we drag and drop files into the program? Do we have to press Enter after every response we make, or can the program read a single keystroke at a time?

This chapter won't discuss *designing* user interfaces: entire bookshelves are filled with books written on the subject. Instead, we focus on *implementing* user interfaces—parsing command-line arguments, reading a character at a time, writing anywhere on the screen, and writing a graphical user interface.

The simplest user interface is what are called *line mode* interfaces. Line mode programs normally read entire lines and write characters or entire lines. Filters like *grep* and utilities like *mail* exemplify this type of interface. We don't really talk much about this type of interface in this chapter, because so much of the rest of the book does.

A more complex interface is what is called *full-screen mode*. Programs such as *vi*, *elm*, and *lynx* have full-screen interfaces. They read single characters at a time and can write to any character position on the screen. We address this type of interface in Recipes 15.4, 15.6, 15.9, 15.10, and 15.11.

Still more complex are the graphical user interfaces (GUIs). Programs with GUIs can address individual pixels, not just characters. GUIs often follow a windowing metaphor, in which a program creates windows that appear on the user's display device. The windows are filled with widgets, which include things like scrollbars to drag or buttons to click. Netscape Navigator provides a full graphical user interface, as does your window manager. Perl can use many GUI toolkits, but here we'll cover the Tk toolkit, since it's the most well-known and portable. See Recipes 15.14, 15.15, and 15.22.

The final class of UIs is one we won't address here—web user interfaces. Increasingly, people are eschewing the complicated programming of a fully responsive GUI whose every pixel is addressable, preferring relatively clunky and plain-looking HTML pages. After all, everyone has a web browser, but not everyone can figure out how to install Perl/Tk. We cover the Web in Chapters 19, 20, and 21.

A program's user interface is different from the environment you run it in. Your environment determines the type of program you can run. If you're logged in through a terminal capable of full-screen I/O, you can run line mode applications but not GUI programs. Let's look briefly at the environments.

Some environments only handle programs that have a bare line mode interface. This includes executing programs with backticks, over *rsh* or *ssh*, or from *cron*. Their simple interface allows them to be combined creatively and powerfully as reusable components in larger scripts. Line mode programs are wonderful for automation, because they don't rely on a keyboard or screen. They rely on STDIN and STDOUT only—if that. These are often the most portable programs because they use nothing but the basic I/O supported by virtually all systems.

The typical login session, where you use a terminal with a screen and keyboard, permits both line mode and full-screen interfaces. Here the program with the full-screen interface talks to the terminal driver and has intimate knowledge of how to make the terminal write to various positions on the screen. To automate such a program, you need to create a pseudo-terminal for the program to talk to, as shown in Recipe 15.13.

Finally, some window systems let you run line mode and full-screen programs as well as programs that use a GUI. For instance, you can run *grep* (line-mode programs) from within *vi* (a full-screen program) from an *xterm* window (a GUI program running in a window system environment). GUI programs are difficult to automate unless they provide an alternative interface through remote procedure calls.

Toolkits exist for programming in full-screen and GUI environments. These toolkits (*curses* for full-screen programs; Tk for GUI programs) increase the portability of your programs by abstracting out system-specific details. A curses program can run on virtually any kind of terminal without the user worrying about which particular escape sequences they need to use. Tk programs will run unmodified on Unix and Windows systems—providing you don't use operating-system specific functions.

There are other ways to interact with a user, most notably through the Web. We cover the Web in Chapters 19, 20, and 21, so we make no further mention of it here.

GUIs, web pages, and printed documents are all enhanced by graphics. We give here a few recipes for working with image files and creating graphs of data. Once again, the environment you're in doesn't preclude creating or manipulating images. You don't need a GUI to create a graph of data (though you'll need one to view it, unless you print the graph out).

15.1 Parsing Program Arguments

Problem

You want to let users change your program's behavior by giving options on the command line. For instance, you want to allow the user to control the level of output that your program produces with a **-v** (verbose) option.

Solution

Use the standard Getopt::Std module to permit single-character options:

```
use Getopt::Std;

# -v ARG, -D ARG, -o ARG, sets $opt_v, $opt_D, $opt_o
getopt("vDo");
# -v ARG, -D ARG, -o ARG, sets $args{v}, $args{D}, $args{o}
getopt("vDo", \%args);

getopts("vDo:");         # -v, -D, -o ARG, sets $opt_v, $opt_D, $opt_o
getopts("vDo:", \%args); # -v, -D, -o ARG, sets $args{v}, $args{D}, $args{o}
```

Or, use the standard Getopt::Long module to permit named arguments:

```
use Getopt::Long;

GetOptions( "verbose"  => \$verbose,    # --verbose
            "Debug"    => \$debug,      # --Debug
            "output=s" => \$output );   # --output=string or --output string
```

Discussion

Most traditional programs like *ls* and *rm* take single-character options (also known as flags or switches), such as **-l** and **-r**. In the case of *ls -l* and *rm -r*, the argument is Boolean: either it is present or it isn't. Contrast this with *gcc -o compiledfile source.c*, where *compiledfile* is a value associated with the option **-o**. We can combine Boolean options into a single option in any order. For example:

```
% rm -r -f /tmp/testdir
```

Another way of saying this is:

```
% rm -rf /tmp/testdir
```

The Getopt::Std module, part of the standard Perl distribution, parses these types of traditional options. Its getopt function takes a single string of characters (each corresponding to an option that takes a value), parses the command-line arguments stored in @ARGV, and sets a global variable for each option. For example, the value for the **-D** option will be stored in $opt_D. All options parsed though getopt are value options, not Boolean options.

Getopt::Std also provides the `getopts` function, which lets you specify whether each option is Boolean or takes a value. Arguments that take a value, such as the **-o** option to *gcc*, are indicated by a "`:`", as in this code:

```
use Getopt::Std;
getopts("o:");
if ($opt_o) {
    print "Writing output to $opt_o";
}
```

Both getopt and getopts can take a second argument, a reference to a hash. If present, option values are stored in $hash{X} instead of $opt_X:

```
use Getopt::Std;

%option = ();
getopts("Do:", \%option);

if ($option{D}) {
    print "Debugging mode enabled.\n";
}

 # if not set, set output to "-".  opening "-" for writing
 # means STDOUT
 $option{o} = "-" unless defined $option{o};

print "Writing output to file $option{o}\n" unless $option{o} eq "-";
open(STDOUT, "> $option{o}")
    or die "Can't open $option{o} for output: $!\n";
```

Some programs' options you specify using full words instead of single characters. These options are (usually) indicated with two dashes instead of one:

```
% gnutar --extract --file latest.tar
```

The value for the **--file** option could also be given with an equals sign:

```
% gnutar --extract --file=latest.tar
```

The Getopt::Long module's `GetOptions` function parses this style of options. It takes a hash whose keys are options and values are references to scalar variables:

```
use Getopt::Long;

GetOptions( "extract" => \$extract,
            "file=s"  => \$file );

if ($extract) {
    print "I'm extracting.\n";
}
```

```
    die "I wish I had a file" unless defined $file;
    print "Working on the file $file\n";
```

If a key in the hash is just an option name, it's a Boolean option. The corresponding variable will be set to false if the option wasn't given, or to 1 if it was. Getopt::Long provides fancier options than just the Boolean and value of Getopt::Std. Here's what the option specifier can look like:

Specifier	Value?	Comment
`option`	No	Given as `--option` or not at all
`option!`	No	May be given as `--option` or `--nooption`
`option=s`	Yes	Mandatory string parameter: `--option=somestring`
`option:s`	Yes	Optional string parameter: `--option` or `--option=somestring`
`option=i`	Yes	Mandatory integer parameter: `--option=35`
`option:i`	Yes	Optional integer parameter: `--option` or `--option=35`
`option=f`	Yes	Mandatory floating point parameter: `--option=3.141`
`option:f`	Yes	Optional floating point parameter: `--option` or `--option=3.141`

See Also

The documentation for the standard Getopt::Long and Getopt::Std modules; the Getopt::Declare module from CPAN; examples of argument parsing by hand can be found in Recipes 1.6, 1.23, 6.21, 7.14, 8.25, and 15.12

15.2 Testing Whether a Program Is Running Interactively

Problem

You want to know whether your program is being called interactively or not. For instance, a user running your program from a shell is interactive, whereas the program being called from *cron* is not.

Solution

Use -t to test STDIN and STDOUT:

```
    sub I_am_interactive {
        return -t STDIN && -t STDOUT;
    }
```

If you're on a POSIX system, test process groups:

```
    use POSIX qw/getpgrp tcgetpgrp/;

    sub I_am_interactive {
```

```
    my $tty;
    open($tty, "<", "/dev/tty")    or die "can't open /dev/tty: $!";
    my $tpgrp = tcgetpgrp(fileno($tty));
    my $pgrp  = getpgrp();
    close $tty;
    return ($tpgrp == $pgrp);
}
```

Discussion

The -t file test operator tells whether the filehandle or file is a tty device. Such devices are signs of interactive use. This only tells you whether your program has been redirected. Running your program from the shell and redirecting STDIN and STDOUT makes the -t version of I_am_interactive return false. Called from *cron*, I_am_interactive also returns false.

The POSIX test tells you whether your program has exclusive control over its tty. A program whose input and output has been redirected still can control its tty if it wants to, so the POSIX version of I_am_interactive returns true. A program run from *cron* has no tty, so I_am_interactive returns false.

Whichever I_am_interactive you choose to use, here's how you'd call it:

```
while (1) {
    if (I_am_interactive()) {
        print "Prompt: ";
    }
    $line = <STDIN>;
    last unless defined $line;
    # do something with the line
}
```

Or, more clearly:

```
sub prompt { print "Prompt: " if I_am_interactive() }
for (prompt(); $line = <STDIN>; prompt()) {
    # do something with the line
}
```

See Also

The documentation for the standard POSIX module, also in Chapter 32 of *Programming Perl*; the -t file test operator in Chapter 3 of *Programming Perl* and in *perlop*(1)

15.3   Clearing the Screen

Problem

You want to clear the screen.

Solution

Use the Term::Cap module to send the appropriate character sequence. Use POSIX::
Termios to get the output speed of the terminal (or guess 9600 bps). Use eval to trap
any exceptions that arise using POSIX::Termios.

```
use Term::Cap;

$OSPEED = 9600;
eval {
    require POSIX;
    my $termios = POSIX::Termios->new( );
    $termios->getattr;
    $OSPEED = $termios->getospeed;
};

$terminal = Term::Cap->Tgetent({OSPEED=>$OSPEED});
$terminal->Tputs('cl', 1, STDOUT);
```

Or, just run the *clear* command:

```
system("clear");
```

Discussion

If you clear the screen a lot, cache the return value from the termcap or *clear* command:

```
$clear = $terminal->Tputs('cl');
$clear = `clear`;
```

Then you can clear the screen a hundred times without running *clear* a hundred
times:

```
print $clear;
```

See Also

Your system's *clear*(1) and *termcap*(5) manpages (if you have them); the documentation for the standard module Term::Cap module, also in Chapter 32 of *Programming Perl*; the documentation for the Term::Lib module from CPAN

15.4 Determining Terminal or Window Size

Problem

You need to know the size of the terminal or window. For instance, you want to format text so that it doesn't pass the righthand boundary of the screen.

Solution

Either use the ioctl described in Recipe 12.17, or else use the CPAN module Term::ReadKey:

```
use Term::ReadKey;

($wchar, $hchar, $wpixels, $hpixels) = GetTerminalSize();
```

Discussion

GetTerminalSize returns four elements: the width and height in characters and the width and height in pixels. If the operation is unsupported for the output device (for instance, if output has been redirected to a file), it returns an empty list.

Here's how you'd graph the contents of @values, assuming no value is less than 0:

```
use Term::ReadKey;

($width) = GetTerminalSize();
die "You must have at least 10 characters" unless $width >= 10;

$max = 0;
foreach (@values) {
    $max = $_ if $max < $_;
}

$ratio = ($width-10)/$max;          # chars per unit
foreach (@values) {
    printf("%8.1f %s\n", $_, "*" x ($ratio*$_));
}
```

See Also

The documentation for the Term::ReadKey module from CPAN; Recipe 12.17

15.5 Changing Text Color

Problem

You want text to appear in different colors on the screen. For instance, you want to emphasize a mode line or highlight an error message.

Solution

Use the CPAN module Term::ANSIColor to send the ANSI color-change sequences to the user's terminal:

```
use Term::ANSIColor;

print color("red"), "Danger, Will Robinson!\n", color("reset");
```

```
print "This is just normal text.\n";
print colored("<BLINK>Do you hurt yet?</BLINK>", "blink");
```

Or, you can use convenience functions from Term::ANSIColor:

```
use Term::ANSIColor qw(:constants);

print RED, "Danger, Will Robinson!\n", RESET;
```

Discussion

Term::ANSIColor prepares escape sequences that some (but far from all) terminals will recognize. For example, if you normally launch a *color-xterm*, this recipe will work. If you normally use the normal *xterm* program, or have a vt100 in your kitchen, it won't.

There are two ways of using the module: either by calling the exported functions color($attribute) and colored($text, $attribute), or by using convenience functions like BOLD, BLUE, and RESET.

Attributes can be a combination of colors and controls. The colors are black, red, green, yellow, blue, magenta, on_black, on_red, on_green, on_yellow, on_blue, on_magenta, on_cyan, and on_white. (Apparently orange and purple don't matter.) The controls are clear, reset, bold, underline, underscore, blink, reverse, and concealed. clear and reset are synonyms, as are underline and underscore. reset restores the colors to the way they were when the program started, and concealed makes foreground and background colors the same.

You can combine attributes:

```
# rhyme for the deadly coral snake
print color("red on_black"),  "venom lack\n";
print color("red on_yellow"), "kill that fellow\n";

print color("green on_cyan blink"), "garish!\n";
print color("reset");
```

We could have written this as:

```
print colored("venom lack\n", "red", "on_black");
print colored("kill that fellow\n", "red", "on_yellow");

print colored("garish!\n", "green", "on_cyan", "blink");
```

or as:

```
use Term::ANSIColor qw(:constants);

print BLACK, ON_WHITE, "black on white\n";
print WHITE, ON_BLACK, "white on black\n";
print GREEN, ON_CYAN, BLINK, "garish!\n";
print RESET;
```

Here, BLACK is a function exported from Term::ANSIColor.

It's important to print RESET or color("reset") at the end of your program if you're not calling colored for everything. Failure to reset your terminal will leave it displaying odd colors. You may want to use:

```
END { print color("reset") }
```

to ensure the colors will be reset when your program finishes.

Attributes that span lines of text can confuse some programs or devices. If this becomes a problem, either manually set the attributes at the start of each line, or use colored after setting the variable $Term::ANSIColor::EACHLINE to the line terminator:

```
$Term::ANSIColor::EACHLINE = $/;
print colored(<< EOF, RED, ON_WHITE, BOLD, BLINK);
This way
each line
has its own
attribute set.
EOF
```

See Also

The documentation for the Term::AnsiColor module from CPAN

15.6   Reading Single Characters
from the Keyboard

Problem

You want to read a single character from the keyboard. For instance, you've displayed a menu of one-character options, and you don't want to require users to press the Enter key to make their selection.

Solution

Use the CPAN module Term::ReadKey to put the terminal into cbreak mode, read characters from STDIN, and then put the terminal back into its normal mode:

```
use Term::ReadKey;

ReadMode 'cbreak';
$key = ReadKey(0);
ReadMode 'normal';
```

Discussion

Term::ReadKey can put the terminal into many modes—cbreak is just one of them. cbreak mode makes each character available to your program as it is typed (see

Example 15-1). It also echoes the characters to the screen; see Recipe 15.10 for an example of a mode that does not echo.

Example 15-1. sascii

```perl
#!/usr/bin/perl -w
# sascii - Show ASCII values for keypresses

use Term::ReadKey;
ReadMode('cbreak');
print "Press keys to see their ASCII values.  Use Ctrl-C to quit.\n";

while (1) {
    $char = ReadKey(0);
    last unless defined $char;
    printf(" Decimal: %d\tHex: %x\n", ord($char), ord($char));
}

ReadMode('normal');
```

Using cbreak mode doesn't prevent the terminal's device driver from interpreting end-of-file and flow-control characters. If you want to be able to read a real Ctrl-C (which normally sends a SIGINT to your process) or a Ctrl-D (which indicates end-of-file under Unix), you want to use raw mode.

An argument of 0 to ReadKey indicates that we want a normal read using getc. If no input is available, the program will pause until there is some. We can also pass -1 to indicate a non-blocking read, or a number greater than 0 to indicate the number of seconds to wait for input to become available; fractional seconds are allowed. Non-blocking reads and timed-out reads return either undef when no input is available or a zero-length string on end-of-file.

Recent versions of Term::ReadKey also include limited support for non-Unix systems.

See Also

The getc and sysread functions in Chapter 29 of *Programming Perl*, and in *perlfunc*(1); the documentation for the Term::ReadKey module from CPAN; Recipe 15.8; Recipe 15.9

15.7   Ringing the Terminal Bell

Problem

You want to sound an alarm on the user's terminal.

Solution

Print the "\a" character to sound a bell:

```
print "\aWake up!\n";
```

Or use the "vb" terminal capability to show a visual bell:

```
use Term::Cap;

$OSPEED = 9600;
eval {
    require POSIX;
    my $termios = POSIX::Termios->new( );
    $termios->getattr;
    $OSPEED = $termios->getospeed;
};

$terminal = Term::Cap->Tgetent({OSPEED=>$OSPEED});
$vb = "";
eval {
    $terminal->Trequire("vb");
    $vb = $terminal->Tputs('vb', 1);
};

print $vb;                              # ring visual bell
```

Discussion

The "\a" escape is the same as "\cG", "\007", and "\x07". They all correspond to the ASCII BEL character and cause an irritating ding. In a crowded terminal room at the end of the semester, this beeping caused by dozens of *vi* novices all trying to get out of insert mode at once can be maddening. The visual bell is a workaround to avoid irritation. Based upon the polite principle that terminals should be seen and not heard (at least, not in crowded rooms), some terminals let you briefly reverse the foreground and background colors to give a flash of light instead of an audible ring.

Not every terminal supports the visual bell, which is why we eval the code that finds it. If the terminal doesn't support it, Trequire will die without having changed the value of $vb from "". If the terminal does support it, the value of $vb will be set to the character sequence to flash the bell.

There's a better approach to the bell issue in graphical terminal systems like *xterm*. Many of these let you enable the visual bell from the enclosing application itself, allowing all programs that blindly output a chr(7) to become less noisy.

See Also

The section on "String Literals" in Chapter 2 of *Programming Perl* or the section on "Quote and Quote-like Operators" in *perlop*(1); the documentation for the standard Term::Cap module

15.8 Using POSIX termios

Problem

You'd like to manipulate your terminal characteristics directly.

Solution

Use the POSIX termios interface.

Description

Think of everything you can do with the *stty* command—you can set everything from special characters to flow control and carriage-return mapping. The standard POSIX module provides direct access to the low-level terminal interface to implement *stty*-like capabilities in your program.

Example 15-2 finds what your tty's erase and kill characters are (probably backspace and Ctrl-U). Then it sets them back to their original values out of antiquity, # and @, and has you type something. It restores them when done.

Example 15-2. demo POSIX termios

```perl
#!/usr/bin/perl -w
# demo POSIX termios

use POSIX qw(:termios_h);

$term = POSIX::Termios->new;
$term->getattr(fileno(STDIN));

$erase = $term->getcc(VERASE);
$kill = $term->getcc(VKILL);
printf "Erase is character %d, %s\n", $erase, uncontrol(chr($erase));
printf "Kill is character %d, %s\n", $kill, uncontrol(chr($kill));

$term->setcc(VERASE, ord('#'));
$term->setcc(VKILL, ord('@'));
$term->setattr(1, TCSANOW);

print("erase is #, kill is @; type something: ");
$line = <STDIN>;
print "You typed: $line";

$term->setcc(VERASE, $erase);
$term->setcc(VKILL, $kill);
$term->setattr(1, TCSANOW);

sub uncontrol {
```

Example 15-2. demo POSIX termios (continued)

```
    local $_ = shift;
    s/([\200-\377])/sprintf("M-%c",ord($1) & 0177)/eg;
    s/([\0-\37\177])/sprintf("^%c",ord($1) ^ 0100)/eg;
    return $_;
}
```

Here's a module called HotKey that implements a readkey function in pure Perl. It doesn't provide any benefit over Term::ReadKey, but it shows POSIX termios in action:

```
# HotKey.pm
package HotKey;

@ISA = qw(Exporter);
@EXPORT = qw(cbreak cooked readkey);

use strict;
use POSIX qw(:termios_h);
my ($term, $oterm, $echo, $noecho, $fd_stdin);

$fd_stdin = fileno(STDIN);
$term     = POSIX::Termios->new();
$term->getattr($fd_stdin);
$oterm    = $term->getlflag();

$echo     = ECHO | ECHOK | ICANON;
$noecho   = $oterm & ~$echo;

sub cbreak {
    $term->setlflag($noecho);  # ok, so i don't want echo either
    $term->setcc(VTIME, 1);
    $term->setattr($fd_stdin, TCSANOW);
}

sub cooked {
    $term->setlflag($oterm);
    $term->setcc(VTIME, 0);
    $term->setattr($fd_stdin, TCSANOW);
}

sub readkey {
    my $key = '';
    cbreak();
    sysread(STDIN, $key, 1);
    cooked();
    return $key;
}

END { cooked() }

1;
```

See Also

POSIX Programmer's Guide, by Donald Lewine; the documentation for the standard POSIX module, also in Chapter 32 of *Programming Perl*; Recipe 15.6; Recipe 15.9

15.9 Checking for Waiting Input

Problem

You want to know whether keyboard input is waiting without actually reading it.

Solution

Use the CPAN module Term::ReadKey, and try to read a key in non-blocking mode by passing it an argument of -1:

```
use Term::ReadKey;

ReadMode ('cbreak');

if (defined ($char = ReadKey(-1)) ) {
    # input was waiting and it was $char
} else {
    # no input was waiting
}

ReadMode ('normal');               # restore normal tty settings
```

Discussion

The -1 parameter to ReadKey indicates a non-blocking read of a character. If no character is available, ReadKey returns undef.

See Also

The documentation for the Term::ReadKey module from CPAN; Recipe 15.6

15.10 Reading Passwords

Problem

You want to read input from the keyboard without the keystrokes being echoed on the screen. For instance, you want to read passwords as *passwd* does, i.e., without displaying the user's password.

Solution

Use the CPAN module Term::ReadKey, set the input mode to noecho, and then use ReadLine:

```
use Term::ReadKey;

ReadMode('noecho');
$password = ReadLine(0);
```

Discussion

Example 15-3 shows how to verify a user's password. If your system uses shadow passwords, only the superuser can get the encrypted form of the password with getpwuid. Everyone else just gets * as the password field of the database, which is useless for verifying passwords.

Example 15-3. checkuser

```
#!/usr/bin/perl -w
# checkuser - demonstrates reading and checking a user's password

use Term::ReadKey;

print "Enter your password: ";
ReadMode 'noecho';
$password = ReadLine 0;
chomp $password;
ReadMode 'normal';

print "\n";

($username, $encrypted) = ( getpwuid $< )[0,1];

if (crypt($password, $encrypted) ne $encrypted) {
    die "You are not $username\n";
} else {
    print "Welcome, $username\n";
}
```

See Also

The documentation for the Term::ReadKey module from CPAN; the crypt and getpwuid functions in Chapter 29 of *Programming Perl* and in *perlfunc*(1), which demonstrate using the *stty*(1) command; your system's *crypt*(3) and *passwd*(5) manpages (if you have them)

15.11 Editing Input

Problem

You want a user to be able to edit a line before sending it to you for reading.

Solution

Use the standard Term::ReadLine library along with the Term::ReadLine::Gnu module from CPAN:

```
use Term::ReadLine;

$term = Term::ReadLine->new("APP DESCRIPTION");
$OUT = $term->OUT || *STDOUT;

$term->addhistory($fake_line);
$line = $term->readline($prompt);

print $OUT "Any program output\n";
```

Discussion

The program in Example 15-4 acts as a crude shell. It reads a line and passes it to the shell to execute. The `readline` method reads a line from the terminal, with editing and history recall. It automatically adds the user's line to the history.

Example 15-4. vbsh

```
#!/usr/bin/perl -w
# vbsh - very bad shell
use strict;

use Term::ReadLine;
use POSIX qw(:sys_wait_h);

my $term = Term::ReadLine->new("Simple Shell");
my $OUT = $term->OUT( ) || *STDOUT;
my $cmd;

while (defined ($cmd = $term->readline('$ ') )) {
    my @output = `$cmd`;
    my $exit_value  = $? >> 8;
    my $signal_num  = $? & 127;
    my $dumped_core = $? & 128;
    printf $OUT "Program terminated with status %d from signal %d%s\n",
            $exit_value, $signal_num,
            $dumped_core ? " (core dumped)" : "";
    print @output;
    $term->addhistory($cmd);
}
```

If you want to seed the history with your own functions, use the addhistory method:

```
$term->addhistory($seed_line);
```

You can't seed with more than one line at a time. To remove a line from the history, use the remove_history method, which takes an index into the history list. 0 is the first (least recent) entry, 1 the second, and so on up to the most recent history lines.

```
$term->remove_history($line_number);
```

To get a list of history lines, use the GetHistory method, which returns a list of the lines:

```
@history = $term->GetHistory;
```

See Also

The documentation for the standard Term::ReadLine module and the Term::Read-Line::Gnu from CPAN

15.12 Managing the Screen

Problem

You want to control the screen layout or highlighting, detect when special keys are pressed, or present full-screen menus, but you don't want to think about what kind of display device the user has.

Solution

Use the Curses module from CPAN, which makes use of your native *curses*(3) library.

Description

The *curses* library provides easy access to the full-screen display in an efficient and device-independent fashion. (By display, we mean any cursor-addressable monitor.) With Curses, you write high-level code to put data on the logical display, building it up character by character or string by string. When you want output to show up, call the refresh function. The library generates output consisting only of the changes on the virtual display since the last call to refresh. This is particularly appreciated on a slow connection.

The example program in Example 15-5, called *rep*, demonstrates this. Call it with arguments of the program to run, like any of these:

```
% rep ps aux
% rep netstat
% rep -2.5 lpq
```

The *rep* script will repeatedly call the listed command, printing its output to the screen, updating only what changed since the previous run. This is most effective when the changes between runs are small. It maintains the current date in reverse video at the bottom-right corner of your screen.

By default, *rep* waits 10 seconds before rerunning the command. You can change this delay period by calling it an optional number of seconds (which can be a decimal number) as shown in the previous example when calling *lpq*. You may also hit any key during the pause for it to run the command right then.

Example 15-5. rep

```perl
#!/usr/bin/perl -w
# rep - screen repeat command
use strict;
use Curses;

my $timeout = 10;
if (@ARGV && $ARGV[0] =~ /^-(\d+\.?\d*)$/) {
    $timeout = $1;
    shift;
}

die "usage: $0 [ -timeout ] cmd args\n" unless @ARGV;

initscr();          # start screen
noecho();
cbreak();
nodelay(1);         # so getch() is non-blocking

$SIG{INT} = sub { done("Ouch!") };
sub done { endwin(); print "@_\n"; exit; }

while (1) {
    while ((my $key = getch()) ne ERR) {      # maybe multiple keys
        done("See ya") if $key eq 'q'
    }
    my @data = `(@ARGV) 2>&1`;                 # gather output+errors
    for (my $i = 0; $i < $LINES; $i++) {
        addstr($i, 0, $data[$i] || ' ' x $COLS);
    }

    standout();
    addstr($LINES-1, $COLS - 24, scalar localtime);
    standend();

    move(0,0);
    refresh();                                 # flush new output to display

    my ($in, $out) = ('', '');
    vec($in,fileno(STDIN),1) = 1;              # look for key on stdin
    select($out = $in,undef,undef,$timeout);   # wait up to this long
}
```

Curses lets you tell whether the user typed one of the arrow keys or those other funny keys, like HOME or INSERT. This is normally difficult, because those keys send multiple bytes. With Curses, it's easy:

```
keypad(1);                  # enable keypad mode
$key = getch();
if ($key eq 'k'      ||     # vi mode
    $key eq "\cP"    ||     # emacs mode
    $key eq KEY_UP)         # arrow mode
{
    # do something
}
```

Other Curses functions let you read the text at particular screen coordinates, control highlighting and standout mode, and even manage multiple windows.

The perlmenu module, also from CPAN, is built on top of the lower-level Curses module. It provides high-level access to menus and fill-out forms. Here's a sample form from the perlmenu distribution:

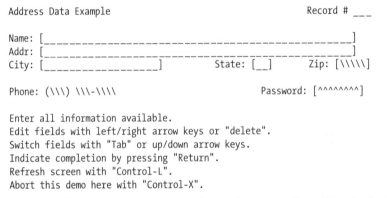

```
                    Template Entry Demonstration

    Address Data Example                          Record # ___

    Name: [_____]
    Addr: [_____]
    City: [_____]   State: [__]   Zip: [\\\\\]

    Phone: (\\\) \\\-\\\\              Password: [^^^^^^^^]

    Enter all information available.
    Edit fields with left/right arrow keys or "delete".
    Switch fields with "Tab" or up/down arrow keys.
    Indicate completion by pressing "Return".
    Refresh screen with "Control-L".
    Abort this demo here with "Control-X".
```

The user types in the areas indicated, with regular text indicated by underline fields, numeric data by backslashed fields, and starred-out data with circumflexed fields. This is reminiscent of Perl's formats, except that forms are used for output, not input.

See Also

Your system's *curses*(3) manpage (if you have it); the documentation for the Curses and the perlmenu modules from CPAN; Chapter 7 of *Programming Perl*, or *perlform*(1); Recipe 3.10

15.13 Controlling Another Program with Expect

Problem

You want to automate interaction with a full-screen program that expects to have a terminal behind STDIN and STDOUT.

Solution

Use the Expect module from CPAN:

```
use Expect;

$command = Expect->spawn("program to run")
    or die "Couldn't start program: $!\n";

# prevent the program's output from being shown on our STDOUT
$command->log_stdout(0);

# wait 10 seconds for "Password:" to appear
unless ($command->expect(10, "Password")) {
    # timed out
}

# wait 20 seconds for something that matches /[lL]ogin: ?/
unless ($command->expect(20, -re => '[lL]ogin: ?')) {
    # timed out
}

# wait forever for "invalid" to appear
unless ($command->expect(undef, "invalid")) {
    # error occurred; the program probably went away
}

# send "Hello, world" and a carriage return to the program
print $command "Hello, world\r";

# if the program will terminate by itself, finish up with
$command->soft_close();

# if the program must be explicitly killed, finish up with
$command->hard_close();
```

Discussion

This module requires two other modules from CPAN: IO::Pty and IO::Stty. It sets up a pseudo-terminal to interact with programs that insist on talking to the terminal device driver. People often use this for talking to *passwd* to change passwords. *telnet* (Net::Telnet, described in Recipe 18.6, is probably more suitable and portable) and *ftp* are also programs that expect a real tty.

Start the program you want to run with Expect->spawn, passing a program name and arguments either in a single string or as a list. Expect starts the program and returns an object representing that program, or undef if the program couldn't be started.

To wait for the program to emit a particular string, use the expect method. Its first argument is the number of seconds to wait for the string, or undef to wait forever. To wait for a string, give that string as the second argument to expect. To wait for a regular expression, give "-re" as the second argument and a string containing the pattern as the third argument. You can give further strings or patterns to wait for:

```
$which = $command->expect(30, "invalid", "success", "error", "boom");
if ($which) {
    # found one of those strings
}
```

In scalar context, expect returns the number of arguments it matched. In the previous example, expect would return 1 if the program emitted "invalid", 2 if it emitted "success", and so on. If none of the patterns or strings matches, expect returns false.

In list context, expect returns a five-element list. The first element is the number of the pattern or string that matched, which is the same as its return value in scalar context. The second argument is a string indicating why expect returned. If there were no error, the second argument would be undef. Possible errors are "1:TIMEOUT", "2:EOF", "3:spawn id(...)died", and "4:...". (See the *Expect*(3) manpage for the precise meaning of these messages.) The third argument of expect's return list is the string matched. The fourth argument is text before the match, and the fifth argument is text after the match.

Sending input to the program you're controlling with Expect is as simple as using print. The only catch is that terminals, devices, and sockets all vary in what they send and expect as the line terminator—we've left the sanctuary of the C standard I/O library, so the behind-the-scenes conversion to "\n" isn't taking place. We recommend trying "\r" at first. If that doesn't work, try "\n" and "\r\n".

When you're finished with the spawned program, you have three options. One, you can continue with your main program, and the spawned program will be forcibly killed when the main program ends. This will accumulate processes, though. Two, if you know the spawned program will terminate normally either when it has finished sending you output or because you told it to stop—for example, *telnet* after you exit the remote shell—call the soft_close method. If the spawned program could continue forever, like *tail -f*, then use the hard_close method; this kills the spawned program.

See Also

The documentation for the Expect, IO::Pty, and IO::Stty modules from CPAN; *Exploring Expect*, by Don Libes (O'Reilly)

15.14 Creating Menus with Tk

Problem

You want to create a window that has a menu bar at the top.

Solution

Use the Tk Menubutton and Frame widgets:

```
use Tk;

$main = MainWindow->new( );

# Create a horizontal space at the top of the window for the
# menu to live in.
$menubar = $main->Frame(-relief              => "raised",
                        -borderwidth         => 2)
                 ->pack (-anchor             => "nw",
                         -fill               => "x");

# Create a button labeled "File" that brings up a menu
$file_menu = $menubar->Menubutton(-text      => "File",
                                  -underline => 1)
                     ->pack    (-side        => "left" );
# Create entries in the "File" menu
$file_menu->command(-label    => "Print",
                    -command  => \&Print);
```

This is considerably easier if you use the -menuitems shortcut:

```
$file_menu = $menubar->Menubutton(-text           => "File",
                                  -underline       => 1,
                                  -menuitems       => [
                [ Button => "Print",-command       => \&Print ],
                [ Button => "Save",-command        => \&Save  ] ])
                       ->pack(-side               => "left");
```

Discussion

Menus in applications can be viewed as four separate components working together: Frames, Menubuttons, Menus, and Menu Entries. The Frame is the horizontal bar at the top of the window that the menu resides in (the *menubar*). Inside the Frame are a set of Menubuttons, corresponding to Menus: File, Edit, Format, Buffers, and so on. When the user clicks on a Menubutton, the Menubutton brings up the corresponding Menu, a vertically arranged list of Menu Entries.

Options on a Menu are *labels* (Open, for example) or *separators* (horizontal lines dividing one set of entries from another in a single menu).

The *command* entry, like Print in the File menu shown earlier, has code associated with it. When the entry is selected, the command is run by invoking the callback. These are the most common:

```
$file_menu->command(-label   => "Quit Immediately",
                     -command => sub { exit } );
```

Separators don't have any action associated with them:

```
$file_menu->separator( );
```

A *checkbutton* menu entry has an on value, an off value, and a variable associated with it. If the variable has the on value, the checkbutton menu entry has a check beside its label. If the variable has the off value, it does not. Selecting the entry on the menu toggles the state of the variable.

```
$options_menu->checkbutton(-label    => "Create Debugging File",
                           -variable => \$debug,
                           -onvalue  => 1,
                           -offvalue => 0);
```

A group of *radiobuttons* is associated with a single variable. Only one radiobutton associated with that variable can be on at any time. Selecting a radiobutton gives the variable the value associated with it:

```
$debug_menu->radiobutton(-label    => "Level 1",
                         -variable => \$log_level,
                         -value    => 1);

$debug_menu->radiobutton(-label    => "Level 2",
                         -variable => \$log_level,
                         -value    => 2);

$debug_menu->radiobutton(-label    => "Level 3",
                         -variable => \$log_level,
                         -value    => 3);
```

Create nested menus with the *cascade* menu entry. For instance, under *Netscape Navigator*, the File menu button at the left has a cascade menu entry New that brings up a selection of new windows. Creating a cascading menu entry is trickier than creating the other menu entries. You must create a cascade menu entry, fetch the new menu associated with that menu entry, and create entries on that new menu.

```
# step 1: create the cascading menu entry
$format_menu->cascade      (-label   => "Font");

# step 2: get the new Menu we just made
$font_menu = $format_menu->cget("-menu");

# step 3: populate that Menu
$font_menu->radiobutton    (-label    => "Courier",
                            -variable => \$font_name,
                            -value    => "courier");
$font_menu->radiobutton    (-label    => "Times Roman",
```

```
                         -variable => \$font_name,
                         -value    => "times");
```

A *tear-off* menu entry lets the user move the menu that it is on. By default, all Menubuttons and cascade menu entries make Menus that have a tear-off entry at the top of them. To create Menus without that default, use the -tearoff option:

```
$format_menu = $menubar->Menubutton(-text     => "Format",
                                    -underline => 1
                                    -tearoff   => 0)
                 ->pack;

$font_menu  = $format_menu->cascade(-label   => "Font",
                                    -tearoff => 0);
```

The -menuitems option to Menubutton is a shorthand for creating these menubuttons. Pass it an array reference representing the options on the Menubutton. Each option is itself an anonymous array. The first two elements of the option array are the button type ("command", "radiobutton", "checkbutton", "cascade", or "tearoff") and the menu name.

Here's how to use menuitems to make an Edit menu:

```
my $f = $menubar->Menubutton(-text => "Edit", -underline => 0,
                             -menuitems =>
    [
     [Button => 'Copy',          -command => \&edit_copy ],
     [Button => 'Cut',           -command => \&edit_cut ],
     [Button => 'Paste',         -command => \&edit_paste  ],
     [Button => 'Delete',        -command => \&edit_delete ],
     [Separator => ''],
     [Cascade => 'Object ...',   -tearoff => 0,
                                 -menuitems => [
        [ Button => "Circle",   -command => \&edit_circle ],
        [ Button => "Square",   -command => \&edit_square ],
        [ Button => "Point",    -command => \&edit_point ] ] ],
    ])->grid(-row => 0, -column => 0, -sticky => 'w');
```

See Also

The documentation for the Tk module from CPAN; *Mastering Perl/Tk*, by Stephen Lidie and Nancy Walsh

15.15 Creating Dialog Boxes with Tk

Problem

You want to create a dialog box, i.e., a new top-level window with buttons to make the window go away. The dialog box might also have other items, such as labels and text entry widgets for creating a fill-out form. You could use such a dialog box to collect registration information, and you want it to go away when registration is sent or if the user chooses not to register.

Solution

For simple jobs, use the Tk::DialogBox widget:

```
use Tk::DialogBox;

$dialog = $main->DialogBox( -title   => "Register This Program",
                            -buttons => [ "Register", "Cancel" ] );

# add widgets to the dialog box with $dialog->Add( )

# later, when you need to display the dialog box
$button = $dialog->Show( );
if ($button eq "Register") {
    # ...
} elsif ($button eq "Cancel") {
    # ...
} else {
    # this shouldn't happen
}
```

Discussion

A DialogBox has two parts: the bottom is a set of buttons, and the top has the widgets of your choosing. Showing a DialogBox pops it up and returns the button the user selected.

Example 15-6 contains a complete program demonstrating the DialogBox.

Example 15-6. tksample3

```
#!/usr/bin/perl -w
# tksample3 - demonstrate dialog boxes

use Tk;
use Tk::DialogBox;

$main = MainWindow->new( );

$dialog = $main->DialogBox( -title   => "Register",
                            -buttons => [ "Register", "Cancel" ],
                          );

# the top part of the dialog box will let people enter their names,
# with a Label as a prompt

$dialog->add("Label", -text => "Name")->pack( );
$entry = $dialog->add("Entry", -width => 35)->pack( );
```

Example 15-6. tksample3 (continued)

```
    # we bring up the dialog box with a button
    $main->Button( -text    => "Click Here For Registration Form",
                   -command => \&register)    ->pack(-side => "left");
    $main->Button( -text    => "Quit",
                   -command => sub { exit } ) ->pack(-side => "left");

MainLoop;

#
# register
#
# Called to pop up the registration dialog box
#

sub register {
    my $button;
    my $done = 0;

    do {
        # show the dialog
        $button = $dialog->Show;

        # act based on what button they pushed
        if ($button eq "Register") {
            my $name = $entry->get;

            if (defined($name) && length($name)) {
                print "Welcome to the fold, $name\n";
                $done = 1;
            } else {
                print "You didn't give me your name!\n";
            }
        } else {
            print "Sorry you decided not to register.\n";
            $done = 1;
        }
    } until $done;
}
```

The top part of this DialogBox has two widgets: a label and a text entry. To collect more information from the user, we'd have more labels and text entries.

A common use of dialog boxes is to display error messages or warnings. The program in Example 15-7 demonstrates how to display Perl's warn function in a DialogBox.

Example 15-7. tksample4

```
#!/usr/bin/perl -w
# tksample4 - popup dialog boxes for warnings

use Tk;
```

Example 15-7. tksample4 (continued)

```perl
use Tk::DialogBox;

my $main;

# set up a warning handler that displays the warning in a Tk dialog box

BEGIN {
    $SIG{__WARN__} = sub {
        if (defined $main) {
            my $dialog = $main->DialogBox( -title   => "Warning",
                                          -buttons => [ "Acknowledge" ]);
            $dialog->add("Label", -text => $_[0])->pack;
            $dialog->Show;
        } else {
            print STDOUT join("\n", @_), "n";
        }
    };
}

# your program goes here

$main = MainWindow->new();

$main->Button( -text    => "Make A Warning",
               -command => \&make_warning) ->pack(-side => "left");
$main->Button( -text    => "Quit",
               -command => sub { exit } )  ->pack(-side => "left");

MainLoop;

# dummy subroutine to generate a warning

sub make_warning {
    my $a;
    my $b = 2 * $a;
}
```

See Also

The Tk::DialogBox manpage in the documentation for the Tk module from CPAN; the *menu*(n) manpage (if you have it); *Mastering Perl/Tk*

15.16 Responding to Tk Resize Events

Problem

You've written a Tk program, but your widget layout goes awry when the user resizes their window.

Solution

You can prevent the user from resizing the window by intercepting the Configure event:

```
use Tk;

$main = MainWindow->new( );

$main->bind('<Configure>' => sub {
    $xe = $main->XEvent;
    $main->maxsize($xe->w, $xe->h);
    $main->minsize($xe->w, $xe->h);
});
```

Or you can use pack to control how each widget resizes and expands when the user resizes its container:

```
$widget->pack( -fill => "both", -expand => 1 );
$widget->pack( -fill => "x",    -expand => 1 );
```

Discussion

By default, packed widgets resize if their container changes size—they don't scale themselves or their contents to the new size. This can lead to empty space between widgets, or cropped or cramped widgets if the user resizes the window.

One solution is to prevent resizing. We bind to the Configure event, which is sent when a widget's size or position changes, registering a callback to reset the window's size. This is how you'd ensure a pop-up error-message box couldn't be resized.

You often want to let the user resize the application's windows. You must then define how each widget will react. Do this through the arguments to the pack method: -fill controls the dimensions the widget will resize in, and -expand controls whether the widget's size will change to match available space. The -expand option takes a Boolean value, true or false. The -fill option takes a string indicating the dimensions the widget can claim space in: "x", "y", "both", or "none".

The solution requires both options. Without -fill, -expand won't claim space to grow into. Without -expand, -fill will claim empty space but won't expand in it.

Different parts of your application will behave differently. The main area of a web browser, for example, should probably change size in both dimensions when the window is resized. You'd pack the widget like this:

```
$mainarea->pack( -fill => "both", -expand => 1 );
```

The menubar above the main area, though, should expand horizontally but not vertically. You'd pack the widget thus:

```
$menubar->pack( -fill => "x", -expand => 1 );
```

Associated with resizing is the need to anchor a widget to part of its container. Here's how you'd anchor the menubar to the top-left corner of its container when you call pack:

```
$menubar->pack (-fill    => "x",
                -expand  => 1,
                -anchor  => "nw" );
```

Now when you resize it, the menubar stays at the top of the window where it belongs, instead of being centered in wide open space.

See Also

The *pack*(n), *XEvent*(3), and *XConfigureEvent*(3) manpages (if you have them); *Tcl and the Tk Toolkit*, by John Ousterhout (Addison-Wesley); *Mastering Perl/Tk*

15.17 Removing the DOS Shell Window with Windows Perl/Tk

Problem

You have written a Perl program for the Windows port of Perl and Tk, but you get a DOS shell window every time you start your program.

Solution

Add this to the start of your program:

```
BEGIN {
  if ($^O eq 'MSWin32') {
    require Win32::Console;
    Win32::Console::Free( );
  }
}
```

Description

The Win32::Console module lets you control the terminal window that launched your program. All you need to do is close that window (or Free it in, in the peculiar parlance of the Windows API) and voilà—no pesky DOS shell window.

See Also

The documentation for the Win32::Console module, which is included with distributions of Perl destined for Microsoft systems

15.18 Graphing Data

Problem

You have numerical data that you want to represent as a bar, pie, or line chart.

Solution

Use the GD::Graph::* modules from CPAN:

```
use GD::Graph::lines;                        # bars, lines, points, pie
$chart = GD::Graph::lines->new(480,320);
$chart->set(x_label => $X_AXIS_LABEL,        # no axes for pie chart
            y_label => $Y_AXIS_LABEL,
            title   => $GRAPH_TITLE,
            # ... more options possible
           );
$plot = $chart->plot($DATA_REF) or die $chart->error;
# do something with $plot->png which is the image in PNG form
```

Here is a sample data structure (every row must have the same number of values):

```
$DATA_REF = [
              [ 1990, 1992, 1993, 1995, 2002 ],     # X values
              [ 10,   15,   18,   20,   25   ],     # first dataset
              [ 9,    undef,17,   undef,12   ],     # second dataset
              # ...
            ];
```

Discussion

The GD::Graph module requires you to have the GD module installed, which itself depends on a C library available from *http://www.boutell.com/gd/*. Early versions of this library created GIF images, but since the owners of the GIF patent are cracking down, the library now emits PNG and JPEG images:

```
$png_data = $plot->png;
$jpg_data = $plot->jpeg;
```

The documentation for GD::Graph lists a large number of options you can fine-tune (colors, fonts, placement), but the most important ones are labels and the image title. There are no axes to label in pie charts, so the x_label and y_label options are not available. By default, pie charts are drawn with a pseudo-3D look, which you can disable by setting the 3d option to a false value.

Recipe 15.23 contains a program that (crudely) extracts the day of the week on which each mail message in a mailbox was sent, and then graphs that data.

See Also

Documentation for the GD and GD::Graph modules; *Perl Graphics Programming*, by Shawn Wallace (O'Reilly)

15.19 Thumbnailing Images

Problem

You have a large image and you want to create a smaller version of that image, the *thumbnail*. For example, on a web site you might use a thumbnail as a preview to let readers see the basic image before they decide whether to download the larger original.

Solution

Use the Image::Magick module from CPAN:

```
use Image::Magick;

$image = Image::Magick->new();
$image->Read($ORIGINAL_FILENAME);
$image->Resize(geometry => '120x90');
$image->Write($THUMBNAIL_FILENAME);
```

Discussion

The Image::Magick module is a frontend to the ImageMagick suite, available from *http://imagemagick.sourceforge.net*. It handles many complex and powerful image manipulations, but here we're only concerned with the very simple resizing.

The Resize method's geometry parameter indicates the new geometry (*widthxheight*). You can also specify percentages: '75%' to resize each axis proportionally to 3/4 of its original size, or '10%x30%' to resize the X axis to 10% of its original value and the Y axis to 30%.

You can also specify a filter to use and how much to blur or sharpen the image with that filter:

```
$image->Resize(geometry => '120x90',
               filter   => 'Gaussian',
               blur     => 2);
```

A blur value greater than 1 indicates blurring; a value less than 1 indicates sharpening. The valid filters are Point, Box, Triangle, Hermite, Hanning, Hamming, Blackman, Gaussian, Quadratic, Cubic, Catrom, Mitchell, Lanczos, Bessel, and Sinc.

See Also

The documentation for the Image::Magick modules; *Perl Graphics Programming*

15.20 Adding Text to an Image

Problem

You want to write text onto an existing image. For example, you want to add a small copyright message to all photos on your web site.

Solution

Use the GD module from CPAN:

```
use GD;
$image = GD::Image->new($FILENAME);
$blue = $image->colorAllocate(0,0,255);
$image->string(gdTinyFont, 10, 10, "Copyright Me, 2037", $blue);
# write $image->png() to file
```

Discussion

The GD module can load only certain file formats; precisely which depends on the C libraries available when the underlying C library of GD was built. At the time of this writing, GD could read and write PNG, JPEG, XBM, XPM, and WBMP (Windows Bitmap), as well as its own GD2 and GD formats.

The arguments to the string method are: the font to use, the *x* and *y* coordinates to draw at, the string to draw, and the color to draw the text in.

GD comes with five fonts: gdTinyFont, gdSmallFont, gdMediumBoldFont, gdLargeFont, and gdGiantFont. If your GD was compiled to handle TrueType fonts, you can write with a TrueType font using:

```
$image->stringFT($color, $font, $point_size, $angle, $x, $y, $string);
```

Here, $font is the absolute pathname of the *.ttf* file containing the TrueType font. The $point_size and $angle parameters indicate the size (in points; fractions are acceptable) and rotation from horizontal (in radians). For example:

```
$image->stringFT($blue, '/Users/gnat/fonts/arial.ttf', 8, 0,
                 10, 20, 'Copyright Me Me Me');
```

See Also

The documentation for the GD module; *Perl Graphics Programming*

15.21 Program: Small termcap Program

Description

This program clears your screen and scribbles all over it until you interrupt it. It shows how to use Term::Cap to clear the screen, move the cursor, and write anywhere on the screen. It also uses Recipe 16.6.

The program text is shown in Example 15-8.

Example 15-8. tcapdemo

```perl
#!/usr/bin/perl -w
# tcapdemo - show off direct cursor placement

use POSIX;
use Term::Cap;

init();                 # Initialize Term::Cap.
zip();                  # Bounce lines around the screen.
finish();               # Clean up afterward.
exit();

# Two convenience functions.  clear_screen is obvious, and
# clear_end clears to the end of the screen.
sub clear_screen { $tcap->Tputs('cl', 1, *STDOUT) }
sub clear_end    { $tcap->Tputs('cd', 1, *STDOUT) }

# Move the cursor to a particular location.
sub gotoxy {
    my($x, $y) = @_;
    $tcap->Tgoto('cm', $x, $y, *STDOUT);
}

# Get the terminal speed through the POSIX module and use that
# to initialize Term::Cap.
sub init {
    $| = 1;
    $delay = (shift() || 0) * 0.005;
    my $termios = POSIX::Termios->new();
    $termios->getattr;
    my $ospeed = $termios->getospeed;
    $tcap = Term::Cap->Tgetent ({ TERM => undef, OSPEED => $ospeed });
    $tcap->Trequire(qw(cl cm cd));
}

# Bounce lines around the screen until the user interrupts with
# Ctrl-C.
sub zip {
    clear_screen();
    ($maxrow, $maxcol) = ($tcap->{_li} - 1, $tcap->{_co} - 1);
```

Example 15-8. tcapdemo (continued)

```perl
@chars = qw(* - / | \ _ );
sub circle { push(@chars, shift @chars); }

$interrupted = 0;
$SIG{INT} = sub { ++$interrupted };

$col = $row = 0;
($row_sign, $col_sign) = (1,1);

do {
    gotoxy($col, $row);
    print $chars[0];
    select(undef, undef, undef, $delay);

    $row += $row_sign;
    $col += $col_sign;

    if    ($row == $maxrow) { $row_sign = -1; circle; }
    elsif ($row == 0 )      { $row_sign = +1; circle; }

    if    ($col == $maxcol) { $col_sign = -1; circle; }
    elsif ($col == 0 )      { $col_sign = +1; circle; }

} until $interrupted;

}

# Clean up the screen.
sub finish {
    gotoxy(0, $maxrow);
    clear_end();
}
```

This is what it looks like in mid-run:

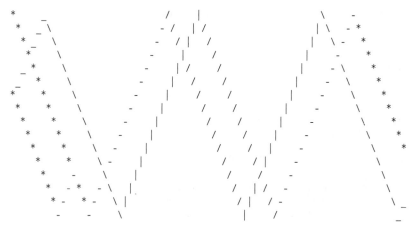

See Also

termcap(5) (if you have it); the documentation for the standard Term::Cap module

15.22 Program: tkshufflepod

This short program uses Tk to list the =head1 sections in the file using the Listbox widget, and it lets you drag the sections around to reorder them. When you're done, press "s" or "q" to save or quit. You can even double-click a section to view it with the Pod widget. It writes the section text to a temporary file in */tmp* and removes the file when the Pod widget is destroyed.

Call it with the name of the Pod file to view:

```
% tkshufflepod chap15.pod
```

We used this a lot when we wrote this book.

The program text is shown in Example 15-9.

Example 15-9. tkshufflepod

```
#!/usr/bin/perl -w
# tkshufflepod - reorder =head1 sections in a pod file

use Tk;
use Tk::Pod;
use strict;

# declare variables

my $podfile;        # name of the file to open
my $m;              # main window
my $l;              # listbox
my ($up, $down);    # positions to move
my @sections;       # list of pod sections
my $all_pod;        # text of pod file (used when reading)

# read the pod file into memory, and split it into sections.

$podfile = shift || "-";

undef $/;
open(F, " < $podfile")
    or die "Can't open $podfile : $!\n";
$all_pod = <F>;
close(F);
@sections = split(/(?==head1)/, $all_pod);

# turn @sections into an array of anonymous arrays.  The first element
# in each of these arrays is the original text of the message, while
# the second element is the text following =head1 (the section title).

foreach (@sections) {
```

Example 15-9. tkshufflepod (continued)

```perl
        /(.*)/;
        $_ = [ $_, $1 ];
    }

    # fire up Tk and display the list of sections.

    $m = MainWindow->new( );
    $l = $m->Listbox('-width' => 60)->pack('-expand' => 1, '-fill' => 'both');

    foreach my $section (@sections) {
        $l->insert("end", $section->[1]);
    }

    # permit dragging by binding to the Listbox widget.
    $l->bind( '<Any-Button>'        => \&down );
    $l->bind( '<Any-ButtonRelease>' => \&up );

    # permit viewing by binding double-click
    $l->bind( '<Double-Button>'     => \&view );

    # 'q' quits and 's' saves
    $m->bind( '<q>'                 => sub { exit } );
    $m->bind( '<s>'                 => \&save );

    MainLoop;

    # down(widget): called when the user clicks on an item in the Listbox.

    sub down {
        my $self = shift;
        $down = $self->curselection;;
    }

    # up(widget): called when the user releases the mouse button in the
    # Listbox.

    sub up {
        my $self = shift;
        my $elt;

        $up = $self->curselection;;

        return if $down == $up;

        # change selection list
        $elt = $sections[$down];
        splice(@sections, $down, 1);
        splice(@sections, $up, 0, $elt);

        $self->delete($down);
        $self->insert($up, $sections[$up]->[1]);
    }
```

Example 15-9. tkshufflepod (continued)

```
 # save(widget): called to save the list of sections.

sub save {
    my $self = shift;

    open(F, "> $podfile")
      or die "Can't open $podfile for writing: $!";
    print F map { $_->[0] } @sections;
    close F;

    exit;
}

# view(widget): called to display the widget.  Uses the Pod widget.

sub view {
    my $self = shift;
    my $temporary = "/tmp/$$-section.pod";
    my $popup;

    open(F, "> $temporary")
      or warn ("Can't open $temporary : $!\n"), return;
    print F $sections[$down]->[0];
    close(F);
    $popup = $m->Pod('-file' => $temporary);

    $popup->bind('<Destroy>' => sub { unlink $temporary } );




}
```

15.23 Program: graphbox

The *graphbox* program shown in Example 15-10 generates a bar graph of how many email messages were sent on each day of the week, using the GD::Graph::Bars module (see Recipe 15.18). It extracts the day of the week from the Date: headers and then plots the results.

Example 15-10. graphbox

```
#!/usr/bin/perl -w
# graphbox - graph number of messages by day of week they were sent

use GD::Graph::bars;
use Getopt::Std;
use strict;

my %count;  # running total of messages for each day of the week
```

Example 15-10. graphbox

```perl
my $chart;  # the GD::Graph::bars object
my $plot;   # the GD object containing the actual graph

my @DAYS = qw(Mon Tue Wed Thu Fri Sat Sun);
my $day_re = join("|", @DAYS);
$day_re = qr/$day_re/;

# process options

my %Opt;
getopts('ho:', \%Opt);
if ($Opt{h} or !$Opt{o}) {
  die "Usage:\n\t$0 -o outfile.png < mailbox\n";
}

# extract dates from Date headers (guessing!)

while (<>) {
  if (/^Date: .*($day_re)/) {
    $count{$1}++;
  }
}

# build graph

$chart = GD::Graph::bars->new(480,320);
$chart->set(x_label => "Day",
            y_label => "Messages",
            title   => "Mail Activity");
$plot = $chart->plot([ [ @DAYS ],
                       [ @count{@DAYS} ],
                     ]);

# save it

open(F, "> $Opt{o}")
  or die "Can't open $Opt{o} for writing: $!\n";
print F $plot->png;
close F;
```

## CHAPTER 16

Process Management and Communication

*It is quite a three-pipe problem, and I beg that you
won't speak to me for fifty minutes.*
—Sherlock Holmes, *The Red-Headed League*

16.0 Introduction

Perl may be many things to many people, but to most of us it is the glue that connects diverse components. This chapter is about launching commands and connecting separate processes together. It's about managing their creation, communication,
and ultimate demise. It's about systems programming.

When it comes to systems programming, Perl, as usual, makes easy things easy and
hard things possible. If you want to use it as you would the shell, Perl is happy to
assist you. If you want to roll up your sleeves for low-level hacking like a hardcore C
programmer, you can do that, too.

Because Perl lets you get so close to the system, portability issues can sneak in. This
chapter is the most Unix-centric chapter of the book. It will be tremendously useful
to those on Unix systems, but of limited use to others. (If you're not on Unix, consult the *perlport*(3) manpage that came with Perl to see which of the techniques we
describe are available on other operating systems or emulated by Perl.) We deal with
features that aren't as universal as strings and numbers and basic arithmetic. Most
basic operations work more or less the same everywhere. But if you're not using
some kind of Unix or other POSIX conformant system, most of the interesting features in this chapter may work differently for you—or not at all. Check the documentation that came with your Perl port if you aren't sure.

You might even be pleasantly surprised. Windows users, for example, are often
astonished to learn that Perl's fork function, long unique to Unix, is supported on
their platform. See *perlfork*(1).

Process Creation

In this chapter, we cover the proper care and feeding of your own child processes. Sometimes this means launching a standalone command and letting it have its own way with the world (using system). Other times it means keeping a tight rein on your child, feeding it carefully filtered input or taking hold of its output stream (backticks and piped opens). Without even starting a new process, you can use exec to replace your current program with a completely different program.

We first show how to use the most portable and commonly used operations for managing processes: backticks, system, open, and the manipulation of the %SIG hash. Those are the easy things, but we don't stop there. We also show what to do when the simple approach isn't good enough.

For example, you might want to interrupt your program while it's running a different program. Maybe you need to process a child program's standard error separately from its standard output. Perhaps you need to control both the input and output of a program simultaneously. When you tire of having just one thread of control and begin to take advantage of multitasking, you'll want to learn how to split your current program into several, simultaneously running processes that all talk to each other.

For tasks like these, you have to drop back to the underlying syscalls: pipe, fork, and exec. The pipe function creates two connected filehandles, a reader and writer, whereby anything written to the writer can be read from the reader. The fork function is the basis of multitasking, but unfortunately it has not been supported on all non-Unix systems. It clones off a duplicate process identical in virtually every aspect to its parent, including variable settings and open files. The most noticeable changes are the process ID and parent process ID. New programs are started by forking, then using exec to replace the program in the child process with a new one. You don't always both fork and exec together, so having them as separate primitives is more expressive and powerful than if all you could do is run system. In practice, you're more apt to use fork by itself than exec by itself.

When a child process dies, its memory is returned to the operating system, but its entry in the process table isn't freed. This lets a parent check the exit status of its child processes. Processes that have died but haven't been removed from the process table are called *zombies*, and you should clean them up lest they fill the whole process table. Backticks and the system and close functions automatically take care of this, and will work on most non-Unix systems. You have more to worry about when you go beyond these simple portable functions and use low-level primitives to launch programs. One thing to worry about is signals.

Signals

Your process is notified of the death of a child it created with a *signal*. Signals are a kind of notification delivered by the operating system. They are used for errors (when the kernel says, "Hey, you can't touch that area of memory!") and for events (death of a child, expiration of a per-process timer, interrupt with Ctrl-C). If you're launching processes manually, you normally arrange for a subroutine of your choosing to be called whenever one of your children exits.

Each process has a default disposition for each possible signal. You may install your own handler or otherwise change the disposition of most signals. Only SIGKILL and SIGSTOP cannot be changed. The rest you can ignore, trap, or block.

Briefly, here's a rundown of the more important signals:

SIGINT

Normally triggered by Ctrl-C. This requests that a process interrupt what it's doing. Simple programs like filters usually just die, but more important ones like shells, editors, or FTP programs usually use SIGINT to stop long-running operations so you can tell them to do something else.

SIGQUIT

Also normally generated by a terminal, usually Ctrl-\. Its default behavior is to generate a core dump.

SIGTERM

Sent by the *kill* shell command when no signal name is explicitly given. Think of it as a polite request for a process to die.

SIGUSR1 *and* SIGUSR2

Never caused by system events, so user applications can safely use them for their own purposes.

SIGPIPE

Sent by the kernel when your process tries to write to a pipe or socket when the process on the other end has closed its connection, usually because it no longer exists.

SIGALRM

Sent when the timer set by the alarm function expires, as described in Recipe 16.21.

SIGHUP

Sent to a process when its controlling terminal gets a hang-up (e.g., the modem lost its carrier), but it also often indicates that a program should restart or reread its configuration.

SIGCHLD

Probably the most important signal when it comes to low-level systems programming. The system sends your process a SIGCHLD when one of its child processes stops running—or, more likely, when that child exits. See Recipe 16.19 for more on SIGCHLD.

Signal names are a convenience for humans. Each signal has an associated number that the operating system uses instead of names. Although we talk about SIGCHLD, your operating system knows it only as a number, like 20 (these numbers vary across operating systems). Perl translates between signal names and numbers for you, so you can think in terms of signal names.

Recipes 16.15, 16.17, 16.21, 16.18, and 16.20 run the full gamut of signal handling.

16.1 Gathering Output from a Program

Problem

You want to run a program and collect its output into a variable.

Solution

Either use backticks:

```
$output = `program args`;   # collect output into one multiline string
@output = `program args`;   # collect output into array, one line per element
```

or use Recipe 16.4:

```
open(my $fh, "-|", "program", @args)
    or die "Can't run program: $!\n";
while (<$fh>) {
    $output .= $_;
}
close $fh;
```

Discussion

The backticks are a convenient way to run other programs and gather their output. The backticks do not return until the called program exits. Perl goes to some trouble behind the scenes to collect the output, so it is inefficient to use the backticks and ignore their return value:

```
`fsck -y /dev/rsd1a`;       # BAD AND SCARY
```

The backtick operator calls the shell to run the command. This makes it unsafe when used in a program with special privileges, but lets you use shell wildcards in the command:

```
@files = `ls -1 /music/*.mp3`;
```

If you want to read the output of a wildcarded command line as it's generated (and don't mind the potential security problems), use this form of open:

```
open(README, "ls -1 /music/*.mp3 |") or die "Can't run program: $!\n";
while(<README>) {
    # the latest line is in $_
}
close(README);
```

In versions of Perl before 5.8, this two-argument form of open was the only one available to you. In those versions of Perl, you wrote the solution as:

```
open(FH, "program @args |")
    or die "Can't run program: $!\n";
```

Here's a low-level workaround, using pipe (to create two connected filehandles), fork (to split off a new process), and exec (to replace the new process with the program to read from):

```
use POSIX qw(:sys_wait_h);

my  ($readme, $writeme);
pipe $readme, $writeme;
if ($pid = fork) {
    # parent
    $SIG{CHLD} = sub { 1 while ( waitpid(-1, WNOHANG)) > 0 };
    close $writeme;
} else {
    die "cannot fork: $!" unless defined $pid;
    # child
    open(STDOUT, ">&=", $writeme)    or die "Couldn't redirect STDOUT: $!";
    close $readme;
    exec($program, $arg1, $arg2)    or die "Couldn't run $program : $!\n";
}

while (<$readme>) {
    $string .= $_;
    # or  push(@strings, $_);
}
close($readme);
```

There's no reason to prefer this over the open "-|" code in the Solution, except that the low-level workaround lets you change signal disposition before you launch the new program. For example, you could disable the INT signal in the child so that only the parent process receives it.

See Also

The section on "Talking to Yourself" in Chapter 16 of *Programming Perl* or *perlsec*(1); Recipe 16.2; Recipe 16.4; Recipe 16.10; Recipe 16.19; Recipe 19.5

16.2 Running Another Program

Problem

From one program you want to run another, pause until it is done, and then continue with the original program. The other program should have the same STDIN and STDOUT as you have.

Solution

Call system with a string to have the shell interpret the string as a command line:

```
$status = system("vi $myfile");
```

If you don't want the shell involved, pass system a list:

```
$status = system("vi", $myfile);
```

Discussion

The system function is the simplest and most generic way to run another program in Perl. It doesn't gather the program's STDOUT like backticks or open. Instead, its return value is (essentially) that program's exit status. While the new program is running, your main program is suspended, so the new program can read from your STDIN and write to your STDOUT so users can interact with it.

Like open, exec, and backticks, system uses the shell to start the program whenever it's called with one argument. This is convenient when you want to do redirection or other tricks:

```
system("cmd1 args | cmd2 | cmd3 >outfile");
system("cmd args < infile >outfile 2>errfile");
```

To avoid the shell, call system with a list of arguments:

```
$status = system($program, $arg1, $arg);
die "$program exited funny: $?" unless $status == 0;
```

The returned status value is not just the exit value: it includes the signal number (if any) that the process died from. This is the same value that wait sets $? to. See Recipe 16.19 to learn how to decode this value.

The system function ignores SIGINT and SIGQUIT while child processes are running. That way those signals will kill only the child process. If you want your main program to die as well, check the return value of system or the value of the $? variable.

```
if (($signo = system(@arglist)) &= 127) {
    die "program killed by signal $signo\n";
}
```

To get the effect of a system that ignores SIGINT, install your own signal handler and then manually fork and exec:

```
if ($pid = fork) {
    # parent catches INT and berates user
    local $SIG{INT} = sub { print "Tsk tsk, no process interruptus\n" };
    waitpid($pid, 0);
} else {
    die "cannot fork: $!" unless defined $pid;
    # child ignores INT and does its thing
    $SIG{INT} = "IGNORE";
    exec("summarize", "/etc/logfiles")          or die "Can't exec: $!\n";
}
```

A few programs examine their own program name. Shells look to see whether they were called with a leading minus to indicate interactivity. The *expn* program at the end of Chapter 18 behaves differently if called as *vrfy*, which can happen if you've installed the file under two different links as suggested. This is why you shouldn't trust that $0 is really the pathname to the invoked program—you could have been lied to in a number of ways.

If you want to fib to the program you're executing about its own name, specify the real path as the "indirect object" in front of the list passed to system. (This also works with exec.) The indirect object has no comma following it, just like using printf with a filehandle or making object methods without the pointer arrow.

```
$shell = '/bin/tcsh';
system $shell '-csh';          # pretend it's a login shell
```

Or, more directly:

```
system {'/bin/tcsh'} '-csh';   # pretend it's a login shell
```

In the next example, the program's real pathname is supplied in the indirect object slot as {'/home/tchrist/scripts/expn'}. The fictitious name 'vrfy' is given as the first real function argument, which the program will see stored in $0.

```
# call expn as vrfy
system {'/home/tchrist/scripts/expn'} 'vrfy', @ADDRESSES;
```

Using an indirect object with system is also more secure. This usage forces interpretation of the arguments as a multivalued list, even if the list had just one argument. That way you're safe from the shell expanding wildcards or splitting up words with whitespace in them.

```
@args = ( "echo surprise" );

system @args;# subject to shell escapes if @args == 1
system { $args[0] } @args;  # safe even with one-arg list
```

The first version, the one without the indirect object, ran the *echo* program, passing it "surprise" as an argument. The second version didn't—it tried to run a program literally called "echo surprise", didn't find it, and set $? to a non-zero value indicating failure.

See Also

The section on "Talking to Yourself" in Chapter 16 of *Programming Perl* or *perlsec*(1); the waitpid, fork, exec, system, and open functions in Chapter 29 of *Programming Perl*, or *perlfunc*(1); Recipe 16.1; 16.4; 16.19; Recipe 19.5; *Advanced Programming in the UNIX Environment*, by Richard W. Stevens (Addison-Wesley)

16.3 Replacing the Current Program with a Different One

Problem

You want to replace the running program with another, as when checking parameters and setting up the initial environment before running another program.

Solution

Use the built-in exec function. If exec is called with a single argument containing metacharacters, the shell will be used to run the program:

```
exec("archive *.data")
    or die "Couldn't replace myself with archive: $!\n";
```

If you pass exec more than one argument, the shell will not be used:

```
exec("archive", "accounting.data")
    or die "Couldn't replace myself with archive: $!\n";
```

If called with a single argument containing no shell metacharacters, the argument will be split on whitespace and then interpreted as though the resulting list had been passed to exec:

```
exec("archive accounting.data")
    or die "Couldn't replace myself with archive: $!\n";
```

Discussion

The exec function in Perl is a direct interface to the *execlp*(2) syscall, which replaces the current program with another, leaving the process intact. The program that calls exec gets wiped clean, and its place in the operating system's process table is taken by the program specified in the arguments to exec. As a result, the new program has the same process ID ($$) as the original program. If the specified program couldn't be run, exec returns a false value and the original program continues. Be sure to check for this.

As with system (see Recipe 16.2), an indirect object identifies the program to be run:

```
exec { '/usr/local/bin/lwp-request' } 'HEAD', $url;
```

The first real argument ('HEAD' here) is what the new program will be told it is. Some programs use this to control their behavior, and others use it for logging. The main use of this, however, is that exec called with an indirect object will never use the shell to run the program.

If you exec yourself into a different program, neither your END blocks nor any object destructors will be automatically run as they would if your process actually exited.

See Also

The exec function in Chapter 29 of *Programming Perl*, and in *perlfunc*(1); your system's *execlp*(2) manpage (if you have it); Recipe 16.2

16.4 Reading or Writing to Another Program

Problem

You want to run another program and either read its output or supply the program with input.

Solution

Use open with a pipe symbol at the beginning or end. To read from a program, put the pipe symbol at the end:

```
$pid = open $readme, "-|", "program", "arguments"
                                    or die "Couldn't fork: $!\n";
while (<$readme>) {
    # ...
}
close $readme                      or die "Couldn't close: $!\n";
```

To write to the program, put the pipe at the beginning:

```
$pid = open $writeme, "|-", "program", "arguments"
                                    or die "Couldn't fork: $!\n";
print $writeme "data\n";
close $writeme                     or die "Couldn't close: $!\n";
```

Discussion

In the case of reading, this is similar to using backticks, except you have a process ID and a filehandle, and the shell is never involved. If you want Perl to use the shell when it sees shell-special characters in its argument—for example, to let the shell do filename wildcard expansion and I/O redirection—then you must use the two-argument form of open:

```
open($writeme, "| program args");
open($readme, "program args |");
```

However, sometimes this isn't desirable. Piped opens that include unchecked user data would be unsafe while running in taint mode or in untrustworthy situations.

Notice how we specifically call close on the filehandle. When you use open to connect a filehandle to a child process, Perl remembers this and automatically waits for the child when you close the filehandle. If the child hasn't exited by then, Perl waits until it does. This can be a very, very long wait if your child doesn't exit:

```
$pid = open $f, "-|", "sleep", "100000";  # child goes to sleep
close $f;                                 # and the parent goes to lala land
```

To avoid this, you can save the PID returned by open to kill your child, or use a manual pipe-fork-exec sequence as described in Recipe 16.10.

If you attempt to write to a process that has gone away, your process will receive a SIGPIPE. The default disposition for this signal is to kill your process, so the truly paranoid install a SIGPIPE handler just in case.

If you want to run another program and be able to supply its STDIN yourself, a similar construct is used:

```
$pid = open $writeme, "|-", "program", "args";
print $writeme "hello\n";            # program will get hello\n on STDIN
close $writeme;                      # program will get EOF on STDIN
```

The second argument to open ("|-") tells Perl to start another process instead. It connects the opened filehandle to the process's STDIN. Anything you write to the filehandle can be read by the program through its STDIN. When you close the filehandle, the opened process will get EOF when it next tries to read from STDIN.

You can also use this technique to change your program's normal output path. For example, to automatically run everything through a pager, use something like:

```
$pager = $ENV{PAGER} || '/usr/bin/less';  # XXX: might not exist
open(STDOUT, "|-", $pager);
```

Now, without changing the rest of your program, anything you print to standard output will go through the pager automatically.

As before, the parent should also be wary of close. If the parent closes the filehandle connecting it to the child, the parent will block while waiting for the child to finish. If the child doesn't finish, neither will the close. The workaround as before is to either kill your child process prematurely, or else use the low-level pipe-fork-exec scenario.

When using piped opens, always check return values of both open and close, not just of open. That's because the return value from open does not indicate whether the command was successfully launched. With a piped open, you fork a child to execute the command. Assuming the system hasn't run out of processes, the fork immediately returns the PID of the child it just created.

By the time the child process tries to exec the command, it's a separately scheduled process. So if the command can't be found, there's effectively no way to communicate this back to the open function, because that function is in a different process!

Check the return value from close to see whether the command was successful. If the child process exits with non-zero status—which it will do if the command isn't found—the close returns false and $? is set to the wait status of that process. You can interpret its contents as described in Recipe 16.19.

In the case of a pipe opened for writing, you should also install a SIGPIPE handler, since writing to a child that isn't there will trigger a SIGPIPE.

See Also

The open function in Chapter 29 of *Programming Perl*, and in *perlfunc*(1); Recipe 16.10; Recipe 16.15; Recipe 16.19; Recipe 19.5

16.5 Filtering Your Own Output

Problem

You want to postprocess your program's output without writing a separate program to do so.

Solution

Use the forking form of open to attach a filter to yourself. For example, this will restrict your program to a hundred lines of output:

```
head(100);
while (<>) {
    print;
}

sub head {
    my $lines = shift || 20;
    return if $pid = open STDOUT, "|-";
    die "cannot fork: $!" unless defined $pid;
    while (<STDIN>) {
        print;
        last unless --$lines;
    }
    exit;
}
```

Discussion

It's easy to add an output filter. Just use the forking *open* on your own STDOUT, and let the child filter STDIN to STDOUT, performing whatever alterations you care about. Notice that we install the output filter *before* we generate the output. This makes sense—you can't filter your output if it has already left your program. Any such filters should be applied in LIFO order—the last one inserted is the first one run.

Here's an example that uses two output filters. One numbers lines; the other quotes the lines like a mail reply. When run on */etc/motd*, you get something like:

```
1:  > Welcome to Linux, version 2.0.33 on a i686
2:  >
```

```
3:   >     "The software required `Windows 95 or better',
4:   >        so I installed Linux."
```

If you reversed the order of the two filters, you'd get:

```
> 1: Welcome to Linux, Kernel version 2.0.33 on a i686
> 2:
> 3:     "The software required `Windows 95 or better',
> 4:        so I installed Linux."
```

The program is in Example 16-1.

Example 16-1. qnumcat

```perl
#!/usr/bin/perl
# qnumcat - demo additive output filters

number();                    # push number filter on STDOUT
quote();                     # push quote filter on STDOUT

while (<>) {                  # act like /bin/cat
    print;
}
close STDOUT;                # tell kids we're done--politely
exit;

sub number {
    my $pid;
    return if $pid = open STDOUT, "|-";
    die "cannot fork: $!" unless defined $pid;
    while (<STDIN>) { printf "%d: %s", $., $_ }
    exit;
}

sub quote {
    my $pid;
    return if $pid = open STDOUT, "|-";
    die "cannot fork: $!" unless defined $pid;
    while (<STDIN>) { print "> $_" }
    exit;
}
```

As with all process forks, doing this a zillion times has some cost, but it's fine for a couple of processes, or even a couple dozen. If the system was actually designed to be multitasking right from the start, as Unix was, this is far cheaper than you might imagine. Virtual memory and copy-on-write makes this efficient. Forking is an elegant and inexpensive solution to many, if not most, multitasking needs.

See Also

The open function in Chapter 29 of *Programming Perl* and in *perlfunc*(1); Recipe 16.4

16.6 Preprocessing Input

Problem

You'd like your programs to work on files with funny formats, such as compressed files or remote web documents specified with a URL, but your program only knows how to access regular text in local files.

Solution

Take advantage of Perl's easy pipe handling by changing your input files' names to pipes before opening them.

To autoprocess gzipped or compressed files by decompressing them with *gzip*, use:

```
@ARGV = map { /\.(gz|Z)$/ ? "gzip -dc $_ |" : $_  } @ARGV;
while (<>) {
    # .......
}
```

To fetch URLs before processing them, use the *GET* program from LWP (see Chapter 20):

```
@ARGV = map { m#^\w+://# ? "GET $_ |" : $_ } @ARGV;
while (<>) {
    # .......
}
```

You might prefer to fetch just the text, of course, not the HTML. That just means using a different command, perhaps *lynx -dump*.

Discussion

As shown in Recipe 16.1, Perl's built-in open function is magical: you don't have to do anything special to get Perl to open a pipe instead of a file. (That's why it's sometimes called *magic open* and, when applied to implicit ARGV processing, *magic ARGV*.) If it looks like a pipe, Perl will open it like a pipe. We take advantage of this by rewriting certain filenames to include a decompression or other preprocessing stage. For example, the file "09tails.gz" becomes "gzcat -dc 09tails.gz|".

This technique has further applications. Suppose you wanted to read */etc/passwd* if the machine isn't using NIS, and the output of *ypcat passwd* if it is. You'd use the output of the *domainname* program to decide if you're running NIS, and then set the filename to open to be either "</etc/passwd" or "ypcat passwd|":

```
$pwdinfo = `domainname` =~ /^(\(none\))?$/
                ? '</etc/passwd'
                : 'ypcat  passwd |';

open(PWD, $pwdinfo)              or die "can't open $pwdinfo: $!";
```

The wonderful thing is that even if you didn't think to build such processing into your program, Perl already did it for you. Imagine a snippet of code like this:

```
print "File, please? ";
chomp($file = <>);
open (FH, $file)                          or die "can't open $file: $!";
```

The user can enter a regular filename—or something like "webget http://www.perl.com |" instead—and your program would suddenly be reading from the output of some *webget* program. They could even enter -, a lone minus sign, which, when opened for reading, interpolates standard input instead.

This also comes in handy with the automatic ARGV processing we saw in Recipe 7.14.

See Also

Recipe 7.14; 16.4

16.7 Reading STDERR from a Program

Problem

You want to run a program as you would with system, backticks, or open, but you don't want its STDERR to be sent to your STDERR. You would like to be able to either ignore or read the STDERR.

Solution

Use the shell's numeric redirection and duplication syntax for file descriptors. (We don't check the return value from open here in order to make the examples easier to read, but you should always check it in your programs!)

To capture a command's STDERR and STDOUT together:

```
$output = `cmd 2>&1`;                       # with backticks
# or
$pid = open(PH, "cmd 2>&1 |");              # with an open pipe
while (<PH>) { }                            # plus a read
```

To capture a command's STDOUT and discard its STDERR:

```
$output = `cmd 2>/dev/null`;                # with backticks
# or
$pid = open(PH, "cmd 2>/dev/null |");       # with an open pipe
while (<PH>) { }                            # plus a read
```

To capture a command's STDERR and discard its STDOUT:

```
$output = `cmd 2>&1 1>/dev/null`;           # with backticks
# or
$pid = open(PH, "cmd 2>&1 1>/dev/null |");  # with an open pipe
while (<PH>) { }                            # plus a read
```

To exchange a command's STDOUT and STDERR, i.e., capture the STDERR but have its STDOUT come out on our old STDERR:

```
$output = `cmd 3>&1 1>&2 2>&3 3>&-`;          # with backticks
# or
$pid = open(PH, "cmd 3>&1 1>&2 2>&3 3>&-|");  # with an open pipe
while (<PH>) { }                              # plus a read
```

To read both a command's STDOUT and its STDERR separately, it's easiest and safest to redirect them separately to files, and then read from those files when the program is done:

```
system("program args 1>/tmp/program.stdout 2>/tmp/program.stderr");
```

Discussion

When you launch a command with backticks, a piped open, or system on a single string, Perl checks for characters special to the shell. These allow you to redirect the new program's file descriptors. STDIN is file descriptor number 0, STDOUT number 1, and STDERR number 2. You can then use 2>*file* to redirect STDERR to a file. The special notation &N where N is a file descriptor number is used to redirect to a file descriptor. Therefore, 2>&1 points STDERR at STDOUT.

Table 16-1 lists some interesting shell file descriptor redirections.

Table 16-1. Redirections and their meanings

Redirection	Meaning
0</dev/null	Make STDIN give immediate EOF
1>/dev/null	Discard STDOUT
2>/dev/null	Discard STDERR
2>&1	Send STDERR to STDOUT instead
2>&-	Close STDERR (not recommended)
3<>/dev/tty	Open fd 3 to */dev/tty* in read-write mode

Using this, let's examine the most complicated of the redirection sequences from the Solution:

```
$output = `cmd 3>&1 1>&2 2>&3 3>&-`;
```

There are four steps here:

Step A: 3>&1
> Make a new file descriptor, number 3, be a copy of number 1. This saves the destination of STDOUT in the new file descriptor we've just opened.

Step B: 1>&2
> Make STDOUT go wherever STDERR had been going. We still have the saved destination squirreled away in descriptor 3.

Step C: 2>&3

Make file descriptor 2 a copy of number 3. That means that STDERR is now going out where STDOUT originally had been going.

Step D: 3>&-

Since we're done moving streams around, keep everything nice and tidy and close our temporary file descriptor. This avoids file descriptor leaks.

If that's confusing, it might help to think in terms of regular variables and a sequence of assignment statements, with $fd1 representing STDOUT and $fd2 representing STDERR. If you wanted to exchange the two variables, you'd use a temporary file to hold one value. That's all we're doing here.

```
$fd3 = $fd1;
$fd1 = $fd2;
$fd2 = $fd3;
$fd3 = undef;
```

When all's said and done, the string returned from the backticks is the command's STDERR, and its STDOUT has been diverted to the original STDERR.

Ordering is important in all of these examples because the shell processes file descriptor redirections in strictly left to right order.

```
system("prog args 1>tmpfile 2>&1");
system("prog args 2>&1 1>tmpfile");
```

The first command sends both standard out and standard error to the temporary file. The second command sends only the old standard output there, and the old standard error shows up on the old standard out. If that's confusing, think in terms of assignments to variables representing file descriptors. For example:

```
# system ("prog args 1>tmpfile 2>&1");
$fd1 = "tmpfile";        # change stdout destination first
$fd2 = $fd1;             # now point stderr there, too
```

is very different from:

```
# system("prog args 2>&1 1>tmpfile");
$fd2 = $fd1;             # stderr same destination as stdout
$fd1 = "tmpfile";        # but change stdout destination
```

See Also

Your system's *sh*(1) manpage (if you have one) for details about file descriptor redirection; the system function in Chapter 29 of *Programming Perl* and in *perlfunc*(1)

16.8 Controlling Input and Output of Another Program

Problem

You want to both write to and read from another program. The open function lets you do one or the other, but not both.

Solution

Use the standard IPC::Open2 module:

```
use IPC::Open2;

$pid = open2(*README, *WRITEME, $program);
print WRITEME "here's your input\n";
$output = <README>;
close(WRITEME);
close(README);
waitpid($pid, 0);
```

Discussion

Wanting simultaneous read and write access to another program is very common, but surprisingly perilous. That's one reason the built-in open doesn't permit:

```
open(my $double_handle, "| program args |")    # WRONG
```

The big problem here is buffering. Because you can't force the other program to unbuffer its output, you can't guarantee that your reads won't block. If you block trying to read at the same time the other process blocks waiting for you to send something, you've achieved the unholy state of deadlock. There you'll both stay, wedged, until someone kills your process or the machine reboots.

If you control the other process's buffering because you wrote the other program and know how it works, then IPC::Open2 may be the module for you. If you pass undefined scalar values as the first two arguments, open2 creates new filehandles:

```
use IPC::Open2;

$pid = open2(my $reader, my $writer, $program);
```

Alternatively, you can pass in arguments that look like "<&OTHERFILEHANDLE" or ">&OTHERFILEHANDLE", which specify existing filehandles for the child process to read from or write to. These filehandles don't have to be controlled by your program—they may be connected to other programs, files, or sockets.

You can specify the program either as a list (where the first element is the program name and the remaining elements are arguments to the program) or as a single string (which is passed to the shell as a command to start the program). If you also want control over the process's standard error, use the IPC::Open3 module and see the next recipe.

If an error occurs, open2 and open3 do not return. Instead, they die with an error message that begins with "open2" or "open3". To test for failure, use the eval BLOCK construct:

```
eval {
    $pid = open2($readme, $writeme, @program_and_arguments);
};
if ($@) {
    if ($@ =~ /^open2/) {
        warn "open2 failed: $!\n$@\n";
        return;
    }
    die;            # reraise unforeseen exception
}
```

You must call waitpid, as we do in the Solution, because IPC::Open2 doesn't reap the child process after it exits. See Recipe 16.19 for details.

See Also

The documentation for the IPC::Open2 and IPC::Open3 modules; Recipe 10.12; the eval function in Chapter 29 of *Programming Perl* and in *perlfunc*(1); the $@ variable in the section on "Special Variables in Alphabetical Order" in Chapter 28 of *Programming Perl* and in *perlvar*(1)

16.9 Controlling the Input, Output, and Error of Another Program

Problem

You want full control over a command's input, output, and error streams.

Solution

Carefully use the standard IPC::Open3 module, possibly in conjunction with the standard IO::Select module.

Discussion

If you're interested in only one of the program's STDIN, STDOUT, or STDERR, the task is simple. When you want to manage two or more of these, however, it abruptly stops being simple. Multiplexing multiple I/O streams is never a pretty picture. Here's an easy workaround:

```
@all = `($cmd | sed -e 's/^/stdout: /' ) 2>&1`;
for (@all) { push @{ s/stdout: // ? \@outlines : \@errlines }, $_ }
print "STDOUT:\n", @outlines, "\n";
print "STDERR:\n", @errlines, "\n";
```

If you don't have *sed* on your system, you'll find that for simple cases like this, *perl -pe* works just as well as *sed -e*.

However, that's not really simultaneous processing. All we're doing is marking STDOUT lines with "stdout:" and then stripping them back out once we've read all the STDOUT and STDERR the program produced.

You can use the standard IPC::Open3 module for this. Mysteriously, the argument order is different for IPC::Open3 than for IPC::Open2.

```
open3($write_me, $read_me, $errors, "program to run");
```

Using this has even *more* potential for chaos than using open2. If you're reading the program's STDERR as it is trying to write more than one buffer's worth to its STDOUT, the program will block on the write because its buffers are full, and you will block on the read because there's nothing available.

You can avoid this deadlock by mimicking open3 with fork, open, and exec; making all filehandles unbuffered; and using sysread, syswrite, and select to decide which readable filehandle to read a byte from. This makes your program slower and bulkier, though, and it doesn't solve the classic open2 deadlock where each program is expecting the other to say something.

```
use IPC::Open3;
$pid = open3($child_in, $child_out, $child_err, $cmd);
close $child_in;  # give end-of-file to kid
@outlines = <$child_out>;              # read till EOF
@errlines = <$child_err>;              # XXX: block potential if massive
print "STDOUT:\n", @outlines, "\n";
print "STDERR:\n", @errlines, "\n";
```

As if deadlock weren't bad enough, this approach is subtly error-prone. There are at least three worrisome situations: both the child and the parent trying to read at the same time, causing deadlock; full buffers causing the child to block as it tries to write to STDERR while the parent is blocked trying to read from the child's STDOUT; and full buffers causing the parent to block writing to the child's STDIN while the child is blocked writing to either its STDOUT or STDERR. The first problem is generally unsolvable, although you can work around it by setting timers with alarm and preventing blocking operations from restarting if a SIGALRM is received.

We use the IO::Select module (you could also do this with the built-in function select) to learn which filehandles (if any) can be read from. This solves the second problem, but not the third. To solve the third, you also need alarm and non-restarting SIGALRM.

If you want to send input to the program, read its output, and either read or ignore its error, you need to work much harder. (See Example 16-2.)

Example 16-2. cmd3sel

```perl
#!/usr/bin/perl
# cmd3sel - control all three of kids in, out, and error.
use IPC::Open3;
use IO::Select;

$cmd = "grep vt33 /none/such - /etc/termcap";
$pid = open3($cmd_in, $cmd_out, $cmd_err, $cmd);

$SIG{CHLD} = sub {
    print "REAPER: status $? on $pid\n" if waitpid($pid, 0) > 0
};

print $cmd_in "This line has a vt33 lurking in it\n";
close $cmd_in;

$selector = IO::Select->new( );
$selector->add($cmd_err, $cmd_out);

while (@ready = $selector->can_read) {
    foreach $fh (@ready) {
        if (fileno($fh) == fileno($cmd_err)) {print "STDERR: ", scalar <$cmd_err>}
        else                                 {print "STDOUT: ", scalar <$cmd_out>}
        $selector->remove($fh) if eof($fh);
    }
}
close $cmd_out;
close $cmd_err;
```

We sent only a short line as input, then closed the handle. This avoids the deadlock situation of two processes each waiting for the other to write something.

See Also

The documentation for the standard IO::Select, IPC::Open2, and IPC::Open3 modules; the alarm function in Chapter 29 of *Programming Perl* or *perlfunc*(1); Recipe 16. 8; 16.15; 16.16

16.10 Communicating Between Related Processes

Problem

You have two related processes that need to communicate, and you need better control than you can get from open, system, and backticks.

Solution

Use pipe and then fork:

```
my ($reader, $writer);
pipe $reader, $writer;
if (fork) {
    # run parent code, either reading or writing, not both
} else {
    # run child code, either reading or writing, not both
}
```

Or use a special forking form of open:

```
if ($pid = (open $child, "|-")) {
        # run parent code, writing to child
} else {
    die "cannot fork: $!" unless defined $pid;
    # otherwise run child code here, reading from parent
}
```

Or, going the other way:

```
if ($pid = open ($child, "-|")) {
    # run parent code, reading from child
} else {
    die "cannot fork: $!" unless defined $pid;
    # otherwise run child code here, writing to parent
}
```

Discussion

Pipes are simply two connected filehandles, where data written to one filehandle can be read by the other. The pipe function creates two filehandles linked in this way, one writable and one readable. Even though you can't take two already existing filehandles and link them, pipe can be used for communication between processes. One process creates a pair of filehandles with the pipe functions, then forks off a child, resulting in two distinct processes both running in the same program, each with a copy of the connected filehandles. As with open, if pipe is passed undefined scalars instead of filehandles, it creates filehandles in those scalars.

It doesn't matter which process is the reader and which is the writer, so long as one of them takes one role and its peer process takes the other. You can only have one-way communication. (But read on.)

We'll pull in the IO::Handle module so we can call its autoflush method. (You could instead play the select games described in Chapter 7, if you prefer a lightweight solution.) If we didn't, our single line of output would get lodged in the pipe and not make it through to the other side until we closed that handle.

The version of the parent writing to the child is shown in Example 16-3.

Example 16-3. pipe1

```
#!/usr/bin/perl -w
# pipe1 - use pipe and fork so parent can send to child

use IO::Handle;
my ($reader, $writer);
pipe $reader, $writer;
$writer->autoflush(1);

if ($pid = fork) {
    close $reader;
    print $writer "Parent Pid $$ is sending this\n";
    close $writer;
    waitpid($pid,0);
} else {
    die "cannot fork: $!" unless defined $pid;
    close $writer;
    chomp($line = <$reader>);
    print "Child Pid $$ just read this: `$line'\n";
    close $reader;  # this will happen anyway
    exit;
}
```

In the examples in this recipe, most error checking has been left as an exercise for the reader. This is so you can more clearly see how the functions interact. In real life, test the return values of all syscalls.

The version of the child writing to the parent is shown in Example 16-4.

Example 16-4. pipe2

```
#!/usr/bin/perl -w
# pipe2 - use pipe and fork so child can send to parent

use IO::Handle;
my ($reader, $writer);
pipe($reader, $writer);
$writer->autoflush(1);

if ($pid = fork) {
    close $writer;
    chomp($line = <$reader>);
    print "Parent Pid $$ just read this: `$line'\n";
    close $reader;
    waitpid($pid,0);
} else {
    die "cannot fork: $!" unless defined $pid;
    close $reader;
    print $writer "Child Pid $$ is sending this\n";
    close $writer;  # this will happen anyway
    exit;
}
```

In most code, both halves would go into loops, with the reader continuing to read until end-of-file. This happens when the writer closes or exits.

Because piped filehandles are not bidirectional, each process uses just one of the pair and closes the filehandle it doesn't use. The reason is subtle; picture the situation where the reader does not close the writable filehandle. If the writer then exits while the reader is trying to read something, the reader will hang forever. This is because the system won't tell the reader that there's no more data to be read until all copies of the writable filehandle are closed.

The open function, when passed as its second argument either "-|" or "|-", will implicitly pipe and fork. This makes the piping code shown earlier slightly easier. The child talks to the parent over STDIN or STDOUT, depending on whether "-|" or "|-" was used.

Using open this way, if the parent wants to write to the child, it does something like what's shown in Example 16-5.

Example 16-5. pipe3

```perl
#!/usr/bin/perl -w
# pipe3 - use forking open so parent can send to child

use IO::Handle;
if ($pid = open ($child, "|-")) {
    $child->autoflush(1);
    print $child "Parent Pid $$ is sending this\n";
    close $child;
} else {
    die "cannot fork: $!" unless defined $pid;
    chomp($line = <STDIN>);
    print "Child Pid $$ just read this: `$line'\n";
    exit;
}
```

Since the child already has STDIN set to the parent, the child could exec some other program that expects to read from standard input, such as *lpr*. In fact, this is useful and commonly done.

If the child wants to write to the parent, it does something like what's shown in Example 16-6.

Example 16-6. pipe4

```perl
#!/usr/bin/perl -w
# pipe4 - use forking open so child can send to parent

use IO::Handle;
if ($pid = open $child, "-|") {
    chomp($line = <$child>);
    print "Parent Pid $$ just read this: `$line'\n";
    close $child;
```

Example 16-6. pipe4 (continued)

```
} else {
    die "cannot fork: $!" unless defined $pid;
    STDOUT->autoflush(1);
    print STDOUT "Child Pid $$ is sending this\n";
    exit;
}
```

Again, since the child already has its STDOUT connected to the parent, this child could exec some other program to produce something interesting on its standard output. That output would be available to the parent as input from <CHILD>.

When using open this way, we don't have to manually call waitpid since we didn't do a manual fork. We do have to call close, though. In both cases, the $? variable will have the child's wait status in it (see Recipe 16.19 to see how to interpret this status value).

The preceding examples were unidirectional. What if you want both processes talking to each other? Just make two calls to pipe before forking. You must be careful about who tells whom what and when, though, or you're apt to deadlock. (See Example 16-7.)

Example 16-7. pipe5

```
#!/usr/bin/perl -w
# pipe5 - bidirectional communication using two pipe pairs
#           designed for the socketpair-challenged
use IO::Handle;
my ($parent_rdr, $child_wtr, $child_rdr, $parent_wtr);
pipe $parent_rdr, $child_wtr;
pipe $child_rdr,  $parent_wtr;
$child_wtr->autoflush(1);
$parent_wtr->autoflush(1);

if ($pid = fork) {
    close $parent_rdr; close $parent_wtr;
    print $child_wtr "Parent Pid $$ is sending this\n";
    chomp($line = <$child_rdr>);
    print "Parent Pid $$ just read this: `$line'\n";
    close $child_rdr; close $child_wtr;
    waitpid($pid,0);
} else {
    die "cannot fork: $!" unless defined $pid;
    close $child_rdr; close $child_wtr;
    chomp($line = <$parent_rdr>);
    print "Child Pid $$ just read this: `$line'\n";
    print $parent_wtr "Child Pid $$ is sending this\n";
    close $parent_rdr; close $parent_wtr;
    exit;
}
```

That's getting complicated. It just so happens that there's a special syscall, shown in Example 16-8, that makes the last example simpler. It's called socketpair, and it works like pipe, except that both handles can be used for reading and for writing.

Example 16-8. pipe6

```
#!/usr/bin/perl -w
# pipe6 - bidirectional communication using socketpair
#   "the best ones always go both ways"

use Socket;
use IO::Handle;
# We say AF_UNIX because although *_LOCAL is the
# POSIX 1003.1g form of the constant, many machines
# still don't have it.
socketpair($child, $parent, AF_UNIX, SOCK_STREAM, PF_UNSPEC)
    or  die "socketpair: $!";

$child->autoflush(1);
$parent->autoflush(1);

if ($pid = fork) {
    close $parent;
    print $child "Parent Pid $$ is sending this\n";
    chomp($line = <$child>);
    print "Parent Pid $$ just read this: `$line'\n";
    close $child;
    waitpid($pid,0);
} else {
    die "cannot fork: $!" unless defined $pid;
    close $child;
    chomp($line = <$parent>);
    print "Child Pid $$ just read this: `$line'\n";
    print $parent "Child Pid $$ is sending this\n";
    close $parent;
    exit;
}
```

In fact, some systems have historically implemented pipes as two half-closed ends of a socketpair. They essentially define pipe($reader, $writer) this way:

```
socketpair($reader, $writer, AF_UNIX, SOCK_STREAM, PF_UNSPEC);
shutdown($reader, 1);      # no more writing for reader
shutdown($writer, 0);      # no more reading for writer
```

See Also

Chapter 29 of *Programming Perl* or *perlfunc*(1) for all functions used here; the documentation for the standard IPC::Open2 module; *Advanced Programming in the UNIX Environment*; Recipe 16.8; Recipe 19.5

16.11 Making a Process Look Like a File with Named Pipes

Problem

You want a process to intercept all access to a file. For instance, you want to make your ~/.plan file a program that returns a random quote.

Solution

Use named pipes. First create one, probably from your shell:

```
% mkfifo /path/to/named.pipe
```

Here's a reader for it:

```
open($fifo, "<", "/path/to/named.pipe")        or die $!;
while (<$fifo>) {
    print "Got: $_";
}
close $fifo;
```

Here's a writer for it:

```
open($fifo, ">", "/path/to/named.pipe")        or die $!;
print $fifo "Smoke this.\n";
close $fifo;
```

Discussion

A named pipe, or FIFO as they are also known, is a special file that acts as a buffer to connect processes on the same machine. Ordinary pipes also allow processes to communicate, but those processes must have inherited the filehandles from their parents. To use a named pipe, a process need know only the named pipe's filename. In most cases, processes don't even need to be aware that they're reading from a FIFO.

Named pipes can be read from and written to just as though they were ordinary files (unlike Unix-domain sockets as discussed in Chapter 17). Data written into the FIFO is buffered up by the operating system, then read back in the order it was written in. Because a FIFO acts as a buffer to connect processes, opening one for reading will block until another process opens it for writing, and vice versa. If you open for read and write using the +< mode to open, you won't block (on most systems), because your process could be both reader and writer.

Let's examine how to use a named pipe so people will get a different file each time they *finger* you. To create a named pipe, use *mkfifo* or *mknod* to create a named pipe called *.plan* in your home directory:

```
% mkfifo ~/.plan          # isn't this everywhere yet?
% mknod  ~/.plan p        # in case you don't have mkfifo
```

On some systems, you must use *mknod*(8). The location and names of these programs aren't uniform or necessarily obvious, so consult your system documentation to find out where these programs are.

The next step is to create a program to feed data to the programs that read from your *~/.plan* file. We'll just print the date and time, as shown in Example 16-9.

Example 16-9. dateplan

```perl
#!/usr/bin/perl -w
# dateplan - place current date and time in .plan file
while (1) {
    open($fifo, "> $ENV{HOME}/.plan")
        or die "Couldn't open $ENV{HOME}/.plan for writing: $!\n";
    print $fifo "The current time is ", scalar(localtime), "\n";
    close $fifo;
    sleep 1;
}
```

Unfortunately, this won't always work, because some *finger* programs and their attendant daemons check the size of the *.plan* file before trying to read it. Because named pipes appear as special files of zero size on the filesystem, such clients and servers will not try to open or read from our named pipe, and the trick will fail.

In our *.plan* example, the writer was a daemon. It's not uncommon for readers to be daemons as well. Take, for instance, the use of a named pipe to centralize logging from many processes. The log server reads log messages from the named pipe and can send them to a database or file. Clients write their messages to the named pipe. This removes the distribution logic from the clients, making changes to message distribution easy to implement.

Example 16-10 is a simple program to read two-line messages where the first line is the name of the service and the second line is the message being logged. All messages from httpd are ignored, while all messages from login are saved to */var/log/login*.

Example 16-10. fifolog

```perl
#!/usr/bin/perl -w
# fifolog - read and record log msgs from fifo

$SIG{ALRM} = sub { close(FIFO) };    # move on to the next queued process

while (1) {
    alarm(0);                        # turn off alarm for blocking open
    open($fifo, "</tmp/log")         or die "Can't open /tmp/log : $!\n";
    alarm(1);                        # you have 1 second to log

    $service = <$fifo>;
    next unless defined $service;    # interrupted or nothing logged
    chomp $service;
```

Example 16-10. fifolog (continued)

```
    $message = <$fifo>;
    next unless defined $message;    # interrupted or nothing logged
    chomp $message;

    alarm(0);                        # turn off alarms for message processing

    if ($service eq "http") {
        # ignoring
    } elsif ($service eq "login") {
        # log to /var/log/login
        if ( open($log, ">> /tmp/login") ) {
            print $log scalar(localtime), " $service $message\n";
            close $log;
        } else {
            warn "Couldn't log $service $message to /var/log/login : $!\n";
        }
    }
}
```

This program is more complicated than the *.plan* program for several reasons. First and foremost, we don't want our logging server to block would-be writers for long. It's easy to imagine a situation where an attacker or misbehaving writer opens the named pipe for writing, but doesn't send a complete message. To prevent this, we use alarm and SIGALRM to signal us if we get stuck reading.

Only two exceptional conditions can happen when using named pipes: a writer can have its reader disappear, or vice versa. If a process is reading from a named pipe and the writer closes its end, the reading process will get an end-of-file (<> returns undef). If the reader closes the connection, though, the writer will get a SIGPIPE when it next tries to write there. If you disregard broken pipe signals with $SIG{PIPE} = 'IGNORE', your print will return a false value and $! will be set to EPIPE:

```
use POSIX qw(:errno_h);

$SIG{PIPE} = 'IGNORE';
# ...
$status = print $fifo "Are you there?\n";
if (!$status && $! == EPIPE) {
    warn "My reader has forsaken me!\n";
    next;
}
```

You may be asking "If I have 100 processes all trying simultaneously to write to this server, how can I be sure that I'll get 100 separate entries and not a jumbled mish-mash with characters or lines from different processes?" That's a good question. The POSIX standard says that writes of less than PIPE_BUF bytes in size will be delivered atomically, i.e., not jumbled. You can get the PIPE_BUF constant from POSIX:

```
use POSIX;
print PIPE_BUF, "\n";
```

Fortunately, the POSIX standard also requires PIPE_BUF to be *at least* 512 bytes. This means that all we have to do is ensure that our clients don't try to log more than 512 bytes at a time.

What if you want to log more than 512 bytes at a time? Then you split each large message into several smaller (fewer than 512 bytes) messages, preface each with the unique client identifier (process ID, say), and have the server reassemble them. This is similar to the processing involved in TCP/IP message fragmentation and reassembly.

Because a single named pipe doesn't allow bidirectional access between writer and reader, authentication and similar ways of preventing forged messages are hard to do (if not impossible). Rather than struggle to force such things on top of a model that doesn't accommodate them, you are better off using the filesystem's access control to restrict access to the file through the owner and group permissions on the named pipe.

See Also

mkfifo(8) or *mknod*(8) (if you have them); Recipe 17.6

16.12 Sharing Variables in Different Processes

Problem

You want to share variables across forks or between unrelated processes.

Solution

Use SysV IPC if your operating system supports it.

Discussion

While SysV IPC (shared memory, semaphores, etc.) isn't as widely used as pipes, named pipes, and sockets for interprocess communication, it still has some interesting properties. Normally, however, you can't expect to use shared memory via shmget or the *mmap*(2) syscall to share a variable among several processes. That's because Perl would reallocate your string when you weren't wanting it to.

The CPAN module IPC::Shareable takes care of that. Using a clever tie module, SysV shared memory, and the Storable module from CPAN allows data structures of arbitrary complexity to be shared among cooperating processes on the same machine. These processes don't even have to be related to each other.

Example 16-11 is a simple demonstration of the module.

Example 16-11. sharetest

```perl
#!/usr/bin/perl
# sharetest - test shared variables across forks
use IPC::Shareable;

$handle = tie $buffer, 'IPC::Shareable', undef, { destroy => 1 };
$SIG{INT} = sub { die "$$ dying\n" };

for (1 .. 10) {
    unless ($child = fork) {          # i'm the child
        die "cannot fork: $!" unless defined $child;
        squabble();
        exit;
    }
    push @kids, $child;  # in case we care about their pids
}

while (1) {
    print "Buffer is $buffer\n";
    sleep 1;
}
die "Not reached";

sub squabble {
    my $i = 0;
    while (1) {
        next if $buffer =~ /^$$\b/o;
        $handle->shlock();
        $i++;
        $buffer = "$$ $i";
        $handle->shunlock();
    }
}
```

The starting process creates the shared variable, forks off 10 children, and then sits back and prints out the value of the buffer every second or so, forever, or until you hit Ctrl-C.

Because the SIGINT handler was set before any forking, it got inherited by the squabbling children as well, so they'll also bite the dust when the process group is interrupted. Keyboard interrupts send signals to the whole process group, not just one process.

What do the kids squabble over? They're bickering over who gets to update that shared variable. Each one looks to see whether someone else was here or not. So long as the buffer starts with their own signature (their PID), they leave it alone. As soon as someone else has changed it, they lock the shared variable using a special method call on the handle returned from the tie, update it, and release the lock.

The program runs much faster by commenting out the line that starts with next where each process is checking that they were the last one to touch the buffer.

The /^$$\b/o may look suspicious, since /o tells Perl to compile the pattern once only, but then went and changed the variable's value by forking. Fortunately, the value isn't locked at program compile time, but only the first time the pattern is itself compiled in each process, during whose own lifetime $$ does not alter.

The IPC::Sharable module also supports sharing variables among unrelated processes on the same machine. See its documentation for details.

See Also

The semctl, semget, semop, shmctl, shmget, shmread, and shmwrite functions in Chapter 29 of *Programming Perl*, and in *perlfunc*(1); the documentation for the IPC:: Shareable module from CPAN

16.13 Listing Available Signals

Problem

You want to know the signals your operating system provides.

Solution

If your shell has a built-in *kill -l* command, use it:

```
% kill -l
HUP INT QUIT ILL TRAP ABRT BUS FPE KILL USR1 SEGV USR2 PIPE
ALRM TERM CHLD CONT STOP TSTP TTIN TTOU URG XCPU XFSZ VTALRM
PROF WINCH POLL PWR
```

Or using just Perl, print the keys in %SIG if you have release 5.004 or later:

```
% perl -e 'print join(" ", keys %SIG), "\n"'
XCPU ILL QUIT STOP EMT ABRT BUS USR1 XFSZ TSTP INT IOT USR2 INFO TTOU
ALRM KILL HUP URG PIPE CONT SEGV VTALRM PROF TRAP IO TERM WINCH CHLD
FPE TTIN SYS
```

Before Version 5.004, you had to use the Config module:

```
% perl -MConfig -e 'print $Config{sig_name}'
ZERO HUP INT QUIT ILL TRAP ABRT EMT FPE KILL BUS SEGV SYS PIPE ALRM
TERM URG STOP TSTP CONT CHLD TTIN TTOU IO XCPU XFSZ VTALRM PROF WINCH
INFO USR1 USR2 IOT
```

Discussion

If your version of Perl is before 5.004, you have to use signame and signo in Config to find the list of available signals, since keys %SIG wasn't implemented then.

The following code retrieves by name and number the available signals from Perl's standard Config.pm module. Use @signame indexed by number to get the signal name, and %signo indexed by name to get the signal number.

```
use Config;
defined $Config{sig_name} or die "No sigs?";
$i = 0;                       # Config prepends fake 0 signal called "ZERO".
foreach $name (split(' ', $Config{sig_name})) {
    $signo{$name} = $i;
    $signame[$i] = $name;
    $i++;
}
```

See Also

The documentation for the standard Config module, also in Chapter 32 of *Programming Perl*; the "Signals" sections in Chapter 16 of *Programming Perl* and in *perlipc*(1)

16.14 Sending a Signal

Problem

You want to send a signal to a process. This could be sent to your own process or to another on the same system. For instance, you caught SIGINT and want to pass it on to your children.

Solution

Use kill to send a signal by name or number to the process IDs listed in the remaining arguments:

```
kill 9    => $pid;            # send $pid a signal 9
kill -1   => $pgrp;           # send whole job a signal 1
kill USR1 => $$;              # send myself a SIGUSR1
kill HUP  => @pids;           # send a SIGHUP to processes in @pids
```

Discussion

Perl's kill function is an interface to the syscall of the same name. The first argument is the signal to send, identified by number or by name; subsequent arguments are process IDs to send the signal to. It returns the count of processes successfully signaled. You can only send signals to processes running under the same real or saved UID as your real or effective UID—unless you're the superuser.

If the signal number is negative, Perl interprets remaining arguments as process group IDs and sends that signal to all those groups' processes using the *killpg*(2) syscall.

A process group is essentially a job. It's how the operating system ties related processes together. For example, when you use your shell to pipe one command into another, you've started two processes, but only one job. When you use Ctrl-C to interrupt the current job or Ctrl-Z to suspend it, this sends the appropriate signals to the entire job, which may be more than one process.

kill can also check whether a process is alive. Sending the special pseudo-signal number 0 checks whether it's legal for you to send a signal to the process—without actually sending one. If it returns true, the process is still alive. If it returns false, the process either has changed its effective UID (in which case $! will be set to EPERM) or no longer exists (and $! is ESRCH). Zombie processes (as described in Recipe 16.19) also report back as ESRCH.

```
use POSIX qw(:errno_h);

if (kill 0 => $minion) {
    print "$minion is alive!\n";
} elsif ($! == EPERM) {              # changed uid
    print "$minion has escaped my control!\n";
} elsif ($! == ESRCH) {
    print "$minion is deceased.\n";  # or zombied
} else {
    warn "Odd; I couldn't check on the status of $minion: $!\n";
}
```

See Also

The "Signals" sections in Chapter 16 of *Programming Perl* and in *perlipc*(1); your system's *sigaction*(2), *signal*(3), and *kill*(2) manpages (if you have them); the kill function in Chapter 29 of *Programming Perl* and *perlfunc*(1)

16.15 Installing a Signal Handler

Problem

You want to control how your program responds to signals. You need to do this if you want to catch Ctrl-C, avoid accumulating finished subprocesses, or prevent your process from dying when it writes to a child that has gone away.

Solution

Use the %SIG hash to install your own handler by name or by code reference:

```
$SIG{QUIT} = \&got_sig_quit;    # call &got_sig_quit for every SIGQUIT
$SIG{PIPE} = 'got_sig_pipe';    # call main::got_sig_pipe for every SIGPIPE
$SIG{INT}  = sub { $ouch++ };   # increment $ouch for every SIGINT
```

%SIG also lets you ignore a signal:

```
$SIG{INT} = 'IGNORE';           # ignore the signal INT
```

It also restores handling for that signal to the default:

```
$SIG{STOP} = 'DEFAULT';         # restore default STOP signal handling
```

Discussion

Perl uses the %SIG hash to control what happens when signals are received. Each key in %SIG corresponds to a signal. Each value is the action to take when Perl receives the corresponding signal. Perl provides two special behaviors: "IGNORE" to take no action when a particular signal is received, and "DEFAULT" to perform the default Unix action for that signal.

Although a C programmer might think of a signal as SIGINT, Perl uses just INT. Perl figures you only use signal names in functions that deal with signals, so the SIG prefix is redundant. This means that you'll assign to $SIG{CHLD} to change what your process does when it gets a SIGCHLD.

If you want to run your own code when a given signal is received, you have two choices of what to put in the hash: either a code reference or a subroutine name. (This means you can't name a signal handler IGNORE or DEFAULT if you store the string, but they'd be mighty strange names for signal handlers anyway.) If you use a subroutine name that isn't qualified by a package, Perl will interpret this name to be a function in the main:: package, not one in the package in which the handler was installed. A code reference refers to a subroutine in a particular package, so it is a better choice.

Perl calls your handler code with a single argument: the name of the signal that triggered it, such as "INT" or "USR1". Returning from a signal handler takes you back to whatever you were doing when the signal hit.

Perl defines two special signals, __DIE__ and __WARN__, whose handlers are called whenever a Perl program emits warnings through warn or dies through die. This lets you catch such warnings, and selectively trap or propagate them. The die and warn handlers are disabled while they run, so you can safely die from a __DIE__ handler or warn from a __WARN__ handler without fear of recursion.

See Also

The "Signals" sections in Chapter 16 of *Programming Perl* and in *perlipc*(1); your system's *sigaction*(2), *signal*(3), and *kill*(2) manpages (if you have them)

16.16 Temporarily Overriding a Signal Handler

Problem

You want to install a signal handler only for a particular subroutine. For instance, your subroutine catches SIGINT, and you don't want to disturb SIGINT handling outside the subroutine.

Solution

Use local to temporarily override a signal's behavior:

```
# the signal handler
sub ding {
    $SIG{INT} = \&ding;
    warn "\aEnter your name!\n";
}

# prompt for name, overriding SIGINT
sub get_name {
    local $SIG{INT} = \&ding;
    my $name;

    print "Kindly Stranger, please enter your name: ";
    chomp( $name = <> );
    return $name;
}
```

Discussion

You must use local rather than my to save away one value out of %SIG. The change remains in effect throughout the execution of that block, including in anything called from it. In this case, that's the get_name subroutine. If the signal is delivered while another function that your function calls is running, your signal handler is triggered—unless the called subroutine installs its own signal handler. The previous value of the hash is automatically restored when the block exits. This is one of the (few) places where dynamic scoping is more convenient than confusing.

See Also

Recipe 10.13; Recipe 16.15; Recipe 16.18

16.17 Writing a Signal Handler

Problem

You want to write a subroutine that will be called whenever your program receives a signal.

Solution

A signal handler is just a subroutine. With some risk, you can do anything in a signal handler you'd do in any Perl subroutine, but the more you do, the riskier it gets.

Some systems require you to reinstall your signal handler after each signal:

```
$SIG{INT} = \&got_int;
sub got_int {
    $SIG{INT} = \&got_int;              # but not for SIGCHLD!
    # ...
}
```

Some systems restart blocking operations, such as reading data. In such cases, you must call die within the handler and trap it with eval:

```
my $interrupted = 0;

sub got_int {
    $interrupted = 1;
    $SIG{INT} = 'DEFAULT';              # or 'IGNORE'
    die;
}

eval {
    $SIG{INT} = \&got_int;
    # ... long-running code that you don't want to restart
};

if ($interrupted) {
    # deal with the signal
}
```

Discussion

At the C level, signals can interrupt just about anything. Unfortunately, this means that signals could interrupt Perl while Perl is changing its own internal data structures, leaving those data structures inconsistent and leading to a core dump. As of Perl 5.8, Perl tries very hard to ensure that this doesn't happen—when you install a signal handler, Perl installs a C-level signal handler that says "Perl received this signal." When Perl's data structures are consistent (after each operation it performs), the Perl interpreter checks to see whether a signal was received. If one was, your signal handler is called.

This prevents core dumps, but at the cost of slightly delaying signals in cases where one of Perl's built-in operations takes a long time to finish. For example, building a long list like this:

```
@a = 1..5_000_000;
```

might take 10 seconds on a heavily loaded system, but you won't be able to interrupt it because Perl will not check whether a signal was received while the list is being built. There are two operations in this statement, list generation and assignment, and Perl checks for signals only after each operation completes.

Signals have been implemented in many different operating systems, often in slightly different flavors. The two situations where signal implementations vary the most are when a signal occurs while its signal handler is active (*reliability*), and when a signal interrupts a blocking syscall such as read or accept (*restarting*).

The initial Unix implementation of signals was unreliable, meaning that while a handler was running, further occurrences of the same signal would cause the default action, likely aborting the program. Later systems addressed this (each in their own subtly different way, of course) by providing a way to block the delivery of further signals of that number until the handler has finished. If Perl detects that your system can use reliable signals, it generates the proper syscalls needed for this saner, safer behavior. You can use POSIX signals to block signal delivery at other times, as described in Recipe 16.20.

For truly portable code, the paranoid programmer will assume the worst case (unreliable signals) and reinstall the signal handler manually, usually as the first statement in a function:

```
$SIG{INT} = \&catcher;
sub catcher {
    $SIG{INT} = \&catcher;
    # ...
}
```

In the special case of catching SIGCHLD, see Recipe 16.19. System V has bizarre behavior that can trip you up.

Use the Config module to find out whether you have reliable signals:

```
use Config;
print "Hurrah!\n" if $Config{d_sigaction};
```

Just because you have reliable signals doesn't mean you automatically get reliable programs. But without them, you certainly won't.

The first implementation of signals interrupted slow syscalls, functions that require the cooperation of other processes or device drivers. If a signal comes in while those syscalls are still running, they (and their Perl counterparts) return an error value and set the error to EINTR, "Interrupted system call". Checking for this condition made programs so complicated that most didn't check, and therefore misbehaved or died if a signal interrupted a slow syscall. Most modern versions of Unix allow you to change this behavior. Perl will always make syscalls restartable if it is on a system that supports it. If you have a POSIX system, you can control restarting using the POSIX module (see Recipe 16.20).

To determine whether your interrupted syscalls will automatically restart, look at your system's C *signal.h* include file:

```
% egrep 'S[AV]_(RESTART|INTERRUPT)' /usr/include/*/signal.h
```

Two signals are untrappable and unignorable: SIGKILL and SIGSTOP. Full details of the signals available on your system and what they mean can be found in the *signal*(3) manpage.

Finally, if you have a hostile operating system, you can still have signal problems. In particular, some operating systems have library calls that themselves intercept signals. For example, *gethostbyname*(3) on some systems uses SIGALRM signals to manage timeouts and restarts. There can be only one timer running, and so you can't say "stop looking up this hostname after five seconds," because your five-second timer is replaced by gethostbyname's timer as soon as Perl calls the library routine. This means you can't interrupt a wedged hostname lookup on such systems, because the signals don't get through. Fortunately, such situations are rare.

See Also

The "Signals" sections in Chapter 16 of *Programming Perl* and in *perlipc*(1); your system's *sigaction*(2), *signal*(3), and *kill*(2) manpages (if you have them); *Advanced Programming in the UNIX Environment*

16.18 Catching Ctrl-C

Problem

You want to intercept Ctrl-C, which would otherwise kill your whole program. You'd like to ignore it or run your own function when the signal is received.

Solution

Set a handler for SIGINT. Set it to "IGNORE" to make Ctrl-C have no effect:

```
$SIG{INT} = 'IGNORE';
```

Or set it to a subroutine of your own devising to respond to Ctrl-C:

```
$SIG{INT} = \&tsktsk;

sub tsktsk {
    $SIG{INT} = \&tsktsk;           # See ``Writing A Signal Handler''
    warn "\aThe long habit of living indisposeth us for dying.\n";
}
```

Discussion

Ctrl-C isn't directly affecting your program. The terminal driver processing your keystrokes recognizes the Ctrl-C combination (or whatever you've set your terminal to recognize as the interrupt character), and sends a SIGINT to every process in the foreground process group (*foreground job*) for that terminal. The foreground job normally comprises all programs started from the shell on a single command line, plus any other programs run by those programs. See "Signals" in the Introduction to this chapter for details.

The interrupt character isn't the only special character interpreted by your terminal driver. Type stty -a to find out your current settings:

```
% stty -a
speed 9600 baud; 38 rows; 80 columns;
```

```
lflags: icanon isig iexten echo echoe -echok echoke -echonl echoctl
        -echoprt -altwerase -noflsh -tostop -flusho pendin -nokerninfo
        -extproc
iflags: -istrip icrnl -inlcr -igncr ixon -ixoff ixany imaxbel -ignbrk
        brkint -inpck -ignpar -parmrk
oflags: opost onlcr oxtabs
cflags: cread cs8 -parenb -parodd hupcl -clocal -cstopb -crtscts -dsrflow
        -dtrflow -mdmbuf
cchars: discard = ^O; dsusp = ^Y; eof = ^D; eol = <undef;>
        eol2 = <undef; erase = ^H; intr = ^C; kill = ^U; lnext = ^V;>
        min = 1; quit = ^\; reprint = ^R; start = ^Q; status = <undef;>
        stop = ^S; susp = ^Z; time = 0; werase = ^W;
```

The last section, cchars:, is the list of special characters. Recipe 15.8 shows you how to change these from your script without calling the *stty* program.

See Also

Your system's *stty*(1) manpage (if you have one); Recipe 15.8; Recipe 16.17

16.19 Avoiding Zombie Processes

Problem

Your program forks children, but the dead children accumulate, fill up your process table, and aggravate your system administrator.

Solution

If you don't need to record the children that have terminated, use:

```
$SIG{CHLD} = 'IGNORE';
```

To keep better track of deceased children, install a SIGCHLD handler to call waitpid:

```
use POSIX ":sys_wait_h";

$SIG{CHLD} = \&REAPER;
sub REAPER {
    my $stiff;
    while (($stiff = waitpid(-1, WNOHANG)) > 0) {
        # do something with $stiff if you want
    }
    $SIG{CHLD} = \&REAPER;                # install *after* calling waitpid
}
```

Discussion

When a process exits, the system keeps it in the process table so the parent can check its status—whether it terminated normally or abnormally. Fetching a child's status

---

(thereby freeing it to drop from the system altogether) is rather grimly called *reaping* dead children. (This entire recipe is full of ways to harvest your dead children. If this makes you queasy, we understand.) It involves a call to wait or waitpid. Some Perl functions (piped opens, system, and backticks) will automatically reap the children they make, but you must explicitly wait when you use fork to manually start another process.

To avoid accumulating dead children, simply tell the system that you're not interested in them by setting $SIG{CHLD} to "IGNORE". If you want to know which children die and when, you'll need to use waitpid.

The waitpid function reaps a single process. Its first argument is the process to wait for—use -1 to mean any process—and its second argument is a set of flags. We use the WNOHANG flag to make waitpid immediately return 0 if there are no dead children. A flag value of 0 is supported everywhere, indicating a blocking wait. Call waitpid from a SIGCHLD handler, as we do in the Solution, to reap the children as soon as they die.

The wait function also reaps children, but it does not have a non-blocking option. If you inadvertently call it when there are running child processes but none have exited, your program will pause until there is a dead child.

Because the kernel keeps track of undelivered signals using a bit vector, one bit per signal, if two children die before your process is scheduled, you will get only a single SIGCHLD. You must always loop when you reap in a SIGCHLD handler, and so you can't use wait.

Both wait and waitpid return the process ID that they just reaped and set $? to the wait status of the defunct process. This status is actually two 8-bit values in one 16-bit number. The high byte is the exit value of the process. The low 7 bits represent the number of the signal that killed the process, with the 8th bit indicating whether a core dump occurred. Here's one way to isolate those values:

```
$exit_value  = $? >> 8;
$signal_num  = $? & 127;
$dumped_core = $? & 128;
```

The standard POSIX module has macros to interrogate status values: WIFEXITED, WEXITSTATUS, WIFSIGNALLED, and WTERMSIG. Oddly enough, POSIX doesn't have a macro to test whether the process core dumped.

Beware of two things when using SIGCHLD. First, the operating system doesn't send a SIGCHLD just when a child exits; it also sends one when the child stops. A process can stop for many reasons—waiting to be foregrounded so it can do terminal I/O, being sent a SIGSTOP (it will wait for the SIGCONT before continuing), or being suspended from its terminal. You need to check the status with the WIFEXITED* function from the

---

* Not SPOUSEXITED, even on a PC.

POSIX module to make sure you're dealing with a process that really died, and isn't just suspended.

```
use POSIX qw(:signal_h :errno_h :sys_wait_h);

$SIG{CHLD} = \&REAPER;
sub REAPER {
    my $pid;

    $pid = waitpid(-1, &WNOHANG);

    if ($pid == -1) {
        # no child waiting.  Ignore it.
    } elsif (WIFEXITED($?)) {
        print "Process $pid exited.\n";
    } else {
        print "False alarm on $pid.\n";
    }
    $SIG{CHLD} = \&REAPER;          # in case of unreliable signals
}
```

The second trap with SIGCHLD is related to Perl, not the operating system. Because system, open, and backticks all fork subprocesses and the operating system sends your process a SIGCHLD whenever any of its subprocesses exit, you could get called for something you weren't expecting. The built-in operations all wait for the child themselves, so sometimes the SIGCHLD will arrive before the close on the filehandle blocks to reap it. If the signal handler gets to it first, the zombie won't be there for the normal close. This makes close return false and set $! to "No child processes". Then, if the close gets to the dead child first, waitpid will return 0.

Most systems support a non-blocking waitpid. Use Perl's standard Config.pm module to find out:

```
use Config;
$has_nonblocking = $Config{d_waitpid} eq "define" ||
                   $Config{d_wait4}   eq "define";
```

System V defines SIGCLD, which has the same signal number as SIGCHLD but subtly different semantics. Use SIGCHLD to avoid confusion.

See Also

The "Signals" sections in Chapter 16 of *Programming Perl* and in *perlipc*(1); the wait and waitpid functions in Chapter 29 of *Programming Perl* and in *perlfunc*(1); the documentation for the standard POSIX module in Chapter 32 of *Programming Perl*; your system's *sigaction*(2), *signal*(3), and *kill*(2) manpages (if you have them); Recipe 16.17

16.20 Blocking Signals

Problem

You'd like to delay the reception of a signal, possibly to prevent unpredictable behavior from signals that can interrupt your program at any point.

Solution

Use the POSIX module's interface to the *sigprocmask*(2) syscall. This is available only if your system is POSIX conformant.

To block a signal around an operation:

```
use POSIX qw(:signal_h);

$sigset = POSIX::SigSet->new(SIGINT);      # define the signals to block
$old_sigset = POSIX::SigSet->new;          # where the old sigmask will be kept

sigprocmask(SIG_BLOCK, $sigset, $old_sigset)
    or die "Could not block SIGINT\n";
```

To unblock:

```
defined sigprocmask(SIG_UNBLOCK, $old_sigset)
    or die "Could not unblock SIGINT\n";
```

Discussion

The POSIX standard introduced `sigaction` and `sigprocmask` to give you better control over how signals are delivered. The `sigprocmask` function controls delayed delivery of signals, and `sigaction` installs handlers. If available, Perl uses `sigaction` when you change %SIG.

To use `sigprocmask`, first build a signal set using `POSIX::SigSet->new`. This takes a list of signal numbers. The POSIX module exports functions named after the signals, which return their signal numbers.

```
use POSIX qw(:signal_h);

$sigset = POSIX::SigSet->new( SIGINT, SIGKILL );
```

Pass the POSIX::SigSet object to `sigprocmask` with the SIG_BLOCK flag to delay signal delivery, SIG_UNBLOCK to restore delivery of the signals, or SIG_SETMASK to block only signals in the POSIX::SigSet. The most paranoid of programmers block signals for a fork to prevent a signal handler in the child process being called before Perl can update the child's $$ variable, its process id. If the signal handler were called immediately and reported $$ in that handler, it could possibly report its parent's $$, not its own. This issue does not arise often.

See Also

Your system's *sigprocmask*(2) manpage (if you have one); the documentation for the standard POSIX module in Chapter 32 of *Programming Perl*

16.21 Timing Out an Operation

Problem

You want to make sure an operation doesn't take more than a certain amount of time. For instance, you're running filesystem backups and want to abort if it takes longer than an hour. Or, you want to give the user a limited amount of time to respond to a query.

Solution

To interrupt a long-running operation, set a SIGALRM handler to call die, in effect transforming the signal into an exception. Set an alarm with alarm, then eval your code:

```
eval {
    local $SIG{ALRM} = sub { die "alarm clock restart" };
    alarm 10;                   # schedule alarm in 10 seconds
    eval {
        ########
        # long-running operation goes here
        ########
    };
    alarm 0;                    # cancel the alarm
};
alarm 0;                        # race condition protection
die if $@ && $@ !~ /alarm clock restart/; # reraise
```

Discussion

The alarm function takes one argument: the integer number of seconds before the kernel sends your process a SIGALRM, that is, an alarm signal. It may be delivered after that time in busy time-sharing systems. The default action for SIGALRM is to terminate your program, so you should install your own signal handler.

Because this example should work no matter what operation is being timed out, we take some special precautions in case your long-running operation contains a slow syscall. Slow syscalls are those that don't return immediately, but await some external event, such as for I/O to happen or some sort of timer to go off. These external events include read (including readline, the <FH> operator), write, and open on certain devices, fifos, and sockets, as well as accept, connect, send, recv, flock, wait, waitpid, and of course, sleep. If the alarm hits while you're in a slow syscall and you simply catch the signal and return, you'll go right back into that syscall. That's because Perl automatically restarts syscalls where it's able to. The only way out of them is to raise an exception through die and then let eval catch it. (This works because the exception winds up calling the C library's *longjmp*(3) function, which is what really gets you out of the restarting syscall.)

The nested exception trap is because you cannot be sure that arbitrary code in your long-running operation isn't going to raise some exception of its own. If it did, then that would pop you out of the inner eval with the alarm still pending. You need to make sure to clear the alarm anyway. The second alarm 0 is in case the signal comes in after running the long-running operation, but before getting to the first alarm 0. If you don't do that, you would risk a tiny race condition—but size doesn't matter in race conditions; they either exist or they don't. And we prefer that they don't.

You cannot (usefully) give the alarm function a fractional number of seconds; if you try, it will be truncated to an integer. For precise timers, see Recipe 3.9.

See Also

The "Signals" sections in Chapter 16 of *Programming Perl* and in *perlipc*(1); the section on "Handling Race Conditions" in Chapter 23 of *Programming Perl*; the alarm function in Chapter 29 of *Programming Perl* and in *perlfunc*(1); Recipe 3.9

16.22 Turning Signals into Fatal Errors

Problem

END blocks aren't run when your program dies from an uncaught signal. Your program gets such signals, and you'd like your END blocks to have a chance to clean up.

Solution

Use the sigtrap pragma:

```
use sigtrap qw(die untrapped normal-signals);
```

Discussion

Untrapped signals cause your program to die without running END blocks. Although you could manually install signal handlers that call die, this becomes tedious for a lot of signals:

```
$SIG{INT} = $SIG{HUP} = $SIG{PIPE} = $SIG{TERM} = sub { die };
```

The sigtrap pragma provides a convenient shorthand for installing such handlers:

```
use sigtrap qw(die untrapped normal-signals);
```

The die import tells `sigtrap` to call die (you can also import stack-trace to install handlers that trigger stack traces). The untrapped import tells `sigtrap` to install handlers only for signals that don't already have them, so if you handle SIGPIPE yourself, `sigtrap` won't replace your handler.

normal-signals is one of several imports that specify predefined lists of useful signals to trap. The signal lists are given in Table 16-2.

Table 16-2. Signal lists

List	Signals
normal-signals	HUP, INT, PIPE, TERM
error-signals	ABRT, BUS, EMT, FPE, ILL, QUIT, SEGV, SYS, TRAP
old-interface-signals	ABRT, BUS, EMT, FPE, ILL, PIPE, QUIT, SEGV, SYS, TERM, TRAP

You can combine signal lists:

```
use sigtrap qw(die untrapped normal-signals error-signals);
```

You can even combine different handler types in one import list. Here we use untrapped to specify only the normal signals for which there is not already a handler installed, then use any to revert to `sigtrap`'s default behavior of installing handlers for all signals in the named list:

```
use sigtrap qw(
    die         untrapped   normal-signals
    stack-trace any         error-signals
);
```

See Also

Recipe 12.7; the documentation for the standard module `sigtrap`; Recipe 16.15

16.23 Program: sigrand

The following program gives you random signatures by using named pipes. It expects the signatures file to have records in the format of the *fortune* program—that is, each possible multiline record is terminated with "%%\n". Here's an example:

```
Make is like Pascal: everybody likes it, so they go in and change it.
                        --Dennis Ritchie
%%
I eschew embedded capital letters in names; to my prose-oriented eyes,
they are too awkward to read comfortably. They jangle like bad typography.
                        --Rob Pike
%%
God made the integers; all else is the work of Man.
                        --Kronecker
%%
I'd rather have :rofix than const.          --Dennis Ritchie
```

```
%%
If you want to program in C, program in C.  It's a nice language.
I use it occasionally...   :-)            --Larry Wall
%%
Twisted cleverness is my only skill as a programmer.
                                        --Elizabeth Zwicky
%%
Basically, avoid comments. If your code needs a comment to be understood,
it would be better to rewrite it so it's easier to understand.
                                        --Rob Pike
%%
Comments on data are usually much more helpful than on algorithms.
                                        --Rob Pike
%%
Programs that write programs are the happiest programs in the world.
                                        --Andrew Hume
%%
```

We check whether we're already running by using a file with our PID in it. If sending a signal number 0 indicates that PID still exists (or, rarely, that something else has reused it), we just exit. We also look at the current Usenet posting to decide whether to look for a per-newsgroup signature file. That way, you can have different signatures for each newsgroup you post to. For variety, a global signature file is still on occasion used even if a per-newsgroup file exists.

You can even use *sigrand* on systems without named pipes if you remove the code to create a named pipe and extend the sleep interval before file updates. Then *.signature* would just be a regular file. Another portability concern is that the program forks itself in the background, which is almost like becoming a daemon. If you have no fork call, just comment it out.

The full program is shown in Example 16-12.

Example 16-12. sigrand

```perl
#!/usr/bin/perl -w
# sigrand - supply random fortunes for .signature file

use strict;

# config section variables
use vars qw( $NG_IS_DIR $MKNOD $FULLNAME $FIFO $ART $NEWS $SIGS $SEMA
                    $GLOBRAND $NAME );

# globals
use vars qw( $Home $Fortune_Path @Pwd );

###############################################################
# begin configuration section
# should really read from ~/.sigrandrc

gethome();
```

Example 16-12. sigrand (continued)

```
# for rec/humor/funny instead of rec.humor.funny
$NG_IS_DIR      = 1;

$MKNOD          = "/bin/mknod";
$FULLNAME       = "$Home/.fullname";
$FIFO           = "$Home/.signature";
$ART            = "$Home/.article";
$NEWS           = "$Home/News";
$SIGS           = "$NEWS/SIGNATURES";
$SEMA           = "$Home/.sigrandpid";
$GLOBRAND       = 1/4;  # chance to use global sigs anyway

# $NAME should be (1) left undef to have program guess
# read address for signature maybe looking in ~/.fullname,
# (2) set to an exact address, or (3) set to empty string
# to be omitted entirely.

$NAME           = '';               # means no name used
## $NAME        = "me\@home.org\n";

# end configuration section -- HOME and FORTUNE get autoconf'd
##############################################################

setup();                # pull in inits
justme();               # make sure program not already running
fork && exit;           # background ourself and go away

open(SEMA, "> $SEMA")               or die "can't write $SEMA: $!";
print SEMA "$$\n";
close SEMA                          or die "can't close $SEMA: $!";

# now loop forever, writing a signature into the
# fifo file.  if you don't have real fifos, change
# sleep time at bottom of loop to like 10 to update
# only every 10 seconds.
for (;;) {
    open(FIFO, "> $FIFO")                   or die "can't write $FIFO: $!";
    my $sig = pick_quote();
    for ($sig) {
        s/^((:?[^\n]*\n){4}).*$/$1/s;   # trunc to 4 lines
        s/^(.{1,80}).*? *$/$1/gm;       # trunc long lines
    }
    # print sig, with name if present, padded to four lines
    if ($NAME) {
        print FIFO $NAME, "\n" x (3 - ($sig =~ tr/\n//)), $sig;
    } else {
        print FIFO $sig;
    }
    close FIFO;

    # Without a microsleep, the reading process doesn't finish before
    # the writer tries to open it again, which since the reader exists,
```

Example 16-12. sigrand (continued)

```
    # succeeds.  They end up with multiple signatures.  Sleep a tiny bit
    # between opens to give readers a chance to finish reading and close
    # our pipe so we can block when opening it the next time.

    select(undef, undef, undef, 0.2);   # sleep 1/5 second
}
die "XXX: NOT REACHED";          # you can't get here from anywhere

################################################################

# Ignore SIGPIPE in case someone opens us up and then closes the fifo
# without reading it; look in a .fullname file for their login name.
# Try to determine the fully qualified hostname.  Look our for silly
# ampersands in passwd entries.  Make sure we have signatures or fortunes.
# Build a fifo if we need to.

sub setup {
    $SIG{PIPE} = 'IGNORE';

    unless (defined $NAME) {           # if $NAME undef in config
        if (-e $FULLNAME) {
                $NAME = `cat $FULLNAME`;
                die "$FULLNAME should contain only 1 line, aborting"
                    if $NAME =~ tr/\n// > 1;
        } else {
                my($user, $host);
                chop($host = `hostname`);
                ($host) = gethostbyname($host) unless $host =~ /\./;
                $user = $ENV{USER} || $ENV{LOGNAME} || $Pwd[0]
                    or die "intruder alert";
                ($NAME = $Pwd[6]) =~ s/,.*//;
                $NAME =~ s/&/\u\L$user/g; # can't believe some folks still do this
                $NAME = "\t$NAME\t$user\@$host\n";
        }
    }

    check_fortunes() if !-e $SIGS;

    unless (-p $FIFO) {        # -p checks whether it's a named pipe
        if (!-e _) {
                system($MKNOD, $FIFO, "p") && die "can't mknod $FIFO";
                warn "created $FIFO as a named pipe\n";
        } else {
                die "$0: won't overwrite file .signature\n";
        }
    } else {
        warn "$0: using existing named pipe $FIFO\n";
    }

    # get a good random number seed.  not needed if 5.004 or better.
    srand(time() ^ ($$ + ($$ << 15)));
}
```

Example 16-12. sigrand (continued)

```perl
# choose a random signature
sub pick_quote {
    my $sigfile = signame();
    if (!-e $sigfile) {
        return fortune();
    }
    open(SIGS, "< $sigfile")                      or die "can't open $sigfile";
    local $/  = "%%\n";
    local $_;
    my $quip;
    rand($.) < 1 && ($quip = $_) while <SIGS>;
    close SIGS;
    chomp $quip;
    return $quip || "ENOSIG: This signature file is empty.\n";
}

# See whether ~/.article contains a Newsgroups line.  if so, see the first
# group posted to and find out whether it has a dedicated set of fortunes.
# otherwise return the global one.  also, return the global one randomly
# now and then to spice up the sigs.
sub signame {
    (rand(1.0) > ($GLOBRAND) && open ART) || return $SIGS;
    local $/  = '';
    local $_  = <ART>;
    my($ng)   = /Newsgroups:\s*([^,\s]*)/;
    $ng =~ s!\.!/!g if $NG_IS_DIR;       # if rn -/,  or SAVEDIR=%p/%c
    $ng = "$NEWS/$ng/SIGNATURES";
    return -f $ng ? $ng : $SIGS;
}

# Call the fortune program with -s for short flag until
# we get a small enough fortune or ask too much.
sub fortune {
    local $_;
    my $tries = 0;
    do {
        $_ = `$Fortune_Path -s`;
    } until tr/\n// < 5 || $tries++ > 20;
    s/^/ /mg;
    $_ || " SIGRAND: deliver random signals to all processes.\n";
}

# Make sure there's a fortune program.  Search
# for its full path and set global to that.
sub check_fortunes {
    return if $Fortune_Path;     # already set
    for my $dir (split(/:/, $ENV{PATH}), '/usr/games') {
        return if -x ($Fortune_Path = "$dir/fortune");
    }
    die "Need either $SIGS or a fortune program, bailing out";
}
```

Example 16-12. sigrand (continued)

```perl
# figure out our directory
sub gethome {
    @Pwd = getpwuid($<);
    $Home = $ENV{HOME} || $ENV{LOGDIR} || $Pwd[7]
                    or die "no home directory for user $<";
}

# "There can be only one."  --the Highlander
sub justme {
    if (open SEMA) {
        my $pid;
        chop($pid = <SEMA>);
        kill(0, $pid)           and die "$0 already running (pid $pid), bailing out";
        close SEMA;
    }



}
```

CHAPTER 17

Sockets

Glendower: I can call spirits from the vasty deep.
Hotspur: Why so can I, or so can any man, But will
they come when you do call for them?
—Shakespeare, *Henry IV, part I, Act III scene 1*

17.0 Introduction

Sockets are endpoints for communication. Some types of sockets provide reliable communications. Others offer few guarantees, but consume low system overhead. Socket communication can be used to let processes talk on just one machine or over the Internet.

In this chapter we consider the two most commonly used types of sockets: *streams* and *datagrams*. Streams provide a bidirectional, sequenced, and reliable channel of communication—similar to pipes. *Datagram* sockets do not guarantee sequenced, reliable delivery, but they do guarantee that message boundaries will be preserved when read. Your system may support other types of sockets as well; consult your *socket*(2) manpage or equivalent documentation for details.

We also consider both the Internet and Unix domains. The Internet domain gives sockets two-part names: a host (an IP address in a particular format) and a port number. In the Unix domain, sockets are named using files (e.g., */tmp/mysock*).

In addition to domains and types, sockets also have a *protocol* associated with them. Protocols are not very important to the casual programmer, as there is rarely more than one protocol for a given domain and type of socket.

Domains and types are normally identified by numeric constants (available through functions exported by the Socket and IO::Socket modules). Stream sockets have the type SOCK_STREAM, and datagram sockets have the type SOCK_DGRAM. The Internet domain is PF_INET, and the Unix domain PF_UNIX. (POSIX uses PF_LOCAL instead of PF_UNIX, but PF_UNIX will almost always be an acceptable constant simply because of the preponderance of existing software that uses it.) You should use these symbolic names instead of numbers because the numbers may change (and historically, have).

Protocols have names such as tcp and udp, which correspond to numbers that the operating system uses. The getprotobyname function (built into Perl) returns the number when given a protocol name. Pass protocol number 0 to socket functions to have the system select an appropriate default.

Perl has built-in functions to create and manipulate sockets; these functions largely mimic their C counterparts. While this is good for providing low-level, direct access to every part of the system, most of us prefer something more convenient. That's what the IO::Socket::INET and IO::Socket::UNIX classes are for—they provide a high-level interface to otherwise intricate system calls.

Let's look at the built-in functions first. They all return undef and set $! if an error occurs. The socket function makes a socket, bind gives a socket a local name, connect connects a local socket to a (possibly remote) one, listen readies a socket for connections from other sockets, and accept receives the connections one by one. You can communicate over a stream socket with print and <> as well as with syswrite and sysread, or over a datagram socket with send and recv. (Perl does not currently support *sendmsg*(2).)

A typical server calls socket, bind, and listen, then loops in a blocking accept call that waits for incoming connections (see Recipes 17.2 and 17.5). A typical client calls socket and connect (see Recipes 17.1 and 17.4). Datagram clients are special. They don't have to connect to send data, because they can specify the destination as an argument to send.

When you bind, connect, or send to a specific destination, you must supply a socket name. An Internet domain socket name is a host (an IP address packed with inet_aton) and a port (a number), packed into a C-style structure with sockaddr_in:

```
use Socket;

$packed_ip   = inet_aton("208.201.239.37");
$socket_name = sockaddr_in($port, $packed_ip);
```

A Unix domain socket name is a filename packed into a C structure with sockaddr_un:

```
use Socket;

$socket_name = sockaddr_un("/tmp/mysock");
```

To take a packed socket name and turn it back into a filename or host and port, call sockaddr_un or sockaddr_in in list context:

```
($port, $packed_ip) = sockaddr_in($socket_name);    # for PF_INET sockets
($filename)         = sockaddr_un($socket_name);    # for PF_UNIX sockets
```

Use inet_ntoa to turn a packed IP address back into an ASCII string. It stands for "numbers to ASCII," and inet_aton stands for "ASCII to numbers."

```
$ip_address = inet_ntoa($packed_ip);
$packed_ip  = inet_aton("208.201.239.37");
$packed_ip  = inet_aton("www.oreilly.com");
```

Most recipes use Internet domain sockets in their examples, but nearly everything that applies to the Internet domain also applies to the Unix domain. Recipe 17.6 explains the differences and pitfalls.

Sockets are the basis of network services. We provide three ways to write servers: one where a child process is created for each incoming connection (Recipe 17.11), one where the server forks in advance (Recipe 17.12), and one where the server process doesn't fork at all (Recipe 17.13).

Some servers need to listen to many IP addresses at once, which we demonstrate in Recipe 17.16. Well-behaved servers clean up and restart when they get a HUP signal; Recipe 17.18 shows how to implement that behavior in Perl. We also show how to put a name to both ends of a connection; see Recipes 17.7 and 17.8.

UNIX Network Programming (Prentice Hall) and the three-volume *TCP/IP Illustrated* (Addison-Wesley) by W. Richard Stevens are indispensable for the serious socket programmer. If you want to learn the basics about sockets, it's hard to beat the original and classic reference, *An Advanced 4.4BSD Interprocess Communication Tutorial*. It's written for C, but almost everything is directly applicable to Perl. It's available in */usr/share/doc* on most BSD-derived Unix systems. We also recommend you look at *The Unix Programming Frequently Asked Questions List* (Gierth and Horgan), and *Programming UNIX Sockets in C—Frequently Asked Questions* (Metcalf and Gierth), both of which are posted periodically to the *comp.unix.answers* newsgroup.

17.1 Writing a TCP Client

Problem

You want to connect to a socket on a remote machine.

Solution

This solution assumes you're using the Internet to communicate. For TCP-like communication within a single machine, see Recipe 17.6.

Either use the standard IO::Socket::INET class:

```
use IO::Socket;

$socket = IO::Socket::INET->new(PeerAddr => $remote_host,
                                PeerPort => $remote_port,
                                Proto    => "tcp",
                                Type     => SOCK_STREAM)
```

```
        or die "Couldn't connect to $remote_host:$remote_port : $@\n";

    # ... do something with the socket
    print $socket "Why don't you call me anymore?\n";

    $answer = <$socket>;

    # and terminate the connection when we're done
    close($socket);
```

or create a socket by hand for better control:

```
    use Socket;

    # create a socket
    socket(TO_SERVER, PF_INET, SOCK_STREAM, getprotobyname('tcp'));

    # build the address of the remote machine
    $internet_addr = inet_aton($remote_host)
        or die "Couldn't convert $remote_host into an Internet address: $!\n";
    $paddr = sockaddr_in($remote_port, $internet_addr);

    # connect
    connect(TO_SERVER, $paddr)
        or die "Couldn't connect to $remote_host:$remote_port : $!\n";

    # ... do something with the socket
    print TO_SERVER "Why don't you call me anymore?\n";

    # and terminate the connection when we're done
    close(TO_SERVER);
```

Discussion

While coding this by hand requires a lot of steps, the IO::Socket::INET class wraps them all in a convenient constructor. The important things to know are where you're going (the PeerAddr and PeerPort parameters) and how you're getting there (the Type parameter). IO::Socket::INET tries to determine these things from what you've given it. It deduces Proto from the Type and Port if possible, and assumes tcp otherwise.

PeerAddr is a string containing either a hostname ("www.oreilly.com") or an IP address ("208.201.239.36"). PeerPort is an integer, representing the port number to connect to. You can embed the port number in the address by giving an address like "www.oreilly.com:80". Type is the kind of socket to create: SOCK_DGRAM for datagrams or SOCK_STREAM for streams.

If you want a SOCK_STREAM connection to a port on a particular machine with no other options, pass a single string to IO::Socket::INET->new consisting of the hostname and port separated by a colon:

```
    $client = IO::Socket::INET->new("www.yahoo.com:80")
        or die $@;
```

If an error occurs, IO::Socket::INET will return undef and $@ (*not* $!) will be set to the error message.

```
$s = IO::Socket::INET->new(PeerAddr => "Does not Exist",
                           Peerport => 80,
                           Type     => SOCK_STREAM )
    or die $@;
```

If your packets are disappearing into a network void, it can take a while for your inability to connect to a port to be recognized. You can decrease this time by specifying a Timeout parameter to IO::Socket::INET->new( ):

```
$s = IO::Socket::INET->new(PeerAddr => "bad.host.com",
                           PeerPort => 80,
                           Type     => SOCK_STREAM,
                           Timeout  => 5 )
    or die $@;
```

If you do this, though, there's no way to tell from $! or $@ whether you couldn't connect or whether you timed out. Sometimes it's better to set it up by hand instead of using a module.

If you have several network interfaces, the kernel decides which one to use based on your current routes. If you wish to override this default, add a Local parameter to your call to IO::Socket::INET->new. If coding by hand, do this:

```
$inet_addr = inet_aton("208.201.239.37");
$paddr     = sockaddr_in($port, $inet_addr);
bind(SOCKET, $paddr)        or die "bind: $!";
```

If you know only the name, do this:

```
$inet_addr = gethostbyname("www.yahoo.com")
                        or die "Can't resolve www.yahoo.com: $!";
$paddr     = sockaddr_in($port, $inet_addr);
bind(SOCKET, $paddr)        or die "bind: $!";
```

See Also

The socket, bind, connect, and gethostbyname functions in Chapter 29 of *Programming Perl* and in *perlfunc*(1); the documentation for the standard Socket, IO::Socket, and Net::hostent modules; the section on "Networking Clients" in Chapter 16 of *Programming Perl* and in *perlipc*(1); *UNIX Network Programming*; Recipe 17.2; Recipe 17.3

17.2 Writing a TCP Server

Problem

You want to write a server that waits for clients to connect over the network to a particular port.

Solution

This recipe assumes you're using the Internet to communicate. For TCP-like communication within a single Unix machine, see Recipe 17.6.

Use the standard IO::Socket::INET class:

```
use IO::Socket;

$server = IO::Socket::INET->new(LocalPort => $server_port,
                                Type      => SOCK_STREAM,
                                Reuse     => 1,
                                Listen    => 10 )   # or SOMAXCONN
    or die "Couldn't be a tcp server on port $server_port : $@\n";

while ($client = $server->accept()) {
    # $client is the new connection
}

close($server);
```

Or craft it by hand for better control:

```
use Socket;

# make the socket
socket(SERVER, PF_INET, SOCK_STREAM, getprotobyname('tcp'));

# so we can restart our server quickly
setsockopt(SERVER, SOL_SOCKET, SO_REUSEADDR, 1);

# build up my socket address
$my_addr = sockaddr_in($server_port, INADDR_ANY);
bind(SERVER, $my_addr)
    or die "Couldn't bind to port $server_port : $!\n";

# establish a queue for incoming connections
listen(SERVER, SOMAXCONN)
    or die "Couldn't listen on port $server_port : $!\n";

# accept and process connections
while (accept(CLIENT, SERVER)) {
    # do something with CLIENT
}

close(SERVER);
```

Discussion

Setting up a server is more complicated than being a client. The optional listen function tells the operating system how many pending, unanswered connections can queue up while waiting for your server. The setsockopt function used in the Solution allows you to avoid waiting two minutes after killing your server before you restart it again (valuable in testing). The bind call registers your server with the kernel so others can find you. Finally, accept takes the incoming connections one by one.

The numeric argument to listen is the number of unaccepted connections that the operating system should queue before clients start getting "connection refused" errors. Historically, the maximum listen value was 5, and even today, many operating systems silently limit this queue size to around 20. With busy web servers becoming commonplace, many vendors have increased this value. Your documented system maximum can be found in the SOMAXCONN constant from the Socket module.

The accept function takes two arguments: the filehandle to connect to the remote client and the server filehandle. It returns the client's port and IP address, as packed by inet_ntoa:

```
use Socket;

while ($client_address = accept(CLIENT, SERVER)) {
    ($port, $packed_ip) = sockaddr_in($client_address);
    $dotted_quad = inet_ntoa($packed_ip);
    # do as thou wilt
}
```

With the IO::Socket classes, accept is a method of the server filehandle:

```
while ($client = $server->accept()) {
    # ...
}
```

If you call the accept method in list context, it returns the client socket and its address:

```
while (($client,$client_address) = $server->accept()) {
    # ...
}
```

If no connection is waiting, your program blocks in the accept until a connection comes in. If you want to ensure that your accept won't block, use non-blocking sockets:

```
use Fcntl qw(F_GETFL F_SETFL O_NONBLOCK);

$flags = fcntl(SERVER, F_GETFL, 0)
            or die "Can't get flags for the socket: $!\n";

$flags = fcntl(SERVER, F_SETFL, $flags | O_NONBLOCK)
            or die "Can't set flags for the socket: $!\n";
```

Now when you accept and nothing is waiting for you, accept will return undef and set $! to EWOULDBLOCK.

You might fear that when the return flags from F_GETFL are 0, this would trigger the die just as a failure from undef would. Not so—as with ioctl, a non-error return from fcntl is mapped by Perl to the special value "0 but true". This special string is even exempt from non-numeric warnings, so feel free to use it in your functions when you want to return a value that's numerically zero yet still true. It probably should have been "0 and sneaky" instead.

See Also

The socket, bind, listen, accept, fcntl, and setsockopt functions in Chapter 29 of *Programming Perl* and in *perlfunc*(1); your system's *fcntl*(2), *socket*(2), and *setsockopt*(2) manpages (if you have them); the documentation for the standard Socket, IO::Socket, and Net::hostent modules; the section on "Networking Servers" in Chapter 16 of *Programming Perl* and in *perlipc*(1); *UNIX Network Programming*; *Beej's Guide to Network Programming* at *http://www.ecst.csuchico.edu/~beej/guide/net*; Recipe 7.22; Recipe 7.20; Recipe 17.1; Recipe 17.3; Recipe 17.7

17.3 Communicating over TCP

Problem

You want to read or write data over a TCP connection.

Solution

This recipe assumes you're using the Internet to communicate. For TCP-like communication within a single machine, see Recipe 17.6.

Use print or <> :

```
print SERVER "What is your name?\n";
chomp ($response = <SERVER>);
```

Or use send and recv :

```
defined (send(SERVER, $data_to_send, $flags))
    or die "Can't send : $!\n";

recv(SERVER, $data_read, $maxlen, $flags)
    or die "Can't receive: $!\n";
```

Or use the corresponding methods on an IO::Socket object:

```
use IO::Socket;

$server->send($data_to_send, $flags)
    or die "Can't send: $!\n";

$server->recv($data_read, $maxlen, $flags)
    or die "Can't recv: $!\n";
```

To find out whether data can be read or written, use the select function, which is nicely wrapped by the standard IO::Socket class:

```
use IO::Select;

$select = IO::Select->new();
```

```
$select->add(*FROM_SERVER);
$select->add($to_client);

@read_from = $select->can_read($timeout);
foreach $socket (@read_from) {
    # read the pending data from $socket
}
```

Discussion

Sockets handle two completely different types of I/O, each with attendant pitfalls and benefits. The normal Perl I/O functions used on files (except for seek and sysseek) work for stream sockets, but datagram sockets require the system calls send and recv, which work on complete records.

Awareness of buffering issues is particularly important in socket programming. That's because buffering, while designed to enhance performance, can interfere with the interactive feel that some programs require. Gathering input with <> may try to read more data from the socket than is yet available as it looks for a record separator. Both print and <> use stdio buffers, so unless you've changed autoflushing (see the Introduction to Chapter 7) on the socket handle, your data won't be sent to the other end as soon as you print it. Instead, it will wait until a buffer fills up.

For line-based clients and servers, this is probably okay, so long as you turn on autoflushing for output. Newer versions of IO::Socket do this automatically on the anonymous filehandles returned by IO::Socket->new.

But stdio isn't the only source of buffering. Output (print, printf, or syswrite—or send on a TCP socket) is further subject to buffering at the operating system level under a strategy called the *Nagle Algorithm*. When a packet of data has been sent but not acknowledged, further to-be-sent data is queued and is sent as soon as another complete packet's worth is collected or the outstanding acknowledgment is received. In some situations (mouse events being sent to a windowing system, keystrokes to a real-time application) this buffering is inconvenient or downright wrong. You can disable the Nagle Algorithm with the TCP_NODELAY socket option:

```
use Socket;
require "sys/socket.ph";    # for &TCP_NODELAY

setsockopt(SERVER, SOL_SOCKET, &TCP_NODELAY, 1)
    or die "Couldn't disable Nagle's algorithm: $!\n";
```

Re-enable it with:

```
setsockopt(SERVER, SOL_SOCKET, &TCP_NODELAY, 0)
    or die "Couldn't enable Nagle's algorithm: $!\n";
```

In most cases, TCP_NODELAY isn't something you need. TCP buffering is there for a reason, so don't disable it unless your application is one of the few real-time packet-intensive situations that need to.

Load in TCP_NODELAY from *sys/socket.ph*, a file that isn't automatically installed with Perl, but can be easily built. See Recipe 12.17 for details.

Because buffering is such an issue, you have the select function to determine which filehandles have unread input, which can be written to, and which have "exceptional conditions" pending. The select function takes three strings interpreted as binary data, each bit corresponding to a filehandle. A typical call to select looks like this:

```
$rin = '';                            # initialize bitmask
vec($rin, fileno(SOCKET), 1) = 1;     # mark SOCKET in $rin
# repeat calls to vec( ) for each socket to check

$timeout = 10;                        # wait ten seconds

$nfound = select($rout = $rin, undef, undef, $timeout);
if (vec($rout, fileno(SOCKET),1)){
    # data to be read on SOCKET
}
```

The four arguments to select are: a bitmask indicating which filehandles to check for unread data; a bitmask indicating which filehandles to check for safety to write without blocking; a bitmask indicating which filehandles to check for exceptional conditions; and a time in seconds indicating the maximum time to wait (this can be a floating-point number).

The function changes the bitmask arguments passed to it, so that when it returns, the only bits set correspond to filehandles ready for I/O. This leads to the common strategy of assigning an input mask ($rin in the previous example) to an output one ($rout in the example), so that select can only affect $rout, leaving $rin alone.

You can specify a timeout of 0 to *poll* (check without blocking). Some beginning programmers think that blocking is bad, so they write programs that "busy-wait"—they poll and poll and poll and poll. When a program blocks, the operating system recognizes that the process is pending on input and gives CPU time to other programs until input is available. When a program busy-waits, the system can't let it sleep, because it's always doing something—checking for input! Occasionally, polling is the right thing to do, but far more often it's not. A timeout of undef to select means "no timeout," and your program will patiently block until input becomes available.

Because select uses bitmasks, which are tiresome to create and difficult to interpret, we use the standard IO::Select module in the Solution. It bypasses bitmasks and is generally the easier route.

A full explanation of the exceptional data that is tested for with the third bitmask in select is beyond the scope of this book. Consult Stevens's *UNIX Network Programming* for a discussion of out-of-band and urgent data.

Other send and recv flags are listed in the manpages for those system calls.

See Also

The send, recv, fileno, vec, setsockopt, and select functions in Chapter 29 of *Programming Perl* and in *perlfunc*(1); the sections on "I/O Operators" and on "Bitwise String Operators" in *perlop*(1); your system's *setsockopt*(2) manpage (if you have one); the documentation for the standard Socket and IO::Socket modules; the section on "Sockets" in Chapter 16 of *Programming Perl* and in *perlipc*(1); *UNIX Network Programming*; Recipe 17.1; Recipe 17.2

17.4 Setting Up a UDP Client

Problem

You want to exchange messages with another process using UDP (datagrams).

Solution

To set up a UDP socket handle, use either the low-level Socket module on your own filehandle:

```
use Socket;
socket(SOCKET, PF_INET, SOCK_DGRAM, getprotobyname("udp"))
    or die "socket: $!";
```

or else IO::Socket, which returns an anonymous one:

```
use IO::Socket;
$handle = IO::Socket::INET->new(Proto => 'udp')
    or die "socket: $@";      # yes, it uses $@ here
```

Then to send a message to a machine named $HOSTNAME on port number $PORTNO, use:

```
$ipaddr   = inet_aton($HOSTNAME);
$portaddr = sockaddr_in($PORTNO, $ipaddr);
send(SOCKET, $MSG, 0, $portaddr) == length($MSG)
        or die "cannot send to $HOSTNAME($PORTNO): $!";
```

To receive a message of length no greater than $MAXLEN, use:

```
$portaddr = recv(SOCKET, $MSG, $MAXLEN, 0)      or die "recv: $!";
($portno, $ipaddr) = sockaddr_in($portaddr);
$host = gethostbyaddr($ipaddr, AF_INET);
print "$host($portno) said $MSG\n";
```

Discussion

Datagram sockets are unlike stream sockets. Streams provide sessions, giving the illusion of a stable connection. You might think of them as working like a telephone call—expensive to set up, but once established, reliable and easy to use. Datagrams, though, are more like the postal system—it's cheaper and easier to send a letter to your friend on the other side of the world than to call them on the phone. Datagrams are easier on the system than streams. You send a small amount of information one message at a time. But your messages' delivery isn't guaranteed, and they might arrive in the wrong order. Like a small post box, the receiver's queue might fill up and cause further messages to be dropped.

Why then, if datagrams are unreliable, do we have them? Because some applications are most sensibly implemented in terms of datagrams. For instance, in streaming audio, it's more important that the stream as a whole be preserved than that every packet get through, especially if packets are being dropped because there's not enough bandwidth for them all. Another use for datagrams is broadcasting, which corresponds to mass mailing of advertisements in the postal model, and is equally popular in most circles. One use for broadcast packets is to send out a message to your local subnet saying, "Hey, is there anybody around here who wants to be my server?"

Because datagrams don't provide the illusion of a lasting connection, you get a little more freedom in how you use them. You don't have to connect your socket to the remote end that you're sending data. Instead, address each datagram individually when you send. Assuming $remote_addr is the result of a call to sockaddr_in, do this:

```
send(MYSOCKET, $msg_buffer, $flags, $remote_addr)
    or die "Can't send: $!\n";
```

The only flag argument used much is MSG_OOB, which lets you send and receive out-of-band data in advanced applications.

The remote address should be a port and Internet address combination returned by the Socket module's sockaddr_in function. If you want, call connect on that address instead. Then you can omit the last argument to your sends, after which they'll all go to that recipient. Unlike streams, you are free to reconnect to another machine with the same datagram socket.

Example 17-1 is a small example of a UDP program. It contacts the UDP time port of the machine whose name is given on the command line, or of the local machine by default. This doesn't work on all machines, but those with a server will send you back a 4-byte integer packed in network byte order representing the time that machine thinks it is. The time returned, however, is in the number of seconds since 1900. You have to subtract the number of seconds between 1900 and 1970 to feed that time to the localtime or gmtime conversion functions.

Example 17-1. clockdrift

```perl
#!/usr/bin/perl
# clockdrift - compare another system's clock with this one
use strict;
use Socket;

my ($host, $him, $src, $port, $ipaddr, $ptime, $delta);
```

Example 17-1. clockdrift (continued)

```
my $SECS_of_70_YEARS      = 2_208_988_800;

socket(MsgBox, PF_INET, SOCK_DGRAM, getprotobyname("udp"))
    or die "socket: $!";
$him = sockaddr_in(scalar(getservbyname("time", "udp"))),
defined(send(MsgBox, 0, 0, $him))
    or die "send: $!";
defined($src = recv(MsgBox, $ptime, 4, 0))
    or die "recv: $!";
($port, $ipaddr) = sockaddr_in($src);
$host = gethostbyaddr($ipaddr, AF_INET);
my $delta = (unpack("N", $ptime) - $SECS_of_70_YEARS) - time();
print "Clock on $host is $delta seconds ahead of this one.\n";
```

If the machine you're trying to contact isn't alive or if its response is lost, you'll only know because your program will get stuck in the recv waiting for an answer that will never come.

See Also

The send, recv, gethostbyaddr, and unpack functions in Chapter 29 of *Programming Perl* and in *perlfunc*(1); the documentation for the standard Socket and IO::Socket modules; the section on "Message Passing" in Chapter 16 of *Programming Perl* and in *perlipc*(1); *UNIX Network Programming*; Recipe 17.5

17.5   Setting Up a UDP Server

Problem

You want to write a UDP server.

Solution

First bind to the port on which the server is to be contacted. With IO::Socket, this is easily accomplished:

```
use IO::Socket;
$server = IO::Socket::INET->new(LocalPort => $server_port,
                                Proto      => "udp")
    or die "Couldn't be a udp server on port $server_port : $@\n";
```

Then, go into a loop receiving messages:

```
while ($him = $server->recv($datagram, $MAX_TO_READ, $flags)) {
    # do something
}
```

Discussion

Life with UDP is much simpler than life with TCP. Instead of accepting client connections one at a time and committing yourself to a long-term relationship, take messages from clients as they come in. The recv function returns the address of the sender, which you must then decode.

Example 17-2 is a small UDP-based server that just sits around waiting for messages. Every time a message comes in, we find out who sent it, send that person a message based on the previous message, and then save the new message.

Example 17-2. udpqotd

```perl
#!/usr/bin/perl -w
# udpqotd - UDP message server
use strict;
use IO::Socket;
my ($sock, $oldmsg, $newmsg, $hisaddr, $hishost, $MAXLEN, $PORTNO);
$MAXLEN = 1024;
$PORTNO = 5151;
$sock = IO::Socket::INET->new(LocalPort => $PORTNO, Proto => 'udp')
    or die "socket: $@";
print "Awaiting UDP messages on port $PORTNO\n";
$oldmsg = "This is the starting message.";
while ($sock->recv($newmsg, $MAXLEN)) {
    my($port, $ipaddr) = sockaddr_in($sock->peername);
    $hishost = gethostbyaddr($ipaddr, AF_INET);
    print "Client $hishost said ``$newmsg''\n";
    $sock->send($oldmsg);
    $oldmsg = "[$hishost] $newmsg";
}
die "recv: $!";
```

This program is easier using IO::Socket than the raw Socket module. We don't have to say where to send the message, because the library keeps track of who sent the last message and stores that information away on the $sock object. The peername method retrieves it for decoding.

You can't use the *telnet* program to talk to this server. You have to use a dedicated client. One is shown in Example 17-3.

Example 17-3. udpmsg

```perl
#!/usr/bin/perl -w
# udpmsg - send a message to the udpquotd server
use IO::Socket;
use strict;
my($sock, $server_host, $msg, $port, $ipaddr, $hishost,
    $MAXLEN, $PORTNO, $TIMEOUT);
$MAXLEN  = 1024;
$PORTNO  = 5151;
$TIMEOUT = 5;
```

Example 17-3. udpmsg (continued)

```
$server_host = shift;
$msg        = "@ARGV";
$sock = IO::Socket::INET->new(Proto    => 'udp',
                              PeerPort => $PORTNO,
                              PeerAddr => $server_host)
    or die "Creating socket: $!\n";
$sock->send($msg) or die "send: $!";
eval {
    local $SIG{ALRM} = sub { die "alarm time out" };
    alarm $TIMEOUT;
    $sock->recv($msg, $MAXLEN)       or die "recv: $!";
    alarm 0;
    1;  # return value from eval on normalcy
} or die "recv from $server_host timed out after $TIMEOUT seconds.\n";
($port, $ipaddr) = sockaddr_in($sock->peername);
$hishost = gethostbyaddr($ipaddr, AF_INET);
print "Server $hishost responded ``$msg''\n";
```

This time when we create the socket, we supply a peer host and port at the start, allowing us to omit that information in the send.

We've added an alarm timeout in case the server isn't responsive, or maybe not even alive. Because recv is a blocking system call that may not return, we wrap it in the standard eval block construct for timing out a blocking operation.

See Also

The send, recv, and alarm functions in Chapter 29 of *Programming Perl* and in *perlfunc*(1); the documentation for the standard Socket and IO::Socket modules; the section on "Message Passing" in Chapter 16 of *Programming Perl* and in *perlipc*(1); *UNIX Network Programming*; Recipe 16.21; Recipe 17.4

17.6   Using Unix Domain Sockets

Problem

You want to communicate with other processes on only the local machine.

Solution

Use domain sockets. You can use the code and techniques from the preceding Internet domain recipes, with the following changes:

- Because the naming system is different, use sockaddr_un instead of sockaddr_in.
- Use IO::Socket::UNIX instead of IO::Socket::INET, and use Peer and Local instead of PeerAddr/PeerPort and LocalAddr/LocalPort.

- Use PF_UNIX instead of PF_INET, and give PF_UNSPEC as the last argument to socket.

- SOCK_STREAM clients don't have to bind to a local address before they connect.

Discussion

Unix domain sockets have names like files on the filesystem. In fact, most systems implement them as special files; that's what Perl's -S filetest operator looks for—whether the file is a Unix domain socket.

Supply the filename as the Peer argument to IO::Socket::UNIX->new, or encode it with sockaddr_un and pass it to connect. Here's how to make server and client Unix domain stream sockets with IO::Socket::UNIX:

```
use IO::Socket;

unlink "/tmp/mysock";
$server = IO::Socket::UNIX->new(LocalAddr => "/tmp/mysock",
                                Type      => SOCK_STREAM,
                                Listen    => 5 )
    or die $@;

$client = IO::Socket::UNIX->new(PeerAddr  => "/tmp/mysock",
                                Type      => SOCK_STREAM,
                                Timeout   => 10 )
    or die $@;
```

Here's how to use the traditional functions to make stream sockets:

```
use Socket;

socket(SERVER, PF_UNIX, SOCK_STREAM, 0);
unlink "/tmp/mysock";
bind(SERVER, sockaddr_un("/tmp/mysock"))
    or die "Can't create server: $!";

socket(CLIENT, PF_UNIX, SOCK_STREAM, 0);
connect(CLIENT, sockaddr_un("/tmp/mysock"))
    or die "Can't connect to /tmp/mysock: $!";
```

Unless you know what you're doing, set the protocol (the Proto argument to IO::Socket::UNIX->new and the last argument to socket) to 0 for PF_UNIX sockets. You can use both SOCK_DGRAM and SOCK_STREAM types of communication in the Unix domain, with the same semantics as we saw for Internet sockets. Changing the domain doesn't change the characteristics of the socket type.

Because many systems actually create a special file in the filesystem, you should delete the file before you try to bind the socket. Even though there is a race condition (somebody could create a file with the name of your socket between your calls to unlink and bind), this isn't a security problem, because bind won't overwrite an existing file.

See Also

Recipes 17.1 through 17.5

17.7 Identifying the Other End of a Socket

Problem

You have a socket and want to identify the machine at the other end.

Solution

If you're only interested in the IP address of the remote machine, use:

```
use Socket;

$other_end          = getpeername(SOCKET)
    or die "Couldn't identify other end: $!\n";
($port, $iaddr)     = unpack_sockaddr_in($other_end);
$ip_address         = inet_ntoa($iaddr);
```

If you want its actual hostname, use:

```
use Socket;

$other_end          = getpeername(SOCKET)
    or die "Couldn't identify other end: $!\n";
($port, $iaddr)     = unpack_sockaddr_in($other_end);
$actual_ip          = inet_ntoa($iaddr);
$claimed_hostname   = gethostbyaddr($iaddr, AF_INET);
@name_lookup        = gethostbyname($claimed_hostname)
    or die "Could not look up $claimed_hostname : $!\n";
@resolved_ips       = map { inet_ntoa($_) }
    @name_lookup[ 4 .. $#name_lookup ];
```

Discussion

For a long time, figuring out who connected to you was considered more straightforward than it really is. The getpeername function returns the IP address of the remote machine in a packed binary structure (or undef if an error occurred). To unpack it, use inet_ntoa. If you want the name of the remote end, call gethostbyaddr to look up the name of the machine in the DNS tables, right?

Not really. That's only half the solution. Because a name lookup goes to the name's owner's DNS server and a lookup of an IP address goes to the address's owner's DNS server, you have to contend with the possibility that the machine that connected to you is giving incorrect names. For instance, the machine evil.crackers.org could belong to malevolent cyberpirates who tell their DNS server that its IP address (1.2.3.4) should be identified as trusted.dod.gov. If your program trusts trusted.dod.gov, a connection from evil.crackers.org will cause getpeername to return the right IP address (1.2.3.4), but gethostbyaddr will return the duplicitous name.

To avoid this problem, we take the (possibly deceitful) name returned by gethostbyaddr and look it up again with gethostbyname. In the case of evil.crackers.org, the lookup of trusted.dod.gov will be done through dod.gov's DNS servers, and will return the real IP address(es) for trusted.dod.gov. Because many machines have more than one IP address (multihomed web servers are the obvious example), we can't use the simplified form of gethostbyname:

```
$packed_ip  = gethostbyname($name) or die "Couldn't look up $name : $!\n";
$ip_address = inet_ntoa($packed_ip);
```

So far we've assumed we're dealing with an Internet domain application. You can also call getpeername on a Unix domain socket. If the other end called bind, you'll get the filename they bound to. If the other end *didn't* call bind, however, getpeername may return an empty string (unpacked), a packed string with oddball garbage in it, or undef to indicate an error, or your computer may reboot. (These possibilities are listed in descending order of probability and desirability.) This is what we in the computer business call "undefined behavior."

Even this level of paranoia and mistrust isn't enough. It's still possible for people to fake out DNS servers they don't directly control, so don't use hostnames for identification or authentication. True paranoiacs and misanthropes use cryptographically secure methods.

See Also

The gethostbyaddr, gethostbyname, and getpeername functions in Chapter 29 of *Programming Perl* and in *perlfunc*(1); the inet_ntoa function in the standard Socket module; the documentation for the standard IO::Socket and Net::hostnet modules

17.8 Finding Your Own Name and Address

Problem

You want to find your (fully qualified) hostname.

Solution

First, get your (possibly qualified) hostname. Try either the standard Sys::Hostname module:

```
use Sys::Hostname;

$hostname = hostname();
```

or POSIX's uname function:

```
use POSIX qw(uname);
($kernel, $hostname, $release, $version, $hardware) = uname( );

$hostname = (uname)[1];             # or just one
```

Then turn it into an IP address and convert to its canonical name:

```
use Socket;                         # for AF_INET
$address = gethostbyname($hostname)
    or die "Couldn't resolve $hostname : $!";
$hostname = gethostbyaddr($address, AF_INET)
    or die "Couldn't re-resolve $hostname : $!";
```

Discussion

Sys::Hostname tries to be portable by using knowledge about your system to decide how best to find the hostname. It tries many different ways of getting the hostname, but several involve running other programs. This can lead to tainted data (see Recipe 19.1).

POSIX::uname, on the other hand, works only on POSIX systems and isn't guaranteed to provide anything useful in the nodename field that we are examining. That said, the value *is* useful on many machines and doesn't suffer from the tainted data problem that Sys::Hostname does.

Once you have the name, though, you must consider that it might be missing a domain name. For instance, Sys::Hostname may return you guanaco instead of guanaco.camelids.org. To fix this, convert the name back into an IP address with gethostbyname and then back into a name again with gethostbyaddr. By involving the domain name system, you are guaranteed of getting a full name.

See Also

The gethostbyname and gethostbyaddr functions in Chapter 29 of *Programming Perl* and in *perlfunc*(1); the documentation for the standard Net::hostent and Sys::Hostname modules

17.9   Closing a Socket After Forking

Problem

Your program has forked and you want to tell the other end that you're done sending data. You've tried close on the socket, but the remote end never gets an EOF or SIGPIPE.

Solution

Use shutdown:

```
shutdown(SOCKET, 0);          # I/we have stopped reading data
shutdown(SOCKET, 1);          # I/we have stopped writing data
shutdown(SOCKET, 2);          # I/we have stopped using this socket
```

On an IO::Socket object, you could also write:

```
$socket->shutdown(0);         # I/we have stopped reading data
```

Discussion

When a process forks, the child has copies of the parent's open filehandles, including sockets. When you close a file or socket, you close only the current process's copy. If another process (parent or child) still has the socket open, the operating system doesn't consider their file or socket closed.

Take the case of a socket that data is being sent to. If two processes have this socket open, one can close it but, because the other still has it open, the socket isn't considered closed by the operating system. Until the *other* process closes the socket, the process reading from the socket won't get an end-of-file. This can lead to confusion and deadlock.

To avoid this, either close unused filehandles after a fork or use shutdown. The shutdown function is a more insistent form of close—it tells the operating system that even though other processes have copies of this filehandle, it should be marked as closed, and the other end should get an end-of-file if the processes read from it or a SIGPIPE if they write to it.

The numeric argument to shutdown lets you specify which sides of the connection are closed. An argument of 0 says that we're done reading data, so the other end of the socket will get a SIGPIPE if they try writing. 1 says that we're done writing data, so the other end of the socket will get an end-of-file if they try reading. 2 says we're done reading and writing.

Imagine a server that wants to read its client's request until end-of-file, and then send an answer. If the client calls close, that socket is now invalid for I/O, so no answer would ever come back. Instead, the client should use shutdown to half-close the connection.

```
print SERVER "my request\n";   # send some data
shutdown(SERVER, 1);           # send eof; no more writing
$answer = <SERVER>;            # but you can still read
```

See Also

The close and shutdown functions in Chapter 29 of *Programming Perl* and in *perlfunc*(1); your system's *shutdown*(2) manpage (if you have it)

17.10 Writing Bidirectional Clients

Problem

You want set up a fully interactive client so you can type a line, get the answer, type a line, get the answer, etc., somewhat like *telnet*.

Solution

Once you've connected, fork off a duplicate process. One twin reads only your input and passes it on to the server, and the other reads only the server's output and sends it to your own output.

Discussion

In a client-server relationship, it is difficult to know whose turn it is to talk. Single-threaded solutions involving the four-argument version of select are hard to write and maintain. But there's no reason to ignore multitasking solutions. The fork function dramatically simplifies this problem.

Once you've connected to the service you'd like to chat with, call fork to clone a twin. Each of these two (nearly) identical processes has a simple job. The parent copies everything from the socket to standard output, and the child simultaneously copies everything from standard input to the socket.

The code is in Example 17-4.

Example 17-4. biclient

```perl
#!/usr/bin/perl -w
# biclient - bidirectional forking client
use strict;
use IO::Socket;
my ($host, $port, $kidpid, $handle, $line);

unless (@ARGV == 2) { die "usage: $0 host port" }
($host, $port) = @ARGV;

# create a tcp connection to the specified host and port
$handle = IO::Socket::INET->new(Proto     => "tcp",
                                PeerAddr  => $host,
                                PeerPort  => $port)
    or die "can't connect to port $port on $host: $!";

$handle->autoflush(1);              # so output gets there right away
print STDERR "[Connected to $host:$port]\n";

# split the program into two processes, identical twins
die "can't fork: $!" unless defined($kidpid = fork());
```

Example 17-4. biclient (continued)

```
if ($kidpid) {
    # parent copies the socket to standard output
    while (defined ($line = <$handle>)) {
        print STDOUT $line;
    }
    kill("TERM" => $kidpid);          # send SIGTERM to child
}
else {
    # child copies standard input to the socket
    while (defined ($line = <STDIN>)) {
        print $handle $line;
    }
}
exit;
```

To accomplish the same thing using just one process is remarkably more difficult. It's easier to code two processes, each doing a single task, than it is to code one process to do two different tasks. Take advantage of multitasking by splitting your program into multiple threads of control, and some of your bewildering problems will become much easier.

The kill function in the parent's if block is there to send a signal to the child (currently running in the else block) as soon as the remote server has closed its end of the connection. The kill at the end of the parent's block is there to eliminate the child process as soon as the server on the other end goes away.

If the remote server sends data a byte at time and you need that data immediately without waiting for a newline (which may never arrive), you may wish to replace the while loop in the parent with the following:

```
my $byte;
while (sysread($handle, $byte, 1) == 1) {
    print STDOUT $byte;
}
```

Making a system call for each byte you want to read is not very efficient (to put it mildly), but it is the simplest to explain and works reasonably well.

See Also

The sysread and fork functions in Chapter 29 of *Programming Perl* and in *perlfunc*(1); the documentation for the standard IO::Socket module; Recipe 16.5; Recipe 16.10; Recipe 17.11

17.11 Forking Servers

Problem

You want to write a server that forks a subprocess to handle each new client.

Solution

Fork in the accept loop, and use a $SIG{CHLD} handler to reap the children.

```
# set up the socket SERVER, bind and listen ...
use POSIX qw(:sys_wait_h);

sub REAPER {
    1 until (-1 == waitpid(-1, WNOHANG));
    $SIG{CHLD} = \&REAPER;                  # unless $]>= 5.002
}

$SIG{CHLD} = \&REAPER;

while ($hisaddr = accept(CLIENT, SERVER)) {
    next if $pid = fork;                    # parent
    die "fork: $!" unless defined $pid;     # failure
    # otherwise child
    close(SERVER);                          # no use to child
    # ... do something
    exit;                                   # child leaves
} continue {
    close(CLIENT);                          # no use to parent
}
```

Discussion

This approach is very common for SOCK_STREAM servers in the Internet and Unix domains. Each incoming connection gets a cloned server of its own. The model is:

1. Accept a stream connection.
2. Fork off a duplicate to communicate over that stream.
3. Return to 1.

This technique isn't used with SOCK_DGRAM sockets, because their method of communication is different. The time it takes to fork makes the forking model impractical for UDP-style servers. Instead of working with a series of stateful, long-running connections, SOCK_DGRAM servers work with a bunch of sporadic datagrams, usually statelessly. With them, the model must become:

1. Read a datagram.
2. Handle the datagram.
3. Return to 1.

The child process deals with the new connection. Because it will never use the SERVER socket, we immediately close it. This is partly to keep a tidy house, but mainly so that the server socket is closed when the parent (server) process exits. If the children do not close the SERVER socket, the operating system considers the socket still open even when the parent dies. For more on this, see Recipe 17.9.

%SIG ensures that we clean up after our children when they exit. See Chapter 16 for details.

See Also

The fork and accept functions in Chapter 29 of *Programming Perl* and in *perlfunc*(1); Recipe 16.15; Recipe 16.19; Recipe 17.12; Recipe 17.13

17.12 Pre-Forking Servers

Problem

You want to write a server that concurrently processes several clients (as in Recipe 17.11), but connections are coming in so fast that forking slows the server too much.

Solution

Have a master server maintain a pool of pre-forked children, as shown in Example 17-5.

Example 17-5. preforker

```perl
#!/usr/bin/perl
# preforker - server who forks first
use IO::Socket;
use Symbol;
use POSIX;

# establish SERVER socket, bind and listen.
$server = IO::Socket::INET->new(LocalPort => 6969,
                                Type     => SOCK_STREAM,
                                Proto    => 'tcp',
                                Reuse    => 1,
                                Listen   => 10 )
  or die "making socket: $@\n";

# global variables
$PREFORK               = 5;      # number of children to maintain
$MAX_CLIENTS_PER_CHILD = 5;      # number of clients each child should process
%children              = ();     # keys are current child process IDs
$children              = 0;      # current number of children

sub REAPER {                     # takes care of dead children
```

Example 17-5. preforker (continued)

```
        $SIG{CHLD} = \&REAPER;
    my $pid = wait;
    $children --;
    delete $children{$pid};
}

sub HUNTSMAN {                          # signal handler for SIGINT
    local($SIG{CHLD}) = 'IGNORE';       # we're going to kill our children
    kill 'INT' => keys %children;
    exit;                               # clean up with dignity
}

# Fork off our children.
for (1 .. $PREFORK) {
    make_new_child();
}

# Install signal handlers.
$SIG{CHLD} = \&REAPER;
$SIG{INT}  = \&HUNTSMAN;

# And maintain the population.
while (1) {
    sleep;                              # wait for a signal (i.e., child's death)
    for ($i = $children; $i < $PREFORK; $i++) {
        make_new_child();               # top up the child pool
    }
}

sub make_new_child {
    my $pid;
    my $sigset;

    # block signal for fork
    $sigset = POSIX::SigSet->new(SIGINT);
    sigprocmask(SIG_BLOCK, $sigset)
        or die "Can't block SIGINT for fork: $!\n";

    die "fork: $!" unless defined ($pid = fork);

    if ($pid) {
        # Parent records the child's birth and returns.
        sigprocmask(SIG_UNBLOCK, $sigset)
            or die "Can't unblock SIGINT for fork: $!\n";
        $children{$pid} = 1;
        $children++;
        return;
    } else {
        # Child can *not* return from this subroutine.
        $SIG{INT} = 'DEFAULT';          # make SIGINT kill us as it did before

        # unblock signals
```

Example 17-5. preforker (continued)

```
        sigprocmask(SIG_UNBLOCK, $sigset)
            or die "Can't unblock SIGINT for fork: $!\n";

        # handle connections until we've reached $MAX_CLIENTS_PER_CHILD
        for ($i=0; $i < $MAX_CLIENTS_PER_CHILD; $i++) {
            $client = $server->accept()      or last;
            # do something with the connection
        }

        # tidy up gracefully and finish

        # this exit is VERY important, otherwise the child will become
        # a producer of more and more children, forking yourself into
        # process death.
        exit;
    }
}
```

Discussion

Whew. Although this is a lot of code, the logic is simple: the parent process never deals with clients but instead forks $PREFORK children to do that. The parent keeps track of how many children it has and forks more to replace dead children. Children exit after having handled $MAX_CLIENTS_PER_CHILD clients.

The code is a reasonably direct implementation of this logic. The only trick comes with signal handlers: we want the parent to catch SIGINT and kill its children, so we install our signal handler &HUNTSMAN to do this. But we then have to be careful that the child doesn't have the same handler after we fork. We use POSIX signals to block the signal for the duration of the fork (see Recipe 16.20).

When you use this code in your programs, be sure that make_new_child never returns. If it does, the child will return, become a parent, and spawn off its own children. Your system will fill up with processes, your system administrator will storm down the hallway to find you, and you may end up tied to four horses wondering why you hadn't paid more attention to this paragraph.

On some operating systems, notably Solaris, you cannot have multiple children doing an accept on the same socket. You have to use file locking to ensure that only one child can call accept at any particular moment. Implementing this is left as an exercise for the reader.

See Also

The select function in Chapter 29 of *Programming Perl* or *perlfunc*(1); your system's *fcntl*(2) manpage (if you have one); the documentation for the standard Fcntl, Socket, IO::Select, IO::Socket, and Tie::RefHash modules; Recipe 17.11; Recipe 17.12

17.13 Non-Forking Servers

Problem

You want a server to deal with several simultaneous connections, but you don't want to fork a process to deal with each connection.

Solution

Keep an array of open clients, use select to read information when it becomes available, and deal with a client only when you have read a full request from it, as shown in Example 17-6.

Example 17-6. nonforker

```perl
#!/usr/bin/perl -w
# nonforker - server who multiplexes without forking
use POSIX;
use IO::Socket;
use IO::Select;
use Socket;
use Fcntl;
use Tie::RefHash;

$port = 1685;                    # change this at will

# Listen to port.
$server = IO::Socket::INET->new(LocalPort => $port,
                                Listen    => 10 )
    or die "Can't make server socket: $@\n";

# begin with empty buffers
%inbuffer  = ();
%outbuffer = ();
%ready     = ();

tie %ready, 'Tie::RefHash';

nonblock($server);
$select = IO::Select->new($server);

# Main loop: check reads/accepts, check writes, check ready to process
while (1) {
    my $client;
    my $rv;
    my $data;

    # check for new information on the connections we have

    # anything to read or accept?
    foreach $client ($select->can_read(1)) {
```

Example 17-6. nonforker (continued)

```perl
        if ($client == $server) {
            # accept a new connection

            $client = $server->accept();
            $select->add($client);
            nonblock($client);
        } else {
            # read data
            $data = '';
            $rv   = $client->recv($data, POSIX::BUFSIZ, 0);

            unless (defined($rv) && length $data) {
                # This would be the end of file, so close the client
                delete $inbuffer{$client};
                delete $outbuffer{$client};
                delete $ready{$client};

                $select->remove($client);
                close $client;
                next;
            }

            $inbuffer{$client} .= $data;

            # test whether the data in the buffer or the data we
            # just read means there is a complete request waiting
            # to be fulfilled.  If there is, set $ready{$client}
            # to the requests waiting to be fulfilled.
            while ($inbuffer{$client} =~ s/(.*\n)//) {
                push( @{$ready{$client}}, $1 );
            }
        }
    }

    # Any complete requests to process?
    foreach $client (keys %ready) {
        handle($client);
    }

    # Buffers to flush?
    foreach $client ($select->can_write(1)) {
        # Skip this client if we have nothing to say
        next unless exists $outbuffer{$client};

        $rv = $client->send($outbuffer{$client}, 0);
        unless (defined $rv) {
            # Whine, but move on.
            warn "I was told I could write, but I can't.\n";
            next;
        }
        if ($rv == length $outbuffer{$client} ||
```

Example 17-6. nonforker (continued)

```
            $!  == POSIX::EWOULDBLOCK )
    {
        substr($outbuffer{$client}, 0, $rv) = '';
        delete $outbuffer{$client} unless length $outbuffer{$client};
    } else {
        # Couldn't write all the data, and it wasn't because
        # it would have blocked.  Shutdown and move on.
        delete $inbuffer{$client};
        delete $outbuffer{$client};
        delete $ready{$client};

        $select->remove($client);
        close($client);
        next;
    }
}


# Out of band data?
foreach $client ($select->has_exception(0)) {  # arg is timeout
    # Deal with out-of-band data here, if you want to.
}
}

# handle($socket) deals with all pending requests for $client
sub handle {
    # requests are in $ready{$client}
    # send output to $outbuffer{$client}
    my $client = shift;
    my $request;

    foreach $request (@{$ready{$client}}) {
        # $request is the text of the request
        # put text of reply into $outbuffer{$client}
    }
    delete $ready{$client};
}

# nonblock($socket) puts socket into nonblocking mode
sub nonblock {
    my $socket = shift;
    my $flags;

    $flags = fcntl($socket, F_GETFL, 0)
            or die "Can't get flags for socket: $!\n";
    fcntl($socket, F_SETFL, $flags | O_NONBLOCK)
            or die "Can't make socket nonblocking: $!\n";
}
```

Discussion

As you see, handling multiple simultaneous clients within one process is more complicated than forking dedicated clones. You end up having to do a lot of operating system–like work to split your time between different connections and to ensure you don't block while reading.

The select function tells which connections have data waiting to be read, which can have data written to them, and which have unread out-of-band data. We could use the select function built into Perl, but it would take more work to find out which filehandles are available. So we use the standard IO::Select module.

We use fcntl to turn on the non-blocking option for the server socket. Without it, a single client whose socket buffers filled up would cause the server to pause until the buffers emptied. Using non-blocking I/O, however, means that we have to deal with the case of partial reads and writes—we can't simply use <> to block until an entire record can be read, or use print to send an entire record with print. %inbuffer holds the incomplete command read from clients, %outbuffer holds data not yet sent, and %ready holds arrays of unhandled messages.

To use this code in your program, do three things. First, change the IO::Socket:: INET call to specify your service's port. Second, change the code that moves records from the inbuffer to the ready queue. Currently it treats each line (text ending in \n) as a request. If your requests are not lines, you'll want to change this.

```
while ($inbuffer{$client} =~ s/(.*\n)//) {
    push( @{$ready{$client}}, $1 );
}
```

Finally, change the middle of the loop in handler to actually create a response to the request. A simple echoing program would say:

```
$outbuffer{$client} .= $request;
```

Error handling is left as an exercise to the reader. At the moment, we assume any read or write that caused an error is reason to end that client's connection. This is probably too harsh, because "errors" like EINTR and EAGAIN don't warrant termination (although you *should* never get an EAGAIN when using select( )).

See Also

The select function in Chapter 29 of *Programming Perl* or *perlfunc*(1); your system's *fcntl*(2) manpage (if you have one); the documentation for the standard Fcntl, Socket, IO::Select, IO::Socket, and Tie::RefHash modules; Recipe 17.11; Recipe 17.12

17.14 Multitasking Server with Threads

Problem

You want to write a server that handles multiple clients from within the one process using your operating system's threads.

Solution

Use Perl v5.8.1 or later and threads.pm:

```
use threads;
use IO::Socket;
my $listen = IO::Socket::INET->new(
                                    LocalPort => $SERVER_PORT,
                                    ReuseAddr => 1,
                                    Listen => 10,
                                    );
sub handle_connection {
    my $socket = shift;
    my $output = shift || $socket;
    my $exit = 0;
    while (<$socket>) {
        # work with $_,
        # print to $output
        # set $exit to true when connection is done
        last if $exit;
    }
}
while (my $socket = $listen->accept) {
    async(\&handle_connection, $socket)->detach;
}
```

Discussion

Threading in Perl is still evolving, but it became functional as of v5.8.1. The code in the Solution will not work in earlier versions of Perl. In particular, earlier versions of Perl implemented an entirely different threading model than the current "interpreter threads" system that threads.pm assumes.

The hard work of handling the connection to the client is done in the handle_connection subroutine. It is given the client socket as a parameter, and can call blocking routines like <$socket> because it runs in its own thread. If one thread blocks while reading, other threads can still run.

The master thread in the program creates the socket and accepts connections on it. When a new client connects, the master thread spawns a new thread (with the async call) to handle the connection. The thread runs until the subroutine it is called with (handle_connection in this case) returns.

We detach the newly created thread to ensure that its variables are garbage collected (closing the socket to the client) when the thread ends. If we didn't call detach, our process would accumulate dead threads until we could no longer spawn new threads.

See Also

The documentation for the standard module threads.pm; Recipe 17.15

17.15 Writing a Multitasking Server with POE

Problem

You want to write a server that handles multiple clients from within the one process, without using Perl 5.8's threads or the complexity of non-blocking I/O.

Solution

Use the cooperative multitasking framework POE (available from CPAN) and the accompanying POE::Component::Server::TCP module to create the server for you:

```
#!/usr/bin/perl

use warnings;
use strict;

use POE qw(Component::Server::TCP);

# Start a TCP server.  Client input will be logged to the console and
# echoed back to the client, one line at a time.

POE::Component::Server::TCP->new
  ( Port => $PORT_NUMBER,          # port to listen on
    ClientInput => \&handle_input, # method to call with input
  );

# Start the server.

$poe_kernel->run( );
exit 0;

sub handle_input {
  my ( $session, $heap, $input ) = @_[ SESSION, HEAP, ARG0 ];
  # $session is a POE::Session object unique to this connection,
  # $heap is this connection's between-callback storage.
  # New data from client is in $input.  Newlines are removed.
  # To echo input back to the client, simply say:
  $heap->{client}->put($input);
  # and log it to the console
  print "client ", $session->ID, ": $input\n";
}
```

Solution

POE is a cooperatively multitasking framework for Perl built entirely out of software components. POE doesn't require you to recompile the Perl interpreter to support threads, but it does require you to design your program around the ideas of events and callbacks. Documentation for this framework is available at *http://poe.perl.org/*.

It helps to think of POE as an operating system: there's the kernel (an object responsible for deciding which piece of code is run next) and your processes (called *sessions*, implemented as objects). POE stores the kernel object in the variable $poe_kernel, which is automatically imported into your namespace. Each process in your operating system has a *heap*, memory where the variables for that process are stored. Sessions have heaps as well. In an operating system, I/O libraries handle buffered I/O. In POE, a *wheel* handles accepting data from a writer and sending it on to a reader.

There are dozens of prebuilt sessions (called *components*) for servers, clients, parsers, queues, databases, and many other common tasks. These components do the hard work of understanding the protocols and data formats, leaving you to write only the interesting code—what to do with the data or what data to serve.

When you use POE::Component::Server::TCP, the component handles creating the server, listening, accepting connections, and receiving data from the client. For each bit of data it receives, the component calls back to your code. Your code is responsible for parsing the request and generating a response.

In the call to POE::Component::Server::TCP's constructor, specify the port to listen on with Port, and your code to handle input with ClientInput. There are many other options and callbacks available, including Address to specify a particular interface address to listen on and ClientFilter to change its default line parser.

Your client input subroutine is called with several parameters, but we use only three: the POE session object representing this connection, the heap for this session, and the latest chunk of input from the client. The first two are standard parameters supplied by POE to all session calls, and the last is supplied by the server component.

The strange assignment line at the start of handle_input merely takes a slice of @_, using constants to identify the position in the method arguments of the session, heap, and first real argument. It's a POE idiom that lets the POE kernel change the actual method parameters and their order, without messing up code that was written before such a change.

```
my ( $session, $heap, $input ) = @_[ SESSION, HEAP, ARG0 ];
```

The session's heap contains a client shell that you use for communicating with the client: $heap->{client}. The put method on that object sends data back to the client. The client's IP address is accessible through $heap->{remote_ip}.

If the action you want to perform in the callback is time-consuming and would slow down communication with other clients that are connected to your server, you may want to use POE sessions. A session is an event-driven machine: you break the time-consuming task into smaller (presumably quicker) chunks, each of which is implemented as a callback. Each callback has one or more events that trigger it.

It's the responsibility of each callback to tell the kernel to queue more events, which in turn pass execution to the next callback (e.g., in the "connect to the database" function, you'd tell the kernel to call the "fetch data from the database" function when you're done). If the action cannot be broken up, it can still be executed asynchronously in another process with POE::Wheel::Run or POE::Component::Child.

POE includes non-blocking timers, I/O watchers, and other resources that you can use to trigger callbacks on external conditions. Wheels and Components are ultimately built from these basic resources.

Information on POE programming is given at *http://poe.perl.org*, including pointers to tutorials given at various conferences. It can take a bit of mental adjustment to get used to the POE framework, but for programs that deal with asynchronous events (such as GUIs and network servers) it's hard to beat POE for portability and functionality.

See Also

The documentation for the CPAN modules POE, POE::Session, POE::Wheel, and POE::Component::Server::TCP; *http://poe.perl.org/*; Recipe 17.14

17.16 Writing a Multihomed Server

Problem

You want to write a server that knows that the machine it runs on has multiple IP addresses, and that it should possibly do different things for each address.

Solution

Don't bind your server to a particular address. Instead, bind to INADDR_ANY. Then once you've accepted a connection, use getsockname on the client socket to find out which address the client connected to:

```
use Socket;

socket(SERVER, PF_INET, SOCK_STREAM, getprotobyname('tcp'));
setsockopt(SERVER, SOL_SOCKET, SO_REUSEADDR, 1);
bind(SERVER, sockaddr_in($server_port, INADDR_ANY))
    or die "Binding: $!\n";

# accept loop
while (accept(CLIENT, SERVER)) {
    $my_socket_address = getsockname(CLIENT);
    ($port, $myaddr)   = sockaddr_in($my_socket_address);
}
```

Discussion

Whereas getpeername (as discussed in Recipe 17.7) returns the address of the remote end of the socket, getsockname returns the address of the local end. When we've bound to INADDR_ANY, thus accepting connections on any address the machine has, we need to use getsockname to identify which address the client connected to.

If you're using IO::Socket::INET, your code will look like this:

```
$server = IO::Socket::INET->new(LocalPort => $server_port,
                                Type      => SOCK_STREAM,
                                Proto     => 'tcp',
                                Listen    => 10)
    or die "Can't create server socket: $@\n";

while ($client = $server->accept()) {
    $my_socket_address = $client->sockname();
    ($port, $myaddr)   = sockaddr_in($my_socket_address);
    # ...
}
```

If you don't specify a local port to IO::Socket::INET->new, your socket will be bound to INADDR_ANY.

If you want your server to listen only for a *particular* virtual host, don't use INADDR_ANY. Instead, bind to a specific host address:

```
use Socket;

$port = 4269;                           # port to bind to
$host = "specific.host.com";            # virtual host to listen on

socket(Server, PF_INET, SOCK_STREAM, getprotobyname("tcp"))
    or die "socket: $!";
bind(Server, sockaddr_in($port, inet_aton($host)))
    or die "bind: $!";
while ($client_address = accept(Client, Server)) {
    # ...
}
```

See Also

The getsockname function in Chapter 29 of *Programming Perl* and in *perlfunc*(1); the documentation for the standard Socket and IO::Socket modules; the section on "Sockets" in Chapter 16 of *Programming Perl* or *perlipc*(1)

17.17 Making a Daemon Server

Problem

You want your program to run as a daemon.

Solution

If you are paranoid and running as root, chroot to a safe directory:

```
chroot("/var/daemon")
    or die "Couldn't chroot to /var/daemon: $!";
```

Fork once, and let the parent exit:

```
$pid = fork;
exit if $pid;
die "Couldn't fork: $!" unless defined($pid);
```

Close the three standard filehandles by reopening them to */dev/null*:

```
for my $handle (*STDIN, *STDOUT, *STDERR) {
    open($handle, "+<", "/dev/null")
        || die "can't reopen $handle to /dev/null: $!";
}
```

Dissociate from the controlling terminal that started us and stop being part of whatever process group we had been a member of:

```
use POSIX;

POSIX::setsid( )
    or die "Can't start a new session: $!";
```

Trap fatal signals, setting a flag to indicate that we need to gracefully exit:

```
$time_to_die = 0;

sub signal_handler {
    $time_to_die = 1;
}

$SIG{INT} = $SIG{TERM} = $SIG{HUP} = \&signal_handler;
# trap or ignore $SIG{PIPE}
```

Wrap your actual server code in a loop:

```
until ($time_to_die) {
    # ...
}
```

Discussion

Before POSIX, every operating system had its own way for a process to tell the operating system "I'm going it alone, please interfere with me as little as possible." POSIX makes it much cleaner. That said, you can still take advantage of any operating system–specific calls if you want to.

The chroot call is one of those non-POSIX calls. It makes a process change where it thinks the directory / is. For instance, after chroot "/var/daemon", if the process tries to read the file */etc/passwd*, it will read */var/daemon/etc/passwd*. A chrooted process needs copies of any files it will run made available inside its new /, of course. For instance, our chrooted process would need */var/daemon/bin/csh* if it were going to glob files. For security reasons, only the superuser may chroot. This is done by FTP servers if you log into them anonymously. It isn't really necessary to become a daemon.

The operating system expects a child's parent to wait when the child dies. Our daemon process has no particular parent to do this, so we need to disinherit it. This we do by forking once and having our parent exit, so that the child is not associated with the process that started the parent. The child then closes the filehandles it got from its parent (STDIN, STDERR, and STDOUT) by reopening them to */dev/null*, and then calls POSIX::setsid to ensure that it is completely dissociated from its parent's terminal.

If you want to make sure any higher numbered file descriptors are also closed, you can use the +<&=*NUMBER* notation to connect up an existing system file descriptor to a Perl filehandle, and then call close on that handle. Here we'll hit all descriptors above 2 and below 256:

```
for (my $fd = 3; $fd < 256; $fd++) {
    open(my $handle, "+<&=$fd");        # XXX: no error checking
    close $handle;                      # XXX: no error checking
}
```

Instead of guessing the highest possible file descriptor number, the "correct" way to handle that would be to write a C extension that called *getdtablesize*(3). This is an exercise we leave up to the user.

Now we're almost ready to begin. We don't want signals like SIGINT to kill us immediately (its default behavior), so we use %SIG to catch them and set a flag saying it's time to exit. Then our main program simply becomes: "While we weren't killed, do something."

The signal SIGPIPE is a special case. It's easy to get (by writing to a filehandle whose other end is closed) and has unforgiving default behavior (it terminates your process). You probably want to either ignore it ($SIG{PIPE} = 'IGNORE') or define your own signal handler to deal with it appropriately.

See Also

Your system's *setsid*(2) and *chroot*(1) manpage (if you have them); the chroot function in Chapter 29 of *Programming Perl* and in *perlfunc*(1); the Unix Socket FAQ at *http://www.ibrado.com/sock-faq/*; *UNIX Network Programming*

17.18 Restarting a Server on Demand

Problem

You want your server to shut down and restart when it receives a HUP signal, just like inetd or httpd.

Solution

Catch the SIGHUP. Within the handler, set harmless signal handlers, unblock signals, and re-execute your program:

```
use POSIX qw(:signal_h sigprocmask);

my $SELF = "/path/to/my/program";
my @ARGS = @ARGV;    # save for later

$SIG{HUP} = \&phoenix;

# your program

sub phoenix {
  # make signals harmless
  for my $nal (qw[ALRM CHLD HUP INT PIPE TERM]) {
    $SIG{$nal} = sub { };
  }

  # reenable them
  my $s = POSIX::SigSet->new;
  my $t = POSIX::SigSet->new;
  sigprocmask(SIG_BLOCK, $s, $t);

  # and restart
  print "Restarting\n";
  exec $SELF => @ARGS;
  die "Couldn't exec $SELF => @ARGS\n";
}
```

Discussion

It sounds simple ("when I get a HUP signal, restart"), but it's tricky. You must know your own program name, and that isn't easy to find out. You could use $0 or the FindBin module. For normal programs, this is fine, but critical system utilities must be more cautious, as there's no guarantee that $0 is valid. You can hardcode the filename and arguments into your program, as we do here. That's not necessarily the most convenient solution, however, so you might want to read the program and arguments from an external file (using the filesystem's protections to ensure it hasn't been tampered with).

Be sure to install your signal handler *after* you define $SELF and @ARGS; otherwise there's a race condition when a SIGHUP could run restart but you don't know the program to run. This would cause your program to die.

Signals are tricky beasts. When you exec to restart your program, the reborn version inherits a set of blocked signals from its parent. Inside a signal handler, that signal is blocked. So if your signal handler simply called exec right away, the new process would have SIGHUP blocked. You could only restart your program once!

But it's not as simple as unblocking SIGHUP using the POSIX module's sigaction. Your program might have blocked other signals (ALRM, CHLD, and the others listed in the phoenix subroutine in the Solution), and those would also be blocked. If you simply unblocked them, your SIGHUP handler might be interrupted by delivery of those signals, so you must first give those signals a harmless handler. That's the purpose of the foreach loop in phoenix.

Some servers don't want to restart on receiving a SIGHUP—they just want to reread their configuration file.

```
$CONFIG_FILE = "/usr/local/etc/myprog/server_conf.pl";
$SIG{HUP} = \&read_config;
sub read_config {
    do $CONFIG_FILE;
}
```

Some observant servers even autoload their configuration files when they notice that those files have been updated. That way you don't have to go out of your way to signal them.

See Also

The exec function in Chapter 29 of *Programming Perl* and in *perlfunc*(1); Recipe 8.16; Recipe 8.17; Recipe 16.15

17.19 Managing Multiple Streams of Input

Problem

The next input to your program could be coming from any number of filehandles, but you don't know which. You've tried using select(), but the need to then do unbuffered I/O is more than you can deal with (and it's making your code very difficult to follow).

Solution

Use the IO::Multiplex module from CPAN. It calls a mux_input() function when input is received over a socket, and handles input and output buffering for you:

```
use IO::Multiplex;
$mux = IO::Multiplex->new();
$mux->add($FH1);
$mux->add($FH2); # ... and so on for all the filehandles to manage
$mux->set_callback_object(__PACKAGE__);  # or an object
$mux->Loop();

sub mux_input {
  my ($package, $mux, $fh, $input) = @_;
```

```
    # $input is ref to the filehandle's input buffer
    # ...
}
```

Discussion

Although you can use select to manage input coming at you from multiple directions, there are many tricks and traps. For example, you can't use <> to read a line of input, because you never know whether the client has sent a full line yet (or will ever finish sending a line). You can't print to a socket without the risk of the output buffer being full and your process blocking. You need to use non-blocking I/O and maintain your own buffers, and, consequently, life rapidly becomes unmanageably complex.

Fortunately, we have a way of hiding complexity: modules. The IO::Multiplex module from CPAN takes care of non-blocking I/O and select for you. You tell it which filehandles to watch, and it tells you when new data arrives. You can even print to the filehandles, and it'll buffer and non-blockingly output it. An IO::Multiplex object manages a pool of filehandles.

Use the add method to tell IO::Multiplex to manage a filehandle. This enables non-blocking I/O and disables the stdio buffering. When IO::Multiplex receives data on one of its managed filehandles, it calls a mux_input method on an object or class of your choosing. Specify where mux_input is by passing a package name (if your callback is a class method) or object value (if your callback is an object method) to the IO::Multiplex set_callback_object method. In the example in the Solution, we pass in the current package name so that IO::Multiplex will call the current package's mux_input method.

Your mux_input callback is called with four parameters: the object or package name that you gave to set_callback_object, the IO::Multiplex object that dispatched the callback, the filehandle from which data was received, and a reference to the input buffer. The callback should delete data from the buffer once it has been processed. For example, to process line by line:

```
sub mux_input {
    my ($obj, $mux, $fh, $buffer) = @_;
    my ($line) = $$buffer =~ s{^(.*)\n}{} or return;
    # ...
}
```

The IO::Multiplex module also takes care of accepting incoming connections on server sockets. Once you have a socket bound and listening (see Recipe 17.2), pass it to the listen method of an IO::Multiplex object:

```
use IO::Socket;
$server = IO::Socket::INET->new(LocalPort => $PORT, Listen => 10)
    or die $@;
$mux->listen($server);
```

When new incoming connections are accepted, the mux_connection callback is called. There are other callbacks, such as for full and partial closure of a filehandle, time-outs, and so on. For a full list of the methods you can use to control an IO::Multiplex object and a full list of the callbacks, see the IO::Multiplex documentation.

Example 17-7 is a rudimentary chat server that uses IO::Multiplex. It listens on port 6901 of the local host address and implements a very rudimentary chat protocol. Every client (see Example 17-8) has a "name," which they can change by sending a line that looks like /nick newname. Every other incoming line of text is sent out to all connected machines, prefaced with the name of the client that sent it.

To test this out, run the server in one window, then start a few clients in other windows. Type something into one and see what appears in the others.

Example 17-7. chatserver

```perl
#!/usr/bin/perl -w
# chatserver - very simple chat server
use IO::Multiplex;
use IO::Socket;
use strict;
my %Name;
my $Server = IO::Socket::INET->new(LocalAddr => "localhost:6901",
                                   Listen    => 10, Reuse => 1,
                                   Proto     => 'tcp') or die $@;
my $Mux = IO::Multiplex->new();
my $Person_Counter = 1;
$Mux->listen($Server);
$Mux->set_callback_object(__PACKAGE__);
$Mux->loop();
exit;
sub mux_connection {
  my ($package, $mux, $fh) = @_;
  $Name{$fh} = [ $fh, "Person " . $Person_Counter++ ];
}
sub mux_eof {
  my ($package, $mux, $fh) = @_;
  delete $Name{$fh};
}
sub mux_input {
  my ($package, $mux, $fh, $input) = @_;
  my $line;
  my $name;
  $$input =~ s{^(.*)\n+}{} or return;
  $line = $1;
  if ($line =~ m{^/nick\s+(\S+)\s*}) {
    my $oldname = $Name{$fh};
    $Name{$fh} = [ $fh, $1 ];
    $line = "$oldname->[1] is now known as $1";
  } else {
    $line = "<$Name{$fh}[1]> $line";
  }
  foreach my $conn_struct (values %Name) {
```

Example 17-7. chatserver (continued)

```
      my $conn = $conn_struct->[0];
      $conn->print("$line\n");
    }
  }
```

Example 17-8. chatclient

```
#!/usr/bin/perl -w
# chatclient - client for the chat server
use IO::Multiplex;
use IO::Socket;
use strict;
my $sock = IO::Socket::INET->new(PeerAddr => "localhost:6901",
                                 Proto    => "tcp") or die $@;
my $Mux = IO::Multiplex->new( );
$Mux->add($sock);
$Mux->add(*STDIN);
$Mux->set_callback_object(__PACKAGE__);
$Mux->loop( );
exit;
sub mux_input {
  my ($package, $mux, $fh, $input) = @_;
  my $line;
  $line = $$input;
  $$input = "";
  if (fileno($fh) == fileno(STDIN)) {
    print $sock $line;
  } else {
    print $line;
  }
}
```

See Also

The documentation for the CPAN module IO::Multiplex; Recipes 17.1, 17.2, 17.20, and 17.21

17.20 Program: backsniff

This program logs attempts to connect to ports. It uses the Sys::Syslog module to log the connection attempt through a Unix socket, with logging level LOG_NOTICE and facility LOG_DAEMON. It uses getsockname to find out what port was connected to and getpeername to find out what machine made the connection. It uses getservbyport to convert the local port number (e.g., 7) into a service name (e.g, "echo").

It produces entries in the system log file like this:

```
May 25 15:50:22 coprolith sniffer: Connection from 207.46.131.141 to
207.46.130.164:echo
```

Install it in the *inetd.conf* file with a line like this:

```
echo    stream  tcp nowait  nobody /usr/scripts/snfsqrd sniffer
```

The program is shown in Example 17-9.

Example 17-9. backsniff

```perl
#!/usr/bin/perl -w
# backsniff - log attempts to connect to particular ports
use strict;
use Sys::Syslog qw(:DEFAULT setlogsock);
use Socket;
# identify my port and address
my $sockname       = getsockname(STDIN)
                       or die "Couldn't identify myself: $!\n";
my ($port, $iaddr) = sockaddr_in($sockname);
my $my_address     = inet_ntoa($iaddr);
# get a name for the service
my $service = (getservbyport ($port, "tcp"))[0] || $port;
# now identify remote address
$sockname          = getpeername(STDIN)
                           or die "Couldn't identify other end: $!\n";
($port, $iaddr)    = sockaddr_in($sockname);
my $ex_address     = inet_ntoa($iaddr);
# and log the information
setlogsock("unix");
openlog("sniffer", "ndelay", "daemon");
syslog("notice", "Connection from %s to %s:%s\n", $ex_address,
       $my_address, $service);
closelog();
```

17.21 Program: fwdport

Imagine that you're nestled deep inside a protective firewall. Somewhere in the outside world is a server that you'd like access to, but only processes on the firewall can reach it. You don't want to log into the firewall machine each time to access that service.

For example, this might arise if your company's ISP provides a news-reading service that seems to come from your main firewall machine, but rejects any NNTP connections from any other address. As the administrator of the firewall, you don't want dozens of people logging onto it, but you would like to let them read and post news from their own workstations.

The program in Example 17-10, *fwdport*, solves this problem in a generic fashion. You may run as many of these as you like, one per outside service. Sitting on the firewall, it can talk to both worlds. When someone wants to access the outside service, they contact this proxy, which connects on their behalf to the external service. To that outside service, the connection is coming from your firewall, so it lets it in. Then your proxy forks off twin processes, one only reading data from the external server and writing that data back to the internal client, the other only reading data from the internal client and writing that data back to the external server.

For example, you might invoke it this way:

```
% fwdport -s nntp -l fw.oursite.com -r news.bigorg.com
```

That means that the program will act as the server for the NNTP service, listening for local connections on the NNTP port on the host *fw.oursite.com*. When one comes in, it contacts *news.bigorg.com* (on the same port), and then ferries data between the remote server and local client.

Here's another example:

```
% fwdport -l myname:9191 -r news.bigorg.com:nntp
```

This time we listen for local connections on port 9191 of the host *myname*, and patch those connecting clients to the remote server *news.bigorg.com* on its NNTP port.

In a way, *fwdport* acts as both a server and a client. It's a server from the perspective of inside the firewall and a client from the perspective of the remote server outside. The program summarizes this chapter well because it demonstrates just about everything we've covered here. It has server activity, client activity, collecting of zombie children, forking and process management, plus much more thrown in.

Example 17-10. fwdport

```perl
#!/usr/bin/perl -w
# fwdport -- act as proxy forwarder for dedicated services

use strict;                 # require declarations
use Getopt::Long;           # for option processing
use Net::hostent;           # by-name interface for host info
use IO::Socket;             # for creating server and client sockets
use POSIX ":sys_wait_h";    # for reaping our dead children

my (
    %Children,              # hash of outstanding child processes
    $REMOTE,                # whom we connect to on the outside
    $LOCAL,                 # where we listen to on the inside
    $SERVICE,               # our service name or port number
    $proxy_server,          # the socket we accept() from
    $ME,                    # basename of this program
);

($ME = $0) =~ s,.*/,,;      # retain just basename of script name

check_args();               # processing switches
start_proxy();              # launch our own server
service_clients();          # wait for incoming
die "NOT REACHED";          # you can't get here from there
```

Example 17-10. fwdport (continued)

```perl
# process command line switches using the extended
# version of the getopts library.
sub check_args {
    GetOptions(
        "remote=s"    => \$REMOTE,
        "local=s"     => \$LOCAL,
        "service=s"   => \$SERVICE,
    ) or die << EOUSAGE;
    usage: $0 [ --remote host ] [ --local interface ] [ --service service ]
EOUSAGE
    die "Need remote"              unless $REMOTE;
    die "Need local or service"    unless $LOCAL || $SERVICE;
}

# begin our server
sub start_proxy {
    my @proxy_server_config = (
      Proto      => 'tcp',
      Reuse      => 1,
      Listen     => SOMAXCONN,
    );
    push @proxy_server_config, LocalPort => $SERVICE if $SERVICE;
    push @proxy_server_config, LocalAddr => $LOCAL    if $LOCAL;
    $proxy_server = IO::Socket::INET->new(@proxy_server_config)
                    or die "can't create proxy server: $@";
    print "[Proxy server on ", ($LOCAL || $SERVICE), " initialized.]\n";
}

sub service_clients {
    my (
        $local_client,        # someone internal wanting out
        $lc_info,             # local client's name/port information
        $remote_server,       # the socket for escaping out
        @rs_config,           # temp array for remote socket options
        $rs_info,             # remote server's name/port information
        $kidpid,              # spawned child for each connection
    );

    $SIG{CHLD} = \&REAPER;        # harvest the moribund

    accepting();

    # an accepted connection here means someone inside wants out
    while ($local_client = $proxy_server->accept()) {
        $lc_info = peerinfo($local_client);
        set_state("servicing local $lc_info");
        printf "[Connect from $lc_info]\n";

        @rs_config = (
            Proto      => 'tcp',
            PeerAddr   => $REMOTE,
        );
```

Example 17-10. fwdport (continued)

```perl
    push(@rs_config, PeerPort => $SERVICE) if $SERVICE;

    print "[Connecting to $REMOTE...";
    set_state("connecting to $REMOTE");                  # see below
    $remote_server = IO::Socket::INET->new(@rs_config)
                    or die "remote server: $@";
    print "done]\n";

    $rs_info = peerinfo($remote_server);
    set_state("connected to $rs_info");

    $kidpid = fork();
    die "Cannot fork" unless defined $kidpid;
    if ($kidpid) {
        $Children{$kidpid} = time();             # remember his start time
        close $remote_server;                    # no use to master
        close $local_client;                     # likewise
        next;                                    # go get another client
    }

    # at this point, we are the forked child process dedicated
    # to the incoming client.  but we want a twin to make i/o
    # easier.

    close $proxy_server;                          # no use to slave

    $kidpid = fork();
    die "Cannot fork" unless defined $kidpid;

    # now each twin sits around and ferries lines of data.
    # see how simple the algorithm is when you can have
    # multiple threads of control?

    # this is the fork's parent, the master's child
    if ($kidpid) {
        set_state("$rs_info --> $lc_info");
        select($local_client); $| = 1;
        print while <$remote_server>;
        kill('TERM', $kidpid);      # kill my twin cause we're done
        }
    # this is the fork's child, the master's grandchild
    else {
        set_state("$rs_info <-- $lc_info");
        select($remote_server); $| = 1;
        print while <$local_client>;
        kill('TERM', getppid());    # kill my twin cause we're done
    }
    exit;                           # whoever's still alive bites it
} continue {
    accepting();
    }
}
```

Example 17-10. fwdport (continued)

```perl
# helper function to produce a nice string in the form HOST:PORT
sub peerinfo {
    my $sock = shift;
    my $hostinfo = gethostbyaddr($sock->peeraddr);
    return sprintf("%s:%s",
                    $hostinfo->name || $sock->peerhost,
                    $sock->peerport);
}

# reset our $0, which on some systems make "ps" report
# something interesting: the string we set $0 to!
sub set_state { $0 = "$ME [@_]" }

# helper function to call set_state
sub accepting {
    set_state("accepting proxy for " . ($REMOTE || $SERVICE));
}

# somebody just died.  keep harvesting the dead until
# we run out of them.  check how long they ran.
sub REAPER {
    my $child;
    my $start;
    while (($child = waitpid(-1,WNOHANG))> 0) {
        if ($start = $Children{$child}) {
            my $runtime = time() - $start;
            printf "Child $child ran %dm%ss\n",
                $runtime / 60, $runtime % 60;
            delete $Children{$child};
        } else {
            print "Bizarre kid $child exited $?\n";
        }
    }
    # If I had to choose between System V and 4.2, I'd resign. --Peter Honeyman
    $SIG{CHLD} = \&REAPER;
};
```

See Also

Getopt::Long(3), *Net::hostent*(3), *IO::Socket*(3), and *POSIX*(3); Recipe 16.19; Recipe 17.10

## CHAPTER 18

Internet Services

This "telephone" has too many shortcomings to be
seriously considered as a means of communication.
The device is inherently of no value to us.
—Western Union internal memo, 1876

18.0 Introduction

Correct use of sockets is only part of writing programs that communicate over the network. Once you have a way for two programs to talk, you still need a *protocol* for communication. This protocol lets each party know when to talk, and it precisely defines who is responsible for which part of the service.

Common Internet protocols are listed in Table 18-1.

Table 18-1. Common Internet protocols

Protocol	Meaning	Action
FTP	File Transfer Protocol	Copying files between remote machines
telnet		Remote login
rsh and rcp	Remote shell and Remote copy	Remote login and remote file copying
NNTP	Network News Transfer Protocol	Reading and posting USENET news
HTTP	Hypertext Transfer Protocol	Transferring documents on the Web
SMTP	Simple Mail Transfer Protocol	Sending mail
POP3	Post Office Protocol	Reading mail

Even something as relatively simple as connecting to a remote computer requires intricate negotiations between client and server. If you had to write the Perl code to implement these protocols each time you wanted to use a network service, you'd probably end up writing a lot of buggy programs, trying to get demoted into a management position, or both.

Fortunately, Perl has modules for these protocols. Most modules implement the client side of the protocol rather than the server side. This is because most clients make one query at a time, whereas a server must be prepared to deal with multiple clients and that code can get quite tricky. That said, there are FTP (Net::FTPServer), HTTP (HTTP::Daemon, POE::Component::Server::HTTP), SMTP (POE::Component: Server::SMTP), and IRC (POE::Component::Server::IRC) servers on CPAN.

Most of these modules fall under the Net:: hierarchy, a common subset of which has been included standard with Perl since v5.8. We use Net::FTP to send and receive files using FTP, Net::NNTP to read and post Usenet news, Net::Telnet (from CPAN) to simulate a connection to another machine, Net::Ping to check whether a machine is alive, and Net::POP3 and Mail::Mailer (from CPAN) to receive and send mail. We cover the CGI protocol in Chapter 19, and with HTTP in Chapter 20.

Recent years have seen a growth in *web services*, i.e., services offered through the web's HTTP protocol. Chapters 19, 20, and 21 address the Web in more detail, but we cover web services in this chapter. The three main ways of offering web services are XML-RPC, SOAP, and REST.

XML-RPC is a simple way to make remote procedure calls. You can transport XML-RPC requests ("I want to call this method with these arguments") and responses ("this fault occurred" or "this is what the method returned") across protocols like HTTP, SMTP, Jabber, and so on. The XMLRPC::Lite modules handle translation between Perl function calls and the XML representation that goes across the wire.

SOAP is more complex than XML-RPC, providing more OO and exception support. It also offers a "document mode," where the response is an XML document rather than an encoded data structure; for example, you might submit an order and get back an XML receipt. SOAP has more built-in data types than XML-RPC and lets you define custom data types using W3C Schema. Like XML-RPC, SOAP runs over a variety of protocols. Both SOAP and XML-RPC are implemented in the SOAP-Lite distribution.

Representational State Transfer (REST) is a different way of viewing web services. Rather than writing remote procedure calls and encoding arguments, which exposes the implementation, REST offers a way to separate implementation from how the client accesses a particular resource. In REST, a URL is an object's address. You can use GET, POST, PUT, and DELETE methods to fetch, change state, create, update, and delete. Because it's more a design philosophy than an API or encoding, we don't cover it here. The book *Programming Web Services with Perl*, by Randy Ray and Pavel Kulchenko (O'Reilly), gives an introduction to REST.

You can thank Graham Barr, whose IO::Socket modules we used for low-level network communication in Chapter 17, for most of these modules. He also wrote Net:: FTP, Net::NNTP, Net::POP3, and Mail::Mailer. Jay Rogers wrote Net::Telnet, and

Paul Kulchenko developed the SOAP-Lite toolkit. Thank these folks that you don't have to reinvent these tricky wheels!

18.1 Simple DNS Lookups

Problem

You want to find the IP address of a host or turn an IP address into a name. Network servers do this to authenticate their clients, and clients do it when the user gives them a hostname. But Perl's socket library requires an IP address. Furthermore, many servers produce log files containing IP addresses, but hostnames are more useful to analysis software and humans.

Solution

If you have a name like www.perl.com, use gethostbyname if you want all addresses:

```
use Socket;

@addresses = gethostbyname($name)    or die "Can't resolve $name: $!\n";
@addresses = map { inet_ntoa($_) } @addresses[4 .. $#addresses];
# @addresses is a list of IP addresses ("208.201.239.48", "208.201.239.49")
```

Or use inet_aton if you need only the first address:

```
use Socket;

$address = inet_ntoa(inet_aton($name));
# $address is a single IP address "208.201.239.48"
```

If you have an IP address like "208.201.239.48", use:

```
use Socket;

$name = gethostbyaddr(inet_aton($address), AF_INET)
            or die "Can't resolve $address: $!\n";
# $name is the hostname ("www.perl.com")
```

Discussion

This process is complicated because the functions are mere wrappers for C system calls, so you have to convert IP addresses from ASCII strings ("208.146.240.1") into C structures. The standard Socket module provides inet_aton to convert from ASCII to the packed numeric format and inet_ntoa to convert back:

```
use Socket;
$packed_address = inet_aton("208.146.140.1");
$ascii_address  = inet_ntoa($packed_address);
```

The gethostbyname function takes a string containing the hostname (or IP address). In scalar context, it returns the remote IP address suitable for passing to inet_ntoa (or undef on error). In list context, it returns a list of at least five elements (or an empty list on error). The returned list is:

Index	Meaning
0	Official name of host
1	Aliases (space-separated string)
2	Address type (normally AF_INET)
3	Length of address structure (irrelevant)
4,5, ...	Address structures

A hostname may have more than one address, as often seen for busy web sites where many machines serve identical web pages to share the load. In such situations, the DNS server that provides addresses rotates them to balance the load. If you need to pick an IP address to connect to, just select the first. But if it doesn't work, try the rest as well.

```
$packed = gethostbyname($hostname)
            or die "Couldn't resolve address for $hostname: $!\n";
$address = inet_ntoa($packed);
print "I will use $address as the address for $hostname\n";
```

If you're using hostnames to permit or deny access to a service, be careful. Anyone can set their DNS server to identify their machine as www.whitehouse.gov, www.yahoo.com, or this.is.not.funny. You can't know whether the machine really has the name it claims to have until you use gethostbyname and check that the original address is in the address list for the name.

```
# $address is the IP address I'm checking, like "128.138.243.20"
use Socket;
$name   = gethostbyaddr(inet_aton($address), AF_INET)
            or die "Can't look up $address : $!\n";
@addr   = gethostbyname($name)
            or die "Can't look up $name : $!\n";
$found  = grep { $address eq inet_ntoa($_) } @addr[4..$#addr];
```

It turns out that even with this algorithm, you can't be absolutely sure of the name due to a variety of mechanisms that can circumvent this technique. Even the IP address from which packets appear to be coming can be spoofed, so you should never rely on the network layer for authentication. Always do authentication yourself (with passwords or cryptographic challenges) when it matters, because the IPv4 network was not designed to provide security.

More information is kept about a host than just addresses and aliases. To access this information, use the Net::DNS module from CPAN. For instance, Example 18-1 shows how to retrieve the MX (mail exchange) records for an arbitrary host.

Example 18-1. mxhost

```perl
#!/usr/bin/perl -w
# mxhost - find mx exchangers for a host
use Net::DNS;
use strict;
my ($host, $res, @mx);
$host = shift or die "usage: $0 hostname\n";
$res = Net::DNS::Resolver->new( );
@mx = mx($res, $host)
    or die "Can't find MX records for $host (".$res->errorstring.")\n";
foreach my $record (@mx) {
    print $record->preference, " ", $record->exchange, "\n";
}
```

Here's some output:

```
% mxhost cnn.com
10 atlmail1.turner.com
10 atlmail4.turner.com
20 atlmail2.turner.com
30 nymail1.turner.com
```

The inet_aton function takes a string containing a hostname or IP address, as does gethostbyname, but it returns only the first IP address for the host. To find them all, you'll need to add more code. The Net::hostent module provides by-name access for that; Example 18-2 shows an example of its use.

Example 18-2. hostaddrs

```perl
#!/usr/bin/perl -w
# hostaddrs - canonize name and show addresses
use Socket;
use Net::hostent;
use strict;
my ($name, $hent, @addresses);
$name = shift || die "usage: $0 hostname\n";
if ($hent = gethostbyname($name)) {
    $name       = $hent->name;              # in case different
    my $addr_ref = $hent->addr_list;
    @addresses = map { inet_ntoa($_) } @$addr_ref;
}
print "$name => @addresses\n";
```

Here's the output:

```
% hostaddrs www.oreilly.com
www.oreilly.com => 208.201.239.37 208.201.239.36

% hostaddrs www.whitehouse.gov
a1289.g.akamai.net => 216.241.36.232 216.241.36.230
```

See Also

The gethostbyname and gethostbyaddr functions in Chapter 29 of *Programming Perl* and in *perlfunc*(1); the documentation for the Net::DNS module from CPAN; the documentation for the standard Socket and Net::hostent modules

18.2 Being an FTP Client

Problem

You want to connect to an FTP server and transfer files. For example, you might want to automate the one-time transfer of many files or automatically mirror an entire section of an FTP server.

Solution

Use the Net::FTP module:

```
use Net::FTP;

$ftp = Net::FTP->new("ftp.host.com")   or die "Can't connect: $@\n";
$ftp->login($username, $password)      or die "Couldn't login\n";
$ftp->cwd($directory)                  or die "Couldn't change directory\n";
$ftp->get($filename)                   or die "Couldn't get $filename\n";
$ftp->put($filename)                   or die "Couldn't put $filename\n";
```

Discussion

Using the Net::FTP module is a three-part process: *connect* to a server, identify and *authenticate* yourself, and *transfer* files. All interaction with the FTP server happens through method calls on a Net::FTP object. If an error occurs, methods return undef in scalar context or the empty list in list context.

The connection is established with the new constructor. If an error occurs, $@ is set to an error message and new returns undef. The first argument is the hostname of the FTP server, optionally followed by named options:

```
$ftp = Net::FTP->new("ftp.host.com",
                     Timeout => 30,
                     Debug   => 1)
    or die "Can't connect: $@\n";
```

The Timeout option gives the number of seconds all operations wait before giving up. Debug sets the debugging level (non-zero sends copies of all commands to STDERR). Firewall takes a string as an argument, specifying the machine acting as an FTP proxy. Port lets you select an alternate port number (the default is 21, the standard port for FTP). Finally, if the Passive option is set to true, all transfers are done passively (some firewalls and proxies require this). The Firewall and Passive options override the environment variables FTP_FIREWALL and FTP_PASSIVE.

Having connected, the next step is to authenticate. Normally, you'll want to call login with up to three arguments: username, password, and account.

```
$ftp->login( )
    or die "Couldn't authenticate.\n";

$ftp->login($username)
    or die "Still couldn't authenticate.\n";

$ftp->login($username, $password)
    or die "Couldn't authenticate, even with explicit username
            and password.\n";

$ftp->login($username, $password, $account)
    or die "No dice.  It hates me.\n";
```

If you call login with no arguments, Net::FTP uses the Net::Netrc module to find settings for the host you've connected to. If none are found, anonymous login is attempted (username anonymous, password -anonymous@). If no password is given and the username anonymous is used, the user's mail address is supplied as the password. The optional account argument is not used on most systems. If the authentication fails, login returns undef.

Once authenticated, the usual FTP commands are available as methods called on your Net::FTP object. The get and put methods fetch and send files, respectively. To send a file, use:

```
$ftp->put($localfile, $remotefile)
    or die "Can't send $localfile: $!\n";
```

If you omit the second argument, the remote file will have the same name as the local file. You can also send from a filehandle (in which case the remote filename must be given as the second argument):

```
$ftp->put(*STDIN, $remotefile)
    or die "Can't send from STDIN: $!\n";
```

If the transfer is interrupted, the remote file is not automatically deleted. The put method returns the remote filename if it succeeded, or undef on error.

To fetch a file, use the get method, which returns the local filename, or undef on error:

```
$ftp->get($remotefile, $localfile)
    or die "Can't fetch $remotefile : $!\n";
```

You can also get into a filehandle, in which case the filehandle is returned (or undef on error):

```
$ftp->get($remotefile, *STDOUT)
    or die "Can't fetch $remotefile: $!\n";
```

Pass get an optional third argument, representing an offset into the remote file, to begin the transfer at that offset. Received bytes are appended to the local file.

The type method changes the file translation mode. Pass it a string ("A", "I", "E", or "L") and it will return the previous translation mode. The ascii, binary, ebcdic, and byte methods call type with the appropriate string. If an error occurs (the FTP server does not do EBCDIC, for example), type and its helper methods return undef.

Use cwd($remotedir) and pwd to set and fetch the current remote directory. Both return true if successful, false otherwise. If you cwd(".."), the cdup method is called to change the directory to the parent of the current directory. Call cwd without an argument to change to the root directory.

```
$ftp->cwd("/pub/perl/CPAN/images/g-rated");
print "I'm in the directory ", $ftp->pwd( ), "\n";
```

mkdir($remotedir) and rmdir($remotedir) make and delete directories on the remote machine. You have the built-in mkdir and rmdir functions to make and delete empty directories on the local machine. To create all directories up to the given directory, pass a true second argument to mkdir. For instance, to create /pub, /pub/gnat, and /pub/gnat/perl directories, say:

```
$ftp->mkdir("/pub/gnat/perl", 1)
    or die "Can't create /pub/gnat/perl recursively: $!\n";
```

If mkdir succeeds, the full path to the newly created directory is returned; otherwise, it returns undef.

The ls and dir methods retrieve a list of files in a remote directory. Traditionally, dir gives you a more verbose listing than ls, but neither has a standard format. Most Unix FTP servers return the output of *ls* and *ls -l* respectively, but you can't guarantee that behavior from every FTP server. In list context, these methods return the list of lines returned by the server. In scalar context, they return a reference to an array containing those lines.

```
@lines = $ftp->ls("/pub/gnat/perl")
    or die "Can't get a list of files in /pub/gnat/perl: $!";
$ref_to_lines = $ftp->dir("/pub/perl/CPAN/src/latest.tar.gz")
    or die "Can't check status of latest.tar.gz: $!\n";
```

When you're done and want to finish gracefully, use the quit method:

```
$ftp->quit( )    or warn "Couldn't quit.  Oh well.\n";
```

Other methods rename, change ownership and permissions of remote files, check the size of the remote file, and so on. Read the Net::FTP documentation for details.

To mirror files between machines, use the excellent *mirror* program written in Perl by Lee McLoughlin. Look for it on the Web at *http://sunsite.doc.ic.ac.uk/packages/mirror/*.

See Also

Your system's *ftp*(1) and *ftpd*(8) manpages (if you have them); the documentation for the Net::FTP module

18.3 Sending Mail

Problem

You want your program to send mail. Some programs monitor system resources like disk space and notify appropriate people when disk space becomes dangerously low. CGI script authors may not want programs to report errors like "the database is down" to the user, preferring instead to send mail to the database administrator about the problem.

Solution

Use the CPAN module Mail::Mailer:

```
use Mail::Mailer;

$mailer = Mail::Mailer->new("sendmail");
$mailer->open({ From    => $from_address,
                To      => $to_address,
                Subject => $subject,
              })
    or die "Can't open: $!\n";
print $mailer $body;
$mailer->close();
```

Or use the sendmail program directly:

```
open(SENDMAIL, "|/usr/lib/sendmail -oi -t -odq")
                    or die "Can't fork for sendmail: $!\n";
print SENDMAIL <<"EOF";
From: User Originating Mail <me\@host>
To: Final Destination <you\@otherhost>
Subject: A relevant subject line

Body of the message goes here, in as many lines as you like.
EOF
close(SENDMAIL)     or warn "sendmail didn't close nicely";
```

Discussion

You have three choices for sending mail from your program. You can call another program normally used to send mail, such as *Mail* or *mailx*; these are called MUAs or *Mail User Agents*. You can use a system-level mail program, such as *sendmail*; this is an MTA, or *Mail Transport Agent*. Or you can connect to an Simple Mail Transfer Protocol (SMTP) server. Unfortunately, there's no standard user-level mail program, *sendmail* doesn't have a standard location, and SMTP isn't particularly simple. The CPAN module Mail::Mailer hides these complexities from you.

Create a Mail::Mailer object with Mail::Mailer->new. If you don't pass any arguments, it uses the default mail sending method (probably a program like *mail*).

Arguments to new select an alternate way to send the message. The first argument is the type of delivery method ("mail" for a Unix mail user agent, "sendmail" for sendmail, and "smtp" to connect to an SMTP server). The optional second argument is that program's path.

For instance, to instruct Mail::Mailer to use *sendmail* instead of its default:

```
$mailer = Mail::Mailer->new("sendmail");
```

Here's how to tell it to use */u/gnat/bin/funkymailer* instead of *mail*:

```
$mailer = Mail::Mailer->new("mail", "/u/gnat/bin/funkymailer");
```

Here's how to use SMTP with the machine *mail.myisp.com* as the mail server:

```
$mailer = Mail::Mailer->new("smtp", "mail.myisp.com");
```

If an error occurs at any part of Mail::Mailer, die is called. To check for these exceptions, wrap your mail-sending code in eval and check $@ afterward:

```
eval {
    $mailer = Mail::Mailer->new("bogus", "arguments");
    # ...
};
if ($@) {
    # the eval failed
    print "Couldn't send mail: $@\n";
} else {
    # the eval succeeded
    print "The authorities have been notified.\n";
}
```

The new constructor raises an exception if you provide arguments it doesn't understand, or if you specify no arguments and it doesn't have a default method. Mail:: Mailer won't run a program or connect to the SMTP server until you call the open method with the message headers:

```
$mailer->open( { From    => 'Nathan Torkington <gnat@frii.com>',
                 To      => 'Tom Christiansen <tchrist@perl.com>',
                 Subject => 'The Perl Cookbook' } );
```

The open method raises an exception if the program or server couldn't be opened. If open succeeds, you may treat $mailer as a filehandle and print the body of your message to it:

```
print $mailer << EO_SIG;
Are we ever going to finish this book?
My wife is threatening to leave me.
She says I love EMACS more than I love her.
Do you have a recipe that can help me?

Nat
EO_SIG
```

When you're done, call the close function on the Mail::Mailer object:

```
close($mailer)                    or die "can't close mailer: $!";
```

If you want to go it alone and communicate with *sendmail* directly, use something like this:

```
open(SENDMAIL, "|/usr/sbin/sendmail -oi -t -odq")
            or die "Can't fork for sendmail: $!\n";
print SENDMAIL << "EOF";
From: Fancy Chef <chef@example.com>
To: Grubby Kitchenhand <hand@example.com>
Subject: Re: The Perl Cookbook

(1) We will never finish the book.
(2) No man who uses EMACS is deserving of love.
(3) I recommend coq au vi.

Frank Wah
EOF
close(SENDMAIL);
```

This is a straightforward use of open to run another program (see Recipe 16.4). You need to specify the full path to sendmail because its location varies from machine to machine. It is often found in places like */usr/lib* or */usr/sbin*. The flags we give to *sendmail* say not to exit when a line with only a dot is read (-oi), to read the message headers to decide whom to send it to (-t), and to queue the message instead of attempting immediate delivery (-odq). This last option is important only when sending many messages (in bulk); omitting it would quickly swamp the machine with *sendmail* processes. For immediate delivery of your message (for instance, you're testing your program or the mail is urgent), remove -odq from the command line.

We print an entire message, headers and then body, separated by a blank line. There are no special escapes to insert newlines (as some user mail programs have), so all text is literal. *sendmail* adds headers like Date and Message-ID, which you shouldn't generate yourself anyway.

Some ports of Perl (Windows and Mac OS 9 particularly) don't have *sendmail* or *mail*. In these cases, you should find yourself a receptive SMTP server.

See Also

The open function in Chapter 29 of *Programming Perl* and in *perlfunc*(1); Recipe 16. 4; Recipe 16.10; Recipe 16.19; Recipe 19.5; the RFCs dictating the SMTP protocol, RFC 821, *Simple Mail Transfer Protocol*, as amended by later RFCs; the documentation for the Mail::Mailer module from CPAN

18.4 Reading and Posting Usenet News Messages

Problem

You want to connect to a Usenet news server to read and post messages. Your program could send a periodic posting to a newsgroup,* summarize a newsgroup, or identify first-time contributors in a newsgroup so you can send them a helpful welcome message.

Solution

Use the Net::NNTP module:

```
use Net::NNTP;

$server = Net::NNTP->new("news.host.dom")
    or die "Can't connect to news server: $@\n";
($narticles, $first, $last, $name) = $server->group( "misc.test" )
    or die "Can't select misc.test\n";
$headers  = $server->head($first)
    or die "Can't get headers from article $first in $name\n";
$bodytext = $server->body($first)
    or die "Can't get body from article $first in $name\n";
$article  = $server->article($first)
    or die "Can't get article $first from $name\n";

$server->postok( )
    or warn "Server didn't tell me I could post.\n";

$server->post( [ @lines ] )
    or die "Can't post: $!\n";
```

Discussion

Usenet is a distributed bulletin board system. Servers exchange messages to ensure that each server gets all messages for the newsgroups it carries. Each server sets its own expiration criteria for how long messages stay on the server. Client newsreaders connect to their designated server (usually belonging to their company, ISP, or university) and can read existing postings and contribute new ones.

Each message (or article, as they're also known) has a set of headers and a body, separated by a blank line. Articles are identified in two ways: the *message ID* header and an *article number* within a newsgroup. An article's message ID is stored in the message itself and is guaranteed unique no matter which news server the article was read

---

* If so, be sure to check out Ian Kluft's *auto-faq* program at *http://www.novia.net/~pschleck/auto-faq/*.

from. When an article references others, it does so by message ID. A message ID is a string like:

```
<0401@jpl-devvax.JPL.NASA.GOV>
```

An article can also be identified by its newsgroup and article number within the group. Each news server assigns its own article numbers, so they're valid only for the news server you got them from.

The Net::NNTP constructor connects to the specified news server. If the connection couldn't be made, it returns undef and sets $@ to an error message. If the connection was successful, new returns a new Net::NNTP object:

```
$server = Net::NNTP->new("news.mycompany.com")
    or die "Couldn't connect to news.mycompany.com: $@\n";
```

Once connected, fetch a list of newsgroups with the list method. This returns a reference to a hash whose keys are newsgroup names. Each value is a reference to an array consisting of the first valid article number in the group, the last valid article number in the group, and a string of flags. Flags are typically "y", meaning you may post, but could be "m" for moderated or "=NAME", meaning that the group is an alias for the newsgroup "NAME". Your server might carry over 60,000 newsgroups, so fetching a list of all groups can take a while.

```
$grouplist = $server->list()
    or die "Couldn't fetch group list\n";

foreach $group (keys %$grouplist) {
    if ($grouplist->{$group}->[2] eq 'y') {
        # I can post to $group
    }
}
```

Much as FTP has the concept of a current directory, the Network News Transfer Protocol (NNTP) has the concept of a current group. Set the current group with the group method:

```
($narticles, $first, $last, $name) = $server->group("comp.lang.perl.misc")
    or die "Can't select comp.lang.perl.misc\n";
```

The group method returns a four-element list: the number of articles in the group, the first article number, the last article number, and the name of the group. If the group does not exist, it returns an empty list.

There are two ways to retrieve articles: call article with a message ID, or select a group with group and then call article with an article number. In scalar context, article returns a reference to an array of lines. In list context, it returns a list of lines. If an error occurs, article returns false:

```
@lines = $server->article($message_id)
    or die "Can't fetch article $message_id: $!\n";
```

Fetch an article's header or body with the head and body methods. Like article, these methods take an article number or message ID and return a list of lines or an array reference.

```
@group = $server->group("comp.lang.perl.misc")
    or die "Can't select group comp.lang.perl.misc\n";
@lines = $server->head($group[1])
    or die "Can't get headers from first article in comp.lang.perl.misc\n";
```

To post an article, give the post method a list of lines or a reference to an array of lines. It returns true if the post succeeded, false otherwise.

```
$server->post(@message)
    or die "Can't post\n";
```

Use the postok method to find out whether you may post to that server:

```
unless ($server->postok()) {
    warn "You may not post.\n";
}
```

Read the manpage for Net::NNTP for a complete list of methods.

See Also

The documentation for the Net::NNTP module; RFC 977, *Network News Transfer Protocol*; your system's *trn*(1) and *innd*(8) manpages (if you have them)

18.5   Reading Mail with POP3

Problem

You want to fetch mail from a POP3 server. This lets you write a program to summarize your unread mail, move it from a remote server to a local mailbox, or toggle between Internet and local mail systems.

Solution

Use the Net::POP3 module:

```
$pop = Net::POP3->new($mail_server)
    or die "Can't open connection to $mail_server : $!\n";
defined ($pop->login($username, $password))
    or die "Can't authenticate: $!\n";
$messages = $pop->list
    or die "Can't get list of undeleted messages: $!\n";
foreach $msgid (keys %$messages) {
    $message = $pop->get($msgid);
    unless (defined $message) {
        warn "Couldn't fetch $msgid from server: $!\n";
        next;
    }
```

```
    # $message is a reference to an array of lines
    $pop->delete($msgid);
}
```

Discussion

Traditionally, mail has been a three-party system: the *MTA* (Mail Transport Agent, a system program like *sendmail*) delivers mail to the *spool*, where it is read by the *MUA* (Mail User Agent, a program like *mail*). This dates from the days of big servers holding mail and users reading it through dumb terminals. As PCs and networks entered the picture, the need arose for MUAs like Pine to run on different machines than the one housing the spool. The Post Office Protocol (POP) implements efficient message listing, reading, and deleting over a TCP/IP session.

The Net::POP3 module is a POP client. That is, it lets your Perl program act as an MUA. The first step in using Net::POP3 is to create a new Net::POP3 object. Pass new the name of the POP3 server:

```
$pop = Net::POP3->new( "pop.myisp.com" )
    or die "Can't connect to pop.myisp.com: $!\n";
```

All Net::POP3 functions return undef or the empty list upon error, depending on the calling context. If an error occurs, the fickle $! variable just might contain a meaningful error message—but also might not.

You may optionally pass further arguments to new using named-parameter pairs. The "Timeout" parameter specifies a timeout value in seconds for all network operations.

```
$pop = Net::POP3->new( "pop.myisp.com",
                       Timeout => 30 )
    or die "Can't connect to pop.myisp.com : $!\n";
```

Authenticate yourself to the POP3 server with the login method. It takes two arguments, username and password, but both are optional. If the username is omitted, the current username is used. If the password is omitted, Net::POP3 tries to use Net::Netrc to find a password:

```
defined ($pop->login("gnat", "S33kr1T Pa55wOrD"))
    or die "Hey, my username and password didn't work!\n";

defined ($pop->login( "midget" ))          # use Net::Netrc to find password
    or die "Authentication failed.\n";

defined ($pop->login( ))                    # current username and Net::Netrc
    or die "Authentication failed.  Miserably.\n";
```

The login method sends the password in plain text across the network. This is virtually always undesirable, so you can use the apop method instead. It works exactly like login, except that it encrypts the password:

```
$pop->apop( $username, $password )
    or die "Couldn't authenticate: $!\n";
```

Once authenticated, you may then access the spool with `list`, `get`, and `delete`. The `list` method gives you a list of undeleted messages in the spool. It returns a hash where each key is a message number and each value the size in bytes of the corresponding message:

```
%undeleted = $pop->list( );
foreach $msgnum (keys %undeleted) {
    print "Message $msgnum is $undeleted{$msgnum} bytes long.\n";
}
```

To retrieve a message, call `get` with the message number. It returns a reference to an array of lines in the message:

```
print "Retrieving $msgnum : ";
$message = $pop->get($msgnum);
if ($message) {
    # succeeded
    print "\n";
    print @$message;                    # print the message
} else {
        # failed
    print "failed ($!)\n";
}
```

The `delete` method marks a message as deleted. When you call `quit` to terminate your POP3 session, the messages marked as deleted are removed from the mailbox. The `reset` method undoes any `delete` calls made during the session. If the session is terminated by the Net::POP3 object being destroyed (e.g., the only reference to the object went out of scope), `reset` is called automatically.

You have probably noticed there's no way to *send* mail. POP3 only supports reading and deleting existing messages. To send new ones, you still have to use programs like *mail* or *sendmail*, or do SMTP. In other words, you still need Recipe 18.3.

The task attempted by POP3—connecting mail clients and mail servers—is also attempted by the IMAP protocol. IMAP has more features and is more typically seen on very large sites.

See Also

The documentation for the Net::POP3 module; RFC 1734, *POP3 AUTHentication command*; RFC 1957, *Some Observations on Implementations of the Post Office Protocol*

18.6   Simulating Telnet from a Program

Problem

You want to simulate a *telnet* connection from your program by logging into a remote machine, issuing commands, and reacting to what is returned. This has many applications, from automating tasks on machines you can telnet to but which don't support scripting or *rsh*, to simply testing whether a machine's Telnet daemon is still running properly.

Solution

Use the CPAN module Net::Telnet:

```
use Net::Telnet;

$t = Net::Telnet->new( Timeout => 10,
                       Prompt  => '/%/',
                       Host    => $hostname );

$t->login($username, $password);
@files = $t->cmd("ls");
$t->print("top");
(undef, $process_string) = $t->waitfor('/\d+ processes/');
$t->close;
```

Discussion

Net::Telnet provides an object-oriented interface to the Telnet protocol. Create a connection with `Net::Telnet->new`, then interact with the remote machine using method calls on the resulting object.

Give the `new` method a list of named-parameter pairs, much like initializing a hash. We'll cover only a few possible parameters. The most important is `Host`, the machine you're telnetting to. The default host is `localhost`. To connect to a port other than the one Telnet normally uses, specify this in the `Port` option. Error handling is done through the function whose reference is specified in the `Errmode` parameter.

Another important option is `Prompt`. When you log in or run a command, Net::Telnet uses the `Prompt` pattern to determine when the login or command has completed. The default `Prompt` is:

```
/[\$%#>] $/
```

which matches the common Unix shell prompts. If the prompt on the remote machine doesn't match the default pattern, you have to specify your own. Remember to include slashes.

`Timeout` lets you control how long (in seconds) network operations wait before they give up. The default is 10 seconds.

An error or timeout in the Net::Telnet module raises an exception by default, which, if uncaught, prints a message to `STDERR` and exits. To change this, pass `new` a subroutine reference to the `Errmode` argument. If instead of a code subroutine you specify the string `"return"` as the `Errmode`, methods return undef (in scalar context) or an empty list (in list context) on error, with the error message available via the errmsg method:

```
$telnet = Net::Telnet->new( Errmode => sub { main::log(@_) }, ... );
```

The login method sends a username and password to the remote machine. It uses the Prompt to decide when the login is complete and times out if the machine doesn't reply with a prompt:

```
$telnet->login($username, $password)
    or die "Login failed: @{[ $telnet->errmsg( ) ]}\n";
```

To run a program and gather its output, use the cmd method. Pass it the string to send; it returns the command output as one line per list element in list context, or as one long line in scalar context. It waits for the Prompt before returning.

Separate sending the command from reception of its output with the print and waitfor methods, as we do in the Solution. The waitfor method takes either a single string containing a Perl regular expression in slashes:

```
$telnet->waitfor('/--more--/')
```

or named arguments. Timeout specifies a timeout to override the default, Match is a string containing a match operator as shown earlier, and String is a literal string to find:

```
$telnet->waitfor(String => 'greasy smoke', Timeout => 30)
```

In scalar context, waitfor returns true if the pattern or string was found. Otherwise, the Errmode action is performed. In list context, it returns two strings: any text before the match and the matching text itself.

See Also

The documentation for the Net::Telnet module from CPAN; RFCs 854–856, as amended by later RFCs

18.7 Pinging a Machine

Problem

You want to test whether a machine is alive. Network- and system-monitoring software often use the ping program as an indication of availability.

Solution

Use the standard Net::Ping module:

```
use Net::Ping;

$p = Net::Ping->new( )
```

```
        or die "Can't create new ping object: $!\n";
print "$host is alive" if $p->ping($host);
$p->close;
```

Discussion

Testing whether a machine is up isn't as easy as it sounds. It's not only possible but
also unpleasantly common for machines to respond to the *ping* command when they
have no working services. It's better to think of *ping* as testing whether a machine is
reachable, rather than whether the machine is doing its job. To check the latter, you
must try its services (Telnet, FTP, web, NFS, etc.).

In the form shown in the Solution, Net::Ping attempts to connect to the TCP *echo*
port (port number 7) on the remote machine. The ping method returns true if the
connection could be made, false otherwise.

You can also ping using other protocols by passing the protocol name to new. Valid
protocols are *tcp*, *udp*, *syn*, and *icmp* (all lowercase). A UDP ping attempts to connect to the echo port (port 7) on the remote machine, sends a datagram, and
attempts to read the response. The machine is considered unreachable if it can't connect, if the reply datagram isn't received, or if the reply differs from the original datagram. An ICMP ping uses the ICMP protocol, just like the *ping*(8) command. On
Unix machines, you must be the superuser to use the ICMP protocol:

```
# use TCP if we're not root, ICMP if we are
$pong = Net::Ping->new( $> ? "tcp" : "icmp" );

(defined $pong)
    or die "Couldn't create Net::Ping object: $!\n";

if ($pong->ping("kingkong.com")) {
    print "The giant ape lives!\n";
} else {
    print "All hail mighty Gamera, friend of children!\n";
}
```

A SYN ping is asynchronous: you first send out many pings and then receive
responses by repeatedly invoking the ack method. This method returns a list containing the hostname, round-trip time, and the IP address that responded:

```
$net = Net::Ping->new('syn');
foreach $host (@hosts) {
    $net->ping($host);
}
while (($host, $rtt, $ip) = $net->ack()) {
    printf "Response from %s (%s) in %d\n", $host, $ip, $rtt;
}
```

Of course, most machines don't take a second or more to set up a TCP connection. If
they did, you'd find web browsing painfully slow! To get anything but 0 second
round-trip times back from this test, you need more granularity in your time

measurements. The hires method uses Time::HiRes (see Recipe 3.9) to measure ACK times. The following code snippet enables high-resolution timers (changed code appears in bold):

```
$net = Net::Ping->new('syn');
$net->hires();               # enable high-resolution timers
foreach $host (@hosts) {
  $net->ping($host);
}
while (($host, $rtt, $ip) = $net->ack()) {
  printf "Response from %s (%s) in %.2f\n", $host, $ip, $rtt;
}
```

The value in $rtt is still in seconds, but it might have a decimal portion. The value is accurate to milliseconds.

If using TCP to ping, set the port that Net::Ping uses. This might mean a service is present although any industrial-grade monitoring system will also test whether the service responds to requests:

```
$test = Net::Ping->new('tcp');
$test->{port_num} = getservbyname("ftp", "tcp");
if (! $test->ping($host)) {
  warn "$host isn't serving FTP!\n";
}
```

All these ping methods are prone to failure. Some sites filter the ICMP protocol at their router, so Net::Ping would say such machines are down even though you could connect using other protocols. Similarly, many machines disable the TCP and UDP *echo* services, causing TCP and UDP pings to fail. There is no way to know whether the ping failed because the service is disabled or filtered, or because the machine is actually down.

See Also

The documentation for the Net::Ping module from CPAN; your system's *ping*(8), *tcp*(4), *udp* (4), and *icmp*(4) manpages (if you have them); RFCs 792 and 950

18.8   Accessing an LDAP Server

Problem

You want to fetch or maintain information from a Lightweight Directory Access Protocol (LDAP) server. For example, you have a list of email addresses in your company, and you want correct names for those people.

Solution

Use the Net::LDAP module from CPAN. For example, to search, use:

```
use Net::LDAP;

$ldap = Net::LDAP->new("ldap.example.com") or die $@;
$ldap->bind( );
$mesg = $ldap->search(base => $base_dn,
                      filter => $FILTER);

$mesg->code( ) && die $mesg->error;

foreach $result ($mesg->all_entries) {
    # do something with $result
}
$ldap->unbind( );
```

Discussion

The Net::LDAP module manages an LDAP session. It is a pure Perl module, so it doesn't require a C compiler to install. To use it effectively, though, you'll need to know a little about LDAP in general and the query syntax in particular. If you're new to LDAP, you might want to read the articles at *http://www.onlamp.com/topics/apache/ldap*.

The four steps to working with an LDAP server are connecting, authenticating, interacting, and logging off. Interacting includes searching, adding, deleting, and altering records.

The connect method establishes a connection to the LDAP server and is immediately followed by a call to the bind method. If you give no argument to bind, you log into the LDAP server anonymously. You can give a fully qualified Distinguished Name (DN) and password to authenticate yourself:

```
$ldap->bind("cn=directory manager,ou=gurus,dc=oreilly,dc=com",
            password => "timtoady") or die $@;
```

This sends the username and password unencrypted over the wire. For encrypted access, pass a sasl parameter to bind to use an Authen::SASL object to authenticate with.

The search method returns an object containing a set of entries. You can fetch that entire set of entries with all_entries as shown in the Solution, or one by one thus:

```
$num_entries = $mesg->count( );
for ($i=0; $i < $num_entries; $i++) {
  my $entry = $mesg->entry($i);
  # ...
}
```

You can even pop entries off the results stack:

```
while (my $entry = $mesg->shift_entry) {
  # ...
}
```

Each entry is an object with methods for querying attributes:

```
foreach $attr ($entry->attributes) {
  @values = $entry->get($attr);
  print "$attr : @values\n";
}
```

For a complete list of valid entry methods, see the Net::LDAP::Entry documentation. The DN is not an attribute of an entry, so to obtain the DN for an entry, use the dn method:

```
$dn = $entry->dn;
```

The basic components of a search are the base and the filter. The *base* marks the top of the tree being searched, and *filter* indicates which records you're interested in:

```
$mesg = $ldap->search(base => "o=oreilly.com",
                      filter => "uid=gnat");
```

You can limit how much of the tree is searched with an additional scope parameter: setting it to "base" searches only the base node of the tree. A value of "one" searches only nodes directly beneath the named node. The default value is "sub", meaning every node under the one named.

You can also administrate as well as search. For example, the add method inserts a record into the LDAP database:

```
$res = $ldap->add("cn=Sherlock Holmes, o=Sleuths B Us, c=gb",
       attr => [ cn     => ["Sherlock Holmes", "S Holmes"],
                 sn     => "Holmes",
                 mail   => 'sherlock@221b.uk',
                 objectclass => [qw(top person organizationalPerson
                                     inetOrgPerson)] ]);

$res->code && warn "Couldn't add record: " . $res->error;
```

Similarly, you can delete records:

```
$res = $ldap->delete($DN);
$res && warn "Couldn't delete: " . $res->error;
```

The powerful modify method lets you make substantial changes to the information on a particular DN. See the documentation for Net::LDAP for information beyond these examples:

```
$res = $ldap->modify("cn=Sherlock Holmes, o=Sleuths B Us, c=gb",
       add     => { phone => '555 1212' },
       replace => { mail  => 'sholmes@braintrust.uk' },
       delete  => { cn => [ 'S Holmes' ] });
```

See Also

The documentation for the CPAN module Net::LDAP; the Net::LDAP home page at *http://perl-ldap.sourceforge.net/*

18.9 Sending Attachments in Mail

Problem

You want to send mail that includes attachments; for example, you want to mail a PDF document.

Solution

Use the MIME::Lite module from CPAN. First, create a MIME::Lite object representing the multipart message:

```
use MIME::Lite;

$msg = MIME::Lite->new(From    => 'sender@example.com',
                       To      => 'recipient@example.com',
                       Subject => 'My photo for the brochure',
                       Type    => 'multipart/mixed');
```

Then, add content through the attach method:

```
$msg->attach(Type     => 'image/jpeg',
             Path      => '/Users/gnat/Photoshopped/nat.jpg',
             Filename  => 'gnat-face.jpg');

$msg->attach(Type     => 'TEXT',
             Data      => 'I hope you can use this!');
```

Finally, send the message, optionally specifying how to send it:

```
$msg->send();             # default is to use sendmail(1)
# alternatively
$msg->send('smtp', 'mailserver.example.com');
```

Discussion

The MIME::Lite module creates and sends mail with MIME-encoded attachments. MIME stands for Multimedia Internet Mail Extensions, and is the standard way of attaching files and documents. It can't, however, extract attachments from mail messages—for that you need to read Recipe 18.10.

When creating and adding to a MIME::Lite object, pass parameters as a list of named parameter pairs. The pair conveys both mail headers (e.g., From, To, Subject) and those specific to MIME::Lite. In general, mail headers should be given with a trailing colon:

```
$msg = MIME::Lite->new('X-Song-Playing:' => 'Natchez Trace');
```

However, MIME::Lite accepts the headers in Table 18-2 without a trailing colon. * indicates a wildcard, so Content-* includes Content-Type and Content-ID but not Dis-Content.

Table 18-2. MIME::Lite headers

Approved	Encrypted	Received	Sender
Bcc	From	References	Subject
Cc	Keywords	Reply-To	To
Comments	Message-ID	Resent-*	X-*
Content-*	MIME-Version	Return-Path	
Date	Organization		

The full list of MIME::Lite options is given in Table 18-3.

Table 18-3. MIME::Lite options

Data	FH	ReadNow
Datestamp	Filename	Top
Disposition	Id	Type
Encoding	Length	
Filename	Path	

The MIME::Lite options and their values govern what is attached (the data) and how:

Path
> The file containing the data to attach.

Filename
> The default filename for the reader of the message to save the file as. By default this is the filename from the Path option (if Path was specified).

Data
> The data to attach.

Type
> The Content-Type of the data to attach.

Disposition
> Either inline or attachment. The former indicates that the reader should display the data as part of the message, not as an attachment. The latter indicates that the reader should display an option to decode and save the data. This is, at best, a hint.

FH
> An open filehandle from which to read the attachment data.

There are several useful content types: TEXT means text/plain, which is the default; BINARY similarly is short for application/octet-stream; multipart/mixed is used for a message that has attachments; application/msword for Microsoft Word files; application/vnd.ms-excel for Microsoft Excel files; application/pdf for PDF files; image/gif, image/jpeg, and image/png for GIF, JPEG, and PNG files, respectively;

audio/mpeg for MP3 files; video/mpeg for MPEG movies; video/quicktime for Quicktime (*.mov*) files.

The only two ways to send the message are using *sendmail*(1) or using Net::SMTP. Indicate Net::SMTP by calling send with a first argument of "smtp". Remaining arguments are parameters to the Net::SMTP constructor:

```
# timeout of 30 seconds
$msg->send("smtp", "mail.example.com", Timeout => 30);
```

If you plan to make more than one MIME::Lite object, be aware that invoking send as a class method changes the default way to send messages:

```
MIME::Lite->send("smtp", "mail.example.com");
$msg = MIME::Lite->new(%opts);
# ...
$msg->send();                    # sends using SMTP
```

If you're going to process multiple messages, also look into the ReadNow parameter. This specifies that the data for the attachment should be read from the file or filehandle immediately, rather than when the message is sent, written, or converted to a string.

Sending the message isn't the only thing you can do with it. You can get the final message as a string:

```
$text = $msg->as_string;
```

The print method writes the string form of the message to a filehandle:

```
$msg->print($SOME_FILEHANDLE);
```

Example 18-3 is a program that mails filenames given on the command line as attachments.

Example 18-3. mail-attachment

```
#!/usr/bin/perl -w
# mail-attachment - send files as attachments

use MIME::Lite;
use Getopt::Std;

my $SMTP_SERVER = 'smtp.example.com';        # CHANGE ME
my $DEFAULT_SENDER = 'sender@example.com';      # CHANGE ME
my $DEFAULT_RECIPIENT = 'recipient@example.com';# CHANGE ME

MIME::Lite->send('smtp', $SMTP_SERVER, Timeout=>60);

my (%o, $msg);

# process options

getopts('hf:t:s:', \%o);
```

Example 18-3. mail-attachment (continued)

```
$o{f} ||= $DEFAULT_SENDER;
$o{t} ||= $DEFAULT_RECIPIENT;
$o{s} ||= 'Your binary file, sir';

if ($o{h} or !@ARGV) {
    die "usage:\n\t$0 [-h] [-f from] [-t to] [-s subject] file ...\n";
}

# construct and send email

$msg = new MIME::Lite(
    From => $o{f},
    To   => $o{t},
    Subject => $o{s},
    Data => "Hi",
    Type => "multipart/mixed",
);

while (@ARGV) {
  $msg->attach('Type' => 'application/octet-stream',
               'Encoding' => 'base64',
               'Path' => shift @ARGV);
}

$msg->send( );
```

See Also

The documentation for MIME::Lite

18.10 Extracting Attachments from Mail

Problem

You have one or more mail messages with MIME attachments, and you want to process these messages with a Perl program to extract files or otherwise manipulate attachments.

Solution

Use the MIME-Tools bundle from CPAN:

```
use MIME::Parser;

$parser = MIME::Parser->new( );
$parser->output_to_core(1);        # don't write attachments to disk

$message = $parser->parse_data($MESSAGE);    # die( )s if can't parse
# OR
```

```
$message   = $parser->parse($FILEHANDLE);      # die()s if can't parse

$head      = $message->head();                 # object--see docs
$preamble  = $message->preamble;               # ref to array of lines
$epilogue  = $message->epilogue;               # ref to array of lines

$num_parts = $message->parts;
for (my $i=0; $i < $num_parts; $i++) {
  my $part         = $message->parts($i);
  my $content_type = $part->mime_type;
  my $body         = $part->as_string;
}
```

Discussion

Formally, a MIME message has only two parts: the head (containing headers such as From and Subject) and the body (containing the message, rather than its metadata). The body, however, has three parts: the preamble (text before the first attachment), a series of parts (the attachments), and the epilogue (text after the last attachment). This is shown in Figure 18-1.

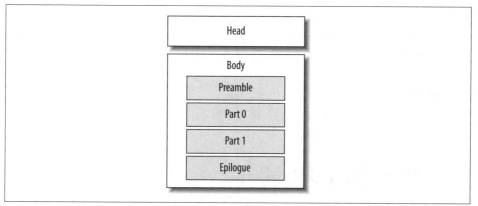

Figure 18-1. Composition of a MIME message

In the Solution, we disable the default behavior of MIME::Parser that writes the attachments to disk. Doing so increases memory consumption because now the decoded attachments must be stored in memory, but prevents the need to clean up temporary files and directories once the attachments are no longer needed.

To write attachments to a file, replace the call to output_to_core with calls to methods that specify the directory in which to store the attachments and what to name the files. The output_under method specifies a directory under which each message will get its own subdirectory; those subdirectories will contain the decoded attachments:

```
$parser->output_under("/tmp");
# parsing creates files like /tmp/msg-1048509652-16134-0/foo.png
```

Alternatively, output_dir specifies a directory into which all attachment files go:

```
$parser->output_dir("/tmp");
# parsing creates files like /tmp/foo.png
```

To clean up temporary files once parsing is done, say:

```
$parser->filer->purge;
```

Because parsing can trigger exceptions, catch the exceptions if you want to clean up:

```
eval { $message = $parser->parse($FILEHANDLE) };
# ...
$parser->filer->purge;
```

Whether you create files on disk, you can still treat the attachments as files by using the open method on an individual part:

```
for (my $i=0; $i < $num_parts; $i++) {
  my $part = $message->parts($i);
  my $fh = $part->open("r") or die "Can't open for reading: $!\n";
  while (<$fh>) {
    # reading lines from the current attachment
  }
}
```

There are actually six different classes that form part of the MIME-Tools distribution, and each is well-documented. Start with the MIME::Tools manpage and explore from there.

See Also

The MIME::Tools manpage and other documentation for the MIME-Tools distribution

18.11 Writing an XML-RPC Server

Problem

You want to write a server for an XML-RPC web service.

Solution

Use the SOAP-Lite distribution from CPAN, which supports XML-RPC. Your server can be either standalone:

```
use XMLRPC::Transport::HTTP;

$daemon = XMLRPC::Transport::HTTP::Daemon
        ->new(LocalPort => $PORT)
        ->dispatch_to('ClassName')
        ->handle();
```

or a CGI script:

```
use XMLRPC::Transport::HTTP;

$daemon = XMLRPC::Transport::HTTP::CGI
        ->dispatch_to('ClassName')
        ->handle();
```

In both cases, incoming methods will be invoked on the class named in the dispatch_
to method (it will be required if it is not already loaded):

```
package ClassName;

sub handler {
  my ($class, $arg_hash_ref) = @_;
  # ...
}
```

Discussion

The SOAP-Lite toolkit's modules take care of translating between Perl's native data
structures and the XML representation of those values. However, it's up to you how
the server decides which method to invoke when a request arrives. This process of
matching an XML-RPC request to a Perl function is known as *dispatching*.

It looks strange to see all those chained method invocations in the Solution. When
used to set a value, XMLRPC::Lite methods return their invocation, which lets you
chain methods rather than repeat $daemon over and over again:

```
$daemon = XMLRPC::Transport::HTTP::Daemon;
$daemon->new(LocalPort => $PORT);
$daemon->dispatch_to('ClassName');
$daemon->handle();
```

The new constructor takes IO::Socket::INET's constructor parameters as well, so you
can say ReuseAddr => 1, for example.

When you give the dispatch_to method a class name argument (as in the Solution),
the XML-RPC server looks for methods in that class. If the server in the Solution
receives a request for the ClassName.hasBeen method (XML-RPC methods are typically in IntraCaps), it invokes the ClassName->hasBeen method for a response.

Give dispatch_to a method name or list of method names, optionally qualified with a
package name. This tells Perl that only those methods should be invoked. For example, the following code ensures that only the hasBeen and willBe methods from the
main package and the canDo method from the MonkeySea class are valid:

```
$daemon->dispatch_to('hasBeen', 'willBe', 'MonkeySea::canDo')
```

Finally, give dispatch_to a pathname (optionally, as with method names or class
names), and XMLRPC::Lite will load modules as needed from that directory at runtime:

```
$daemon->dispatch_to('/path/to/exposed/modules', 'MyClass::API');
```

This means "all modules in */path/to/exposed/modules* and MyClass::API can be called through XML-RPC." MyClass::API might have been preloaded, or it might be found in @INC. This specifically does *not* mean "only dispatch to the MyClass::API in */path/to/exposed/modules.*"

See Also

Recipe 18.12; Recipe 18.13

18.12 Writing an XML-RPC Client

Problem

You want to write a client for an XML-RPC service.

Solution

Use the XMLRPC::Lite module from the SOAP-Lite distribution:

```
use XMLRPC::Lite;

$server = XMLRPC::Lite->proxy("http://server.example.com/path");
$result = $server->call('ClassName.handler', @ARGS);
die $call->faultstring if $call->fault;
print $call->result;
```

Discussion

A single XML-RPC server may run many services, differentiated by their method name: ClassName.handler corresponds to ClassName->handler on the server side; A.B.method corresponds to A::B->method; and a call to handler corresponds to main->handler.

The proxy is the actual URL of the server. If you're using a CGI server, the proxy method looks something like this:

```
$server->proxy("http://server.example.com/path/to/server.cgi")
```

There are three ways to invoke remote methods. The first way is to use the call method on your XMLRPC::Lite object. The first argument to call is the remote method name, and the remaining arguments are parameters for the remote method:

```
$returned = $server
        -> call("getRecordByNumber", 12, { format => "CSV" })
        -> result;
```

The second way to invoke a remote method is to call that method on the XMLRPC::Lite object. This works only when the remote method name isn't the same as a method provided by the XMLRPC::Lite object. For example:

```
$returned = $server
        -> getRecordByNumber(12, { format => "CSV" })
        -> result;
```

The last way to invoke a remote method is with *autodispatch*, turning unrequired function calls and method invocations in your Perl program into XML-RPC requests. Enable autodispatch with:

```
use XMLRPC::Lite +autodispatch =>
  proxy => "http://server.example.com/path";

$returned = getRecordByNumber(12, { format => "CSV" });
```

A critical difference between autodispatch and the other styles is that autodispatch automatically decodes the result into a Perl value for you. When you use an XML-RPC::Lite object, you must explicitly invoke the result method to decode the XML-RPC response into a Perl value.

See Also

Recipe 18.11; Recipe 18.14

18.13 Writing a SOAP Server

Problem

You want to write a web service where SOAP is the transport.

Solution

Use the SOAP-Lite distribution from CPAN. Your server can be either standalone:

```
use SOAP::Transport::HTTP;

$daemon = SOAP::Transport::HTTP::Daemon
        ->new(LocalPort => $PORT)
        ->dispatch_to('ClassName')
        ->handle();
```

or a CGI script:

```
use SOAP::Transport::HTTP;

$daemon = SOAP::Transport::HTTP::CGI
        ->dispatch_to('ClassName')
        ->handle();
```

In both cases, the only methods that SOAP clients are permitted to invoke are those in the classes named in the argument to dispatch_to (those classes will be required if not already loaded):

```
package ClassName;

sub handler {
  my ($class, $arg_hash_ref) = @_;
  # ...
}
```

Discussion

The SOAP-Lite toolkit contains SOAP and XML-RPC modules. Writing a SOAP service is similar to writing an XML-RPC service. Control method dispatch in SOAP as in XML-RPC. See Recipe 18.11 for details.

See Also

Recipe 18.14; Recipe 18.11

18.14 Writing a SOAP Client

Problem

You want to write a client for a SOAP web service.

Solution

Use the SOAP::Lite module from the SOAP-Lite distribution:

```
use SOAP::Lite;

$server = SOAP::Lite
        -> uri("http://localhost/Namespace")
        -> proxy("http://server.example.com/path");
$result = $server->call('ClassName.handler', @ARGS);
die $call->faultstring if $call->fault;
print $call->result;
```

Discussion

A single SOAP server may offer remote access to the methods of many classes. A client identifies the class upon which it wishes to invoke methods with the uri parameter. The hostname in the argument is irrelevant; only the path portion (the class name) matters. For example, these two URIs are equivalent:

```
http://modacrylic.clue.com/GimpyMod
http://weenies.mit.edu/GimpyMod
```

As with XML-RPC, the proxy argument is the server's URL. For example, if your SOAP server is implemented as a CGI script, the proxy call looks like this:

```
$server->proxy("http://server.example.com/path/to/server.cgi");
```

Invoke remote methods as you do with XML-RPC, either with the call method:

```
$returned = $server
        -> call("getRecordByNumber", 12, { format => "CSV" })
        -> result;
```

or by invoking the method on a SOAP::Lite object directly:

```
$returned = $server
        -> getRecordByNumber(12, { format => "CSV" })
        -> result;
```

or using autodispatch:

```
use SOAP::Lite +autodispatch =>
  uri   => "http://identifier.example.com/Namespace",
  proxy => "http://server.example.com/path";

$returned = getRecordByNumber(12, { format => "CSV" });
```

You can also use this with OO syntax:

```
$returned = Some::Remote::Module->getRecordByNumber(12, { format => "CSV" });
```

See Also

There's a *lot* more to SOAP than we can explain here. The books *Programming Web Services with SOAP*, by James Snell, Pavel Kulchenko, and Doug Tidwell (O'Reilly), and *Programming Web Services with Perl*, by Randy Ray and Pavel Kulchenko (O'Reilly), form a comprehensive guide to the standards and implementations. Also see Recipe 18.11; Recipe 18.13

18.15 Program: rfrm

This program fetches a list of messages waiting on a POP3 server and summarizes that list:

```
# ./rfrm
Nathan Torkington     Re: YAPC
Rob Brown             Re: Net::Ping syn round trip time
Rael Dornfest         Re: Book Proposal - Blosxom in a Nutshell
spam@example.com      Extend your ping times 633%!!!!
```

Tell the program which POP3 server to contact and the username and password to authenticate with using a *~/.rfrmrc* file like this:

```
SERVER=pop3.example.com
USER=gnat
PASS=I(heart)Perl
```

The program verifies that your *.rfrmrc* file isn't readable or writable by anyone but you, and stops if it is.

The program is shown in Example 18-4.

Example 18-4. rfrm

```perl
#!/usr/bin/perl -w
# rfrm - get a list of mail messages waiting on a pop server

use Net::POP3;
use strict;

my ($Pop_host, $Pop_user, $Pop_pass) = read_conf() or usage();

my $pop = Net::POP3->new($Pop_host)
  or die "Can't connect to $Pop_host: $!\n";
defined ($pop->login($Pop_user, $Pop_pass))
  or die "Can't authenticate\n";

my $messages = $pop->list
  or die "Can't get a list of messages\n";

foreach my $msgid (sort { $a <=> $b } keys %$messages) {
  my ($msg, $subject, $sender, $from);

  $msg = $pop->top($msgid, 0); # returns ref to array
  $msg = join "\n", @$msg;      # now it's one big string

  # extract From and Subject lines, and boil From down
  $subject = $sender = '';
  if ($msg =~ /^Subject: (.*)/m) { $subject = $1 }
  if ($msg =~ /^From: (.*)/m)    { $sender  = $1 }
  ($from = $sender) =~ s{<.*>}{};
  if ($from =~ m{\((.*\))}) { $from = $1 }
  $from ||= $sender;

  # print boiled down summary of this message
  printf("%-20.20s %-58.58s\n", $from, $subject);
}

sub usage {
  die <<EOF ;
usage: rfrm
Configure with ~/.rfrmrc thus:
  SERVER=pop.mydomain.com
  USER=myusername
  PASS=mypassword
EOF
}

sub read_conf {
  my ($server, $user, $pass, @stat);
```

Example 18-4. rfrm (continued)

```perl
    open(FH, "< $ENV{HOME}/.rfrmrc") or return;

    # paranoia check
    @stat = stat(FH) or die "Can't stat ~/.rfrmrc: $!\n";
    if ($stat[2] & 177) {
        die "~/.rfrmrc should be mode 600 or tighter\n";
    }

    # read config file
    while (<FH>) {
        if (/SERVER=(.*)/) { $server = $1 }
        if (/USER=(.*)/)   { $user   = $1 }
        if (/PASS=(.*)/)   { $pass   = $1 }
    }
    close FH;

    # must have something for every value
    return unless $server && $user && $pass;

    return ($server, $user, $pass);
}
```

18.16 Program: expn and vrfy

This program uses Net::SMTP to talk to an SMTP server and uses the EXPN and VRFY commands to figure out whether an address is going to work. It isn't perfect, because it relies on the remote SMTP giving meaningful information with the EXPN and VRFY commands—they are common ways for spammers to harvest email addresses, and so many servers have disabled these options. It uses Net::DNS if available, but can also work without it.

This program inspects $0 (the program name) to see how it was called. If run as *expn*, it uses the EXPN command; if called as *vrfy*, it uses the VRFY command. Use links to install it with two names (on a system without links, simply copy the program code in Example 18-5):

```
% cat > expn
#!/usr/bin/perl -w
...
^D
% ln expn vrfy
```

When given an email address as an argument, the program reports what the mail server says when you try to EXPN or VRFY the address. If you have Net::DNS installed, it tries all hosts listed as mail exchangers in the DNS entry for the address.

Here's what it looks like without Net::DNS:

```
% expn gnat@frii.com
Expanding gnat at frii.com (gnat@frii.com):
```

> *calisto.frii.com Hello coprolith.frii.com [207.46.130.14],*
> *   pleased to meet you*
> *gnat@mail.frii.com*

And here's the same address with Net::DNS installed:

```
% expn gnat@frii.com
Expanding gnat at mail.frii.net (gnat@frii.com):
deimos.frii.com Hello coprolith.frii.com [207.46.130.14],
    pleased to meet you
Nathan Torkington <gnat@deimos.frii.com>

Expanding gnat at mx1.frii.net (gnat@frii.com):
phobos.frii.com Hello coprolith.frii.com [207.46.130.14],
    pleased to meet you
gnat@mail.frii.com

Expanding gnat at mx2.frii.net (gnat@frii.com):
europa.frii.com Hello coprolith.frii.com [207.46.130.14],
    pleased to meet you
gnat@mail.frii.com

Expanding gnat at mx3.frii.net (gnat@frii.com):
ns2.winterlan.com Hello coprolith.frii.com [207.46.130.14],
    pleased to meet you
550 gnat... User unknown
```

The program is shown in Example 18-5.

Example 18-5. expn

```
#!/usr/bin/perl -w
# expn -- convince smtp to divulge an alias expansion
use strict;
use Net::SMTP;
use Sys::Hostname;
my $fetch_mx = 0;
# try loading the module, but don't blow up if missing
eval {
    require Net::DNS;
    Net::DNS->import('mx');
    $fetch_mx = 1;
};
my $selfname = hostname();
die "usage: $0 address\@host ...\n" unless @ARGV;
# Find out whether called as "vrfy" or "expn".
my $VERB = ($0 =~ /ve?ri?fy$/i)  ? 'VRFY' : 'EXPN';
my $multi = @ARGV > 1;
my $remote;
# Iterate over addresses given on command line.
foreach my $combo (@ARGV) {
    my ($name, $host) = split(/\@/, $combo);
    my @hosts;
    $host ||= 'localhost';
    @hosts = map { $_->exchange } mx($host)     if $fetch_mx;
```

Example 18-5. expn (continued)

```
    @hosts = ($host)    unless @hosts;
    foreach my $host (@hosts) {
        print $VERB eq 'VRFY' ? "Verify" : "Expand",
            "ing $name at $host ($combo):";
        $remote = Net::SMTP->new($host, Hello => $selfname);
        unless ($remote) {
            warn "cannot connect to $host\n";
            next;
        }
        print "\n";
        if ($VERB eq 'VRFY') {
            $remote->verify($name);
        } elsif ($VERB eq 'EXPN') {
            $remote->expand($name);
        }
        last if $remote->code == 221;
        next if $remote->code == 220;
        print $remote->message;
        $remote->quit;
        print "\n" if $multi;
    }
}
```

CHAPTER 19

CGI Programming

A successful tool is one that was used to do something undreamt of by its author.
—Stephen C. Johnson

19.0 Introduction

Changes in the environment or the availability of food can make certain species more successful than others at finding food or avoiding predators. Many scientists believe a comet struck the Earth millions of years ago, throwing an enormous cloud of dust into the atmosphere. Subsequent radical changes to the environment proved too much for some organisms, say dinosaurs, and hastened their extinction. Other creatures, such as mammals, found new food supplies and freshly exposed habitats to compete in.

Much as the comet altered the environment for prehistoric species, the Web has altered the environment for modern programming languages. It's opened up new vistas, and although some languages have found themselves eminently unsuited to this new world order, Perl has positively thrived. Because of its strong background in text processing and system glue, Perl has readily adapted itself to the task of providing information using text-based protocols.

Architecture

The Web is driven by plain text. Web servers and web browsers communicate using a text protocol called HTTP, Hypertext Transfer Protocol. Many of the documents exchanged are encoded in a text markup system called HTML, Hypertext Markup Language. This grounding in text is the source of much of the Web's flexibility, power, and success. The only notable exception to the predominance of plain text is the Secure Socket Layer (SSL) protocol that encrypts other protocols like HTTP into binary data that snoopers can't decode.

Web pages are identified using the Uniform Resource Locator (URL) naming scheme. URLs look like this:

```
http://www.perl.com/CPAN/
http://www.perl.com:8001/bad/mojo.html
ftp://gatekeeper.dec.com/pub/misc/netlib.tar.Z
ftp://anonymous@myplace:gatekeeper.dec.com/pub/misc/netlib.tar.Z
file:///etc/motd
```

The first part (http, ftp, file) is called the *scheme*, which identifies how the file is retrieved. The next part (://) means a hostname will follow, whose interpretation depends on the scheme. After the hostname comes the *path* identifying the document. This path information is also called a *partial URL*.

The Web is a client-server system. Client browsers like Netscape and Lynx request documents (identified by a partial URL) from web servers like Apache. This browser-to-server dialog is governed by the HTTP protocol. Most of the time, the server merely sends back the file contents. Sometimes, however, the web server runs another program to return a document that could be HTML text, binary image, or any other document type.

The server-to-program dialog can be handled in two ways. Either the code to handle the request is part of the web server process, or else the web server runs an external program to generate a response. The first scenario is the model of Java servlets and mod_perl (covered in Chapter 21). The second is governed by the Common Gateway Interface (CGI) protocol, so the server runs a *CGI program* (sometimes known as a *CGI script)*. This chapter deals with CGI programs.

The server tells the CGI program what page was requested, what values (if any) came in through HTML forms, where the request came from, whom they authenticated as (if they authenticated at all), and much more. The CGI program's reply has two parts: headers to say "I'm sending back an HTML document," "I'm sending back a GIF image," or "I'm not sending you anything; go to this page instead," and a document body, perhaps containing image data, plain text, or HTML.

The CGI protocol is easy to implement wrong and hard to implement right, which is why we recommend using Lincoln Stein's excellent CGI.pm module. It provides convenient functions for accessing the information the server sends you, and for preparing the CGI response the server expects. It's so useful, it's included in the standard Perl distribution, along with helper modules such as CGI::Carp and CGI::Fast. We show it off in Recipe 19.1.

Some web servers come with a Perl interpreter embedded in them. This lets Perl generate documents without starting a new process. The system overhead of reading an unchanging page isn't noticeable on infrequently accessed pages, even when it's happening several times a second. CGI accesses, however, bog down the machine running the web server. Chapter 21 shows how to use mod_perl, the Perl interpreter embedded in the Apache web server to get the benefits of CGI programs without the overhead.

Behind the Scenes

CGI programs are called each time the web server needs a dynamic document generated. It is important to understand that your CGI program doesn't run continuously, with the browser calling different parts of the program. Each request for a partial URL corresponding to your program starts a new copy. Your program generates a page for that request, then quits.

A browser can request a document in several distinct ways called *methods*. (Don't confuse HTTP methods with the methods of object-orientation. They have nothing to do with each other). The GET method is the most common, indicating a simple request for a document. The HEAD method supplies information about the document without actually fetching it. The POST method submits form values.

Form values can be encoded in both GET and POST methods. With the GET method, values are encoded directly in the URL, leading to ugly URLs like this:

```
http://www.perl.com/cgi-bin/program?name=Johann&born=1685
```

With the POST method, values are encoded in a separate part of the HTTP request that the client browser sends the server. If the form values in the previous example URL were sent with a POST request, the user, server, and CGI script would all see the URL:

```
http://www.perl.com/cgi-bin/program
```

The GET and POST methods differ in another respect: *idempotency*. This simply means that making a GET request for a particular URL once or multiple times should be no different. The HTTP protocol definition says that a GET request may be cached by the browser, the server, or an intervening proxy. POST requests cannot be cached, because each request is independent and matters. Typically, POST requests any changes or depends on the state of the server (query or update a database, send mail, or purchase a computer).

Most servers log requests to a file (the *access log*) for later analysis by the webmaster. Error messages produced by CGI programs don't by default go to the browser. Instead they are logged to a file on the server (the *error log*), and the browser simply gets a "500 Server Error" message, which means that the CGI program didn't uphold its end of the CGI bargain.

Error messages are useful in debugging any program, but they are especially so with CGI scripts. Sometimes, though, the authors of CGI programs either don't have access to the error log or don't know where it is. Sending error messages to a more convenient location is discussed in Recipe 19.2. Tracking down errors is covered in Recipe 19.3.

Recipe 19.8 shows how to learn what your browser and server are really saying to one another. Unfortunately, some browsers do not implement the HTTP specification correctly, and this recipe helps you determine whether your program or your browser is the cause of a problem.

Security

CGI programs let anyone run a program on your system. Sure, you get to pick the program, but the anonymous user from Out There can send unexpected values, hoping to trick it into doing the wrong thing. Thus security is a big concern on the Web.

Some sites address this concern by banning CGI programs. Sites that can't do without the power and utility of CGI programs must find ways to secure their CGI programs. Recipe 19.4 gives a checklist of considerations for writing a secure CGI script, briefly covering Perl's tainting mechanism for guarding against accidental use of unsafe data. Recipe 19.5 shows how your CGI program can safely run other programs.

HTML and Forms

Some HTML tags let you create forms, where the user can fill in values to submit to the server. The forms are composed of widgets, such as text entry fields and check boxes. CGI programs commonly return HTML, so the CGI module has helper functions to create HTML for everything from tables to form widgets.

In addition to Recipe 19.6, this chapter also has Recipe 19.10, which shows how to create forms that retain values over multiple calls. Recipe 19.11 shows how to make a single CGI script that produces and responds to a set of pages, such as a product catalog and ordering system.

Web-Related Resources

Unsurprisingly, some of the best references on the Web are found on the Web:

WWW Security FAQ
   http://www.w3.org/Security/Faq/

Web FAQ
   http://www.boutell.com/faq/

CGI FAQ
   http://www.webthing.com/tutorials/cgifaq.html

HTTP Specification
   http://www.w3.org/pub/WWW/Protocols/HTTP/

HTML Specification
   http://www.w3.org/TR/REC-html40/
   http://www.w3.org/pub/WWW/MarkUp/

CGI Specification
   http://www.w3.org/CGI/

CGI Security FAQ
   http://www.go2net.com/people/paulp/cgi-security/safe-cgi.txt

We recommend *CGI Programming with Perl*, by Scott Guelich, Shishir Gundavaram, and Gunther Birznieks (O'Reilly); *HTML & XHTML: The Definitive Guide*, by Chuck Musciano and Bill Kennedy (O'Reilly); and *HTTP: The Definitive Guide*, by David Gourley and Brian Totty, et al (O'Reilly).

19.1 Writing a CGI Script

Problem

You want to write a CGI script to process the contents of an HTML form. In particular, you want to access the form contents and produce valid output in return.

Solution

A CGI script is a server-side program launched by a web server to generate dynamic content. It receives encoded information from the remote client (user's browser) via STDIN and environment variables, and it must produce a valid HTTP header and body on STDOUT. The standard CGI module, shown in Example 19-1, painlessly manages input and output encoding.

Example 19-1. hiweb

```
#!/usr/bin/perl -w
# hiweb - load CGI module to decode information given by web server
use strict;

use CGI qw(:standard escapeHTML);

# get a parameter from a form
my $value = param('PARAM_NAME');

# output a document
print header(), start_html("Howdy there!"),
     p("You typed: ", tt(escapeHTML($value))),
     end_html();
```

Discussion

CGI is just a protocol, a formal agreement between a web server and a separate program. The server encodes the client's form input data, and the CGI program decodes the form and generates output. The protocol says nothing regarding which language the program must be written in; programs and scripts that obey the CGI protocol have been written in C, shell, Rexx, C++, VMS DCL, Smalltalk, Tcl, Python, and of course Perl.

The full CGI specification lays out which environment variables hold which data (such as form input parameters) and how it's all encoded. In theory, it should be easy to follow the protocol to decode the input, but in practice, it is surprisingly tricky to get right. That's why we *strongly* recommend using the CGI module. The hard work of handling the CGI requirements correctly and conveniently has already been done, freeing you to write the core of your program without getting bogged down in network protocols.

CGI scripts are called in two main ways, referred to as *methods*—but don't confuse HTTP methods with Perl object methods! The HTTP GET method is used in document retrievals where an identical request will produce an identical result, such as a dictionary lookup. A GET stores form data in the URL. This means it can be conveniently bookmarked for canned requests, but has limitations on the total request size. The HTTP POST method sends form data separate from the request. It has no size limitations, but cannot be bookmarked. Forms that update information on the server, such as mailing in feedback or modifying a database entry, should use POST. Client browsers and intervening proxies are free to cache and refresh the results of GET requests behind your back, but they may not cache POST requests. GET is suitable only for short read-only requests, whereas POST works for forms of any size, as well as for updates and feedback responses. By default, therefore, the CGI module uses POST for all forms it generates.

With few exceptions, mainly related to file permissions and highly interactive work, CGI scripts can do nearly anything other programs can do. They can send results back in many formats: plain text, HTML documents, XML files, sound files, pictures, or anything else specified in the HTTP header. Besides producing plain text or HTML text, they can also redirect the client browser to another location, set server cookies, request authentication, and give errors.

The CGI module provides two different interfaces: a procedural one for casual use, and an object-oriented one for power users with complicated needs. Virtually all CGI scripts should use the simple procedural interface, but unfortunately, most of CGI.pm's documentation uses examples with the original object-oriented approach. Due to backward compatibility, if you want the simple procedural interface, you need to specifically ask for it using the :standard import tag. See Chapter 12 for more on import tags.

To read the user's form input, pass the param function a field name. If you have a form field named "favorite", then param("favorite") returns its value. With some types of form fields, such as scrolling lists, the user can choose more than one option. For these, param returns a list of values, which you could assign to an array.

For example, here's a script that pulls in values of three form fields, the last one having many return values:

```
use CGI qw(:standard);
$who   = param("Name");
$phone = param("Number");
@picks = param("Choices");
```

Called without arguments, param returns a list of valid form parameters in list context or how many form parameters there were in scalar context.

That's all there is to accessing the user's input. Do with it whatever you please, then generate properly formatted output. This is nearly as easy. Remember that unlike regular programs, a CGI script's output must be formatted in a particular way: it must first emit a set of headers followed by a blank line before any normal output.

As shown in the Solution, the CGI module helps with output as well as input. The module provides functions for generating HTTP headers and HTML code. The header function builds the header for you. By default, it produces headers for a text/html document, but you can change the Content-Type and supply other optional header parameters as well:

```
print header( -TYPE    => 'text/plain',
              -EXPIRES => '+3d' );
```

CGI.pm can also be used to generate HTML. It may seem trivial, but this is where the CGI module shines: the creation of dynamic forms, especially stateful ones such as shopping carts. The CGI module even has functions for generating forms and tables.

When printing form widgets, the characters &, <, >, and " in HTML output are automatically replaced with their entity equivalents. This is not the case with arbitrary user output. That's why the Solution imports and makes use of the escapeHTML function—if the user types any of those special characters, they won't cause formatting errors in the HTML.

For a full list of functions and their calling conventions, see CGI.pm's documentation.

See Also

The documentation for the standard CGI module; *http://www.w3.org/CGI/*; Recipe 19.6

19.2   Redirecting Error Messages

Problem

You're having trouble tracking down your script's warnings and error messages, or your script's STDERR output is confusing your server.

Solution

Use the CGI::Carp module from the standard Perl distribution to prefix each line on STDERR with the program name and current date. You can also send warnings and errors to a file or the browser if you wish.

Discussion

Tracking down error messages from CGI scripts is notoriously annoying. Even if you manage to find the server error log, you still can't determine which message came from which script, or at what time. Some unfriendly web servers even abort the script if it has the audacity to emit anything out its STDERR before the Content-Type header is generated on STDOUT, so warnings can get you into trouble.

Enter the CGI::Carp module. It replaces warn and die—plus the normal Carp module's carp, croak, cluck, and confess functions—with more verbose and safer versions. It still sends them to the normal server error log.

```
use CGI::Carp;
warn "This is a complaint";
die "But this one is serious";
```

The following use of CGI::Carp also redirects errors to a file of your choice, placed in a BEGIN block to catch compile-time warnings as well:

```
BEGIN {
    use CGI::Carp qw(carpout);
    open(LOG, ">>/var/local/cgi-logs/mycgi-log")
        or die "Unable to append to mycgi-log: $!\n";
    carpout(*LOG);
}
```

You can even arrange for fatal errors to show up at the client browser, which is nice for your own debugging but might confuse the end user.

```
use CGI::Carp qw(fatalsToBrowser);
die "Bad error here";
```

Even if the error happens before you get the HTTP header out, the module will try to detect this and avoid the dreaded 500 Server Error. Normal warnings still go to the server error log (or wherever you've sent them with carpout) with the program name and date stamp prepended.

See Also

The documentation for the standard CGI::Carp module; the discussion on BEGIN in Recipe 12.3

19.3   Fixing a 500 Server Error

Problem

Your CGI script gives you a 500 Server Error.

Solution

Follow the checklist given in the discussion.

Discussion

This checklist is aimed at a Unix audience, but the general principles embodied in the questions apply to all systems.

Make sure the web server can run the script

Check ownership and permissions with *ls -l*. The appropriate read and execute bits must be set on the script before the web server can run it. The script should be readable and executable by everyone (or at least by whomever the server runs scripts as). Use *chmod 0755 scriptname* if it's owned by you, or otherwise *chmod 0555 scriptname* if owned by the designated anonymous web user, assuming you are running as that user or the superuser. All directories in the path must also have their execute bit set (most FTP clients support changing protections on uploaded files if you don't have shell access to your server).

Make sure the script can be identified as a script by the web server. Most web servers have a system-wide *cgi-bin*, and all files in that directory will be run as scripts. Some servers identify a CGI script as any file whose name ends in a particular extension, such as *.cgi* or *.plx*. Some servers have options to permit access via the GET method alone, not through the POST method that your form likely uses. Consult your web server documentation, configuration files, webmaster, and (if all else fails) technical support.

If you're running on Unix, do you have the right path to the Perl executable on the #! line? The #! line must be the first line in the script; you can't even have blank lines before the #! line. Some operating systems have ridiculously short limits on the number of characters that can be in this line, so you may need to make a link (e.g., from */home/richh/perl* to */opt/installed/third-party/software/perl-5.004/bin/perl*, to pick a hypothetical, pathological example).

If you're running on Win32, have you associated your Perl scripts with the correct Perl executable? Or, if your server uses #! lines, have you given the correct path in the #! line?

Make sure the script has permissions to do what it's trying to do

Identify the user the script runs as with the simple code shown in Example 19-2.

Example 19-2. webwhoami

```
#!/usr/bin/perl
# webwhoami - show web users id
print "Content-Type: text/plain\n\n";
print "Running as ", scalar getpwuid($>), "\n";
```

This prints the username the script is running as.

Identify the resources the script is trying to access. List files, network connections, system calls, and so on, that require special privilege. Then make sure they can be accessed by the user the script is running as. Are there disk or network quotas? Do protections on the file allow access? Are you trying to get the encrypted password field using getpwent on a shadow password system (since usually only the superuser can get shadow passwords)?

Set permissions on any files the script needs to write to at 0666, or better yet to 0644 if they're owned by the effective user ID the script is running under. If new files are to be created or old ones moved or removed, write and execute permission on the enclosing directory of those files is also needed.

Is the script valid Perl?

Try to run it from a shell prompt. CGI.pm lets you run and debug your scripts from the command line or from standard input. Here, ^D represents whatever you type to get an end-of-file.

```
% perl -wc cgi-script                    # just compilation

% perl -w  cgi-script                    # parms from stdin
(offline mode: enter name=value pairs on standard input)
name=joe
number=10
^D

% perl -w  cgi-script name=joe number=10    # run with mock form input
% perl -d  cgi-script name=joe number=10    # ditto, under the debugger

# POST method script in csh
% (setenv HTTP_METHOD POST; perl -w cgi-script name=joe number=10)
# POST method script in sh
% HTTP_METHOD=POST perl -w cgi-script name=joe number=10
```

Check the server's error log. Most web servers redirect CGI process's STDERR into a file. Find that file (try */usr/local/etc/httpd/logs/error_log*, */usr/local/www/logs/error_log*, or just ask your administrator) and see whether any warnings or error messages are showing up there.

Are you using an old version of Perl? Type *perl -v* to find out. If you're not using 5.004 or better, you or your admins should upgrade because 5.003 and earlier releases were not protected against buffer overruns. This is a grave security matter.

Are you using an old version of the libraries? You can *grep -i version* in the library file (probably in */usr/lib/perl5/*, */usr/local/lib/perl5/*, */usr/lib/perl5/site_perl*, or some such). For CGI.pm, and in fact, with any module, you can do this to figure out which version you're using:

```
% perl -MCGI -le 'print CGI->VERSION'
2.49
```

Are you running the latest version of your web server? It's not often that it happens, but sometimes a web server has bugs that can interfere with your scripts.

Are you running with the **-w** switch or use warnings? This makes Perl gripe about things like using uninitialized variables, reading from a write-only filehandle, and so on.

Are you running with the **-T** flag? If Perl complains about insecure actions, you might be assuming things about your script's input and environment that aren't true. Make it taint-clean (read Recipe 19.4, see the *perlsec* manpage or Chapter 23 of *Programming Perl* to find out about tainting and its consequences for your program, and check the CGI Security FAQ for particular web traps to avoid) and you may sleep easier at night as well as have a working script.

Are you running with use strict? It makes you declare variables before you use them and quote your strings to avoid any confusion with subroutines, and in doing so finds a lot of errors.

Are you checking return values from every system call? Many people blindly believe that every open or system or rename or unlink in their programs will work all the time. These functions return a value so you can find out whether they worked or not—check them!

Can Perl find the libraries you're using? Write a small script that just prints @INC (Perl's array of directories it looks for modules and libraries in). Check permissions on the libraries (they must be readable by the user the script runs as). Don't copy modules from one machine to another—a lot of them have compiled and autoloaded components hidden in the Perl library directory. Install them yourself from scratch.

Is Perl giving you warnings or errors? Try using CGI::Carp (see Recipe 19.2) to send Perl's error messages and warnings to the browser or a file you have access to.

Is the script upholding its end of the CGI protocol?

The HTTP header must come before the text or image you return. Don't forget the blank line between the header and body. Also, because STDOUT is not automatically autoflushed but STDERR is, if your script generates warnings or errors to STDERR, the web server might see them before it sees your HTTP header and can generate an error on some servers. Add this at the top of your script (after the #! line) to also flush STDOUT:

```
$| = 1;
```

Don't ever try to decode the incoming form data by parsing the environment and standard input yourself. There are just too many places where it can go wrong. Use the CGI module and spend your time writing cool programs or reading slashdot instead of tracking down bugs in your implementation of an arcane protocol.

Asking for help elsewhere

Check the FAQs and other documents mentioned at the end of the Introduction to this chapter. There is still a chance that you have made a common mistake on whatever system you're using—read the relevant FAQs to make sure you don't embarrass yourself by asking the CGI equivalent of "why doesn't my car run when it's out of gas and oil?"

Ask a friend. Almost everyone knows somebody they can ask for help. You'll probably get a reply much sooner than if you asked the Net.

Post to `comp.infosystems.www.authoring.misc` if your question is about a CGI script (the CGI module, decoding cookies, finding out where the user is coming from, etc.).

See Also

Recipe 19.2; the discussion on buffering in the Introduction of Chapter 8; the CGI FAQ at *http://www.webthing.com/tutorials/cgifaq.html*

19.4   Writing a Safe CGI Program

Problem

Because CGI programs allow external users to run programs on systems they would not otherwise have access on, all CGI programs represent a potential security risk. You want to minimize your exposure.

Solution

- Use taint mode (the **-T** switch on the #! line).
- Don't blindly untaint data. (See the Discussion.)
- Sanity-check everything, including all form widget return values, even hidden widgets or values generated by JavaScript code. Many people naïvely assume that just because they tell JavaScript to check the form's values before the form is submitted, the form's values will actually be checked. Not at all! The user can trivially circumvent this by disabling JavaScript in their browser, by downloading the form and altering the JavaScript, or quit by talking HTTP without a browser using any of the examples in Chapter 20.
- Check return conditions from system calls.
- Be conscious of race conditions (described in the Discussion).
- Run with use `warnings` and use `strict` to make sure Perl isn't assuming things incorrectly.
- Don't run anything setuid unless you absolutely must. If you must, think about running setgid instead if you can. Certainly avoid setuid root at all costs. If you must run setuid or setgid, use a wrapper unless Perl is convinced your system has secure setuid scripts and you know what this means.

- Always encode login passwords, credit card numbers, social security numbers, and anything else you'd not care to read pasted across the front page of your local newspaper. Use a secure protocol like SSL when dealing with such data. Ensuring that a CGI only ever runs as HTTPS can be as simple as:

  ```
  croak "This CGI works only over HTTPS"
      if $ENV{'SERVER_PORT'} && !$ENV{'HTTPS'};
  ```

  Moreover, never pass secure data through email. If you need to mail a user some secure data, instead mail them an *https*: URL to a page that will display the secure data only if the user provides the correct password—a password that has never been sent over an insecure protocol like email or *http*. Keep secure data around only as needed, and consider the likelihood and consequences of anyone wrongly accessing the secure data.

Discussion

Many of these suggestions are good ideas for any program—using warnings and checking the return values of your system calls are obviously applicable even when security isn't the first thing on your mind. The use warnings pragma makes Perl issue warnings about dubious constructs, like using an undefined variable as though it had a legitimate value, or writing to a read-only filehandle.

Apart from unanticipated shell escapes, the most common security threat lies in forged values in a form submission. It's trivial for anyone to save the source to your form, edit the HTML, and submit the altered form. Even if you're certain that a field can return only "yes" or "no", they can always edit it up to return "maybe" instead. Even fields marked as type HIDDEN in the form can be tampered with. If the program at the other end blindly trusts its form values, it can be fooled into deleting files, creating new user accounts, mailing password or credit card databases, or innumerable other malicious abuses. This is why you must never blindly trust data (like prices) stored in hidden fields when writing CGI shopping cart applications.

Even worse is when the CGI script uses a form value as the basis of a filename to open or a command to run. Bogus values submitted to the script could trick it into opening arbitrary files. Situations like this are precisely why Perl has a taint mode. If a program runs setuid or in taint mode, data from program arguments, environment variables, directory listings, or files are considered tainted, and cannot be used directly or indirectly to affect the outside world.

Running under taint mode, Perl insists that you set your path variable first, even if specifying a complete pathname to call a program. That's because you have no assurance that the command you run won't turn around and invoke some other program using a relative pathname. You must also untaint any externally derived data for safety.

For instance, when running in taint mode:

```
#!/usr/bin/perl -T
open(FH, "> $ARGV[0]") or die;
```

Perl warns with:

Insecure dependency in open while running with -T switch at ...

This is because $ARGV[0] (having come from outside your program) is not trustworthy. The only way to change tainted data into untainted data is by using regular expression backreferences:

```
$file = $ARGV[0];                          # $file tainted
unless ($file =~ m#^([\w.-]+)$#) {         # $1 is untainted
    die "filename '$file' has invalid characters.\n";
}
$file = $1;                                # $file untainted
```

Tainted data can come from anything outside your program, such as from your program arguments or environment variables, the results of reading from filehandles or directory handles, and stat or locale information. Operations considered insecure with tainted data include system(*STRING*), exec(*STRING*), backticks, glob, open with any access mode except read-only, unlink, mkdir, rmdir, chown, chmod, umask, link, symlink, the **-s** command-line switch, kill, require, eval, truncate, ioctl, fcntl, socket, socketpair, bind, connect, chdir, chroot, setpgrp, setpriority, and syscall.

A common attack exploits what's known as a *race condition*. That's a situation where, between two actions of yours, an attacker can race in and change something to make your program misbehave. A notorious race condition occurred in the way older Unix kernels ran setuid scripts: between the kernel reading the file to find which interpreter to run and the now-setuid interpreter reading the file, a malicious person could substitute their own script.

Race conditions crop up even in apparently innocuous places. Consider what would happen if not one but many copies of the following code ran simultaneously.

```
unless (-e $filename) {                    # WRONG!
    open(FH, "> $filename");
    # ...
}
```

There's a race between testing whether the file exists and opening it for writing. Similar race conditions can occur in such common situations as reading data from a file, updating the data, and writing it back out to that file.

Still worse, if someone replaced the file with a link to something important, like one of your personal configuration files, the code just shown would erase that file. The correct way to do this is to do a non-destructive create with the sysopen function, described in Recipe 7.1.

A setuid CGI script runs with different permissions than the web server does. This lets the CGI script access resources (files, shadow password databases, etc) that it otherwise could not. This can be convenient, but it can also be dangerous. Weaknesses in setuid scripts may let crackers access not only files that the low-privilege web server user can access, but also any that could be accessed by the user the script runs as. For a poorly written setuid root script, this could let anyone change passwords, delete files, read credit card records, and other malicious acts. Always make sure your programs run with the lowest privilege possible, normally the user the web server runs as: nobody.

Finally (and this recommendation may be the hardest to follow), be conscious of the physical path your network traffic takes. Are you sending passwords over an unencrypted connection? Do these unencrypted passwords travel through insecure networks? A form's PASSWORD input field only protects you from someone looking over your shoulder. Always use SSL when real passwords are involved. If you're serious about security, fire up your browser and a packet sniffer to see how easily your traffic is decoded.

See Also

The section on "Talking to Yourself" in Chapter 16 of *Programming Perl*; the section on "Accessing Commands and Files Under Reduced Privilege" in Chapter 23 of *Programming Perl*; *perlsec*(1); the CGI and HTTP specs and the CGI Security FAQ, all mentioned in the Introduction to this chapter; the section on "Avoiding Denial of Service Attacks" in the standard CGI module documentation; Recipe 19.5

19.5   Executing Commands Without Shell Escapes

Problem

You need to use a user's input as part of a command, but you don't want to allow the user to trick the shell into running other commands or looking at other files. If you just blindly call the system function or backticks on a single string containing a command line derived from untested user input, the shell might be used to run the command. This would be unsafe.

Solution

Unlike its single-argument version, the list form of the system function is safe from shell escapes. When the command's arguments involve user input from a form, never use this:

```
system("command $input @files");          # UNSAFE
```

Write it this way instead:

```
system("command", $input, @files);        # safer
```

Discussion

Because Perl was designed as a glue language, it's easy to use it to call other programs—too easy, in some cases.

If you're merely trying to run a shell command but don't need to capture its output, it's easy enough to call system using its multiple argument form. But what happens if you're using the command in backticks or as part of a piped open? Now you have a real problem, because those don't permit the multiple argument form that system does. The solution (prior to v5.8; see later in this Discussion) is to manually fork and exec the child processes on your own. It's more work, but at least stray shell escapes won't be ruining your day.

It's safe to use backticks in a CGI script only if the arguments you give the program are internally generated, as in:

```
chomp($now = `date`);
```

But if the command within the backticks contains user-supplied input, perhaps like this:

```
@output = `grep $input @files`;
```

you have to be much more careful.

```
die "cannot fork: $!" unless defined ($pid = open(SAFE_KID, "-|"));
if ($pid == 0) {
    exec('grep', $input, @files) or die "can't exec grep: $!";
} else {
    @output = <SAFE_KID>;
    close SAFE_KID;                 # $? contains status
}
```

This works because exec, like system, permits a calling convention that's immune to shell escapes. When passed a list, no shell is called, and so no escapes can occur.

Similar circumlocutions are needed when using open to start up a command. Here's a safe backtick or piped open for read. Instead of using this unsafe code:

```
open(KID_TO_READ, "$program @options @args |");    # UNSAFE
```

use this more complicated but safer code:

```
# add error processing as above
die "cannot fork: $!" unless defined($pid = open(KID_TO_READ, "-|"));

if ($pid) {    # parent
    while (<KID_TO_READ>) {
        # do something interesting
    }
    close(KID_TO_READ)              or warn "kid exited $?";

} else {        # child
    # reconfigure, then
```

```
        exec($program, @options, @args)  or die "can't exec program: $!";
    }
```

Here's a safe piped open for writing. Instead of using this unsafe code:

```
    open(KID_TO_WRITE, "|$program $options @args");    # UNSAFE
```

use this more complicated but safer code:

```
    die "cannot fork: $!" unless defined($pid = open(KID_TO_WRITE, "-|"));
    $SIG{PIPE} = sub { die "whoops, $program pipe broke" };

    if ($pid) {   # parent
        for (@data) { print KID_TO_WRITE $_ }
        close(KID_TO_WRITE)                 or warn "kid exited $?";

    } else {      # child
        # reconfigure, then
        exec($program, @options, @args)  or die "can't exec program: $!";
    }
```

Put any extra security measures you'd like where the comment in the code says
reconfigure. You can change environment variables, reset temporary user or group
ID values, change directories or umasks, etc. You're in the child process now, where
changes won't propagate back to the parent.

If you don't have any reconfiguration to do in the child process, and you're running
at least the v5.8 release of Perl, open supports a list of separate parameters that works
as system and exec do when passed a list; that is, it avoids the shell altogether. Those
two calls would be:

```
    open(KID_TO_READ, "-|", $program, @options, @args)
        || die "can't run $program: $!";
```

and:

```
    open(KID_TO_WRITE, "|-", $program, $options, @args)
        || die "can't run $program: $!";
```

This doesn't help you, of course, if you run a setuid program that can be exploited
with the data you give it. The mail program *sendmail* is a setuid program commonly
run from CGI scripts. Know the risks before you call *sendmail* or any other setuid
program.

See Also

The system, exec, and open functions in Chapter 29 of *Programming Perl* and in
perlfunc(1); the section on "Talking to Yourself" in Chapter 16 of *Programming Perl*;
the section on "Accessing Commands and Files Under Reduced Privilege" in Chapter 23 of *Programming Perl*; *perlsec*(1); Recipe 16.1; Recipe 16.2; Recipe 16.3

19.6 Formatting Lists and Tables with HTML Shortcuts

Problem

You have several lists and tables to generate and wish they were easier to output.

Solution

The CGI module provides HTML helper functions that, when passed array references, apply themselves to each element of the referenced array:

```
print ol( li([ qw(red blue green)]) );
<OL><LI>red</LI><LI>blue</LI><LI>green</LI></OL>
@names = qw(Larry Moe Curly);
print ul( li({ -TYPE => "disc" }, \@names) );
<UL><LI TYPE="disc">Larry</LI> <LI TYPE="disc">Moe</LI>
    <LI TYPE="disc">Curly</LI></UL>
```

Discussion

The HTML-generating functions in CGI.pm can make it easy to generate lists and tables. Passed a simple string, these functions produce HTML for that string. But passed an array reference, they work on all strings in that array.

```
print li("alpha");
<LI>alpha</LI>
print li( [ "alpha", "omega"] );
<LI>alpha</LI> <LI>omega</LI>
```

The shortcut functions for lists are loaded when you use the :standard import tag, but you need to ask for :html3 explicitly to get helper functions for tables. There's also a conflict between the <TR> tag, which would normally make a tr( ) function, and Perl's built-in tr/// operator. Therefore, to make a table row, use the Tr( ) function.

This example generates an HTML table starting with a hash of arrays. The keys will be the row headers, and the array of values are the columns.

```
use CGI qw(:standard :html3);

%hash = (
    "Wisconsin"  => [ "Superior", "Lake Geneva", "Madison" ],
    "Colorado"   => [ "Denver", "Fort Collins", "Boulder" ],
    "Texas"      => [ "Plano", "Austin", "Fort Stockton" ],
    "California" => [ "Sebastopol", "Santa Rosa", "Berkeley" ],
);

$\ = "\n";

print "<TABLE><CAPTION>Cities I Have Known</CAPTION>";
```

```
print Tr(th [qw(State Cities)]);
for $k (sort keys %hash) {
    print Tr(th($k), td( [ sort @{$hash{$k}} ] ));
}
print "</TABLE>";
```

That generates text like this:

```
<TABLE> <CAPTION>Cities I Have Known</CAPTION>
    <TR><TH>State</TH> <TH>Cities</TH></TR>
    <TR><TH>California</TH> <TD>Berkeley</TD> <TD>Santa Rosa</TD>
        <TD>Sebastopol</TD> </TR>
    <TR><TH>Colorado</TH> <TD>Boulder</TD> <TD>Denver</TD>
        <TD>Fort Collins</TD> </TR>
    <TR><TH>Texas</TH> <TD>Austin</TD> <TD>Fort Stockton</TD>
        <TD>Plano</TD> </TR>
    <TR><TH>Wisconsin</TH> <TD>Lake Geneva</TD> <TD>Madison</TD>
        <TD>Superior</TD></TR>
</TABLE>
```

You can produce the same output using one print statement, although it is slightly trickier because you have to use a map to create the implicit loop. This print statement produces output identical to that displayed previously:

```
print table
        caption('Cities I have Known'),
        Tr(th [qw(State Cities)]),
        map { Tr(th($_), td( [ sort @{$hash{$_}} ] )) } sort keys %hash;
```

This is especially useful for formatting the results of a database query, as in Example 19-3 (see Chapter 14 for more on databases).

Example 19-3. salcheck

```
#!/usr/bin/perl
# salcheck - check for salaries
use DBI;
use strict;
use CGI qw(:standard :html3);

my $limit = param("LIMIT");

print header(), start_html("Salary Query"),
    h1("Search"),
    start_form(),
    p("Enter minimum salary", textfield("LIMIT")),
    submit(),
    end_form();

if (defined $limit) {
    my $dbh = DBI->connect("dbi:mysql:somedb:server.host.dom:3306",
        "username", "password")
        or die "Connecting: $DBI::errstr";
    my $sth = $dbh->prepare("SELECT name,salary FROM employees
        WHERE salary > $limit")
        or die "Preparing: ", $dbh->errstr;
```

Example 19-3. salcheck (continued)

```
    $sth->execute
        or die "Executing: ", $sth->errstr;

    print h1("Results"), "<TABLE BORDER=1>";

    while (my $row = $sth->fetchrow_arrayref()) {
            print Tr( td( $row ) );
    }

    print "</TABLE>\n";
    $sth->finish;
    $dbh->disconnect;
}

print end_html();
```

See Also

The documentation for the standard CGI module; Recipe 14.9

19.7 Redirecting to a Different Location

Problem

You need to tell the client's browser to look elsewhere for a page.

Solution

Instead of a normal header, just issue a location redirect and exit. Don't forget the extra newline at the end of the header.

```
    $url = "http://www.perl.com/CPAN/";
    print "Location: $url\n\n";
    exit;
```

Discussion

Sometimes your CGI program doesn't need to generate the document on its own. It only needs to tell the client at the other end to fetch a different document instead. In that case, the HTTP header needs to include this directive as a Location line followed by the URL you want to send them to. Make sure to use an absolute URL, not a relative one.

The direct and literal solution given in the Solution is usually sufficient, but if you already have the CGI module loaded, use the redirect function. You might use this code for building and setting a cookie, as shown in Example 19-4.

Example 19-4. oreobounce

```perl
#!/usr/bin/perl -w
# oreobounce - set a cookie and redirect the browser
use CGI qw(:cgi);
use strict;

my $oreo = cookie( -NAME    => 'filling',
                   -VALUE   => "vanilla crème",
                   -EXPIRES => '+3M',     # M for month, m for minute
                   -DOMAIN  => '.perl.com');

my $whither = "http://somewhere.perl.com/nonesuch.html";

print redirect( -URL     => $whither,
                -COOKIE  => $oreo);
```

That would produce:

```
Status: 302 Moved Temporarily
Set-Cookie: filling=vanilla%20cr%E4me; domain=.perl.com;
    expires=Tue, 21-Jul-1998 11:58:55 GMT
Date: Tue, 21 Apr 1998 11:55:55 GMT
Location: http://somewhere.perl.com/nonesuch.html
Content-Type: text/html
<<blank line here>>
```

Example 19-5 is a complete program that looks at the client browser name and redirects it to a page in Eric Raymond's edition of the *Jargon File* that talks about the user's browser. It's also a nice example of a different approach to building a switch statement in Perl (see Recipe 10.17).

Example 19-5. os_snipe

```perl
#!/usr/bin/perl
# os_snipe - redirect to a Jargon File entry about current OS
$dir = 'http://www.wins.uva.nl/%7Emes/jargon';
for ($ENV{HTTP_USER_AGENT}) {
    $page =    /Mac/              && 'm/Macintrash.html'
            || /Win(dows )?NT/    && 'e/evilandrude.html'
            || /Win|MSIE|WebTV/   && 'm/MicroslothWindows.html'
            || /Linux/            && 'l/Linux.html'
            || /HP-UX/            && 'h/HP-SUX.html'
            || /SunOS/            && 's/ScumOS.html'
            ||                       'a/AppendixB.html';
}
print "Location: $dir/$page\n\n";
```

The *os_snipe* program uses dynamic redirection because you don't always send every user to the same place. If you did, it would usually make more sense to arrange for a static redirect line in the server's configuration file, since that would be more efficient than running a CGI script for each redirection.

Telling the client's browser that you don't plan to produce any output is not the same as redirecting nowhere:

```
use CGI qw(:standard);
print header( -STATUS => '204 No response' );
```

That produces this:

```
Status: 204 No response
Content-Type: text/html
<<blank line here>>
```

Use this, for instance, when the user submits a form request but you don't want their page to change or even update.

It may seem silly to provide a content type and then no content, but that's what the module does. If you were hand-coding this, the content type wouldn't be required, but the blank line still would be.

```
#!/bin/sh

cat <<EOCAT
Status: 204 No response

EOCAT
```

See Also

The documentation for the standard CGI module

19.8   Debugging the Raw HTTP Exchange

Problem

Your CGI script is misbehaving strangely with your browser, and you suspect something in the HTTP header is missing. You want to find out exactly what your browser is sending to the server in the HTTP header.

Solution

Create your own fake web server and point your browser at it, as shown in Example 19-6.

Example 19-6. dummyhttpd

```
#!/usr/bin/perl -w
# dummyhttpd - start an HTTP daemon and print what the client sends

use strict;
use LWP 5.32;  # minimal good version
use HTTP::Daemon;
```

Example 19-6. dummyhttpd (continued)

```perl
my $server = HTTP::Daemon->new(Timeout => 60, LocalPort => 8989);
print "Please contact me at: <URL:", $server->url, ">\n";

while (my $client = $server->accept) {
  CONNECTION:
    while (my $answer = $client->get_request) {
        print $answer->as_string;
        $client->autoflush;
  RESPONSE:
        while (<STDIN>) {
            last RESPONSE   if $_ eq ".\n";
            last CONNECTION if $_ eq "..\n";
            print $client $_;
        }
        print "\nEOF\n";
    }
    print "CLOSE: ", $client->reason, "\n";
    $client->close;
    undef $client;
}
```

Discussion

It's hard to keep track of which versions of all browsers still have which bugs. The fake server program can save you days of head scratching, because sometimes a misbehaving browser doesn't send the server the right thing. Historically, we have seen aberrant browsers lose their cookies, mis-escape a URL, send the wrong status line, and other blunders even less obvious.

The fake server is best run on the same machine as the real server. That way your browser still sends any cookies destined for that domain. Then instead of pointing your browser at:

```
http://somewhere.com/cgi-bin/whatever
```

use the alternate port given in the new constructor in the Solution. You don't need to be the superuser to run the server if you use the alternate port.

```
http://somewhere.com:8989/cgi-bin/whatever
```

If you convince yourself that the client is behaving properly but wonder about the server, it's easiest to use the *telnet* program to manually talk to the remote server.

```
% telnet www.perl.com 80
GET /bogotic HTTP/1.0
<<blank line here>>
HTTP/1.1 404 File Not Found
Date: Tue, 21 Apr 1998 11:25:43 GMT
Server: Apache/1.2.4
Connection: close
Content-Type: text/html
```

```
<HTML><HEAD>
<TITLE>404 File Not Found </TITLE>
</HEAD><BODY>
<H1>File Not Found</H1>
The requested URL /bogotic was not found on this server.<P>
</BODY></HTML>
```

If you have LWP installed on your system, you can use the *GET* alias for the *lwp-request* program. This will follow any redirection chains, which can shed light on your problem. For example:

```
% GET -esuSU http://mox.perl.com/perl/bogotic
GET http://language.perl.com/bogotic
Host: mox.perl.com
User-Agent: lwp-request/1.32

GET http://mox.perl.com/perl/bogotic --> 302 Moved Temporarily
GET http://www.perl.com/perl/bogotic --> 302 Moved Temporarily
GET http://language.perl.com/bogotic --> 404 File Not Found
Connection: close
Date: Tue, 21 Apr 1998 11:29:03 GMT
Server: Apache/1.2.4
Content-Type: text/html
Client-Date: Tue, 21 Apr 1998 12:29:01 GMT
Client-Peer: 208.201.239.47:80
Title: Broken perl.com Links

<HTML>
<HEAD><TITLE>An Error Occurred</TITLE></HEAD>
<BODY>
<H1>An Error Occurred</h1>
404 File Not Found
</BODY>
</HTML>
```

See Also

The documentation for the standard CGI module; Recipe 19.9; *lwp-request*(1)

19.9   Managing Cookies

Problem

You want to get or set a cookie to help manage sessions or user preferences.

Solution

Using CGI.pm, retrieve an existing cookie like this:

```
$preference_value = cookie("preference name");
```

To prepare a cookie, do this:

```
$packed_cookie = cookie( -NAME    => "preference name",
                         -VALUE   => "whatever you'd like",
                         -EXPIRES => "+2y");
```

To save a cookie back to the client browser, you must include it in the HTTP header, probably using either the header or redirect functions:

```
print header(-COOKIE => $packed_cookie);
```

Discussion

Cookies store information on the client's browser. If you're using Netscape under Unix, you can inspect your own *~/.netscape/cookies* file, although this doesn't show your current cookies. It holds only those cookies present when you last exited the browser. Think of them as per-application user preferences or a way to help with transactions. Benefits of cookies are that they can be shared between several different programs on your server, and they persist even across browser invocations.

However, cookies can be used for dubious purposes like traffic analysis and click tracing. This makes some folks very nervous about who is collecting their personal data and what use will be made of their page viewing habits. Cookies don't travel well, either. If you use a browser at home or in someone else's office, it won't have the cookies from the browser at your office. For this reason, do not expect every browser to accept the cookies you give it. As if that weren't bad enough, browsers can't guarantee they'll keep cookies around forever. Here's an excerpt from the HTTP State Management Mechanism RFC (number 2109):

> Because user agents have finite space in which to store cookies, they may also discard older cookies to make space for newer ones, using, for example, a least-recently-used algorithm, along with constraints on the maximum number of cookies that each origin server may set.

While in theory a browser can delete cookies at any time, a browser that freely did so with session cookies or with recently used longer-term cookies would quite annoy its users.

Due to their unreliability, you should probably not place too much faith in cookies. Use them for simple, stateful transactions, and avoid traffic analysis for reasons of privacy.

Example 19-7 is a complete program that remembers the user's last choice.

Example 19-7. ic_cookies

```
#!/usr/bin/perl -w
# ic_cookies - sample CGI script that uses a cookie
use CGI qw(:standard);

use strict;
```

Example 19-7. ic_cookies (continued)

```
my $cookname = "favorite ice cream";
my $favorite = param("flavor");
my $tasty    = cookie($cookname) || 'mint';

unless ($favorite) {
    print header(), start_html("Ice Cookies"), h1("Hello Ice Cream"),
        hr(), start_form(),
            p("Please select a flavor: ", textfield("flavor",$tasty)),
                end_form(), hr();
    exit;
}

my $cookie = cookie(
                -NAME    => $cookname,
                -VALUE   => $favorite,
                -EXPIRES => "+2y",
            );

print header(-COOKIE => $cookie),
    start_html("Ice Cookies, #2"),
    h1("Hello Ice Cream"),
    p("You chose as your favorite flavor `$favorite'.");
```

A more extensible approach is to send a single cookie containing a unique semi-random session identifier (such as `sprintf "%x-%x-%x", time(), $$, int rand 0x10000`) and use that to map to a file (or database record) on the server that maintains any state you associate with that session. Just be sure that accessing that file or record doesn't create a race condition, as described in Recipe 19.4. Also be sure to occasionally purge old session files on the server, and gracefully cope with session cookies that no longer exist on the server. There are already Perl modules for intelligently implementing just this kind of server-side data, such as CGI::Session.

See Also

The documentation for the standard CGI module; the documentation for the CGI::Session module; Recipe 19.4; RFC 2109

19.10 Creating Sticky Widgets

Problem

You want form fields to default to the last values submitted. For instance, you want a search form like Google (*http://www.google.com/*) where the keywords you searched for appear in the search dialog above the results.

Solution

Use CGI.pm's HTML shortcuts to create your form, which automatically provides previous values as defaults:

```
print textfield("SEARCH");          # previous SEARCH value is the default
```

Discussion

Example 19-8 is a simple script for producing the list of users currently logged in.

Example 19-8. who.cgi

```perl
#!/usr/bin/perl -wT
# who.cgi - run who(1) on a user and format the results nicely

$ENV{IFS}='';
$ENV{PATH}='/bin:/usr/bin';

use CGI qw(:standard);

# print search form
print header(), start_html("Query Users"), h1("Search");
print start_form(), p("Which user?", textfield("WHO")); submit(), end_form();

# print results of the query if we have someone to look for
$name = param("WHO");
if ($name) {
    print h1("Results");
    $html = '';

    # call who and build up text of response
    foreach (`who`) {
        next unless /^$name\s/o;          # only lines matching $name
        s/&/&amp;/g;                      # escape HTML
        s/</&lt;/g;
        s/>/&gt;/g;
        $html .= $_;
    }
    # nice message if we didn't find anyone by that name
    $html = $html || "$name is not logged in";

    print pre($html);
}

print end_html();
```

The call to `textfield` generates HTML for a text entry field whose parameter name is WHO. After printing the form, we check whether we were called with a value for the WHO parameter. If so, we try to find lines in the output from *who* for that user.

See Also

The documentation for the standard CGI module; Recipe 19.4; Recipe 19.6

19.11 Writing a Multiscreen CGI Script

Problem

You want a single CGI script that can return several different pages to the browser. For instance, you want a single script for administering a database of products. The script will be called to display the form to add a product, to process the add-product form, to display a list of products to delete, to process the delete-product form, to display a list of products to edit, to display a form of the product's attributes for the user to change, and to process the edit-product form. You can use these multiscreen CGI scripts to form an elementary shopping-cart application.

Solution

Use a hidden field to encode the current screen.

Discussion

It is easy to generate sticky hidden fields with the CGI module. The `hidden` function returns HTML for a hidden widget and uses the widget's current value if you pass `hidden` only the widget name:

```
use CGI qw(:standard);
print hidden("bacon");
```

To determine which page ("display product list", "display all items in shopping cart", "confirm order") to display, use another hidden field. We'll call this one `.State` so it won't conflict with any field we might have called `State` (for instance, in credit card billing information). To let the user move from page to page, use submit buttons that set `.State` to the name of the page to go to. For instance, to make a button to take the user to the "Checkout" page, use:

```
print submit(-NAME => ".State", -VALUE => "Checkout");
```

We wrap this in a function to make it easier to type:

```
sub to_page { return submit( -NAME => ".State", -VALUE => shift ) }
```

To decide what code to display, check the `.State` parameter:

```
$page = param(".State") || "Default";
```

Put the code to generate each page in separate subroutines. You could decide which subroutine to call with a long `if ... elsif ... elsif`:

```
if ($page eq "Default") {
    front_page( );
```

```
    } elsif ($page eq "Checkout") {
        checkout( );
    } else {
        no_such_page( );          # when we get a .State that doesn't exist
    }
```

This is tedious and clumsy. Instead use a hash that maps a page name to a subroutine. This is another strategy for implementing a C-style switch statement in Perl:

```
%States = (
    'Default'    => \&front_page,
    'Shirt'      => \&shirt,
    'Sweater'    => \&sweater,
    'Checkout'   => \&checkout,
    'Card'       => \&credit_card,
    'Order'      => \&order,
    'Cancel'     => \&front_page,
);

if ($States{$page}) {
    $States{$page}->( );   # call the correct subroutine
} else {
    no_such_page( );
}
```

Each page will have some persistent widgets. For instance, the page that lets the user order t-shirts will want the number of t-shirts to persist even when the user continues and orders shoes as well. We do this by calling the page-generating subroutines with a parameter that lets them know whether they're the active page. If they're not the active page, they should only send back hidden fields for any persistent data:

```
while (($state, $sub) = each %States) {
    $sub->( $page eq $state );
}
```

The eq comparison returns true if the page is the current page, false otherwise. The page-generating subroutine then looks like this:

```
sub t_shirt {
    my $active = shift;

    unless ($active) {
        print hidden("size"), hidden("color");
        return;
    }

    print p("You want to buy a t-shirt?");
    print p("Size: ", popup_menu('size', [ qw(XL L M S XS) ]));
    print p("Color:", popup_menu('color', [ qw(Black White) ]));

    print p( to_page("Shoes"), to_page("Checkout") );
}
```

Because the subroutines all generate HTML, we have to print the HTTP header and start the HTML document and form before we call the subroutines. This lets us print a standard header and footer for all pages. Here, we assume we have subroutines standard_header and standard_footer for printing headers and footers:

```
print header("Program Title"), start_html();
print standard_header(), begin_form();
while (($state, $sub) = each %States) {
    $sub->( $page eq $state );
}
print standard_footer(), end_form(), end_html();
```

Don't make the mistake of encoding prices in the forms. Calculate prices based on the values of the hidden widgets, and sanity-check the information where you can. For example, compare against known products to make sure they're not trying to order a burgundy XXXXXXL t-shirt. You can identify items by any string, whether it's a text string like "sweater_xl_plain" that's a key to a hash of prices, or whether you want to use a product "SKU" number that you look up in an external database.

Using hidden data is more robust than using cookies, because you can't rely on the browser supporting or accepting cookies. A full explanation is in Recipe 19.9. On the other hand, using hidden data means that every link the user follows must be a form submit button instead of a normal hyperlink.

We show a simple shopping cart application as the program *chemiserie* at the end of this chapter.

See Also

The documentation for the standard CGI module.

19.12 Saving a Form to a File or Mail Pipe

Problem

Your CGI script needs to save or mail the entire form contents to a file.

Solution

To store a form, use the CGI module's save_parameters function or save method, which take a filehandle argument. You can save to a file:

```
# first open and exclusively lock the file
open(FH, ">>/tmp/formlog")          or die "can't append to formlog: $!";
flock(FH, 2)                        or die "can't flock formlog: $!";

# either using the procedural interface
use CGI qw(:standard);
save_parameters(*FH);               # with CGI::save

# or using the object interface
```

```
use CGI;
$query = CGI->new( );
$query->save(*FH);

close(FH)                                    or die "can't close formlog: $!";
```

or save to a pipe, such as one connected to a mailer process:

```
use CGI qw(:standard);
open(MAIL, "|/usr/lib/sendmail -oi -t") or die "can't fork sendmail: $!";
print MAIL <<EOF;
From: $0 (your cgi script)
To: hisname\@hishost.com
Subject: mailed form submission

EOF
save_parameters(*MAIL);
close(MAIL)                                  or die "can't close sendmail: $!";
```

Discussion

Sometimes all you want to do with form data is to save it for later use. The save_
parameters function and save method in CGI.pm write form parameters to an open
filehandle. That filehandle can be attached to an open file (preferably one opened in
append mode and locked, as in the Solution), or to a pipe whose other end is a mail
program.

File entries are stored one per line as variable=value pairs, with any funny characters URL-escaped. Each record is separated by a line with a single equals sign. These
are typically read back by invoking the CGI->new method with a filehandle argument
that manages all of the unescaping automatically, as described later.

If you want to add extra information to your query before you save it, the param function (or method, if you're using the object-oriented interface) can take more than one
argument, setting the value(s) of a form parameter. For example, here's how to save
a time stamp and the entire environment:

```
param("_timestamp", scalar localtime);
param("_environs", %ENV);
```

Once you have the forms in a file, process them by using the object interface.

To load a query object from a filehandle, call the new method with a filehandle argument. Each time you do this, it returns a complete form. When end of file is hit, the
returned form has no parameters. The following code demonstrates this approach. It
keeps a running total of all "items request" parameters, but only if the form was not
submitted from a *perl.com* site. Remember, we added the _environs and _timestamp
parameters when we wrote the file.

```
use CGI;
open(FORMS, "< /tmp/formlog")        or die "can't read formlog: $!";
flock(FORMS, 1)                      or die "can't lock formlog: $!";
```

```
while ($query = CGI->new(*FORMS)) {
    last unless $query->param();       # means end of file
    %his_env = $query->param('_environs');
    $count   += $query->param('items requested')
                unless $his_env{REMOTE_HOST} =~ /(^|\.)perl\.com$/
}
print "Total orders: $count\n";
```

File ownership and access permissions are an issue here, as for any files created by CGI scripts.

See Also

Recipe 18.3; Recipe 19.3

19.13 Program: chemiserie

The CGI script in Example 19-9 lets people order t-shirts and sweaters over the Web, using techniques described in Recipe 19.11. Its output isn't elegant or beautiful, but illustrating the multiscreen technique in a short program was challenging enough without trying to make it pretty as well.

The shirt and sweater subroutines check their widget values. If the user somehow submits an invalid color or size, the value is reset to the first in the list of allowable colors or sizes.

Example 19-9. chemiserie

```
#!/usr/bin/perl -w
# chemiserie - simple CGI shopping for shirts and sweaters

use strict;
use CGI qw(:standard);
use CGI::Carp qw(fatalsToBrowser);

my %States;                    # state table mapping pages to functions
my $Current_Screen;            # the current screen
croak "This CGI works only over HTTPS"
  if $ENV{'SERVER_PORT'} && !$ENV{'HTTPS'};
# Since we deal with sensitive data like credit card numbers
# Hash of pages and functions.

%States = (
    'Default'    => \&front_page,
    'Shirt'      => \&shirt,
    'Sweater'    => \&sweater,
    'Checkout'   => \&checkout,
    'Card'       => \&credit_card,
    'Order'      => \&order,
    'Cancel'     => \&front_page,
);
```

Example 19-9. chemiserie (continued)

```perl
$Current_Screen = param(".State") || "Default";
die "No screen for $Current_Screen" unless $States{$Current_Screen};

# Generate the current page.

standard_header();

while (my($screen_name, $function) = each %States) {
    $function->($screen_name eq $Current_Screen);
}
standard_footer();
exit;

#################################
# header, footer, menu functions
#################################

sub standard_header {
    print header(), start_html(-Title => "Shirts", -BGCOLOR=>"White");
    print start_form(); # start_multipart_form() if file upload
}

sub standard_footer { print end_form(), end_html() }

sub shop_menu {
    print p(defaults("Empty My Shopping Cart"),
        to_page("Shirt"),
        to_page("Sweater"),
        to_page("Checkout"));
}

#############################
# subroutines for each screen
#############################

# The default page.
sub front_page {
    my $active = shift;
    return unless $active;

    print "<H1>Hi!</H1>\n";
    print "Welcome to our Shirt Shop!  Please make your selection from ";
    print "the menu below.\n";

    shop_menu();
}

# Page to order a shirt from.
sub shirt {
    my $active = shift;
    my @sizes  = qw(XL L M S);
    my @colors = qw(Black White);
```

Example 19-9. chemiserie (continued)

```perl
    my ($size, $color, $count) =
      (param("shirt_size"), param("shirt_color"), param("shirt_count"));

    # sanity check
    if ($count) {
        $color = $colors[0] unless grep { $_ eq $color } @colors;
        $size  = $sizes[0]  unless grep { $_ eq $size  } @sizes;
        param("shirt_color", $color);
        param("shirt_size",  $size);
    }

    unless ($active) {
        print hidden("shirt_size")  if $size;
        print hidden("shirt_color") if $color;
        print hidden("shirt_count") if $count;
        return;
    }

    print h1("T-Shirt");
    print p("What a shirt!  This baby is decked out with all the options.",
        "It comes with full luxury interior, cotton trim, and a collar",
        "to make your eyes water!  Unit price: \$33.00");

    print h2("Options");
    print p("How Many?", textfield("shirt_count"));
    print p("Size?",  popup_menu("shirt_size",  \@sizes ),
        "Color?", popup_menu("shirt_color", \@colors));

    shop_menu( );
}

# Page to order a sweater from.
sub sweater {
    my $active = shift;
    my @sizes  = qw(XL L M);
    my @colors = qw(Chartreuse Puce Lavender);

    my ($size, $color, $count) =
      (param("sweater_size"), param("sweater_color"), param("sweater_count"));

    # sanity check
    if ($count) {
        $color = $colors[0] unless grep { $_ eq $color } @colors;
        $size  = $sizes[0]  unless grep { $_ eq $size  } @sizes;
        param("sweater_color", $color);
        param("sweater_size",  $size);
    }

    unless ($active) {
        print hidden("sweater_size")  if $size;
        print hidden("sweater_color") if $color;
        print hidden("sweater_count") if $count;
```

Example 19-9. chemiserie (continued)

```perl
        return;
    }

    print h1("Sweater");
    print p("Nothing implies preppy elegance more than this fine",
        "sweater.  Made by peasant workers from black market silk,",
        "it slides onto your lean form and cries out \"Take me,",
        "for I am a god!\".  Unit price: \$49.99.");

    print h2("Options");
    print p("How Many?", textfield("sweater_count"));
    print p("Size?",  popup_menu("sweater_size",  \@sizes));
    print p("Color?", popup_menu("sweater_color", \@colors));

    shop_menu( );
}

# Page to display current order for confirmation.
sub checkout {
    my $active = shift;

    return unless $active;

    print h1("Order Confirmation");
    print p("You ordered the following:");
    print order_text( );
    print p("Is this right?  Select 'Card' to pay for the items",
        "or 'Shirt' or 'Sweater' to continue shopping.");
    print p(to_page("Card"),
        to_page("Shirt"),
        to_page("Sweater"));
}

# Page to gather credit-card information.
sub credit_card {
    my $active = shift;
    my @widgets = qw(Name Address1 Address2 City Zip State Phone Card Expiry);

    unless ($active) {
        print map { hidden($_) } @widgets;
        return;
    }

    print pre(p("Name:            ", textfield("Name")),
            p("Address:         ", textfield("Address1")),
            p("                 ", textfield("Address2")),
            p("City:            ", textfield("City")),
            p("Zip:             ", textfield("Zip")),
            p("State:           ", textfield("State")),
            p("Phone:           ", textfield("Phone")),
            p("Credit Card #: ", textfield("Card")),
            p("Expiry:          ", textfield("Expiry")));
```

Example 19-9. chemiserie (continued)

```perl
    print p("Click on 'Order' to order the items.  Click on 'Cancel' to return shopping.
");

    print p(to_page("Order"), to_page("Cancel"));
}

# Page to complete an order.
sub order {
    my $active = shift;

    unless ($active) {
        return;
    }

    # you'd check credit card values here

    print h1("Ordered!");
    print p("You have ordered the following toppings:");
    print order_text();

    print p(defaults("Begin Again"));
}

# Returns HTML for the current order ("You have ordered ...")
sub order_text {
    my $html = '';

    if (param("shirt_count")) {
        $html .= p("You have ordered ", param("shirt_count"),
                    " shirts of size ",  param("shirt_size"),
                    " and color ", param("shirt_color"), ".");
    }
    if (param("sweater_count")) {
        $html .= p("You have ordered ",  param("sweater_count"),
                    " sweaters of size ", param("sweater_size"),
                    " and color ", param("sweater_color"), ".");
    }
    $html = p("Nothing!") unless $html;
    $html .= p("For a total cost of ", calculate_price());
    return $html;
}

sub calculate_price {
    my $shirts   = param("shirt_count")   || 0;
    my $sweaters = param("sweater_count") || 0;
    return sprintf("\$%.2f", $shirts*33 + $sweaters * 49.99);
}


sub to_page { submit(-NAME => ".State", -VALUE => shift) }
```

## CHAPTER 20

Web Automation

*The web, then, or the pattern, a web at once sensuous
and logical, an elegant and pregnant texture: that is
style, that is the foundation of the art of literature.*

—Robert Louis Stevenson,
  On some Technical Elements of Style in Literature
  (1885)

20.0   Introduction

Chapter 19 concentrated on responding to browser requests and producing documents using CGI. This chapter approaches the Web from the other side: instead of responding to a browser, you pretend to be one, generating requests and processing returned documents. We make extensive use of modules to simplify this process because the intricate network protocols and document formats are tricky to get right. By letting existing modules handle the hard parts, you can concentrate on the interesting part—your own program.

The relevant modules can all be found under the following URL:

> *http://search.cpan.org/modlist/World_Wide_Web*

There you'll find modules for computing credit card checksums, interacting with Netscape or Apache server APIs, processing image maps, validating HTML, and manipulating MIME. The largest and most important modules for this chapter, though, are found in the libwww-perl suite of modules, referred to collectively as LWP. Table 20-1 lists just a few modules included in LWP.

Table 20-1. LWP modules

Module name	Purpose
LWP::UserAgent	WWW user agent class
LWP::RobotUA	Develop robot applications
LWP::Protocol	Interface to various protocol schemes

Table 20-1. LWP modules (continued)

Module name	Purpose
LWP::Authen::Basic	Handle 401 and 407 responses
LWP::MediaTypes	MIME types configuration (text/html, etc.)
LWP::Debug	Debug logging module
LWP::Simple	Simple procedural interface for common functions
HTTP::Headers	MIME/RFC 822–style headers
HTTP::Message	HTTP-style message
HTTP::Request	HTTP request
HTTP::Response	HTTP response
HTTP::Daemon	HTTP server class
HTTP::Status	HTTP status code (200 OK, etc.)
HTTP::Date	Date-parsing module for HTTP date formats
HTTP::Negotiate	HTTP content negotiation calculation
WWW::RobotRules	Parse *robots.txt* files
File::Listing	Parse directory listings

The HTTP:: and LWP:: modules request documents from a server. The LWP::Simple module offers an easy way to fetch a document. However, the module can't access individual components of the HTTP response. For these, use HTTP::Request, HTTP::Response, and LWP::UserAgent. We show both sets of modules in Recipes 20.1, 20.2, and 20.10.

Once distributed with LWP, but now in distributions of their own, are the HTML:: modules. These parse HTML. They provide the basis for Recipes 20.5, 20.4, 20.6, 20.3, 20.7, and the programs *htmlsub* and *hrefsub*.

Recipe 20.12 gives a regular expression to decode fields in your web server's log files and shows how to interpret the fields. We use this regular expression and the Logfile::Apache module in Recipe 20.13 to show two ways of summarizing data in web server log files.

For detailed guidance on the LWP modules, see Sean Burke's *Perl & LWP* (O'Reilly) This book expands on much of this chapter, picking up where recipes such as Recipe 20.5 on converting HTML to ASCII, Recipe 20.14 on fetching pages that use cookies, and Recipe 20.15 on fetching password-protected pages leave off.

20.1 Fetching a URL from a Perl Script

Problem

You have a URL whose contents you want to fetch from a script.

Solution

Use the get function from the CPAN module LWP::Simple, part of LWP.

```
use LWP::Simple;
$content = get($URL);
```

Discussion

The right library makes life easier, and the LWP modules are the right ones for this task. As you can see from the Solution, LWP makes this task a trivial one.

The get function from LWP::Simple returns undef on error, so check for errors this way:

```
use LWP::Simple;
unless (defined ($content = get $URL)) {
    die "could not get $URL\n";
}
```

When called that way, however, you can't determine the cause of the error. For this and other elaborate processing, you'll have to go beyond LWP::Simple.

Example 20-1 is a program that fetches a remote document. If it fails, it prints out the error status line. Otherwise, it prints out the document title and the number of bytes of content. We use three modules, two of which are from LWP.

LWP::UserAgent

> This module creates a virtual browser. The object returned from the new constructor is used to make the actual request. We've set the name of our agent to "Schmozilla/v9.14 Platinum" just to give the remote webmaster browser-envy when they see it in their logs. This is useful on obnoxious web servers that needlessly consult the user agent string to decide whether to return a proper page or an infuriating "you need Internet Navigator v12 or later to view this site" cop-out.

HTTP::Response

> This is the object type returned when the user agent actually runs the request. We check it for errors and contents.

URI::Heuristic

> This curious little module uses Netscape-style guessing algorithms to expand partial URLs. For example:

Simple	Guess
perl	*http://www.perl.com*
www.oreilly.com	*http://www.oreilly.com*
ftp.funet.fi	*ftp://ftp.funet.fi*
/etc/passwd	*file:/etc/passwd*

Although the simple forms listed aren't legitimate URLs (their format is not in the URI specification), Netscape tries to guess the URLs they stand for. Because Netscape does it, most other browsers do, too.

The source is in Example 20-1.

Example 20-1. titlebytes

```perl
#!/usr/bin/perl -w
# titlebytes - find the title and size of documents
use strict;
use LWP::UserAgent;
use HTTP::Response;
use URI::Heuristic;
my $raw_url = shift                    or die "usage: $0 url\n";
my $url = URI::Heuristic::uf_urlstr($raw_url);
$| = 1;                                # to flush next line
printf "%s =>\n\t", $url;
# bogus user agent
my $ua = LWP::UserAgent->new( );
$ua->agent("Schmozilla/v9.14 Platinum"); # give it time, it'll get there
# bogus referrer to perplex the log analyzers
my $response = $ua->get($url, Referer => "http://wizard.yellowbrick.oz");
if ($response->is_error( )) {
  printf " %s\n", $response->status_line;
} else {
  my $content = $response->content( );
  my $bytes = length $content;
  my $count = ($content =~ tr/\n/\n/);
  printf "%s (%d lines, %d bytes)\n",
    $response->title( ) || "(no title)", $count, $bytes;
}
```

When run, the program produces output like this:

```
% titlebytes http://www.tpj.com/
http://www.tpj.com/ =>
    The Perl Journal (109 lines, 4530 bytes)
```

Yes, "referer" is not how "referrer" should be spelled. The standards people got it wrong when they misspelled HTTP_REFERER. Please use double r's when referring to things in English.

The first argument to the get method is the URL, and subsequent pairs of arguments are headers and their values.

See Also

The documentation for the CPAN module LWP::Simple, and the *lwpcook*(1) and *lwptut*(1) manpages that came with LWP; the documentation for the modules LWP:: UserAgent, HTTP::Response, and URI::Heuristic; Recipe 20.2 and *Perl & LWP*

20.2 Automating Form Submission

Problem

You want to submit form values to a CGI script from your program. For example, you want to write a program that searches Amazon and notifies you when new books with a particular keyword in the title or new books by a particular author appear.

Solution

If you're submitting form values with GET, use the get method on an LWP::User-Agent object:

```
use LWP::Simple;
use URI::URL;

$url = url("http://www.amazon.com/exec/obidos/search-handle-url/index=books");
$url->query_form("field-author" => "Larry Wall"); # more params if needed
$page = get($url);
```

If you're using the POST method, create your own user agent and encode the content appropriately:

```
use LWP::UserAgent;

$ua = LWP::UserAgent->new( );
$resp = $ua->post("www.amazon.com/exec/obidos/search-handle-form",
                  { "url"           => "index-books",
                    "field-keywords" => "perl" });
$content = $resp->content;
```

Discussion

For simple operations, the procedural interface of the LWP::Simple module is sufficient. For fancier ones, the LWP::UserAgent module provides a virtual browser object, which you manipulate using method calls.

The format of a query string is:

```
field1=value1&field2=value2&field3=value3
```

In GET requests, this is encoded in the URL being requested:

```
script.cgi?field1=value1&field2=value2&field3=value3
```

Fields must still be properly escaped, so setting the arg form parameter to "this isn't <EASY> & <FUN>" would yield:

```
http://www.site.com/path/to/
        script.cgi?arg=%22this+isn%27t+%3CEASY%3E+%26+%3CFUN%3E%22
```

The query_form method called on a URL object correctly escapes the form values for you, or you could use the URI::Escape::uri_escape or CGI::escape_html functions on your own. In POST requests, the query string is in the body of the HTTP document sent to the CGI script.

You can use the LWP::Simple module to submit data in a GET request, but there is no corresponding LWP::Simple interface for POST requests. Instead, the $ua->post method creates and submits the request in one fell swoop.

If you need to go through a proxy, construct your user agent and tell it to use a proxy this way:

```
$ua->proxy('http' => 'http://proxy.myorg.com:8081');
```

If a proxy handles multiple protocols, pass an array reference as the first argument:

```
$ua->proxy(['http', 'ftp'] => 'http://proxy.myorg.com:8081');
```

That says that HTTP and FTP requests through this user agent should be routed through the proxy on port 8081 at *proxy.myorg.com*.

See Also

The documentation for the CPAN modules LWP::Simple, LWP::UserAgent, HTTP::Request::Common, URI::Escape, and URI::URL; Recipe 20.1; *Perl & LWP*

20.3 Extracting URLs

Problem

You want to extract all URLs from an HTML file. For example, you have downloaded a page that lists the MP3 files downloadable from some site. You want to extract those MP3s' URLS so you can filter the list and write a program to download the ones you want.

Solution

Use the HTML::LinkExtor module from CPAN:

```
use HTML::LinkExtor;

$parser = HTML::LinkExtor->new(undef, $base_url);
$parser->parse_file($filename);
@links = $parser->links;
foreach $linkarray (@links) {
    my @element = @$linkarray;
    my $elt_type = shift @element;              # element type

    # possibly test whether this is an element we're interested in
    while (@element) {
        # extract the next attribute and its value
        my ($attr_name, $attr_value) = splice(@element, 0, 2);
```

```
        # ... do something with them ...
    }
}
```

Discussion

You can use HTML::LinkExtor in two different ways: either by calling links to get a list of all links in the document once it is completely parsed, or by passing a code reference in the first argument to new. The referenced function is called on each link as the document is parsed.

The links method clears the link list, so call it only once per parsed document. It returns a reference to an array of elements. Each element is itself an array reference with an HTML::Element object at the front followed by a list of attribute name and attribute value pairs. For instance, the HTML:

```
<A HREF="http://www.perl.com/">Home page</A>
<IMG SRC="images/big.gif" LOWSRC="images/big-lowres.gif">
```

would return a data structure like this:

```
[
  [ a,   href   => "http://www.perl.com/" ],
  [ img, src    => "images/big.gif",
         lowsrc => "images/big-lowres.gif" ]
]
```

Here's an example of how to use $elt_type and $attr_name to print out and anchor an image:

```
if ($elt_type eq 'a' && $attr_name eq 'href') {
    print "ANCHOR: $attr_value\n"
        if $attr_value->scheme =~ /http|ftp/;
}
if ($elt_type eq 'img' && $attr_name eq 'src') {
    print "IMAGE:  $attr_value\n";
}
```

To extract links only to MP3 files, you'd say:

```
foreach my $linkarray (@links) {
    my ($elt_type, %attrs) = @$linkarray;

    if ($elt_type eq 'a' && $attrs{'href'} =~ /\.mp3$/i) {
      # do something with $attr{'href'}, the URL of the mp3 file
    }
}
```

Example 20-2 is a complete program that takes as its arguments a URL, such as *file://
/tmp/testing.html* or *http://www.ora.com/*, and produces on standard output an alphabetically sorted list of unique URLs linked from that site.

Example 20-2. xurl

```perl
#!/usr/bin/perl -w
# xurl - extract unique, sorted list of links from URL
use HTML::LinkExtor;
use LWP::Simple;

$base_url = shift;
$parser = HTML::LinkExtor->new(undef, $base_url);
$parser->parse(get($base_url))->eof;
@links = $parser->links;
foreach $linkarray (@links) {
    my @element  = @$linkarray;
    my $elt_type = shift @element;
    while (@element) {
        my ($attr_name , $attr_value) = splice(@element, 0, 2);
        $seen{$attr_value}++;
    }
}
for (sort keys %seen) { print $_, "\n" }
```

This program does have a limitation: if the get of $base_url involves a redirection, links resolve using the original URL instead of the URL after the redirection. To fix this, fetch the document with LWP::UserAgent and examine the response code to find out whether a redirection occurred. Once you know the post-redirection URL (if any), construct the HTML::LinkExtor object accordingly.

Here's an example of the run:

```
% xurl http://www.perl.com/CPAN
ftp://ftp@ftp.perl.com/CPAN/CPAN.html
http://language.perl.com/misc/CPAN.cgi
http://language.perl.com/misc/cpan_module
http://language.perl.com/misc/getcpan
http://www.perl.com/index.html
http://www.perl.com/gifs/lcb.xbm
```

In mail or Usenet messages, you may see URLs written as:

```
<URL:http://www.perl.com>
```

This is supposed to make it easy to pick URLs from messages:

```
@URLs = ($message =~ /<URL:(.*?)>/g);
```

See Also

The documentation for the CPAN modules LWP::Simple, HTML::LinkExtor, and HTML::Entities; Recipe 20.1

20.4   Converting ASCII to HTML

Problem

You want to convert ASCII text to HTML. For example, you have mail you want to display intelligently on a web page.

Solution

Use the simple little encoding filter in Example 20-3.

Example 20-3. text2html

```perl
#!/usr/bin/perl -w -p00
# text2html - trivial html encoding of normal text
# -p means apply this script to each record.
# -00 mean that a record is now a paragraph

use HTML::Entities;
$_ = encode_entities($_, "\200-\377");

if (/^\s/) {
    # Paragraphs beginning with whitespace are wrapped in <PRE>
    s{(.*)$}        {<PRE>\n$1</PRE>\n}s;        # indented verbatim
} else {
    s{^(>.*)}       {$1<BR>}gm;                  # quoted text
    s{<URL:(.*?)>}  {<A HREF="$1">$1</A>}gs       # embedded URL   (good)
                    ||
    s{(http:\S+)}   {<A HREF="$1">$1</A>}gs;      # guessed URL    (bad)
    s{\*(\S+)\*}    {<STRONG>$1</STRONG>}g;       # this is *bold* here
    s{\b_(\S+)\_\b} {<EM>$1</EM>}g;               # this is _italics_ here
    s{^}            {<P>\n};                      # add paragraph tag
}
```

Discussion

Converting arbitrary plain text to HTML has no general solution because there are too many conflicting ways to represent formatting information. The more you know about the input, the better you can format it.

For example, if you knew that you would be fed a mail message, you could add this block to format the mail headers:

```perl
BEGIN {
    print "<TABLE>";
    $_ = encode_entities(scalar <>);
    s/\n\s+/ /g;  # continuation lines
    while ( /^(\S+?:)\s*(.*)$/gm ) {              # parse heading
        print "<TR><TH ALIGN='LEFT'>$1</TH><TD>$2</TD></TR>\n";
    }
    print "</TABLE><HR>";
}
```

The CPAN module HTML::TextToHTML has options for headers, footers, indentation, tables, and more.

See Also

The documentation for the CPAN modules HTML::Entities and HTML::TextToHTML

20.5 Converting HTML to ASCII

Problem

You want to convert an HTML file into formatted, plain ASCII. For example, you want to mail a web document to someone.

Solution

If you have an external formatter like *lynx*, call an external program:

```
$ascii = `lynx -dump $filename`;
```

If you want to do it within your program and don't care about the things that the HTML::FormatText formatter doesn't yet handle well (tables and frames):

```
use HTML::FormatText 3;
$ascii = HTML::FormatText->format_file(
  $filename,
  leftmargin => 0, rightmargin => 50
);
```

Discussion

These examples both assume the HTML is in a file. If your HTML is in a variable, you need to write it to a file for *lynx* to read. With HTML::FormatText, use the format_string( ) method:

```
use HTML::FormatText 3;
$ascii = HTML::FormatText->format_string(
  $filename,
  leftmargin => 0, rightmargin => 50
);
```

If you use Netscape, its "Save as" option with the type set to "Text" does the best job with tables.

See Also

The documentation for the CPAN modules HTML::TreeBuilder and HTML::FormatText; your system's *lynx*(1) manpage; Recipe 20.6

20.6 Extracting or Removing HTML Tags

Problem

You want to remove HTML tags from a string, leaving just plain text. For example, you are indexing a document but don't want your index to show "words" like `<B>` and `<body>`.

Solution

The following oft-cited solution is simple but wrong on all but the most trivial HTML:

```
($plain_text = $html_text) =~ s/<[^>]*>//gs;    # WRONG
```

A correct but slower and slightly more complicated way is to use the technique from Recipe 20.5:

```
use HTML::FormatText 2;
$plain_text = HTML::FormatText->format_string($html_text);
```

Discussion

As with almost everything else in Perl, there is more than one way to do it. Each solution attempts to strike a balance between speed and flexibility. Occasionally you may find HTML that's simple enough that a trivial command-line call works:

```
% perl -pe 's/<[^>]*>//g' file
```

However, this breaks with files whose tags cross line boundaries, like this:

```
<IMG SRC = "foo.gif"
    ALT = "Flurp!">
```

So, you'll see people doing this instead:

```
% perl -0777 -pe 's/<[^>]*>//gs' file
```

or its scripted equivalent:

```
{
    local $/;                # temporary whole-file input mode
    $html = <FILE>;
    $html =~ s/<[^>]*>//gs;
}
```

But even that isn't good enough except for simplistic HTML without any interesting bits in it. This approach fails for the following examples of valid HTML (among many others):

```
<IMG SRC = "foo.gif" ALT = "A > B">

<!-- <A comment> -->
```

```
<script>if (a<b && a>c)</script>

<# Just data #>

<![INCLUDE CDATA [ >>>>>>>>>>> ]]>
```

If HTML comments include other tags, those solutions would also break on text like this:

```
<!-- This section commented out.
    <B>You can't see me!</B>
-->
```

The only solution that works well here is to use the HTML parsing routines from CPAN. The second code snippet shown in the Solution demonstrates this better technique.

For more flexible parsing, subclass the HTML::Parser class and record only the text elements you see:

```
package MyParser;
use HTML::Parser;
use HTML::Entities qw(decode_entities);

@ISA = qw(HTML::Parser);

sub text {
    my($self, $text) = @_;
    print decode_entities($text);
}

package main;
MyParser->new->parse_file(*F);
```

If you're only interested in simple tags that don't contain others nested inside, you can often make do with an approach like the following, which extracts the title from a non-tricky HTML document:

```
($title) = ($html =~ m#<TITLE>\s*(.*?)\s*</TITLE>#is);
```

Again, the regex approach has its flaws, so a more complete solution using LWP to process the HTML is shown in Example 20-4.

Example 20-4. htitle

```
#!/usr/bin/perl
# htitle - get html title from URL
use LWP;
die "usage: $0 url ...\n" unless @ARGV;
foreach $url (@ARGV) {
    $ua = LWP::UserAgent->new();
    $res = $ua->get($url);
    print "$url: " if @ARGV > 1;
    if ($res->is_success) {
        print $res->title, "\n";
```

Example 20-4. htitle (continued)

```
    } else {
        print $res->status_line, "\n";
    }
}
```

Here's an output example:

```
% htitle http://www.ora.com
www.oreilly.com -- Welcome to O'Reilly & Associates!

% htitle http://www.perl.com/ http://www.perl.com/nullvoid
http://www.perl.com/: The www.perl.com Home Page
http://www.perl.com/nullvoid: 404 File Not Found
```

See Also

The documentation for the CPAN modules HTML::TreeBuilder, HTML::Parser, HTML::Entities, and LWP::UserAgent; Recipe 20.5

20.7 Finding Stale Links

Problem

You want to check a document for invalid links.

Solution

Use the technique outlined in Recipe 20.3 to extract each link, and then use LWP:: Simple's head function to make sure that link exists.

Discussion

Example 20-5 is an applied example of the link-extraction technique. Instead of just printing the name of the link, we call LWP::Simple's head function on it. The HEAD method fetches the remote document's metainformation without downloading the whole document. If it fails, the link is bad, so we print an appropriate message.

Because this program uses the get function from LWP::Simple, it is expecting a URL, not a filename. If you want to supply either, use the URI::Heuristic module described in Recipe 20.1.

Example 20-5. churl

```
#!/usr/bin/perl -w
# churl - check urls
use HTML::LinkExtor;
use LWP::Simple;
```

Example 20-5. churl (continued)

```
$base_url = shift
    or die "usage: $0 <start_url>\n";
$parser = HTML::LinkExtor->new(undef, $base_url);
$html = get($base_url);
die "Can't fetch $base_url" unless defined($html);
$parser->parse($html);
@links = $parser->links;
print "$base_url: \n";
foreach $linkarray (@links) {
    my @element  = @$linkarray;
    my $elt_type = shift @element;
    while (@element) {
        my ($attr_name , $attr_value) = splice(@element, 0, 2);
        if ($attr_value->scheme =~ /\b(ftp|https?|file)\b/) {
            print "  $attr_value: ", head($attr_value) ? "OK" : "BAD", "\n";
        }
    }
}
```

Here's an example of a program run:

```
% churl http://www.wizards.com
http://www.wizards.com:
  FrontPage/FP_Color.gif:  OK
  FrontPage/FP_BW.gif:  BAD
  #FP_Map:  OK
  Games_Library/Welcome.html:  OK
```

This program has the same limitation as the HTML::LinkExtor program in Recipe 20.3.

See Also

The documentation for the CPAN modules HTML::LinkExtor, LWP::Simple, LWP::UserAgent, and HTTP::Response; Recipe 20.8

20.8   Finding Fresh Links

Problem

Given a list of URLs, you want to determine which have been modified most recently. For example, you want to sort your bookmarks so those most recently updated are on the top.

Solution

The program in Example 20-6 reads URLs from standard input, rearranges them by date, and prints them to standard output with those dates prepended.

Example 20-6. surl

```
#!/usr/bin/perl -w
# surl - sort URLs by their last modification date
use strict;
use LWP::UserAgent;
use HTTP::Request;
use URI::URL qw(url);
my %Date;
my $ua = LWP::UserAgent->new();
while ( my $url = url(scalar <>) ) {
    my $ans;
    next unless $url->scheme =~ /^(file|https?)$/;
    $ans = $ua->head($url);
    if ($ans->is_success) {
        $Date{$url} = $ans->last_modified || 0;   # unknown
    } else {
        warn("$url: Error [", $ans->code, "] ", $ans->message, "!\n");
    }
}
foreach my $url ( sort { $Date{$b} <=> $Date{$a} } keys %Date ) {
    printf "%-25s %s\n", $Date{$url} ? (scalar localtime $Date{$url})
                                      : "<NONE SPECIFIED>", $url;
}
```

Discussion

The *surl* script works more like a traditional filter program. It reads from standard input one URL per line. (Actually, it uses ARGV to read, which defaults to STDIN when @ARGV is empty.) The last-modified date on each URL is fetched by a HEAD request. That date is stored in a hash with the URL as key. Then a simple sort by value is run on the hash to reorder the URLs by date. On output, the internal date is converted into localtime format.

Here's an example of using the *xurl* program from the earlier recipe to extract the URLs, then running that program's output to feed into *surl*.

```
% xurl http://use.perl.org/~gnat/journal | surl | head
Mon Jan 13 22:58:16 2003  http://www.nanowrimo.org/
Sun Jan 12 19:29:00 2003  http://www.costik.com/gamespek.html
Sat Jan 11 20:57:03 2003  http://www.cpan.org/ports/index.html
Sat Jan 11 09:46:19 2003  http://jakarta.apache.org/gump/
Tue Jan  7 20:27:30 2003  http://use.perl.org/images/menu_gox.gif
Tue Jan  7 20:27:30 2003  http://use.perl.org/images/menu_bgo.gif
Tue Jan  7 20:27:30 2003  http://use.perl.org/images/menu_gxg.gif
Tue Jan  7 20:27:30 2003  http://use.perl.org/images/menu_ggx.gif
Tue Jan  7 20:27:30 2003  http://use.perl.org/images/menu_gxx.gif
Tue Jan  7 20:27:30 2003  http://use.perl.org/images/menu_gxo.gif
```

Having a variety of small programs that each do one thing and can be combined into more powerful constructs is the hallmark of good programming. You could even argue that *xurl* should work on files, and that some other program should actually fetch the URL's contents over the Web to feed into *xurl*, *churl*, or *surl*. That program would probably be called *gurl*, except that program already exists: the LWP module suite has a program called *lwp-request* with aliases *HEAD*, *GET*, and *POST* to run those operations from shell scripts.

See Also

The documentation for the CPAN modules LWP::UserAgent, HTTP::Request, and URI::URL; Recipe 20.7

20.9   Using Templates to Generate HTML

Problem

You want to store a parameterized template in an external file, read that template from your CGI script, and substitute your own variables for escapes embedded in the text. This separates your program from the static parts of the document.

Solution

To expand only variable references, use this `template` function:

```
sub template {
    my ($filename, $fillings) = @_;
    my $text;
    local $/;                   # slurp mode (undef)
    open(my $fh, "<", $filename) or return;
    $text = <$fh>;              # read whole file
    close($fh);                 # ignore retval
    # replace quoted words with value in %$fillings hash
    $text =~ s{ %% ( .*? ) %% }
              { exists( $fillings->{$1} )
                    ? $fillings->{$1}
                    : ""
              }gsex;
    return $text;
}
```

on a data file like this:

```
<!-- simple.template for internal template() function -->
<HTML><HEAD><TITLE>Report for %%username%%</TITLE></HEAD>
<BODY><H1>Report for %%username%%</H1>
%%username%% logged in %%count%% times, for a total of %%total%% minutes.
```

If you can guarantee the data file is secure from tampering, use the CPAN module Text::Template to expand full expressions. A data file for Text::Template looks like this:

```
<!-- fancy.template for Text::Template -->
<HTML><HEAD><TITLE>Report for {$user}</TITLE></HEAD>
<BODY><H1>Report for {$user}</H1>
```

```
    { lcfirst($user) } logged in {$count} times, for a total of
    { int($total / 60) } minutes.
```

For a complete templating solution, see the Template Toolkit's Template module
This offers a scripting language and mod_perl integration, and is covered in Recipe
21.17.

Discussion

Parameterized output for your CGI scripts is a good idea for many reasons. Separating your program from its data lets other people (art directors, for instance) change the HTML but not the program. Even better, two programs can share the same template, so style changes in the template are immediately reflected in both programs' output.

For example, suppose you have the first template from the Solution stored in a file. Then your CGI program contains the definition of the template subroutine shown earlier and makes appropriate settings for variables $username, $count, and $total. You can fill in the template by simply using:

```
%fields = (
            username => $whats_his_name,
            count    => $login_count,
            total    => $minute_used,
);

print template("/home/httpd/templates/simple.template", \%fields);
```

The template file contains keywords surrounded by double percent symbols (%%KEYWORD%%). These keywords are looked up in the %$fillings hash whose reference was passed as the second argument to template. Example 20-7 is a more elaborate example using an SQL database.

Example 20-7. userrep1

```
#!/usr/bin/perl -w
# userrep1 - report duration of user logins using SQL database

use DBI;
use CGI qw(:standard);

# template() defined as in the Solution section above

$user = param("username")                  or die "No username";

$dbh = DBI->connect("dbi:mysql:connections:mysql.domain.com",
    "connections", "seekritpassword")      or die "Couldn't connect\n";
$sth = $dbh->prepare(<<"END_OF_SELECT")    or die "Couldn't prepare SQL";
    SELECT COUNT(duration),SUM(duration)
    FROM logins WHERE username='$user'
END_OF_SELECT
```

Example 20-7. userrep1 (continued)

```
    # this time the duration is assumed to be in seconds
    if (@row = $sth->fetchrow_array( )) {
        ($count, $seconds) = @row;
    } else {
        ($count, $seconds) = (0,0);
    }

    $sth->finish( );
    $dbh->disconnect;

    print header( );
    print template("report.tpl", {
        'username' => $user,
        'count'    => $count,
        'total'    => $total
    });
```

For a fancier, more flexible solution, look at the second template in the Solution section, which relies upon the CPAN module Text::Template. Contents of braces found within the template file are evaluated as Perl code. Ordinarily, these substitutions are just simple variables:

```
    You owe: {$total}
```

but they can also include full expressions:

```
    The average was {$count ?  ($total/$count) : 0}.
```

Example 20-8 is an example of using that template.

Example 20-8. userrep2

```
    #!/usr/bin/perl -w
    # userrep2 - report duration of user logins using SQL database

    use Text::Template;
    use DBI;
    use CGI qw(:standard);

    $tmpl = "/home/httpd/templates/fancy.template";
    $template = Text::Template->new(-type => "file", -source => $tmpl);
    $user = param("username")                    or die "No username";

    $dbh = DBI->connect("dbi:mysql:connections:mysql.domain.com",
        "connections", "secret passwd")         or die "Couldn't db connect\n";
    $sth = $dbh->prepare(<<"END_OF_SELECT")     or die "Couldn't prepare SQL";
        SELECT COUNT(duration),SUM(duration)
        FROM logins WHERE username='$user'
    END_OF_SELECT

    $sth->execute( )                            or die "Couldn't execute SQL";

    if (@row = $sth->fetchrow_array( )) {
```

Example 20-8. userrep2 (continued)

```
    ($count, $total) = @row;
} else {
    $count = $total = 0;
}

$sth->finish();
$dbh->disconnect;

print header();
print $template->fill_in();
```

But this approach raises security concerns. Anyone who can write to the template file can insert code that your program will run. See Recipe 8.17 for ways to lessen this danger.

See Also

The documentation for the CPAN modules Text::Template and Template; Recipe 8.16; Recipe 14.9

20.10 Mirroring Web Pages

Problem

You want a local copy of a web page kept up-to-date.

Solution

Use LWP::Simple's mirror function:

```
use LWP::Simple;
mirror($URL, $local_filename);
```

Discussion

Although closely related to the get function discussed in Recipe 20.1, the mirror function doesn't download the file unconditionally. It adds the If-Modified-Since header to the GET request it creates, so the server does not transfer the file unless the file has been updated.

The mirror function mirrors only a single page, not a full tree. To mirror a set of pages, use this recipe in conjunction with Recipe 20.3. A good solution to mirroring an entire directory hierarchy can be found in the *w3mir* program, also found on CPAN, and the *wget* program from *ftp.gnu.org*.

Be careful! It's possible (and easy) to write programs that run amok and begin downloading all web pages on the net. This is not only poor etiquette, it's also an infinite task, since some pages are dynamically generated. It could also get you into trouble with someone who doesn't want their pages downloaded *en masse*.

See Also

The documentation for the CPAN module LWP::Simple; the HTTP specification at *http://www.w3.org/pub/WWW/Protocols/HTTP/*

20.11 Creating a Robot

Problem

You want to create a script that navigates the Web on its own (i.e., a robot), and you'd like to respect the remote sites' wishes.

Solution

Instead of writing your robot with LWP::UserAgent, use LWP::RobotUA instead:

```
use LWP::RobotUA;
$ua = LWP::RobotUA->new('websnuffler/0.1', 'me@wherever.com');
```

Discussion

To avoid marauding robots and web crawlers hammering their servers, sites are encouraged to create a file with access rules called *robots.txt*. If you're fetching only one document, this is no big deal, but if your script fetches many documents from the same server, you could easily exhaust that site's bandwidth.

When writing scripts to run around the Web, it's important to be a good net citizen: don't request documents from the same server too often, and heed the advisory access rules in their *robots.txt* file.

The easiest way to handle this is to use the LWP::RobotUA module instead of LWP::UserAgent to create agents. This agent automatically knows to fetch data slowly when calling the same server repeatedly. It also checks each site's *robots.txt* file to see whether you're trying to grab a file that is off-limits. If you do, you'll get a response like this:

```
403 (Forbidden) Forbidden by robots.txt
```

Here's an example *robots.txt* file, fetched using the GET program that comes with the LWP module suite:

```
% GET http://www.webtechniques.com/robots.txt
User-agent: *
    Disallow: /stats
    Disallow: /db
    Disallow: /logs
```

```
Disallow: /store
Disallow: /forms
Disallow: /gifs
Disallow: /wais-src
Disallow: /scripts
Disallow: /config
```

A more interesting and extensive example is at *http://www.cnn.com/robots.txt*. This file is so big, they even keep it under RCS control!

```
% GET http://www.cnn.com/robots.txt | head
# robots, scram
# $I d : robots.txt,v 1.2 1998/03/10 18:27:01 mreed Exp $
User-agent: *
Disallow: /
User-agent:     Mozilla/3.01 (hotwired-test/0.1)
Disallow:    /cgi-bin
Disallow:    /TRANSCRIPTS
Disallow:    /development
```

See Also

The documentation for the CPAN module LWP::RobotUA(3); *http://info.webcrawler.com/mak/projects/robots/robots.html* for a description of how well-behaved robots act

20.12 Parsing a Web Server Log File

Problem

You want to extract selected information from a web server log file.

Solution

Pull apart the log file as follows:

```
while (<LOGFILE>) {
  my ($client, $identuser, $authuser, $date, $time, $tz, $method,
      $url, $protocol, $status, $bytes) =
  /^(\S+) (\S+) (\S+) \[([^:]+):(\d+:\d+:\d+) ([^\]]+)\] "(\S+) (.*?) (\S+)"
      (\S+) (\S+)$/;
  # ...
}
```

Discussion

This regular expression pulls apart entries in Common Log Format, an informal standard that most web servers adhere to. The fields are listed in Table 20-2.

Table 20-2. Common Log Format fields

Field	Meaning
client	IP address or hostname of browser's machine
identuser	If IDENT (RFC 1413) was used, what it returned
authuser	If username/password authentication was used, whom they logged in as
date	Date of request (e.g., 01/Mar/1997)
time	Time of request (e.g., 12:55:36)
tz	Time zone (e.g., −0700)
method	Method of request (e.g., GET, POST, or PUT)
url	URL in request (e.g., /~user/index.html)
protocol	HTTP/1.0 or HTTP/1.1
status	Returned status (200 is okay, 500 is server error)
bytes	Number of bytes returned (could be "-" for errors, redirects, and other non-document transfers)

Other formats include the referrer and agent information. The pattern needs only minor changes to work with other log file formats. Beware that spaces in the URL field are not escaped, so we can't use \S* to extract the URL. .* would cause the regex to match the entire string and then backtrack until it could satisfy the rest of the pattern. We use .*? and anchor the pattern to the end of the string with $ to make the regular expression engine initially match nothing but then add characters until the entire pattern is satisfied.

See Also

The CLF spec at *http://www.w3.org/Daemon/User/Config/Logging.html*

20.13 Processing Server Logs

Problem

You need to summarize your server logs, but you don't have a customizable program to do it.

Solution

Parse the error log yourself with regular expressions, or use the Logfile modules from CPAN.

Discussion

Example 20-9 is a sample report generator for an Apache weblog.

Example 20-9. sumwww

```perl
#!/usr/bin/perl -w
# sumwww - summarize web server log activity

$lastdate = "";
daily_logs();
summary();
exit;

# read CLF files and tally hits from the host and to the URL
sub daily_logs {
    while (<>) {
        ($type, $what) = /"(GET|POST)\s+(\S+?) \S+"/ or next;
        ($host, undef, undef, $datetime) = split;
        ($bytes) = /\s(\d+)\s*$/ or next;
        ($date)  = ($datetime =~ /\[([^:]*)/);
        $posts   += ($type eq POST);
        $home++ if m, / ,;
        if ($date ne $lastdate) {
            if ($lastdate) { write_report()    }
            else           { $lastdate = $date }
        }
        $count++;
        $hosts{$host}++;
        $what{$what}++;
        $bytesum += $bytes;
    }
    write_report() if $count;
}

# use *typeglob aliasing of global variables for cheap copy
sub summary  {
    $lastdate = "Grand Total";
    *count    = *sumcount;
    *bytesum  = *bytesumsum;
    *hosts    = *allhosts;
    *posts    = *allposts;
    *what     = *allwhat;
    *home     = *allhome;
    write;
}

# display the tallies of hosts and URLs, using formats
sub write_report {
    write;

    # add to summary data
    $lastdate      = $date;
    $sumcount     += $count;
    $bytesumsum   += $bytesum;
    $allposts     += $posts;
    $allhome      += $home;
```

Example 20-9. sumwww (continued)

```
    # reset daily data
    $posts = $count = $bytesum = $home = 0;
    @allwhat{keys %what}   = keys %what;
    @allhosts{keys %hosts} = keys %hosts;
    %hosts = %what = ( );
}

format STDOUT_TOP =
@|||||||||| @|||||| @||||||| @||||||| @|||||| @|||||| @||||||||||||||
"Date",     "Hosts", "Accesses", "Unidocs", "POST", "Home", "Bytes"
----------- ------- -------- -------- ------- ------- --------------
.

format STDOUT =
@>>>>>>>>>> @>>>>>> @>>>>>>> @>>>>>>> @>>>>>> @>>>>>> @>>>>>>>>>>>>>
$lastdate,  scalar(keys %hosts),
            $count, scalar(keys %what),
                            $posts,  $home,   $bytesum
.
```

Here's sample output from that program:

Date	Hosts	Accesses	Unidocs	POST	Home	Bytes
19/May/1998	353	6447	3074	352	51	16058246
20/May/1998	1938	23868	4288	972	350	61879643
21/May/1998	1775	27872	6596	1064	376	64613798
22/May/1998	1680	21402	4467	735	285	52437374
23/May/1998	1128	21260	4944	592	186	55623059
Grand Total	6050	100849	10090	3715	1248	250612120

Use the Logfile::Apache module from CPAN, shown in Example 20-10, to write a similar, but less specific, program. This module is distributed with other Logfile modules in a single Logfile distribution (*Logfile-0.115.tar.gz* at the time of this writing).

Example 20-10. aprept

```perl
#!/usr/bin/perl -w
# aprept - report on Apache logs

use Logfile::Apache;

$l = Logfile::Apache->new(
    File  => "-",                  # STDIN
    Group => [ Domain, File ]);

$l->report(Group => Domain, Sort => Records);
$l->report(Group => File,   List => [Bytes,Records]);
```

The new constructor reads a log file and builds indices internally. Supply a filename with the parameter named File and the fields to index in the Group parameter. The possible fields are Date (date request), Hour (time of day the request was received),

File (file requested), User (username parsed from request), Host (hostname requesting the document), and Domain (Host translated into "France", "Germany", etc.).

To produce a report on STDOUT, call the report method. Give the index to use with the Group parameter, and optionally say how to sort (Records is by number of hits, Bytes by number of bytes transferred) or how to break it down further (by number of bytes or number of records).

Here's some sample output:

```
Domain                  Records
= == == == == == == == == == == == == == == == ==
US Commercial           222 38.47%
US Educational          115 19.93%
Network                  93 16.12%
Unresolved               54  9.36%
Australia                48  8.32%
Canada                   20  3.47%
Mexico                    8  1.39%
United Kingdom            6  1.04%


File                          Bytes        Records
= == == == == == == == == == == == == == == == == == == == == == == == == == ==
/                             13008  0.89%       6  1.04%
/cgi-bin/MxScreen             11870  0.81%       2  0.35%
/cgi-bin/pickcards            39431  2.70%      48  8.32%
/deckmaster                  143793  9.83%      21  3.64%
/deckmaster/admin             54447  3.72%       3  0.52%
```

See Also

The documentation for the CPAN module Logfile::Apache; *perlform*(1) and Chapter 7 of *Programming Perl*

20.14 Using Cookies

Problem

You want to fetch web pages, but the server is using cookies to track you. For example, some sites use a cookie to remember that you've authenticated. If you don't send the right cookie, you'll never get past the login screen.

Solution

Let LWP::UserAgent handle cookies for you. You can enable cookies for just this program run with:

```
$ua->cookie_jar({ });
```

Or instead store cookies in a file between invocations with:

```
$ua->cookie_jar({ file => "$ENV{HOME}/.cookies" });
```

Discussion

The default behavior of LWP::UserAgent is never to send a Cookie: header, even when the server offers cookies in a response. To keep track of cookies LWP::UserAgent receives and send them when appropriate, provide the user agent object with a special "cookie jar" object to hold the cookies: an HTTP::Cookies object.

Pass the cookie_jar method either an HTTP::Cookies object to use that object as the cookie jar, or else a hash reference whose contents go into a new HTTP::Cookies object.

Without parameters, an HTTP::Cookies object keeps cookies in memory, so they're no longer available once your program exits. The file parameter in the cookie_jar method call specifies a filename to use for initializing the cookie jar and for saving updated or new cookies. This is how you give cookies a shelf life beyond a single run of your program.

To disable cookies, call cookie_jar with no parameters:

```
$ua->cookie_jar();
```

See Also

The documentation for the CPAN modules LWP::UserAgent and HTTP::Cookie

20.15 Fetching Password-Protected Pages

Problem

You want to use LWP to fetch web pages or submit forms, but the web server requires authentication.

Solution

Set the username and password for a particular realm with the user agent's credentials method:

```
$ua->credentials('http://www.perlcabal.com/cabal_only/',
                 'Secret Perl Cabal Files',
                 'username' => 'password');
```

Discussion

To access pages protected by basic authentication, a browser must supply the username and password for the *realm* of the authentication. The realm is just a string that identifies which username and password the user must supply. The credentials method tells the user agent to send the username and password for a particular realm.

A somewhat kludgey solution is to specify URLs with the username and password in them:

```
http://user:password@www.example.com/private/pages/
```

This is kludgey because links within the returned document do not have your username and password encoded in them. Solutions that rely entirely on URL-encoded usernames and passwords often quickly degenerate into code that wishes it had used credentials to begin with.

See Also

The documentation for the CPAN module LWP::UserAgent

20.16 Fetching https:// Web Pages

Problem

You want to work with a web server over a secure (SSL) connection. For example, you want to automate ordering supplies for your company from an online store, and the online store wisely protects its transactions with SSL.

Solution

Install Crypt::SSLeay and https: URLs automatically work with LWP. You do not need to reinstall LWP.

Discussion

When LWP sends a request to an https server, it checks whether there is a module installed to do SSL. The two modules that LWP can use are, in order of preference, Crypt::SSLeay and IO::Socket::SSL. Of the two, Crypt::SSLeay is the more fully featured, but requires the OpenSSL libraries from *http://www.openssl.org*.

See Also

The documentation for the CPAN module Crypt::SSLeay; the *README.SSL* file in the libwww-perl distribution

20.17 Resuming an HTTP GET

Problem

You have part of a file and want to download the rest without refetching the content you already have. For example, your initial download was interrupted, so you want to complete it.

Solution

Use the HTTP 1.1 Range header in your GET request:

```
use LWP;
$have = length($file);
$response = $ua->get($URL,
                     'Range', "bytes=$have-");
# $response->content hold the rest of the file
```

Discussion

The Range header lets you specify which bytes to fetch. The 0th byte is the first in the file, so the range "bytes=0-" fetches the whole file.

You can also specify a range with two endpoints: "0-25", for example, fetches the first 26 bytes of the file. If you want to fetch an interior range, use "26-99".

Some servers don't support ranges, even though they claim to understand HTTP 1.1. In this case you'll be sent the whole file, not the range you asked for. To detect this, use HEAD to see the size of the file and then use a GET with a range to fetch the rest. If the content in the GET response is the same length as the original file, your range was ignored.

Here is the full list of ranges possible in the HTTP 1.1 specification:

[start]-	From start on (inclusive)
[start]-[end]	From start to end (inclusive)
-[num]	The last num bytes
[num]	From offset num on
0-0	The first byte
-1	The last byte

The HTTP specification also permits lists of ranges (e.g., "0-5,10-15,20-"). This returns a multipart response.

See Also

LWP documentation; the HTTP spec at *http://www.ietf.org/rfc/rfc2616.txt*

20.18 Parsing HTML

Problem

You need to extract complex information from a web page or pages. For example, you want to extract news stories from web sites like *CNN.com* or *news.bbc.co.uk*.

Solution

Use regular expressions for data that's well identified:

```
# story is everything from <!-- story --> to <!-- /story -->
if ($html =~ m{<!-- story -->(.*?)<!-- /story -->}s) {
  my $story = $1;
  # ...
} else {
  warn "No story found in the page";
}
```

But for tables and data identifiable only by complex patterns of HTML, use a parser:

```
use HTML::TokeParser;

my $parser = HTML::TokeParser->new($FILENAME)
    or die "Can't open $FILENAME: $!\n";
while (my $token = $parser->get_token()) {
    my $type = $token->[0];
    if    ($type eq 'S')  { ... }   # start tag
    elsif ($type eq 'E')  { ... }   # end tag
    elsif ($type eq 'T')  { ... }   # text
    elsif ($type eq 'C')  { ... }   # comment
    elsif ($type eq 'D')  { ... }   # declaration
    elsif ($type eq 'PI') { ... }   # processing instruction
    else { die "$type isn't a valid HTML token type" }
}
```

Discussion

Regular expressions are a convenient way to extract information from HTML. However, as the complexity of the HTML and the amount of information to be extracted go up, the maintainability of the regular expressions goes down. For a few well-defined fields, regular expressions are fine. For anything else, use a proper parser.

As an example of processing HTML with regular expressions, let's get the list of recent O'Reilly book releases. The list is found on *http://www.oreilly.com/catalog/new.html*, but there's also a navigation bar and a list of upcoming releases, so we can't simply extract all links.

The relevant HTML from the page looks like this:

```
<!-- New titles -->
<h3>New Titles</h3>
```

```
<ul><li><a href="netwinformian/">.NET Windows Forms in a
Nutshell</a> <em>(March)</em></li><li><a href="actscrptpr/">
ActionScript for Flash MX Pocket Reference</a> <em>(March)</em>
</li><li><a href="abcancer/">After Breast Cancer</a> <em>(March)
...
<li><a href="samba2/">Using Samba, 2nd Edition</a> <em>(February)
</em></li><li><a href="vbscriptian2/">VBScript in a Nutshell, 2nd
Edition</a> <em>(March)</em></li><li><a href="tpj2/">Web, Graphics
& Perl/Tk</a> <em>(March)</em></li></ul></td>
<td valign="top">
<!-- Upcoming titles -->
```

In fact, it's even uglier than this at the time of this writing—there are no newlines in the list of new books. It's all on one long line. Fortunately, this turns out to be comparatively simple to match. First we extract the HTML for the new titles, and then we extract the individual book links using the list anchors to anchor the regular expression:

```
($new_titles) = $html =~ m{<!-- New titles -->(.*?)<!-- Upcoming titles -->}s
    or die "Couldn't find new titles HTML";
```

```
while (m{<li>                # list item
        <a\ href="
        ([^\"]+)            # link to book = $1 = everything to next quote
        \">
        ([^<]+)             # book title = $2 = everything up to </a>
        </a>\ <em>\(
        ([^)]+)             # month = $3 = everything in the parentheses
        }gx) {
    printf("%-1010s%s\n", $3, $2); # could use $1 if we wanted
}
```

This produces output like:

```
March       .NET Windows Forms in a Nutshell
March       ActionScript for Flash MX Pocket Reference
March       After Breast Cancer
...
February    Using Samba, 2nd Edition
March       VBScript in a Nutshell, 2nd Edition
March       Web, Graphics & Perl/Tk
```

Regular expressions are difficult for this problem because they force you to work at the level of characters. The CPAN module HTML::TokeParser treats your HTML file as a series of HTML-y things: starting tags, closing tags, text, comments, etc. It decodes entities for you automatically, so you don't have to worry about converting & back into & in your code.

The argument to the new constructor of HTML::TokeParser is either a filename, a filehandle (or any object providing a read method), or a reference to the HTML text to be parsed:

```
$parser = HTML::TokeParser->new("foo.html") or die;
$parser = HTML::TokeParser->new(*STDIN) or die;
$parser = HTML::TokeParser->new(\$html) or die;
```

Each time you invoke get_token on the parser object, you get back a reference to an array. The first element in the array is a string identifying what type of token you have: start tag, end tag, etc. The rest of the array varies depending on what type of token it is. The four types of tokens that most people are interested in are starting tags, ending tags, text, and comments.

Starting tags have four more values in the token array: the tag name (in lowercase), a reference to a hash of attributes (lowercased attribute name as key), a reference to an array containing lowercased attribute names in the order they appeared in the tag, and a string containing the opening tag as it appeared in the text of the document. Parsing the following HTML:

```
<IMg SRc="/perl6.jpg" ALT="Steroidal Camel">
```

creates a token like this:

```
[ 'S',
  'img',
  { "src" => "/perl6.jpg",
    "alt" => "Steroidal Camel"
  },
  [ "src", "alt" ],
  '<IMg SRc="/perl6.jpg" ALT="Steroidal Camel">'
]
```

Since ending tags have fewer possibilities than opening tags, it follows that their tokens have a simpler structure. A token for an end tag contains "E" (identifying it as an end tag), the lowercased name of the tag being closed (e.g., "body"), and the tag as it appeared in the source (e.g., "</BODY>").

A token for a text tag has three values: "T" (to identify it as a text token), the text, and a flag identifying whether you need to decode entities on it (decode only if this flag is false).

```
use HTML::Entities qw(decode_entities);

if ($token->[0] eq "T") {
    $text = $token->[1];
    decode_entities($text) unless $token->[2];
    # do something with $text
}
```

Even simpler, a comment token contains only "C" (to indicate that it is a comment) followed by the comment text.

For a detailed introduction to parsing with tokens, see *Perl & LWP* by Sean Burke (O'Reilly).

See Also

HTML::TokeParser documentation; LWP documentation; *Perl & LWP*

20.19 Extracting Table Data

Problem

You have data in an HTML table, and you would like to turn that into a Perl data structure. For example, you want to monitor changes to an author's CPAN module list.

Solution

Use the HTML::TableContentParser module from CPAN:

```
use HTML::TableContentParser;

$tcp = HTML::TableContentParser->new;
$tables = $tcp->parse($HTML);

foreach $table (@$tables) {
  @headers = map { $_->{data} } @{ $table->{headers} };
  # attributes of table tag available as keys in hash
  $table_width = $table->{width};

  foreach $row (@{ $tables->{rows} }) {
    # attributes of tr tag available as keys in hash
    foreach $col (@{ $row->{cols} }) {
      # attributes of td tag available as keys in hash
      $data = $col->{data};
    }
  }
}
```

Discussion

The HTML::TableContentParser module converts all tables in the HTML document into a Perl data structure. As with HTML tables, there are three layers of nesting in the data structure: the table, the row, and the data in that row.

Each table, row, and data tag is represented as a hash reference. The hash keys correspond to attributes of the tag that defined that table, row, or cell. In addition, the value for a special key gives the contents of the table, row, or cell. In a table, the value for the rows key is a reference to an array of rows. In a row, the cols key points to an array of cells. In a cell, the data key holds the HTML contents of the data tag.

For example, take the following table:

```
<table width="100%" bgcolor="#ffffff">
  <tr>
    <td>Larry &amp; Gloria</td>
    <td>Mountain View</td>
    <td>California</td>
```

```
        </tr>
        <tr>
          <td><b>Tom</b></td>
          <td>Boulder</td>
          <td>Colorado</td>
        </tr>
        <tr>
          <td>Nathan &amp; Jenine</td>
          <td>Fort Collins</td>
          <td>Colorado</td>
        </tr>
      </table>
```

The parse method returns this data structure:

```
[
  {
    'width' => '100%',
    'bgcolor' => '#ffffff',
    'rows' => [
              {
                'cells' => [
                            { 'data' => 'Larry &amp; Gloria' },
                            { 'data' => 'Mountain View' },
                            { 'data' => 'California' },
                           ],
                'data' => "\n        "
              },
              {
                'cells' => [
                            { 'data' => '<b>Tom</b>' },
                            { 'data' => 'Boulder' },
                            { 'data' => 'Colorado' },
                           ],
                'data' => "\n        "
              },
              {
                'cells' => [
                            { 'data' => 'Nathan &amp; Jenine' },
                            { 'data' => 'Fort Collins' },
                            { 'data' => 'Colorado' },
                           ],
                'data' => "\n        "
              }
             ]
  }
]
```

The data tags still contain tags and entities. If you don't want the tags and entities, remove them by hand using techniques from Recipe 20.6.

Example 20-11 fetches a particular CPAN author's page and displays in plain text the modules they own. You could use this as part of a system that notifies you when your favorite CPAN authors do something new.

Example 20-11. Dump modules for a particular CPAN author

```perl
#!/usr/bin/perl -w
# dump-cpan-modules-for-author - display modules a CPAN author owns
use LWP::Simple;
use URI;
use HTML::TableContentParser;
use HTML::Entities;
use strict;
our $URL = shift || 'http://search.cpan.org/author/TOMC/';
my $tables = get_tables($URL);
my $modules = $tables->[4];     # 5th table holds module data
foreach my $r (@{ $modules->{rows} }) {
  my ($module_name, $module_link, $status, $description) =
      parse_module_row($r, $URL);
  print "$module_name <$module_link>\n\t$status\n\t$description\n\n";
}
sub get_tables {
  my $URL = shift;
  my $page = get($URL);
  my $tcp = new HTML::TableContentParser;
  return $tcp->parse($page);
}
sub parse_module_row {
  my ($row, $URL) = @_;
  my ($module_html, $module_link, $module_name, $status, $description);
  # extract cells
  $module_html = $row->{cells}[0]{data};  # link and name in HTML
  $status      = $row->{cells}[1]{data};  # status string and link
  $description = $row->{cells}[2]{data};  # description only
  $status =~ s{<.*?>}{}g; # naive link removal, works on this simple HTML
  # separate module link and name from html
  ($module_link, $module_name) = $module_html =~ m{href="(.*?)".*?>(.*)<}i;
  $module_link = URI->new_abs($module_link, $URL); # resolve relative links
  # clean up entities and tags
  decode_entities($module_name);
  decode_entities($description);
  return ($module_name, $module_link, $status, $description);
}
```

See Also

The documentation for the CPAN module HTML::TableContentParser; *http://search.cpan.org*

20.20 Program: htmlsub

This program makes substitutions in HTML files so changes happen only in normal text. If you had the file *scooby.html* that contained:

```html
<HTML><HEAD><TITLE>Hi!</TITLE></HEAD>
<BODY><H1>Welcome to Scooby World!</H1>
```

```
I have <A HREF="pictures.html">pictures</A> of the crazy dog
himself.  Here's one!<P>
<IMG SRC="scooby.jpg" ALT="Good doggy!"><P>
<BLINK>He's my hero!</BLINK>  I would like to meet him some day,
and get my picture taken with him.<P>
P.S. I am deathly ill.  <A HREF="shergold.html">Please send
cards</A>.
</BODY></HTML>
```

you could use *htmlsub* to change every occurrence of the word "picture" in the document text to read "photo". It prints the new document on STDOUT:

```
% htmlsub picture photo scooby.html
<HTML><HEAD><TITLE>Hi!</TITLE></HEAD>
<BODY><H1>Welcome to Scooby World!</H1>
I have <A HREF="pictures.html">photos</A> of the crazy dog
himself.  Here's one!<P>
<IMG SRC="scooby.jpg" ALT="Good doggy!"><P>
<BLINK>He's my hero!</BLINK>  I would like to meet him some day,
and get my photo taken with him.<P>
P.S. I am deathly ill.  <A HREF="shergold.html">Please send
cards</A>.
</BODY></HTML>
```

The program is shown in Example 20-12.

Example 20-12. htmlsub

```perl
#!/usr/bin/perl -w
# htmlsub - make substitutions in normal text of HTML files
# from Gisle Aas <gisle@aas.no>

sub usage { die "Usage: $0 <from> <to> <file>...\n" }

my $from = shift or usage;
my $to   = shift or usage;
usage unless @ARGV;

# Build the HTML::Filter subclass to do the substituting.

package MyFilter;
use HTML::Filter;
@ISA=qw(HTML::Filter);
use HTML::Entities qw(decode_entities encode_entities);

sub text
{
   my $self = shift;
   my $text = decode_entities($_[0]);
   $text =~ s/\Q$from/$to/go;        # most important line
   $self->SUPER::text(encode_entities($text));
}

# Now use the class.
```

Example 20-12. htmlsub (continued)

```
package main;
foreach (@ARGV) {
    MyFilter->new->parse_file($_);
}
```

20.21 Program: hrefsub

hrefsub makes substitutions in HTML files, so changes apply only to text in <A HREF="..." > tags. For instance, if you had the *scooby.html* file from the previous recipe, and you've moved *shergold.html* to be *cards.html*, you need but say:

```
% hrefsub shergold.html cards.html scooby.html
<HTML><HEAD><TITLE>Hi!</TITLE></HEAD>
<BODY><H1>Welcome to Scooby World!</H1>
I have <A HREF="pictures.html">pictures</A> of the crazy dog
himself.  Here's one!<P>
<IMG SRC="scooby.jpg" ALT="Good doggy!"><P>
<BLINK>He's my hero!</BLINK>  I would like to meet him some day,
and get my picture taken with him.<P>
P.S. I am deathly ill.  <a href="cards.html">Please send
cards</A>.
</BODY></HTML>
```

The HTML::Filter manual page has a BUGS section that says:

> Comments in declarations are removed from the declarations and then inserted as separate comments after the declaration. If you turn on strict_comment( ), then comments with embedded "-\|-" are split into multiple comments.

This version of *hrefsub* (shown in Example 20-13) always lowercases the a and the attribute names within this tag when substitution occurs. If $foo is a multiword string, then the text given to MyFilter->text may be broken such that these words do not come together; i.e., the substitution does not work. There should probably be a new option to HTML::Parser to make it not return text until the whole segment has been seen. Also, some people may not be happy with having their 8-bit Latin-1 characters replaced by ugly entities, so *htmlsub* does that, too.

Example 20-13. hrefsub

```
#!/usr/bin/perl -w
# hrefsub - make substitutions in <A HREF="..."> fields of HTML files
# from Gisle Aas <gisle@aas.no>

sub usage { die "Usage: $0 <from> <to> <file>...\n" }

my $from = shift or usage;
my $to   = shift or usage;
usage unless @ARGV;

# The HTML::Filter subclass to do the substitution.
```

Example 20-13. hrefsub (continued)

```perl
package MyFilter;
use HTML::Filter;
@ISA=qw(HTML::Filter);
use HTML::Entities qw(encode_entities);

sub start {
    my($self, $tag, $attr, $attrseq, $orig) = @_;
    if ($tag eq 'a' && exists $attr->{href}) {
        if ($attr->{href} =~ s/\Q$from/$to/g) {
            # must reconstruct the start tag based on $tag and $attr.
            # wish we instead were told the extent of the 'href' value
            # in $orig.
            my $tmp = "<$tag";
            for (@$attrseq) {
                my $encoded = encode_entities($attr->{$_});
                $tmp .= qq( $_="$encoded ");
            }
            $tmp .= ">";
            $self->output($tmp);
            return;
        }
    }
    $self->output($orig);
}

# Now use the class.

package main;
foreach (@ARGV) {
        MyFilter->new->parse_file($_);
}
```

mod_perl

Speed is good only when wisdom leads the way.
—James Poe

21.0 Introduction

The mod_perl project (*http://perl.apache.org/*) integrates Perl with the Apache web server. That way, you can use Perl to configure Apache, manipulate and respond to requests, write to log files, and much more.

Most people begin using mod_perl to avoid the performance penalty of CGI. With CGI programs, the web server starts a separate process for each request. This can be a costly business on most operating systems, with lots of kernel data structures to copy and file I/O to load the new process's binary. If you serve a lot of requests, the operating system may be unable to keep up with the demand for new processes, leaving your web server (and indeed the whole machine) unresponsive.

By embedding the Perl interpreter within the Apache process, mod_perl removes the need to start a separate process to generate dynamic content. Indeed, the Apache:: Registry and Apache::PerlRun modules provide a CGI environment within this persistent Perl interpreter (and form the basis of Recipe 21.12). This gives you an immediate performance boost over CGI (some report 10–100x performance) but doesn't take full advantage of the integration of Perl with Apache. For that, you need to write your own handlers.

Handlers

Because Apache has access to Perl at every step as it processes a request (and vice versa), you can write code (*handlers*) for every phase of a request-response cycle. There are 13 phases for which you can write handlers, and each phase has a default handler (so you don't have to install a handler for every phase).

You must do three things to install a handler for a specific phase: write the code, load the code into mod_perl, and tell mod_perl to call the code.

Handlers are simply subroutines. They're passed an Apache request object as the first argument, and through that object they can learn about the request, change Apache's information about the request, log errors, generate the response, and more. The return value of a handler determines whether the current phase continues with other handlers, the current phase ends successfully and execution proceeds to the next phase, or the current phase ends with an error. The return values are constants from the Apache::Constants module.

Although you can put your handler code in Apache's *httpd.conf* file, it's tidier to put your handlers in a module:

```perl
# in MyApp/Content.pm
package MyApp::Content;
use Apache::Constants ':common';

sub handler {
  my $r = shift;    # get the request object
  # ...
  return OK;        # for example
}
```

The subroutine can be named anything, but mod_perl makes it convenient to name every handler subroutine `handler` and to store different handlers in different modules. So MyApp::Content holds the handler for content generation, whereas MyApp:: Logging might hold the handler that logs the request.

Because the Perl interpreter doesn't go away after each request, you have to program tidily if you want to use mod_perl. This means using lexical (`my`) variables instead of globals and closing filehandles when done with them (or using lexical filehandles). Unclosed filehandles remain open until the next time that process runs your CGI script (when they are reopened), and global variables whose values aren't undefed will still have those values the next time that process runs your CGI script. The *mod_perl_traps* manpage that comes with mod_perl contains details of common mod_perl gotchas.

Load your handler module with a PerlModule directive in *httpd.conf*:

```
PerlModule MyApp::Content
```

This behaves like use in a Perl script: it loads and runs the module. Now that mod_ perl has your code loaded, tell Apache to call it.

Directives used in *httpd.conf* to install handlers are:

```
PerlChildInitHandler
PerlPostReadRequestHandler
PerlInitHandler
PerlTransHandler
PerlHeaderParserHandler
```

```
PerlAccessHandler
PerlAuthenHandler
PerlAuthzHandler
PerlTypeHandler
PerlFixupHandler
PerlHandler
PerlLogHandler
PerlCleanupHandler
PerlChildExitHandler
PerlDispatchHandler
PerlRestartHandler
```

Apache Phases

Understanding the phases of a request-response transaction requires some knowledge of how Apache works and consequences of the various ways of configuring it. Apache keeps a pool of server processes (*children*) to handle requests in parallel. The ChildInit and ChildExit phases represent the start and end of a child process, respectively.

A PostReadRequestHandler handler is called as soon as Apache reads the request from the client. Apache extracts the URL and virtual host name, but doesn't yet attempt to figure out to which file the request maps. Therefore you can't install such a handler from a *.htaccess* file or the <Location>, <Directory>, or <Files> sections (or their *Match variants) of *httpd.conf*.

The translation phase is responsible for decoding the incoming request and guessing the file that corresponds to the URL. It is here that you could affect your own aliases and redirects. Once Apache knows the requested URL and the corresponding file to look for, it can check the <Location>, <Directory>, and <Files> sections of *httpd.conf* and begin looking for *.htaccess* files. Install a translation handler with PerlTransHandler.

The header parsing phase is misleadingly named. The headers have already been parsed and stored in the request object. The intent of this phase is to give you an opportunity to act based on the headers once you know the file that the URL corresponds to. You can examine headers within a PostReadRequestHandler, but the file isn't known yet. PostReadRequestHandler is per-server, whereas HeaderParserHandler can be per-location, per-file, or per-directory. This is the first phase of the request for which you can install a handler from any part of an *httpd.conf* or *.htaccess* file.

The PerlInitHandler is an alias for "the first available handler." Inside the <Location>, <Directory>, and <Files> sections of *httpd.conf* or anywhere in a *.htaccess* file, it is an alias for PerlHeaderParserHandler. Everywhere else, PerlInitHandler is an alias for PerlPostReadRequestHandler.

Next come the authorization and authentication phases. Add a PerlAccessHandler to limit access without requiring usernames and passwords. The authentication phase decodes the username and password from the request and decides whether the user is a valid one. The authorization phase determines whether the user is allowed to access the requested resource. Apache splits authentication from authorization so separate areas of your web site can share a user database but grant different types of access to each area. We talk about writing authentication and authorization handlers in Recipe 21.1. Most people stick to basic authentication, which trivially encodes the password as part of the request header. If you want more secure authentication, you can use digest authentication (which is tricky to implement in a way that works on all browsers) or simply encrypt the entire request by using *https://* URLs to a secure server.

Once Apache has established that the client is allowed to access the requested document, the type determination phase occurs. Here Apache checks *httpd.conf* and *.htaccess* to see whether a specific content type has been forced on the requested file. If not, it uses the filename and its list of MIME types to figure out the file type. You can install a PerlTypeHandler to determine your own types.

Apache then offers you the chance to make any last-minute changes to the request via PerlFixupHandler. We use it in Recipe 21.10 to reinsert part of the URL removed earlier in a PerlHeaderParserHandler.

Then a handler must generate content. This is such a common use for mod_perl that the directive to install a content handler is simply PerlHandler. Once the content is generated, the logging phase begins, and it is normally here that the access log entry is written. You can, of course, write your own logging code to replace or augment Apache's (for example, logging to a database). This is the subject of Recipe 21.9.

The logging phase occurs before the connection to the client is closed. You can install code to run after the response is sent through a PerlCleanupHandler. Because a slow logging handler keeps the connection open (and thus the child waiting for more responses), a common mod_perl idiom is to use the cleanup phase for logging when the act of logging could take a long time (for example, when it involves a lot of I/O). Using the cleanup phase to actually clean up turns out to be rare.

That concludes the main phases and handlers. There are other handlers you can install. We don't use PerlDispatchHandler in this chapter, but it is an alternative mechanism to the system of registering handlers for every phase. If you register a PerlDispatchHandler, that handler is called for every phase. A PerlRestartHandler lets you run code whenever the Apache server restarts.

Much of the difficulty in getting started with mod_perl resides in learning how to do what you already knew how to do with CGI.pm. Cookies and form parameters are cumbersome to manipulate with pure mod_perl. This is why Recipes 21.2 and 21.3 discuss these seemingly simple topics.

More Documentation

There is a wealth of CPAN modules for mod_perl, and we don't hesitate to use them where possible. People often use an existing module until they run into limitations, then extend or replace the module. The convention is that mod_perl modules begin with Apache::; you can find a list of them at *http://search.cpan.org/modlist/World_Wide_Web/Apache*.

There are many good references for mod_perl developers. There's only one API reference book for mod_perl, *Writing Apache Modules in Perl and C* by Doug MacEachern and Lincoln Stein (O'Reilly). Although it was written for an early version of mod_perl, it is still highly relevant today.

If you're developing in mod_perl, get a copy of *Practical mod_perl* by Stas Bekman and Eric Cholet (O'Reilly). It's a rewrite and expansion of the online mod_perl guide (*http://perl.apache.org/guide*). *Apache Pocket Reference*, by Andrew Ford (O'Reilly), also includes a useful summary of mod_perl directives and methods.

To keep this chapter brief, we answer only initial questions about mod_perl. Deeper questions are answered by the *mod_perl Developer's Cookbook* by Geoffrey Young, Randy Kobes, and Paul Lindner (Sams). This is a great reference book, in a format similar to this book. The authors maintain a web site, *http://www.modperlcookbook.org*, with sample chapters, full source code, and further resources for mod_perl developers.

And, of course, mod_perl comes with its own documentation. Use the *mod_perl*(1) manpage for help with directives, and *Apache*(1) for help with the methods invokable on an Apache request object. Study the *mod_perl_traps*(1) manpage closely when you begin to migrate CGI scripts to mod_perl. If the documentation fails you, the mod_perl mailing list is a great way to get questions answered and keep up with the mod_perl world. See *http://apache.perl.org* for details on how to subscribe to the mailing list.

mod_perl 2

As this chapter goes to press, developers are putting the finishing touches on mod_perl 2.0. This is a major revision and rewrite of mod_perl for the Apache 2.0 system. The changes between 1.0 and 2.0 are too numerous to list: they affect configuration directives and Perl classes. There's an Apache::compat module that emulates the 1.0 handler API, but (as with using Apache::Registry to emulate CGI) there's a cost to the emulation. For maximum performance and flexibility, modify your modules to use the 2.0 API.

One of the biggest changes in 2.0 is the support for threads. Not only can you now have multiple Apache processes running at once, you can also have multiple threads of execution within each process. Some tasks are easier with threads, and you may see better performance with threads. However, it's trickier to write code—especially correct code—under threading.

For more on mod_perl 2.0, see *http://perl.apache.org/docs/2.0/*.

21.1 Authenticating

Problem

You want to verify the username and password supplied by users who are authenticating themselves.

Solution

Get the password with $r->get_basic_auth_pw, and the username with $r->connection->user. Indicate success by returning OK. Indicate failure by calling $r->note_basic_auth_failure and returning AUTH_REQUIRED.

```
package Your::Authentication::Package;
use Apache::Constants ':common';

sub handler {
  my $r = shift;

  return OK unless $r->is_main;    # skip for subrequests

  my ($res, $sent_pw) = $r->get_basic_auth_pw;
  if ($res != OK) {
    $r->note_basic_auth_failure;
    return $res;
  }

  my $user = $r->user;

  # check username and password, setting $failed if they don't match

  if ($failed) {
    $r->note_basic_auth_failure;
    return AUTH_REQUIRED;
  }

  return OK;
}
```

Install the handler for a directory or set of files with:

```
# the realm
AuthName "Holiday Photos"
# next line shouldn't be changed
AuthType Basic
PerlAuthenHandler Your::Authentication::Package
require valid-user
```

Description

The realm is what the user sees when their browser prompts for a username and password. If you set the realm to "Holiday Photos", the user is prompted to "enter username and password for Holiday Photos". You need at least one require directive to trigger the call to the authentication handler.

When you invoke $r->get_basic_auth_pw, Apache processes any authentication information sent by the client. Therefore you can't call $r->user before you call $r->get_basic_auth_pw (well, you can, but you won't get anything back).

The call to $r->get_basic_auth_pw returns two values, a status code and a password. If the status is OK, the browser agreed to authenticate and provided information. If the status is DECLINED, either the area isn't protected by basic authentication or there's no AuthType specified in *httpd.conf*. If the status is SERVER_ERROR, there's no realm defined for this area. If the status is AUTH_REQUIRED, the browser mangled or omitted basic authentication. If you decide to return AUTH_REQUIRED, first call $r->note_basic_auth_failure to ensure Apache sends realm information to the browser.

The status code returned from $r->get_basic_auth_pw tells you whether the browser knows to authenticate these pages. When the browser sends no authentication information, you respond "no password, no access." To do this, note the authentication failure and return the AUTH_REQUIRED that $r->get_basic_auth_pw gave you.

We invoke $r->is_main to learn whether we're the main request. Apache often makes subrequests, and there's no point in doing the (potentially slow) authentication lookup for the subrequests. This doesn't result in less security, since if the authentication fails for the main request, the content handler isn't run. This avoids messy problems like recursion and multiple attempts to parse POST data.

See Also

The Apache.pm manpage; *Writing Apache Modules with Perl and C*; Recipe 13.3 in *mod_perl Developer's Cookbook*

21.2 Setting Cookies

Problem

You want to send a cookie to a client as part of a response.

Solution

Use the Apache::Cookie module from CPAN. From within your content handler, create a new cookie and attach it to the outgoing headers:

```
use Apache::Cookie;
$cookie = Apache::Cookie->new($r,
                              -name   => "cookie name",
                              -value  => "its value",
```

```
                              -expires => "+1d" );
    $cookie->bake;
```

Don't forget to send the headers before generating content:

```
    $r->send_http_header;

    $r->print("...");
```

Description

The Apache::Cookie module builds a string that represents a cookie. To specify an expiration time for your cookie, use one of these formats:

+30s	30 seconds from now
+10m	10 minutes from now
+1h	1 hour from now
-1d	1 day ago
now	Now
+3M	Three months from now
+10y	Ten years from now
Thursday, 25-Apr-1999 00:30:31 GMT	Then

Call the bake method once you finish changing the cookie's parameters. This adds the cookie in its current state to mod_perl's planned response. If you change the cookie object after calling bake, changes won't be reflected in the header sent by mod_perl.

Apache maintains two sets of headers: error headers (which, confusingly, are always sent, regardless of whether the response code indicates an error) and ordinary headers (which are sent only for successful responses). Apache::Cookie sets the cookie in the error headers, so the cookie will be sent even for redirection responses.

The CGI::Cookie module is a slower pure Perl module with the same interface, which should be used only when the XS module Apache::Cookie is unavailable. To use it, substitute "CGI::Cookie" for "Apache::Cookie" in your code and remove the request object from the call to new. You can't call bake either—instead you must say:

```
    $r->err_headers_out->add("Set-Cookie", $cookie->as_string);
```

We use err_headers_out rather than err_header_out because the former method allows for multiple values for a header, whereas the latter does not. That is, err_headers_out lets you build up a header over time by adding to its existing value before it's sent, as we might do here if we independently set three cookies. The err_header_out method always replaces, never augments.

See Also

The documentation for the CGI::Cookie and Apache::Cookie modules on CPAN; the Netscape cookie specification at *http://wp.netscape.com/newsref/std/cookie_spec.html*; Recipe 3.7 in *mod_perl Developer's Cookbook*; the Apache.pm manpage

---

21.3   Accessing Cookie Values

Problem

You want to examine values client sent you in a cookie.

Solution

Use the CPAN module Apache::Cookie to populate a hash of cookie objects derived from the header sent by the client.

```
use Apache::Cookie;
$ac = Apache::Cookie->new($r);
%all_cookies = $ac->parse();
```

Now each element of that hash is an object representing a single cookie:

```
$one_cookie = $all_cookies{COOKIE_NAME};
```

Interrogate the object to learn about that cookie's values:

```
$one_cookie->value()     $one_cookie->name()
$one_cookie->domain()    $one_cookie->path()
$one_cookie->expires()   $one_cookie->secure()
```

Discussion

To test whether a cookie was sent by the browser, use exists on the hash element:

```
unless (exists $all_cookies{chocolate}) {
  $r->header_out(Location => "http://www.site.com/login");
  return REDIRECT;
}
```

Don't simply test for truth:

```
unless ($all_cookies{chocolate}) {  # BAD
```

Valid cookie values include the empty string and 0, both false to Perl. See the Introduction to Chapter 1 for more.

The CGI::Cookie module is a pure Perl substitute for Apache::Cookie. Its strategy for getting a hash of cookies is slightly different from that of Apache::Cookies:

```
use CGI::Cookie;
%all_cookies = CGI::Cookie->fetch;
```

This hash of cookies works the same as the one by Apache::Cookie.

See Also

Writing Apache Modules with Perl and C; Recipe 20.14; Recipe 3.7 in *mod_perl Developer's Cookbook*; the Apache.pm manpage; documentation for the CGI::Cookie and Apache::Cookie modules from CPAN

21.4   Redirecting the Browser

Problem

You want to send a redirection back to the browser.

Solution

Use $r->header_out to set the Location header, then return REDIRECT:

```
$r->header_out(Location => "http://www.example.com/somewhere");
return REDIRECT;
```

Discussion

If you set the Location header and return REDIRECT, the client knows the address of the new page. This is called an external redirection, because the browser (external to the web server) handles the mechanics of requesting the new page. The URL should be a complete URL (with http, etc.), never a partial one.

An internal redirection is one where Apache sends back another page from the same site. The browser never knows that the page has changed, which means relative URLs from the page could be broken. Request an internal redirection with:

```
$r->internal_redirect($new_partial_url);
return OK;
```

Apache treats internal redirections almost as though they were new requests: each phase of the request cycle is called again for the new request. Unlike the Location header, internal_redirect takes only a partial URL. You should have no logic after calling internal_redirect other than to return OK.

See Also

Writing Apache Modules with Perl and C; Recipe 19.7; Recipe 8.5 in *mod_perl Developer's Cookbook*; the Apache.pm manpage

21.5   Interrogating Headers

Problem

You want to learn the value of a header sent by the client.

Solution

Use the $r->header_in method:

```
$value = $r->header_in("Header-name");
```

Discussion

For example, suppose you want to discover the client's preferred language (as sent in the Accept-Language header).

```
if ($r->header_in("Accept-Language") !~ /\ben-US\b/i) {
  $r->print("No furriners!");
  return OK;
}
```

If you want to access more than one header, use the $r->headers_in method, which returns a list of key-value pairs of all clients' request headers, which are typically assigned to a hash:

```
%h = $r->headers_in;
if ($h{"Accept-Language"} !~ /\ben-US\b/i) {
  $r->print("No furriners!");
  return OK;
}
```

See Also

Writing Apache Modules with Perl and C; Recipe 3.4 in *mod_perl Developer's Cookbook*; the Apache.pm manpage

21.6   Accessing Form Parameters

Problem

You want the values for form fields submitted by the client.

Solution

To access the form's various parameters, use $r->content to access POSTed parameters and $r->args to access GET parameters encoded in the URL.

```
%post_parameters = $r->content;
%get_parameters  = $r->args;
```

You can call $r->content only once per request because the first call consumes all POSTed data.

The Apache::Request module from CPAN gives you a $r->param method to access specific parameters, regardless of whether they're from GET or POST:

```
use Apache::Request;

sub handler {
  my $r = Apache::Request->instance(shift);
  my @param_names = $r->param;
  my $value       = $r->param("username");  # single value
```

```
  my @values      = $r->param("toppings");  # multiple values

  # ...
}
```

Discussion

Processing form parameters without Apache::Request is problematic with values that occur multiple times. For example, a SELECT list with MULTIPLE enabled sends repeated entries for the same parameter name. Putting them into a hash preserves only one of those entries. Apache::Request solves this problem by accumulating multiply-submitted parameters in an array.

Form parameters POSTed to your handler can be a problem. The nature of Apache is that once one handler reads the POSTed data, another handler cannot come along later and reread that same information. So if you're going to process POSTed form parameters, you had better keep the decoded parameters around in case another handler wants to access them. The instance constructor handles this for us. When two handlers both call the instance constructor, the second handler gets back the Apache::Request object populated by the first, with form parameters already decoded.

The Apache::Request $r->param interface is based on the CGI module's parameter-parsing interface.

See Also

The Apache.pm manpage; *Writing Apache Modules with Perl and C*; Recipe 3.5 in *mod_perl Developer's Cookbook*; the Apache::Request manpage; Recipe 20.2

21.7   Receiving Uploaded Files

Problem

You want a mod_perl handler that processes an uploaded file. For example, an image gallery might let the owner upload image files to the gallery.

Solution

Use the Apache::Request module's $r->upload and $r->param methods from within your handler (assuming the file upload field was called fileParam):

```
use Apache::Request;

my $TEN_MEG = 10 * 2 ** 20;       # 10 megabytes
sub handler {
  my $r = Apache::Request->new(shift,
```

```
                        DISABLE_UPLOADS => 0,
                        POST_MAX        => $TEN_MEG);
    $r->parse;
    my $uploaded_file = $r->upload("fileParam");
    my $filename      = $uploaded_file->filename;   # filename
    my $fh            = $uploaded_file->fh;         # filehandle
    my $size          = $uploaded_file->size;       # size in bytes
    my $info          = $uploaded_file->info;       # headers
    my $type          = $uploaded_file->type;       # Content-Type
    my $tempname      = $uploaded_file->tempname;   # temporary name
    # ...
}
```

Discussion

By default, Apache::Request won't process uploaded file data. This is because the file is read into memory, which might not be released to the operating system once the request is over. If you do enable uploaded files (by setting DISABLE_UPLOADS to false), set an upper limit on the size of the file you will accept. This prevents a malicious attacker from sending an infinite stream of data and exhausting your system's memory. The POST_MAX value (10M in the Solution code) is that maximum value, specified in bytes.

The $r->upload method processes the POSTed file data and returns an Apache:: Upload object. This object has the following methods for accessing information on the uploaded file:

Method	Returns
fh	Filehandle from which to read the uploaded data
filename	Client-supplied filename
info	Apache::Table object containing HTTP headers sent by the client
name	The name of the form field this file was submitted as
size	Size of the uploaded file in bytes
tempname	Apache::Request's temporary filename
type	Client-supplied content-type of the uploaded file

You can invoke $r->upload only once per request, as the first invocation consumes all POSTed data. Sometimes multiple handlers need access to the same uploaded file but can't coordinate among themselves by designating one handler to read the file and save its name somewhere that the others can access. In this case, make each handler use the Apache::Request module's $r->instance method to get a request object instead of directly shifting it from the argument list:

```
use Apache::Request;
# ...
sub handler {
  my $r = Apache::Request->instance(shift,
```

```
                              DISABLE_UPLOADS => 0,
                              POST_MAX        => 10 * 2**20);
    # ...
    }
```

See Also

Writing Apache Modules with Perl and C; Recipe 3.8 in *mod_perl Developer's Cookbook*; the Apache.pm manpage

21.8 Speeding Up Database Access

Problem

You use the DBI module within your mod_perl handler, but connecting to the database server for each request is slowing down your web application unacceptably.

Solution

To cache database connections transparently, load the Apache::DBI module before the DBI module:

```
use Apache::DBI;
use DBI;
```

Discussion

Many sites load the Apache::DBI module from the *httpd.conf* file to ensure it's loaded before anything else:

```
PerlModule Apache::DBI
```

The Apache::DBI module intercepts the DBI->connect method, returning a previously opened handle if the handle had the same connection parameters as the current request. The module also prevents $dbh->disconnect from closing connections. This lets you add use Apache::DBI to the start of an existing program without having to touch the rest of your code.

The Apache::DBI module uses an open database connection for each different database login in each Apache child process. You might need to change your database server's configuration to increase its maximum number of connections. With commercial database systems, you might even need to buy more client licenses.

This proliferation of connections can lead to situations where Apache::DBI isn't the best choice. For example, if each user of your site has his own database login, you'll need as many concurrent database connections as the number of active users multiplied by however many *httpd* processes are running worth of database connections, which might well be more than your server supports! Similarly, if you have many Apache child processes running concurrently, this could open more simultaneous database connections than your server supports.

One strategy for optimizing database access is to batch requests where possible. For example, if you're logging to a database, consider accumulating log information and updating the database only after every 5 or 10 hits.

Another strategy is to cache information in the client. For example, if you use a database to map user IDs to real names and that mapping never changes, then use a persistent hash in your handler to store real names for user IDs you've encountered—this avoids repeated database lookups on unchanging information. To prevent the hash from consuming too much memory, you might want to use the Tie::Cache::LRU module from CPAN or reimplement some other form of flushing the least-recently-used entries once the cache reaches a particular size.

See Also

Documentation for the Apache::DBI and Tie::Cache::LRU modules from CPAN; the Apache.pm manpage; Recipes 2.11 and 2.12 in *mod_perl Developer's Cookbook*

21.9 Customizing Apache's Logging

Problem

You want to change how Apache logs requests. For example, you want a database of URLs and access counts, or per-user logs.

Solution

Install a handler with PerlLogHandler:

```
PerlModule Apache::MyLogger
PerlLogHandler Apache::MyLogger
```

Within the handler, methods on the request object obtain information about the completed request. In the following code, $r is the request object and $c is the connection object obtained from $r->connection:

```
$r->the_request           GET /roast/chickens.html HTTP/1.1
$r->uri                   /roast/chickens.html
$r->header_in("User-Agent")   Mozilla-XXX
$r->header_in("Referer")      http://gargle.com/?search=h0t%20chix0rz
$r->bytes_sent            1648
$c->get_remote_host       208.201.239.56
$r->status_line           200 OK
$r->server_hostname       www.myserver.com
```

Discussion

Apache calls logging handlers after sending the response to the client. You have full access to the request and response parameters, such as client IP address, headers, status, and even content. Access this information through method calls on the request object.

You'll probably want to escape values before writing them to a text file because spaces, newlines, and quotes could spoil the formatting of the files. Two useful functions are:

```
# return string with newlines and double quotes escaped
sub escape {
  my $a = shift;
  $a =~ s/([\n\"])/sprintf("%%%02x", ord($1))/ge;
 return $a;
}

# return string with newlines, spaces, and double quotes escaped
sub escape_plus {
  my $a = shift;
  $a =~ s/([\n \"])/sprintf("%%%02x", ord($1))/ge;
  return $a;
}
```

Two prebuilt logging modules on CPAN are Apache::Traffic and Apache::DBILogger. Apache::Traffic lets you assign owner strings (either usernames, UIDs, or arbitrary strings) to your web server's directories in *httpd.conf*. Apache::Traffic builds a DBM database as Apache serves files from these directories. For each owner, the database records the number of hits their directories received each day and the total number of bytes transferred by those hits.

Apache::DBILogger is a more general interface, logging each hit as a new entry in a table. The table has columns for data such as which virtual host delivered the data, the client's IP address, the user agent (browser), the date, the number of bytes transferred, and so on. Using this table and suitable indexes and queries, you can answer almost any question about traffic on your web site.

Because the logging handler runs before Apache has closed the connection to the client, don't use this phase if you have a slow logging operation. Instead, install the handler with PerlCleanupHandler so that it runs after the connection is closed.

See Also

Writing Apache Modules with Perl and C; Chapter 16 of *mod_perl Developer's Cookbook*; documentation for the Apache::Traffic and Apache::DBILogger CPAN modules; the Apache.pm manpage

---

21.10 Transparently Storing Information in URLs

Problem

You want to store information like session IDs in the URL, but you don't want to figure out to how work around the extra data when constructing relative URLs.

Solution

Store the ID at the start of the URL:

```
http://www.example.com/ID/12345678/path/to/page
```

Extract it with a PerlTransHandler, and store it in a pnote, a hash entry accessible by other Perl handlers in this request:

```
sub trans {
  my $r = shift;

  my $uri = $r->uri();
  if ($uri =~ s{/ID/(\d{8})}{}) {
    $r->pnotes("ID", $1);
  }
  $r->uri($uri);
  return DECLINED;
}
```

Restore the URL in a PerlFixupHandler:

```
sub fixup {
  my $r = shift;

  my $id = $r->pnotes("ID");
  if ($id) {
    $r->uri("/ID/$id" . $r->uri);
  }
  return DECLINED;
}
```

Consult the pnote in the content handler:

```
use Apache::URI;

sub content {
  my $r = shift;
  my $id = $r->pnotes("ID");

  unless ($id) {
    join(('', map { int rand 10 } (1..8)));
    my $uri = Apache::URI->parse($r);
    $uri->path("ID/$id" . $uri->path);
    $r->header_out(Location => $uri->unparse);
    return REDIRECT;
  }
}
```

```
    # use $id

    return OK;
}
```

Discussion

The client thinks your pages have a URL like *http://www.example.com/ID/12345678/
path/to/page.html*. Your PerlTransHandler intercepts the incoming request and
removes the */ID/12345678* part before Apache tries to translate the request into a file
location. Just before your content handler runs, your PerlFixupHandler reinserts the
ID. When your content handler calls $r->uri, it gets a URI that includes the ID.

We returned DECLINED from our PerlTransHandler and PerlFixupHandler to indicate that any other translation or fixup handlers that were installed should also be
run. If we returned OK in the PerlTransHandler, Apache would not call any subsequent translation handlers. In PerlFixupHandlers, DECLINED and OK both mean a
successful fixup, and that other fixup handlers should also run.

This solution doesn't look at the HTML emitted by your handler, so it only preserves the ID across relative links. If you give absolute links in your HTML (HREF="/
elsewhere/"), then you'll lose the ID and have to re-establish it.

See Also

Recipe 12.3 of *mod_perl Developer's Cookbook*; Recipe 21.11

21.11 Communicating Between mod_perl and PHP

Problem

You want to build your site from both mod_perl and PHP. For example, you might
want to use mod_perl for authentication and logging, while PHP generates the actual
content. However, doing so means that Perl and PHP must share values; for example, so the PHP content handler knows which username successfully authenticated
through mod_perl.

Solution

Use Apache notes. From Perl, you simply say:

```
$main = $r->main || $r;
$main->notes($KEY => $VALUE);
$VALUE = $main->notes($KEY);
```

From PHP, you say:

```
apache_note($KEY, $VALUE);
$VALUE = apache_note($KEY);
```

Discussion

A *note* is a string value attached to an Apache request. They're a perfect way to pass information between handlers, even when those handlers are written in different programming languages. Each request has a different set of notes, so from Perl always identify the main request and use it to communicate with PHP code.

Don't confuse the $r->notes method with the $r->pnotes method. The latter is only available to Perl modules.

See Also

Recipe 21.10

21.12 Migrating from CGI to mod_perl

Problem

Your CGI script is called so often that your web server's performance deteriorates unacceptably. You'd like to use mod_perl to make things faster.

Solution

Use Apache::Registry or Apache::PerlRun:

```
PerlModule Apache::Registry
# or Apache::PerlRun
PerlModule CGI
PerlSendHeader On

Alias /perl/ /real/path/to/perl/scripts/
<Location /perl>
SetHandler  perl-script
PerlHandler Apache::Registry
# or Apache::PerlRun
Options ExecCGI
</Location>
```

Discussion

The Solution tells Apache that requests with URLs starting in */perl/* are in */real/path/ to/perl/scripts/* and that Apache::Registry handles them. This module runs them in a

CGI environment. `PerlModule CGI` preloads the CGI module, and `PerlSendHeader On` makes most CGI scripts work out of the box with mod_perl.

We have configured */perl/* to work analogously to */cgi-bin/*. To make the suffix *.perl* indicate mod_perl CGI scripts, just as the suffix *.cgi* indicates regular CGI scripts, use the following in your Apache configuration file:

```
<Files *.perl>
SetHandler  perl-script
PerlHandler Apache::Registry
Options ExecCGI
</Files>
```

Because the Perl interpreter that runs your CGI script doesn't shut down when your script is done, as would occur when the web server runs your script as a separate program, you cannot rely on global variables being undefined when the script runs repeatedly. The `warnings` and `strict` pragmas check for many bad habits in these kinds of scripts. There are other gotchas, too—see the *mod_perl_traps* manpage.

The Apache::PerlRun handler can work around some of these traps. This is like Apache::Registry, but doesn't cache the compiled module. If your CGI program is sloppy and doesn't initialize variables or close filehandles, you can still gain speed by not starting a new process for every request. To use it, substitute Apache::PerlRun for Apache::Registry.

Your scripts aren't preloaded, so each web server process carries its own copy around. To share the code between processes, load them during Apache configuration with either the Apache::RegistryLoader module, PerlModule sections of *httpd. conf*, or a *startup.pl* file.

See Also

The Apache.pm manpage; the documentation for Bundle::Apache, Apache, Apache::Registry, Apache::RegistryLoader, and Apache::PerlRun from CPAN; *http://perl. apache.org*; the mod_perl FAQ at *http://perl.apache.org/faq/*; the *mod_perl*(3) and *cgi_ to_mod_perl*(1) manpages (if you have them); Recipes 2.1 through 2.5 in *mod_perl Developer's Cookbook*

21.13 Sharing Information Between Handlers

Problem

You want to share information between handlers, but global variables are global to a process and not automatically cleaned up after every request.

Solution

Use Apache pnotes (Perl notes):

```
# in one handler
$r->pnotes("Name", $name);

# in another handler
$name = $r->pnotes("Name");
```

Discussion

Apache modules communicate with each other using notes (see Recipe 21.11). Apache notes act like a hash attached to a request—one handler stores a value for a key in the hash, so that another handler can read it later. The Perl notes features is also a hash attached to the request object, but it's only for the Perl handlers.

To set a pnote, pass a key and a value to the $r->pnotes method. To retrieve a pnote, pass only the key. You can store complex data structures:

```
$r->pnotes("Person", { Name => "Nat",
                       Age  => 30,
                       Kids => 2 });
# later
$person = $r->pnotes("Person");
```

and even objects:

```
$person = new Person;
$person->name("Nat");
$person->age(30);
$person->kids(2);

$r->pnotes(Person => $person);

# later

$person = $r->pnotes("Person");
# $person is a reference to the same object
```

See Also

Recipe 8.11 in *mod_perl Developer's Cookbook*; Apache::Table; pnotes method in the Apache manpage

21.14 Reloading Changed Modules

Problem

You've updated your mod_perl modules, but you have to restart the web server for Apache to notice the change.

Solution

Use Apache::StatINC (standard with mod_perl) to automatically reload any code when it changes on disk:

```
PerlModule Apache::StatINC
PerlInitHandler Apache::StatINC
```

Or use the CPAN module Apache::Reload to limit the monitoring to specific modules:

```
PerlModule Apache::Reload
PerlInitHandler Apache::Reload
PerlSetVar ReloadAll Off
PerlSetVar ReloadModules "Example::One Example::Two Example::Three"
```

Discussion

Apache::Reload includes the functionality of Apache::StatINC. Simply saying:

```
PerlModule Apache::Reload
PerlInitHandler Apache::Reload
```

is enough to duplicate the functionality of Apache::StatINC. That is, at the start of each request, Apache::Reload goes through all currently loaded modules, checking timestamps to see which have changed. Because checking every module on every request is a burden on popular sites, Apache::Reload also lets you specify which modules to check and reload.

See Also

The documentation for the Apache::StatINC and Apache::Reload modules; Recipe 8.1 in *mod_perl Developer's Cookbook*; the mod_perl guide at *http://perl.apache.org/guide*

21.15 Benchmarking a mod_perl Application

Problem

You have an idea to speed up your application, but you're not sure whether your change will help.

Solution

Use Apache::Timeit to time how long your content handler takes to run:

```
PerlModule Apache::Timeit
PerlFixupHandler Apache::Timeit
```

For more detailed analysis, use the Apache::DProf module available from CPAN:

```
PerlModule Apache::DProf
```

Discussion

The Apache::Timeit module is available at *http://perl.apache.org/dist/contrib/Timeit.pm*.

This module records in the error log the amount of time that elapsed while the content handler ran. By scanning the logs and averaging these numbers, you can see which pages take longer to generate, and you can then start to figure out why.

To drill down into your code and figure out which parts of the content handler are taking the most time, use the Apache::DProf module. This module connects the standard (as of v5.8) Devel::DProf module to Apache and mod_perl.

The profiler records time spent in every subroutine the Perl module executes. The record of times is written to a file named *dprof/$$/tmon.out* (*$$* is the process ID of the Apache child process), located under the ServerRoot directory. This file corresponds to every Perl subroutine encountered during the lifetime of the Apache child process. To profile just a single request, set the MaxRequestsPerChild directive in the *httpd.conf* file:

```
MaxRequestsPerChild 1
```

You must create and chmod this directory yourself:

```
cd $APACHE_SERVER_ROOT
mkdir logs/dprof
chmod 777 logs/dprof
```

To analyze the output, use the *dprofpp* program:

```
dprofpp -r dprof/13169/tmon.out
Total Elapsed Time = 89.93962 Seconds
          Real Time = 89.93962 Seconds
Exclusive Times
%Time ExclSec CumulS #Calls sec/call Csec/c  Name
 0.01   0.010  0.010      1   0.0100 0.0100  Apache::Reload::handler
 0.00   0.000 -0.000      1   0.0000      -  Apache::DProf::handler
 0.00   0.000 -0.000      1   0.0000      -  MP002::trans
 0.00   0.000 -0.000      1   0.0000      -  MP002::fixup
 0.00   0.000 -0.000      1   0.0000      -  MP002::content
```

The **-r** option makes *dprofpp* display elapsed time instead of the default CPU time. The difference is important for mod_perl applications, where I/O and other non-CPU tasks are often significant causes of user-perceived delay.

There are a lot of options to *dprofpp* that refine and manipulate timing data. For example, **-R** gives separate timing data for each anonymous subroutine in a package, rather than lumping them together; **-l** sorts by the number of times the subroutine was called, rather than how long it took. See the *dprofpp* manpage for a complete list.

See Also

Recipe 9.12 in *mod_perl Developer's Cookbook*; documentation for the CPAN module Apache::DProf; documentation for the standard module Devel::DProf; the *dprofpp*(1) manpage; the section "The Perl Profiler" in Chapter 20 of *Programming Perl*

21.16 Templating with HTML::Mason

Problem

You want to separate presentation (HTML formatting) from logic (Perl code) in your program. Your web site has a lot of components with only slight variations between them. You'd like to abstract out common elements and build your pages from templates without having a lot of "if I'm in this page, then print this; else if I'm in some other page..." conditional statements in a single master template.

Solution

Use HTML::Mason components and inheritance.

Discussion

HTML::Mason (also simply called Mason) offers the power of Perl in templates. The basic unit of a web site built with Mason is the component—a file that produces output. The file can be HTML, Perl, or a mixture of both. Components can take arguments and execute arbitrary Perl code. Mason has many features, documented at *http://masonhq.com* and in *Embedding Perl in HTML with Mason* by Dave Rolsky and Ken Williams (O'Reilly; online at *http://masonbook.com*).

Mason works equally well with CGI, mod_perl, and non-web programs. For the purposes of this recipe, however, we look at how to use it with mod_perl. The rest of this recipe contains a few demonstrations to give you a feel for what you can do with Mason and how your site will be constructed. There are more tricks, traps, and techniques for everything we discuss, though, so be sure to visit the web site and read the book for the full story.

Configuration

Install the HTML-Mason distribution from CPAN and add the following to your *httpd.conf*:

```
PerlModule HTML::Mason::ApacheHandler
<Location /mason>
  SetHandler perl-script
  PerlHandler HTML::Mason::ApacheHandler
  DefaultType text/html
</Location>
```

This tells mod_perl that every URL that starts with /mason is handled by Mason. So if you request /mason/hello.html, the file *mason/hello.html* in your document directory will be compiled and executed as a Mason component. The DefaultType directive lets you omit the *.html* from component names.

Next create a directory for Mason to cache the compiled components in. Mason does this to speed up execution.

```
cd $SERVER_ROOT
mkdir mason
```

Then make a *mason* directory for components to live in:

```
cd $DOCUMENT_ROOT
mkdir mason
```

Now you're ready for "Hello, World". Put this in *mason/hello*:

```
Hello, <% ("World", "Puny Human")[rand 2] %>
```

Restart Apache and load up the *mason/hello* page. If you reload it, you should see "Hello, World" and "Hello, Puny Human" randomly. If not, look at the Mason FAQ (*http://www.masonhq.com/docs/faq/*), which answers most commonly encountered problems.

Basic Mason syntax

There are four types of new markup in Mason components: substitutions, Perl code, component calls, and block tags. You saw a substitution in the "Hello World" example: <% ... %> evaluates the contents as Perl code and inserts the result into the surrounding text.

Perl code is marked with a % at the start of the line:

```
% $now = localtime;   # embedded Perl
This page was generated on <% $now %>.
```

Because substitutions can be almost any Perl code you like, this could have been written more simply as:

```
This page was generated on <% scalar localtime %>.
```

If either of these variations were saved in *footer.mas*, you could include it simply by saying:

```
<& footer.mas &>
```

This is an example of a component call—Mason runs the component and inserts its result into the document that made the call.

Block tags define different regions of your component. <%perl> ... </%perl> identifies Perl code. While % at the start of a line indicates that just that line is Perl code, you can have any number of lines in a <%perl> block.

A <%init> ... </%init> block is like an INIT block in Perl. The code in the block is executed before the main body of code. It lets you store definitions, initialization, database connections, etc. at the bottom of your component, where they're out of the way of the main logic.

The <%args> ... </%args> block lets you define arguments to your component, optionally with default values. For example, here's *greet.mas*:

```
<%args>
    $name => "Larry"
    $town => "Mountain View"
</%args>
Hello, <% $name %>.  How's life in <% $town %>?
```

Calling it with:

```
<& greet.mas &>
```

emits:

```
Hello, Larry.  How's life in Mountain View?
```

You can provide options on the component call:

```
<& greet.mas, name => "Nat", town => "Fort Collins" &>
```

That emits:

```
Hello, Nat.  How's life in Fort Collins?
```

Because there are default values, you can supply only some of the arguments:

```
<& greet.mas, name => "Bob" &>
```

That emits:

```
Hello, Bob.  How's life in Mountain View?
```

Arguments are also how Mason components access form parameters. Take this form:

```
<form action="compliment">
  How old are you?  <input type="text" name="age"> <br />
  <input type="submit">
</form>
```

Here's a *compliment* component that could take that parameter:

```
<%args>
  $age
</%args>
Hi.  Are you really <% $age %>?  You don't look it!
```

Objects

All Mason components have access to a $m variable, which contains an HTML::Mason::Request object. Methods on this object give access to Mason features. For example, you can redirect with:

```
$m->redirect($URL);
```

The $r variable is the mod_perl request object, so you have access to the information and functions of Apache from your Mason handlers. For example, you can discover the client's IP address with:

```
$ip = $r->connection->remote_ip;
```

Autohandlers

When a page is requested through Mason, Mason can do more than simply execute the code in that page. Mason inspects each directory between the component root and the requested page, looking for components called *autohandler*. This forms a *wrapping chain*, with the top-level autohandler at the start of the chain and the requested page at the end. Mason then executes the code at the start of the chain. Each autohandler can say "insert the output of the next component in the chain here."

Imagine a newspaper site. Some parts don't change, regardless of which article you're looking at: the banner at the top, the random selection of ads, the list of sections down the lefthand side. However, the actual article text varies from article to article. Implement this in Mason with a directory structure like this:

```
/sports
/sports/autohandler
/sports/story1
/sports/story2
/sports/story3
```

The individual story files contain only the text of each story. The autohandler builds the page (the banner, the ads, the navigation bar), and when it wants to insert the content of the story, it says:

```
% $m->call_next;
```

This tells Mason to call the next component in the chain (the story) and insert its output here.

The technique of having a chain of components is called *inheritance*, and autohandlers aren't the only way to do it. In a component, you can designate a parent with:

```
<%flags>
  inherit = 'parent.mas'
</%flags>
```

This lets you have different types of content in the one directory, and each contained component gets to identify its surrounding page (its parent).

Dhandlers

Sometimes it's nice to provide the illusion of a directory full of pages, when in reality they are all dynamically generated. For example, stories kept in a database could be accessed through URLs like:

```
/sports/1
/sports/2
/sports/3
```

The Mason way to dynamically generate the pages at these URLs is with a component called *dhandler* in the *sports* directory. The *dhandler* component accesses the name of the missing page (*123* in this case) by calling:

```
$m->dhandler_arg
```

You could then use this to retrieve the story from the database and insert it into a page template.

See Also

Recipe 15.11 in *mod_perl Developer's Cookbook*; *Embedding Perl in HTML with Mason*; *http://www.masonhq.com* and *http://www.masonbook.com*

21.17 Templating with Template Toolkit

Problem

You want to separate presentation (HTML formatting) from logic (Perl code) in your program. You want designers and other people who don't speak Perl to be able to edit the templates.

Solution

Use the Template Toolkit and Apache::Template.

Discussion

The Template Toolkit (TT2) is a general templating system that can be used not just for web pages, but for any kind of templated text. The Apache::Template module is an Apache content handler that uses TT2 to build the returned page. The biggest benefit of TT2 is that it has a simple language for variables, loops, and data structures, which can be used instead of Perl for presentation logic. This simple language can be read and written by people who don't know Perl.

This recipe documents Version 2 of the Template Toolkit. As with HTML::Mason, there's far more to TT2 that we can possibly cover here. This recipe is just a tour of some of the highlights of TT2's syntax and functionality. The Template Toolkit is well documented at *http://www.template-toolkit.org*, and in the upcoming book *Perl Template Toolkit*, by Darren Chamberlain, Dave Cross, and Andy Wardley (O'Reilly).

Configuration

Install the Template and Apache::Template modules from CPAN. Add this to your *httpd.conf* file:

```
PerlModule Apache::Template

TT2EvalPerl On
TT2Params all

TT2IncludePath /usr/local/apache/htdocs/tt2

<Location /tt2>
  SetHandler perl-script
  PerlHandler Apache::Template
  DefaultType text/html
</Location>
```

The TT2EvalPerl directive lets us embed Perl code in our templates as well as the TT2 language. TT2Params tells Apache::Template to give our templates access to form parameters, Apache environment variables, notes, cookies, and more. TT2IncludePath tells the Template Toolkit where to look for templates that our templates include. Finally, we designate the */tt2* area of our server for pages generated by the Template Toolkit.

Syntax

Templates are regular HTML files with directives embedded in [% ... %] tags. The tag delimiters are customizable, but in practice they're rarely changed. The use of square brackets rather than angle brackets means that templates can be edited in HTML editors without fear that a templating directive will be confused for an HTML tag.

This is a simple template:

```
<b>This is how you count to three:</b>
[% FOREACH i = [1 .. 3] %]
  [% i %] ...
[% END %]
Wasn't that easy?
```

When TT2 executes this template, it will produce:

This is how you count to three: 1 ... 2 ... 3 ... Wasn't that easy?

Store that in the file *tt2/count* and point your browser at the equivalent URL.

The FOREACH loop is an example of a TT2 directive. The i variable is the loop iterator, and it takes each value in turn from the list on the righthand side of the =. Loops, like every TT2 block, are terminated by an END directive. Variables in TT2 code have no type sigil like $, @, or %.

To display the value of a variable or expression, simply enclose it in the [% ... %] tags. You can't put arbitrary Perl code there, though, only TT2 syntax.

Perl code

If you want to execute Perl, use a PERL directive:

```
[% PERL %]
  my @numbers = (1 .. 3);
  print join(" ... ", @numbers);
[% END %]
```

Anything printed from within a PERL block becomes part of the final document. PERL blocks execute under use `strict`, so it pays to use lexical variables.

These lexical variables are separate from the TT2 variables like i, the loop iterator in the earlier example. To make a Perl value accessible to TT2 code, or vice versa, you must use the *stash*. This is the TT2 symbol table, and is accessible through the $stash variable automatically present in PERL blocks:

```
[% PERL %]
  my @numbers = (1 .. 3);
  my $text = join(" ... ", @numbers);
  $stash->set(counting => $text);
[% END %]
Here's how you count to three: [% counting %].  Wasn't that easy?
```

Normally you use Perl code for business logic (e.g., fetching values from databases) and TT2 code for presentation logic (e.g., building tables). The Perl code sets TT2 variables with the results of the business logic (e.g., the values from the database) so that the presentation logic has values to put into the template. In practice, most people prefer to disable TT2EvalPerl and keep Perl code out of their templates. This strict separation of business from presentation logic means a customized version of Apache::Template is needed to load the Perl code and place data in the stash.

You can initialize TT2 variables from TT2 as well:

```
[% text = "1 ... 2 ... 3" %]                    <!-- string -->
[% names = [ "Larry", "Tom", "Tim" ] %]         <!-- array  -->
[% language = { Larry => "Perl 6",              <!-- hash   -->
                Tom   => "Perl 5",
                Tim   => "Latin" } %]
[% people = { Larry => { Language => "Perl 6",  <!-- nested structure -->
                         Town     => "Mountain View" },
              Tom   => { Language => "Perl 5",
                         Town     => "Boulder" } } %]
```

Similarly, you can fetch TT2 values from the stash:

```
[% FOREACH i = [1 .. 3] %]
  [% PERL %]
    my $number = $stash->get("i");
    $stash->set(doubled => 2*$number);
  [% END %]
  [% doubled %] ...
```

```
[% END %]
2 ... 4 ... 6 ...
```

From within a PERL block, you can also use modules. It's more efficient, however, to load the modules when Apache starts up by replacing the PERL block's use `Some::Thing` with a `PerlModule Some::Thing` in *httpd.conf*.

Data structures

The stash lets you put scalars, arrays, hashes, even subroutines into the world of TT2 code. Here's an array definition and access:

```
[% names = [ "Nat", "Jenine", "William", "Raley" ] %]
The first person is [% names.0 %].
The first person is Nat.
```

The period (.) separates the structure name from the field you want to access. This works for hashes as well:

```
[% age = { Nat => 30, Jenine => 36, William => 3, Raley => 1.5 } %]
Nat is [% age.Nat %] (and he feels it!)
Nat is 30 (and feels it!)
```

Unlike Perl, TT2 code doesn't put [ ] or { } around the array position or hash key whose value you're accessing. This is part of the simplicity of TT2 code, and why non-programmers can easily modify it. It also hides the implementation—age.1 could just as easily be implemented through an array, a hash, or an object, without requiring changes in the template.

If your index is stored in another variable, use a $:

```
[% age = { Nat => 30, Jenine => 36, William => 3, Raley => 1.5 } %]
[% name = "Nat" %]
Nat is [% age.$name %] (and he feels it)
Nat is 30 (and feels it!)
```

Loop over an array or hash with FOREACH:

```
[% FOREACH name = names %]
  Hi, [% name %]!
[% END %]
Hi, Nat! Hi, Jenine! Hi, William! Hi, Raley!

[% FOREACH person = age %]
  [% person.key %] is [% person.value %].
[% END %]
Nat is 30. Jenine is 36. William is 3. Raley is 1.5.
```

The key and value methods can be called on a hash loop iterator to get the current key and value, respectively. TT2 also makes a loop variable available in loops, from which you can access the current position, find out whether the current position is the first or last, and more. Table 21-1 lists the loop variable methods and their meanings.

Table 21-1. loop variable methods

Method	Meaning
size	Number of elements in the list
max	Index number of last element (size - 1)
index	Index of current iteration from 0 to max
count	Iteration counter from 1 to size (i.e., index + 1)
first	True if the current iteration is the first
last	True if the current iteration is the last
prev	Return the previous item in the list
next	Return the next item in the list

To build a table with alternating row colors, do the following:

```
[% folks = [ [ "Larry",  "Mountain View" ],
             [ "Tom",    "Boulder"       ],
             [ "Jarkko", "Helsinki"      ],
             [ "Nat",    "Fort Collins"  ] ] %]
<table>
[% FOREACH row = folks %]
  <tr [% IF loop.index % 2 %]
          bgcolor="#ffff00"
      [% ELSE %]
          bgcolor="#ffff80"
      [% END %] >
  [% FOREACH col = row %]
    <td>[% col %]</td>
  [% END %]
  </tr>
[% END %]
</table>
```

Subroutines

If you build a lot of tables like this, you should abstract out the code into a subroutine. In TT2 syntax, a subroutine is a *block*. Here's a simple block that takes no parameters:

```
[% BLOCK greet %]
   Hello, world!
[% END %]
```

To call it, use the INCLUDE directive:

```
[% INCLUDE greet %]
```

Here's how you'd write a generic HTML table routine:

```
[% BLOCK table %]
   <table>
   [% FOREACH row = array %]
     <tr [% IF loop.index % 2 %]
```

```
                bgcolor="#ffff00"
        [% ELSE %]
                bgcolor="#ffff80"
        [% END %] >
    [% FOREACH col = row %]
      <td>[% col %]</td>
    [% END %]
    </tr>
  [% END %]
  </table>
[% END %]
```

To call this table block and tell it to print the array folks, you'd say:

```
[% INCLUDE table array=folks %]
```

Including other templates

The same syntax that you used to call a block defined within a template can be used to load and execute another file:

```
[% INCLUDE "header.tt2" %]
```

An INCLUDEd file is treated as a TT2 template. To insert a file that doesn't contain TT2 directives, it's faster to use INSERT:

```
[% INSERT "header.html" %]
```

INSERTed files are not processed by TT2 in any way. Their contents are simply inserted verbatim into the document being built.

Parameters

Apache::Template provides you with several TT2 variables corresponding to various parts of your web environment. Table 21-2 lists these variables and what they contain.

Table 21-2. Template Toolkit variables provided by Apache::Template

Variable	Contains
uri	String containing URI of current page
env	Hash of environment variables
params	Hash of form parameters
pnotes	Hash of Apache request's pnotes
cookies	Hash of cookies
uploads	Array of Apache::Upload objects

Here's a form:

```
<form action="consult">
  Whose city do you want to look up?
  <select name="person">
    <option value="larry">Larry</option>
```

```
        <option value="tom">Tom</option>
        <option value="nat">Nat</option>
    </select><p>
    <input type="submit">
</form>
```

The person form parameter contains the person's name. Here's the *consult* template:

```
[% cities = { larry => "Mountain View",
              tom   => "Boulder",
              nat   => "Fort Collins" } %]

[% name = params.person %]
[% name %] lives in [% cities.$name %]
```

Plug-ins

The Template Toolkit comes with many plug-ins. The most useful is probably the DBI plug-in:

```
[% USE DBI('dbi:mysql:library', 'user', 'pass') %]

[% FOREACH book = DBI.query( 'SELECT title,authors FROM books' ) %]
  [% book.authors %] wrote [% book.title %]<br>
[% END %]
```

Once the plug-in is loaded with the USE directive, you can use the TT2 variable DBI to issue SQL queries. The query method returns an array of rows, each row is a hash mapping column name to value.

The HTML plug-in is also useful. It offers methods to HTML-escape strings:

```
[% USE HTML %]

[% string = 'Over -----> Here' %]
Look [% HTML.escape(string) %]
Look Over -----> Here
```

See Also

The documentation for the Template and Apache::Template modules from CPAN; *http://www.template-toolkit.org*; *Perl Template Toolkit*; Recipe 15.9 in *mod_perl Developer's Cookbook*

## CHAPTER 22

XML

I am a little world made cunningly
Of elements, and an angelic sprite
—- John Donne, *Holy Sonnets*

22.0 Introduction

The Extensible Markup Language (XML) standard was released in 1998. It quickly became the standard way to represent and exchange almost every kind of data, from books to genes to function calls.

XML succeeded where other past "standard" data formats failed (including XML's ancestor, SGML—the Standard Generalized Markup Language). There are three reasons for XML's success: it is text-based instead of binary, it is simple rather than complex, and it has a superficial resemblance to HTML.

Text

Unix realized nearly 30 years before XML that humans primarily interact with computers through text. Thus text files are the only files any system is guaranteed to be able to read and write. Because XML is text, programmers can easily make legacy systems emit XML reports.

Simplicity

As we'll see, a lot of complexity has arisen around XML, but the XML standard itself is very simple. There are very few things that can appear in an XML document, but from those basic building blocks you can build extremely complex systems.

HTML

XML is *not* HTML, but XML and HTML share a common ancestor: SGML. The superficial resemblance meant that the millions of programmers who had to learn HTML to put data on the web were able to learn (and accept) XML more easily.

Syntax

Example 22-1 shows a simple XML document.

Example 22-1. Simple XML document

```
<?xml version="1.0" encoding="UTF-8"?>
<books>
  <!-- Programming Perl 3ed -->
  <book id="1">
    <title>Programming Perl</title>
    <edition>3</edition>
    <authors>
      <author>
        <firstname>Larry</firstname>
        <lastname>Wall</lastname>
      </author>
      <author>
        <firstname>Tom</firstname>
        <lastname>Christiansen</lastname>
      </author>
      <author>
        <firstname>Jon</firstname>
        <lastname>Orwant</lastname>
      </author>
    </authors>
    <isbn>0-596-00027-8</isbn>
  </book>
  <!-- Perl & LWP -->
  <book id="2">
    <title>Perl &amp; LWP</title>
    <edition>1</edition>
    <authors>
      <author>
        <firstname>Sean</firstname>
        <lastname>Burke</lastname>
      </author>
    </authors>
    <isbn>0-596-00178-9</isbn>
  </book>
  <book id="3">
    <!-- Anonymous Perl -->
    <title>Anonymous Perl</title>
    <edition>1</edition>
    <authors />
    <isbn>0-555-00178-0</isbn>
  </book>
</books>
```

At first glance, XML looks a lot like HTML: there are elements (e.g., <book> </book>), entities (e.g., & and <), and comments (e.g., <!-- Perl & LWP -->). Unlike HTML, XML doesn't define a standard set of elements, and defines only a minimum

---

set of entities (for single quotes, double quotes, less-than, greater-than, and ampersand). The XML standard specifies only syntactic building blocks like the < and > around elements. It's up to you to create the *vocabulary*, that is, the element and attribute names like books, authors, etc., and how they nest.

XML's opening and closing elements are familiar from HTML:

```
<book>
</book>
```

XML adds a variation for empty elements (those with no text or other elements between the opening and closing tags):

```
<author />
```

Elements may have attributes, as in:

```
<book id="1">
```

Unlike HTML, the case of XML elements, entities, and attributes matters: <Book> and <book> start two different elements. All attributes must be quoted, either with single or double quotes (id='1' versus id="1"). Unicode letters, underscores, hyphens, periods, and numbers are all acceptable in element and attribute names, but the first character of a name must be a letter or an underscore. Colons are allowed only in namespaces (see "Namespaces," later in this chapter).

Whitespace is surprisingly tricky. The XML specification says anything that's not a markup character is content. So (in theory) the newlines and whitespace indents between tags in Example 22-1 are text data. Most XML parsers offer the choice of retaining whitespace or sensibly folding it (e.g., to ignore newlines and indents).

XML Declaration

The first line of Example 22-1 is the *XML declaration*:

```
<?xml version="1.0" encoding="UTF-8" ?>
```

This declaration is optional—Version 1.0 of XML and UTF-8 encoded text are the defaults. The encoding attribute specifies the Unicode encoding of the document. Some XML parsers can cope with arbitrary Unicode encodings, but others are limited to ASCII and UTF-8. For maximum portability, create XML data as UTF-8.

Processing Instructions

Similar to declarations are *processing instructions*, which are instructions for XML processors. For example:

```
<title><?pdf font Helvetica 18pt?>XML in Perl</title>
```

Processing instructions have the general structure:

```
<?target data ... ?>
```

When an XML processor encounters a processing instruction, it checks the *target*. Processors should ignore targets they don't recognize. This lets one XML file contain instructions for many different processors. For example, the XML source for this book might have separate instructions for programs that convert to HTML and to PDF.

Comments

XML comments have the same syntax as HTML comments:

```
<!-- ... -->
```

The comment text can't contain --, so comments don't nest.

CDATA

Sometimes you want to put text in an XML document without having to worry about encoding entities. Such a literal block is called *CDATA* in XML, written:

```
<![CDATA[literal text here]]>
```

The ugly syntax betrays XML's origins in SGML. Everything after the initial `<![CDATA[` and up to the `]]>` is literal data in which XML markup characters such as `<` and `&` have no special meaning.

For example, you might put sample code that contains a lot of XML markup characters in a CDATA block:

```
<para>The code to do this is as follows:</para>
<code><![CDATA[$x = $y << 8 & $z]]>
```

Well-Formed XML

To ensure that all XML documents are parsable, there are some minimum requirements expected of an XML document. The following list is adapted from the list in *Perl & XML*, by Erik T. Ray and Jason McIntosh (O'Reilly):

- The document must have one and only one top-level element (e.g., books in Example 22-1).
- Every element with content must have both a start and an end tag.
- All attributes must have values, and those values must be quoted.
- Elements must not overlap.
- Markup characters (<, >, and &) must be used to indicate markup only. In other words, you can't have `<title>Perl & XML</title>` because the & can only indicate an entity reference. CDATA sections are the only exception to this rule.

If an XML document meets these rules, it's said to be "well-formed." Any XML parser that conforms to the XML standard should be able to parse a well-formed document.

Schemas

There are two parts to any program that processes an XML document: the XML parser, which manipulates the XML markup, and the program's logic, which identifies text, the elements, and their structure. Well-formedness ensures that the XML parser can work with the document, but it doesn't guarantee that the elements have the correct names and are nested correctly.

For example, these two XML fragments encode the same information in different ways:

```
<book>
  <title>Programming Perl</title>
  <edition>3</edition>
  <authors>
    <author>
      <firstname>Larry</firstname>
      <lastname>Wall</lastname>
    </author>
    <author>
      <firstname>Tom</firstname>
      <lastname>Christiansen</lastname>
    </author>
    <author>
      <firstname>Jon</firstname>
      <lastname>Orwant</lastname>
    </author>
  </authors>
</book>

<work>
  <writers>Larry Wall, Tom Christiansen, and Jon Orwant</writers>
  <name edition="3">Programming Perl</name>
</work>
```

The structure is different, and if you wrote code to extract the title from one ("get the contents of the book element, then find the contents of the title element within that") it would fail completely on the other. For this reason, it is common to write a specification for the elements, attributes, entities, and the ways to use them. Such a specification lets you be confident that your program will never be confronted with XML it cannot deal with. The two formats for such specifications are DTDs and schemas.

DTDs are the older and more limited format, acquired by way of XML's SGML past. DTDs are not written in XML, so you need a custom (complex) parser to work with them. Additionally, they aren't suitable for many uses—simply saying "the book element must contain one each of the title, edition, author, and isbn elements in any order" is remarkably difficult.

For these reasons, most modern content specifications take the form of schemas. The World Wide Web Consortium (W3C), the folks responsible for XML and a host of related standards, have a standard called XML Schema (*http://www.w3.org/TR/xmlschema-0/*). This is the most common schema language in use today, but it is complex and problematic. An emerging rival for XML Schema is the OASIS group's RelaxNG; see *http://www.oasis-open.org/committees/relax-ng/spec-20011203.html* for more information.

There are Perl modules for working with schemas. The most important action you do with schemas, however, is to *validate* an XML document against a schema. Recipe 22.5 shows how to use XML::LibXML to do this. XML::Parser does not support validation.

Namespaces

One especially handy property of XML is nested elements. This lets one document encapsulate another. For example, you want to send a purchase order document in a mail message. Here's how you'd do that:

```
<mail>
  <header>
    <from>me@example.com</from>
    <to>you@example.com</to>
    <subject>PO for my trip</subject>
  </header>
  <body>
    <purchaseorder>
      <for>Airfare</for>
      <bill_to>Editorial</bill_to>
      <amount>349.50</amount>
    </purchaseorder>
  </body>
</mail>
```

It worked, but we can easily run into problems. For example, if the purchase order used <to> instead of <bill_to> to indicate the department to be charged, we'd have two elements named <to>. The resulting document is sketched here:

```
<mail>
  <header>
    <to>you@example.com</to>
  </header>
  <body>
    <to>Editorial</to>
  </body>
</mail>
```

This document uses to for two different purposes. This is similar to the problem in programming where a global variable in one module has the same name as a global variable in another module. Programmers can't be expected to avoid variable names from other modules, because that would require them to know every module's variables.

The solution to the XML problem is similar to the programming problem's solution: namespaces. A namespace is a unique prefix for the elements and attributes in an XML vocabulary, and is used to avoid clashes with elements from other vocabularies. If you rewrote your purchase-order email example with namespaces, it might look like this:

```
<mail xmlns:email="http://example.com/dtds/mailspec/">
  <email:from>me@example.com</email:from>
  <email:to>you@example.com</email:to>
  <email:subject>PO for my trip</email:subject>
  <email:body>
    <purchaseorder xmlns:po="http://example.com/dtd/purch/">
      <po:for>Airfare</po:for>
      <po:to>Editorial</po:to>
      <po:amount>349.50</po:amount>
    </purchaseorder>
  </email:body>
</mail>
```

An attribute like xmnls:*prefix*="*URL*" identifies the namespace for the contents of the element that the attribute is attached to. In this example, there are two namespaces: email and po. The email:to element is different from the po:to element, and processing software can avoid confusion.

Most of the XML parsers in Perl support namespaces, including XML::Parser and XML::LibXML.

Transformations

One of the favorite pastimes of XML hackers is turning XML into something else. In the old days, this was accomplished with a program that knew a specific XML vocabulary and could intelligently turn an XML file that used that vocabulary into something else, like a different type of XML, or an entirely different file format, such as HTML or PDF. This was such a common task that people began to separate the transformation engine from the specific transformation, resulting in a new specification: XML Stylesheet Language for Transformations (XSLT).

Turning XML into something else with XSLT involves writing a stylesheet. A stylesheet says "when you see *this* in the input XML, emit *that*." You can encode loops and branches, and identify elements (e.g., "when you see the book element, print only the contents of the enclosed title element").

Transformations in Perl are best accomplished through the XML::LibXSLT module, although XML::Sablotron and XML::XSLT are sometimes also used. We show how to use XML::LibXSLT in Recipe 22.7.

Paths

Of the new vocabularies and tools for XML, possibly the most useful is XPath. Think of it as regular expressions for XML structure—you specify the elements you're looking for ("the `title` within a `book`"), and the XPath processor returns a pointer to the matching elements.

An XPath expression looks like:

```
/books/book/title
```

Slashes separate tests. XPath has syntax for testing attributes, elements, and text, and for identifying parents and siblings of nodes.

The XML::LibXML module has strong support for XPath, and we show how to use it in Recipe 22.6. XPath also crops up in the XML::Twig module shown in Recipe 22.8.

History of Perl and XML

Initially, Perl had only one way to parse XML: regular expressions. This was prone to error and often failed to deal with well-formed XML (e.g., CDATA sections). The first real XML parser in Perl was XML::Parser, Larry Wall's Perl interface to James Clark's *expat* C library. Most other languages (notably Python and PHP) also had an *expat* wrapper as their first correct XML parser.

XML::Parser was a prototype—the mechanism for passing components of XML documents to Perl was experimental and intended to evolve over the years. But because XML::Parser was the *only* XML parser for Perl, people quickly wrote applications using it, and it became impossible for the interface to evolve. Because XML::Parser has a proprietary API, you shouldn't use it directly.

XML::Parser is an event-based parser. You register callbacks for events like "start of an element," "text," and "end of an element." As XML::Parser parses an XML file, it calls the callbacks to tell your code what it's found. Event-based parsing is quite common in the XML world, but XML::Parser has its own events and doesn't use the standard Simple API for XML (SAX) events. This is why we recommend you don't use XML::Parser directly.

The XML::SAX modules provide a SAX wrapper around XML::Parser and several other XML parsers. XML::Parser parses the document, but you write code to work with XML::SAX, and XML::SAX translates between XML::Parser events and SAX events. XML::SAX also includes a pure Perl parser, so a program for XML::SAX works on any Perl system, even those that can't compile XS modules. XML::SAX supports the full level 2 SAX API (where the backend parser supports features such as namespaces).

The other common way to parse XML is to build a tree data structure: element A is a child of element B in the tree if element B is inside element A in the XML document.

There is a standard API for working with such a tree data structure: the Document Object Model (DOM). The XML::LibXML module uses the GNOME project's *libxml2* library to quickly and efficiently build a DOM tree. It is fast, and it supports XPath and validation. The XML::DOM module was an attempt to build a DOM tree using XML::Parser as the backend, but most programmers prefer the speed of XML:: LibXML. In Recipe 22.2 we show XML::LibXML, not XML::DOM.

So, in short: for events, use XML::SAX with XML::Parser or XML::LibXML behind it; for DOM trees, use XML::LibXML; for validation, use XML::LibXML.

Further Reading

While the XML specification itself is simple, the specifications for namespaces, schemas, stylesheets, and so on are not. There are many good books to help you learn and use these technologies:

- For help with all of the nuances of XML, try *Learning XML*, by Erik T. Ray (O'Reilly), and *XML in a Nutshell*, Second Edition, by Elliotte Rusty Harold and W. Scott Means (O'Reilly).
- For help with XML Schemas, try *XML Schema*, by Eric van der Vlist (O'Reilly).
- For examples of stylesheets and transformations, and help with the many non-trivial aspects of XSLT, see *XSLT*, by Doug Tidwell (O'Reilly), and *XSLT Cookbook*, by Sal Mangano (O'Reilly).
- For help with XPath, try *XPath and XPointer*, by John E. Simpson (O'Reilly).

If you're the type that relishes the pain of reading formal specifications, the W3C web site, *http://www.w3c.org*, has the full text of all of their standards and draft standards.

22.1 Parsing XML into Data Structures

Problem

You want a Perl data structure (a combination of hashes and arrays) that corresponds to the structure and content of an XML file. For example, you have XML representing a configuration file, and you'd like to say $xml->{config}{server}{hostname} to access the contents of <config><server><hostname>...</hostname>.

Solution

Use the XML::Simple module from CPAN. If your XML is in a file, pass the filename to XMLin:

```
use XML::Simple;
$ref = XMLin($FILENAME, ForceArray => 1);
```

If your XML is in a string, pass the string to XMLin:

```
use XML::Simple;
$ref = XMLin($STRING, ForceArray => 1);
```

Discussion

Here's the data structure that XML::Simple produces from the XML in Example 22-1:

```
{
    'book' => {
      '1' => {
        'authors' => [
          {
            'author' => [
              {
                'firstname' => [ 'Larry' ],
                'lastname'  => [ 'Wall'  ]
              },
              {
                'firstname' => [ 'Tom' ],
                'lastname'  => [ 'Christiansen' ]
              },
              {
                'firstname' => [ 'Jon' ],
                'lastname'  => [ 'Orwant' ]
              }
            ]
          }
        ],
        'edition' => [ '3' ],
        'title'   => [ 'Programming Perl' ],
        'isbn'    => [ '0-596-00027-8' ]
      },
      '2' => {
        'authors' => [
          {
            'author' => [
              {
                'firstname' => [ 'Sean' ],
                'lastname'  => [ 'Burke' ]
              }
            ]
          }
        ],
        'edition' => [ '1' ],
        'title'   => [ 'Perl & LWP' ],
        'isbn'    => [ '0-596-00178-9' ]
      },
      '3' => {
        'authors' => [ {} ],
        'edition' => [ '1' ],
```

```
        'title'   => [ 'Anonymous Perl' ],
        'isbn'    => [ '0-555-00178-0' ]
    },
  }
    }
```

The basic function of XML::Simple is to turn an element that contains other elements into a hash. If there are multiple identically named elements inside a single containing element (e.g., book), they become an array of hashes unless XML::Simple knows they are uniquely identified by attributes (as happens here with the id attribute).

By default, XML::Simple assumes that if an element has an attribute called id, name, or key, then that attribute is a unique identifier for the element. This is controlled by the KeyAttr option to the XMLin function. For example, set KeyAttr to an empty list to disable this conversion from arrays of elements to a hash by attribute:

```
$ref = XMLin($xml, ForceArray => 1, KeyAttr => [ ]);
```

For more fine-grained control, specify a hash that maps the element name to the attribute that holds a unique identifier. For example, to create a hash on the id attribute of book elements and no others, say:

```
$ref = XMLin($xml, ForceArray => 1, KeyAttr => { book => "id" });
```

The ForceArray option creates all of those one-element arrays in the data structure. Without it, XML::Simple compacts one-element arrays:

```
'3' => {
  'authors' => {},
  'edition' => '1',
  'title' => 'Anonymous Perl',
  'isbn' => '0-555-00178-0'
},
```

Although this format is easier to read, it's also harder to program for. If you *know* that no element repeats, you can leave ForceArray off. But if some elements repeat and some don't, you need ForceArray to ensure a consistent data structure. Having the data sometimes directly available, sometimes inside an array, complicates the code.

The XML::Simple module has options that control the data structure built from the XML. Read the module's manpage for more details. Be aware that XML::Simple is only really useful for highly structured data, like the kind used in configuration files. It's awkward to use with XML that represents documents rather than data structures, and doesn't let you work with XML features like processing instructions or comments. We recommend that, for all but the most simple XML, you look to DOM and SAX parsing for your XML parsing needs.

See Also

The documentation for the CPAN module XML::Simple; Recipe 22.10

22.2 Parsing XML into a DOM Tree

Problem

You want to use the Document Object Model (DOM) to access and perhaps change the parse tree of an XML file.

Solution

Use the XML::LibXML module from CPAN:

```
use XML::LibXML;
my $parser = XML::LibXML->new( );
my $dom    = $parser->parse_string($XML);
# or
my $dom    = $parser->parse_file($FILENAME);
my $root   = $dom->getDocumentElement;
```

Discussion

DOM is a framework of classes for representing XML parse trees. Each element is a node in the tree, with which you can do operations like find its children nodes (the XML elements in this case), add another child node, and move the node somewhere else in the tree. The parse_string, parse_file, and parse_fh (filehandle) constructors all return a DOM object that you can use to find nodes in the tree.

For example, given the books XML from Example 22-1, Example 22-2 shows one way to print the titles.

Example 22-2. dom-titledumper

```
#!/usr/bin/perl -w
# dom-titledumper -- display titles in books file using DOM

use XML::LibXML;
use Data::Dumper;
use strict;

my $parser = XML::LibXML->new;
my $dom = $parser->parse_file("books.xml") or die;

# get all the title elements
my @titles = $dom->getElementsByTagName("title");
foreach my $t (@titles) {
    # get the text node inside the <title> element, and print its value
    print $t->firstChild->data, "\n";
}
```

The getElementsByTagName method returns a list of elements as nodes within the document that have the specific tag name. Here we get a list of the title elements, then go through each title to find its contents. We know that each title has only a single piece of text, so we assume the first child node is text and print its contents.

If we wanted to confirm that the node was a text node, we could say:

```
die "the title contained something other than text!"
   if $t->firstChild->nodeType != 3;
```

This ensures that the first node is of type 3 (text). Table 22-1 shows LibXML's numeric node types, which the nodeType method returns.

Table 22-1. LibXML's numeric node types

Node type	Number
Element	1
Attribute	2
Text	3
CDATA Section	4
Entity Ref	5
Entity	6
Processing Instruction	7
Comment	8
Document	9
Document Type	10
Document Fragment	11
Notation	12
HTML Document	13
DTD Node	14
Element Decl	15
Attribute Decl	16
Entity Decl	17
Namespace Decl	18
XInclude Start	19
XInclude End	20

You can also create and insert new nodes, or move and delete existing ones, to change the parse tree. Example 22-3 shows how you would add a randomly generated price value to each book element.

Example 22-3. dom-addprice

```
#!/usr/bin/perl -w
# dom-addprice -- add price element to books

use XML::LibXML;
use Data::Dumper;
```

Example 22-3. dom-addprice (continued)

```perl
use strict;

my $parser = XML::LibXML->new;
my $dom = $parser->parse_file("books.xml") or die;
my $root = $dom->documentElement;

# get list of all the "book" elements
my @books = $root->getElementsByTagName("book");

foreach my $book (@books) {
  my $price = sprintf("\$%d.95", 19 + 5 * int rand 5); # random price
  my $price_text_node = $dom->createTextNode($price);  # contents of <price>
  my $price_element   = $dom->createElement("price");  # create <price>
  $price_element->appendChild($price_text_node);       # put contents into <price>
  $book->appendChild($price_element);                  # put <price> into <book>
}

print $dom->toString;
```

We use createTextNode and createElement to build the new price tag and its contents. Then we use appendChild to insert the tag onto the end of the current book tag's existing contents. The toString method emits a document as XML, which lets you easily write XML filters like this one using DOM.

The XML::LibXML::DOM manpage gives a quick introduction to the features of XML::LibXML's DOM support and references the manpages for the DOM classes (e.g., XML::LibXML::Node). Those manpages list the methods for the objects.

See Also

The documentation for the XML::LibXML::DOM, XML::LibXML::Document, XML::LibXML::Element, and XML::LibXML::Node modules

22.3 Parsing XML into SAX Events

Problem

You want to receive Simple API for XML (SAX) events from an XML parser because event-based parsing is faster and uses less memory than parsers that build a DOM tree.

Solution

Use the XML::SAX module from CPAN:

```perl
use XML::SAX::ParserFactory;
use MyHandler;
```

```
my $handler = MyHandler->new( );
my $parser = XML::SAX::ParserFactory->parser(Handler => $handler);

$parser->parse_uri($FILENAME);
# or
$parser->parse_string($XML);
```

Logic for handling events goes into the handler class (MyHandler in this example), which you write:

```
# in MyHandler.pm
package MyHandler;

use base qw(XML::SAX::Base);

sub start_element {    # method names are specified by SAX
  my ($self, $data) = @_;
  # $data is hash with keys like Name and Attributes
  # ...
}

# other possible methods include end_element( ) and characters( )

1;
```

Discussion

An XML processor that uses SAX has three parts: the XML parser that generates SAX events, the handler that reacts to them, and the stub that connects the two. The XML parser can be XML::Parser, XML::LibXML, or the pure Perl XML::SAX::PurePerl that comes with XML::SAX. The XML::SAX::ParserFactory module selects a parser for you and connects it to your handler. Your handler takes the form of a class that inherits from XML::SAX::Base. The stub is the program shown in the Solution.

The XML::SAX::Base module provides stubs for the different methods that the XML parser calls on your handler. Those methods are listed in Table 22-2, and are the methods defined by the SAX1 and SAX2 standards at *http://www.saxproject.org/*. The Perl implementation uses more Perl-ish data structures and is described in the XML::SAX::Intro manpage.

Table 22-2. XML::SAX::Base methods

start_document	end_document	characters
start_element	end_element	processing_instruction
ignorable_whitespace	set_document_locator	skipped_entity
start_prefix_mapping	end_prefix_mapping	comment
start_cdata	end_cdata	entity_reference
notation_decl	unparsed_entity_decl	element_decl
attlist_decl	doctype_decl	xml_decl

Table 22-2. XML::SAX::Base methods (continued)

`entity_decl`	`attribute_decl`	`internal_entity_decl`
`start_dtd`	`end_dtd`	`external_entity_decl`
`resolve_entity`	`start_entity`	`end_entity`
`warning`	`error`	`fatal_error`

The two data structures you need most often are those representing elements and attributes. The $data parameter to `start_element` and `end_element` is a hash reference. The keys of the hash are given in Table 22-3.

Table 22-3. An XML::SAX element hash

Key	Meaning
`Prefix`	XML namespace prefix (e.g., `email:`)
`LocalName`	Attribute name without prefix (e.g., `to`)
`Name`	Fully qualified attribute name (e.g., `email:to`)
`Attributes`	Hash of attributes of the element
`NamespaceURI`	URI of the XML namespace for this attribute

An attribute hash has a key for each attribute. The key is structured as "{*namespaceURI*}attrname". For example, if the current namespace URI is *http://example.com/dtds/mailspec/* and the attribute is `msgid`, the key in the attribute hash is:

```
{http://example.com/dtds/mailspec/}msgid
```

The attribute value is a hash; its keys are given in Table 22-4.

Table 22-4. An XML::SAX attribute hash

Key	Meaning
`Prefix`	XML namespace prefix (e.g., `email:`)
`LocalName`	Element name without prefix (e.g., `to`)
`Name`	Fully qualified element name (e.g., `email:to`)
`Value`	Value of the attribute
`NamespaceURI`	URI of the XML namespace for this element

Example 22-4 shows how to list the book titles using SAX events. It's more complex than the DOM solution because with SAX we must keep track of where we are in the XML document.

Example 22-4. sax-titledumper

```
# in TitleDumper.pm
# TitleDumper.pm -- SAX handler to display titles in books file
package TitleDumper;
```

Example 22-4. sax-titledumper (continued)

```perl
use base qw(XML::SAX::Base);

my $in_title = 0;

# if we're entering a title, increase $in_title
sub start_element {
  my ($self, $data) = @_;
  if ($data->{Name} eq 'title') {
    $in_title++;
  }
}

# if we're leaving a title, decrease $in_title and print a newline
sub end_element {
  my ($self, $data) = @_;
  if ($data->{Name} eq 'title') {
    $in_title--;
    print "\n";
  }
}

# if we're in a title, print any text we get
sub characters {
  my ($self, $data) = @_;
  if ($in_title) {
    print $data->{Data};
  }
}

1;
```

The XML::SAX::Intro manpage provides a gentle introduction to XML::SAX parsing.

See Also

Chapter 5 of *Perl & XML*; the documentation for the CPAN modules XML::SAX, XML::SAX::Base, and XML::SAX::Intro

22.4   Making Simple Changes to Elements or Text

Problem

You want to filter some XML. For example, you want to make substitutions in the body of a document, or add a price to every book described in an XML document, or you want to change `<book id="1">` to `<book> <id>1</id>`.

Solution

Use the XML::SAX::Machines module from CPAN:

```
#!/usr/bin/perl -w

use MySAXFilter1;
use MySAXFilter2;
use XML::SAX::ParserFactory;
use XML::SAX::Machines qw(Pipeline);

my $machine = Pipeline(MySAXFilter1 => MySAXFilter2); # or more
$machine->parse_uri($FILENAME);
```

Write a handler, inheriting from XML::SAX::Base as in Recipe 22.3, then whenever you need a SAX event, call the appropriate handler in your superclass. For example:

```
$self->SUPER::start_element($tag_struct);
```

Discussion

A SAX filter accepts SAX events and triggers new ones. The XML::SAX::Base module detects whether your handler object is called as a filter. If so, the XML::SAX::Base methods pass the SAX events onto the next filter in the chain. If your handler object is not called as a filter, then the XML::SAX::Base methods consume events but do not emit them. This makes it almost as simple to write events as it is to consume them.

The XML::SAX::Machines module chains the filters for you. Import its `Pipeline` function, then say:

```
my $machine = Pipeline(Filter1 => Filter2 => Filter3 => Filter4);
$machine->parse_uri($FILENAME);
```

SAX events triggered by parsing the XML file go to Filter1, which sends possibly different events to Filter2, which in turn sends events to Filter3, and so on to Filter4. The last filter should print or otherwise do something with the incoming SAX events. If you pass a reference to a typeglob, XML::SAX::Machines writes the XML to the filehandle in that typeglob.

Example 22-5 shows a filter that turns the `id` attribute in book elements from the XML document in Example 22-1 into a new `id` element. For example, `<book id="1">` becomes `<book><id>1</id>`.

Example 22-5. filters-rewriteids

```
package RewriteIDs;
# RewriteIDs.pm -- turns "id" attributes into elements

use base qw(XML::SAX::Base);

my $ID_ATTRIB = "{}id";   # the attribute hash entry we're interested in
```

Example 22-5. filters-rewriteids (continued)

```perl
sub start_element {
    my ($self, $data) = @_;

    if ($data->{Name} eq 'book') {
        my $id = $data->{Attributes}{$ID_ATTRIB}{Value};
        delete $data->{Attributes}{$ID_ATTRIB};
        $self->SUPER::start_element($data);

        # make new element parameter data structure for the <id> tag
        my $id_node = { };
        %$id_node = %$self;
        $id_node->{Name} = 'id';        # more complex if namespaces involved
        $id_node->{Attributes} = { };

        # build the <id>$id</id>
        $self->SUPER::start_element($id_node);
        $self->SUPER::characters({ Data => $id });
        $self->SUPER::end_element($id_node);
    } else {
        $self->SUPER::start_element($data);
    }
}

1;
```

Example 22-6 is the stub that uses XML::SAX::Machines to create the pipeline for processing *books.xml* and print the altered XML.

Example 22-6. filters-rewriteprog

```perl
#!/usr/bin/perl -w
# rewrite-ids -- call RewriteIDs SAX filter to turn id attrs into elements

use RewriteIDs;
use XML::SAX::Machines qw(:all);

my $machine = Pipeline(RewriteIDs => *STDOUT);
$machine->parse_uri("books.xml");
```

The output of Example 22-6 is as follows (truncated for brevity):

```
<book><id>1</id>
    <title>Programming Perl</title>
  ...
<book><id>2</id>
    <title>Perl &amp; LWP</title>
  ...
```

To save the XML to the file *new-books.xml*, use the XML::SAX::Writer module:

```perl
#!/usr/bin/perl -w

use RewriteIDs;
```

```
use XML::SAX::Machines qw(:all);
use XML::SAX::Writer;

my $writer = XML::SAX::Writer->new(Output => "new-books.xml");
my $machine = Pipeline(RewriteIDs => $writer);
$machine->parse_uri("books.xml");
```

You can also pass a scalar reference as the Output parameter to have the XML appended to the scalar; as an array reference to have the XML appended to the array, one array element per SAX event; or as a filehandle to have the XML printed to that filehandle.

See Also

The documentation for the modules XML::SAX::Machines and XML::SAX::Writer

22.5 Validating XML

Problem

You want to ensure that the XML you're processing conforms to a DTD or XML Schema.

Solution

To validate against a DTD, use the XML::LibXML module:

```
use XML::LibXML;
my $parser = XML::LibXML->new;
$parser->validation(1);
$parser->parse_file($FILENAME);
```

To validate against a W3C Schema, use the XML::Xerces module:

```
use XML::Xerces;

my $parser = XML::Xerces::DOMParser->new;
$parser->setValidationScheme($XML::Xerces::DOMParser::Val_Always);

my $error_handler = XML::Xerces::PerlErrorHandler->new( );
$parser->setErrorHandler($error_handler);

$parser->parse($FILENAME);
```

Discussion

The *libxml2* library, upon which XML::LibXML is based, can validate as it parses. The validation method on the parser enables this option. At the time of this writing, XML::LibXML could only validate with DOM parsing—validation is not available with SAX-style parsing.

Example 22-7 is a DTD for the *books.xml* file in Example 22-1.

Example 22-7. validating-booksdtd

```
<!ELEMENT books (book*)>
<!ELEMENT book (title,edition,authors,isbn)>
<!ELEMENT authors (author*)>
<!ELEMENT author (firstname,lastname)>
<!ELEMENT title (#PCDATA)>
<!ELEMENT edition (#PCDATA)>
<!ELEMENT firstname (#PCDATA)>
<!ELEMENT lastname (#PCDATA)>
<!ELEMENT isbn (#PCDATA)>

<!ATTLIST book
  id    CDATA    #REQUIRED
>
```

To make XML::LibXML parse the DTD, add this line to the *books.xml* file:

```
<!DOCTYPE books
   SYSTEM "books.dtd">
```

Example 22-8 is a simple driver used to parse and validate.

Example 22-8. validating-bookchecker

```
#!/usr/bin/perl -w
# bookchecker - parse and validate the books.xml file

use XML::LibXML;

$parser = XML::LibXML->new;
$parser->validation(1);
$parser->parse_file("books.xml");
```

When the document validates, the program produces no output—XML::LibXML successfully parses the document into a DOM structure that is quietly destroyed when the program ends. Edit the *books.xml* file, however, and you see the errors the XML::LibXML emits when it discovers broken XML.

For example, changing the id attribute to unique_id causes this error message:

```
'books.xml:0: validity error: No declaration for attribute unique_id
of element book
    <book unique_id="1">
                  ^
books.xml:0: validity error: Element book does not carry attribute id
    </book>
       ^
' at /usr/local/perl5-8/Library/Perl/5.8.0/darwin/XML/LibXML.pm line
405.
 at checker-1 line 7
```

XML::LibXML does a good job of reporting unknown attributes and tags. However, it's not so good at reporting out-of-order elements. If you return *books.xml* to its correct state, and then swap the order of a title and an edition element, you get this message:

```
'books.xml:0: validity error: Element book content does not follow the
DTD
    </book>
        ^
' at /usr/local/perl5-8/Library/Perl/5.8.0/darwin/XML/LibXML.pm line
405.
 at checker-1 line 7
```

In this case, XML::LibXML says that something in the book element didn't follow the DTD, but it couldn't tell us precisely what it violated in the DTD or how.

At the time of this writing, you must use XML::Xerces to validate while using SAX, or to validate against W3C Schema. Both of these features (and RelaxNG validation) are planned for XML::LibXML, but weren't available at the time of printing.

Here's how you build a DOM tree while validating a DTD using XML::Xerces:

```
use XML::Xerces;

# create a new parser that always validates
my $p = XML::Xerces::DOMParser->new( );
$p->setValidationScheme($XML::Xerces::DOMParser::Val_Always);

# make it die when things fail to parse
my $error_handler = XML::Xerces::PerlErrorHandler->new( );
$p->setErrorHandler($error_handler);

$p->parse($FILENAME);
```

To validate against a schema, you must tell XML::Xerces where the schema is and that it should be used:

```
$p->setFeature("http://xml.org/sax/features/validation", 1);
$p->setFeature("http://apache.org/xml/features/validation/dynamic", 0);
$p->setFeature("http://apache.org/xml/features/validation/schema", $SCHEMAFILE);
```

You can pass three possible values to setValidationScheme:

```
$XML::Xerces::DOMParser::Val_Always
$XML::Xerces::DOMParser::Val_Never
$XML::Xerces::DOMParser::Val_Auto
```

The default is to never validate. Always validating raises an error if the file does not have a DTD or Schema. Auto raises an error only if the file has a DTD or Schema, but it fails to validate against that DTD or Schema.

XML::Xerces requires the Apache Xerces C++ XML parsing library, available from *http://xml.apache.org/xerces-c*. At the time of writing, the XML::Xerces module required an archived, older version of the Xerces library (1.7.0) and was appallingly lacking in documentation—you can learn how it works only by reading the documentation for the C++ library and consulting the examples in the *samples/* directory of the XML::Xerces distribution.

See Also

The documentation for the CPAN module XML::LibXML; *http://xml.apache.org/ xerces-c*; *http://xml.apache.org/xerces-p/*

22.6 Finding Elements and Text Within an XML Document

Problem

You want to get to a specific part of the XML; for example, the href attribute of an a tag whose contents are an img tag with alt text containing the word "monkey".

Solution

Use XML::LibXML and construct an XPath expression to find nodes you're interested in:

```
use XML::LibXML;

my $parser = XML::LibXML->new;
$doc = $parser->parse_file($FILENAME);
my @nodes = $doc->findnodes($XPATH_EXPRESSION);
```

Discussion

Example 22-9 shows how you would print all the titles in the book XML from Example 22-1.

Example 22-9. xpath-1

```
#!/usr/bin/perl -w

use XML::LibXML;

my $parser = XML::LibXML->new;
$doc = $parser->parse_file("books.xml");

# find title elements
my @nodes = $doc->findnodes("/books/book/title");

# print the text in the title elements
foreach my $node (@nodes) {
  print $node->firstChild->data, "\n";
}
```

The difference between DOM's `getElementsByTagName` and `findnodes` is that the former identifies elements only by their name. An XPath expression specifies a set of steps that the XPath engine takes to find nodes you're interested in. In Example 22-9 the XPath expression says "start at the top of the document, go into the books element, go into the book element, and then go into the `title` element."

The difference is important. Consider this XML document:

```
<message>
  <header><to>Tom</to><from>Nat</from></header>
  <body>
    <order><to>555 House St, Mundaneville</to>
        <product>Fish sticks</product>
    </order>
  </body>
</message>
```

There are two to elements here: one in the header and one in the body. If we said `$doc->getElementsByTagName("to")`, we'd get both to elements. The XPath expression `"/message/header/to"` restricts output to the to element in the header.

XPath expressions are like regular expressions that operate on XML structure instead of text. As with regular expressions, there are a lot of things you can specify in XPath expressions—far more than the simple "find this child node and go into it" that we've been doing.

Let's return to the books file and add another entry:

```
<book id="4">
  <!-- Perl Cookbook -->
  <title>Perl Cookbook</title>
  <edition>2</edition>
  <authors>
    <author>
      <firstname>Nathan</firstname>
      <lastname>Torkington</lastname>
    </author>
    <author>
      <firstname>Tom</firstname>
      <lastname>Christiansen</lastname>
    </author>
  </authors>
  <isbn>123-345-678-90</isbn>
</book>
```

To identify all books by Tom Christiansen, we need simply say:

```
my @nodes = $doc->findnodes("/books/book/authors/author/
        firstname[text()='Tom']/../
        lastname[text()='Christiansen']/
        ../../../title/text()");

foreach my $node (@nodes) {
  print $node->data, "\n";
}
```

We find the author with firstname equal to "Tom" and lastname equal to "Christiansen", then back out to the "title" element and get its text child nodes. Another way to write the backing out is "head out until you find the book element again":

```
my @nodes = $doc->findnodes("/books/book/authors/author/
    firstname[text( )='Tom']/../
    lastname[text( )='Christiansen']/
    ancestor::book/title/text( )");
```

XPath is a very powerful system, and we haven't begun to touch the surface of it. For details on XPath, see *XPath and XPointer*, by John E. Simpson (O'Reilly), or the W3C specification at *http://www.w3.org/TR/xpath*. Advanced users should look at the XML::LibXML::XPathContext module (also available from CPAN), which lets you write your own XPath functions in Perl.

See Also

The documentation for the modules XML::LibXML and XML::LibXML::XPathContext; *http://www.w3.org/TR/xpath*; *XPath and XPointer*

22.7   Processing XML Stylesheet Transformations

Problem

You have an XML stylesheet that you want to use to convert XML into something else. For example, you want to produce HTML from files of XML using the stylesheet.

Solution

Use XML::LibXSLT:

```
use XML::LibXSLT;

my $xslt       = XML::LibXSLT->new;

my $stylesheet = $xslt->parse_stylesheet_file($XSL_FILENAME);
my $results    = $stylesheet->transform_file($XML_FILENAME);

print $stylesheet->output_string($results);
```

Discussion

XML::LibXSLT is built on the fast and powerful *libxslt* library from the GNOME project. To perform a transformation, first build a stylesheet object from the XSL source and then use it to transform an XML file. If you wanted to (for example, your

XSL is dynamically generated rather than being stored in a file), you could break this down into separate steps:

```
use XML::LibXSLT;
use XML::LibXML;

my $xml_parser  = XML::LibXML->new;
my $xslt_parser = XML::LibXSLT->new;

my $xml         = $xml_parser->parse_file($XML_FILENAME);
my $xsl         = $xml_parser->parse_file($XSL_FILENAME);

my $stylesheet  = $xslt_parser->parse_stylesheet($xsl);
my $results     = $stylesheet->transform($xml);
my $output      = $stylesheet->output_string($results);
```

To save the output to a file, use output_file:

```
$stylesheet->output_file($OUTPUT_FILENAME);
```

Similarly, write the output to an already-opened filehandle with output_fh:

```
$stylesheet->output_fh($FILEHANDLE);
```

It's possible to pass parameters to the transformation engine. For example, your transformation might use parameters to set a footer at the bottom of each page:

```
$stylesheet->transform($xml, footer => "'I Made This!'");
```

The strange quoting is because the XSLT engine expects to see quoted values. In the preceding example, the double quotes tell Perl it's a string, whereas the single quotes are for the XSLT engine.

You can even retrieve data unavailable to XSL (from a database, etc.) or manipulate runtime XSLT data with Perl. Consider the file in Example 22-10, which has multilingual title tags.

Example 22-10. test.xml

```
<list>
  <title>System</title>
  <TituloGrande>Products</TituloGrande>
  <sublist>
    <SubTitleOne>Book</SubTitleOne>
  </sublist>
</list>
```

You'd like to call a Perl function match_names from the XSLT template, *test.xsl*, given in Example 22-11.

Example 22-11. test.xsl

```
<?xml version="1.0" encoding="UTF-8"?>
<xsl:stylesheet
  xmlns:xsl="http://www.w3.org/1999/XSL/Transform" version="1.0"
```

Example 22-11. test.xsl (continued)

```
    xmlns:test="urn:test">
  <xsl:template match="/">

    <xsl:variable name="matched" select="test:match_names('title |
titulo | titre | titolo', . )" />

    <xsl:for-each select="$matched">
      <xsl:copy-of select="." />
    </xsl:for-each>

  </xsl:template>
  </xsl:stylesheet>
```

The arguments to match_names are a regex and a node list, and the function is expected to return a node list object. Use XML::LibXML::NodeList methods to work with the parameters and create the return value. The match_names subroutine is given in Example 22-12.

Example 22-12. match_names subroutine

```
sub match_names {
  my $pattern = shift;
  my $nodelist = shift;
  my $matches = XML::LibXML::NodeList->new;
  foreach my $context ($nodelist->get_nodelist) {
    foreach my $node ($context->findnodes('//*')) {
      if ($node->nodeName =~ /$pattern/ix) {
        $matches->push($node);
      }
    }
  }
  return $matches;
}
```

Use XML::LibXSLT's register_function method to register your function for use from an XSLT template. Here's how you'd process the template from Example 22-10:

```
use strict;
use XML::LibXML;
use XML::LibXSLT;

my $xml_parser = XML::LibXML->new;
my $xslt_parser = XML::LibXSLT->new;

sub match_names { ... }   # as in example 22-10
$xslt_parser->register_function("urn:test", "match_names", \&match_names);
my $dom = $xml_parser->parse_file('test.xml');
my $xslt_dom = $xml_parser->parse_file('test.xsl');
my $xslt = $xslt_parser->parse_stylesheet($xslt_dom);
my $result_dom = $xslt->transform($dom);
print $result_dom->toString;
```

Use closures to let XSLT access Perl variables, illustrated here with an Apache request object:

```
$xslt->register_function("urn:test", "get_request",
                         sub { &get_request($apache_req,@_) } );
```

The get_request XSLT function (named in the second argument to register_ function calls the Perl subroutine get_request (named in the code that is the third argument) with $apache_req preceding any arguments given to the XSLT function. You might use this to return a node list containing HTTP form parameters, or to wrap DBI database queries.

See Also

The documentation for the modules XML::LibXSLT and XML::LibXML

22.8 Processing Files Larger Than Available Memory

Problem

You want to work with a large XML file, but you can't read it into memory to form a DOM or other kind of tree because it's too big.

Solution

Use SAX (as described in Recipe 22.3) to process events instead of building a tree.

Alternatively, use XML::Twig to build trees only for the parts of the document you want to work with (as specified by XPath expressions):

```
use XML::Twig;

my $twig = XML::Twig->new( twig_handlers => {
                           $XPATH_EXPRESSION => \&HANDLER,
                           # ...
                           });
$twig->parsefile($FILENAME);
$twig->flush();
```

You can call a lot of DOM-like functions from within a handler, but only the elements identified by the XPath expression (and whatever those elements enclose) go into a tree.

Discussion

DOM modules turn the entire document into a tree, regardless of whether you use all of it. With SAX modules, there are no trees built—if your task depends on document structure, you must keep track of that structure yourself. A happy middle ground is XML::Twig, which creates DOM trees only for the bits of the file that you're interested in. Because you work with files a piece at a time, you can cope with very large files by processing pieces that fit in memory.

For example, to print the titles of books in *books.xml* (Example 22-1), you could write:

```
use XML::Twig;

my $twig = XML::Twig->new( twig_roots => { '/books/book' => \&do_book });
$twig->parsefile("books.xml");
$twig->purge( );

sub do_book {
  my($title) = $_->find_nodes("title");
  print $title->text, "\n";
}
```

For each book element, XML::Twig calls do_book on its contents. That subroutine finds the title node and prints its text. Rather than having the entire file parsed into a DOM structure, we keep only one book element at a time.

Consult the XML::Twig manpages for details on how much DOM and XPath the module supports—it's not complete, but it's growing all the time. XML::Twig uses XML::Parser for its XML parsing, and as a result the functions available on nodes are slightly different from those provided by XML::LibXSLT's DOM parsing.

See Also

Recipe 22.6; the documentation for the module XML::Twig

22.9 Reading and Writing RSS Files

Problem

You want to create a Rich Site Summary (RSS) file, or read one produced by another application.

Solution

Use the CPAN module XML::RSS to read an existing RSS file:

```
use XML::RSS;

my $rss = XML::RSS->new;
$rss->parsefile($RSS_FILENAME);

my @items = @{$rss->{items}};
```

```
foreach my $item (@items) {
  print "title: $item->{'title'}\n";
  print "link: $item->{'link'}\n\n";
  }
```

To create an RSS file:

```
use XML::RSS;

my $rss  = XML::RSS->new (version => $VERSION);
$rss->channel( title       => $CHANNEL_TITLE,
               link        => $CHANNEL_LINK,
               description => $CHANNEL_DESC);
$rss->add_item(title       => $ITEM_TITLE,
               link        => $ITEM_LINK,
               description => $ITEM_DESC,
               name        => $ITEM_NAME);
print $rss->as_string;
```

Discussion

There are at least four variations of RSS extant: 0.9, 0.91, 1.0, and 2.0. At the time of this writing, XML::RSS understood all but RSS 2.0. Each version has different capabilities, so methods and parameters depend on which version of RSS you're using. For example, RSS 1.0 supports RDF and uses the Dublin Core metadata (*http:// dublincore.org/*). Consult the documentation for what you can and cannot call.

XML::RSS uses XML::Parser to parse the RSS. Unfortunately, not all RSS files are well-formed XML, let alone valid. The XML::RSSLite module on CPAN offers a looser approach to parsing RSS—it uses regular expressions and is much more forgiving of incorrect XML.

Example 22-13 uses XML::RSSLite and LWP::Simple to download The Guardian's RSS feed and print out the items whose descriptions contain the keywords we're interested in.

Example 22-13. rss-parser

```
#!/usr/bin/perl -w
# guardian-list -- list Guardian articles matching keyword

use XML::RSSLite;
use LWP::Simple;
use strict;

# list of keywords we want
my @keywords = qw(perl internet porn iraq bush);

# get the RSS
my $URL = 'http://www.guardian.co.uk/rss/1,,,00.xml';
my $content = get($URL);
```

Example 22-13. rss-parser (continued)

```perl
# parse the RSS
my %result;
parseRSS(\%result, \$content);

# build the regex from keywords
my $re = join "|", @keywords;
$re = qr/\b(?:$re)\b/i;

# print report of matching items
foreach my $item (@{ $result{items} }) {
  my $title = $item->{title};
  $title =~ s{\s+}{ };   $title =~ s{^\s+}{ };   $title =~ s{\s+$}{ };

  if ($title =~ /$re/) {
    print "$title\n\t$item->{link}\n\n";
  }
}
```

The following is sample output from Example 22-13:

> **UK troops to lead Iraq peace force**
>   *http://www.guardian.co.uk/Iraq/Story/0,2763,989318,00.html?=rss*
>
> **Shia cleric challenges Bush plan for Iraq**
>   *http://www.guardian.co.uk/Iraq/Story/0,2763,989364,00.html?=rss*

We can combine this with XML::RSS to generate a new RSS feed from the filtered items. It would be easier, of course, to do it all with XML::RSS, but this way you get to see both modules in action. Example 22-14 shows the finished program.

Example 22-14. rss-filter

```perl
#!/usr/bin/perl -w
# guardian-filter -- filter the Guardian's RSS feed by keyword
use XML::RSSLite;
use XML::RSS;
use LWP::Simple;
use strict;

# list of keywords we want
my @keywords = qw(perl internet porn iraq bush);

# get the RSS
my $URL = 'http://www.guardian.co.uk/rss/1,,,00.xml';
my $content = get($URL);

# parse the RSS
my %result;
parseRSS(\%result, \$content);

# build the regex from keywords
my $re = join "|", @keywords;
```

Example 22-14. rss-filter (continued)

```
$re = qr/\b(?:$re)\b/i;

# make new RSS feed
my $rss = XML::RSS->new(version => '0.91');
$rss->channel(title       => $result{title},
              link        => $result{link},
              description => $result{description});

foreach my $item (@{ $result{items} }) {
  my $title = $item->{title};
  $title =~ s{\s+}{ };  $title =~ s{^\s+}{ }; $title =~ s{\s+$}{ };

  if ($title =~ /$re/) {
    $rss->add_item(title => $title, link => $item->{link});
  }
}
print $rss->as_string;
```

Here's an example of the RSS feed it produces:

```
<?xml version="1.0" encoding="UTF-8"?>

<!DOCTYPE rss PUBLIC "-//Netscape Communications//DTD RSS 0.91//EN"
          "http://my.netscape.com/publish/formats/rss-0.91.dtd">

<rss version="0.91">

<channel>
<title>Guardian Unlimited</title>
<link>http://www.guardian.co.uk</link>
<description>Intelligent news and comment throughout the day from The Guardian
newspaper</description>

<item>
<title>UK troops to lead Iraq peace force</title>
<link>http://www.guardian.co.uk/Iraq/Story/0,2763,989318,00.html?=rss</link>
</item>

<item>
<title>Shia cleric challenges Bush plan for Iraq</title>
<link>http://www.guardian.co.uk/Iraq/Story/0,2763,989364,00.html?=rss</link>
</item>

</channel>
</rss>
```

See Also

The documentation for the modules XML::RSS and XML::RSSLite

22.10 Writing XML

Problem

You have a data structure that you'd like to convert to XML.

Solution

Use XML::Simple's XMLout function:

```
use XML::Simple qw(XMLout);

my $xml = XMLout($hashref);
```

Discussion

The XMLout function takes a data structure and produces XML from it. For example, here's how to generate part of the book data:

```
#!/usr/bin/perl -w

use XML::Simple qw(XMLout);

$ds =  {
    book => [
            {
              id       => 1,
              title   => [ "Programming Perl" ],
              edition => [ 3 ],
            },
            {
              id       => 2,
              title   => [ "Perl & LWP" ],
              edition => [ 1 ],
            },
            {
              id       => 3,
              title   => [ "Anonymous Perl" ],
              edition => [ 1 ],
            },
            ]
};

print XMLout($ds, RootName => "books" );
```

This produces:

```
<books>
  <book id="1">
    <edition>3</edition>
    <title>Programming Perl</title>
  </book>
```

```
<book id="2">
  <edition>1</edition>
  <title>Perl &amp; </title
</book>
<book id="3">
  <edition>1</edition>
  <title>Anonymous Perl</title>
</book>
</books>
```

The rule is: if you want something to be text data, rather than an attribute value, put it in an array. Notice how we used the RootName option to XMLout to specify that books is the top-level element. Pass undef or the empty string to generate an XML fragment with no top-level fragment. The default value is opt.

The id entry in each hash became an attribute because the default behavior of XMLout is to do this for the id, key, and name fields. Prevent this with:

```
XMLout($ds, RootName => "books", KeyAttr => [ ]);
```

As with XMLin (see Recipe 22.1), you can identify the hash values that are to become attributes for specific elements:

```
XMLout($ds, RootName => "books", KeyAttr => [ "car" => "license" ]);
```

That instructs XMLout to create attributes only for the license field in a car hash.

XML::Simple observes the convention that a hash key with a leading hyphen (e.g., -name) is private and should not appear in the XML output.

See Also

The documentation for the module XML::Simple; Recipe 22.1

Index

Symbols

& (ampersand), && operator, 10
<> (angle brackets), 3
   globbing, 358
   line input operator, 270
   reading strings from binary files, 324
* (asterisk), typeglobs, 255–258
@ (at sign)
   @_ array, 374
   @EXPORT array (use pragma), 450
   @EXPORT_OK array (use pragma), 450
   @EXPORT_TAGS array (use
      pragma), 451
   @INC array, 463
   references to arrays, 413
   splice( ), 134
\ (backslash)
   \1, \2, . . . (backreferences), 215
   \a for terminal bell, 594
   \E string metacharacter, 42
   \G anchor, 211
   \L string escape, 29
   \l string escape, 29
   \Q string metacharacter, 42
   \U string escape, 29
   \u string escape, 29
   \X metacharacter, 21
   creating arrays, 421
   creating references, 409
   escaping characters, 41
   references to arrays, 414
   references to scalars, 420

` (backtick)
   executing commands without shell
      escapes, 771
   expanding, 34
   gathering program output, 625
   running another program, 627
: (colon)
   module names, 446
   package names, 444
, (comma)
   in numbers, 85
   printing lists with, 113
{ } (curly braces), 3
   creating anonymous arrays and
      hashes, 409
$ (dollar sign)
   $! variable, 285
   $#ARRAY variable, 115
   $$ variable, 629, 652, 664
   $& variable, 26, 184
   $* variable (deprecated), 183
   $+ variable, 184
   $. variable, 197, 277
   $/ variable, 302
   $; variable, 356
   $? variable, 627, 662
   $@ variable, 206, 392
   $^F variable, 462
   $^I variable, 277
   $^O variable, 294, 366
   $^W variable, 474
   $_ variable, 120, 301, 319
      accidental clobbering, 121
      outlawing unauthorized use, 542

We'd like to hear your suggestions for improving our indexes. Send email to *index@oreilly.com*.

Numbers

A

---

findnodes( ) vs.
getElementsByTagName( ), 886
FIONREAD call, 286
firewalls, fetching web pages
through, 715–719
fixed-length records, 304
flat-file index program, 343–345
reading, 325
FixNum class, 538–540
fixstyle program, 52–55
flat file index program, 343–345
flattened lists, 111
floating-point numbers, 59
comparing, 67
rounding, 64–67
flock( ), 279
compared to SysV lockf( ), 281
floor( ), 66
flushing output, 281–284
fmt program, 40
fnctl( ), locking files, 281
folded_demo program, 544
fonts, Unicode, support for, 337
foodfind program, 165
=for escape pod directive, 488
ForceArray option, 873
foreach loop, 134
printing to multiple filehandles, 260
renaming files, 363
traversing hashes, 158
fork( ), 642
avoiding zombie processes, 661–663
closing sockets after, 690
forking servers, 694
non-forking servers, 698–701
preforking servers, 695–698
shell escapes, 771
(see also processes)
format_string( ), 801
forms, HTML, 759
saving and emailing, 785
sticky widgets, 781
submitting, 796
forward slash (/)
/e substitution modifier, 27, 183
/g pattern-matching modifier, 183
finding Nth matches, 192
where last pattern ended, 210
/i pattern-matching modifier, 182
/m pattern-matching modifier, 183
multiple lines, 195
/o pattern-matching modifier, 203–205

/s pattern-matching modifier, 183
multiple lines, 195
/x pattern modifier, 28
comments in regular expressions, 190
root directory, 346
Frame widget, Tk, 605
FTP clients, 724–726
full-screen mode, 583
functions
interpolating within strings, 33–35
vs. methods, 526
private for variables, 457
references to, 417–420
types of, 8
fuzzy matching, 209
fwdport program, 715–719

G

\G anchor, 211
/g pattern-matching modifier, 183
finding Nth matches, 192
where last pattern ended, 210
garbage collection, 509
circular data structures and, 532–534
gaussian_rand( ), 75
GD module, 615
GD::Graph modules, 613
GD::Graph::Bars module, 620
GDBM files, 549
db2gdbm program, 553
GDBM_File module, 434
generic classes, 505
GET request, 758, 761
resuming, 819
using HTTP 1.1 Range header, 819
get( ), fetching URLs from Perl scripts, 794
get_request( ), 890
get_token( ), parsing HTML, 822
getElementsByTagName( )
vs. findnodes( ), 886
returning a list of elements by nodes, 875
gethostbyaddr( ), 689
gethostbyname( ), 689
finding IP addresses, 721
getitimer( ), 104
getline( ), 257
gctopt( ), 585
Getopt::Long module, 585
Getopt::Std module, 585
GetOptions( ), 586
getopts( ), 586
getpeername( ), 706, 714

About the Authors

Tom Christiansen is an author and lecturer who's been intimately involved with Perl development since Larry Wall first released it to the general public in 1987. After working for several years for TSR Hobbies (of Dungeons and Dragons fame), he set off for college where he spent a year in Spain and five in America pursuing a classical education in computer science, mathematics, music, linguistics, and Romance philology. He eventually escaped UW-Madison without a PhD, but with a BA in Spanish and in Computer Science, plus an MS in Computer Science specializing in operating systems design and computational linguistics.

Co-author of *Programming Perl*, Tom lives in idyllic Boulder, Colorado, where he gives public seminars on all aspects of Perl programming. When he can be coaxed out of the People's Republic of Boulder, Tom travels around the world giving public and private lectures and workshops on Unix, Perl, and the Web on five continents and in three languages. He takes the summers off to pursue his hobbies of reading, backpacking, gardening, birding, gaming, music making, and recreational programming.

Nathan Torkington has never climbed Mount Kilimanjaro. He adamantly maintains that he was nowhere near the grassy knoll. He has never mustered superhuman strength to lift a burning trolleycar to free a trapped child, and is yet to taste human flesh. Nat has never served as a mercenary in the Congo, line-danced, run away to join the circus, spent a year with the pygmies, finished the Death By Chocolate, or been miraculously saved when his cigarillo case stopped the bullet.

Nat is not American, though he is learning the language. He is from Ti Point, New Zealand. People from Ti Point don't do these things. They grow up on fishing boats and say things like "She'll be right, mate." Nat did. He works as an editor for O'Reilly, selects content for the Open Source Convention, is project manager for Perl 6, and sits on the board of The Perl Foundation. He lives in Colorado and New Zealand with his wife, Jenine, and their children, William and Aurelia. His hobbies are bluegrass music and Perl.

Colophon

Our look is the result of reader comments, our own experimentation, and feedback from distribution channels. Distinctive covers complement our distinctive approach to technical topics, breathing personality and life into potentially dry subjects.

The animal featured on the cover of *Perl Cookbook*, Second Edition is a bighorn sheep. Bighorn sheep (*Ovis canadensis*) are wild sheep noted, not surprisingly, for their large, curved horns. Male bighorns grow to approximately 5 feet long and 40 inches tall to the shoulder and weigh up to 350 pounds. Their horns measure up to 18 inches in circumference and 4 feet long and can weigh up to 30 pounds. Despite their bulk, bighorns are adept at negotiating mountainous terrains. With their sharp, cloven hooves they can walk on ledges as thin as two inches. They have excellent eyesight that enables them to locate footholds and to accurately judge distances between ledges. They can jump as far as 20 feet from ledge to ledge.

Competition for ewes is intense and often leads to fierce battles that can continue for a full day. During the battle two rams race at each other at speeds of up to 20 miles an hour, clashing their horns together. The skull of the bighorn sheep is double-layered to provide protection from these blows. Horn size is a significant factor in determining rank, and rams will only fight other rams with an equivalently sized horn. Mature males usually stay apart from the females and young. In these "bachelor flocks" the lower-ranking males often play the part of ewes and behave in a submissive manner toward the dominant males. The dominant male, in turn, behaves like a courting ram and mounts the lower-ranking male. This behavior is believed to enable the rams to live together without rank disputes that might otherwise drive the lower-ranking males out of the flock.

Bighorns can be found in the Rocky Mountains from Canada to Colorado and in the desert from California to west Texas and Mexico. They are threatened with extinction as a result of disease, habitat reduction, and hunting.

Genevieve d'Entremont was the production editor and copyeditor for *Perl Cookbook*, Second Edition. Phil Dangler, Emily Quill, Matt Hutchinson, and Colleen Gorman provided quality control. Mary Agner and Jamie Peppard provided production assistance. Nancy Crumpton wrote the index.

Edie Freedman designed the cover of this book, using a 19th-century engraving from the Dover Pictorial Archive. Emma Colby produced the cover layout with Quark-XPress 4.1 using Adobe's ITC Garamond font.

David Futato designed the interior layout. This book was converted by Julie Hawks and Andrew Savikas from Pod to FrameMaker 5.5.6 with a format conversion tool created by Erik Ray, Jason McIntosh, Neil Walls, and Mike Sierra that uses Perl and XML technologies. The text font is Linotype Birka; the heading font is Adobe Myriad Condensed; and the code font is LucasFont's TheSans Mono Condensed. The illustrations that appear in the book were produced by Robert Romano and Jessamyn Read using Macromedia FreeHand 9 and Adobe Photoshop 6. The warning icon was drawn by Christopher Bing. This colophon was written by Clairemarie Fisher O'Leary.

Related Titles Available from O'Reilly

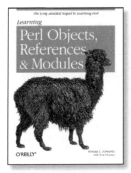

Perl

Advanced Perl Programming

CGI Programming with Perl, *2nd Edition*

Computer Science & Perl Programming:
The Best of the Perl Journal

Embedding Perl in HTML with Mason

Games, Diversions, & Perl Culture:
The Best of the Perl Journal

Learning Perl, *3rd Edition*

Learning Perl Objects, References and Modules

Mastering Algorithms with Perl

Mastering Perl/Tk

Mastering Regular Expressions, *2nd Edition*

Perl & LWP

Perl & XML

Perl 6 Essentials

Perl CD Bookshelf, *Version 4.0*

Perl Debugger Pocket Reference

Perl for System Administration

Perl Graphics Programming

Perl in a Nutshell, *2nd Edition*

Perl Pocket Reference, *4th Edition*

Practical mod_perl

Programming the Perl DBI

Programming Perl, *3rd Edition*

Programming Web Services with Perl

Regular Expression Pocket Guide

Web, Graphics & Perl/Tk: The Best of the Perl Journal

O'REILLY®

Our books are available at most retail and online bookstores.
To order direct: 1-800-998-9938 • *order@oreilly.com* • *www.oreilly.com*
Online editions of most O'Reilly titles are available by subscription at *safari.oreilly.com*

Keep in touch with O'Reilly

1. Download examples from our books

To find example files for a book, go to:

www.oreilly.com/catalog

select the book, and follow the "Examples" link.

2. Register your O'Reilly books

Register your book at *register.oreilly.com*

Why register your books?
Once you've registered your O'Reilly books you can:

- Win O'Reilly books, T-shirts or discount coupons in our monthly drawing.
- Get special offers available only to registered O'Reilly customers.
- Get catalogs announcing new books (US and UK only).
- Get email notification of new editions of the O'Reilly books you own.

3. Join our email lists

Sign up to get topic-specific email announcements of new books and conferences, special offers, and O'Reilly Network technology newsletters at:

elists.oreilly.com

It's easy to customize your free elists subscription so you'll get exactly the O'Reilly news you want.

4. Get the latest news, tips, and tools

www.oreilly.com

- "Top 100 Sites on the Web"—PC Magazine
- CIO Magazine's Web Business 50 Awards

Our web site contains a library of comprehensive product information (including book excerpts and tables of contents), downloadable software, background articles, interviews with technology leaders, links to relevant sites, book cover art, and more.

5. Work for O'Reilly

Check out our web site for current employment opportunities:

jobs.oreilly.com

6. Contact us

O'Reilly & Associates, Inc.
1005 Gravenstein Hwy North
Sebastopol, CA 95472 USA

TEL: 707-827-7000 or 800-998-9938
(6am to 5pm PST)

FAX: 707-829-0104

order@oreilly.com
For answers to problems regarding your order or our products. To place a book order online, visit:

www.oreilly.com/order_new

catalog@oreilly.com
To request a copy of our latest catalog.

booktech@oreilly.com
For book content technical questions or corrections.

corporate@oreilly.com
For educational, library, government, and corporate sales.

proposals@oreilly.com
To submit new book proposals to our editors and product managers.

international@oreilly.com
For information about our international distributors or translation queries. For a list of our distributors outside of North America check out:

international.oreilly.com/distributors.html

adoption@oreilly.com
For information about academic use of O'Reilly books, visit:

academic.oreilly.com